# URBAN SOCIAL GEOGRAPHY
## an introduction
### Second edition

Paul Knox

# Urban Social Geography

## an introduction

### Second edition

Copublished in the United States with
John Wiley & Sons, Inc., New York

**Longman Scientific & Technical,**
Longman Group UK Limited
Longman House, Burnt Mill, Harlow,
Essex CM20 2JE, England
*and Associated Companies throughout the world.*

*Copublished in the United States with*
*John Wiley & Sons, Inc., 605 Third Avenue, New York,*
*NY 10158*

*First published 1982*
*Second edition 1987*
*Reprinted 1989, 1990*

**British Library Cataloguing in Publication Data**
Knox, Paul L.
   Urban social geography: an introduction.
   – 2nd ed.
   1. Cities and towns 2. Anthropo-geography
   1. Title
   307.7 '6'091821 GF125

   ISBN 0-582-30160-2

**Library of Congress Cataloging-in-Publication Data**
Knox, Paul L.
   Urban social geography.

   Bibliography: p.
   Includes index.
   1. Sociology, Urban.   2. Anthropo-geography.
3. Cities and towns.   I. Title.
HT151.K57   1987      307.7′6         86-19067
ISBN 0-470-20780-9 (Wiley, USA only).

Set in Linotron 202 10/11pt Times

Produced by Longman Group (FE) Limited
Printed in Hong Kong

# Contents

# Acknowledgements

This book has emerged from several years of involvement in teaching courses in urban and social geography, mainly at the University of Dundee and Virginia Tech, but also at the University of Stirling, the University of Oklahoma, and the University of Wisconsin at Madison. During this time I have received assistance, advice and encouragement from many sources. Special thanks are due to Mike Barke, Martin Cadwallader, Barry Cottam, Joe Cullen, George Gordon, Briavel Holcomb, Philip Kivell, Ronan Paddison, Bronwen Walker, John Western, Nick Williams and Beverley Wilson for their ideas and constructive criticism at various stages in the preparation of the book, and to the students on my courses who have helped me crystallize my ideas. I also wish to express my debt to Bryan Coates. He it was who encouraged me in my postgraduate career, supervising my first uncertain attempts at research, helping me to present my thoughts to others and generally stimulating my interest in human geography and the social sciences. His interest and encouragement have been much appreciated. Finally, my thanks and appreciation to my wife, Lynne, who has not only suffered my preoccupation in writing (and re-writing) this book but also provided practical help and encouragement.

Paul Knox
Blacksburg, Virginia
February 1986

We are grateful to the following for permission to reproduce copyright material:

Academic Press for fig 7.4 (Baboolal 1981); Academic Press and the author, Professor Agocs for table 7.1 (Agocs 1981); Edward Arnold (Publishers) Ltd and the author, D Herbert for figs 3.11, 3.13 from figs 2, 3 (Herbert 1977a); Associated Book Publishers Ltd for table 3.3 from table 6 (Baldwin & Bottoms 1976); Association of American Geographers for fig 5.10 from fig 15 (Moore 1972); the author, T Baerwald for figs 2.8, 2.9 (Baerwald 1984), figs 6.10, 6.11 (Baerwald 1981); Ballinger Publishing Co for fig 3.9 compiled from figs 7.6a, 7.6b, 7.9 (Pyle 1976), fig 6.9 from fig 4.15 (Mercer & Hultquist 1976) Copyright 1976 Ballinger Publishing Co; Cambridge University Press for figs 2.3, 2.4, 2.5 (Dennis 1984) Copyright Cambridge University Press; Canadian Sociology and Anthropology Association and the author, Professor L Driedger for fig 7.2 (Driedger & Church 1974); Centre for Environmental Studies for fig 4.21 (Brooks 1977), table 4.8 from table 42 (Webber 1975); Centre for Urban and Regional Studies for table 4.1 from Index 7 (Duncan 1971); the author, Professor W A V Clark for fig 5.7 (Clark & Onaka 1983); the author, Professor M Conzen for figs 2.2, 4.3, 4.4 (Conzen 1980); Croom Helm Ltd for table 9.1 (Pressman 1985); Croom Helm Ltd and the author, Professor N Pressman for fig 9.2 (Pressman 1985); the author, Professor W K D Davies for figs 4.11, 4.16, 4.17, 4.18 (Davies 1984); the author, Professor D Dingemans for fig 6.12 (Dingemans 1979); the authors, Professor R M Downs and Professor D Stea for fig 4.24 compiled from figs 7.2, 7.3, 7.4, 7.5 (Orleans 1973) Copyright (c) 1973 by Aldine Publishing Co., New York; the editor and the author, P Salins for fig 4.13 compiled from figs 2.5, 2.10 (Salins 1971); the editor and the author, Professor E H Wohlenberg for fig 3.6 (Wohlenberg 1982); the author, D J Evans for fig 3.10 (Evans & Oulds 1984), fig 3.12 (Evans 1980); the authors, J Forbes and I M L

Robertson for figs 5.5, 5.6 from figs 3.1 (Forbes & Robertson 1978); the author, G Gappert for fig 9.1 (Gappert 1982); Geografiska Annaler for fig 4.5 compiled from figs 2, 13 (Johnston 1969a); the author, Professor P Hall for fig 9.3 (Hall 1984c); the author, D T Herbert for fig 3.5 (Herbert & Raine 1976); Institute of British Geographers for fig 3.3 adapted from fig 2 (Smith & Smith 1978), table 2.1 from table V (Warnes 1973), table 5.3 from table V (Short 1978b), table 5.4 from table 1 (Morgan 1976); the author, Dr P N Jones for fig 7.6 (Jones 1983); Katholieke Universiteit for fig 7.10 from fig 1 (Janelle & Millward 1976); the author, Dr J Kemeny for fig 5.8 (Kemeny 1980); the author, A Kirby for fig 7.13 (Jones & Kirby 1982); the author, P Knox for fig 4.6 (Knox 1984), figs 7.14, 7.15 (Knox 1982); Professor R Lawton for fig 2.6 from fig 12.7 (Dodghson & Butlin 1978); Little, Brown & Co for fig 3.7 (Banfield 1974) Copyright © 1974 by Edward C Banfield; Longman Group UK Ltd for table 7.3 (Knox 1982b); McGraw Hill Book Co for fig 9.4 from fig 7.2 (Pred & Palm 1978); The MIT Press for fig 4.23 from figs 35, 36 (Lynch 1960) Copyright 1960 by The Massachusetts Institute of Technology & the President & Fellowes of Harvard College; New South Wales Department of Environment and Planning for fig 6.7 (Stimpson 1982); Office of Population Censuses & Surveys for table 5.2 from table 5.56 (Office of Population Censuses & Surveys 1978) Crown Copyright; Oxford University Press for fig 5.9 adapted from fig 2.2 (Robson 1975), fig 7.7 from fig 2(2) (Busteed 1975), fig 7.8 adapted from fig 11.5 and table 7.2 adapted from tables 11.4, 11.5, 11.6 (Pinch 1979), table 8.1 (Hampton 1970) © W Hampton 1970; Oxford University Press Inc for table 5.5 from table 5.6 & table 5.6 adapted from tables 5.1, 5.2 (Michelson 1977) Copyright © 1977 by Oxford University Press Inc; Pergamon Journals Ltd and the author, S Pinch for fig 7.1 (Humphreys, Mason & Pinch 1983) Copyright 1983 Pergamon Journals Ltd; Pion Ltd and the authors, W A V Clark & M T Cadwallader for fig 4.27 from fig 3 (Clark & Cadwallader 1973); the author, Professor J P Radford for fig 2.1 (Radford 1979); the author, J H Rae for fig 4.22 (Rae 1983); Royal Scottish Geographical Society for fig 4.8 compiled from figs 1, 2 (Knox 1976); Royal Scottish Geographical Society and the author, Professor E Jones for fig 4.1 slightly adapted from fig 2 (Jones 1958); Shelter for fig 6.13 from fig 2 (Weir 1976); the author, C J Smith for fig 7.9 from fig 10.11 (Smith 1980); Southwark Borough Developing Department for figs 6.3, 6.4, 6.5 from figs 7, 8, 9 & tables 6.2, 6.3 from figs 5, 6 (London Borough of Southwark 1973); Stanford University Press for table 4.2 from table II.I (Shevky & Bell 1955) Copyright 1955 by the Board of Trustees of the Leland Stanford Junior University; the author, P Taylor for figs 6.8, 6.15 (Taylor & Hadfield 1982); Town and Country Planning Association for fig 2.10 from fig 2 (Howard 1965); Universitetsforlaget for fig 4.20 from figs 3, 2 (Aase & Dale 1978); University of California Press for fig 4.10 (Shevky & Bell 1949); University of Chicago Press for fig 3.1 from chart II (Park, Burgess & McKenzie 1925), fig 4.15 (Berry & Rees 1969); University of Chicago Press and the author, R Murdie for figs 4.9, 4.14 from figs 4, 1 (Murdie 1969); University of Chicago Press and the author, Professor O Zunz for table 2.2 (Zunz 1982); University of Florida for fig 4.19 (Smith 1973); the author, D Ward for fig 2.7 (Ward 1983); the author, P White for table 5.1 adapted from table 2 (White 1985); John Wiley & Sons Ltd for fig 3.4 from fig 6.1 (Bell & Newby 1976) Copyright © 1976 John Wiley & Sons Ltd, table 5.7 from table 4.5 (Bourne 1976) Copyright © 1976 John Wiley & Sons Ltd; the author, N J Williams for fig 3.8 (Williams 1985); V H Winston & Sons Inc for figs 6.1, 6.2, 6.14 (Bourne 1981).

We have been unable to trace the author, E Baboolal and the copyright holders in figs 3.2, 4.25, 4.26, 4.28 and 7.3 and would appreciate any information that would enable us to do so.

The photographs at the beginning of each chapter are reproduced by kind permission of the following:

Chapters 1, 2, 3, 5, 6, 8 and 9 – the author, **Paul Knox**
Chapter 4 – US Department of Housing and Urban Development
Chapter 7 – **Ruth Rohr-Zanker.**

# 1 Introduction

At one point in his essay on Boston, Jonathan Raban stops to ask:

why should the Italians all cram themselves behind the expressway in the North End? Why should Negroes live in Roxbury and Jews in Chelsea? By what law do Boston suburbs turn into rigidly circumscribed ghettoes when they look so much alike, so quaintly attractive, so prim, so dull? For it is as if someone had taken a map of the city and, resolutely blind to its topography, had coloured in irregularly-shaped lumps labelled 'Blacks', 'Jews', 'Irish', 'Academics', 'Gentry', 'Italians', 'Chinese', 'Assorted Others' (Raban 1975: 216).

For the geographer, such questions present themselves in more general terms, so that the major issues become: why do city populations get sifted out according to race and social class to produce distinctive neighbourhoods? And how? In addition, the geographer is interested in a number of supplementary issues. Are there, for example, any other criteria by which individuals and households become physically segregated within the city? To what extent is territory relevant to the operation of local social systems? How does a person's area of residence affect his behaviour? How do people choose where to live, and what are the constraints on their choices? What groups, if any, are able to manipulate the 'geography' of the city, and to whose advantage?

As many writers now acknowledge, the answer to most of these questions is ultimately to be found in the wider context of social, economic and political organization. In short, the city must be seen as a reflection of the society which maintains it. It follows that the study of the city should not be abstracted from its historical, cultural and economic matrix. It also follows that a proper understanding of the city requires an interdisciplinary approach, whatever the ultimate focus of attention. In the city, everything is connected to everything else, and the deficiencies of one academic specialism must be compensated for by the emphases of others. The boundaries of 'urban social geography' are therefore ill-defined, and its subject-matter is shared with history, economics, politics, sociology, demography, anthropology, social psychology, planning and social administration. Moreover, because urban social geography is comparatively recent in its development as an academic specialism, it cannot yet be said to represent a coherent or distinctive approach. Rather, it encompasses an eclectic mixture of ideas, theories and empirical research which collectively can be considered to lead (to borrow Jones and Eyles' definition (1977: 6) of social geography) to: (i) an *understanding* 'of the patterns which arise from the use social groups make of space as they see it, and of the processes involved in making and changing such patterns' and; (ii) an *appreciation* 'of the social patterns and processes arising from the distribution of, and access to, scarce resources' in the city.

This eclecticism is compounded by the coexistence, within geography as a whole, of several different approaches to knowledge and understanding. According to Johnston (1977), three main approaches have been identifiable in the recent literature of urban geography. The first is a quantitative and descriptive approach, based on a philosophy in which the geographer's role is to document the spatial organization of society. Its explanatory concepts are derived partly from neoclassical economics and partly from the functional sociology of Talcott Parsons. Second is the so-called behavioural approach, which emerged in the mid-1960s as a reaction to the normative assumptions of neoclassical-functional description. The emphasis here is on the study of people's activities and decision-making processes (where to live, for example) within their perceived worlds. Many of the explanatory concepts are derived from social psychology although phenomenological philosophy, with its emphasis on the ways in which people experience the world around them, has also exerted a considerable influence on behavioural research. Finally there is the 'radical' approach, which stresses the constraints on the behaviour of individuals which are imposed by the organization of society as a whole and by the activities of powerful groups and institutions within it. At its broadest level, this approach looks to political science for its explanatory concepts, focusing on the idea of power and conflict as the main determinants of locational behaviour and resource allocation. In this context, the 'managerialist' ideas of Ray Pahl (1969; 1975) have been influential but the chief source of inspiration has been Marxist theory and its modern derivatives.

Although there is some scope for a rapprochement between these different approaches (Gregory 1978; Hay 1979; Johnston 1979a) it seems likely that urban social geography must continue for some time yet as a rather mixed bag, straddling macro and micro concerns with a wide range of methodological and philosophical perspectives but without a commonly agreed theoretical framework. However, as Johnston (1979a) and others have pointed out, this is not necessarily a bad thing, particularly from the educational point of view, where the objective may be the broad one of developing an empathetic understanding of the city. Meanwhile, it should be emphasized that urban social geography is not merely a collection of subject matter and philosophy culled from other disciplines with a common focus provided by a holistic concern for the city. Geography's traditional concern with inter-relationships between people and their physical and social environments provides a basis for study which, while not comprehensive, is broader than most. Moreover, space itself should not simply be regarded as a medium in which social, economic and political processes are expressed. It is of importance in its own right in contributing both to the pattern of urban development and to the nature of the relationships between different social groups within the city. While not necessarily the dominant factor in shaping patterns of social interaction, distance is undeniably important as a determinant of social networks, friendships and marriages. Similarly, territoriality is frequently the basis for the development of distinctive social milieux which, as well as being of interest in themselves, are important because of their capacity to mould the attitudes and shape the behaviour of their inhabitants. Distance also emerges as a significant determinant of the quality of life in different parts of the city because of variations in physical accessibility to opportunities and amenities such as jobs, shops, schools, clinics, parks and sports centres. Because the benefits conferred by proximity to these amenities contribute so much to people's welfare, locational issues also often form the focus of inter-class conflict within the city, thus giving the spatial perspective a key role in the analysis of urban politics. The partitioning of space through the establishment of de jure territorial boundaries also represents an important spatial attribute which has direct repercussions on several spheres of urban life. The location of local authority boundaries helps to determine their fiscal standing, for example; while the boundaries of school catchment areas have important implications for community status and welfare; and the configuration of electoral districts is crucial to the outcome of formal political contests in the city.

The geographer therefore has a considerable contribution to make to urban social studies. Moreover, the geographer is uniquely placed to provide descriptive analyses of cities. Although it is fashionable to play down the 'mapping' role of geography, the identification of spatial patterns and spatial linkages within the city provides a basic source of material both for educationalists and policymakers. Similarly, the geographer's traditional concern with the 'distinctiveness of place' and areal differentiation is very relevant to the study of the city, for it is widely accepted that, while cities must be seen as wholes and, ultimately, as part of the wider social and economic system, they comprise a 'mosaic' of different neighbourhoods and districts. Here, the geographer's ability to synthesize a wide variety of environmental, social and economic characteristics and to identify distinctive regions is germane both to theory and practice in urban analysis. Thus, for example, the identification of urban 'problem regions' and their salient characteristics has occupied an increasing number of geographers since the concern for 'relevance' in geographic research emerged as a major issue within the discipline in the early 1970s. More recently, there has been a revival of interest in regionalism as an academic approach, emphasizing the locally unique factors which modify the more general forces which shape urban residential structure. Gregory, for example, in his book on *Ideology, Science and Human Geography*, calls for a general revival of the regional approach (which had been discredited because of the low intellectual level of much work done in its name during the 1950s and 1960s) on the simple grounds that 'spatial structures are implicated in social structures and each has to be theorized with the other' (Gregory 1978: 172).

Certainly it is the distinctiveness of particular neighbourhoods and districts and the 'sense of place' associated with them that gives the city its fascination not only to geographers but also to writers from a wide variety of disciplines. Take, for example, the variety of neighbourhoods one finds in a 'typical' medium-sized British city (Harrison 1974). At one end of the spectrum is the run-down inner-city neighbourhood of old terraces where the dwellings, many of them without an inside lavatory, look out on the blackened remains of dead and dying factories. Children play games in the street amid roaming dogs

and old women beating carpets, cleaning windows, or just gossiping. Similar, and yet very different, are the nearby neighbourhoods of terraced housing jammed between railway lines and now occupied by Asian or West Indian immigrants and their families. Even the shops here are immigrant-owned, apart from those run by a few diehard white corner-shopkeepers whose premises betray the poor state of their trade. The houses, having been inherited from the city's indigenous working classes, are now orientalized and caribbeanized by exotic colour schemes: bright pink and dull turquoise, ochre and cobalt blue. Further along the socio-economic spectrum and on the outer edges of the inner city are neighbourhoods of mixed tenure and varied character, where an ageing population struggles to maintain respectability in the midst of a steadily deteriorating environment. Here and there are groups of two or three newer houses, squeezed into gaps in the urban fabric and sporting imitation coach lamps, frosted-glass porches and some young rose bushes in a brave attempt to elevate their status against all the evidence of their surroundings. At about the same distance from the city centre there may be a small neighbourhood of formerly artisan houses which have been 'gentrified' by an influx of prosperous young professionals. The character of such areas is derived more from the life-style of their new inhabitants than from anything else:

Their cars are grimly economic and ecological, as near to bicycles as four wheels and the internal combustion engine will allow – the Deux Cheveaux, the Renault 4L, the baby Fiat and the Volkswagen. Here children play with chunky all-wood Abbatt toys; here girl-wives grill anaemic escalopes of veal; everyone takes the *Guardian* (Raban 1975: 88).

For the most part though, the more prosperous neighbourhoods are suburban. At the top end of the socio-economic scale there is usually a sequestered area of soundly-built, older houses standing in their own plots amid an abundance of trees and shrubbery. With increasing distance from this core of affluence and respectability is a series of neighbourhoods of diminishing status whose individuality is to be found in subtle variations of garage space, garden size and the architectural detail of the houses – all of which are owned, or are at least in the process of being purchased, by their inhabitants. In these neighbourhoods, children definitely do not play in the streets, and the shopping centres are dotted with freezer food centres, fashion shops and boutiques selling cane chairs, paper lamp-shades, herb racks and reproduction tea caddies. Finally, and sharing the fringe of the city with the most recent of the middle-class neighbourhoods, there is a series of public housing estates, graded into distinctive neighbourhoods through a combination of landscape architecture and the age structure, public comportment and social reputation of their inhabitants. Like the newer privately-built estates, they have few neighbourhood amenities. There are few shops or pubs, probably no doctor's surgery, no playgrounds, and a poor bus service into town.

This picture is by no means exhaustive: a full listing would have to include student bed-sitter neighbourhoods, redeveloped inner-city areas, red light districts, and so on. It is also important to remember that although a similar variety of neighbourhoods exists in cities of other countries, their character and *raison d'être* may be quite different. Compare, for example, the description of a typical medium-sized British city given above with this description of 'Anycity USA':

Anycity, USA is laid out on a grid street pattern. At its centre are new glass and steel corporate towers. . . . One of its main retail streets has been converted to a brick surfaced pedestrian mall. It is lined by a mixture of large department stores, older establishments catering to lower income consumers, and a scattering of new boutiques, record stores, health clubs and bookstores with racks of greeting cards. . . . Within the city centre is an imposing city hall, county headquarters, or domed State capitol building surrounded by green lawns and sporting the appropriate flags. Adjacent to downtown are several old industrial districts located near rail lines or canalized rivers. There are still a few active mills, factories and warehouses, but others are boarded up, awaiting 'adaptive reuse' or demolition. Some signs of redevelopment appear in warehouses converted to residential condominium apartments or artists' lofts. Nearby is skid row where homeless people (including an increasing number of women) drink from bottles in paper bags and varieties of 'adult' entertainment are purveyed. Not far from the city centre is an historic district of renovated Victorian homes with shady trees, olive green doors, brass fittings and wrought iron lamp standards. But most of the inner city housing is in apartment blocks and terraced or semi-detached houses in various stages of deterioration and renovation.

Perhaps the most quintessentially American part of Anycity is its postwar suburbs. Sprawling in most directions for several miles are single family ranch style or split level homes on lots of an eighth of an acre. Most have garages, with the second family car (or boat or pickup truck) parked in the driveway. The grid iron street pattern is replaced by a curvilinear one in more affluent neighbourhoods. There are few fences or hedges, nor, compared to the equivalent European neighbourhoods, many flower beds. . . . Anycity's suburbs have local shopping centres with convenience stores and fast food outlets, often close by some apartment complexes. . . . The suburban fringe is also the location of large 'regional' shopping centres . . . surrounded by an ocean of parking lots. Increasingly, industrial parks, seeking cheaper land and lower taxes, locate in suburban tracts – especially those adjacent to interstate highways. The parks are both the site of manufacturing industries and of corporate office buildings. As the outer suburbs or the rural-urban fringe is reached, the lots are larger and land once farmed lies unworked, awaiting the best offer from a developer (Holcomb, forthcoming).

The present book is concerned with cities in Western countries which have 'post-industrial' societies, particularly those of the English-speaking world, where levels of urbanization are amongst the highest anywhere. References to cities elsewhere are included not to redress this bias but to provide contrasting or complementary examples and to place arguments within a wider setting. The principal focus of attention is upon British and North American cities, reflecting the weight and distribution of published research in urban social geography as well as the origins of much of the relevant social, economic and urban theory. Even within this relatively narrow cultural and geographical realm, however, there are important differences in the nature of the urban environment. These will be elaborated in the body of the text but, as Robson (1975) points out, it is important to guard against 'cultural myopia' from the very beginning of any discussion of urban geography. It is, therefore, worth briefly pointing to the principal differences between British and North American cities. For one thing, British cities are generally much older, with a tangible legacy of earlier modes of economic and social organization embedded within their physical structure and, sometimes, carried over into present-day attitudes and behaviour. Another contrast is in the composition of urban populations, for in Britain the significance of ethnic minority groups is much less than in North America. A third major difference stems from the way in which urban government has evolved. Whereas North American cities tend to be fragmented into a number of quite separate and independent municipalities, British cities are less so and their public services are funded to a significant level by the central government, making for a potentially more even-handed allocation of resources within the city as a whole. This is not unrelated to yet another important source of contrast – the existence of a well-developed welfare state in Britain. This not only affects the size and allocation of the 'social wage' within cities but also has had profound effects on the social geography of the city through the operation of the housing market. Whereas fewer than 5 per cent of US urban families live in public housing, over 30 per cent of the families in most British cities live in dwellings rented from public authorities. Finally, it is worth noting that in Britain, where the general ideology of privatism is less pronounced and where there has for some time been an acute awareness of the pressures of urban sprawl on prime agricultural land, the power and influence of the city planning machine is much more extensive. As a result, the morphology and social structure of British cities owes much to planning codes and philosophies. Thus, for example, the decentralization of jobs and homes and the proliferation of out-of-town hypermarkets and shopping malls has

been much less pronounced in Britain than in North America, mainly because of the British planners' policy of urban containment. The corollary of this, of course, is that the central business districts (CBDs) of British cities have tended to retain a greater commercial vitality than many of their North American counterparts. Finally, it should be noted that there are important *regional* and *functional* differences in the social geography of cities within countries and continents: the cities of the American 'Snowbelt' (or 'Rustbelt') are significantly different, in some ways, from those of the 'Sunbelt', for example, as are those of Canada and the United States (Goldberg and Mercer 1986).

The format adopted in this book is mainly thematic, with an emphasis on pattern and empirical analysis which directly reflects the nature of much of the work done in urban social geography. Background theory is introduced where relevant but no particular theoretical perspective or academic approach is given special emphasis because the belief which underlies the book is that no single body of theory and no one approach to knowledge can be expected to provide all the answers to the questions currently of concern to urban geographers. It is also worth pointing out at this stage that because the emphasis of the book is on social activities and processes of residential differentiation, there are some aspects of urban structure (such as the nature and location of urban commercial and industrial activity and the spatial characteristics of the CBD) which are only dealt with indirectly, in so far as they affect people's behaviour, their residential opportunities and their general welfare. The chapter which follows is a brief summary of the principal consequences of the evolution of the modern city from its pre-industrial origins through the crucial transformation of the Victorian era to its current form. This not only provides an essential factual foundation upon which to build an understanding of the social geography of the modern city but also serves to introduce a number of important concepts and processes which are elaborated in subsequent chapters.

CONTRA GIFTS & CRAFTS

# 2 Historical perspectives on the city

An appreciation of urban history is vital to the student of urban social geography. The social relationships, class structures, ideologies and institutions forged during earlier stages of urban development can be directly traced to the modern city, where they continue to shape urban lifestyles and to constrain the behaviour of people, businesses and governments. Moreover, the historic city obtrudes as a visible factor in the contemporary landscape of cities throughout Europe and North America, revealing itself in turn as historic artefact, slum district, or, more subtly, as the morphological template upon which successive waves of urban renewal and land-use change have taken place. By examining the historical development of cities it is therefore possible to identify both the physical and the social bases of modern urbanism which are central to the patterns and processes dealt with in subsequent chapters of this book.

This chapter provides an outline to the development of Western cities from the early pre-industrial/pre-capitalist stages through the transitional stage of the eighteenth and early nineteenth centuries and the crucial Victorian era to the modern capitalist city. The focus of attention is on the changing relationships between people and neighbourhoods in response to changes in economic organization and the consequent effects of changes in technology, social organization, family relationships and people's attitudes towards living in the city. Particular emphasis is given to three themes: the instrumental role of transport technology in the physical development and residential differentiation of cities; the effects of the changing balance of economic power on the ethos and goals of urban government; and the translation of the prevailing spirit and ideology of different groups of people at different times into the bricks and mortar of the built environment. In pursuing this approach it is inevitable that the diversity of individual cities must give way to rather broad generalizations. Yet, as we shall see, cities responded in different ways and at different times to the common economic and social forces to which they were subject, rendering any generalization vulnerable to the specific experience of an individual town or city.

In nineteenth-century England, for example, the social geography of individual cities varied significantly according to: (1) size; (2) demographic characteristics; (3) local socio-political structure; (4) the local strength and diversity of religious adherence; (5) the size and composition of migrant populations; and (6) local land tenure arrangements (Dennis 1984). It is important to bear this variability in mind from the outset, therefore, and the reader is encouraged to set the generalizations made here against the greater detail of urban history portrayed in works such as *Victorian Cities* (Briggs 1968), *The Urban Wilderness* (Warner 1972), *Housing and the Spatial Structure of the City* (Pritchard 1976) and *The Changing Face of Inequality* (Zunz 1982).

## The transformation of urban structure

### The pre-capitalist city

Before the full emergence of capitalistic economies in the eighteenth century and the advent of the Industrial Revolution in the nineteenth century, cities were essentially small-scale settlements based on a mercantile economy and a rigid social order stemming from the tradition of medieval feudalism. The conventional wisdom concerning the social geography of these cities is derived from Sjoberg's (1960) model, in which the spatial expression of the division of pre-industrial society into a small élite and a much larger proletariat was marked by a pleasant and exclusive central core surrounded by a crowded, poorly-built and garbage-strewn periphery (Fig. 2.1). According to Sjoberg, the élite group consisted of those in control of the religious, political, administrative and social functions of the city. Merchants – even wealthy ones – were generally excluded from the élite because a 'pre-occupation with money and other mundane pursuits ran counter to the religious-philosophical value system of the dominant group' (Sjoberg 1960: 83). Responding to these values, the élite tended to favour a residential location close to the administrative, political and religious institutions which were typically located in the centre of the city, thus producing an exclusive, high-status core. In time, the élite came to be increasingly segregated from the rest of urban society, partly because of the repulsiveness of the rest of the city and its inhabitants, and partly because of a clustering reinforced by bonds of kinship and inter-marriage amongst the élite.

Beyond this core area lived the lower classes, although not in an undifferentiated mass. Distinct socio-economic clusters developed as a result of the spatial association of craftsmen of different kinds, reinforced by social organizations such as guilds, which fostered the group cohesion and spatial propinquity of their members. Less well-organized groups, including the poor, members of ethnic and religious minority groups, people engaged in particularly malodorous jobs such as tanning, and people who could only find intermittent menial employment carting, sweeping or peddling, found themselves pushed to the outskirts of the city in extensive but densely inhabited tracts of the very worst housing.

This idea of a social geography characterized by an exclusive central core surrounded by a wider area over which status and wealth steadily diminished with distance from the city centre has been questioned by Vance (1971),

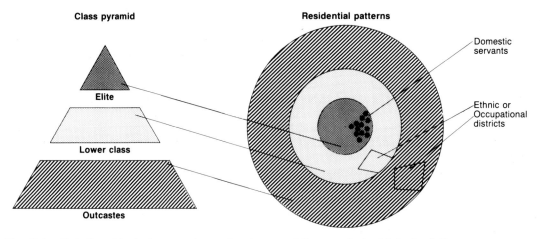

**Fig. 2.1**   Relationship between class structure and the pre-industrial city (after Sjoberg).   *Source*: Radford (1979) Fig. 1, p. 394.

who attaches much greater significance to the *occupational* clustering arising from the inter-relationships between social and economic organization promoted by the craft guilds. For Vance, the early city was 'many centred' in distinct craft quarters – metalworking, wood-working, weaving, and so on – each with its own shops, workplaces and wide social spec-trum of inhabitants. The political, social and economic advantages conferred by guild membership reinforced the external econ-omies derived from spatial association, creating tight clusters of population living under a patriarchal social system headed by the master craftsmen. Within each of the occupational districts, dwellings, workshops and storerooms were arranged with a *vertical* rather than horizontal structuring of space, with workshops on the ground floor, the master's family quarters on the floor above and, higher still, the storerooms and rooms of the journeymen, apprentices and servants. Beyond the specialized craft quarters Vance recognized, like Sjoberg, the existence of a fringe population of the very poorest of the proletariat and a central core area inhabited by the city's élite. Unlike Sjoberg, however, Vance allows these groups only a minor impact on the social geography of the city. The result is a model of the city in which spatial differentiation is dominated by a mosaic of occupational districts, with class and status stratification contributing a secondary dimension which is more important vertically than horizontally.

## The urban transformation

As with much social history, we do not yet have enough evidence from comparative studies to judge which of these two models is the more accurate. A study of ante-bellum Charleston (South Carolina) concluded that Sjoberg had exaggerated and overgeneralized, but that his model was 'plausible' (Radford 1979). In Britain, Jones (1980) and Langton (1975) have tested the ideas of both Sjoberg and Vance against the available statistics on the distribution of wealth in seventeenth-century London and in Dublin, Exeter and Newcastle upon Tyne. Both models were found wanting, though again there was some corroborative support for Sjoberg's model.

For present purposes, however, it is prob-ably more helpful to stress the points of common agreement between the two models. Both portray a city in which everything physical was at a human scale, a 'walking city' in which the distances between home and work were even more tightly constrained by the organization of work into patriarchal and familial groupings. Both portray an immutable social order based on a traditional and essen-tially non-materialistic value system; and both recognize the existence (though with different emphasis) of a patrician élite residing in the core of the city, a number of occupationally distinctive but socially mixed 'quarters' in intermediate locations, and a residual popu-lation of the very poor living on the outskirts of the city.

The modern city has inherited few of these characteristics, social or morphological. Some, like Bologna, Bruges, Norwich and Stirling have been fortunate enough to retain their castles, cathedrals, palaces and other insti-tutional buildings, together, perhaps, with frag-ments of the pre-industrial residential fabric. Others, like Aigues-Mortes, Bernkastel and Tewkesbury have been bypassed by change and have retained much of the appearance of the pre-industrial city, albeit in a sanitized, renovated and picture-postcard way. For the most part, though, cities have altered radi-cally. Not only has most of the older fabric of the city been replaced (often several times), but the relative location of the city's major components and the relationships between them have greatly altered. The social geog-raphy of the city has been turned inside out, with the rich exchanging their central location for the peripheral location of the poor. Occu-pational clustering has given way to residential differentiation in terms of status and family structure; power and status in the city are no longer determined by traditional values but by wealth; ownership of land has become di-vorced from its use; workplace and home have become separated; and family structure has been transformed from an extended, patriarchal system to the small, nuclear family unit.

A social geography has thus evolved which is radically different from Vance's city of socially-mixed occupational districts, and which is the *inverse* of Sjoberg's merchant city: poverty is almost universally concentrated in the inner city, with wealth predominantly on the periphery. The causes of this profound realignment are primarily economic, rooted in the emergence of capitalism as the dominant means of production and exchange and buttressed by the technology which subsequently emerged during the Industrial Revolution. As Radford (1981) notes, the changes in scale, heterogeneity and orientation that accompanied industrialization can largely be accounted for by the operation of three sets of forces:

1. The advent of factory-based industry and the resulting physical and psychological separation of home and work.
2. The impact of intra-urban transportation innovations.
3. The expansion and differentiation of central business districts.

Not surprisingly, this transformation of economies, societies and cities was complex in its development, with inter-related events often occluding cause and effect. Nevertheless, it is worth sketching out the major components of change – insofar as they affected the social geography of cities – in rough sequence.

Probably the most fundamental change to emerge with the rise of capitalism and its new system of production – the factory – was the creation of two *new social groups*: the industrial capitalists and the unskilled factory workers. These two groups respectively formed the basis of a new élite and a new proletariat which replaced the old order. As the accumulation of capital by individuals became not only morally acceptable but also the dominant criterion of status and power, the entrepreneurs introduced a new, materialistic *value system* to urban affairs.

Meanwhile, traditional forms and modes of *culture* were lost or blurred as the collective experience of urban life brought new cultural forms and new social and economic institutions, including the apartment house, the department store, the sports stadium and the vaudeville house (Barth 1980; Bailey 1983). The new economic order also wrought important changes in terms of *age-* and *gender-based social cleavages*. For example, as the apprenticeship of artisans became less common, fewer young men boarded with master craftmen: instead, home residence was prolonged as compulsory education laws were passed (in response to the numeracy and literacy required by the new economy) and schooling became the key to social mobility. As a result, 'a socially defined stage of life called adolescence emerged at the end of the nineteenth century' (Moch 1983: 130), and a new youth culture emerged. Moreover, the novelty and momentum of urban life placed a premium on youthful energy and drive while undermining respect for age and experience: 'In the unending rush for the new, older people were pushed aside . . . long before they had outlived their usefulness' (Barth 1980: 19). More dramatic was the reorganization of family life, and in particular the changing role of women. On the one hand, working-class women were increasingly drawn out of their dominant role in the domestic economy and into subordinate roles in the formal economy of manufacturing and services. On the other hand, middle-class women were increasingly allocated roles as homemakers in the new, privatized lifestyle of the bourgeoisie.

Competition for the best and most accessible sites for the new factories and for the warehouses, shops and offices which depended on them brought about the first crucial change in *land use*. Land was given over to uses which could justify the highest rent, rather than being held by a traditional group of users. The factory and commercial sites secured; there sprang up around them large tracts of housing to accommodate the workers and their families. The new urban structure became increasingly *differentiated*, with homes no longer used as workplaces and residential areas graded according to the rents different sites could command. Social status, newly ascribed in terms of money, became synonymous with rent-paying ability, so that neighbourhoods were, in effect, created along status divisions.

Inevitably, since the size and quality of

dwellings was positively linked with price, and price with builders' profits, housing built for the lowest-paid, lowest-status groups was of the lowest quality, crammed in at high densities in order to cover the costs of the ground rent. At the same time, the wealthy moved to new locations on the urban fringe. Edged out from the inner city by factories and warehouses, the wealthy were in any case anxious to add physical distance to the social distance between themselves and the bleak misery of the growing working-class districts adjacent to the factories. Encouraged by the introduction of *new transport services* in the early nineteenth century, they were, therefore, easily lured to the fashionable new dwellings being built in the *suburbs* by speculators with an eye towards this lucrative new market.

Later, as the full effects of a dramatic excess of births over deaths (which resulted largely from improvements in medical practice and public health) were reinforced by massive *immigration* (in response to the cities' increased range and number of opportunities), the rate of urban growth accelerated. Changes in *building technology* made it possible for cities to grow upwards as well as outwards, and the *cyclical growth* of the capitalist economy, with successive improvements in urban infrastructure produced a sequence of growth phases which endowed the modern city with a series of patchy but distinctive suburban zones.

Thus, although the transformation of urban social geography which paralleled the emergence of capitalism was radical and abrupt, it was a complex process, and it is useful to identify several intermediate stages of urban development, each with its own social geography and each contributing to both the morphological and the social inheritance of the capitalist city of today. Although it is dangerous to be pedantic about the timing of historical epochs, several writers have found Mumford's periodization of 1820 to 1870, 1870 to 1920 and 1920 to the present to be effective in dealing with the different stages of American urban development (Mumford 1934, 1940; Borchert 1967; Warner 1972.) In Europe, and particularly in Britain, the equivalent periods would approximate to the years

1780 to 1830, 1830 to 1920, and 1920 to the present. Nevertheless, generalizations about phases of urban development anywhere are easily confounded. Mill towns in both Britain and the United States, for example, exhibited many of the features of industrial capitalism at a time when most other cities were still dominated by the petty commodity mode of production which was transitional between the pre-capitalist city and the industrial city of Victorian times (Walker 1978). In this chapter, therefore, nominal periods with overlapping and unwritten chronological boundaries are used to categorize the major stages in the development of the capitalist city: the Transitional City, the Victorian City, and the Modern City.

## The transitional city

The last quarter of the eighteenth century and the first half of the nineteenth century were the years of the perfection of machine tools and the development of steam engines. Yet for all the new technology there was little mechanized production, except in textiles and in some aspects of ironworking. More significant for urban development were the new transport networks – canals and railways – which gave impetus to the large regional city and to the consequent organization of the economy around regional marketing and financial centres. Nevertheless, even the biggest cities of the transitional period were relatively compact: most could be comfortably traversed on foot in under one hour. Within these cities, business was still very much on a small scale, and in most cases the artisan competed quite successfully with the sweatshop factory. The modest spatial requirements of most business enterprises meant that workshops and factories tended to be dispersed throughout the city, with only a primitive specialization of land use. Even the more fashionable districts of larger cities contained a variety of factories, workshops and other businesses. In New York's Washington Square area, for example, there were nearly fifty factories, turning out pianos, cabinet furniture, chocolate, carriages, trunks, clothing, and even soap and candles (Burrell 1865, reported in Warner 1972: 82). Burrell's survey also identified over 500 stores in the area, together with 234 'dram shops', 23 'lager bier saloons', 17 gambling saloons, 7 concert saloons, 76 brothels and 22 'policy shops'.

As Warnes (1973) points out, realistic generalizations about the social geography of the emerging industrial city are difficult to make because of this apparent disorganization and because of the strong local influence of valuable cultivable land and of mineral resources, water power, transport facilities and economic specialization. Nevertheless, the transitional city did have a loose internal structure which could be recognized in both small industrial towns and larger commercial cities. Occupation was still the chief influence on residential location, as Warnes, drawing on the example of Chorley (Lancashire), has shown:

. . . non-landed gentry, including professional people, lived near the centre of towns along with shopkeepers and workers, publicans and small manufacturers of consumer goods, all attracted by the point of most profitable exchange. Small-holders, who formed a large proportion of

domestic manufacturers, were necessarily more predominant on the less built-up periphery of the town, as would be those groups working the mineral resources of the area, such as miners and brick-makers. Water-powered factories, and their workers, were also scattered because of the limited number of stream-side sites, but when powered by steam they were attracted to the source of fuel, whether mine or, more often, transport terminal. They were therefore more clustered and often nearer to the centre of the urban area (Warnes 1973: 181).

Johann Kohl, a nineteenth-century observer, summarized this common pattern into the form of an idealized model in which he portrayed the city as being structured both horizontally and vertically, with decreasing desirability of locations above and below the ground floor and first floor of each building and with increasing distance from the city centre (Kohl 1841, reported in Peucker 1968, and Berry and Rees 1969).

Following these observations, the principal features of the social geography of the transitional city are summarized in Table 2.1 and Fig. 2.2 (top). In larger cities, these proto-neighbourhoods had a more pronounced

**Table 2.1**  Residential structure of the emerging industrial city

|  | Centre | Adjacent to centre | Intermediate | Periphery |
|---|---|---|---|---|
| Lower floors | Professional classes | Non-landed gentry |  | Landed nobility and gentry |
|  | Shop and inn keepers | Town houses in larger towns and cities | Unskilled and semi-skilled workers in domestic or non-domestic employment | Smallholders, domestic manufacturers |
|  | Consumer-goods manufacturers, e.g. bankers, tailors, cordwainers |  | Mobile population, with recent immigrants | Workers at water-powered factories |
|  |  |  | Typical employers: workshops, factories, foundries, gasworks, rope works and timber yards | Mineral workers, e.g. brickmakers, miners, quarrymen |
| Upper floors, cellars, yards, back premises | House, shop and office servants | House servants |  | House servants |
| Institutions | Religious and educational establishments | Religious and educational establishments | Old and destitute in workhouse and almshouses |  |

*Source:* Warnes, (1973): 180.

**Fig. 2.2** Changing land use ecology of the nineteenth-century large US city.
*Source*: Conzen (1980) Fig. 1, p. 123.

atmosphere and character. The central, downtown areas were an unlikely mixture of densely-packed workshops, stores, factories and slaughter-houses side by side with the more genteel firms that dealt in law, banking and insurance. Just beyond this area would be a few streets dominated by the homes of the wealthy merchants, manufacturers and professionals who could afford the increasingly valuable land and who wished to enjoy the prominence and convenience of a central address. Belgravia in London, the Rue du Faubourg St Honoré in Paris, Beacon Hill in Boston, Chestnut Street in Philadelphia and Westmount in Montreal survive as reminders of the housing preferences of a large section of the élite. These early versions of 'nob hill' and 'millionaires' row' also set the axes of fashion in their respective cities, so that when subsequent growth drove the wealthy further out, their new homes advanced in the same general direction that had been initiated by their inner-city residences (Firey 1947; Hoyt 1939).

Near to these prestigious areas were the decaying neighbourhoods in which owners subdivided houses into rooms, garrets and cellars for the poor, who crowded in to be near downtown jobs. These formed the basis for the 'rookeries' which expanded during the Victorian era to overwhelm almost the whole of the inner-city area. In some cases, a local neighbourhood served as a tight-knit industrial quarter of its own, given over to shoemaking or metalworking: a legacy from the occupational districts of the pre-industrial city. Indeed, the largest and most rapidly-growing cities of all, being encircled by a 'shanty-town' housing immigrant labour (Ward 1971), bore a superficial resemblance in their spatial structure to the pattern of Sjoberg's pre-industrial city. For the most part, though, the proletariat of the transitional city mingled with middle-class families, renting small rooms and apartments all over the city, in neighbourhoods which were apparently haphazard and disorganized:

Boardinghouses stood beside prosperous homes, mill workers crowded around a suburban establishment. . ., while the owner's home stood alone across a field from the group. Another row

of houses for downtown workers might stand a block away, and back lots were universally crammed with stables and blacksmiths' shops and lumber yards (Warner 1972: 83).

## The Victorian city

The Victorian city was at once the product and the agent of almost cataclysmic economic, social and demographic change. It was, as Briggs has observed 'a characteristic Victorian achievement, impressive in scale but limited in vision, creating new opportunities but also providing massive problems' (Briggs 1968: 16). By the end of the century, cities had changed radically in terms of territorial scale, organizational complexity, population growth, levels of mobility, technology and culture. Geographically, this meant:

specially created areas of uniformly expensive housing, often suburban or fringe in location, and paid for either through low densities on high value land (reasonably central) or distant low densities brought functionally close through transport links. This segregated city pressed the poor into near-central ghettos and relied on housing filtering and neighborhood change to accommodate social mobility. By then, the central business district had become the nerve-centre of the urban economy and cultural activity, and industry conspired with transport corridors to demarcate the residential cells of the metropolis (Conzen 1980: 122) (see Fig. 2.2, bottom).

Central to this whole stage of urban development was the unprecedented *rate* of urban growth, triggered by the movement of immigrants in response to the opportunities and demands of industrialization and reinforced by the growing momentum of the natural increase in population arising from the demographic transition (Lees and Lees 1976; Vance 1977; Lampard 1983). With London already a sprawling commercial city of 900,000 in 1801, British provincial cities were the first to reflect these demographic changes. Between 1821 and 1831, Manchester, Leeds, Glasgow, Liverpool, Dundee, Birmingham and Bradford all grew at astonishing rates of between 45 and 65 per cent; and the increase continued in the following two decades, though at a somewhat diminished rate. By 1851, several of these cities had grown to conurbations of a quarter of a million, while London had grown to 2.5 millions and over half the total population of England and Wales lived in settlements classified as 'urban' (Lawton 1983). Later, London's rate of growth gathered momentum, creating an awesome mass of humanity. Between 1881 and 1891 the four communities with the highest rates of population growth in Britain were all in London: Leyton, Tottenham, West Ham and Willesden; and by 1911 London had growth to nearly five millions (Briggs 1968). Elsewhere – in Europe and North America – comparable rates of growth occurred somewhat later, concentrated in the late Victorian period. In the United States, the proportion of the total population living in cities of 25,000 or more increased from 12 per cent in 1860 to 36 per cent in 1920; and in the same period the number of cities of 250,000 or more inhabitants increased from 3 to 25 (Ward 1971). Moreover, whereas Manchester had been the 'shock city' of the early Victorian period, Chicago became the 'shock city' of the 1860s and 1870s, growing from less than 30,000 in 1850 to nearly 300,000 by 1870.

### Immigrants and ghettos

The immigrant populations which continually shaped and reshaped the character and composition of Victorian urban society created an urban environment – physical, social and political – which was not only of great contemporary concern but which is also of crucial importance to the understanding of many of the legacies and problems of the modern city. In most of the larger cities and conurbations, the numerically dominant working-class population was derived almost entirely from rural migrants and from immigrants from poorer nations. In the United States, foreign immigrants were especially important (Table 2.2). By 1890 New York contained more foreign born residents than any city in the world. The city had half as many Italians as Naples, as many Germans as Hamburg, twice as many Irish as Dublin, and two and a half times the number of Jews in Warsaw. In 1893 Chicago contained the third largest Bohemian community in the world; by the time of the First World War, Chicago ranked only behind Warsaw and Lodz as a city of Poles. Noticeable also was the fact that four out of five people living in New York in 1890 had either been born abroad or were of foreign parentage (Glaab and Brown 1967: 139).

In Britain, the influx of immigrants was less cosmopolitan, consisting chiefly of poor Irish labourers, many of whom might have preferred to emigrate to North America if they could have saved the extra fare. In the mid-nineteenth century they were the biggest group of immigrants in many British cities – especially Glasgow, Liverpool and Manchester (Lawton 1959) – and to them attached the stigma of the ghetto which was attached successively to Irish, German, Jewish, Italian and Eastern European immigrants in the cities of the United States Upper Midwest and eastern seaboard. These 'internal colonies' and ghettos were in fact the first and most conspicuous consequence of the massive immigration of outsiders on the social geography of the city. Confined to the cheap housing of the deteriorating inner city because their lack of skills and experience could command only the lowest-paid jobs, migrants of different races, language, ethnicity and religion tended to cluster together in response to family ties and the bond of common language and culture in a strange and often hostile environment. In Huddersfield, for example, the Irish population was concentrated in two groups of neighbourhoods immediately east and west of the town centre (Fig. 2.3 (i)), where they accounted for up to 25 per cent of the resident population. Within these neighbourhoods, however, there were marked concentrations of Irish families in certain blocks and courts (Fig. 2.3 (ii)). As Dennis (1984) notes, such segregation was sometimes compounded by social segregation as various kinds of institution were established with the intention of promoting cultural solidarity among migrants. It is also important to note that there were important distinctions *within* the Irish population. One was the distinction between pre-Famine migrants, who were socially acceptable to the English population, and Famine migrants, who were generally unskilled, poor, casually or infor-

**Table 2.2**  Ethnic groups, Detroit, 1900

| Ethnicity | Population[a] | Percentage |
|---|---|---|
| Native white American[b] | 60,904 | 21.36 |
| Native black American | 2,604 | .91 |
| Foreign-born Black | 1,707 | .60 |
| Native-born white of mixed American and foreign parentage | 37,030 | 12.99 |
| Canadian (English)[c] | 10,694 | 3.75 |
| Canadian American (English)[d] | 4,939 | 1.73 |
| Canadian (French) | 2,823 | .99 |
| Canadian American (French) | 1,976 | .69 |
| British | 7,916 | 2.78 |
| British American | 5,319 | 1.87 |
| Irish | 6,316 | 2.22 |
| Irish American | 8,561 | 3.04 |
| German | 30,903 | 10.84 |
| German American | 38,436 | 13.48 |
| Polish | 12,177 | 4.27 |
| Polish American | 12,799 | 4.49 |
| Russian | 1,637 | .57 |
| Russian American | 1,155 | .41 |
| Austro-Hungarian | 596 | .21 |
| Austro-Hungarian American | 599 | .21 |
| Italian | 734 | .26 |
| Italian American | 463 | .16 |
| Swiss | 337 | .12 |
| Swiss American | 132 | .05 |
| French | 427 | .15 |
| French American | 620 | .22 |
| Belgian, Dutch, and Luxembourger | 1,083 | .38 |
| Belgian, Dutch, and Luxembourger American | 554 | .19 |
| Norwegian, Swedish, and Danish | 394 | .14 |
| Norwegian, Swedish, and Danish American | 116 | .04 |
| Other foreign-born European | 118 | .04 |
| Other European American | 7 | .00 |
| Oriental | 23 | .01 |
| Native-born white of mixed foreign parentage | 10,834 | 3.80 |
| Foreign-born white of mixed foreign parentage | 20,095 | 7.05 |

a. Estimated number from weighted sample data.
b. Born in the U.S. of two U.S.-born parents.
c. Born in English-speaking Canada of two Canadian parents, born in French-speaking Canada of two Canadian parents, born in Great Britain of two British parents, etc.
d. Born in the U.S. of two parents born in English-speaking Canada, etc.
*Source*: Zunz (1982) Table 5.3, p. 104.

mally employed, and frequently despised by the English. Another was the difference between Catholic and Protestant Irish populations.

While the larger British cities each had their 'Little Ireland', their American counterparts also had their 'Little Deutschland', 'Little Sicily', Chinatown and so on, each with a special character – and notoriety – which often tended to persist for several decades or more. This spatial differentiation of the inner-city slums was not, however, confined to foreign immigrants. American

cities, for example, began to attract large black populations from the rural South soon after 1900. And in Paris, migrants from different regions of France tended to cluster in different parts of the city according to contact patterns among friends and relatives; patterns which were strongly influenced by the location of the chief 'port of entry': the various railway stations serving different regions of France (Ogden and Winchester 1975). In most large cities, these ethnic concentrations tended to overlap one another, with the extremes of residential segregation

**Fig. 2.3** The Irish in Huddersfield in 1851
(i) by enumeration district, (ii) by address.
The principal concentrations of Irish-born are
indicated: PF, Paddock Foot; S, Swallow
Street; K, Kirkmoor Place; W, Windsor
Court; P, Post Office Yard.
*Source*: Dennis (1984) Fig. 7.4, pp. 226–7.

being exhibited only at the scale of individual streets or blocks. In many ways, therefore, immigrant neighbourhoods in the Victorian city should be seen as a reflection of *class* and *occupation* (Burstein 1981; Ward 1982; Zunz 1980). As Greenberg puts it: 'workers in a particular industry lived around workplaces in that industry, and within that larger industrial cluster, small, homogeneous ethnic enclaves may have evolved' (1981: 224).

These immigrant neighbourhoods had an impact on the social geography of the city far beyond their numerical importance. The high densities and dilapidated housing of the inner city, combined with the inadequate byelaws and a lack of medical knowledge, created problems of *public health* which spilled over to affect the whole of the city. Living conditions were seen at their worst in the lodging houses of immigrant neighbourhoods. In the heart of the Irish quarter of Leeds in 1851, for example, a survey of 222 lodging houses showed that 536 rooms were being used by 2,429 people – almost five to a room – with only 1,035 beds, many of them crammed into damp and filthy cellars (Dillon 1973). In early Victorian times, it was quite common for wholesome water to be sold for profit at prices which many could not afford (Gauldie 1974). Infectious diseases of all kinds were endemic in large cities, and rates of infant mortality exceeded those of rural areas by a factor of two or three (Rosen 1973; Weber 1899). So hazardous was the nineteenth-century urban environment that even the gentry of cities like Manchester had a life expectancy considerably shorter than their rural counterparts (Table 2.3). Nevertheless, labourers could expect to live only half as long as the well-to-do, and it was working-class districts that contained the filthiest and most hazardous environment and where epidemics were localized (Fig. 2.4; see also Pooley and Pooley 1984; Woods 1984). Such conditions, together with the high rates of unemployment and decreasing real wages among the working class led in turn to the proliferation of crime and social disorganization: each city had its own geography of social pathology which followed closely the pattern of poor housing and disease.

Moreover, these physical and social path-

**Table 2.3**  Mortality in the Victorian city

| Class | Average age at death | |
| --- | --- | --- |
| | **Manchester** | **Rural England** |
| Professional persons and gentry; and their families | 38 | 52 |
| Tradesmen and their families | 20 | 41* |
| Mechanics and labourers and their families | 17 | 38 |

\* including farmers and graziers

*Source*: Report on the Sanitary Conditions of the Labouring Population of Great Britain (1842).

ologies have also had an important indirect impact on the social geography of the modern city; for it was an abhorrence of the Victorian slum and an appreciation of its implications for public health and social order which prompted liberal-minded reformers to campaign for the provision of basic services and amenities from the public purse. As a result, the dominance of *laissez-faire* doctrine began to decline, and an era of 'municipal socialism' began to emerge, bringing new public services like sewage and water, new social amenities such as schools and hospitals, and new legislation controlling building standards and housing codes.

## Economic specialization and residential segregation

Commercial expansion and, in particular, industrialization, were the driving forces behind these changes. With a more sophisticated technology powered by electricity and with mechanized, in-line production techniques, the Victorians reorganized labour into the factory system of production, seeking the advantages of the division of labour and economies of scale. These advantages not only brought unprecedented opportunities for the mass consumption of all kinds of new products and the collective consumption of new public goods (roads, sewers, parks, schools, and the like), but also brought the opportunity to create and to accumulate personal wealth. In

**Fig. 2.4** Leeds in 1839: mills, 'houses of the first class' and cholera localities (after Baker, in Chadwick 1842).
*Source*: Dennis (1984) Fig. 3.3, p. 68.

realizing these advantages, however, the organization of the economy, of society, and of cities had to be radically altered.

New social and economic relationships emerged, with a new rhythm of life dictated by the factory clock and disciplined by the needs of machinery (Thompson 1967; Gordon 1984). As industrial technology became more complex and production larger in scale, bigger financial outlays were required for both machinery and raw materials, fostering the centralization of ownership and control, and allowing a growing economic exploitation of the workforce. Together with this basic realignment of society into owners and workers, there emerged the need for a secular bureaucracy: an army of clerks and agents to keep accounts, to attend to correspondence and to furnish the news necessary for entrepreneurs to respond to the changing conditions of the market. There thus emerged a third class – the middle class – whose purchasing power, residential preferences and attitudes to the city were soon to have a profound effect on its social geography (Friedrichs 1978).

Urban land, responding to the pressures of changing economic and social organization, became highly specialized. Users of land became spatially separated by their ability to pay for the most attractive sites – whether for industry, businesses or homes – and, as the expanding economy and growing population increased the level of demand for land still more, the extent and intensity of these different urban land-uses also increased, bringing extremely high residential densities to the central area and extending the urban fabric even further into the countryside. Contemporary observers identified two interrelated processes stemming from this new regime of land values: *succession* and *segregation*. With the increased demand for space for non-residential purposes in the downtown areas, there soon emerged a specialized commercial area dominating the whole of the urban core. As commercial activities succeeded the mixed activities of the downtown area, the well-to-do in adjacent inner-city neighbourhoods moved outwards to new homes in the suburbs, creating a second 'specialist' area, quite segregated from other social groups. At the same time, and as a consequence of the vacation of the inner city by the rich, the older housing left behind was subdivided, downgraded and in some areas altogether replaced by terrace-housing and tenements for the families who moved in to be near the factories, warehouses and shops of the commercial core. New spatial concentrations of the working class were thus collected together near large-scale workplaces, whereas previously they had been spatially dispersed, working in their own homes or in small workshops. The succession of the working classes to the inner city thus created a third element of segregation and completed the basic structure of the social geography of the Victorian city.

### Socio-spatial structure

For Victorian observers, one of the most perplexing aspects of their cities was this novel separation of the classes. Nowhere was this more apparent than in Manchester, the first 'shock city' of the age. In 1839 a local clergyman wrote:

There is no town in the world where the distance between the rich and the poor is so great, or the barrier between them so difficult to be crossed . . . The separation between the different classes, and the consequent ignorance of each other's habits and condition, are far more complete in this place than in any other country . . . There is far less personal communication between the master cotton spinner and his workmen . . . than there was between good old George the Third and the meanest errand-boy about his palace (Parkinson 1839, quoted in Briggs 1968: 114).

Probably the best-known and most succinct description of the spatial expression of this segregation is in Engels's work on Manchester in *The Condition of the Working Class in England*, which was written in 1842 and which provided much of the documentation for the theories of his friend Karl Marx. Engels wrote:

Manchester contains, at its heart, a rather extended commercial district, perhaps half a mile long and about as broad, and consisting almost wholly of offices and warehouses. Nearly the whole district is abandoned by dwellers, and is lonely and deserted at night.

This commercial core was surrounded by

unmixed working people's quarters, stretching like a girdle, averaging a mile and a half in breadth . . . Outside, beyond this girdle, lives the upper and middle bourgeoisie, the middle bourgeoisie in regularly laid out streets in the vicinity of the working quarters . . . the upper bourgeoisie in remoter villas with gardens . . . in free, wholesome country air, in fine comfortable homes, passed once every half or quarter hour by omnibuses going into the city (Engels 1844: 80).

The spatial structure described by Engels was broadly echoed by another contemporary observer, Faucher, who emphasized the role of railway termini in delimiting the central area of warehouses, storehouses and commerce from the surrounding factories, machine shops and suburbs (Fig. 2.5). Sixty years later, another observer, Marr, recognized the same general pattern, though by this time the concentric zones had been interrupted by radial sectors of industrial development along major lines of communication (Fig. 2.5).

This pattern of concentric zones, modified by sectoral axes of industrial development, was to become typical of many Victorian cities (Fig. 2.6). By 1900, London could be seen in terms of four zones round the largely unpopulated commercial core of the city. Charles Booth, in his *Life and Labour of the People of London*, provided a series of 'social maps' which showed these zones clearly (Booth 1903). The first zone was characterized by the most severe crowding and extreme poverty, except in the west, where there was a sector of extreme affluence. The second zone was slightly less wealthy in this western sector and rather less crowded and impoverished elsewhere, while the third zone was inhabited by the 'short distance commuter' belonging mainly to the lower middle class. The fourth zone belonged exclusively to the wealthy. This overall pattern of concentric zones was, however, modified by a series of linear features. As competition for central space drove the price of land up and up, industry began to edge outward from the commercial core, following the route of canals, rivers and railways, and so structuring the city into a series of wedges or sectors:

Houses on low-lying land usually, and by rivers, and canals almost invariably, were of poor quality and deteriorated rapidly. In such places the drainage was bad, and the proximity of water, whether as a sewer or as a means of communication, attracted industry. Thus, except in some parts of Westminster, Chelsea and Hammersmith, the Thames was lined with working class and often with slum housing. The valleys of the Wondle, the Lea and the Ravensbourne were disfigured by gasworks, a form of industry that drove away anyone that could afford to live elsewhere, and so attracted building of the cheapest type . . . On the other hand, areas next to parks, as at Clapham or South Hackney, tended to keep their social status longer than those surrounding (McLeod 1974: 5)

North American cities also exhibited a spatial structure with a predominantly zonal pattern but with important sectoral components. In the United States, Chicago was the archetypal example, despite the physical constraints of Lake Michigan. Indeed, the idealized version of the social geography of Chicago in the early decades of the twentieth century has become, for the urban geographer, 'the seed bed of theory, the norm, the source of urban fact and urban fiction' (Robson 1975: 4). In Chicago, both sectors and zones were particularly pronounced because of the effects of the massive inflows of immigrant workers and the radial development of the railroads which fanned outwards from the centre of the city, drawing with them corridors of manufacturing industry (Warner 1972). The residential communities which developed between these radial corridors during successive phases of urban growth were graphically documented by the Chicago 'school' of urban sociology in the 1920s and 1930s (Burgess 1926; Park *et al.* 1925), providing the basis for the ecological ideas which have influenced urban studies ever since (see pp. 57–63).

This rather orderly image of urban spatial structure can be misleading, however, and in many case studies it takes the eye of faith to discern zones and sectors (Dennis 1984). Although sectors and zones were certainly the

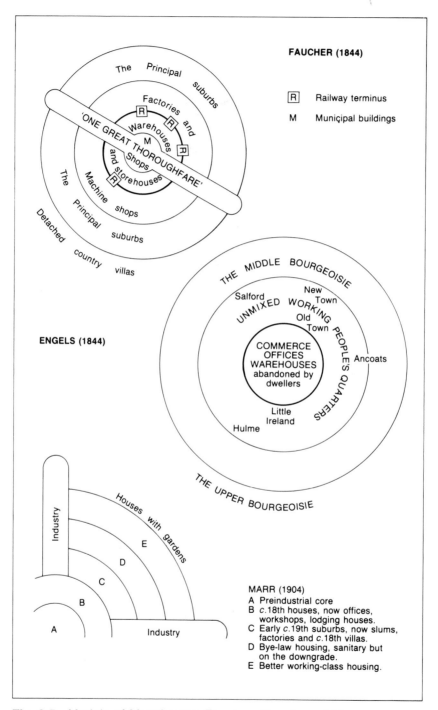

**Fig. 2.5** Models of Manchester: Faucher, Engels and Marr.
*Source*: Dennis (1984) Fig. 3.6, p. 82.

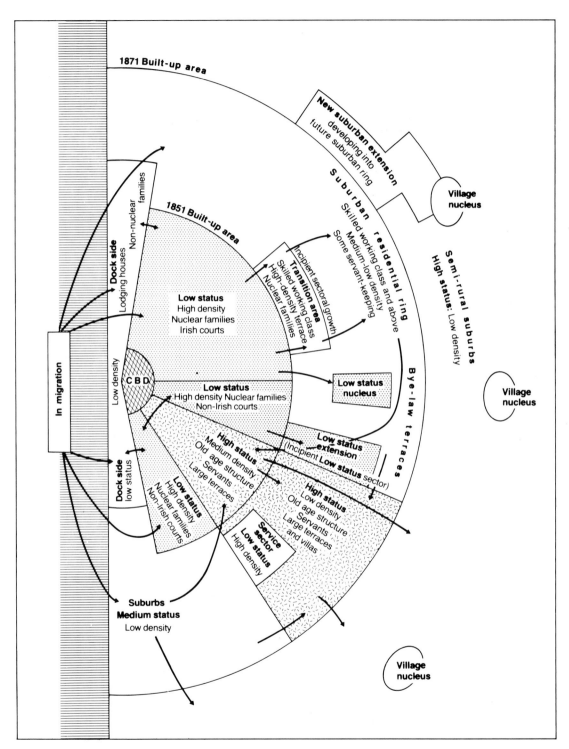

**Fig. 2.6**  The urban structure of mid-Victorian Liverpool. The arrows represent the main streams of migration and residential mobility.   *Source*: Dodghson and Butlin (1978), p. 352.

dominant patterns to emerge from the cumulative processes of urban development during the nineteenth century, it would be more accurate to think of the Victorian city not in terms of a static model but as an evolving system with rather variable outcomes. As Goheen has shown in his detailed analysis of Victorian Toronto, the social geography of the early and mid-Victorian era differed from the later Victorian city not so much in the nature of its social cleavages as in the expression of these cleavages on the map (Goheen 1970). Thus, although economic status, family status, housing tenure and religious adherence can all be shown to be important discriminants of both households and neighbourhoods throughout the 'Victorian' stage of Toronto's development, their territorial expression changed quite significantly. Similarly, Pritchard (1976) has summarized patterns in Victorian Leicester as successively 'early industrial' (1820–1865) and 'ecological' (1865–1914).

It should also be acknowledged that there is considerable debate as to the *degree* of residential segregation underlying these broad patterns (Cannadine 1982; Conzen 1983). In particular, David Ward has argued from research in Leeds that 'modern' levels of residential segregation between social classes did not occur until the late Victorian period. Before then, he argues, only the polar extremes of society were geographically segregated, the rest of the city being characterized by high levels of residential mobility and loose patterns of residential differentiation (Ward 1975, 1980, 1983). Baker's *Sanitary Map* of Leeds in 1839 (Fig. 2.4) provides some support for Ward's argument, for while there was clearly a broad segregation of 'houses of the first class' (to the west) and the 'cholera localities' of the worst slums (to the east), it also illustrates the nature of social mixing in east and west Leeds:

In the east working-class courts and back-to-backs occasionally gave way to a single house or terrace 'of the first class', perhaps occupied by a minor woollen manufacturer or a petty landlord. In the west eighteenth-century efforts to establish a high-class suburb, reflected in the solidly 'first class' streets around Park Square, were soon outflanked by an equally solid block of mills and working-class housing, and subsequent middle-class development was channelled into greenfield sites in Great and Little Woodhouse. In Leeds, . . . it was easy to identify the 'best' parts of town, . . . but it was difficult to discern patterns of segregation *within* working-class areas (Dennis 1984: 67, emphasis added).

Ward's position also seems to be supported by research which shows that mid-Victorian cities were characterized by a residential turnover so high that only 60 to 80 per cent of all households recorded the same address in successive years, and only 13 to 20 per cent were at the same address after ten years (Daunton 1977; Hershberg *et al.* 1981; Pooley 1979). Such volatility, it might be supposed, did not lend itself to the development of highly differentiated communities. Nevertheless, it may be that it was a neighbourhood's *comparative* level of stability that marked it out as a geographical community (Dennis and Daniels 1981); and Pooley (1984) has suggested that residential differentiation in mid-Victorian cities – weak as it may have been by modern standards – represented a very significant social phenomenon for the Victorians themselves. The political implications of this interpretation are very important. McLeod (1974), for example, argues that Victorian working-class London was characterized by an endemic parochialism which made the urban proletariat very inward-looking. This collective introspection, McLeod suggests, was a form of 'psychic self-defence' which enabled the working classes to form their own codes of self-esteem and status. The result was that the proletariat, if not highly fragmented spatially, was highly fragmented in social terms: thereby weakening the potential for class-based urban politics.

The embryonic residential differentiation of Victorian cities was rendered still more complex by a variety of specific influences whose importance varied from place to place according to local economic, social, political and topographic conditions. Thus, for example, recent studies of early- and mid-Victorian Cardiff (Lewis 1979) and late-Victorian Edinburgh (Gordon 1979) have emphasized the transitional nature of their social geography, showing how elements of the pre-industrial urban structure were retained within a spatially reorganized economy and society. Shaw (1979) has pointed to the influence of local physical, environmental and institutional factors in controlling both the general structure of urban development and the detailed pattern of residential differentiation in the Victorian city. In Wolverhampton, for instance, geology exerted a significant influence on the city's social geography through the location of unattractive industrial land uses such as mines, factories and railways (Shaw 1979); and in cities like Leeds, Bradford and Sheffield the preference by the wealthy for better-drained sites with commanding views on higher ground meant that topography was an important determinant of social geography.

The pattern of local land-ownership also had an important role in shaping the nature and direction of urban development in many cities, as Ward (1962) has demonstrated tellingly in relation to Leeds and Cannadine (1977) has shown in relation to Birmingham. Moreover, there were distinctive regional patterns to the style, size and tenure of housing favoured by both landowners and developers (Dennis 1984). In addition, when land was released for building, restrictive conditions often influenced the type of property built, thus subverting the idealized sector-and-zone pattern in yet another way. Many of the high-status areas in Edinburgh and Glasgow, for example, resulted from conditions in leasehold covenants which excluded undesirable uses (Gordon 1979, 1983). Conversely, the absence of restrictions often led to low-standard development and rapid residential deterioration. Finally, Cowlard (1979) has pointed to the influence of residents' behaviour, both active and passive, in perpetuating the individuality of specific neighbourhoods and so influencing the character of urban development. It is prudent, therefore, to end this section on a note of caution, noting Briggs's assertion that Victorian cities were not all alike, not 'the same place with different alibis: Dickens's Coketown, alias Smokeover, Mechanicsville, Manchester, Leeds, Birmingham, Elberfeld, Essen, Lyons, Pittsburgh and Youngstown.

. . . Below the surface, . . . nineteenth century cities not only had different topography [and] different economic . . . structures . . . but they responded differently to the urban problems which they shared in common' (Briggs 1968: 33–4).

### Family, home and suburb in the new social order

Many of the new social relationships that were forged in the Victorian city have made an important contribution to patterns of urban life in the modern city. The kinship ties and extended family system which helped to alleviate the hardships of urban life in working-class areas, for example, could be identified in communities living in the depressed inner areas of modern cities (Coates and Silburn 1970; Young and Willmott 1962). Similarly, the modern suburban ethos of 'minding one's own business' and the culture of privatism centred on the nuclear family unit can be traced to the new social relationships which emerged in Victorian middle-class suburbs.

For working-class households in the Victorian city, the demands of industrialization and urbanization required a rationalization of everyday life, while the discipline of time imposed by the division of labour was exacerbated by the geographical separation of home and workplace, making it increasingly difficult for the family to fulfill some traditional roles. At the same time, increased residential mobility tended to isolate the nuclear family from the larger network of kin, so that fewer relatives could perform informal service functions. Therefore, in order to accommodate the routine of the new economic order, families not only gave up their economic function as a unit of production but also shed many of the responsibilities for educating children, supporting the elderly, and caring for the sick. The corollary of this change was the importance of a whole range of new service professions and establishments such as tailors, barbers, doctors, restaurants, laundries and dispensaries. Similarly, a much sharper distinction between 'work' and 'leisure' began to emerge – though the ability to participate in leisure pursuits outside the home was closely circumscribed by stringent 'coupling constraints': the sheer difficulties of getting to and from leisure-related locations, given the new time discipline and family organization required by industrial capitalism (Pred 1981a). In practical terms, therefore, the major distinction was between 'work' and 'home'. It must be acknowledged, however, that this distinction was much clearer for men than for women. Although women were drawn increasingly into the formal economy, their participation was often transitory, depending on the stage of the family life cycle and on the cyclical fluctuations of the industrial economy. In these circumstances, the only ways that women could obtain money to supplement family income were through outwork – ranging from squalid, miserably-paid occupations such as fur-pulling to more respectable work such as tinting Christmas cards – or through surrogate family activities like casual cleaning, child minding, taking in washing, or providing houseroom and domestic services to lodgers and boarders (Davidoff 1979; Goldin 1981; Tilly 1981). Within the home, the task of 'home making' also fell to women (Loyd 1982). One result of this could be seen in 'the growing institutionalization of the Sunday suit and the elaborately furnished front parlour' (Jones 1974, pp. 486–7). In short, the working-class house came to encapsulate an increasingly private, independent and consumption-oriented lifestyle (Daunton 1983), thus setting the framework for the family life of 'modern' working-class households.

For middle-class households the framework for family life was established in a new setting: the suburbs. Here, the separation of home and work and the pursuit of a private, independent and consumption-oriented lifestyle were developed to a much greater degree. For the middle classes, the flight to the suburbs involved a temporary rejection of the rest of society: the most satisfactory neighbourhood was one that provided the maximum of privacy and the minimum of outside distraction (Carter 1984). This, of course, was essentially a male view of the attractions of suburbia, since it was the man who went out

to work and then sought daily relief from the strains of business and the 'outside' world by escaping to the supposedly undemanding comforts of the family home, while women, left to make what they could of day-long isolation, busied themselves with creating an uplifting environment, filled with the conveniences and fashionable objects that were being made available by the industrial economy (Davidoff and Hall 1983; Miller 1983; Wright 1981). As Thompson puts it (1982: 13):

The clear separation of work and home, the insistence on social distancing, the treatment of the home as a feminine domain, the importance attached to domestic privacy and the exclusion of the vulgar prying multitude, can all be seen as parts of a code of individual responsibility, male economic dominance and female domestic subordination, and family-nurtured morality which served to give the bourgeoisie a social identity and mark them off from the upper class and the lower orders.

In other words, the suburbs are not middle class because the middle class lives there: the middle class lives there because the suburbs could be *made* middle class (Walker 1981).

In detail, the development of Victorian suburbs was also shaped by:

1. pre-development features (that influenced the shape, form, character and timing of suburbanization);
2. the limitations which market forces placed on the power of landowners and developers to decide what should be built;
3. the varying role of different kinds of transport systems; and
4. the specific strata of middle-class society being catered to (see, for example, Carr 1982; Jahn 1982; Treen 1982).

In general, the development of Victorian suburbs must be seen as a product not only of middle-class privacy and territoriality but also of several broad sets of economic and political imperatives:

1. increasing tax burdens in central city areas (a result of the huge demand for

public services and infra-structural improvements);

2. the challenge to the political control of the middle classes in central city areas that came with the combination of massive levels of immigration and minor improvements in urban democracy; and

3. the incipient decentralization of industry in response to the physical congestion and escalating class hostilities of central areas (Ashton 1984).

The catalyst which translated all of these imperatives into reality was the advent of inexpensive urban transport (see pp. 30–36), but the whole process was greatly facilitated by public investment in the suburbs. Both industrialists and private households demanded public expenditure on roads, public utilities and services for the suburbs, and they were reinforced by lobbyists for construction, real estate and transportation interests. In practice, the ability of local governments to provide such support for suburban development was dependent on the availability of capital that came towards the end of business cycles (Moore 1983).

Walker (1981) has argued that the whole process of suburbanization was a critical mechanism through which the capitalist city was able to resolve its own inner conflicts and contradictions. According to this (neo-marxist) kind of interpretation, the growth of suburban settings:

1. provided *spatial differentiation* that (a) defused potential conflict between the new social classes produced by the new division of labour and (b) facilitated the search for monopolistic rents;

2. allowed both industry and upper-middle class residents to *decentralize* in response to the negative externalities generated by industrial capitalism in inner-city neighbourhoods;

3. provided an arena and a focus for the pursuit of *consumption* (so stimulating the circulation of capital);

4. provided outlets for investment capital which had 'overaccumulated' during the *growth phases* of business cycles; and

5. provided an arena in which the 'cult of domesticity' and fragmented local politics were able to flourish and thereby foster the *social reproduction* of the middle classes: 'to send the working father back into the fray rejuvenated, to optimize the life-chances of children, to avoid falling back into the working class, and to reproduce a mode of life' (Walker 1981: 392; see also Mackenzie 1980; Pred 1981b; Women and Geography Study Group 1984).

The development of Victorian suburbs, then, was an interactive process, with each element – family, home, neighbourhood, class, capital, and state – both nourishing and feeding from the others.

## The modern city

Since the modern city is the central concern of the remaining chapters of this book, it would be pointless to indulge here in a detailed summary of its characteristics and the mechanisms and processes which have produced them. It is, however, instructive to set out the principal aspects of the transformation of urban structure in the modern period alongside those we have noted in relation to precapitalist, transitional and Victorian cities.

Like cities of earlier times, the modern city can be seen as the product of changing economic organization, reflecting the social relationships inherent to these changes, moulded by the prevailing means of transport, and continually reshaped by the public policies (or lack of them) and personal life-styles which stem from the dominant spirit of the age. There has, however, been no single shift in economic organization in the modern period equivalent to the rise of industrialism during the nineteenth century. Rather, change has been more complex, with successive 'quantum jumps' in technology bringing a greater range of products for mass consumption, new means of transport freeing production from fixed locations, and high levels of personal mobility generating large areas of low-density suburban development. At the same time, more and more of the Western economy has switched from farming, mining and heavy manufacturing into the provision of services, the organization of international business, and the administration and provision of all kinds of public goods and social welfare services. These changes, in turn, have helped to increase levels of economic security and social mobility, producing a hierarchically differentiated labour force that is increasingly dominated by those described as the 'new' or the 'lower' middle class. But although the 'post-industrial' or 'corporate' capitalism of the modern era requires a smaller proletariat, there has remained a significant residuum of endemically impoverished households, the majority of whom have become concentrated in homogeneous inner-city neighbourhoods or in decentralized municipal housing estates (Fig. 2.7).

The modern era has also brought new extremes of urbanization – megalopolitan regions: multi-city, multi-centred urban regions characterized by a high proportion of low-density settlement and complex networks of economic specialization – public as well as private – to facilitate the production and consumption of sophisticated products and services. Gottman coined the term megalopolis in relation to the urbanized north-eastern seaboard of the United States stretching from Boston through New York and Philadelphia to Baltimore and Washington (Gottman 1961), but other megalopolitan areas can be identified in the American Upper Midwest (Chicago-Detroit-Pittsburgh), the Rhine-Ruhr axis (Köln-Dusseldorf-Duisburg-Bochum-Dortmund), the Randstad region of the Netherlands (Rotterdam-The Hague-IJmuiden-Amsterdam-Utrecht), and in the belt of urban development stretching from Liverpool, Manchester, Sheffield and Leeds through Birmingham to London and the Home Counties. Indeed, the whole of England may be compared in size and intensity of urbanization with Gottman's original megalopolis (Hall *et al.* 1973). In addition, there are three emergent megalopolitan regions: the Canadian urban corridor stretching from Windsor along Lake Erie, Lake Ontario and the St Lawrence Valley to Quebec; the metropolitan West Coast of America between San Diego and the San Francisco Bay area; and the rapidly-urbanizing sector of Mediterranean Europe that stretches from Avignon through Marseilles, Milan, Turin and Genoa to Pisa.

Within the modern city and throughout these megalopolitan areas, the pattern of urban life is shaped by the contradictory forces of *centralization* and *decentralization*. On the one hand, the concentration of economic and political power in giant corporations and in larger and larger public authorities has made for a centralization of administrative and bureaucratic activity in the central business districts of cities. On the other hand, the new locational freedom of many shops and business enterprises has prompted a further decentralization of jobs; and the vast increase in the number of white-collar workers, together with the consequent rise in average incomes and the more widespread availability of automobiles, has decentralized the residential structure of the city, creating enormous tracts of low-density suburban development. As a result, land use in the city has become even more specialized and segregated. 'Shopping strips, one-class suburbs, black ghettos and industrial parks dot the urbanized region. Even the old industrial metropolis's downtown, so formidable a monument fifty years ago, has turned into an office and financial center, while its retailing, wholesaling and manufacturing have been scattered over the whole megalopolis' (Warner 1972: 64). This, in turn, has revolutionized people's daily activity patterns. The decentralization of the city, together with the increased personal mobility afforded by the automobile, has increased the range of opportunities available to the affluent urbanite for employment, shopping, recreation and socializing.

In contrast to the advantages which the modern city confers upon the affluent, the poor have neither physical nor economic access to the city's new 'opportunity space'. The unskilled urban worker remains trapped in a localized cycle of poverty in which the inter-related effects of poor housing, ill-health, poorly equipped schools, low educational achievement, restricted job

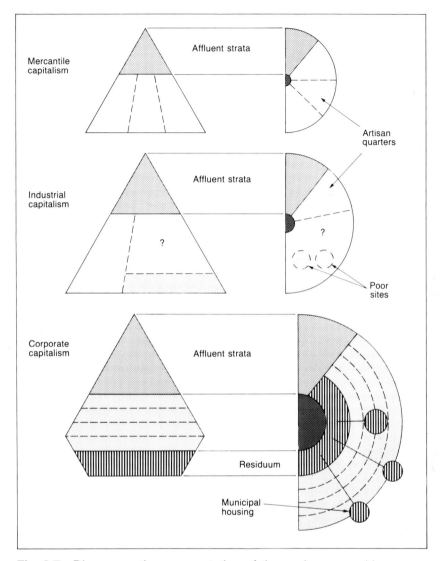

**Fig. 2.7**  Diagrammatic representation of the socio-geographic outcomes of Mercantile (pre-industrial) Capitalism, Industrial Capitalism and Corporate Capitalism.
*Source*: Ward (1983) Fig. 4, p. 372.

opportunities, low wages and unemployment generate an environment of deprivation and social malaise. The persistence of these problems, together with the changing social climate and the increased economic and political powers of urban governments in the twentieth century, have fostered the development of public intervention in order to 'manage' the economic, social and physical environment of the city. Town planning, environmental control and the provision of public housing are three of the more important aspects of this intervention, the origins of which can be traced back to the philanthropic and reformist movements of the nineteenth century (see pp. 47–53).

Municipal involvement in urban development is particularly important in European
countries, where public housing programmes
and compensatory planning (the provision of
public goods and services in 'deprived' neighbourhoods) have a very marked effect on the
social geography of cities. Indeed, the existence of a large public sector in the housing
markets of most European cities is probably
the single most important factor in
distinguishing European cities from the 'norm'
derived from the North American urban
experience. This is not to say that municipal
involvement in planning and housing policies
has been unimportant in North America.
Some cities have established a reputation for
progressive action while many more have
assembled large teams of highly qualified
planners which would be the envy of many
European city planning departments. The
chief difference between these planners and
their European counterparts is that they do
not have the legislative power to implement
their plans and strategies, and so must be
content with a more advisory role, or a role
in which they are the junior partners in joint
ventures with private developers.

These, then, are the principal aspects of
urban development in the modern stage. Yet
modern cities defy an easy type-casting even
more than the Victorian city and, as we shall
see, generalizations about structure, form and
social geography are often hedged with
numerous qualifications and sometimes
seriously disputed. In most circumstances –
city, conurbation or metropolis – the characteristics of modern urbanism have been
grafted on to a physical and social fabric
created in the nineteenth century or before,
creating problems of analysis which only an
historical perspective can unravel. In a
number of cities in the trans-Mississippi West
of the United States, however, almost all the
urban fabric and urban way of life belongs to
the modern period, and if there is an archetypal modern city it must be found in this
region. Most people would probably nominate
Los Angeles, the automobile city *par excel-
lence*, with a metropolitan population of ten
millions spread out at low densities in rather
uniform single-family dwellings over the best
part of 2,500 square kilometres: an apparent
formlessness which contrasts strikingly with
the sectors and zones of older cities (Banham
1973; Nelson and Clark 1976; Wachs 1984).

So much for the general chronology of
urban development. The remaining sections of
this chapter retrace in detail the development
and implications of three of the principal
aspects of change which recur throughout the
period from the pre-capitalist city onwards:
the role of local transport systems in shaping
the physical development and residential
differentiation of cities, the nature and role of
urban government, and the role of new ideas
and changing public attitudes in modifying the
nature of urban environments.

## Transport systems and urban residential differentiation

The fundamental determinants of urban
growth and the timing of these major phases
of urban development, as noted above, have
been economic, stemming from the emergence of capitalism as the dominant mode of
production. Generally speaking, the major
growth phases of individual cities have been
governed by the response of labour and
capital to the cycles of national and international prosperity inherent in the capitalist
economy, with the production of new residential buildings following effective demand and
the availability of capital (Adams 1970;
Gottlieb 1976; Lewis 1965; Whitehand 1972,
1975). These growth phases have generated
successive areas of new housing which are
largely responsible for the zonal component
of the morphology of many cities. The *nature*
of these concentric zones, however, is a result
of several factors besides the age and condition of housing built during different growth
phases. Whitehand cites innovations in
building materials, construction techniques,
building standards, architectural styles, methods
of house purchase, town planning and intra-
urban transport as important morphogenetic
factors, and suggests that they also are subject
to the periodicity of the overall economy
(Whitehand 1977).

Within each growth phase, changes in transport systems are considered by many to have been the single most important determinant of urban morphology and residential differentiation (Hume 1983; Isard 1942; Ward 1964, 1971; Warner 1962). As these authors point out, the transport technology that prevailed during each boom not only controlled the density and areal extent of urban development but also influenced the suburbanization of the middle classes. Moreover, urban transport systems have also been instrumental in contributing a distinctive sectoral pattern to many cities as the radial routes of successive transport systems have pinned down areas socially and intersected them physically, creating corridors of commercial and industrial land use between which there developed wedges of residential development. The precise effect of transport systems on urban form depends, of course, on the transport technology and growth phase in question. In this section, the effects of each of the major innovations in transport technology are examined in rough chronological order: railways, horse-drawn systems, electric tramways and rapid transit systems, and automobiles.

## Railways

Although railways were principally developed for inter-urban transport, they have had a very marked effect on the internal structure of cities. In addition to their general role in stimulating economic expansion (and so accelerating urban growth), railways have affected the development of cities in two main ways. First, the intrusion of railway tracks and termini had the effect of polarizing land use and increasing residential differentiation in inner-city areas. With the start of the railway boom in the 1830s there began a steady realignment of land uses around the central termini and along the railway routes through the built-up area. Retail shopkeepers, transit warehouses and hotels were attracted to the termini, while residential users were repelled. The new rail terminus in Portsmouth, England, unable to reach the existing city centre because of a ring of barracks and parks

encircling the old city, effectively relocated the centre of gravity of the city by drawing the central business district over 1 km from its old site – a phenomenon which was repeated in several other cities (Smailes 1966). Beyond the immediate vicinity of the termini, the criss-crossing of branch lines tended to create shadow areas of middens, claypits, scrapyards and derelict land. In addition, the huge new viaducts needed to carry the railways into the heart of the city tended to isolate small areas, cutting them off from shops and amenities, depressing land values and encouraging dereliction and marginal uses. Equally significant were the broad swathes created by the main-line tracks and their assorted stockyards, warehouses and factories as they passed through the rest of the city, repelling all but the lowest grade of housing and establishing marked linear features which served as formers for the subsequent development of the city. The most powerful symbol of railway blight was the viaduct, 'intended to save land and avoid street closures, but in practice creating a belt of unsavoury land uses, underneath the arches and on land in their shadow. Even if roads continued to pass under the arches of the viaduct, an impermeable mental barrier between districts on either side was established' (Dennis 1984: 130).

These effects were greatest in British cities, where competing railway companies were unwilling to share terminus facilities. Thus, in contrast to the single central station of many large cities in continental Europe and North America, many British cities had two or more termini, together with the extra mileage of approach tracks and sidings. London had as many as 15 termini by the end of the nineteenth century, while Glasgow and Manchester each had four, Belfast, Leeds, Leicester, and Liverpool had three, and Birmingham, Bradford, Dundee, Edinburgh and Sheffield each had two (Simmons 1973). Kellett has shown that in the scuffle for access to British cities the railway companies became the owners of up to 10 per cent of central land and often indirectly influenced the functions of another 20 per cent (Kellett 1969). The exact location of termini and approach routes depended largely on the availability of sufficiently large tracts of land, so that an important controlling factor was the pattern of land ownership. The cost of land was also an important consideration, leading to a preference for the redevelopment of slum areas, where land values were lowest. Fortunately for the railway companies, slum areas and large landholdings often coincided, as in Southwark and Lambeth, where the purchase of parts of the vast slum holdings of the Archbishop of Canterbury and the Lord Bishop of Winchester enabled a railway route to be driven through south London (Kellett 1969). Large numbers of people found themselves displaced in this way, much to the approval of municipal authorities who were glad to be rid of the 'hovels and brothels' which were replaced by the railway infrastructure. Nevertheless, the displaced inhabitants of these areas had to live somewhere, and one of the important secondary effects of railway construction was therefore to increase the congestion of low-income housing areas. As Engels observed of Little Ireland, a slum in the path of the Manchester South Junction Railway, it 'had not been abolished at all, but had simply been shifted from the south side of Oxford Road to the north side' (1887; quoted in Dennis 1984: 128).

The second main way in which railway development affected the geography of cities was through the growth of commuter traffic. In this respect, American cities experienced a greater impact than European cities, although railway companies everywhere found it difficult to make very large profits from commuter services. Only the most prosperous of the middle classes could afford to commute over the considerable distances between railway stations, and their numbers were relatively small. Nevertheless, both railway travel and out-of-town residences were considered to be genteel, and high status dormitory settlements or 'exurbs' eventually developed around many of the larger cities. According to Kennedy (1962), 20 per cent of Boston's businessmen travelled to work by train in 1848 from exurbs located between 20 and 25 km from central Boston. Similarly, Vance (1964) cites the communities of Burlingame, San Mateo and Belmont as examples of the

wealthy exurbs which developed around San Francisco in the 1860s. In addition, railway companies operating from large cities soon began to offer services to intermediate, suburban stations, attracting substantial numbers of commuters of more modest means. The Illinois Central Railroad, for example, carried nearly 14,000 commuters a day from the southern sector of Chicago in 1893 (Yeates and Garner 1976).

In Britain, it was only belatedly that the railways affected suburban development. As in the United States, the railway companies catered mainly for the prosperous middle classes but, in contrast to the development of new exurbs, the suburbanization sustained by the railways in Britain tended to take the form of accretions of low-density villa settlement located at a discreet distance from the railway stations of long-established villages, resorts, market towns and spas which fell within the hinterland of larger cities (Pollins 1964). The railway companies seemed uninterested in exploiting the potential market for passengers from more modest suburban developments nearer to the cities themselves, except where conditions were especially favourable: an attractive location, an established group of commuters, landowners ambitious to become developers, and a propitious moment in the trade cycle. Such circumstances did occur, for example, in the London exurb of Bromley, where local landowners were the chief promoters of the railway that was opened in 1858, ushering in a decade of rapid local growth (Rawcliffe 1982).

Only the Great Eastern Railway actively wooed commuter traffic on the scale of the large American cities of the time, leaving other companies to be accused by contemporary critics of running the railways for the exclusive benefit of the rich (Costelloe 1899). The government, in an attempt to ease the pressure on crowded central areas, sponsored the Cheap Trains Act (1883), which required the railway companies to provide accommodation at fares not exceeding 1d per mile on certain suburban trains, in return for some tax relief. But, although the existence of 'workmen's trains' eventually helped to sustain the growth of new zones of relatively cheap suburban housing – the north London suburbs occupied by large populations of city clerks, for example – the railways did not have their heart in the scheme.

Kellett (1969) has suggested that the reluctance of the companies to exploit the large-scale suburbanization of the lower-middle and working classes was the product of several inter-related factors. First, the railway managers took upon themselves the role of 'gate-keepers', deliberately restricting working-class neighbourhoods to certain parts of the city because they believed that 'throwing open' suburban areas to the working classes would not only 'drive out' the richer and more profitable classes but would also 'spoil' large parts of the city for good. Reinforcing this class prejudice were certain economic factors which made suburban services unattractive to the railway companies. One was that short-haul suburban services always failed to attract goods traffic, which was the staple of the railways; most goods tended to be carted to the suburbs by road. Another factor was connected with the operation of local rates (property taxes). Being large landowners, the railway companies were inevitably liable to high tax bills; but this was aggravated if a rural area became a suburb, for taxes had to be increased on all properties in order to pay for essential public services such as sewage and paving. The most significant point, however, is that if the suburban development was of low quality – and therefore of low taxable value – the overall level of taxation had to be increased much more in order to raise the necessary revenue. Low grade suburban development thus represented a substantial financial burden to companies whose railway lines passed through the area.

## Horse-drawn systems

Two of the earliest innovations in intra-urban transport technology were the horse-drawn omnibus (a simple passenger wagon) and the horse-drawn streetcar, or horsecar (a passenger wagon on rails). Together with cable cars and various steam-driven enterprises, these provided the first systems designed especially

to cater for the daily ebb and flow of the growing number of people wanting to live in new suburban homes but work in the city centre. The effect of these systems on the fabric of the city was moderated, however, by disadvantages which limited the market for their services. Most serious was the relatively high cost to the passenger. Horses, in the numbers needed to operate a system based on omnibuses or streetcars, were expensive to buy and look after; while cablecars and steam engines also incurred high capital and maintenance costs which were, inevitably, borne by passengers. In addition, all four systems tended to be relatively slow, and the mechanically propelled systems had the added disadvantage of frightening horses, people, or both. As Yeates and Garner observe, 'One of the chief problems confronting the widespread use of [steam driven systems] seems to have been that the centre of gravity of the engine and carriages was rather high, resulting in unfortunate mishaps on curved and sharp turns. For example, at a later date, the elevated railway curve 73 feet above 110th Street in New York was known as "suicide corner"' (Yeates and Garner 1976: 184).

Nevertheless, these were the only mass transit systems available to commuters for most of the nineteenth century, and much of the earliest suburban development was dependent on their existence. The most popular systems were the horse-drawn omnibuses and streetcars, operating on a few routes radiating from the city centre. The example of Boston's early experience of mass transit, drawn from Ward (1964) and Warner (1962) illustrates how these horse-drawn systems began to modify the morphology and social geography of cities during the third quarter of the nineteenth century. In Boston, as in many cities, it was the horsecar which had the greatest spatial impact, for although horse-drawn omnibuses served areas up to ten miles from the city centre their slow speeds and high fares made them unattractive to potential commuters. Horsecars were introduced by several companies during the 1850s, most of them operating, at first, a single route leading from the centre to the edge of town. These installations prompted a crucial change in Boston's social geography, as the wealthier members of the city's middle classes were attracted to large new brownstone terraced dwellings built along the horsecar routes in the outer fringes of the city, reinforcing the idea of suburban living pioneered by the residents of the railway exurbs and endowing previously dull suburban locations with the cachet of social status.

Despite the new attractiveness and feasibility of suburban living, few people seemed willing to spend more than an hour a day travelling to and from work. Given the speed of the horsecar (6 to 8 kph), this restricted its suburbanizing effects to a radius of about 7 km. Moreover, since people were also reluctant to walk very far from their homes to the streetcar stops, much of the suburban expansion took the form of discontinuous ribbon development. Later, crosstown and branch routes were introduced to areas within 4 km of the city centre but in the area between 4 and 7 km from the city the large interstitial areas between the ribbons of upper-middle income residences remained largely untouched by residential development.

## Electric tramways and rapid transit

The electric tram, alias the streetcar or trolley, was the electrically-driven version of the horsecar, powered by way of overhead cables. First introduced in 1887 in Richmond, Virginia, the tram had an immediate and dramatic effect on the fabric of cities. In the United States, more than 200 cities had adopted the system by 1892. In Germany, the total length of electric tramways increased from 102 km in 1893 to 3,692 km ten years later; in France and Britain the equivalent figures were 41 km and 71 km in 1893 and 1,995 km and 2,354 km in 1903 (McKay 1976). The reasons for the popularity of electric tramways were several. Electricity was quieter and more efficient than alternative sources of power, and enabled trams to travel twice as fast at horsecars. Most significant of all though was the fact that the large carrying capacity of their rolling stock made them cheaper to operate per passenger mile than

horsecars, thus allowing a policy of low fares to attract a high volume of passengers. McKay (1976) estimates that the transition from horse-powered systems to electrically-powered systems involved a decline in real costs to passengers of about 50 per cent in the United Kingdom and 60 per cent in France. Speculative developers were not slow to realize the potential of the tram in opening up the suburbs to a much wider sector of the middle classes than before, and in most cities there was a flurry of activity as developers and tram operators worked together to promote suburban growth (often as different parts of the same company) during the cyclical boom of the early twentieth century.

The increased speed of the tram doubled the distance that people were able to commute within the critical time of 30 minutes and thus quadrupled the area available for residential development (Adams 1970; Ward 1971). As the suburbs extended and more housing was built the middle classes withdrew almost completely from the inner city, leaving behind a residual population of the poor, together with minority groups of various kinds. As with the horsecar, however, passengers were reluctant to live more than a few minutes walk from the tram stops, and the capital cost of providing branch lines and crosstown routes meant that most suburban expansion continued to be channelled along the major radial routeways.

Meanwhile, the promotion of streetcar suburbs also precipitated other changes in urban structure. Thus, for example, tramway systems in the US:

not only extended the growing space available to growing cities of median size, enabling them to preserve the small-town pattern of detatched houses, but also spurred the development of specialized factory and business districts, which permitted the reconstruction of many shabby old districts. In large and long-established metropolitan centers, on the other hand, the same facilities tended to spread the traditional pattern of tenements or row houses; the heavier traffic brought by longer lines added to the congestion of the older streets, further blighting the dwellings of their teeming residents (McKelvey 1963: 84)

In Britain, the impact of electric tramways on suburban development arrived somewhat later than in the United States, and was generally much more modest in scale. Ward (1964) suggests that the less buoyant demographic and economic conditions prevailing in Britain during the late nineteenth century, together with the more stringent building controls of British municipalities, were responsible for limiting the growth of 'streetcar suburbs'. Nevertheless, it would be misleading to suggest that the tram had little effect on the structure of British cities. Tramways in Leeds, for example, carried 94 million passengers a year by 1916, sustaining the development of large but select suburban estates in Potternewton, Lidgett Park, Headingley and Upper Armley (Ward 1964). In Leeds, as elsewhere, the expansion of the tramway system was accomplished by municipal enterprise, motivated by a desire to rationalize intra-urban transport and to ease inner-city congestion by providing a cheap means of transportation for the working classes. By 1906, tramway investments by local authorities in the United Kingdom amounted to £41.7 m, whereas private investments amounted to only £22.4 m (McKay 1976). As a result, the tramway was able to facilitate the movement of artisans, mechanics, and clerks from the inner city to more salubrious housing further out. This movement was generally constrained, however, by the lack of modestly-priced housing in the outer suburbs; so that the tramways brought the best bargains to the more affluent middle classes who could afford to live in more distant but more expensive suburban housing.

In the larger cities of both Europe and North America the congestion of the core area tended to nullify the efficiency of the tramways, thus prompting the development of elevated tracks and subway systems in structures quite separate from other traffic. These rapid transit systems could travel faster while carrying more passengers, and their effect was to stretch ribbon development even further into the countryside, reinforcing and extending the radial form of the city (Davies 1965). Elevated tracks were introduced in New York City as early as 1878 and in Chicago in 1892, while subway systems were opened in London in 1863, Glasgow in 1897, Boston in 1895, Paris in 1900 and New York City in 1904. The presence of rapid transit stations soon influenced the local pattern of residential construction, land values and population density in the suburbs, with nodes of commercial and residential activity focusing on outlying stations, especially the outer termini. The full effects were delayed until the inter-war period, however, when many of the systems were extended outwards. In London, for example, the subway lines were extended to Edgware (in 1924), Stanmore (1932) and Cockfosters (1933) at a time when suburban house prices were cheaper than ever before (or since) in relation to personal incomes (Hall 1974). This, combined with a sustained publicity campaign by London Transport about the advantages of life in 'Metroland', triggered one of London's most significant phases of suburban sprawl.

## The automobile

The personal mobility conferred by the automobile increased yet again the area within acceptable commuting time of people's workplace. Moreover, by increasing the mobility of goods and raw materials, the internal combustion engine facilitated the decentralization of many jobs, thus increasing even more the potential extent of urban residential development. Car ownership grew rapidly after the introduction of mass production techniques in the 1910s, and the widespread use of cars by commuters had begun by the late 1930s, bringing a low-density sprawl of single-family dwellings to the periphery of the city. Meanwhile, the impact of the automobile was further reinforced by the decline of mass transit systems (both tramways and rapid transit) in response not only to competition from the automobile but also as a result of public policies that were steered more by pressure from the auto, oil, rubber and construction industries than by the urban planning movement (Foster 1981; Yago 1984). Low-density development thus rapidly filled the wedge-shaped spaces between the linear development associated with tramways and rapid transit routes, subsequently (since the Second World War) spreading outwards to produce cities 15, 30, or even (in the case of Los Angeles) 80 km across.

As the incidence of car ownership increased and traffic became more congested, the automobile has also been responsible for reshaping the geography of inner areas. Much of the older fabric of the city has given way to parking lots, and traffic engineering has created 'hot spots' of commercial development while separating residential neighbourhoods from one another with arterial roads. In particular, the parkways, freeways and motorway systems which need gentle curves, 100 metre widths of tarmac and a minimum of intersections in order to cope with contemporary volumes of traffic have imposed a broad, sweeping geometry on the existing fabric of the city, isolating some communities and depressing the environment in much the same way as the railway approaches did 100 years before.

In the United States, where levels of car ownership are significantly higher than in Europe, the automobile has also had a profound effect on the commercial structure of the city. Ribbon developments containing drive-in banks, fast-food outlets, supermarkets and retail stores of all kinds (Berry 1959) have produced characteristic conformations of commercial activity including 'automobile rows' dominated by new- and used-car lots; and 'hamburger rows' containing the ubiquitous McDonald's, Burger King, Pizza Hut, Dunkin Donut and Kentucky Fried Chicken franchises. The more recent development of out-of-town shopping malls housing air-conditioned avenues of consumer goods shops and department stores has reinforced the trend of retail decentralization, leaving the central business district of many younger cities of offices, hotels and a few specialist shops and department stores (Muller 1981).

Parallel developments in the decentralization of industry have made for the emergence of the multi-centred city, with a more complex social geography composed around a series of secondary commercial and industrial foci. The journey to work is therefore no longer dominated by the daily movement of workers from suburb to core, so much as from one suburb to another or from a suburb to a secondary business district or industrial estate.

The automobile has also altered patterns of socio-economic segregation, facilitating the settling-out of the middle classes into finely differentiated suburban estates and creating a complex mosaic of neighbourhoods. Within these neighbourhoods though, marriage and friendship patterns have become more diffuse, prompting some writers to announce the end of 'community' and the advent of the 'non-place urban realm' (Webber 1964; see also pp. 65–67). At the same time, poor, car-less families have become increasingly isolated in cheap accommodation near to the low-paid service jobs of the inner city, sustaining the legacy of the Victorian slum within the framework of the modern city. Indeed, the problems associated with the congestion and inequalities of the automobile era have prompted an increasing number of cities – Munich, Newcastle upon Tyne, San Francisco, Seattle, Vienna, Washington DC, for example – to invest in new or extended mass transit systems.

Meanwhile, urban decentralization associated with the automobile era has had important secondary effects in terms of the differential rate of change induced in existing neighbourhoods. The most striking contrasts are often to be found in the experience of former middle-class neighbourhoods and that of some of the neighbourhoods initially developed for working-class households. The latter have tended to be relatively stable, with their residents, unable to afford the costs of decentralization, channelling rises in real incomes into modest home improvements. In contrast, many of the middle-class neighbourhoods of the 'fixed rail' era of tramways and rapid transit have experienced a relative deterioration as the initial cohort of residents have decentralized and been replaced by households of lower status (Fig. 2.8).

Finally, it is important to emphasize the differential impact of successive transport technologies on cities in different regions. In the United States, for example, Baerwald (1983) has shown how the evolution of the internal structure of Eastern port cities differed from that of mid-continent river cities

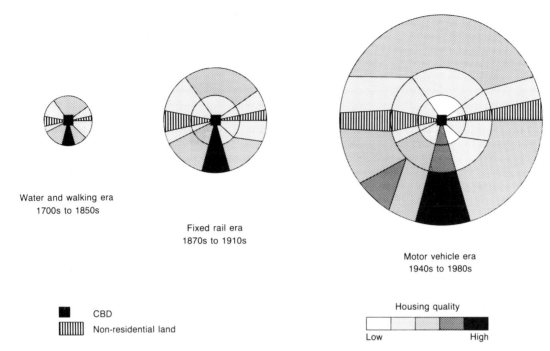

Water and walking era
1700s to 1850s

Fixed rail era
1870s to 1910s

Motor vehicle era
1940s to 1980s

■ CBD

▥ Non-residential land

Housing quality

Low ———— High

**Fig. 2.8** Changing patterns of housing quality in the North American city. *Source*: Baerwald (1984) Fig. 1, p. 5.

and of 'Sunbelt' cities because of the differential timing and interaction of urban growth and transport technologies (Fig. 2.9).

## The changing role of urban government

As cities became larger and more complex in their evolution from the pre-capitalist to the modern stage, so the scope of urban government broadened to include the regulation and provision of all kinds of goods and services, from roads, storm drainage channels, street lighting, water supplies and sewage systems to law enforcement, fire prevention, schools, clinics, transport systems and housing. All these activities have a direct and often fundamental effect on the social geography as well as on the physical morphology of cities, and the contribution of successive generations of urban government can clearly be seen today in the detail of the residential structure and

environmental quality of cities. Moreover, the economic and legislative power of modern local authorities makes them a potent factor in moulding and recasting the urban environment. This stands in stark contrast to the situation in the nineteenth century, when local governments had relatively small budgets and played only a minor role in the economic, cultural and social life of cities.

The changing role of urban governments in regulating and subsidizing different aspects of urban life is not only the result of the increased needs and expectations of city dwellers associated with industrialization and urbanization, but also the product of the changing objectives and orientations of the power-holders within local government. *As the economic base of cities shifted, the fortunes of different groups changed, cities themselves threw up new problems and challenges, and urban government attracted different types of people with different motivations and objectives.* The ethos and orientations of urban government, reflecting these changes, in turn provided the catalyst for further changes in the nature and direction

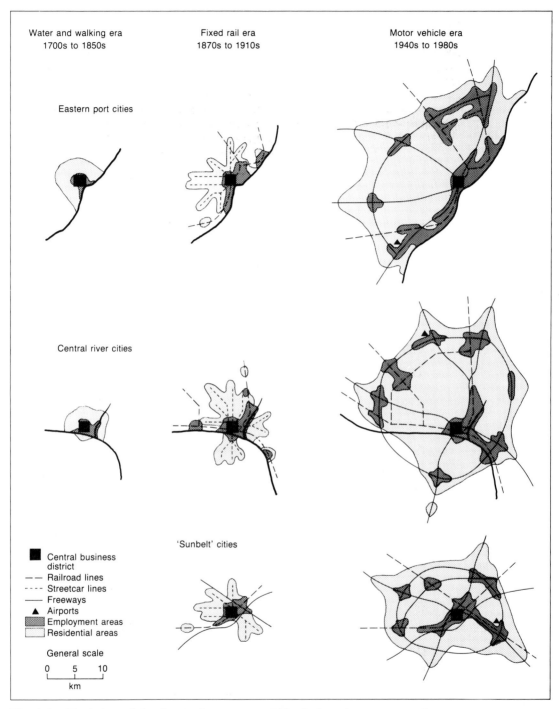

**Fig. 2.9**   Evolution of the internal structure of North American metropolises.
*Source*: Baerwald (1984) Fig. 2, p. 16.

of urban development. The two examples taken here – Britain and the United States – show how the functions of urban government are at once the product of the distribution of economic power and the agent of social and economic change in the city. In addition, both examples show broad parallels in terms of four principal phases in the evolution of urban government.

1. The earliest phase, dating to the first half of the nineteenth century, was a phase of virtual non-government, based on the doctrine of utilitarianism. This *laissez-faire* philosophy rested on the assumption that the maximum public benefit will arise from unfettered market forces. In practice, an oligarchy of merchants and patricians presided over urban affairs but did little to modify the organic growth of cities.

2. The second phase, between 1850 and 1910, saw the introduction of 'municipal socialism' by social leaders in response to the epidemics, urban disorder and congestion of the Victorian city. Urban government in this period developed a strong ethos of public service and paternalism, expressed in a wide range of liberal reforms. At the same time, the increasing power and responsibility of office-holders facilitated the widespread development of corruption in urban affairs.

3. Between 1910 and 1940 the Depression helped to generate a climate of opinion more favourable to the provision of public goods and social welfare services and, as a result, the legal powers and responsibilities of local government were futher widened.

4. In the most recent phase, since 1940, the many roles of urban government have generated large, vertically segregated bureaucracies of professional administrators geared to managing the city and its environment. The professional and the party politician now rule as a duumvirate, the balance of power between the two being variable from function to function and from city to city.

## Britain: 'Fit and Proper Persons', shopocracy and bureaucracy

In Britain, the task of exercising municipal government in an increasingly complex urban society arrived at the beginning of the nineteenth century with no precedent to which people could turn. For a long time, the most successful of the urban élite had graduated into the rural gentry and aristocracy, enriching the upper ranks of society with new talent and ideas but leaving the towns with a relatively stagnant leadership (Hennock 1973). During the early nineteenth century, however, an urban aristocracy emerged from the ranks of the rising industrial capitalists: the cotton lords of Manchester, the textile kings of Leeds, the metal magnates of Birmingham, and the jute barons of Dundee, all keen to obtain political power to match and enhance their economic weight (Cannadine 1982). This new urban élite was estranged from the upper echelons of traditional British 'society', however, by its collective struggle against the landed gentry over the Corn Laws, which kept up grain prices to the benefit of Tory landed interests while increasing the costs of food for industrial workers. The city was, in any case, the natural focus of industrialists, who clearly saw that their own fortunes and those of the city were closely inter-related. As it became apparent that municipal government could be the means of promoting local prosperity while increasing the value and productivity of their own capital through civic improvements, businessmen simply could not afford to be left out of civic affairs. So, instead of aspiring towards the squirearchy and a seat on the county bench, the industrialists founded a new local oligarchy with a strong attachment to the town.

As the pace of urban development accelerated and the problems facing municipal government multiplied, more of the successful industrialists, businessmen and *petite bourgeoisie* were attracted to office by the same combination of self interest and public service. Meanwhile, revolutionary working-class politics organized under the Chartist movement led to outbreaks of civil disorder which were quickly and heavily repressed with the help of troops (Thompson 1968). For the most part, however, the prevailing climate of opinion continued to endorse the ancient principle that those with the greatest stake in society should have the loudest voice in its affairs; and a large proportion of the people simply expected to be governed by a leadership of educated gentlemen. In this respect, the accelerated elevation of the *nouveaux riches* and *petite bourgeoisie* to municipal office gave rise to widespread complaint about the calibre of councillors and aldermen (Hennock 1973; Newton 1968). Victorians demanded 'station', 'respectability', 'intelligence' and 'education' in their leaders, as well as 'substance' and 'wealth'; and it was widely believed that many of the new recruits to urban government lacked the qualities of 'fit and proper persons'.

Nevertheless, it was the emerging middle classes which increasingly dominated urban affairs, and, at least until the 1880s, the politics of city life were characterized more by the contest for power within the middle classes than by a class struggle between the old aristocracy, the bourgeoisie and the proletariat (Fraser 1976; 1979). Mid-Victorian urban politics was dominated by the struggle for power between the old and the new families of the middle class, between Anglicans, Evangelicals and Dissenters, between Tories and Liberals. In Manchester, for example, the bourgeoisie evidently did not feel threatened politically by the proletariat; rather, their outlook was overwhelmingly 'self-referential' (Gatrell 1982). Meanwhile, the unpropertied working classes were systematically excluded from power by the legal framework of Victorian society. Under the 1835 Municipal Corporations Act, for example, the list of qualified voters was limited to occupiers of taxable property, and candidates for election to the borough council had to own real or personal property worth £1,000 or else occupy a property with a rateable value of at least £30. Even later, when these formal restrictions were relaxed, the vast majority of social groups in the city remained outside the corridors of local power. In Wolverhampton between 1888 and 1890, as many as 33 per cent of council members were owners or controllers of substantial manufacturing enterprises, while manufacturers, professionals and shopkeepers made up 72 per cent of the total. Only 6 per cent were 'workers' (Hennock 1973; Jones 1969). Few workmen, of course,

would have had time for council activity (especially with council meetings held during normal working hours) even if they were not alienated from or indifferent to the 'democratic' machinery of local government.

There is, however, some evidence that the proletariat exercised a significant *indirect* effect on the functions of urban government in the mid-nineteenth century. Foster, for instance, has argued that the liberalization of urban politics in the late nineteenth century was the collective response of the ruling classes to a crisis in the social system which was integrally related to the period of working-class consciousness and unrest in the first half of the nineteenth century (Foster 1974; see also Jones 1981). Although the extent of this class consciousness seems to have been rather variable from town to town (it was more pronounced in smaller industrial towns with a narrow economic base than in larger and economically more diversified cities), the deprivation, inherent unhealthiness and potential violence of 'the mob' undoubtedly had a lot to do with the steady abandonment of the *laissez-faire* doctrine and the corresponding increase in liberal reform during the nineteenth century (see pp. 47–53). Legislation relating to roads, water, sewage and housing all helped to ease the sanitary problems of the Victorian city and to defuse the revolutionary mood of the slums. At the same time, the improved conditions made for economic efficiency and higher productivity, so that what was good for public health and inter-class harmony was also, happily, good for business (A. Sutcliffe 1982). For a similar mixture of reasons, civic leaders introduced street lighting, paving, tramways, gas and electricity, transforming urban government itself into a great undertaking on the scale of a large business.

The professional skills and entrepreneurial attitudes developed in the everyday occupations of many councillors now became very appropriate to the job of running the city, and the inspired leadership of a few individuals enabled some cities to become the pacesetters of change. Birmingham, for example, gained a reputation as the 'best-governed city in the world' under the leadership of Joseph

Chamberlain, who pursued a municipal doctrine which relied heavily on business principles (Hennock 1973). Nevertheless, the expansion of municipal enterprise did not proceed without check. The demands of 'municipal socialism' on the pockets of ratepayers soon resulted in the election of representatives of small businessmen and the 'shopocracy', who brought a new, prudential disposition to the council chamber; and for the rest of the nineteenth century the debate between 'improvers' and 'economists' over the nature and extent of municipal spending became a central issue of urban politics.

As in the United States, it was the widespread privations of the Depression which finally swung public opinion in favour of a permanent and more fundamental municipal role in providing for many aspects of social well-being. The liberal reforms of the nineteenth century were consolidated, and cities everywhere expanded their activities in health, welfare, housing, education, security and leisure. At the same time, the composition and character of city councils shifted once more. The 75 per cent de-rating of industry by the Local Government Act (1929) and the central government's policy of industrial protection in the 1930s combined to remove from many businessmen the incentive to participate in local affairs (Cox 1976). In contrast, members of the working and lower-middle classes found a new rationale for being on the council: to speak for the city's growing number of salaried officials and blue-collar employees. These developments led to the replacement of paternalistic businessmen and social leaders by 'public persons' drawn from a wider social spectrum (Lee 1963). In addition, representatives of the working class were installed on city councils through the agency of the Labour party, and party politics soon became an important new facet of urban government. One of the most significant developments to emerge from this was the formulation of coherent policies for urban development by the major parties as part of their respective political platforms, which meant that the subsequent implementation of these policies introduced a new strategic component to the role of urban government

and brought even greater demands of judgement, foresight and expertise upon the elected members of the council.

Inevitably, these demands have led to an escalation in the number of professional officers employed to assist councillors in their decision-making. At the same time, however, the effective power of councillors to formulate policy initiatives had decreased. As the technical complexities of municipal finance, public health, educational administration and town planning have increased, councillors have become more and more dependent on the expertise of the professional officers and their staff. Consequently, the activities of urban government are increasingly influenced by the ideologies of the various administrative professions – the conservatism of accountants, the environmental determinism of town planners, and so on – rather than the inclinations of office-bearers or the preferences of the electorate. As is shown in Chapter 8, the behaviour and activities of these 'evangelistic bureaucrats' constitute one of the major influences in the social geography of contemporary British cities.

## The United States: city bosses and city managers

The system of local government in most of the United States dates from the nineteenth century, when counties, municipalities and school districts were set up in order to assist state governments in carrying out their responsibilities. Municipalities were established in order to provide essential local services for the inhabitants of urban settlements, whereas counties were given a wider set of administrative functions together with responsibility for basic rural services such as farm roads and policing; school districts were established as independent units because of a strong conviction that public education was of such importance to society as to warrant its economic and political freedom from other local governments (Bollens and Schmandt 1975). The most important exception to this system of local government is the township, which originated during the colonial period and is still prevalent in New England. In addition to the principle of elected representatives guiding urban affairs in the light of their interpretation of the 'public good', an important feature of the New England township system is the element of participatory democracy provided by town meetings, which are held in order to help resolve controversial policy issues.

In the early nineteenth century, neither townships nor municipalities regarded their role as extending beyond the provision of a reasonably sanitary and lawful environment, and city government was quietly dominated by 'natural' leaders drawn from 'established' local families. Later, as in Britain, the intensification of urban problems prompted local authorities to undertake a much greater range of activities, and the creation of a new economic order resulted in a broadened community leadership with a quite different tone. Robert Dahl has documented the best-known model of the political life-cycle of the growing American city. He portrays three successive dynasties in local affairs: the oligarchic 'Patricians' rule first, until they are pushed aside by ambitious 'Entrepreneurs', who are in turn replaced by the rising immigrants and working classes – the 'Ex-Plebes' (Dahl 1961). Nevertheless, it should be borne in mind that this schema often needs considerable modifications in order to match to experience of particular cities, as Frisch (1969), for example, has shown in his research on urban politics in nineteenth-century Springfield, Massachusetts.

Moreover, the governments of different cities developed quite different attitudes towards their responsibilities according to their different social composition and municipal backgrounds. The two principal systems of political ethics to emerge during the nineteenth century have been identified by Hofstadter:

One, founded upon the indigenous Yankee-Protestant political traditions, and upon middle-class life, assumed and demanded the constant, disinterested activity of the citizens in public affairs, argued that political life ought to be run, to a greater degree than it was, in accordance with general principles and abstract laws apart from and superior to personal needs, and expressed a common feeling that government

should be in good part an effort to moralize the lives of individuals . . .

The other system was associated with the background of European immigrant populations, and was founded

upon their unfamiliarity with independent political action, their familiarity with hierarchy and authority . . . [It] took for granted that the political life of the individual would arise out of family needs, interpreted political and civic relations chiefly in terms of personal obligations, and placed strong loyalties above allegiance to abstract codes of law or morals. It was chiefly upon this system of values that the political life of the immigrant, the boss and the urban machine was based (Hofstadter 1955: 9; see also Banfield and Wilson 1963).

The second of these situations was evident in most of the larger cities, which all contained large immigrant populations; and it was this political environment which propagated the widespread corruption which is held by some to be characteristic of American metropolitan affairs (Gardiner and Olson 1974). While petty corruption associated with the jobbing of contracts for public works was also prevalent in Victorian Britain, the patronage, bribery and organized corruption characteristic of large US cities was never paralleled except, perhaps, in Liverpool (Hennock 1973). The central feature of the system was the political 'machine' whose leaders clearly regarded the conduct of municipal affairs as a personal commercial venture or, more simply, as a source of exploitation and plunder (Callow 1976). The best-known of these machines is probably the Tammany organization in New York, which was set up in the 1970s as a Jeffersonian political club. Initially its power base was derived from the urban poor, whose approval of its stance against imprisonment for debt was consolidated during the depression of 1837–42 by the distribution of food, clothing and fuel by Tammany members. As it became increasingly involved in the local affairs of the Democratic party, the organization acquired patronage and was 'consulted' in the choice of candidates for political office who, when elected, deferred to the wishes of Tammany Hall in the distribution of city jobs. In return, these grateful job-holders donated a portion of their salary to the organization, thus lubricating the wheels of corruption with the vital ingredient of money.

The chief beneficiary of the system, of course, was the mayor, or 'city boss'. In New York, the most notorious of the city bosses was Boss Tweed (Mandelbaum 1982), but nearly every major city hosted a series of such despots and their collective impact on urban affairs has been fundamental. Besides introducing a diathesis of wholesale corruption to urban government, they also played an important part in bringing immigrant communities into the mainstream of economic and political life by way of the patronage which helped, in turn, to keep the bosses in office. In addition, many of the bosses operating in the late nineteenth and early twentieth centuries were astute enough to appreciate the general economic benefits associated with improvements to the city's infra-structure as well as the personal kudos associated with Great Works. Moreover, the more housing codes, building regulations and municipal ordinances that were passed, the more opportunities there were to solicit graft in return for not enforcing them. As a result, it was often the bosses who were responsible for extending the role of urban government in the provision of public services and amenities. They were also responsible, albeit indirectly, for the introduction of more widespread liberal reform, for, as a consequence of their personal excesses and the connection of the political machines with bootlegging, prostitution and gambling, the climate of public opinion began to swing in favour of progressive candidates sponsored by middle-class reform groups. Only in cities where the majority of the upper-middle classes had moved out to suburban municipalities, taking with them their interest in urban affairs, did the machine system continue to dominate urban politics – as in Chicago, Detroit and Philadelphia (McCarthy 1977; Stave and Stave 1981).

Elsewhere, reform groups took steps towards eliminating the worst effects of machine politics. In this context, one of the most significant developments was the modification of the mayor/council system of government through the appointment of a 'manager' who would be directly responsible to the city council for the administration of municipal functions of all kinds. First introduced in Staunton, Virginia, in 1908, and widely publicized by its adoption in Dayton, Ohio, in 1914, the city manager/council system is now in operation in a majority of municipalities of between 23,000 and 250,000 population, and in one in four of all larger cities (Bollens and Schmandt 1982). Much of the attractiveness of the system must be attributed to the need for professional assistance in handling the increasing scope and complexity of municipal affairs, especially given the expansion of urban social welfare programmes since the Depression. For the same reason, most cities have become dependent on large bureaucracies staffed by specialist professionals. These include members of research teams and planning departments whose functions are centred on the formulation of strategic policies relevant to the various social and economic problems which afflict the contemporary city. Compared to their counterparts in Britain, however, US city planners have much less weight in influencing the actual outcome of events, with the major exceptions of transport planning and land-use zoning. Warner (1972) believes that the strong American tradition of private property rights and the consequent reluctance to give planners the power to deal with land as a social resource lies at the heart of many urban dilemmas, including environmental degradation, housing problems, and the inefficient and inequitable location of schools, hospitals and other public facilities. The idea of combating urban problems by means of coercive, regulatory and redistributive policies did gain some momentum after the Second World War (particularly during the Kennedy and Johnson administrations), to the extent that some aspects of the social geography of American cities began to alter. Recently, however, the return to free-enterprise principles imposed by the Reagan administration has prompted severe cut-backs in public expenditure and a significant retreat in the ambitions of city planners (Ahlbrandt 1984).

## Spirit and matter: ideology and the built environment

Just as the functions of urban government can be seen as a reflection of the interaction between the orientation of successive groups of power-holders and the problems and opportunities which confronted them, so can the general layout and townscape of cities be seen as a reflection of the prevailing ideology (in the sense of a political climate, *zeitgeist*, or 'spirit') of a particular period. Of course, the political climate of an age, together with its dominant economic and social formations, its technology, and the functions of contemporary local government, should really be seen as inter-related components of a broader process of urban development (Knox 1984), and attempts to link them within a theoretical framework are considered in some detail in subsequent chapters. For the moment, however, it is convenient to focus specifically on the interaction between 'spirit' and 'matter'.

The idea of urban fabric being seen – in part, at least – as the outcome of broad political, socio-economic and cultural forces has been explicit in much writing on urban history (see, for example, Mumford 1961; Curl 1970; King 1980a). As Curl puts it, 'The argument, briefly, is that the political climate is determined by the dominant members of a society, that is, by the ruling classes, and that the political climate thus created in turn influences the design of urban settlements profoundly' (Curl 1970: 1). The best-known examples of the influence of ideology on urban form are non-Western, relating to the influence of religious and cosmological beliefs on town plans. Many Chinese and south-east Asian cities, for example, were laid out as images of the universe (Wheatley 1975; Carter 1975), and there is evidence to suggest that Roman cities were also laid out according to cosmological beliefs (Rykwert 1976). Other examples are not difficult to find, however. Despotism, nationalism, colonialism, and paternalism (i.e. what passes for socialism in most Western cities) have all been shown to have produced distinctive urban environments

which can still be identified in the bricks and mortar left over from earlier stages in the development of the Western city.

The centralized power associated with colonialism, for example, has been connected with a characteristic morphology. Here, the *zeitgeist* is concerned with imposing order as quickly and efficiently as possible, with a minimum of embellishment. The result, remarkably often, is a settlement whose layout is dominated by a grid or chequerboard system: easy to survey and thus quickly established (Stanislawski 1946). It was the standard form for new towns established in the aftermath of Alexander's conquest of the Middle East, and was adopted by the Romans for their colonial towns, the grid sometimes surviving in the modern street pattern, as in Chichester, Colchester, Orleans and Zaragoza. With the urban revival of the Middle Ages the grid appeared in Slav towns planted by Germans, in the *bastide* towns of southern France, and in the towns established by the Christian kings of Spain as they reconquered territory from the Moors (Smailes 1966). More recently, the grid appeared with the Jacobean colonization of Ulster and the British colonization of North America. Even after the British had left the United States, the grid spread with the administrative colonization of the West, for the federal survey system was based on a six-mile square subdivided into 36 square sections of 640 acres each. As a result, rectilinear layout has become a prominent feature of the American urban landscape.

One of the most striking examples is the symbolization of power in the urban environments created by despotic rulers and nationalistic governments. Renaissance and Baroque cities like Versailles, Richelieu, St Petersburg and Karlsruhe were built in the grand manner – with piazzas, boulevards and monumental architecture – by autocratic rulers, displaying a unity of design which resulted from having been built under the complete control of one hand with the express purpose of reflecting the power and the glory of the secular princes and kings of the emerging nation states of Europe (Lavedan 1941). Similarly, the majestic ground plan and imposing architecture of central Washington can be seen as the result of a deliberate attempt to symbolize the power and self-image of a new nation (Craig 1978; Reps 1965).

With the rise of capitalism and the advent of the nation state, the symbolism of public and ceremonial architecture became more varied. The purpose of the symbolism, nevertheless, was the same: to legitimize a particular ideology or power system by providing a physical focus to which sentiments could be attached. One way in which public architecture was deliberately used in promoting the new ideology of an industrializing nation state has been detailed by Schroeter (1978) using the example of the Pallazzo delle Finanze in Rome. Although unexceptional in terms of 'high' architecture, this building for the Ministry of Finance in the fledgling Italian state of the 1880s was of prime significance in expressing the rejection of the intellectual leadership of the church in favour of a new leadership committed to technology and efficiency. By commissioning a building with a 'minimum of embellishment' and locating it in an undeveloped tract well away from the historic core and the Vatican City, the new government hoped to signal its commitment to a clean break with tradition and a fresh start based on the rationalism of industrial capitalism.

More recently, the nationalistic ideologies fostered by the fascist regimes in Italy and Germany during the 1930s have produced more forthright symbols of power and destiny. Among the better-known examples is Mussolini's attempt to create 'La Terza Roma' in a style which Hughes (1980) has described as having 'a jackboot in either camp: one in the vision of Ancient Rome and the other in the vision of a technocratic future'. Even more symbolic of power and ruthless strength is the ceremonial architecture of the Third Reich: the House of German Art in Munich and the Zeppelin Field and Congress Hall in Nuremburg, for example (Gloag 1979). In addition to these centrepieces, however, both regimes deliberately imprinted their ideology throughout the fabric of the urban system. Mussolini, enraptured by modernism, technology and the cult of masculinity, adopted

Marinetti's Futurism as the official style for Italian Fascism: not only for major projects such as New Towns (Millon 1978), but also for hundreds of smaller structures. In Germany, where party ideologists condemned the Modern Movement as alien and culturally degenerate, the most striking legacy of Fascist ideology is to be found in the domestic architecture of the period: variants of the Hansel and Gretel cottage and of Tyrolean, *Heimatstil* and *Fachwerk* designs, which were intended to reinforce the idea of a distinctive German culture rooted in the virtues of rural peasantry (Mullin 1981, 1982).

These are somewhat larger-than-life examples. More important – though more elusive and less well documented – is the 'meaning' of the various architectural ecologies comprising the modern city. In contemporary Western democracies, power is not only fragmented but also ebbs and flows between different factions of capital (commercial, industrial, international, small businesses, etc.), the central government, local government, and coalitions of special interest groups. It follows that the symbolic content of the built environment will be multi-layered and, often, ambiguous. There are, however, certain themes that are common to the built environment of most modern cities. The ideology of civics and the power of local government, for example, are frequently symbolized in civic architecture:

Town Halls seem to have been built at the point when a city felt it had finally 'arrived' and had a new consciousness of its place in the world. The great steel city of Sheffield built its town hall in the late 1890s while Liverpool, which was a port of considerable wealth when most of the other towns were mere villages, built one in the mid-eighteenth century and added St George's Hall, a fine public place of assembly combined with law courts, in the 1840s (Tarn 1980: 73).

Much of this civic architecture, like the town halls of Manchester, Rochdale and Leeds, was lavish and palatial, intended to impress neighbouring cities as well as their own electorate. In the modern setting, the 'spirit' of municipal pride and boosterism is reflected in a variety of virility symbols ranging from high rise housing projects to redevelopment schemes and urban freeways.

As we have seen, two competing ideologies have dominated urban affairs since the early nineteenth century: *laissez-faire* capitalism, and liberalism. The remainder of this section is concerned with the ramification of these two ideologies on the built environment, with particular emphasis on the implications of the development of the increasingly important paternalistic and idealistic value systems associated with the 'liberal' political climate.

## The environments of capitalism

There are two ways in which the spirit of capitalism has been clearly imprinted on the fabric of modern cities. The first is connected with the symbolization of wealth and achievement by groups of prosperous merchants and industrialists. Early examples of this include the splendid architecture of Edinburgh's New Town, the elegant Georgian squares and crescents of Bath and London, and the urbane town houses of ante-bellum Boston and New York, built for a 'confident and privileged class' of merchant capitalists (Bell and Bell 1972). The industrial capitalists of Victorian times also felt the compulsion to express their achievements in buildings:

Individual commercial firms, banks and insurance companies, the family shops which grew into new department stores, and the railway companies with their stations and hotels, whose scale was more in keeping with the new system of transport than the old coaching inn, all strove for an image which epitomized pride in achievement, individuality and personal success, and a sense of stability which the great piles of stone, brick and terracotta seemed to symbolize. For them architects scoured Ancient Rome and the medieval world as well as their own fantastic imaginations for artistic languages which would adequately express the stature of the newly-rich merchants and bankers of Victorian Britain; men who were intensely proud but not a little insecure, who sought to create the right impression through the acquisition of tangible riches; men who desperately patronized the fashionable artists of the new age from the pre-Raphaelites onwards, and founded art collections which are the pride of many a northern city art gallery to which they were very often bequeathed. . . . Rarely, as in Newcastle upon Tyne was there a consistency of development . . . more often the pattern of land ownership produced a picturesque effect with a Grecian bank, a Renaissance palazzo office or a Jacobean style hotel jostling one another, and on occasion Gothic design for good measure (Tarn 1980: 73)

The Cross Street area of central Manchester is still dominated by the imposing gothic architecture commissioned by the city's Victorian élite who, preoccupied with the accumulation and display of wealth but with a rather philistine attitude towards aesthetics, left a clear impression of their values on the central area of the city. Manchester, as Kennedy observes, 'was a confident city, and that confidence was expressed in bricks and mortar, in edifices built to last, to show future ages all was well' (Kennedy 1970: 86).

As the petite bourgeoisie of small-scale merchant and industrial capital has lost ground to corporate and international capital, so the symbolization of achievement and prosperity has become dominated by corporate structure. Huge office blocks such as the Prudential Building in Boston and the Pirelli Building in Paris are clearly intended as statements of corporate power and achievement, notwithstanding any administrative or speculative functions. Ford, for example, has described how the 'skyscraper infatuation' that spread through the Midwest in the 1920s and 1930s was a result of 'the desire on the part of many companies to construct monuments to themselves' (Ford 1973: 324). These skyscrapers affected the downtown area of cities both from a functional and a visual standpoint: even single buildings such as the Terminal Tower in Cleveland and the AIU Citadel in Columbus (adorned with statues and lanterns and containing within it a copy of the Hall of Mirrors at Versailles and the Bridge of Sighs in Venice) were able to relocate the focal point of a central business district, blighting adjacent residential areas through the increase in local taxes that their presence brought about while attracting, instead, new commercial and administrative buildings. At a more general level, of course, the whole complex of offices and stores in entire downtown areas can be interpreted as symbolic of the power of the 'central district élite' in relation to the rest of the city (Cox 1973). Meanwhile, other institutions have added their particular statements to the palimpsest of the urban fabric. The sponsors of universities, trade union headquarters, cultural centres and the like, unable (or unwilling) to make use of the rude message of high-rise building, have generally fallen back on the combination of neoclassicism and modernism favoured by Mussolini: a style which has become 'as if by osmosis' the reigning international style for any building aspiring to carry authority through an image of high-mindedness rather than raw power (Hughes 1980).

The second way in which the spirit of capitalism can be said to have directly affected the fabric of cities is related to the activities of speculative developers, who have been responsible for the design and layout of a large proportion of the housing stock of cities. Their search for profit – surely the essence of the 'spirit' of capitalism – has produced a large amount of working- and lower-middle class housing based on a repetitive layout (often gridded) and characterized by uniformity and regimentation. It should be emphasized that this is a generalization which applies only to housing built for families with low or modest incomes, for whom the cost of housing (whether for rent or purchase) was a critical factor: the housing produced by speculative developers for the more affluent middle classes has always reflected their ability to pay for a sounder and more varied environment. In the present context, this could be seen as a reflection of another element of capitalist ideology: that of consumer sovereignty. But it is in the lower end of the market that the most direct expression of capitalism's inherent search for profit is to be found (Warner 1984).

Faced with a large but relatively impoverished market, the speculative developers of the nineteenth and early twentieth centuries could only make a satisfactory profit by giving themselves to a high-volume, low-cost product. The latter could only be achieved by producing large tracts of standardized dwellings on rectilinear plots, taking advantage of the divison of labour and economies of scale. Thus emerged the brick terraces of English cities, the tall tenements of Glasgow, Edinburgh, Paris, New York, Berlin and Genoa, the wooden 'three-deckers' of New England towns, and the two- and three-storey walk-up apartment buildings of Philadelphia, Chicago and St Louis. (Later these were joined, on the same principle, by the semi-detached and detached single-family dwellings of lower-middle class suburbs in cities everywhere.) Architecture was superseded by pattern books containing plans of known profitability, and houses were built to minimal standards, soon inducing widespread deterioration. The most profitable shape – deep, narrow buildings – allowed only minimum light and air; and the grid pattern which saved so much on survey, construction and administrative costs soon proved a hindrance to traffic as well as being unsuited to the development of centred and bounded neighbourhoods in which 'community' could flourish.

## Paternalism and idealism

The paternalistic and idealistic value systems associated with liberalism and the development of 'municipal socialism' are, in part, the product of such shortcomings in housing standards. As a number of writers have shown, these value systems are the result of a complex interaction between social, religious, political and environmental factors, leavened by the originality of a few individuals (Ashworth 1954; Sutcliffe 1980; Tarn 1973; Philpott 1978). Because of this, the influence of paternalism and idealism on the built environment is best understood in relation to events in one country, with only occasional sideways glances at what was going on elsewhere. The example taken here in based on events in Britain, where the two ideologies have probably had more influence on urban form than anywhere in the western world. (For a comparison of events elsewhere, see Bollerey and Hartmann 1980; Boyer 1978; Calabi 1980; Marcuse 1980; Ward 1984.)

## The context

The general background to the liberal value systems of the nineteenth century has already been outlined in the discussion of urban government. In particular, it has been suggested that the liberalization of urban politics in the late nineteenth century was essentially a pragmatic response by the ruling classes to the dangers associated with the 'condition' of the working classes. The heart of the problem facing adherents to the *laissez-faire* ideology of unrestrained capitalism (and its corollary of non-government) was to be found in the squalor, overcrowding and disease of the inner city slums. For a long time these areas remained *terra incognita* to the great majority of the Victorian middle classes who were, in consequence, unaware of the extent and intensity of the misery to be found there (Wohl 1977). Throughout the second half of the nineteenth century this ignorance was assailed by a series of mordant and alarming commentaries based on the surveys of a few individuals who had become committed to liberal reform. It was not their compassion which dented the spirit of *laissez-faire*, however, so much as the palpable dangers of the slums to the rest of the city's inhabitants (Jones 1971). The regular outbreaks of cholera, typhoid and dysentery were clearly related to conditions in the slums; and in addition there was the constant danger of large-scale fires. Even more important was the Victorian fear of 'the mob', which was greatly reinforced by the revolutionary events throughout Europe in 1848. Even the New World did not escape proletarian unrest: more than twenty major riots occurred in New York City between 1834 and 1871, mostly attributed to 'riffraff' from Europe (Warner 1972). So, with property as well as physical well-being under threat, the middle classes began to accede to the reformist ideas advanced by the liberal pamphleteers.

## 1840–1870: Private paternalism

The early liberal reformers capitalized on the idea of the 'dangerous classes' in their attempts to promote their cause, but a good deal of careful documentation was also necessary in order to convince Victorians of the need for reform of any kind. One of the most influential figures in this context was Edwin Chadwick who, as First Secretary of the Poor Law Board, was largely responsible for the Board's Report on *The Sanitary Conditions of the Labouring Population and the Means of Its Improvement* (1842), which drew widespread publicity because of its sheer weight of evidence. This document, together with similar publications, played a significant part in changing the climate of opinion about liberal reform for, reinforced by a particularly widespread outbreak of cholera in 1848, it had the effect of focusing the latent sense of *noblesse oblige* among the aristocracy as well as stimulating the Presbyterian sense of guilt which affected many successful Victorian businessmen. The interested parties formed themselves into associations whose *zeitgeist* is reflected in their titles: the Health of Towns Association, the Association for Promoting Cleanliness Amongst the Poor, the Society for Improving the Conditions of the Labouring Classes, the Metropolitan Association for Improving the Dwellings of the Industrious Classes, and so on. At first they were limited to passing pious resolutions; but they soon began to lead by example, commissioning model housing in order to demonstrate the feasibility of building sound housing for the poor at a profit (Chapman 1971). Although they met with some success, it became evident that decent tenement buildings could not be built as cheaply as had been envisaged, with the result that the rents which had to be charged in order to make even a modest return on capital were beyond the pocket of casual labourers. Meanwhile, the efforts of these paternalistic associations were easily outpaced by the feverish activities of speculative developers who employed 'the builder of walls without footing, the bricklayer who knew how to mix mortar without cement, the carpenter who could lay floors over green joists, the plumber who knew just how to lay drains without traps or how to install cold water systems which had a positive, intimate and lethal acquaintance with the sewage arrangements' (Dyos 1968a: 685).

There followed a period of intellectual

debate about housing and public health. Although there was a broad consensus as to the extent and urgency of the problem, observers disagreed both as to its causes and the appropriate remedies. Pons, for example, has shown how contemporary analyses of Manchester ranged from the radical views of Friedrich Engels through the liberal views of Dr James Kay to the eulogistic writings of the Rev. Robert Lamb, who saw the problems of the slums as an unavoidable by-product of the unfolding Destiny of Man (Pons 1978; see also Anderson 1977). Parallel to this debate there emerged a separate, idealistic movement with an underlying anti-urban ideology. The antecedents of this movement had been established earlier in the century with Robert Owen's social experiment at New Lanark (which inspired an ill-fated community at New Harmony in Indiana), and in the 1850s it came to fruition in a series of small communities built by paternalistic factory owners in a spirit of enlightened self-interest (Bell and Bell 1972). These communities, complete with a variety of housing, public baths, wash houses and elevating institutions (like New Lanark's Institute for the Formation of Character) were carefully planted away from towns in the belief that the semi-rural environment would be ideal for the physical and moral welfare of the workers, who would repay the owner not only in grateful loyalty but also in higher productivity. The best-known of these communities is Saltaire, built by Titus Salt in the Aire valley outside Bradford.

During the 1860s the movement lost momentum and was overshadowed by philanthropic housing organizations whose activities were focused on the production of sanitary housing for the poor in large cities. This philanthropy, however, was constrained by the still-dominant ideology of capitalism. Profit still had to be made from such ventures, even if it was only a profit of 5 per cent or so: 'a penance for more fulsome success elsewhere' (Tarn 1973: 43). Like all such movements, the numbers willing to make such a gesture were few; but several wealthy individuals and philanthropic foundations made important contributions to the housing stock of larger cities. In London, for example, the George Peabody Trust completed over 5,000 dwellings for the poor between 1862 and 1895, many of which have survived into the 1980s. Like the earlier demonstration projects, however, these philanthropic ventures were only accessible to the 'respectable poor' who could afford the rents which made profit possible; and, despite the efforts of men like Peabody, the housing problem continued to grow faster than philanthropic contributions.

### 1870–1910: Public paternalism

The political climate of the 1870s was still generally hostile towards any kind of public paternalism, even though most local authorities had acquired powers to undertake essential services such as sewage and water. Indeed, many prominent 'liberal' reformers – such as Octavia Hill – firmly believed in the power of private enterprise and self-help to improve slums without government help. The problems of the poor were widely believed to stem from their 'character' and morals (much blame was attached to the influence of Irish immigrants in this respect), and so the proper solution was seen in terms of amateur social work and educational propaganda. Nevertheless, the failure of model housing, model communities, philanthropic and self-help movements to cope with the potentially dangerous problems of the slums, together with a growing 'crisis of profitability' in inner-city housing markets (Foster 1979), prompted a series of Royal Commissions which led to two Acts of Parliament in 1875. These became landmarks in the history of liberal reform, for they introduced aspects of public intervention with far-reaching effects on the quality of the built environment. The first of these Acts was the Public Health Act, which enabled local authorities to establish model byelaws (i.e. minimum standards for housing development) and to alter or pull down any work which contravened the byelaws. Thus emerged the principle of social control over building activity. The second important Act of 1875 was the Artisans' Dwellings Act which, among other things, allowed local authorities to acquire powers to demolish slum areas if they were considered to be a health hazard. The

Act thus took public paternalism an important step towards area planning and urban renewal, although the immediate success of the Act was limited by the high costs of compensation won by slum landlords (Chapman 1971; Yelling 1982).

Again there followed a period of intellectual debate about the housing question, this time extending to popular newspapers and ladies' tea clubs. One of the most influential publications of this period was Andrew Mearns's *The Bitter Cry of Outcast London* (1883), which drew attention to the continuing moral and sanitary problems caused by overcrowding and called for state and local governments to shoulder more responsibility for housing and environmental problems (Wohl 1977). Almost inevitably, there followed another Royal Commission, this time required to consider the 'Housing of the Working Classes'. It reported in 1885, by which time Parliament was rather distracted by the Irish question. One important outcome of the Commission's report, however, was the Local Government Act of 1888 which reorganized local government into counties and county boroughs, giving them a considerable amount of autonomy. Their creation helped to promote a strong sense of civic pride, and in the more liberal environment that prevailed towards the turn of the century many local authorities began to take full advantage of byelaw and slum clearance legislation. Before long, powers were sought from the Secretary of State to build public housing in areas where neither speculative developers nor philanthropists could profitably build housing for the poor. Some of the first housing schemes were in Scotland, where a long tradition of cultural and economic discipline based on the philosophies of Stewart, Brown, Ferrier and Carlyle had created a *zeitgeist* which made for a firmer and more positive civic government. It was Glasgow, as Allan observes, that first recognized 'that a free market, private philanthropy and public health regulations could not provide an adequate solution . . . and that the City Fathers must at least supervise and plan redevelopment' (Allan 1965: 613); and it was Dundee and Edinburgh, not London or Birmingham, that quickly followed suit. At this stage of municipal development, however, ideological and financial constraints meant that even the best-intentioned schemes to house the 'poorest of the poor' were effectively translated into housing for a working-class élite (Pooley 1985).

The last years of the nineteenth century also saw a resurgence of idealism and the model communities movement, which produced two important developments: Port Sunlight, across the Mersey from Liverpool, and Bournville, outside Birmingham. Both were built by industrialists (W. H. Lever and George Cadbury respectively) seeking room to expand business, but neither were intended to be merely an employer's village. Port Sunlight was intended to demonstrate the viability of profit-sharing at the community level, and Bournville was established as a 'social example', with half of its working population working elsewhere than at the Cadbury Brothers' Factory. Both communities successfully took root, grew and became strong enough to stand by themselves (unlike George Pullman's ill-fated venture south of Chicago, where the townspeople rebelled against the degree of paternalistic control insisted upon by their benefactor), showing that low-density 'garden-suburb' planning was a feasible strategy. Within a few years this idealism was given extra momentum with the publication of Ebenezer Howard's *Garden Cities of Tomorrow* (1902) which codified a great mass of ideas and experience. Howard himself was closely involved in the Garden City Pioneer Co. Ltd, which promoted the development of Letchworth, the first full Garden City. Using Howard's schematic plans (Fig. 2.10), the company laid out roads, parks and factory sites and invited private developers to build carefully regulated housing on prepared sites. The scheme was supported by radicals and liberals because it involved land-use control and centralized planning; and by conservatives because it gave private enterprise the scope to provide housing. More important, it proved to be an economic success. Thus reinforced, Howard's ideas quickly spread, achieving concrete form in several places. New Earswick, near York, had already been commissioned by Joseph Rowntree as a result of Howard's

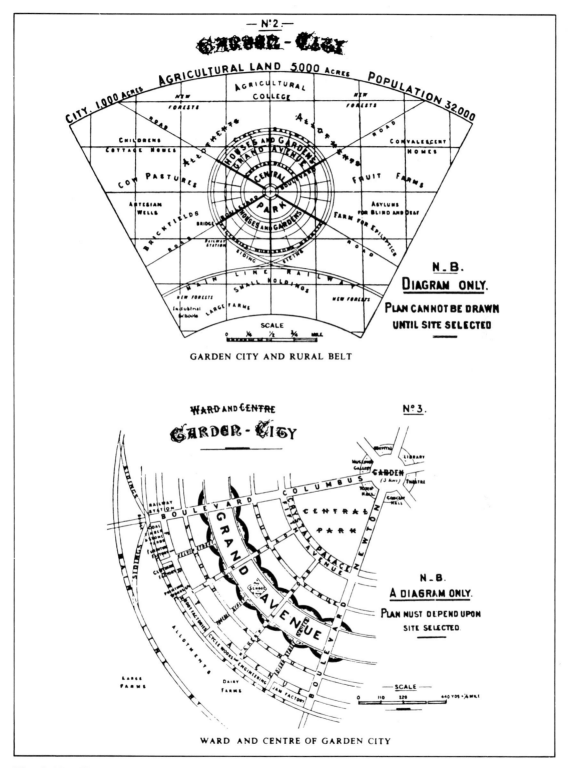

**Fig. 2.10** Ebenezer Howard's ideas for a garden city.
*Source*: Howard (1902) pp. 52 and 53.

*Garden Cities*, and it was quickly followed by Hampstead Garden Suburb (1907–14) and numerous smaller garden suburbs such as Woodlands in Donscaster, Fallings Park in Wolverhampton and Altrincham and Manchester (Edwards 1981; Tarn 1973).

### 1910–1945: Professionalized paternalism

The combination of this movement with the framework of housing legislation and the increasingly liberal political climate provided the background for the emergence of the town planning movement (Cherry 1979), which has become one of the most important single factors in shaping the morphology and social geography of the British city. After seeing the undernourished and undersized recruits for the Boer War, even the most rigid of conservatives were ready to shelve some of their most prized social theories in favour of a more widespread, formalized system of paternalism. An important catalyst in the emergence of such a system was Patrick Geddes, a professor of botany at Dundee, an amateur urban social geographer and an active campaigner for social and housing reform. Geddes had formal or informal affiliations with all of the relevant societies and was in touch with most of the prominent planners and architects of the day, and so came to be one of the leading figures behind the formulation of the first Town Planning Act (1909). This Act encapsulated all of the paternalistic and idealistic value systems which had developed during the nineteenth century, and clearly subscribed to the environmental determinism which has underlain the ideology of the planning profession ever since. In the words of the Bill introducing the Act:

The object of the Bill is to provide a domestic condition for the people in which their physical health, their morals, their character and their whole social condition can be improved . . . The Bill aims in broad outline at, and hopes to secure, the home healthy, the house beautiful, the town pleasant, the city dignified, and the suburb salubrious. It seeks, and hopes to secure, more and better homes, better houses, prettier streets, so that the character of a great people, in towns and cities and villages, can be still further

improved and strengthened by the conditions under which they live. . .

It was not until the interwar period, however, that town planning received the impetus which has made it such an important factor in contemporary urban geography. The impetus came from an unlikely alliance between three different movements, each concerned, for their own reasons, about urban sprawl. Rural conservationists were worried about the loss of prime agricultural land (about 25,000 hectares per annum in the 1930s), and their case was given some urgency by the impending threat of war. Urban idealists were also concerned about the degeneration of the garden city idea into the semi-detached ribbon development which characterized much of the sprawal; and the lobby for the depressed regions of the country had a keen interest in curbing the energy of the big cities in order to promote growth elsewhere. There thus developed a strong anti-urban alliance, epitomized in a collection of essays entitled *Britain and the Beast* (Williams-Ellis 1938): the 'beast' in question being urbanization. This anti-urban school of thought had a profound influence on subsequent planning strategy, largely as a result of the inspired efforts of Patrick Abercrombie, who had interests in each of the allied anti-urban movements and who was responsible for introducing the influential concepts of green belts and overspill policies to town planning in his plan for London in 1944 (King 1980b). These ideas, together with the garden city idealism, the paternalism and evangelical zeal inherited from the nineteenth century, and the new ideas of men like Clarence Perry (on planned neighbourhoods), Vandervelde and Kropotkin (on deurbanization), and Le Corbusier (on high-rise living) have dominated the ideology of the planning profession ever since (Hall 1984a). Their impact on the postwar British city has been substantial, and a detailed consideration of the spatial outcomes associated with their application is presented in Chapter 8. What is most important to bear in mind is that the liberalism and philanthropy which spawned the town planning movement in Victorian Britain was founded on a deep paradox which persists in the make-up of modern planning (Knox and Cullen 1981a). The paradox was this. Although urbanization was the vehicle which capitalism needed in order to marshal goods and labour efficiently, it created dangerous conditions under which the losers and the exploited could organize themselves and consolidate. Planning, as a response to this paradox, was born a hybrid creature, dedicated on the one hand to humanistic reform, but charged on the other with the management of cities according to a particular kind of economic and social organization. Its task was to create and maintain conditions in which workers could flourish and enjoy good health, without flourishing to such a degree that the established social and political order was seriously challenged.

# 3 The social dimensions of modern urbanism

An important part of the geographer's task of illuminating the nature and causes of spatial differentiation is to lay bare the inter-relationships between people and their environments. In urban social geography, this involves a consideration of the complex interaction between individuals, social groups and the diverse physical and socio-economic environments of the city. The objective in this chapter is to provide some commentary on the theories and ideas relevant to this task. Many of the ideas described are derived from other disciplines – chiefly urban sociology and environmental psychology – although the focus throughout is on their spatial implications. This chapter is thus based on the contention that the spatial order of the city can only be properly understood against the background of the underlying dimensions of social organization and human behaviour in the city. The suggestion is not, however, that the spatial order of the city is completely subordinate to social factors; the influence of space and distance on individual behaviour and social organization will be a recurring theme in this chapter.

## Urban life in Western culture

In general, the overall relationship between man and the physical and social environments afforded by cities has traditionally been viewed as bad. Cultural expressions, public opinion and social theories about city life have all erred towards negative impressions and have tended to be highly deterministic,

blaming the ills of city life on the inherent attributes of urban environments (an important exception here is the strand of social thought represented by Marxist social theory, which is considered in detail in subsequent chapters).

Evidence from a sizeable number of attitudinal surveys suggests that most people believe city environments to be unsatisfactory. A recent survey by the United States Department of Housing and Urban Development (Roettger 1980) showed that only 1 in 5 Americans thought that cities represented the best kind of environment in which to live; 30 per cent nominated suburban environments, and 44 per cent nominated small town or rural environments. Data from European surveys show a similar anti-urban leaning. Moreover, these attitudes show up not only in hypothetical residential preferences but also in evaluations of actual communities. Satisfaction with the overall 'quality of life' and with several major components of well-being tends to decline steadily with the transition from rural to metropolian environments (Table 3.1; see also Dahmann 1983). Such data, however, are notoriously difficult to interpret. A case in point is the apparent ambiguity of results which show people professing to prefer rural or small-town living but whose behaviour has brought them to the city, presumably in pursuit of a higher material level of living. The city thus emerges as neither good nor bad, but as a 'necessary evil'.

This lop-sided ambivalence towards the city – a grudging functional attraction accompanied by an intellectual dislike – has long been reflected in the literature and art of Western

**Table 3.1**  Perceived quality of life by community size, European Community, *c.* 1978

| Per cent completely satisfied with | Community Size | | | | |
|---|---|---|---|---|---|
| | <20,000 | 20,000–100,000 | 20,000–100,000 | 100,000–500,000 | 500,000–1 million |
| Employment | 22.0 | 18.6 | 20.0 | 10.0 | 13.1 |
| Income | 24.6 | 22.1 | 25.6 | 16.6 | 14.3 |
| Housing | 11.4 | 11.1 | 12.5 | 5.8 | 3.6 |
| Leisure activities | 20.4 | 16.6 | 18.6 | 10.9 | 6.0 |
| Amount of leisure | 20.4 | 16.4 | 21.9 | 11.8 | 0.0 |
| Welfare benefits | 17.4 | 14.9 | 12.2 | 4.1 | 3.6 |
| Transport | 24.7 | 21.2 | 19.7 | 14.9 | 10.7 |
| Health | 31.3 | 24.0 | 28.1 | 21.0 | 21.4 |
| Social environment | 9.1 | 6.0 | 6.3 | 4.8 | 1.2 |
| Life as a whole | 12.7 | 10.0 | 10.1 | 6.8 | 4.8 |

*Source:* 'Eurobarometer' survey data from the commission of the European communities. Data made available by the Inter-University Consortium for Political and Social Research (USA).

society (including the idiom of popular songs: e.g. the work of Joan Armatrading, Bob Dylan, Joni Mitchell, Paul Simon and Pete Townshend). Raymond Williams, for example, has clearly shown that while British literature has occasionally celebrated the positive attributes of city life, there has been a much greater emphasis on its defects, paralleled by the persistence of a romanticist portrayal of country life: for every urban thrill and sophistication there are several urban laments and rural yearnings (Williams 1973; see also King 1980b). Surveys of American literature and intellectual thought have also emphasized the image of the city as an arena of conflict and desolation (Jaye and Watts 1981; Kazin 1983; Lees 1985; Siegel 1981; Tuan 1978), though others have been able to demonstrate how the city has in addition been variously regarded as a catalyst, a challenge and a 'stage' for the enactment of human drama and personal lifestyle by certain schools of thought (Marx 1984; Paterson 1976). The idea of the city in Western culture is thus 'a montage of mixed and clashing elements: . . . of senseless, brutal crime; of personal freedom and boundless hopes; of variety, choice, excitement; of callous and uncaring people; of social groups diverse enough to satisfy each individual's unique needs; of crass and crushing materialism; of experiment, innovation and creativity; of anxious days and frightful nights' (Fischer 1976: 17).

New York, to most people, is probably the best exemplar of this diversity. On the one hand it is able to prompt the horrific stereotype of urban life portrayed in Feiffer's play *Little Murders*, in which the principal character asks:

You know how I get through the day? . . . in planned segments. I get up in the morning and think, O.K. a sniper didn't get me for breakfast, let's see if I can go for a walk without being mugged.
O.K., I finished my walk, let's see if I can make it back home without having a brick dropped on my head from the top of a building. O.K., I'm safe in the lobby, let's see if I can go up in the elevator without getting a knife in my ribs.
O.K., I made it to the front door, let's see if I can open it without finding burglars in the hall. O.K. I made it to the hall, let's see if I can walk into the living room and not find the rest of my family dead (Feiffer 1968: 88).

On the other hand, the advantages of life in a city like New York include accessibility to a tremendous variety of opportunities. Fischer cites the reaction of a 'refugee' New Yorker living in Vermont:

I kept hearing this tempting ad for a Czechoslovakian restaurant . . . When the ad went on to say that this particular place had been chosen by the critic of the *Times* out of all the Czech restaurants in New York as the very best, I could have broken down and cried. I hardly get a choice of doughnut stands in Vermont; New Yorkers idly pick and choose among Czech restaurants (Fischer 1976: 59)

Fischer suggests that it is possible to recognize four basic themes within this ambivalent imagery of cities, each expressed as polarities:

| Rural | | Urban |
|---|---|---|
| Nature | versus | Art |
| Familiarity | versus | Strangeness |
| Community | versus | Individualism |
| Tradition | versus | Change |

Fischer points out that there is a 'tension' in these pairings which derives from the fact that neither half is universally 'better' or 'worse' than the other. Instead, they pose dilemmas of personal choice. Depending on which horn of the dilemma they have grasped, philosophers and poets have become either pro-urbanists or (as is usually the case) anti-urbanists.

## Urbanism and social theory

These polarities are also present in the stock of social theories concerning city life. The strangeness, artificiality, individualism and diversity of urban environments have been seen by many social scientists as fundamental influences on human behaviour and social organization. This deterministic and environmentalist perspective has had a profound effect on urban social geography as well as on sociology and all the cognate disciplines. It stems from the writings of European social philosophers such as Durkheim, Weber, Simmel and Tönnies, who were seeking to understand the social and psychological implications of the urbanism and urbanization associated with the Industrial Revolution of the nineteenth century.

The kernel of this classic sociological analysis is the association between the scale of society and its 'moral order'. Basically, the argument runs as follows. In pre-industrial society small, fairly homogenous populations contain people who know each other, perform the same kind of work and have the same kind of interests: they thus tend to look, think and behave alike, reflecting a consensus of values

and norms of behaviour. In contrast, the inhabitants of large cities constitute part of what Durkheim called a 'dynamic density' of population subject to new forms of economic and social organization as a result of economic specialization and innovations in transport and communications technology. In this urbanized, industrial society there is contact with more people but close 'primary' relationships with family and friends are less easily sustained. At the same time, social differentiation brings about a divergence of life styles, values and aspirations, thus weakening social consensus and cohesion and threatening to disrupt social order. This, in turn, leads to attempts to adopt 'rational' approaches to social organization, a proliferation of formal controls and, where these are unsuccessful, to an increase in social disorganization and deviant behaviour.

The impact of these ideas on urban geography came chiefly by way of their adoption and modification by the various research orientations which sprang from the Department of Sociology in the University of Chicago under the leadership of R. E. Park, a former student of Georg Simmel. Park gave a timely impetus to the study of urban communities in the rapidly changing urban scene of Chicago in the early decades of the twentieth century. Like earlier theorists, he believed that urbanization produced new environments, new types of people and new ways of life which were manifested in 'a mosaic of little worlds which touch but do not interpenetrate' (Park 1916: 608). He encouraged the 'exploration' and empirical documentation of these social worlds by his colleagues and, as a result, there developed an influential series of 'natural histories' of the distinctive groups and areas of Chicago in the 1920s: juvenile gangs, hobos, the rooming house area, prostitutes, taxi-hall dancers, the Jewish ghetto, and so on (Short 1971; Theodorson 1961). These studies represented part of an approach to urban sociology which became known as *human ecology*, the nature of which is discussed below.

A closely related and equally influential approach to urban sociology also sprang from Chicago a few years later: the so-called

Wirthian theory of urbanism as a way of life. Wirth's ideas, although they contained much of the thinking inherent to human ecology, synthesized a wide range of deterministic principles relevant to individual as well as group behaviour. Wirth, like Park, had studied under Georg Simmel and was heavily influenced by Simmel's work on 'The Metropolis and Mental Life' (1905). Putting Simmel's ideas together with subsequent work from the human ecologists, Wirth produced his classic essay, 'Urbanism as a way of life' (1938), which became one of the most often quoted and reprinted articles in the literature of the city. Wirth attributed the social and psychological consequences of city life (i.e. urbanism) to the combined effects of three factors which he saw as the products of increasing urbanization: (1) the increased size of populations; (2) the increased density of populations; and (3) the increased heterogeneity, or differentiation, of populations. At the *personal* level the effect of these factors, Wirth suggested, is as follows: faced with the abundant and varied physical and social stimuli experienced in the large, dense and highly diverse city environment, the individual has to adapt 'normal' behaviour in order to cope. City dwellers thus become, for example, aloof, brusque and impersonal in their dealings with others: emotionally buffered in their relationships. Nevertheless, the intense stimuli of city environments will sometimes generate what has subsequently been dubbed a 'psychic overload' (Milgram 1970), leading to anxiety and nervous strain. Furthermore, the loosening of personal bonds through this adaptive behaviour tends to leave people both *unsupported* in times of crisis and *unrestrained* in pursuing ego-centred behaviour. The net result, Wirth argues, is an increase in the incidence, on the one hand, of social incompetence, loneliness and mental illness and, on the other, of deviant behaviour of all kinds: from the charmingly eccentric to the dangerously criminal.

At the same time, Wirth draws a parallel picture of *social* change associated with the increased size, density and heterogeneity of urban populations. The specialized neighbourhoods and social groupings resulting from economic competition and the division of labour result in a fragmentation of social life between home, school, workplace, friends and relatives; and so people's time and attention are divided among unconnected people and places. This weakens the social support and control of primary social groups such as family, friends and neighbours, leading to a lack of social order and an increase in 'social disorganization'. Moreover, these trends are reinforced by the weakening of social norms (the rules and conventions of proper and permissible behaviour) resulting from the divergent interests and life-styles of the various specialized groups in the city. The overall societal response is to replace the support and controls formerly provided by primary social groups with 'rational' and impersonal procedures and institutions (welfare agencies, criminal codes supported by police forces, etc.). According to Wirth, however, such an order can never replace a communal order based on consensus and the moral strength of small primary groups. As a result, situations develop in which social norms are so muddled and weak that a social condition known as *anomie* develops: people, unclear or unhappy about norms, tend to challenge or ignore them, thus generating a further source of deviant behaviour. The influence of these ideas in urban sociology, environmental psychology and urban geography has been very great, even to the point of straitjacketing subsequent research orientations (Cullen and Knox 1982). Wirthian theory and its derivations recur throughout this chapter in discussions of social interaction, community studies, territoriality and the geography of deviant behaviour but, as will be shown, his determinism has by no means remained unchallenged.

## The public and private worlds of city life

One of the persistent problems associated with Wirthian theory has been that the results of empirical research have been ambivalent. Most of the evidence can be divided into four avenues of research: studies of helpfulness, conflict, social ties and psychological states. In general, the first two tend to support Wirthian theory, while the second two undermine it. Studies of *helpfulness* have typically involved field experiments designed to gauge reactions to 'strangers' who, for example, reach 'wrong' telephone numbers with their 'last' coin, who have 'lost' addressed letters, who ask for directions, and so on. The general drift of the results has been that city dwellers tend to be significantly less helpful than small-town residents (Korte 1978). Studies of *conflict* show that both group conflict – racial, social, and economic – and interpersonal conflict – certain categories of crime – are disproportionately likely to occur in large communities (Lincoln 1978; Skogan 1977). On the other hand, studies which have attempted to compare the number or quality of friendships or *personal relations* have generally shown no difference between different-sized communities, or have shown greater social integration among urbanites. Similarly, studies of *psychological states* such as stress and alienation show that the incidence of such phenomena is just as great, if not greater, in smaller communities (Srole 1972; Webb and Colette 1979).

Accepting the validity of all these findings, how might they be reconciled? One way is to re-examine the idea of urban environments, recognizing the distinction between the public and the private spheres of urban life (Lofland 1973). The former consists of settings where people are strangers, in which it requires a special etiquette: reserved, careful, non-intrusive. In the public sphere, people must be – or at least appear to be – indifferent to other people. But this is situational behaviour, not a psychological state, and says nothing about people's attitudes and actions in the private sphere. The city dweller 'did not *lose* the capacity for the deep, long-lasting, multi-faceted relationship. But he *gained* the capacity for the surface, fleeting, restricted relationship' (Lofland 1973: 178, emphases added). Fischer (1981) has drawn on this distinction, suggesting that urbanism is not characterized by distrust, estrangement and alienation among neighbours although it is associated with estrangement and alienation from 'other people' in the wider community. In other

words, 'urbanism produces fear and distrust of "foreign" groups in the public sphere, but does not affect private social worlds' (Fischer 1981: 306). In Wirthian terminology, this means that urbanism accommodates both 'moral order' and 'social disorganization' (Jackson 1984).

## Human ecology

Thanks largely to the impetus of the deterministic urban sociologists based in Chicago there is now a considerable literature relating specific geographical phenomena to their environmental context and which could collectively be classified under the general banner of ecological studies. In this section, however, attention is limited to the ecological studies associated with the early writings of the Chicago school: studies of 'human ecology'. This work is associated in particular with Park, together with E. W. Burgess and R. D. McKenzie, and is concerned, at the most general level, with the study of 'the spatial and sustenance relationships in which human beings are organized . . . in response to the operation of a complex of environmental and cultural forces' (McKenzie 1968: 19).

The distinctive feature of the approach adopted by the human ecologists, however, is the conception of the city as a kind of social organism, with individual behaviour and social organization governed by a 'struggle for existence'. The biological analogy provided Park and his colleagues with an attractive general framework in which to place their studies of the 'natural histories' and 'social worlds' of different groups in Chicago. Just as in plant and animal communities, Park concluded, order in human communities must emerge through the operation of 'natural' processes such as dominance, segregation, impersonal competition and succession. If the analogy now seems somewhat naïve, it should be remembered that it was conceived at a time when the appeal of Social Darwinism and classical economic theory was strong. Moreover, ecological studies of plants and animals provided a rich source of concepts and a graphic terminology with which to portray the sociology of the city.

One of the central concepts was that of *impersonal competition* between individuals for favourable locations within the city. This struggle was acted out primarily through market mechanisms, resulting in a characteristic pattern of land rents and the consequent *segregation* of different types of people according to their ability to meet the rents associated with different sites and situations. Economic differentiation was thus seen as the basic mechanism of residential segregation, and the local *dominance* of a particular group was ascribed to its relative competitive power. Functional relationships between different individuals and social groups were seen as *symbiotic* and, where such relationships could be identified as being focused within a particular geographical area, the human ecologists identified *communities*, or *natural areas*: 'territorial units whose distinctive characteristics – physical, economic and cultural – are the result of the unplanned operation of ecological and social processes' (Burgess 1964: 458). As the competitive power of different groups altered and the relative attractiveness

of different locations changed in the course of time, these territories were seen to shift. Once more, ecological concepts were invoked to describe the process, this time using the ideas of *invasion* and *succession* derived from the study of plant communities.

These concepts were all brought together by Burgess in his model of residential differentiation and neighbourhood change in Chicago (Burgess 1925). Observations on the location and extent of specific communities formed the basis for the identification of an urban spatial structure consisting of a series of concentric zones (Fig. 3.1). These zones were seen by Burgess as reflections of the differential economic competitive power of broad groups within society, whereas the further segregation of smaller areas within each zone – such as the ghetto, Chinatown and Little Sicily within the zone of transition – were seen as reflections of symbiotic relationships forged on the basis of language, culture and race. The model was set out in terms of dynamic change as well as the spatial disposition of different groups. Zones I to V represent, in Burgess's words, 'both the

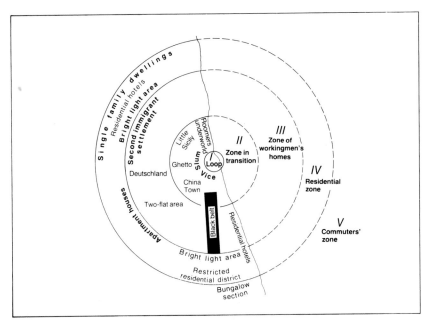

**Fig. 3.1** Burgess's zonal model applied to Chicago.
*Source*: Park, Burgess and McKenzie (1925), p. 53.

successive zones of urban extension and the types of areas differentiated in the process of expansion' (Burgess 1924: 88). As the city grew, the changing occupancy of each zone was related to the process of invasion and succession, and Burgess was able to point to many examples of this in Chicago in the early 1900s as successive waves of immigrants worked their way from their initial quarters in the zone of transition (Zone II) to more salubrious neighbourhoods elsewhere. In his diagrammatic model, some of the early immigrant groups – the Germans are explicitly noted – have already 'made it' to the area of superior accommodation in Zone III and become the dominant group, replacing second-generation American families who had moved out to colonize the outer residential zone (Zone IV).

Within this broad framework a wide range of studies was produced by the 'school' of human ecologists. Berry and Kasarda (1977) suggest that their work can be classified into three types:

1. Studies focusing on the process of competition, dominance and succession and their consequences for the spatial distribution of populations and land use. Such work is best represented by the early writings of Park, Burgess and McKenzie described above.

2. Detailed descriptions of the physical features of 'natural' areas along with the social, economic and demographic characteristics of their inhabitants. Well-known examples of this type of work include Wirth's study of *The Ghetto* (1928) and Zorbaugh's portrayal of Chicago's 'near' North Side in *The Gold Coast and the Slum* (Zorbaugh 1929). Zorbaugh's work provides a good example of the intimate portrayal of individual social worlds set in the framework of the broader ecological theory. The near North Side area was part of the zone in transition and contained four distinctive natural areas: the Gold Coast, a wealthy neighbourhood adjacent to the lakeshore; a rooming house area with a top-heavy demographic structure and a high population turnover; a bright-lights district – Towertown – with brothels, dance-halls and a 'bohemian' population; and a slum area containing clusters of immigrant groups. Zorbaugh showed how the personality of these different quarters related to their physical attributes – the 'habitat' they offered – as well as to the attributes and ways of life of their inhabitants. Moreover, he was also able to illustrate the dynamism of the area, charting the territorial shifts of different groups resulting from the process of invasion and succession.

3. Studies of the ecological context of specific social phenomena such as delinquency, prostitution, and mental disorders. A central concern was the investigation of ecologies which seemed to generate high levels of deviant behaviour, and typical examples include the work by Shaw *et al.* on *Delinquency Areas* (1929) and Faris and Dunham's work on *Mental Disorders in Urban Areas* (1939). Much of this work had a clear 'geographical' flavour since it often involved mapping exercises. It also provided the stimulus for a number of the more recent studies discussed below in the section on Deviant behaviour (pp. 80–96).

Despite its far-reaching effects on the orientation of a great deal of subsequent work in urban sociology and urban geography, traditional human ecology has been abandoned in favour of a much-modified ecological approach based on the idea of identifying key social variables and examining their relationships within an 'ecosystem' or 'ecological complex'. This resurgence of ecological research took place after a long period of neglect during the 1940s and 1950s following a series of theoretical and empirical critiques, including those of Alihan (1938), Davie (1937), Gettys (1940) and Firey (1945). The most general criticism was directed towards the biological analogies. As Timms observes: 'At times the Chicago school seems to have been unduly dazzled by the brilliance of their biological analogies and to have ignored the substance with which they worked' (Timms 1976: 27). Moreover, such analogies had been brought into great disrepute by parallel concepts such as *Lebensraum*, which were given great emphasis by the *geopolitics* used to justify some of the territorial claims of Germany's Third Reich. Other criticisms were more specific, centring on the excessive reliance on competition as the basis of social organization, the failure of its general structural concepts (such as the natural area and concentric zonation) to hold up under comparative examination, and its almost complete exclusion of cultural and motivational factors in explaining residential behaviour.

This last criticism was perhaps the most damaging of all. The first (and therefore best-known) critic of the Chicago school on the grounds that they overlooked the role of 'sentiment' and 'symbolism' in people's behaviour was Walter Firey, who pointed to the evidence of social patterns in Boston where, although there were 'vague concentric patterns', it was clear that the persistence of the status and social characteristics of distinctive neighbourhoods such as Beacon Hill, The Common and the Italian North End could be attributed in large part to the 'irrational' and 'sentimental' values attached to them by different sections of the population (Firey 1947). In short, social values could – and often did – override impersonal, economic competition as the basis for socio-spatial organization. It is also worth noting here that Firey's work is of further significance in that it directed the attention of geographers and sociologists to the importance of the subjective world in the understanding of social patterns in cities: a theme which has only recently begun to be fully explored (see pp. 149–162).

In fairness to the Chicago school, it should be acknowledged that they themselves did not regard their ideas on human ecology as either comprehensive or universally applicable. Park, for instance, clearly distinguished two levels of social organization: the *biotic* and the *cultural* (Park 1936). The former, he argued, was governed by impersonal competition whereas the latter was shaped by the consensus of social values. These cultural aspects of social organization clearly encompass Firey's notions of sentiment and symbolism, and Park and his colleagues were well aware of their influence. Park believed, however, that it was possible to study the biotic level of social organization separately, treating social values and communications as a kind of superstructure of the more basic level of the community (Robson 1969). It is thus not so much the denial of non-biotic factors as the inadequacy of their treatment which led to the unpopularity of traditional human ecology.

Since the demise of traditional human ecology in the 1940s there have been several reformulations of the original ideas and concepts and, with the consequent excision of the crude mechanistic and biotic analogies, there has been a considerable revival of interest in ecological approaches (Entrikin 1980; Jackson 1985a; Jackson and Smith 1981). Saunders (1981) interprets these developments as a response to conceptual and methodological difficulties stemming from the assumption that social organization and territorial organization were intimately related. In the light of criticism, Saunders argues:

human ecology was confronted with two options. Either it could retain its foundation in a positivist methodology while rejecting attempts to theorize the underlying forces determining the mode of human organization, or it could attempt to develop and justify the concept of the ecological community as an abstraction while rejecting the search for an observable and physical reference point. Human ecology could no longer have its cake and eat it, and the two questions of spatial form and functional process, which Park had attempted to unite, had at last to be severed (Saunders 1981: 66).

Different analysts, faced with this apparent dilemma, chose different options.

Wirth's synthesis of the effects of urban life on individual and social behaviour represented the first significant shift away from the biotic approach. Later, the concept of natural areas was reformulated by Hatt (1946), who emphasized that natural areas, defined as discrete territories containing a homogeneous population with distinctive social characteristics, could offer a useful framework for further social analysis. This is a strategy which has been adopted subsequently by social geographers in many avenues of investigation, even though the term 'natural area' has been abandoned in favour of less deterministic terminology such as 'social areas' or 'neighbourhood types'. Further important contributions to the refinement of the ecological approach were made by Hawley (1950) and Schnore (1965). Hawley presented the ecological approach as the study of the form and development of community structure, emphasizing the functional inter-dependence within communities that results from the collective adaptation competition. Schnore, building on Quinn's work (1939), was able to place human ecology in perspective by elaborating in detail the preconditions and assumptions implicit in the work of Burgess and others. Schnore's own preference, like Hawley and Duncan (Duncan and Schnore 1959) is for an approach in which the notion of ecology is used as a conceptual or statistical framework within which to analyse the internal structure of the city. Theodorson (1961) classified these writers as 'neo-orthodox' ecologists and their work, modified sufficiently to avoid the worst shortcomings of traditional human ecology, has been an important link with much of the more recent work on social patterns in cities. Meanwhile, many researchers began to describe and analyse the external characteristics of urban communities in ways that were divorced from any rigorous framework. Mills (1959) described this as 'abstracted empiricism', and it became very well represented within urban geography – reaching its apotheosis in studies of factorial ecology (see pp. 126–139).

The re-emergence of ecological approaches during the 1960s is exemplified by Suttles's work (1968) on the Addams area of Chicago. More recently, Kearsley (1983) has attempted to modify Burgess's model of urban structure in such a way as to incorporate contemporary aspects of urbanization such as inner-city decline, gentrification, and decentralization (Fig. 3.2). For a general review of the role of contemporary ecological studies in research on social and spatial organization, see Berry and Kasarda (1977).

## Social interaction in urban environments

A quite different approach to the study of social organization in urban environments has developed from the pursuit of another of Georg Simmel's suggestions: that the essentials of social organization are to be found in the forms of interaction among individuals (Simmel 1905). As Irving has shown in a lengthy review of the subject (Irving 1978), empirical studies of social interaction really stem from the work of Arensberg, Chapple and Warner some decades later (Arensberg 1937; Chapple 1942; Warner and Lunt 1941; Warner and Srole 1945). This work has provided inspiration for a continuing stream of empirical social research of considerable interest to geographers, and provides a logical preface to the consideration of the more complex and elusive properties of neighbourhoods and communities.

At the most fundamental level, interactionist research seeks to establish the nature of non-random interaction patterns at the 'dyadic' or 'triadic' level: that is, between two or three individuals. A good deal of this research has involved the temporal and sequential characteristics of personal relationships, focusing on considerations of initiative, role and status (Irving 1978), but it is the qualities of the *nature* and *intensity* of interaction which hold most interest for geographers. It is common for the nature of interaction to be classified according to whether it takes place in the context of primary or secondary settings. *Primary* relationships include those between kinfolk – based on ties of blood and duty – and those between friends – based on ties of attraction and mutual interest. Beyond this distinction, the nature of primary relationships may be further qualified. For example, family relationships may be differentiated according to whether the setting is a 'nuclear' unit – husband, wife and offspring – or an 'extended' unit which includes members of more than two generations. Interaction between friends may be differentiated according to whether the friendship is based on age, culture, locality, and so on.

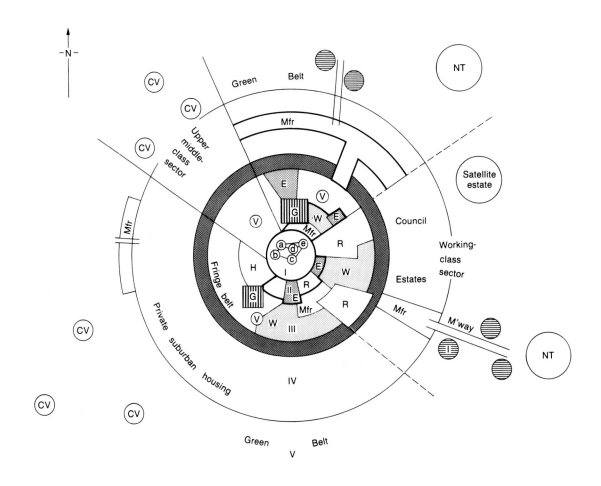

**Key**

| | | | | | |
|---|---|---|---|---|---|
| R | : | Local body development scheme | I | : | Central Business District |
| Mfr | : | Manufacturing district located on radial and concentric routeways or in Twilight Zone | II | : | Zone in Transition: Twilight Zone |
| | | | III | : | Pre-1918 residential development |
| V | : | Encapsulated village | IV | : | Post-1918 suburban development |
| G | : | Area of gentrification | V | : | Exurban zone of commuter settlement |
| W | : | Area of stable working-class communities | NT | : | New Town |
| CV | : | Commuter village | | | The divide between Inner City and Outer |
| E | : | Area of residence of ethnic minority | | | Suburbs – often marked by a fringe belt of |
| I | : | Inter-urban commercial/industrial site | | | institutional land uses. |
| a, b, c, d, e | : | Specialized nodes of activity within the CBD | | | |

- I : Central Business District — Inner City
- II : Zone in Transition: Twilight Zone — Inner City
- III : Pre-1918 residential development — Inner City
- IV : Post-1918 suburban development — Outer Suburbs
- V : Exurban zone of commuter settlement — Outer Suburbs

**Fig. 3.2** A modified Burgess model. *Source*: Kearsely (1983) Fig. 1, p. 12.

*Secondary* relationships are more purposive, involving individuals who group together to achieve particular ends. Such relationships are conveniently subdivided into those in which there is some intrinsic satisfaction in the interaction involved – known as 'expressive' interaction – and those in which the interaction is merely a means of achieving some common goal – 'instrumental' interaction. Both kinds are normally set within a broad group framework. Expressive interaction, for example, is typically facilitated by voluntary associations of various kinds: sports, hobby and social clubs, and 'do-gooding' associations. Instrumental interaction, on the other hand, normally takes place within the framework of business associations, political parties, trade unions and pressure groups. In addition, some writers would include interaction between members of ethnic, religious, and even cultural groups under the label of purposive secondary relationships. Jones and Eyles (1977), for example, argue that such relationships exist essentially to protect or advance the interests of individuals who are similarly placed on cultural, economic or political spectra.

## Social distance and physical distance

This perspective illustrates the complexity of reality and the difficulty of pigeon-holing human behaviour. Moreover, the difficulties of conceptual and empirical classifications of different types of interaction are compounded by the fact that the propensity for, and intensity of, interaction of all kinds is strongly conditioned by the effects of distance: both *social distance* and *physical distance*. There is, however, some overlap in practice between these two concepts of distance; and a further level of complexity is introduced by the fact that patterns of interaction are not only affected by the physical and social structure of cities but that they themselves also have an effect on city structure. Unravelling the processes involved in this apparently indivisible chain of events is a central concern of urban social geography. Before proceeding to a consideration of more complex situations, however, some initial clarification of the role of social and physical distance is in order.

The idea of *social distance* has a long history, and is graphically illustrated by Bogardus's attempt (1962) to measure the perceived social distance between native-born white Americans and other racial, ethnic and linguistic groups. He suggested that social distance could be reflected by a ranked scale of social relationships which people would be willing to sanction: the further up the scale, the closer the perceived distance between people:

1. to admit to close kinship by marriage;
2. to have as a friend;
3. to have as a neighbour on the same street;
4. to admit as a member of one's occupation within one's country;
5. to admit as a citizen of one's country;
6. to admit only as a visitor to one's country;
7. to exclude entirely from one's country.

It is now generally accepted that the less social distance there is between individuals, the greater the probability of interaction of some kind. Similarly, the greater the physical proximity between people – their 'residential propinquity' – the more likelihood of interaction of some kind. The exact influence of social and physical distance depends to some extent on the nature of the interaction concerned, however. Instrumental interaction related to trade unions or political parties, for instance, will clearly be less dependent on physical distance than instrumental interaction which is focused on a local action group concerned with the closure of a school, the construction of a power station, or the organization of a Coronation or Jubilee party. In most cases, of course, the influences of social and physical distance are closely interwoven and difficult to isolate. Research has shown, for example, that voluntary associations tend to reflect class and lifestyle, with membership depending largely on social distance. Middle-class groups, in particular, have been shown to have a propensity to use voluntary associations as a means of establishing and sustaining social relationships. But, because of the close correspondence between social and residential segregation, membership of such associations is also strongly correlated with locational factors (Bottomore 1954; Stacey 1960; Willmott and Young 1960).

Geographers, of course, have a special interest in the role of distance, space and location. There is, however, no real consensus on the role of propinquity in stimulating or retarding social interaction. One well-known study which is often quoted in support of the importance of distance at the micro-scale is that conducted by Festinger, Schacter and

Back on the friendship patterns within two housing projects, in which it was found that friendship patterns appeared to be governed by 'the mere physical arrangement of the houses' (Festinger, Schacter and Back 1950: 10). Their results, however, were based on a sample drawn from a very special case – the interaction between married engineering students studying at the Massachusetts Institute of Technology – and so the generality of their findings must remain in doubt. Indeed, subsequent studies have shown that the more diverse the inhabitants of housing projects, the less dominant the role of propinquity seems to be (Kuper 1953; Priest and Sawyer 1967). Some writers have suggested that propinquity is only of importance during the settling-down phase of a new housing development (Mowrer 1958; Simey 1954). Others, like Gans (1961; 1967) have stressed that social distance and a communality of values are always the major determinants of friendship patterns.

This view has been reinforced by the writings of Melvin Webber and his followers who, while acknowledging the effects of propinquity, suggest that the constraints of distance are rapidly diminishing in the 'shrinking world' of modern technology and mass communications (Webber 1963; 1964). They argue that improvements in personal mobility, combined with the spatial separation of home, workplace and recreational opportunities, have released people from neighbourhood ties. Not everyone, of course, benefits from mobility to the same extent: some people are 'localites', with restricted 'urban realms'; others are 'cosmopolites', for whom distance is elastic and who inhabit a social world without finite geographical borders. This tendency towards an aspatial basis for social interaction has been seen by others as a result not so much of increased personal mobility as a product of modern city planning and social values. Ward, for example, in his book on *The Child in the City* (1978), argues that modern housing estates have 'annihilated' community spirit and replaced it with a parental authoritarianism which restricts the outdoor activities of children and so retards the development of locality-based friendships from the earliest

years of a person's life. Similarly, Keller (1968) claimed that there had been a widespread decline of both organized and spontaneous 'neighbouring' in America because of the combined effects of changes in economic organization and social values. She attributed the decline in neighbouring to four factors:

1. The presence of multiple sources of information and opinion via mass media, travel, voluntary organizations, and employment away from the local area.
2. Better transport beyond local boundaries.
3. Increased differentiation in people's interests and desires, and greater differentiation in rhythms of work, resulting in less inclination and ability, respectively, to interact with neighbours.
4. Better social services and greater economic security.

Against such arguments must be set the work of writers such as Carey and Mapes (1972), Homans (1950; 1961), Mogey (1956) and Warren (1963), who point out that the residential neighbourhood must continue to provide much raw material for social life, especially for relatively immobile groups such as the poor, the aged, and mothers with young children. Even the more mobile must be susceptible to chance local encounters and the subsequent interaction which may follow; and most householders will establish some contact with neighbours from the purely functional point of view of mutual security. Moreover, the most telling argument in support of the role of propinquity, as Irving (1978) observes, is the way in which residential patterns – whether defined in terms of class, race, ethnicity, life-style, kinship, family status or age – have persistently exhibited a strong tendency towards spatial differentiation. In a pioneering study, Duncan and Duncan (1955b) showed that the residential segregation of occupational groups in Chicago closely paralleled their social distance and that the most segregated categories were those possessing the clearest rank, i.e. those at the top and the bottom of the socio-economic scale. Subsequent studies of socio-economic groups elsewhere (Fine, Glenn and Monts 1971; Laumann 1966; Tilly 1961) and of ethnic groups (Kantrowitz 1973; Taeuber 1965; Timms 1969) and religious groups (Poole and Boal 1973) in a number of different cities have all reported a similar degree of residential segregation, though there is some evidence that the traditional cleavages between occupational groups has been breaking down (Morgan 1980; Simkus 1978).

There are several good reasons why segregation should persist within urban society. As Suttles (1968; 1972) has emphasized, the spatial segregation of different 'communities' helps to minimize conflict between social groups while facilitating a greater degree of social control and endowing specific social groups with a more cohesive political voice. Moreover, as Beshers (1962) noted, an important reason for the residential clustering of such groups is the desire of its members to preserve their own group identity or life-style. One of the basic mechanisms by which this segregation can be achieved is through group norms which support marriage within the group and oppose marriage between members of different social, religious, ethnic or racial groups. The organization of groups into different territories facilitates the operation of this mechanism by restricting the number of 'outside' contacts. Thus 'people marry their equals in social status; neighbours tend to be social equals; they marry their neighbours' (Ramsøy 1966; 783). But while Ramsøy was able, in her study of Oslo, to substantiate the correlation between distance and mate selection first observed in Philadelphia and New Haven by Abrams (1943) and Kennedy (1943), she was not able to tease out the causal relationships between distance, segregation and endogamy. She poses the question:

Is it the *workplace* which brings together men and women doing the same kind of work, is it the *family*, urging manipulating or encouraging its offspring to find a 'suitable', *i.e.* socially equal, mate, or is it the *neighbourhood*, putting into daily contact persons belonging to the same economic stratum? (Ramsøy 1966: 779).

Research by Morgan (1979, 1981) on marriage patterns in Christchurch, New Zealand, has at least confirmed that distance and neighbourhood social segregation are important variables in their own right. Distance is important because of its time- and cost-imposing qualities, but it seems that the probability of first meeting is not a simple function of distance. Rather, 'the residential mosaic appears to exert the major influence on the probability of initial contact through its effect on the pattern of social contacts' (Morgan 1981: 919).

It should by now be clear that the debate as to whether physical or social distance is the more decisive factor in influencing patterns of social interaction is rather academic. As Irving observes, 'the two have become mutually reinforcing in a modern urban context' (Irving 1978: 268). In order to make further progress in understanding patterns of social interaction in cities we must now turn to a closer examination of their *structure* and go on to grasp the rather thorny issue of 'community'.

## Social networks, neighbourhoods and communities

It will be clear by now that interpersonal relations extend well beyond a series of dyadic or triadic interactions of different kinds. Most people are involved in several different relationships which may be inter-connected to a greater or lesser extent. We not only have friends, but know friends-of-friends; and kinfolk do not exist in isolation: we may get to know a complete stranger because he or she is a member of the same club or organization as an uncle, an aunt, or a cousin. The way in which these social linkages are structured is often very complex and, *in toto*, they represent the foundations of social organization. Not surprisingly, therefore, the analysis of these linkages has attracted a good deal of attention. Most of the research associated with this approach – known as *social network analysis* – can be traced back to the work of Elizabeth Bott, which was in turn influenced by Barnes's (1954) study of social networks on a Norwegian island. Basically, social network analysis attempts to illustrate the structure of social interaction by treating persons as points and relationships as connecting lines (Granovetter 1976). The analysis of social networks thus allows the researcher to 'map out the complex reality of the interpersonal worlds surrounding specific individuals' (Smith 1978: 108), and has the advantage of not being confined, *a priori*, to any specific level of analysis such as the family or the neighbourhood. As with the analysis of other kinds of network – in transport geography (Taafe and Gauthier 1973) and physical geography (Haggett and Chorley 1969) – this approach facilitates not only the 'mapping' of the 'morphology' of networks (Fig. 3.3), but also the quantification of certain key characteristics such as their 'connectedness', 'centrality', 'proximity' and 'range' (Boissevain 1974; Roistacher 1974).

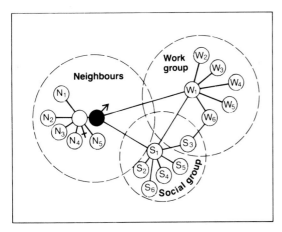

**Fig. 3.3** The morphology of a husband's social network. *Source*: Smith and Smith (1978), p. 106.

Any one person may belong to several different and non-overlapping social networks at the same time, and each of these networks may well have different properties: some may be spatially bounded while others are not; some may have dendritic structures while others are web-like, with interlocking ties, clusters, knots or sub-graphs. Bott's original formulation of types of social network was based on the notion of a continuum of

networks ranging from *looseknit* (where few members of the network know each other independently) to *closeknit* (where most members of the network know each other); but this, like the more sophisticated typologies developed by Mitchell and others (Mitchell 1969) presents practical difficulties in operationalizing a definition of linkage. Should it extend beyond kinship and friendship to acquaintance or 'knowledge of' another person, or what? And how is friendship, for instance, to be measured? In an attempt to minimize such confusion, Bell and Newby (1976) have proposed a typology of social situations which incorporate the notion of the complexity as well as the structure of social networks (Fig. 3.4). They illustrate the typology by way of the extreme and limiting cases: 'A' and 'B' in the diagram:

A is the traditional community as normally understood: social relationships are multiplex in that, for example, neighbours are workmates are kinsmen are leisure-time companions, and the social network has a dense structure in that everyone knows everyone else. B is the situation of idealized urban anonymous anomie: social relationships are uniplex (the taxidriver and his fare), fleeting, impersonal and anonymous, and the social network structure is single-stranded in that only one person knows the others (Bell and Newby 1976: 198–9).

| Plexity | Structure | | |
|---|---|---|---|
| | Dense | Looseknit | Single |
| Multiplex | A | | |
| Simplex | | | |
| Uniplex | | | B |

**Fig. 3.4** A typology of social situations. *Source*: Bell and Newby (1976), p. 109.

This incorporation of the overlap and complexity of different networks brings us away from abstraction and a step nearer to reality. One person who has illustrated the practical relevance of network analysis is Christopher Smith, who has investigated the 'pro-social' behaviour of informal self-help networks which exist in modern cities (Smith 1978; Smith and Smith 1978). Smith suggests – in contrast to the postulates of Wirthian theory – that self-help networks emerge in cities in order to provide help in many different contexts, and that their existence prevents formal welfare agencies from being swamped.

In the mental health area, for example, help is being provided every hour of the day by people from all walks of life, including neighbours, relatives, ministers and shopkeepers. Dozens of helping hands and sympathetic ears are called on each day . . . Instead of going to an agency for help, many people prefer to search out someone in their own social network. It is quicker and cheaper; it is often more successful; and it is certainly less humiliating than going to a mental health centre (Smith and Smith 1978: 102).

The focus of these self-help networks is often the 'natural neighbour' (Collins and Pancoast 1976): a person with a propensity to become involved or make himself available in resolving the problems of other people, whether for self-aggrandizement, altruism, or some other motive. They are usually untrained amateurs who may not consciously recognize their own role in helping others. Indeed, they may not actually provide any direct help themselves but act as 'brokers', putting people in touch with someone who can help (Gartner and Riessman 1980; Gottlieb 1981; Naparstek *et al.* 1982). In a study of neighbourhoods in the Detroit area, Warren (1981) was able to trace the patterns of helping networks used by people when high levels of expertise were not thought to be necessary: for problems related to tension or mild depression, for example, or for advice about retirement decisions, changing jobs, etc. Married persons turned most frequently to their spouse (82 per cent), while those with jobs often turned to co-workers (42 per cent). Other helpers were friends (41 per cent), relatives not living in the same household (37 per cent), neighbours (27 per cent), and a variety of professional workers such as police, clergy, doctors, counsellors and teachers (none more than 8 per cent). Except for co-workers, most of these helpers were found *within the neighbourhood*. When respondents were asked if they had been

helped by a neighbour during a 'life crisis' in the previous year (e.g. personal injury, serious illness, death of a close family member, change of job, crime victimization), 56 per cent said they had.

A major problem in illuminating the structure of these networks, like any others, is the difficulty of empirical social research which necessarily involves a great deal of fieldwork. Moreover, the study of social networks, although a step in the right direction, does not provide the geographer with a sufficiently holistic approach: there remain the fundamental questions of the extent to which social networks of various kinds are spatially defined, and at what scales: questions which have as yet received little attention (Wellman and Crump 1978; Wellman 1979). This brings us to a consideration of the ideas of 'neighbourhood' and 'community'. The concept of community is elusive. It has a long history in all of the disciplines concerned with individual or group behaviour and has generated a huge literature, much of which is plagued by circular argument and semantic ambiguities. These difficulties are more acute for the geographer, who must also pursue the question of whether 'community' can be synonymous with 'neighbourhood' or 'locality', and in what circumstances.

## Community lost

According to classic sociological theory, communities should not exist at all in cities; or, at best, only in a weakened form. This idea first entered sociological theory by way of the writings of Ferdinand Tonnies (1887), who argued that two basic forms of human association could be recognized in all cultural systems. The first of these, *Gemeinschaft*, he related to an earlier period in which the basic unit of organization was the family or kin-group, with social relationships characterized by depth, continuity, cohesion and fulfilment. The second, *Gesellschaft*, was seen as the product of urbanization and industrialization which resulted in social and economic relationships based on rationality, efficiency and contractual obligations amongst individuals whose roles had become specialized. This perspective was reinforced by the writings of sociologists such as Durkheim (1893), Simmel (1905), Sumner (1906) and, as we have seen, Wirth (1938), and has become part of the conventional wisdom about city life: it is not conducive to 'community', however it might be defined. This view has been characterized as the 'community lost' argument (Wellman 1979; Wellman and Leighton 1979), and recent examples of work from this perspective include that of Alexander (1967), Packard (1972) and Lee *et al.* (1984).

## Urban villages and the mutuality of the oppressed: 'community saved'

There is, however, a good deal of evidence to support the idea of socially cohesive communities in cities. Writers such as Jane Jacobs (1961) have portrayed the city as an inherently human place, where sociability and friendliness are a natural consequence of social organization at the neighbourhood level. Moreover, this view is sustained by empirical research in sociology and anthropology. Studies such as those by Liebow (1967) and Suttles (1968) have demonstrated the existence of distinctive social worlds which are territorially bounded and have a vitality which is focused on local 'institutions' such as taverns, pool halls and laundromats. Herbert Gans, following his study of the West End of Boston, suggested that we need not mourn the passing of the cohesive social networks and sense of self-identity associated with village life (Gans 1962), for he found that these properties existed within the inner city in a series of 'urban villages'. This perspective has become known as 'community saved'. The focus of Gans's study was an ethnic village (the Italian quarter), but studies in other cities have described urban villages based on class rather than ethnicity. The most frequently cited example of an urban village of any kind is Young and Willmott's description of life in Bethnal Green, the residents of which have become something of a sociological stereotype. Young and Willmott found 'a *sense* of community . . . a feeling of solidarity between

people who occupy the common territory' (Young and Willmott 1957: 89, emphasis added) which was based on a strong local network of kinship, reinforced by the localized patterns of employment, shopping and leisure activities.

A similar situation was described in Leeds by Hoggart (1958), in Swansea by Rosser and Harris (1965) and in a series of subsequent studies of inner city life on both sides of the Atlantic. Although Pahl (1970b) has cautioned that the utility of these studies is limited by their rather different objectives, by the diversity of the cities themselves, and by the pace of change in people's life styles (Young and Willmott's classic study, for example, was executed at a time when fewer people had cars and when the homogenizing influence of television was still quite weak), the localized social networks they describe do tend to have common origins. In short, urban villages are most likely to develop in long-established working-class areas with a relatively stable population and a narrow range of occupations.

The importance of permanence and immobility in fostering the development of local social systems has been stressed by Stacey (1969), who suggests that the minimum period required for the development of a distinctive locally-based social system is between 50 and 80 years, assuming the majority of the population to have been born and bred in the area; and most writers agree that the relative immobility of the working classes (in every sense: personal mobility, occupational mobility and residential mobility) is an important factor. Immobility results in a strengthening of *vertical* bonds of kinship and *horizontal* bonds of friendship. The high degree of residential propinquity between family members in working-class areas not only makes for a greater intensity of interaction between kinfolk but also facilitates the important role of the matriarch in reinforcing kinship bonds. As sociologists such as Young and Willmott (1957) and Klein (1965) stress, the matriarch plays a key role by providing practical support (e.g. looking after grandchildren, thus enabling a daughter or daughter-in-law to take a job) and by passing on attitudes, information, beliefs and norms of behaviour. Primary social interaction between friends is also reinforced by the residential propinquity which results from immobility. Relationships formed among a cohort of children at school are carried over into street life, courtship and, later on, the pursuit of social activities in pubs, clubs and bingo halls (Guest and Lee 1983).

Another important factor in fostering the development of close-knit and overlapping social networks in working class areas is the economic division of society which leaves many people vulnerable to the cycle of poverty, as Jackson (1968) suggests in his *Working Class Community*. He argues that the shared and repeated experience of hard times, together with the cohesion and functional interdependence resulting from the tight criss-crossing of kinship and friendship networks, generates a mutuality of feeling and purpose in working-class areas: a mutuality which is the mainspring of the social institutions, ways of life and 'community spirit' associated with the urban village.

### The fragility of communality

The cohesiveness and communality arising from immobility and economic deprivation is a fragile phenomenon, however. The mutuality of the urban village is underlain by stresses and tensions which follow from social intimacy and economic insecurity, and several studies of working-class neighbourhoods have described as much conflict and disorder as cohesion and communality. The one factor which has received most attention in this respect is the stress resulting from the simple shortage of space in working-class areas. High densities lead to noise problems, inadequate play space and inadequate drying facilities and are associated with personal stress and fatigue. Children, in particular, are likely to suffer from the psychological effects of the lack of privacy, as Walter Greenwood observed so acutely in his *Love on the Dole*. Jackson notes that 'The only place which is private in the way that a professional worker's "study" might be, is the lavatory . . . The lavatory is the place where the man studies his wage chit, or the woman a new and daring purchase' (Jackson 1968: 157). Where even the lavatory must be shared with other households privacy

is still further eroded, and stress or conflict is even more likely. As Coates and Silburn drily observe: 'In St. Ann's, sharing an outdoor lavatory, as did many of our respondents, may be conducive to heightened social contact, but not always in an entirely happy way' (Coates and Silburn 1970: 94). The fragility of working-class communality also stems from other sources. Coates and Silburn, for example, identified three other stressors in the St Ann's area of Nottingham. The first was the conflict of values which arose from the juxtaposition of people from a variety of ethnic and cultural backgrounds, notwithstanding their common economic experiences. The second was the disruption of social relationships arising as one cohort of inhabitants aged, died and was replaced by younger families, who, even though they were essentially of the same class and life-style, represented an unwitting intrusion on the quieter lives of older folk. Finally, they noted the disruption associated with the presence of undesirable elements – 'problem families', transients and prostitutes – in the midst of an area of respectable families. It seems likely that the relative strength of these stressors may be the crucial factor in tipping the balance between an inner-city neighbourhood of the 'urban village' type and one characterized by the anomie and social disorganization postulated by Wirthian theory.

## Suburban neighbourhoods: community transformed

In contrast to the close-knit social networks of the urban village, suburban life is seen by many observers as the antithesis of 'community'. Lewis Mumford, for example, wrote that the suburbs represent 'a collective attempt to lead a private life' (Mumford 1940: 215), and this view was generally endorsed by a number of early studies of suburban life, including the Lynds' (1956) study of Muncie, Indiana, and Warner's study of 'Yankee City' (New Haven) (Warner and Lunt 1941, 1942; Warner and Srole 1945). Further sociological work such as Whyte's *The Organization Man* (1956) and Stein's *The Eclipse of Community*

(1960) reinforced the image of the suburbs as an area of loose-knit, secondary ties where lifestyles were focused squarely on the nuclear family's pursuit of money, status and consumer durables and the privacy in which to enjoy them. Subsequent investigation, however, has shown the need to revise the 'suburban myth' of 'non-community' (Berger 1960; Donaldson 1969). Although there is little evidence for the existence of suburban villages comparable to the urban villages of inner-city areas (Connell 1973), it is evident that many suburban neighbourhoods do contain localized social networks with a considerable degree of cohesion as Gans showed, for example, in his study of Levittown (Gans 1967).

At the same time, suburban neighbourhoods can be thought of as 'communities of limited liability' – one of a series of social constituencies in which urbanites may choose to participate (Connerly 1985; Kasarda and Janowitz 1974). This view has been translated as 'community transformed' or 'community liberated'. Instead of urban communities *breaking up*, they can be thought of as *breaking down* into an ever-increasing number of independent sub-groups, only some of which are locality-based.

It has been suggested by some that the social networks of suburban residents are in fact more localized and cohesive than those of inner-city residents, even if they lack something in *feelings* of mutuality (Fischer 1976).

Fischer, like others, points to the high levels of 'neighbouring' in American suburbs and suggests that this may be due to one or more of a number of factors:

1. that the detached house is conducive to local social life;
2. that the suburbs tend to be more homogeneous, socially and demographically, than other areas;
3. that there is a 'pioneer eagerness' to make friends in new suburban developments;
4. that suburban residents are a self-selected group having the same preferences for social and leisure activities;
5. that physical distance from other social contacts forces people to settle for local contacts.

The cohesiveness of suburban communities is further reinforced by social networks related to voluntary associations of various kinds. Americans, as de Tocqueville (1946) observed, have a pronounced habit of joining, of organizing social contacts around some cause or activity, and this is especially true of middle-class suburbanites. Furthermore, it appears from the evidence at hand that suburban relationships are neither more nor less superficial than those found in central city areas (Baldassare and Fischer 1975; Fischer and Jackson 1976).

Nevertheless, there are some groups for whom suburban living does result in an attenuation of social contact. Members of minority groups of all kinds and people with slightly atypical values or life-styles will not easily be able to find friends or to pursue their own interests in the suburbs (Gans 1967; Tomeh 1964). This often results in such people having to travel long distances to maintain social relationships. Those who cannot or will not travel must suffer a degree of social isolation as part of the price of suburban residence. The elderly provide a case in point; a study of the elderly in San Antonio, Texas, found that the further out they lived, the fewer friends they reported, the less active they were socially, and the lonelier they were (Carp 1975).

## The mosaic culture of American suburbs

It should also be acknowledged that the nature and intensity of social interaction in suburban neighbourhoods tends to vary according to the *type* of suburb concerned. Muller (1981) argues that American suburbs have become differentiated as a result of two complementary trends. The first of these is the general reorganization of 'cultural space' around different lifestyles related variously to careerist orientations, family orientations, 'ecological' orientations, etc., and constrained by income and life cycle characteristics (see, for example, Feldman and Thielbar 1975). The second is the increasing tendency for people to want to withdraw into a 'territorially defended enclave' inhabited by like-minded people, in an attempt to find refuge from potentially antagonistic rival groups. The net result of the two trends is the emergence of distinctive 'voluntary regions' in the suburbs (see also Zelinsky 1975), a process which has been reinforced by the proliferation of suburban housing types which now extend from the 'normal' detached single-family dwelling to include specialist condominium apartments, 'townhouse' developments and exclusive retirement communities. As a result, 'archipelagos' of similar suburban communities, with outliers in every metropolitan ring, now extend from coast to coast. Muller sees this as the emergence of a 'mosaic culture', a new form of macrosocial organization consisting of a number of subcultures distinguished by sharply contrasting lifestyles which, although divisive for society as a whole, produces harmonious, homogeneous communities at the local level.

Following Berry (1973) and Suttles (1975), Muller recognizes four major types of suburban neighbourhood, each with a rather different pattern of social interaction.

1. *Exclusive upper income suburbs*: These neighbourhoods are typically situated in the outermost parts of the city and consist of large detached houses built in extensive grounds, screened off by trees and shrubbery. This makes casual neighbouring rather difficult, and so local social networks tend to be based more on voluntary associations such as churches and country clubs.

2. *Middle-class family suburbs*: The dominant form of the middle-class American suburb is the detached single-family dwelling, and the dominant pattern of social interaction is based on the nuclear family. As in the more exclusive suburbs, socializing with relatives is infrequent, and emphasis on family privacy tends to inhibit neighbouring. Since the care of children is a central concern, much social contact occurs through family-orientated organizations such as the PTA, the Scouts, and organized sports; and the social cohesion of the neighbourhood derives to a large extent from the overlap of the social networks resulting from these organizations. However, with the tendency for young people to defer marriage, for young couples to defer child rearing, and for land and building costs to escalate, there has recently emerged a quite different type of middle-class suburb based on apartment living. Social interaction in these neighbourhoods tends to be less influenced by

local ties, conforming more to Webber's (1963) idea of an aspatial community of interest.

3. *Suburban cosmopolitan centres*: This apparently contradictory label is given to the small but rapidly increasing number of suburban neighbourhoods which serve as voluntary residential enclaves for 'professionals, intellectuals, students, artists, writers and mutually tolerated misfits' (Muller 1976a: 17): people with broad rather than local horizons, but whose special interests and lifestyle nevertheless generate a cohesive community through a series of overlapping social networks based on cultural activities and voluntary organizations such as bridge clubs, theatre groups and meditation classes. These neighbourhoods are very much a contemporary phenomenon, and are chiefly associated with suburbs adjacent to large universities and colleges.

4. *Working-class suburbs*: Blue-collar suburban neighbourhoods have multiplied greatly in number since the 1940s to the point where they are almost as common as middle-class family suburbs in many American cities. But although these neighbourhoods are also dominated by single-family dwellings, patterns of social interaction are quite different. An intensive use of communal outdoor space makes for a high level of primary local social interaction, and community cohesion is reinforced by a 'person-orientated' rather than a material- or status-orientated lifestyle. Moreover, the tendency for blue-collar workers to be geographically less mobile means that people's homes are more often seen as a place of permanent settlement, with the result that people are more willing to establish local ties (Berger 1971).

Table 3.2 shows the very different socio-economic characteristics of some well-known representative examples of these four categories.

## Suburbs in West European cities

European suburban neighbourhoods do not conform particularly well to this typology, largely because of the greater economic constraints on the elaboration of different life-styles. Exclusive upper income suburbs are sustained by fewer cities; and there are very few examples to be found of the 'suburban cosmopolitan centre'. Moreover, the magnitude of the public housing sector in many European countries means that a large

**Table 3.2**   Selected socioeconomic characteristics of representative suburban lifestyle community types, 1980

| Variable | Exclusive upper income | Middle-income | | Working class | Cosmopolitan suburb |
|---|---|---|---|---|---|
| | Grosse Pointe Shores, Michigan | Upper Darien, Connecticut | Lower Levittown, N.Y. | Milpitas, California | Stanford, California |
| Median household income | 57,951 | 43,459 | 25,493 | 24,950 | 18,393 |
| Per cent households > $25,000 | 81.4 | 71.5 | 51.6 | 49.8 | 39.3 |
| Per cent households < $15,000 | 10.8 | 13.5 | 19.2 | 21.0 | 43.0 |
| Per cent families in poverty | 2.7 | 2.4 | 4.2 | 5.2 | 18.3 |
| Per cent black | 0.3 | 0.1 | 0.1 | 7.3 | 4.9 |
| Median age | 44.4 | 36.9 | 30.3 | 26.3 | 21.2 |
| Per cent population < 18 | 25.4 | 28.4 | 28.9 | 34.1 | 13.6 |
| Per cent population > 65 | 14.9 | 10.8 | 6.0 | 3.8 | 2.1 |
| Per cent same address, 1975 | 71.4 | 59.4 | 76.8 | 42.5 | 15.8 |
| Per cent population 3–34 and in school | 29.0 | 30.2 | 28.8 | 30.7 | 74.2 |
| Per cent high school graduates (persons 25 and over) | 89.2 | 89.7 | 78.5 | 77.2 | 99.1 |
| Per cent women in labour force | 30.8 | 38.6 | 41.2 | 44.5 | 42.5 |
| Per cent managerial and professional workers | 61.6 | 47.8 | 19.6 | 20.4 | 47.2 |
| Per cent technical, sales and administrative support workers | 27.5 | 33.6 | 41.3 | 32.0 | 34.1 |
| Per cent operators, fabricators and labourers | 0.6 | 5.0 | 13.0 | 19.9 | 1.5 |

proportion of the suburbs are publicly-owned working-class neighbourhoods: altogether different to the North American suburban working-class neighbourhood.

Paul White (1984) recognizes four distinctive suburban types:

1. *Industrial suburbs*, with origins that can be traced to the late nineteenth century, typically display a mixture of housing with old industrial cottages, terraces or courtyard dwellings adjacent to more recent, publicly-financed apartment blocks. These suburbs have traditionally exhibited an intimate relationship between homes and workplaces and a strong sense of community, but public housing allocation procedures combined with the 'deindustrialization' of many cities, has disrupted this relationship. Meanwhile, many working-class households have moved to newer, peripheral, publicly-financed suburbs, leaving the industrial suburbs to the elderly and to migrant workers.

2. *Middle-class suburbs*, which are dominated by single-family dwellings, but at relatively high densities. Because of the long-standing cultural preference in continental Europe for in-town, apartment living, the middle-class suburbs of many West European cities form a relatively small proportion of the total suburban realm.

3. *Commuter villages*, which often contain a considerable mixture of social groups – working-class natives as well as middle-class newcomers. In general, they are a recent and accelerating phenomenon, with growth being dominated by private housing for more affluent social groups. They are, however, almost totally absent from Mediterranean Europe. White points out that it should not be assumed that in these settlements 'newcomer' equals 'commuter', or that 'native' can be equated with local employment: 'Continued agricultural labour shedding, coupled with increased urban employment opportunities, have conspired to encourage long-standing residents of peri-urban settlements to take urban employment, sometimes on the basis of a "worker-peasantry" retaining a smallholding as a part-time activity' (White 1984: 225).

4. *New working-class suburbs*, predominantly publicly-financed and typically consisting of high-rise, high-density *grands ensembles*. They are characterized by extremely large-scale developments, by a high degree of homogeneity in terms of demographic and social composition (as a result of housing allocation rules), a general lack of local amenities, and poor accessibility within their respective metropolitan areas.

In Britain, such suburbs have been the focus of a great deal of sociological research, much of which was originally motivated by a concern for the effects on the extended family system and old locality-based social networks which were expected to result from the suburbanization of working-class families. This approach dovetailed nicely with the idea of *embourgeoisment* (Merton 1957; Parsons 1951), which held that increased affluence among the working class results in conformity with the traditional norms and patterns of social interaction of the middle classes. It was

thus expected that the suburbanization of relatively affluent working-class families would result in a loosening of social networks of all kinds. The credibility of the *embourgeoisment* thesis has been much weakened, however, by a series of studies of the 'affluent worker' and working-class suburbs which have shown that, despite a greater relative affluence than before and despite suburban living, there is little evidence that working-class households are adopting middle-class ways of life (Goldthorpe *et al.* 1967, 1968). On the other hand, it is clear that resettling working-class families in suburban estates does result in some disruption of primary social ties with the result that, for a time at least, social cohesion is reduced (Goldthorpe *et al.* 1967, 1968; Willmott and Young 1960). An important contributory factor in this respect is the aloofness generated by status uncertainty as the result of movement to a new and socially unknown environment (see, for example, Willmott and Young 1960). This, together with the reduction in the frequency of contact with kinfolk, leads to the development of a more home-centred way of life, so that many suburban public housing estates are characterized by low levels of neighbouring and a lack of social participation in organized activities in clubs and societies. Not every household is equally affected by status uncertainty and home-centredness, however; and not every household is of the same socio-economic status. There often emerges, therefore, a social polarization within council estates between the 'roughs' and the 'respectables'; and it is often the relationship between these two groups which determines the nature of social networks within the community. In a study of a Liverpool estate, for example, the 'rough' group dominated the area's organized social activities while the 'respectable' group withdrew from this kind of interaction (Lupton and Mitchell 1954). In a study of Watling, the position was reversed (Durant 1959).

## Status panic and crisis communality

One thing which suburban neighbourhoods everywhere seem to have in common is a lack of the mutuality, the permanent but intangible 'community spirit' that is characteristic of the urban village. An obvious explanation for this is the newness of most suburban communities: they have not had time to fully develop a locality-based social system (Stacey 1969). An equally likely explanation, however, is that the residents of suburban neighbourhoods are simply not likely to develop a sense of mutuality in the same way as urban villagers because they are not exposed to the same levels of deprivation or stress. This reasoning is borne out to a certain extent by the 'crisis communality' exhibited in suburban neighbourhoods at times when there is an unusually strong threat to territorial exclusivity, amenities, or property values. Examples of the communality generated in the wake of status panic are well documented, and the best-known is probably the case of the Cutteslowe walls (Collinson 1963). In 1932 Oxford City Council set up a housing estate on a suburban site to the north of the city and directly adjacent to a private middle-class estate. The home owners, united by their fear of a drop both in the status of their neighbourhood and in the value of their property and drawn together by their mutual desire to maintain the social distance between themselves and their new proletarian neighbours, went to the length of building an unscalable wall as a barrier between the two estates. A more recent example is provided by Robson's (1982) chronicle of the Bodley barricade: a conflict which ostensibly revolved around local traffic plans but which was largely motivated by a 'hidden agenda' concerned with the socially-motivated cleavage between private and public households. Other documented examples have mostly been related to the threat posed by urban motorways, airports, or the zoning of land for business use (Molotch 1972; Wolf and Lebeaux 1969), although in North America public housing is still sufficiently controversial to generate crisis communality among middle-class suburbanites.

## Communities and neighbourhoods: definitions and classifications

Whatever the stimulus, however, suburban communality rarely seems to survive the resolution – one way or another – of the central issue. This raises once more the problem of defining communities. As we have seen, the nature and cohesiveness of social networks vary a lot from one set of socio-spatial circumstances to another, and it is not easy to say which situations, if any, reflect the existence of 'community', let alone which of these are also congruent with a discrete geographical territory. Various attempts have been made to establish the spatial expression of community social interaction. Herbert and Raine (1976), following Buttimer (1972), have used the technique of standard deviational ellipses to depict patterns of friendship and local service utilization in Cardiff (Fig. 3.5). Friendship patterns have also been analysed by Lewis (1980) for Leicester; while Walmsley's (1976) analysis of Sydney neighbourhoods was based on patterns of visits to shops, clubs, and churches as well as friends, and Pacione (1984) has extended the approach by attempting to quantify the degree of community cohesion in Glasgow via measures of resident satisfaction, participation in neighbourhood organizations, residential commitment and personal attachment to the neighbourhood in addition to patterns of friendship and the use of neighbourhood facilities. More than 25 years ago Hillery (1955) unearthed over 90 definitions of 'community' in the social sciences, but found that the nearest he could get to common agreement was the presence, in most definitions, of some reference to: (1) area; (2) common ties; and (3) social interaction.

Since Hillery's survey there have been numerous attempts to resolve the problem (see, for example, Bell and Newby 1971; Scherer 1973) and, although there is still no real consensus, it is increasingly clear that both 'community' and 'neighbourhood' should be regarded simply as general terms for a cluster of inter-related situations relating to specific aspects of social organization. Blowers (1973) has offered a typology of neighbourhoods which reflects this approach. He postulates a continuum of neighbourhoods, the extremes of which are determined by the extent of social interaction and common ties. At one end of the continuum are *arbitrary*

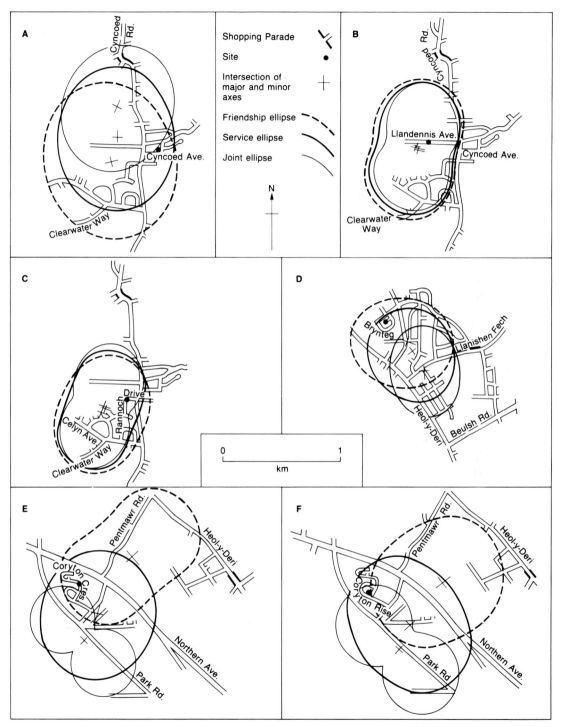

**Fig. 3.5**  Social interaction (friendship) and service ellipses for six sites in Cardiff.
*Source*: Herbert and Raine (1976), Fig. 1, p. 331.

*neighbourhoods*: general localities with definite names but imprecise limits; *physical neighbourhoods* are distinctive environments with clear boundaries; *homogeneous neighbourhoods* are distinctive and internally homogeneous in terms of both environmental and physical characteristics; *functional neighbourhoods* are areas united by particular activity patterns – working or learning, for example; and finally, *community neighbourhoods* are those which contain close-knit groups engaged in primary social interaction.

Bell and Newby (1976) also recognize the multidimensional nature of local social organization. They suggest that it is useful to think in terms of a loose hierarchial relationship between neighbourhood, community and communality. Thus *neighbourhoods* are territories containing people of broadly similar demographic, economic and social characteristics, but are not necessarily significant as a basis for social interaction. *Communities* exist where a degree of social coherence develops on the basis of interdependence, which in turn produces a uniformity of custom, taste and modes of thought and speech. Communities are 'taken-for-granted' worlds defined by reference groups which may be locality-based, school-based, work-based or media-based. *Communality*, or 'communion', exists as a form of human association based on affective bonds. It is 'community experience at the level of consciousness' (Bell and Newby 1976: 197), but it requires an intense mutual involvement that is difficult to sustain and so only appears under conditions of stress.

In the final analysis, 'each neighbourhood is what its inhabitants think it is' (US National Commission on Neighbourhoods 1979: 7). As Downs (1981) points out, this means that definitions and classifications of neighbourhoods and communities must depend on the geographic scales of reference used by people. In this context, it may be helpful to think of *immediate* neighbourhoods (which are small, which may overlap one another, and which are characterized by personal association rather than interaction through formal groups, institutions, or organizations), *traditional* neighbourhoods (which are characterized by social interaction that is consolidated by the sharing of local facilities and the use of local organizations), and *emergent* neighbourhoods (which are large, diverse, and characterized by relatively low levels of social interaction) (Hojnacki 1979).

A rather different, way of approaching neighbourhoods and communities is to focus on their *functions* (Hunter 1979; Smith 1980). It is possible, for example, to think in terms of neighbourhoods' *existential* functions (related to people's affective bonds and sense of belonging), *economic* functions (geared to consumption), *administrative* functions (geared to the organization and use of public services), *locational* functions (relating to the social and material benefits of relative location), *structural* functions (related to the social outcomes of urban design), *political* functions (geared to the articulation of local issues), and *social reproduction* functions (related to the broader political economy of urbanization). All are themes which will surface in subsequent sections of this book.

## Home and neighbourhood as experiential settings

The more closely we examine these questions of neighbourhood and community, the more it becomes apparent that the subjective features of people's residential environment are critical (Cohen 1985). As Ley puts it:

The social reality of the city is not simply given. It is also constructed and maintained intersubjectively in a semiclosed world of communication and shared symbolization. The routines of daily life create a particular view of the world and a mandate for action. It is the unself-conscious, taken-for-granted character of the life-world that makes it so binding on its members, that ensures that its realities will remain secure (Ley 1983: 203).

Some writers, borrowing from the philosophical traditions of phenomenology and existentialism, have begun to explore these aspects of urban social geography. Central to phenomenological approaches is the idea of the *lifeworld*, 'the taken-for-granted pattern and context for everyday living through which people conduct their day-to-day lives without having to make it an object of conscious attention' (Seamon 1979). In this context, Buttimer (1976) has developed the notions of 'insideness' and 'outsideness', arguing that the need is to understand community and locality in terms of the insider, the person who normally lives in and uses the place or setting. Relph (1976) has also explored these notions, viewing them as ends of a continuum along which various modes of place-experience can be identified. Relph's key argument is that places have meaning in direct proportion to the degree that people feel 'inside' that place: 'here rather than there, enclosed rather than exposed, secure rather than threatened'. He also argues that 'placelessness' – the weakening of distinct and diverse experiences of places – is now a dominant force in Western urban societies. Tuan (1974, 1975, 1977), on the other hand, emphasizes the pervasiveness of 'topophilia' and 'sense of place' in human experience. Indeed, sense of place is often interpreted to cover all the affective ties between individuals or groups and their home areas, including their housing (see Duncan 1982).

Seamon (1979) has pursued a rather different theme, using 'environmental experience groups' to explore 'movement' (day-to-day environmental dealings), 'rest' (person-place attachments) and 'encounter' (observation of the world). Together, he claims, the three constitute a 'place-ballet', a 'regularity of individual habits and routines in terms of space, as in an outdoor market place, local diner or street neighbourhood'. Ley (1974, 1977), on the other hand, has emphasized the role of daily verbal communication in creating and maintaining the taken-for-granted lifeworld of city neighbourhoods. Somewhat different again are existential approaches, which are based on the contention that man originates in an alienated condition and defines himself, among other ways, spatially. His 'creation' of space provides him with roots, so that homes and localities are biographies of that creation, statements of the 'existential origins of spatial arrangements, relations and attachments' (Samuels 1981).

Yet, while many geographers have conceded the relevance of experiential approaches to an understanding of urban communities, few have actively pursued the theme (though see Ley 1983 for some illustrative examples). Rather, there has been a tendency towards programmatic writing. Here, a major theme has been the contribution which experiential approaches might make to an 'encounter' between structuralist and humanistic theoretical frameworks (Buttimer 1979; Eyles 1981; Cullen and Knox 1982; Gregory 1978).

# Environment and behaviour in urban settings

In addition to the variations in social organization which occur among different social groups in different parts of the city, geographers have for a long time been interested in the relationships between urban settings and certain aspects of people's behaviour. It should be stressed at the outset that these relationships are reciprocal: 'a neighbourhood takes its character from the values and lifestyles of its residents; however, reciprocally, is personality is also a context that acts to reinforce and narrow a range of human responses' (Ley 1983: 143). The emphasis of most research in this area, though, has been on the way in which the 'personality' of urban settings influences individual and group behaviour and, in particular, the way in which 'deviant' behaviour is related to urban settings.

Central to this whole perspective is the idea of *environmental conditioning*. A classic example is provided by Newson and Newson's work (1965) on patterns of infant care. Impoverished neighbourhoods, they argued, are characterized by a poverty of sensory stimulation, by crowded environments that inhibit play, and by unenlightened attitudes towards child rearing. The net result, it is argued, is that the environmental conditioning experienced by children growing up in such settings produces 'under-socialized' individuals with a competitive nature attuned only to the immediate social group, leaving them ill-equipped to cope with the more subtle forms of competition which prevail in the world beyond. By extension, it is argued that this kind of environmental conditioning tends to curtail creativity, adaptability and flexibility. The result is doubly-disadvantaged individuals who, on the one hand, seek short-term gratification and are weakly attuned to the established norms and rules of society at large while, on the other, are unable to articulate a coherent alternative or opposition to these norms and rules. This kind of argument begs all sorts of questions about the mechanisms and processes involved. How, for example, are distinctive local values sustained in local settings; and to what extent do localized values and attitudes affect the incidence of particular patterns of behaviour? How important is the built environment? And what is the role of broader, class-based factors? As we shall see from an examination of ideas about deviant behaviour, there is a broad spectrum of theories.

## Theories about deviant behaviour

The notion of deviance covers a multitude of social sins, but geographers have been most interested in behaviour with a distinctive pattern of intra-urban variation, such as prostitution, suicide, truancy, delinquency and drug addiction. In fact, most aspects of deviant behaviour seem to exhibit a definite spatial pattern of some sort, rather than being randomly distributed across the city. But, whereas there is little disagreement about the nature of the patterns themselves, theory and research in geography, sociology and environmental psychology are less conclusive about explanations of the patterns. Some writers, for instance, see deviant behaviour as a pathological response to a particular social and/or physical environment. Others argue that certain physical or social attributes act as environmental cues for certain kinds of behaviour; others still that certain environments simply attract certain kinds of people. Until very recently, almost all the theorizing about spatial variations in deviant behaviour shared a common element of environmental deter-

minism, usually traceable to the determinists of the Chicago school. In this section the more influential aspects of this theory are outlined before going on to examine briefly the intra-urban geography of one kind of deviant behaviour – crime and delinquency – as an illustration of the complexity of the actual relationships between urban environments and human behaviour.

### Determinist theory

There is no need to reiterate at length the relationships between urban environments and deviant behaviour postulated by adherents to Wirthian theory (see pp. 57–58). The general position is that deviant behaviour is a product either of adaptive behaviour or maladjustment to city life, or to life in certain parts of the city. Thus the aloofness and impersonality which are developed in response to the competing stimuli and conflicting demands of different social situations are felt to lead to a breakdown of interpersonal relationships and social order and to an increase in social isolation, which in turn facilitates the emergence of ego-centred, unconventional behaviour and precipitates various kinds of deviant behaviour.

Evidence to support these tenets of determinist theory has been assembled on several fronts. The idea of psychological overload resulting from complex or unfamiliar environments has been investigated by environmental psychologists and popularized by Toffler (1970), who suggests that the need to 'scoop up and process' additional information in such situations can lead to 'future-shock': the human response to overstimulation. The nature of this response has been shown by psychologists to take several forms: 'Dernier's strategy', for example, involves the elimination from perception of unwelcome reality, and in an extreme form can result in the construction of a mythological world which becomes a substitute for the real world (Smith 1977) and in which deviant behaviour may be seen by the person concerned as 'normal'. Another response is for people to 'manage' several distinct roles or identities at once (Goffman 1959, 1971). According to determinist theory, this is characteristic of urban environments because of the physical and functional separation of the 'audiences' to which different roles are addressed: family, neighbours, co-workers, club members, and so on. Thus, people tend to be able to present very different 'selves' in different social contexts. Again, the extreme form of this behaviour may lead to deviancy. The city, with its wide choice of different roles and identities becomes a 'magic theatre', and 'emporium of styles' (Raban 1975), and the anonymity afforded by the ease of slipping from one role to another clearly facilitates the emergence of unconventional and deviant behaviour. Moreover, as Berger *et al.* (1973) and Goffman (1971) have pointed out, further deviancy or pathology may result from the strain of having to sustain different and perhaps conflicting identities over a prolonged period.

Most interest, however, has centred on the impersonality and aloofness which apparently results from the psychological overload associated with certain urban environments. Milgram (1970) has illustrated various manifestations of this impersonality, the most striking of which is the collective paralysis of social responsibility which seems to occur in central city areas in crisis situations. Milgram cites the well-known example of the murder of Catherine Genovese in illustrating this phenomenon. Ms Genovese was stabbed to death in a respectable district of Queens in New York, and her murder was evidently witnessed by nearly 40 people, none of whom attempted even to call the police. Other evidence of the lack of 'bystander intervention' and of an unwillingness to assist strangers comes from experiments contrived by psychologists (see, for example, Berkowitz and McCauly 1972; Korte 1978; Korte and Kerr 1975. Such asocial behaviour is itself deviant to some extent, of course; but its significance to determinist theory lies in the way in which it fosters the spread of more serious forms of deviancy by eroding social responsibility and social control.

The net result of these various forms of adaptive behaviour is thus a weakening of personal supports and social constraints and a confusion of behavioural norms. This, in turn, gives a further general impetus to deviant behaviour. Feelings of isolation among the 'lonely crowd' are associated with neurosis, alcoholism and suicide (Riesman 1950); and the anomic state induced by the weakening of behavioural norms is associated with various forms of crime and delinquency. Academic opinion, however, is by no means unanimous as to the utility of determinist theory in explaining patterns of deviant behaviour. It is difficult to establish either proof or refutation of the connections between stress, adaptive behaviour, social isolation, social disorganization, anomie and deviancy because of the difficulty of controlling for the many intervening variables such as age, class, education and personality. Nevertheless, many investigations of intra-urban variations in deviant behaviour have found it useful to invoke determinist theory in at least partial explanation of the patterns encountered. The geography of looting during electricity blackouts in New York City in 1977 (Fig. 3.6), for example, was closely correlated with patterns of poverty. 'Apparently, people excluded from effective participation in the affluent society did not, and cannot be expected to, act with restraint when the enforcement of law and order is immobilized' (Wohlenberg 1982: 42). (See also Mintz and Schwartz (1964) on mental illness, Maris (1969) on suicide, Castle and Gittus (1957) on 'social defects' and Johnston (1979c) on the use of telephone counselling services). To the extent that determinist theory is founded on the effects of urbanism on human behaviour, the inference must be that some parts of the city are more 'urban' (in the Wirthian sense) than others, with more social disorganization, a greater incidence of anomie and, consequently, a higher incidence of deviant behaviour.

### Crowding theory

There is now a considerable literature linking high residential densities, irrespective of other characteristics or urbanism, with a wide range of deviant behaviour. High densities and a sense of crowding, it is argued, create strains

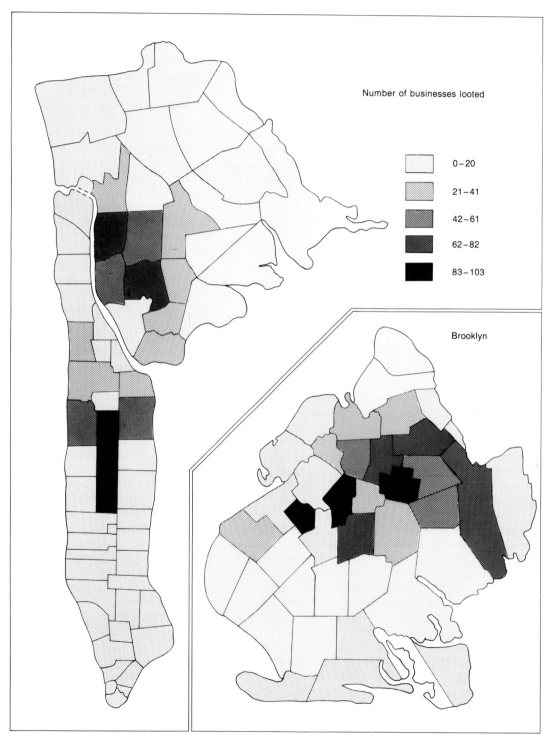

**Fig. 3.6** Looting in New York: businesses approved for Reestablishment Grants by Mayor's Emergency Aid Commission.    *Source*: Wohlenberg (1982) Fig. 2, p. 36.

and tensions which modify behaviour, inducing aggression, withdrawal or, if these strategies are unsuccessful, mental or physical illness. The initial link between crowding and stress is attributed by many to an innate sense of *territoriality*. This idea has been popularized by ethologists such as Ardrey (1966, 1970) and Morris (1967) who believe that humans, like many other animals, are subject to a genetic trait which is produced by the species' need for territory as a source of safety, security and privacy. According to Ardrey (1966), territoriality also satisfies the need for stimulation (provided by 'border disputes') and for a physical expression of personal identity. These needs are believed to add up to a strong 'territorial imperative': a natural component of behaviour which will clearly be disrupted by crowding (Gold 1982; Sack 1980).

The whole approach draws heavily on behavioural research with animals, where the links between crowding, stress and abnormal behaviour can be clearly established under laboratory conditions (Esser 1971). Calhoun, for example, in his celebrated studies of rat behaviour, showed that crowding led to aggression, listlessness, promiscuity, homosexuality, and the rodent equivalent of juvenile delinquency (Calhoun 1962). Projecting these ideas directly to human behaviour leads to the idea of crowded urbanites as 'killer apes'. One sociologist, for example, writes that 'We have caged ourselves in zoos of our own creation; and like caged animals we have developed pathological forms of behaviour' (van den Berghe 1974: 787.) Critics of crowding theory have emphasized the obvious dangers involved in extending animal behaviour to humans: people are not rats; it is by no means certain that humans possess any innate sense of territoriality; and in any case even the most crowded slums do not approach the levels of crowding to which experimental animals have been subjected (Freedman 1975; Reiser 1973). It is difficult, however, to establish conclusively whether or not there is any connection among humans between territoriality, crowding and deviant behaviour. Territoriality may exist in humans through cultural acquisition even if it is not an innate instinct for, as Edney (1976) has pointed out, territoriality in the form of property rights does provide

society with a means of distinguishing social rank and of regulating social interaction. Moreover, there is a considerable body of evidence to support the idea of territorial behaviour in urban men and women, whatever the source of this behaviour may be. Rainwater (1966) and Porteous (1976), for example, have illustrated the function of individuals' home territory as a haven, while Agnew (1982), Cooper (1976), and Duncan and Duncan (1976) have speculated on the home as an expression of identity. Others have demonstrated the existence of what seems to amount to a territorial imperative at the societal level. The simplest example of this is the existence of gang 'turfs' which are rigorously and ceremonially defended by gang members (Patrick 1973; Yablonsky 1970). More complex and sophisticated social groups also seem to exhibit territorial behaviour. Suttles, for example, has documented the 'foreign relations' of different social groups occupying 'defended neighbourhoods, in American inner-city areas (Suttles 1968, 1972); and Boal has illustrated the extreme territoriality that exists in the area around the Shankhill/Falls divide in Belfast, where aggression between members of rival Catholic and Protestant communities has resulted in complete segregation (Boal 1978).

Accepting that humans do acquire some form of territoriality, it does seem plausible that crowding could induce stress and so precipitate a certain amount of deviant behaviour. The evidence, however, is ambiguous. Some studies report a clear association between crowding and social and physical pathology (Carstairs 1966; Sharrod and Downs 1974); others report contradictory findings (Baldassare and Fischer 1976; Cassel 1972), and the whole debate continues to attract controversy in all of the social and environmental disciplines (see, for example, Baum and Epstein 1979; Booth 1976; Boots 1979; Choldin 1978; Galle and Gove 1983; Kirmeyer 1978; McCarthy and Saegert 1978; Schmitt *et al.* 1978).

### Design determinism

In addition to the general debate on crowding theory, a growing amount of attention has been directed towards the negative effects of architecture and urban design on people's behaviour (Kaplan and Kaplan 1978; Mercer 1975; Rapoport 1977). In broad terms the suggestion is that the design and configuration of buildings and spaces sometimes creates micro-environments which discourage 'normal' patterns of social interaction and encourage deviant behaviour of various kinds. A considerable amount of evidence has been accumulated in support of this idea. The inhibiting effects of high-rise and deck-access apartment dwellings on social interaction and child development, for example, have been documented in a number of different studies (Jephcott 1971; Newson and Newson 1965; Rainwater 1966; Yancey 1971); and from these it is a short step to studies which point to the correlation between certain aspects of urban design and the incidence of particular aspects of deviancy such as mental illness and suicide (Wing 1974).

The nature of these relationships is not entirely clear. One interesting proposition has been put forward by Peter Smith (1977), who suggests that the configuration of buildings and spaces creates a 'syntax' of images and symbolism to which people respond through a synthesis of 'gut reactions' and intellectual reactions. Environments which are dominated by an unfamiliar or illogical visual language are thus likely to appear threatening or confusing: qualities which may well precipitate certain aspects of malaise or deviant behaviour. This, however, is a comparatively new notion, and requires more empirical investigation before its utility can be confirmed. A better-known and more thoroughly examined link between urban design and deviant behaviour is Oscar Newman's concept of 'defensible space'. Newman (1972) suggested that much of the petty crime, vandalism, mugging and burglary in moden housing developments is related to an attenuation of community life and a withdrawal of local social controls caused by the inability of residents to identify with, or exert any control over, the space beyond their own front door. This, he argued, was a result of the 'designing out' of territorial definition and delineation in new housing developments, in accordance with popular

taste among architects. Once the space immediately outside the dwelling becomes public, Newman suggested, nobody will feel obliged to 'supervise' it or 'defend' it against intruders. Newman's ideas have been supported by some empirical work (see, for example, Mawby 1977; Tata *et al.* 1975) and enthusiastically received in the professions concerned with urban design, where they have created a new conventional wisdom of their own: defensible space is now an essential component in the praxis of urban design (Rand 1984). On the other hand, Newman's work has been heavily criticized for the quality of his statistical analysis and for his neglect of the interplay of physical and social variables (Mayhew 1979; Gold 1982).

### Alienation

The concept of alienation is a central construct of Marxian theory, where it is seen as a mechanism of social change contributing towards the antithesis of the dominant mode of production. It also has wider socio-political connotations, however, with some relevance to the explanation of deviant behaviour (Fischer 1973; Schacht 1971; Seeman 1971). In its wider sense, alienation is characterized by feelings of powerlessness, dissatisfaction, distrust, and a rejection of the prevailing distribution of wealth and power. These feelings usually stem from people's experience of some aspect of the social, political or economic system. Some people may be alienated because they feel the structure of these systems prevents their effective participation; others may be alienated because they disagree with the very nature of the systems – perhaps because of their ineffectiveness in satisfying human needs (Olsen 1968). Whatever the source, such feelings are clearly experience-based and therefore spatially focused, to a certain extent, on people's area of residence. This makes alienation an attractive explanatory factor when considering spatial variations in people's behaviour, as the early deterministic theorists were quick to note (Park 1916; Wirth 1938). The major interest in this respect has been the relationship between alienation and political behaviour, but it has also been suggested that certain aspects of deviant behaviour may be related to feelings of alienation (Philliber 1977; Schacht 1971). Such behaviour may be manifested in apathy: mildly unconventional in itself but more significant if it is prevalent enough to erode social order. Alternatively, alienation may precipitate deviance directly through some form of activism – which can range from eccentric forms of protest to violence and terrorism.

## Compositional theory

Compositional theory is the product of another school of thought which has developed out of the writings of the Chicago determinists. Compositionalists emphasize the cohesion and intimacy of distinctive social worlds based on ethnicity, kinship, neighbourhood, occupation, or lifestyle, rejecting the idea that these social networks are in any way diminished by urban life (Gans 1962, 1967; Lewis 1952; Reiss 1955). They also minimize the psychological effects of city life on people's behaviour, suggesting, instead, that behaviour is determined largely by economic status, cultural characteristics, family status, and so on: the same attributes that determine which social worlds they live in.

Compositional theory is not framed explicitly to analyse deviant behaviour, but it does offer a distinctive perspective on the question. Deviancy, like other forms of behaviour, is seen as a product of the composition of local populations, with the social mores, political attitudes and cultural traits of certain groups being more productive of unconventional or deviant behaviour than others. The pattern of sexually transmitted disease in London serves to illustrate this compositionalist perspective. The incidence of this particular manifestation of deviant behaviour has a very marked peak in the bed-sitter land of West-Central London, especially around Earls Court. The explanation, in compositionalist terms, is the high proportion of young transients in the area – mostly young single people living in furnished rooms – whose sexual mores are different from those of the rest of the population and whose vulnerability to VD and other sexually transmitted diseases is increased

by the presence of a significant proportion of young males who have themselves been infected before arriving in London. According to London's urban folklore, much of the blame in this respect is attached to Australians who arrive in London having visited Bangkok (Phillips 1977).

## Subcultural theory

Subcultural theory is closely related to compositional theory. Like the latter, subcultural theory subscribes to the idea of social worlds with distinctive socio-demographic characteristics and distinctive lifestyles which propagate certain forms of behaviour. In addition, however, subcultural theory holds that these social worlds, or subcultures, will be *intensified* by the conflict and competition of urban life; and that *new* subcultures will be spawned as specialized groups generated by the arrival of immigrants and by the structural differentiation resulting from industrialization and urbanization reach the 'critical mass' required to sustain cohesive social networks (Fischer 1975). Fischer suggests that 'Among the subcultures spawned or intensified by urbanism are those which are considered to be either downright deviant by the larger society – such as delinquents, professional criminals, and homosexuals; or to be at least 'odd' – such as artists, missionaries of new religious sects, and intellectuals; or to be breakers of tradition – such as life-style experimenters, radicals and scientists' (Fischer 1976: 38). What is seen as deviancy by the larger society, however, is seen by the members of these subcultural groups as a normal form of activity and part of the group's internal social system.

Subcultural theory does not in itself carry any explicitly spatial connotations but, as Karp *et al.* point out, the continued existence of subcultural groups depends to a large extent on avoiding conflict with other groups. Conflict may be avoided, they suggest, by implicit *behavioural* boundaries beyond which groups 'promise' not to trespass: a kind of social contract; but the most effective means of maintaining inter-group tolerance is through *spatial* seregation (Karp, Stone and Yoels 1977). This idea makes subcultural theory attractive in explaining spatial variations in deviant behaviour. It has proved useful, for example, in studies of delinquent behaviour (Cohen 1955; Herbert 1976b; Mays 1963; Phillipson 1971).

Subcultural theory also fits in conveniently with the idea of *cultural transmission*, whereby deviant norms are passed from one generation to another within a local environment. This process was identified over 100 years ago by Mayhew (1862) in the 'rookeries' of London, where children were 'born and bred' to the business of crime; and it was given prominence by Shaw and McKay (1942) in their study of delinquency in Chicago. Another concept relevant to the understanding of deviant behaviour within a localized subculture is the so-called *neighbourhood effect*, whereby people tend to conform to what they perceive as local norms in order to gain the respect of their local peer group. Empirical evidence for this phenomenon has been presented in a number of studies. One well-known example comes from Brian Robson's study of attitudes towards education in different parts of Sunderland, where 'No matter what the area, the attitudes of individual families were more familiar to those prevailing around them than to those of their objective social class' (Robson 1969: 244). People's behaviour also seems directly susceptible to a neighbourhood effect: Hoivik, for example, suggests that the paradoxical syndrome of 'suburban poverty' in new owner-occupier estates is largely a product of neighbourhood effects which serve to impose middle-class consumption patterns on incoming families, many of whom have incomes which are really insufficient to 'keep up with the Jones's' but who nevertheless feel obliged to conform with their neighbours' habits (Hoivik 1973; see also Tallman and Morgner 1970). A similar process has been observed in relation to voting behaviour. Rumley (1981), for example, has shown that the percentage of West Australian manual workers who vote Labour in a given area increases as the percentage of manual workers in that area increases (see also Cox 1969; Johnston 1974, 1979c). It seems likely that many deviant attitudes and deviant forms of behaviour will also be subject to a neighbourhood effect,

although few studies have investigated the idea in this context. Important exceptions include the investigations of crime and delinquency in British cities by Baldwin, Bottoms and Walker (1976) and Herbert (1976b) which are discussed in more detail below.

### Structuralist theory

This perspective, based on a neo-marxist interpretation of urban society, views the rules of social behaviour and the definitions of deviant behaviour as part of society's *superstructure*, the framework of social and philosophical organization that stems from the economic relationships on which society is based. The definitions of deviance, it is argued, protect the interests of the dominant class, thereby helping that class to continue its domination. In modern capitalist society, deviant behaviour can be seen as a direct result of stresses associated with the contradictions that are inherent to the operation of the economic system. One major contradiction in this context involves the existence of a 'reserve army' of surplus labour that is both vulnerable, in the sense of being powerless, but at the same time dangerous, because its members represent a potentially volatile group. The need to maintain this reserve army and to defuse unrest among its members explains the substantial social expenditure of modern welfare states; while the need to control the behaviour of its members explains the rules and definitions attached to many aspects of 'deviant' behaviour associated with the stress of unemployment and the repression and degradation of being supported at a marginal level by the welfare state (Peet 1975; Quinney 1980; Smith 1984).

Another important contradiction, it is argued, is that while capital accumulation requires fit and healthy workers, it also tends to debilitate them through the effects of the stresses that result from the various controls that are exerted on the labour force (Eyer 1977). Examples of these controls include the patterns of socialization that are part of the superstructure of capitalism, in which individuals are rewarded for being competitive but not too individualistic, and in which they are encouraged to spend their rewards on the acquisition of material possessions. As Smith observes:

These sources of stress are endemic in the capitalist system, but they are unequally allocated between the classes: workers experience more than their share of the costs or stresses, and less than their share of the benefits. It is no surprise, therefore, that the working classes are disproportionately represented in the prevalence data for mental illness, drug and alcohol abuse, and crime (Smith 1984: 194).

### Multi-factor explanations: the example of crime and delinquency

The difficulty of reconciling the apparently conflicting evidence relating to these different theories has, inevitably, led to a more flexible approach in which multi-factor explanations of deviant behaviour are admitted without being attached to a specific theoretical perspective. This, as Herbert (1976a) observes, is common to all branches of social deviance research, although it is probably best illustrated in relation to crime and delinquency. Empirical studies of spatial variations in crime and delinquency have lent support, variously, to theories of crowding, social disorganization, anomie, design determinism and deviant subcultures; but, as West (1967) points out, it is difficult to assemble evidence in support of any one theory in preference to the rest. In the absence of any alternative all-embracing theoretical perspective, an eclectic multi-factor approach thus becomes an attractive framework of explanation.

The evidence which can be drawn from studies of spatial variations in crime and delinquency is, like much social geographical research, subject to important qualifications relating to the nature of the data and methods of research which have been employed. It is, therefore, worth noting the more important difficulties and pitfalls involved in such research before going on to illustrate the complexity of inter-relationships between environment and behaviour which is suggested by the results of empirical research. One of the most fundamental problems concerns the quality of data. David Smith (1974b) has emphasized the fragility of data relating to

crime and delinquency, pointing to several sources of error and confusion. Most research has to rely on official data derived from law enforcement agencies, and these data are usually far from comprehensive in their coverage. Many offences do not enter official records because they are not notified to the police; and data on offenders are further diluted by the relatively low detection rate for most offences (Fig. 3.7). More disconcerting is the possibility that the data which are recorded do not provide a representative sample. Many researchers have argued that official data are biased against working-class offenders, suggesting that the police are more likely to allow parental sanctions to replace legal sanctions in middle-class areas, that working-class areas are more intensively policed, and that crime reporting by adults is similarly biased. Conversely, 'white-collar' crimes – fraud, tax evasion, expense account 'fiddles', and so on – tend to be under-reported and are more difficult to detect, even

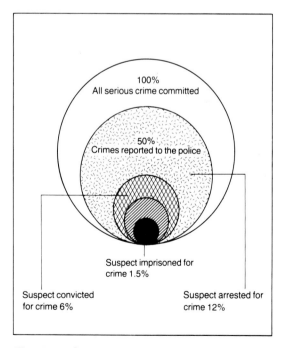

**Fig. 3.7** Crime and law enforcement in the United States. *Source*: Banfield (1974) p. 202.

where large amounts of money are involved. Some critics have suggested that this bias has been compounded by the predilection in empirical research for data relating to blue-collar crimes. This may be attributable in part to the differential availability of data on different kinds of offence, but it also seems likely that data on white-collar crimes have been neglected because they are, simply, less amenable to deterministic hypotheses. Finally, Harries (1981) has argued that the usual form of crime data – frequency counts of popu-lation-based rates – are inappropriate to many research problems. Rather, he suggests, the denominator for crime rates should be indica-tive of the environments with which they are typically associated.

In any event, the net result may well be that empirical studies present only a partial picture of intra-urban patterns of crime and delinquency. As Smith observes, the geo-graphy of crime in Washington, DC, changes dramatically according to whether or not the definition of 'crime' includes the white-collar 'suite crimes' of the business district and middle-class suburbs, the political crimes associ-ated with the Watergate Centre, and the war crimes which may be associated with the Pentagon (Smith 1974b). Because data for many important crime and crime-related vari-ables are only available for groups of people rather than individuals, many studies have pursued an ecological approach, examining variations in crime between territorial groups. Such an approach is inherently attractive to geographers but it does involve certain limi-tations and pitfalls. The chief limitation of ecological studies is that they cannot provide conclusive evidence of causal links. Thus, although certain categories of offenders may be found in crowded and/or socially disorgan-ized areas, their criminal behaviour may actu-ally be related to other causes – alienation or personality factors, for example – and the ecological correlation may simply result from their gravitation to a certain kind of neigh-bourhood. The chief pitfall associated with ecological studies is the so-called 'ecological fallacy': the mistake of drawing inferences about *individuals* on the basis of correlations calculated for areas. One pertinent example

is the frequently-encountered association within British cities between crime rates and neighbourhoods containing large numbers of coloured immigrants. The inference drawn by many is that coloured immigrants and their subcultures are particularly disposed towards crime and delinquency; but research at the level of the individual has in fact shown that 'coloured immigrants are very much less involved in the crime and disorder that surround them in the areas where they live than their white neighbours' (Lambert 1970: 124).

Bearing these limitations in mind, what conclusions can be drawn from empirical studies about the factors which precipitate crime and delinquency? It is not possible to do justice to the extensive literature on criminology and the geography of crime in a text such as this: the serious student should consult the specialist work of Baldwin, Bottoms and Walker (1976), Davidson (1981), Herbert (1982) or Pyle (1974). Nevertheless, it is possible to give some indication of the current state of the art. Following Herbert (1976a, 1977a; 1979; Herbert and Hyde 1985), it is useful to distinguish between factors influ-encing the pattern of *occurrence* of crime and delinquency and those influencing the pattern of *residence* of offenders.

Most cities exhibit very distinctive areas where the occurrence of crime and delin-quency is well above average. Many, in fact, conform to the archetypal pattern identified in Chicago in the 1920s (Shaw *et al.* 1929), with low rates in the suburbs increasing steadily to a peak in the inner city and CBD; though this pattern is often modified, as in Aberdeen (Fig. 3.8), where substantial numbers of low-income, 'problem' households have become localized in suburban public housing estates. Patterns of occurrence vary consider-ably, however, by the type of offence. In Cleveland, for example, the geography of murder differs considerably from the geo-graphy of assault, while the geography of larceny is different from both (Fig. 3.9) Ecological analyses of occurrence patterns for different offences provide some clues as to the relationships between crime and urban environments, and there are several studies

**Fig. 3.8** Patterns of crime in Aberdeen, Scotland. *Source*: Williams (1985) Fig. 3, pp. 55 and 65.

**Fig. 3.9** The distribution of murders, larcenies and assaults in Cleveland, Ohio.
*Source*: Pyle 1976 pp. 273 and 275.

**Fig. 3.9**    (continued)

which are useful in this context. In his pioneering study of crime in Seattle, Schmid (1960) demonstrated the concentration of shoplifting and cheque fraud offences in the CBD, of larceny and burglary in suburban areas, and of robbery and female drunkeness in the 'skid row' area of the city. In a later study of the same city, the dominant pattern of crime occurrence was found to be associated with inner-city areas of low social cohesion, where there was a concentration of burglary, car theft and handbag snatching (Schmid and Schmid 1972). In Akron, Ohio, Pyle (1974) found a similar general association between the occurrence of crime and poverty; and the nature of this relationship has been further elaborated in studies of US cities and suburbs (Brown 1982; Corsi and Harvey 1975; Dunstan and Roberts 1980; Pyle 1976; Stahura, Huff and Smith 1980), where

detailed ecological analysis has revealed a distinct association between low-income neighbourhoods and crimes of violence, including murder, rape and assault. Pyle (1976) also found evidence to suggest that transitional areas – with a high proportion of land devoted to manufacturing and wholesaling, a decaying physical environment, and an ageing population – are associated with a separate and equally distinctive concentration of offences which includes larceny, robbery and car theft as well as assault and murder. Other important relationships to emerge from these studies are the correlation between property crimes – burglary, larceny and car theft – and stable, mid- and upper-income suburban neighbourhoods, and between violent crimes and black neighbourhoods.

These findings lend some support to the emphasis given to spatial variations in *oppor-*

**Table 3.3**  Households subject to house-breaking offences according to rateable value

| Rateable value | Number of house-breaking offences (estimated) | Number of dwellings in Sheffield | Rate per 1,000 dwellings |
|---|---|---|---|
| <£31 | 350 | 58,342 | 6.0 |
| £31–56 | 440 | 66,357 | 6.6 |
| £57–100 | 200 | 35,372 | 5.9 |
| £101–200 | 144 | 6,165 | 23.4 |
| >£200 | 28 | 539 | 51.9 |
| Not known | 44 | – | – |
| Total | 1,214 | 166,775 | 7.0 |

*Source:* Baldwin and Bottoms 1976: 63.

tunities for crime by Boggs, (1965) in her study of St. Louis and by Baldwin, Bottoms and Walker (1976) in their study of Sheffield. Both studies were able to demonstrate the importance of the 'opportunity factor' in explaining occurrence patterns of several offences. In the Sheffield study, for example, a marked relationship between property values and house-breaking offences was revealed (Table 3.3). The ecology of other offences also seemed to confirm the general importance of opportunity factors, although the evidence was not always conclusive. As Herbert (1977a) observes, this uncertainty derives in part from the scale of analysis: ecological studies are simply not able to reflect the environmental nuances which influence the exact location of offences. The importance of the micro-environment has been emphasized by the US National Commission on the Causes and Prevention of Violence (1969), which concluded that accessibility, visibility, control of property, residential density and state of physical repair are the most signficant aspects of the micro-environment of violent crime. Other studies have illustrated the importance of micro-environmental features in explaining other kinds of offence. Brantingham and Brantingham (1975), for example, showed that the incidence of burglary in Tallahassee was higher in peripheral blocks of housing estates, where burglars could benefit from the weaker social control of 'anonymous' boundary areas; and Ley and

Cybriwsky (1974) found that the occurrence of abandoned and stripped cars in Philadelphia, which appeared to have a random spatial distribution at the 'micro' scale, was closely related to vacant land, doorless sides of buildings, and institutional land use. Also relevant at this scale, of course, is Newman's concept of defensible space. Evans and Oulds (1984), for example, found that the uneven micro-pattern of burglary victims in Newcastle-under-Lyme (Fig. 3.10) was explained by the distribution of open and recreational space, playgrounds, garage space and disused railway lines that gave rear access to properties.

David Herbert has provided a useful summary of the general relationship between environmental features and the location of criminal offences in his review of urban crime and delinquency (Fig. 3.11). As he observes, 'there are qualities attached to the offence location which relate to the *built* environment – its design, detailed land use – and to the *social* environment – status, local activity patterns, local control systems' (Herbert 1977a: 224, emphasis added). To these might be added certain features of the *perceived* environment: the offender's image of the attractiveness or vulnerability of particular neighbourhoods, streets and buildings (see, for example, Carter and Hill 1976).

Patterns of *residence* of offenders are subject to a much wider range of explanatory factors although, like patterns of occurrence, they display a consistent social order and clustering which makes them suitable for ecological analysis. Although there are variations by type of offence and age of offender, the classic pattern is the one described by Shaw and McKay (1942) for Chicago and other American cities: a regular gradient, with low rates in the suburbs and a peak in the inner city. In his review of intra-urban variations in crime and delinquency, Scott (1972) asserted that such gradients typify not only North American cities, but virtually all Western cities for which evidence is available. Recently, however, departures from this pattern have become more apparent as the spatial structure of the Western city has changed. Many cities have experienced an outward shift of offenders' residences with changes in residential mobility

**Fig. 3.10** Distribution of burglary victims in two study areas, Newcastle-under-Lyme, 1978–81.
*Source*: Evans and Oulds (1984) Fig. 5, p. 349.

and housing policies. British studies, in particular, have identified localized clusters of offenders in peripheral local authority housing estates (Baldwin 1975; Herbert 1975; 1976b; Timms 1965), which suggests that the social environment is at least as important as the physical environment in explaining offenders' patterns. In Cardiff, for example, the residences of juvenile delinquents tend to be localized not only among inner-city terrace areas around the docks and in middle-ring rooming-house areas, but also in certain suburban local authority housing estates (Fig. 3.12).

Ecological analyses have been useful in specifying the social and environmental contexts of crime and delinquency residence areas, although it should be emphasized that few studies have been able to incorporate, or control for, all of the factors which might affect individual behaviour. Most geographical research has set aside the possible influence of personal factors (such as physical and mental make-up) and factors associated with the family, school and workplace in order to concentrate on the social and physical context provided by the neighbourhood (Pillai 1981). From these studies there is an overwhelming

weight of evidence connecting known offenders with inner-city neighbourhoods characterized by crowded and substandard housing, poverty, unemployment and demographic imbalance. Schmid, for example, concluded that crime areas in Seattle 'are generally characterized by all or most of the following factors: low social cohesion, weak family life, low socio-economic status, physical deterioration, high rates of population mobility and personal disorganization' (Schmid 1960; 678). This general finding has been confirmed in subsequent studies of the city (Gittus and Stephens 1973; Schmid and Schmid 1972) and has been replicated in studies of other cities (see, for example, Herbert 1977b; Scott 1972; and Wallis and Maliphant 1967). In cities where peripheral clusters of offenders are found, there appears to be an additional syndrome linking offenders with public housing developments containing high proportions of families of particularly low social and economic status, many of whom have been 'dumped' in 'problem estates' through the housing allocation mechanisms of public authorities (Baldwin, Bottoms and Walker 1976; see also pp. 217–224).

A few studies have followed up this general

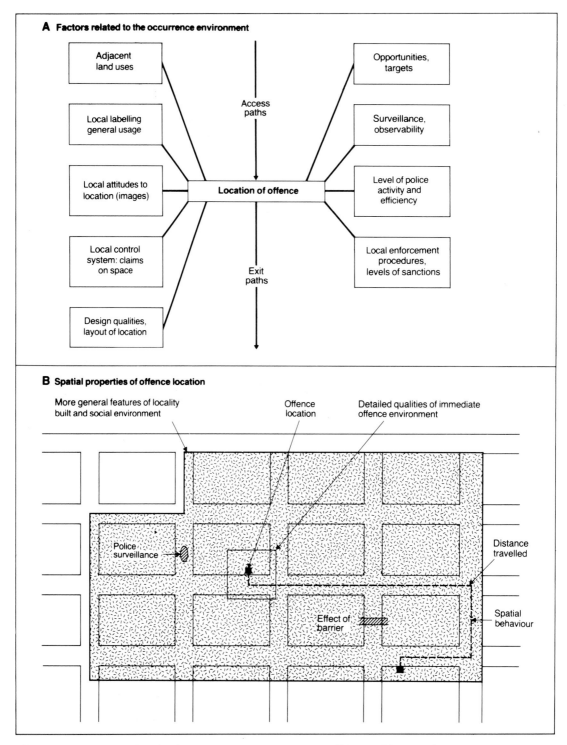

**Fig. 3.11** An analysis of crime occurrence patterns. *Source*: Herbert (1977), p. 223.

**Fig. 3.12**  Juvenile delinquency: offenders' residences in Cardiff, 1977.
*Source*: Evans (1980) Fig. 25, p. 18.

ecological approach with an examination of the less tangible local factors which may be related to crime and delinquency: the dominant values and attitudes associated with different areas. Susan Smith, for example, has argued that the distribution of crime reflects the lifestyle and activity patterns of a community and that the effects of crime, in turn, help to shape these routine urban behaviours (Smith 1984). Herbert and Evans, in their work on juvenile delinquency in Cardiff, have attempted to illustrate the ways in which attitudes and values actually vary between neighbourhoods (Herbert 1976b; Evans 1980). By administering a questionnaire survey to residents of several 'delinquent' neighbourhoods and several 'non-delinquent' neighbourhoods, they were able to show that 'spatial order in the incidence of delinquency is underlain by systematic variations in related attitudes and behaviour' (Herbert 1976b:

490). Significant differences were found in the way in which people 'labelled' areas in their own mind as either delinquent or non-delinquent. Differences between delinquent and non-delinquent areas were also found in relation to people's conception of what amounts to delinquent behaviour: residents of the former were much less disposed towards reporting petty theft and damage to public property than were residents of non-delinquent areas. Similarly, parents in non-delinquent areas were much more inclined to administer sanctions in the home when it came to dealing with misbehaviour. Parents in delinquent areas tended to refer truancy to school authorities, for example, rather than deal with issue themselves. Evans (1980) concludes that these results tend to support subcultural theory more than any other.

But, while it is tempting to cite evidence such as this in support of particular theories

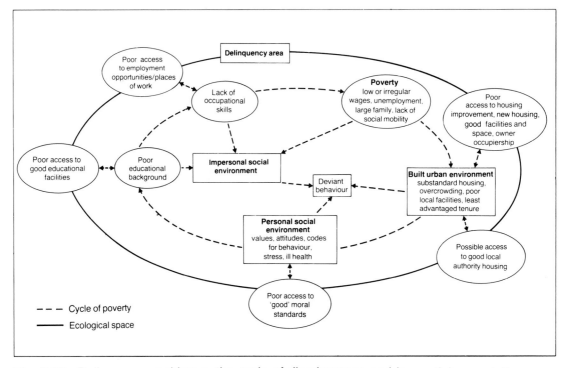

**Fig. 3.13** Delinquency residence: the cycle of disadvantage and its spatial connotations. *Source*: Herbert (1977), p. 277.

and concepts, past experience shows that it is possible to find support for quite different theories within the same pool of evidence. In this situation it seems sensible to accept a multi-factor explanation. Again, Herbert has provided a useful framework within which to subsume the various factors which appear to be involved (Fig. 3.13). Areas of crime and delinquency are linked to several local environmental contexts and generally related to a nexus of social problems. Poverty is the central focus of the model, and is seen as the product of structural factors which, through differential access to educational facilities and employment opportunities, produce an 'impersonal social environment' (i.e. local population) consisting of 'losers' – the aged, the unemployed, misfits and members of minority groups:

. . . poverty limits individuals to particular types of built environment; at worst to the most

disadvantaged housing classes, at best to local authority tenure; both may mean inadequate spatial access to facilities. Disadvantages of the impersonal *social* environment may be compounded by a poor *personal* social environment in which the prevalence of 'unfavourable' values and attitudes may have deleterious effects (Herbert 1977b: 226–7).

While it does not directly further social or geographical theory, Herbert's model does illustrate the complexity of man–environment relationships in the city. Moreover, it also has the advantage of being able to accommodate not only the more deterministic ideas which have been outlined in this section but also the structural explanations of spatial order which are outlined in subsequent chapters and which are favoured by critics of environmental explanations of deviancy (Peet 1975, 1976; Quinney 1980; Taylor, Walton and Young 1973).

# 4 Overviews of spatial differentiation

Areal differentiation has for many years been one of the dominant paradigms of urban social geography. Following the tradition of regionalization within the discipline as a whole, urban geographers have sought to regionalize towns and cities in attempts to produce high-level generalizations about urban form and structure. These generalizations provide useful models with which to generate and test hypotheses and theories concerning urban growth processes and patterns of social interaction in cities. Moreover, many geographers regard the 'regionalization' of cities, like regionalizations of countries or continents, as a basic task of geographical analysis, providing an overall descriptive synthesis which is of fundamental utility in its own right. Whatever the perspective, the initial objective is to identify areas within cities which exhibit distinctive characteristics and which can be shown to be relatively homogeneous. Such areas may be termed neighbourhoods, neighbourhood types, residential areas, urban sub-areas, urban social areas, or urban regions, according to the semantic tastes of the researcher and the type of analysis employed. As in other fields of geographical enquiry, a wide range of techniques and methodologies is available to the researcher concerned with areal differentiation and there is an increasing tendency to adopt more quantitative forms of analysis. There are, however, several distinctive approaches to the identification of urban sub-areas, each with a rather different criterion of areal differentiation. In this chapter three of the most important approaches are examined. These are concerned, respectively, with aspects of the built environment, the socio-economic environment, and the perceived environment. It should be emphasized, however, that these different approaches are significant only because they represent, for the purposes of analysis, a convenient simplification of reality. A comprehensive 'regionalization' of the city would encompass aspects to all three approaches in a more holistic approach. Moreover, the separation of the morphological, socio-economic and perceived environments is seldom complete: many studies of social areas include the physical condition of housing as a variable, for example, while studies of urban morphology frequently rely on class-based categorizations of housing type.

## The built environment

The study of the physical qualities of the urban environment is one of the longest-established components of urban geography, especially in Britain, where the study of 'townscapes' and 'morphological regions' has occupied a prominent place in urban studies. Morphological studies are concerned, by convention, with variations in the style, layout and function of buildings; and they are most logically related to historical aspects of urban growth. As demonstrated in Chapter 2, the built environment is to a large extent a product of the social, economic and techno-logical conditions prevailing at the time of its construction. It has also been noted (p. 30) that most cities experience distinct cycles of building activity which tend to be governed by general economic trends. It therefore makes sense to analyse urban morphology in an historical context, relating the various characteristics of style, layout and function to specific growth phases. This, in fact, is the traditional approach to the analysis of morphological regions in the city. But, although several writers have made major contributions to the description of the general characteristics of morphologies associated with major historical periods (see, for example, Burke 1976; Hiorns 1965; Lavedan 1926–52; Morris 1972; Reps 1965), the use of growth phases as a tool for illustrating the internal structure of cities has been of limited value, largely because simple age categorizations tend to obscure important deviations from the dominant morphological expression of a particular period but also because of the difficulty of accurately establishing the timing of past economic booms and the associated urban growth phases.

More successful have been studies which have incorporated aspects of style, function and layout as explicit criteria in identifying morphological regions, such as Emrys Jones's (1958) study of townscapes in Belfast, in which the principal features of the built environment were mapped using a simple classification based on age (before and after 1896), function (residential areas with and without local shops) and style (detached and terrace housing) which effectively descriminated between five kinds of townscape in addition to the CBD area (Fig. 4. 1). Arthur Smailes, in a series of publications (1955, 1964, 1966), stressed the need for rigorous field surveys and for generalizations about townscape patterns. The core of the urban area, he argued, provided a distinctive townscape unit in towns and cities of all sizes, although its features – the internal specialization of commercial land uses and the dominance of display frontage on most streets – are much more fully developed in larger cities. Smailes recognized that the surrounding tracts of residential development – the 'integuments' of the city – are the product of successive phases of urban growth, each

subject to the influence of different social, economic and cultural forces; and he also allowed for processes of change *within* the city. The growth of every town, he suggests, 'is a *twin process* of outward *extension* and internal *reorganization*. Each phase adds new fabric – outside in the form of accretions, within in the form of replacements. At any time, many of the existing structures are obsolescent and in their deterioration are subject to functional changes; they are converted for new uses' (Smailes 1966: 87, emphasis added).

The older, innermost zones of the city are especially subject to this internal reorganization, with the result that a distinctive townscape element is created, containing a mixture of residential, commercial and industrial functions within physically deteriorating structures. Small factories and workshops make an important contribution to the ambience of such areas. Some of these factories may be residual, having resisted the centrifugal tendency to move out to new sites, but a majority are 'invaders' that have colonized sites vacated by earlier industries or residents. Typically, they occupy old property that has become available in side streets off the shopping thoroughfares in the crowded but decaying residential zone surrounding the CBD. They are thus able to enjoy the advantages of proximity to a relatively cheap labour force as well as to the retail outlets and transport termini of the CBD.

Beyond this inner zone, Smailes suggests, industrial, commercial and residential townscape elements are clearly differentiated. Terrace and villa-type development, associated in different sectors of the city with different social and economic groups, are contiguous with radial prongs and suburban enclaves of industry, but do not intermingle with them. Similarly, shopping and central services present localized townscapes in outlying clusters amid tracts of housing. The 'outer integuments' of the city thus contain several distinctive townscapes, not least of which are several kinds of residential townscape, including:

1.   residential hotels and boarding houses;
2.   blocks of flats or apartments;

**Fig. 4.1** The townscapes of Belfast. *Source*: Jones (1958), p. 154.

3. terrace houses with front gardens;
4. terrace houses without front gardens;
5. detached or semi-detached villas and bungalows with garage or adequate garage space;
6. detached or semi-detached villas and bungalows without garage space;
7. large detached houses in extensive grounds.

Smailes was, cautious, however, about attributing any spatial symmetry to these townscapes. Rather, he suggested, townscapes will be arranged in an imperfect zonation, interrupted by radial arteries of commercial and industrial development, by major roads and railway tracks, and distorted by the peculiarities of site and situation. In addition, he pointed out that most urban development is characterized by the persistence of *enclaves* of relict townscapes which tend to impair the symmetrical pattern which may otherwise emerge: palaces, castles, cathedrals, university precincts, boulevards, public parks and common lands all tend to resist the logic of market forces and so survive as vestigial features amid newly developed or redeveloped neighbourhoods.

## Fixation lines, fringe belts, cadastral patterns and the diffusion of townscape elements

Such attempts to establish the distribution and characteristics of morphological regions in cities, though providing a useful starting point for further study, were not particularly incisive. By the early 1960s, urban geographers had become acutely aware of the lack of theoretical, conceptual and methodological devices available in morphological analysis (Norborg 1962) and these shortcomings, together with a general shift in interest towards economic and social phenomena, relegated morphological studies to an unfashionable status from which they have still not fully recovered.

There have, however, been several significant contributions to the study of intra-urban variations in the built environment. One person who is credited with advancing the status of morphological studies is M. R. G. Conzen, who was able to illustrate the process of townscape development from the evidence of an examination of the growth of Alnwick, in Northumberland (Conzen 1960). Conzen's work was very detailed, involving 49 categories of morphological elements in a town of only 7,500 inhabitants; but from his detailed observations he was able to extract some useful generalizations which had been, at best, only implicit in previous studies. He also emphasized the marked difference in stability of the three major elements of townscape – building style, layout and function – showing that while the function of buildings is relatively volatile, the street plan of a town tends to persist over long periods. Thus, despite the constant reorganization and renewal of the built environment, the plan (and, often, parts of the fabric) of earlier townscapes tends to remain, forming a template upon which new townscapes must emerge.

In describing the process of townscape development, Conzen introduced the concepts of *fringebelts* and *fixation lines* to the vocabulary of morphological study. Conzen argued that the growth phases used in traditional analyses of urban morphology were often selected arbitrarily and so tended to give a false impression of the pattern of townscape development. A more sensitive approach, he suggested, must involve the identification of structural features which act as physical barriers to construction – 'fixation lines' which govern the pattern of urban development. These fixation lines may take the form of physical features such as rivers; they may be man-made features such as railways and fortifications; or even intangible features such as the pattern of land ownership. Eventually, it is argued, pressure for urban development will overcome these fixation lines and building will spill over to create a fringe belt. Such features, according to Conzen, exhibit an inner zone characterized by higher density development and an outer zone where development is more piecemeal and varied in character. With successive phases of urban growth, these fringe belts will either be *preserved*, with undeveloped ground being retained as open spaces; or they will be *translated* into a different townscape element as succeeding land uses invade the area.

Although Conzen's observations do not by any means amount to a theory or even a model of urban morphology, they do help to explain the broad pattern of urban development. The control exerted over urban morphology by the inertia of ground plan and the influence of fixation lines is clearly reflected in the morphology of Köln, for example (Fig. 4.2). The old town, or *Altstadt*, consisting of a Roman grid nucleus with irregular mediaeval extensions, was enclosed by fortifications erected by the Prussians in the early nineteenth century, when the city was developed as a fortress against the French. These fortifications created a marked fixation

**Fig. 4.2**  The morphology of Köln.

line which was only breached later in the century with the construction of a new residential zone some 500 metres wide known as the *Neustadt*. This area, in turn, was surrounded by new fortifications in the 1880s, creating a new fixation line which was reinforced by the route of the railway. Subsequent fringe belt development was displaced by a military regulation proscribing building of any kind in the area immediately outside the city walls, so that late- nineteenth-century growth tended to take the form either of high density internal redevelopment or new building in the daughter settlements of Deutz, Weidenpesch, Dickendorf, Klettenberg, and Zollstock, which have now become engulfed by Köln itself, but with further outward growth currently constrained by a new fixation line in the form of the autobahn. Although the fortifications were demolished between 1907 and 1911, their influence on Köln's morphology is still apparent, for their site is now occupied by a sinuous green belt (Fig. 4.3). After the demilitarization of the city in 1918 there followed a rapid sprawl of residential and industrial development, with the classic radial-concentric plan of the city being accentuated by the focusing of major routeways on the bridges near the centre of the city. During the Second World War over 75 per cent of the city's fabric was destroyed by Allied bombing, and so most of the pre-war townscapes have disappeared. The basic morphological pattern embodied in the city's layout has been retained, however, partly because of a lack of initiative in the city's planning office in the immediate post-war period, but mainly because of the intrinsic stability of the street pattern: even badly damaged roads, tramlines and the associated subterranean services (sewage and electricity lines, etc.) represent an enormous capital asset, and such assets are not lightly set aside by urban governments at any time.

One of the most significant outcomes of Conzen's work is that it has prompted further research by others. Whitehand, for instance, has pursued the idea of fringe belts in some detail and has been able to add to Conzen's ideas on morphogenesis (Whitehand 1967, 1972, 1974). In particular, he has amplified the relationship between residential and non-residential development within fringe areas, showing how 'institutional' land uses (public parks, gardens and playing fields, cemeteries, schools, hospitals, sewage plant, etc.) dominate fringe areas until an economic boom period, when housebuilders outbid institutional users for land:

> . . . we must envisage a situation in which, by the end of a boom period, a zone of housing will have been added to the built-up area, but, scattered beyond it and sometimes lying within it, will be the sites of institutions. During a housing slump, while the house builder is largely inactive, institutions will develop the majority of the most accessible sites which, added to what were outlying institutional sites created during the previous housing boom period, will form a zone with a strongly institutional character. Repeated cycles of booms and slumps are likely to result in a series of alternating zones characterized by different proportions of institutions and housing (Whitehand 1974: 110).

Within the overall structural parameters of fringe belts and fixation lines, one of the major components of urban morphology is the *cadastral pattern*, or layout of landholdings. This is an aspect of morphogenesis that has been considered in some detail by M. P. Conzen (1980) for American cities. The dominant pattern, stemming from the influence of the national land survey system, was of course a grid layout. But the size and orientation of the plats (or subdivisions) varied a great deal, and Conzen has shown how urban morphology often reflects the accretions and modifications that result as earlier components of the cadastral framework become outmoded. Thus, while most American towns started with a grid plan of 30 to 60 blocks, with 8 to 16 lots per block, some city founders thought in more grandiose terms. Detroit, for example, was conceived on a vast scale, with a layout that has been called 'backwoods baroque': an intricate lattice of squares and diagonal streets. Nevertheless, initial plat size generally had little influence on subsequent urban growth. Rather, it was the nature and pace of urban growth that conditioned morphological development through 'accretion', 'repletion' and 'replacement'.

*Accretions* are additions of new plats of land to the built-up zones of urban areas within the morphological frames inherited from the process of land preparation (Fig. 4.3), in which large parcels of agricultural land are broken down through exchange to sizes suitable for urban platting. Sometimes, this process may be so premature that lack of demand for house lots may lead to the subdivision design being abandoned ('abortive platting') for long periods. Meanwhile, 'open' plats of 5 or 10 acre lots might be laid out, to be marketed, perhaps, as country estates. Later, when demand caught up with this speculative activity, these lots would likely be converted to individual, 'closed' plats. Depending on the timing and the circumstances of this land preparation process, a given edge of a city could be incorporated into the urban fabric with considerable integrity or in a disorderly fashion, the distinction being crucial to future neighbourhood prestige and development potential. Conzen asserts that 'on a grand scale, this distended geographical pattern of fringe absorption profoundly influenced vast tracts of land in large cities. . . . Throughout the nineteenth century the boom mentality in real estate led to thousands of acres being subdivided into urban plats far in advance of solid demand, and therefore of actual building construction' (Conzen 1980: 136). And 'to the extend that the prophesy many times failed, the typical urban fringe has become a monument to the city-building values and style of society at large' (p. 135).

Conzen also points out that the process of accretion may have been so drawn out that selective *repletion* – the filling up of interstitial space – set in before basic accretion was complete. In any event, repletion eventually becomes the key process in the transition of districts from 'fringe' to 'inner' urban status; by which time a further process – *replacement* – will begin to contribute to morphogenesis. In general, replacement can be seen as taking one of two forms: the substitution of buildings within existing lot lines, or the redevelopment of parcels of land accumulated from two or more previous lots (re-platting). At the same time, the broader morphological framework

is often modified – as in nineteenth-century Boston (Fig. 4.4) – as parts of the street system are *streamlined* in response to changing transport technology and the increasing scale of social and economic organization.

Another advance in morphological analysis has been provided by Johnston's work on residential building styles. Johnston showed how the diffusion of architectural styles results in distinctive morphological regions. The key mechanism in this process, he argues, is the spread of building styles originally introduced to one area of the city for a specific social group to other parts of the city as the style is adopted and modified by other social groups. The general case, as Johnston sees it, is for a specific style to be introduced

as a new fashion (probably architect-designed) on the periphery of the built-up area in the high-status sector, at which time building in the low-status sector would be in styles developed at an earlier date. By the time lower status inhabitants had adopted the new fashion the city would have extended further and even newer styles would be under development in the more fashionable residential areas. The low status residential areas will always lag behind the more fashionable (Johnston 1969a: 22).

Assuming an idealized urban structure consisting of four concentric zones of progressively newer housing subdivided into three sections inhabited respectively by low-, intermediate- and high-status families, Johnston presents a model of townscape development which reflects the significance of any given building style within each of the twelve areal subdivisions of the city. Figure 4.5a illustrates the type of situation described above. In this example a townscape element is introduced in the second zone of the high-status sector but is adopted by only a few residents of that zone. In the next period of urban growth (represented by zone 3) it becomes very popular among high-status residents and is copied (perhaps in a modified form) by some of the inhabitants of the intermediate- and low-status sectors. The element is much more widely adopted in these sectors in the next period of growth (zone 4), by which time it has been largely abandoned by higher-status residents in favour of newer styles pioneered

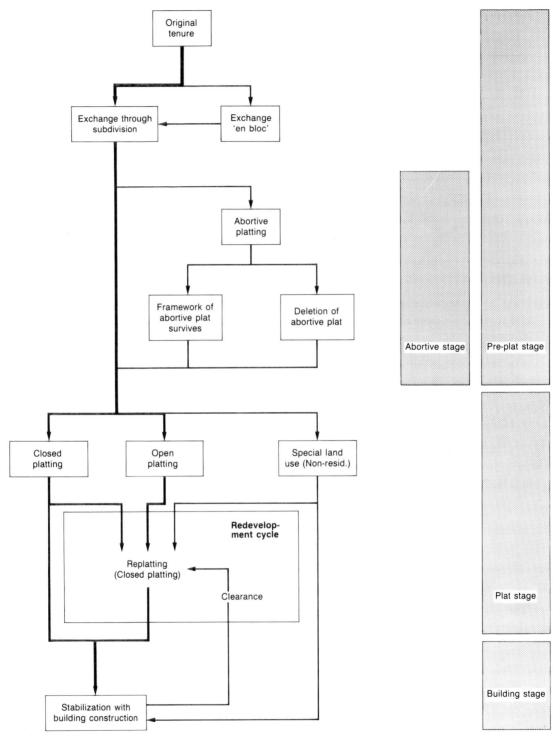

**Fig. 4.3**   The process of urban land preparation.   *Source*: Conzen (1980) Fig. 7, p. 131.

**Fig. 4.4** Nineteenth century streamlining in central Boston.
*Source*: Conzen (1980) Fig. 14, p. 139.

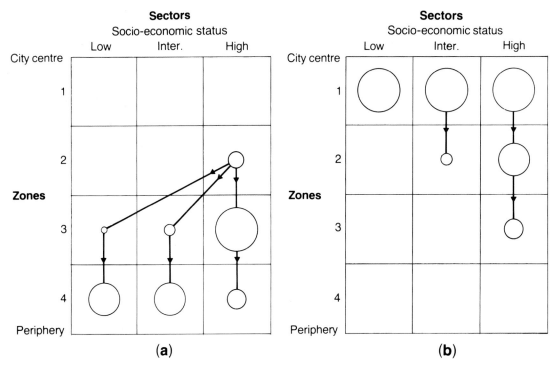

**Fig. 4.5** The spatial diffusion of townscape elements: (A) the stepped model, and (B) the reverse-stepped model with carry-through to high-status sector. The size of the circles is in proportion to the significance of a given element within an area's overall townscape. *Source*: Johnston (1969a), p. 26.

in zone 3 of their sector. This situation, which Johnston calls the *stepped* model, clearly summarizes the spatial impact of the diffusion of townscape elements such as the terraces and villas of British cities described above.

Other situations may also occur, however, such as the outward spread of tenements in Scottish cities from working-class inner-city areas of the early nineteenth century to middle- and higher-status areas of the late nineteenth and early twentieth century. Such situations can also be accommodated in Johnston's framework: in this particular instance Johnston's *reverse stepped* model with a carry-through in the high-status sector (Fig. 4.5b) seems most appropriate. Johnston tested the utility of his own models using data from Melbourne, and found that 74 of a total of 114 different building characteristics (including measures of building height, building mate-

rials, building plan, and architectural style) appeared to fit either the stepped model or the reverse stepped model, with a carry-through in either the high- or low-status sector. The spatial pattern of L-shaped houses, for example, was found to conform to the stepped model, while the pattern of semi-detached houses and flats matched the reverse stepped model with a carry-through in low- and high-status sectors respectively. But, as Johnston points out, it is the more complex pattern of townscapes resulting from the *inter-relationships* of the variables which is of most significance in delimiting morphological regions. When architectural styles are classified according to their building materials, for instance, the complexity of the real townscape becomes apparent. Thus, although the general pattern of L-shaped houses exhibits the characteristics of the stepped model, L-shaped houses in weatherboard and tile are found in all sectors of the outer zones (indicating a general middle-class usage) while L-shaped houses in weatherboard and corrugated iron are mainly characteristic of the outer zones of the low-status sector.

## The social production of the built environment

In reality, the chronology and diffusion of architectural styles is the product of complex relationships between economic and social conditions, population pressures, the cost and availability of construction materials, and changes in technical options and the supply of 'design'. This is a fertile area for research, with obvious linkages to the relationships between 'spirit' and 'matter' outlined in Chapter 2. Rubin (1977), for example, has detailed the chronology of architecture in Los Angeles, viewing the outcome as a 'record of a plural society'. She has also been able to show how 'good taste' in urban design generally has become part of an ideology that has been used to control and exploit urban space. 'In the ideology of American aesthetics, it is understood that those who make taste make money, and those who make money make taste' (Rubin 1979: 360). This points to the key role of major actors and institutions within the land development and building construction industries – landowners, developers, financial institutions, architects, engineers, and the like (Vance 1978; Whitehand 1983). In this context, Whitehand and Whitehand (1983, 1984; Whitehand 1984) have conducted some pioneer research into the changing roles of – and relationships between – architects, consultants, builders and contractors in the evolution of the physical fabric of British town centres.

It is clear from this work, and from the discussion in Chapter 2, that, while the built environment is heavily endowed with social meaning, this meaning is rarely simple, straightforward or unidimensional. The following discussion, based on material from Knox (1984: 112–114, 116–120), attempts to draw together some of the ideas and evidence relevant to an understanding of the built environment as a social product. To begin with, there is an important distinction between the *intended* meaning of architecture and the *perceived* meaning of the built environment as seen by others. This distinction is essential to a proper understanding of the social meaning of the built environment. Harvey's study of the Sacre-Coeur in Paris, for example, demonstrates how the intended symbolism of the building – a re-affirmation of Monarchism in the wake of the Paris Commune – 'was for many years seen as a provocation to civil war' (1979: 362), and is still interpreted by the predominantly republican population of Paris as a provocative rather than a unifying symbol. At a more general level, Lasswell (1979: 57) has claimed that while the 'architecture of opulence' – sleek office buildings and imposing private residences – 'operates on a worldwide scale to reassure the rich, strong and self-confident', it also serves 'to provoke and radicalize the poor and the weak'. Another possibility, of course, is that it reinforces feelings of deference among certain sections of the poor and the weak. The point is that much of the social meaning of the built environment depends on the *audience*. In turn, the concepts of audience held by the producers and managers of the built environment will help to determine the kinds of messages that are sent in the first place (Appleyard 1979a).

Another critical point is that the social meaning of the built environment is not static. The meanings associated with particular symbols and symbolic environments tend to be modified as social values change in response to changing lifestyles and changing patterns of socio-economic organization. At the same time, powerful symbols and motifs from earlier periods are often borrowed in order to legitimize a new social order, as in Mussolini's co-opting of the symbols of Augustan Rome in an attempt to legitimize Fascist urban reorganization (Kostof 1978); and (ironically) in the adoption of a selection of motifs from the classical revival in Europe by Jefferson and the founding fathers responsible for commissioning public and ceremonial architecture in Washington, DC (Craig 1978).

It is also clear that the style of symboliz-ation can vary according to the intentions of the 'producers' of the built environment and the social context of the building. The 'signa-ture of power', according to Lasswell (1979), is manifest in two ways: (i) through a 'strategy of awe', intimidating the audience with majestic diplays of power, and (ii) through a 'strategy of admiration' aimed at diverting the audience with spectacular and histrionic pro-jects. It should be recognized, however, that not everyone wishes to display power. The symbolism of tbe built environment may, therefore, involve 'modest' or 'low profile' architecture; or carry deliberately misleading messages for the purpose of maintaining social harmony (Hill 1980). Neither is power the only kind of message to convey. As we have seen, various elements of the counter-ideology generate their own symbolic structures and environments. Similarly, there is a variety of messages which stem from the self rather than group identity. The commonest are simple 'I-am-here' messages; and these, in turn, are most frequent amongst the socially mobile, the *nouveaux riches*, new migrants, and tran-sients (Duncan and Duncan 1976; Goffman 1959).

How can all these observations be accom-modated within a coherent framework of analysis? Let us consider first the various attempts to develop a systematic approach to the symbolic meaning of the built environ-ment. Gutman (1972: 299) observes that the literature on architectural symbolism conven-tionally distinguishes three levels of symbolic meaning: 'syntactical meaning, or the meaning that an element of form or style acquires by virtue of its location in a chain of form or style elements; semantic meaning, or the meaning it acquires because of the norm, idea or atti-tude that it represents or designates; and prag-matic meaning, or the meaning that is understood in relation to the architect, client or social group that invents or interprets the buildings's form or style'. The first of these has involved a highly abstract approach in an attempt to develop a general theory of symbols and signs: semiology. Working on the assumption that there exist innate conventions through which human artifacts convey meaning,

writers such as Broadbent (1980), Eco (1980) and Krampen (1979) have attempted to explore the 'deep structures' of architecture and urban form. Much of this work, however, is highly codified and mechanistic, deliberately and systematically abstracting symbols from their historical and social context. It has thus sustained what Dickens (1980) calls the 'fetishism' of design, focusing attention on buildings and architects rather than on the sets of social relations that surround the production and meaning of buildings.

There have been some tentative attempts to link the 'syntax' of the built environment to the wider context, moving, in Gutman's terms, towards the study of syntactical and semantic meaning. Hillier *et al.*, for example, have been attempting to develop a theory relating spatial syntax and architectural form to 'social syntax': the patterns of encounters and relationships that hold within society (Hillier *et al.* 1981). Despite their concern with the built environment as a medium of communication, however, none of these approaches directly confronts the fundamental questions of communication *by whom*, to *what audience*, to *what purpose* and to *what effect?* These are the questions which have prompted a number of writers to build on Marxian social theory in such a way as to accommodate the social production of the built environment. According to this perspective, the built environment, as part of the socio-economic superstructure stemming from the dominant mode of production (feudalism, merchant capitalism, industrial capitalism, etc.), reflects the *zeitgeist* of the prevailing system; it also serves, like other components of the super-structure, as one of the means through which the necessary conditions for the continuation of the system are reproduced. One of the first people to sketch out these relationships between social process and urban form was Harvey (1973, 1978), who emphasized the danger of thinking in terms of simple causal relationships, stressing the need for a flexible approach which allows urbanism to exhibit a variety of forms within any dominant mode of production, while similar forms may exist as products of different modes of production.

Within the broad framework sketched by

Harvey, others have begun to contribute detailed studies of the form, interior layout and exterior design of various components of the built environment as a response to the reorganization of society under industrial capitalism. The British prison system, for example, has received a good deal of attention because of the clear relationship it exhibits between ideology, social organization and architectural form (Foucault 1977; Ingnatieff 1978; Tomlinson 1980). In a similar vein, Thorn (1980) has related the appearance of public eating facilities to the social and economic reorganization consequent upon modern urbanization, Rubin (1979) has documented the emergence of 'signature' structures and franchise architecture, Duffy (1980) has examined office buildings and Hancock (1980) has described the development of the apartment house.

Nevertheless, Marxian theory is still very weakly developed in relation to the built environment. Indeed, some recent attempts to relate Marxian theory to architectural design (Krier *et al.* 1978; Tafuri 1976) have not only failed to demonstrate an understanding of traditional Marxist thought but have also overlooked several key issues which have been hotly debated by contemporary interpreters of Marxist theory (Dickens 1979; King 1984). Among other things, these include the consequences of conflict between different factions of capital, the function of the state in relation to capitalism, and the extent to which the dynamic of industrial capitalism is different from, or constrained by, the dynamic of urbanization. Equally, the whole field has yet to develop an adequate framework with which to consider the role and degree of autonomy exercised by the urban design professions in shaping the built environment of modern cities (Knesl 1984; Pipkin, La Gory and Blau 1982).

The architect's role as an arbiter, creator and manipulator of style can be interpreted at two inter-related levels: (i) as part of the process whereby changing relationships within society at large become expressed in the 'superstructure' of ideas, institutions and objects, and (ii) as part of the process through which the dominant mode of production is able to sustain itself and protect itself from opposing social or ideological forces. The first of these perspectives allows us to see major shifts in architectural style as a dialectical response to the evolving *zeitgeist* of urban-industrial society – as part of a series of broad intellectual and artistic reactions rather than the product of isolated innovations wrought by inspired architects. Thus, for example, the Art Nouveau and Jugendstil architecture of the late nineteenth century can be seen as the architectural expression of the romantic reaction to what Mumford (1961) called the 'palaeotechnic' era of the industrial revolution: a reaction that was first expressed in the Arts and Crafts movement and in Impressionist painting. By 1900 the Art Nouveau style was firmly established as the snobbish style, consciously élitist, for all 'high' architecture. The dialectic response was a series of artistic and intellectual movements, beginning with Cubism, which went out of their way to dramatize modern technology, seeking an anonymous and collective method of design in an attempt to divorce themselves from 'capitalist' canons of reputability and power. Thus emerged the Constructivist and Futurist movements, the Bauhaus school and, later, Les Congrès Internationaux d'Architecture Moderne (CIAM) and the Modern Architecture Research Group (MARS), who believed that 'their new architecture and their new concepts of urban planning were expressing not just a new aesthetic image but the very substance of new social conditions which they were helping to create' (Carter 1979: 324).

The subsequent fusion and transformation of these movements into the glib 'Esperanto' of the International Style and the simultaneous adoption of the style as the preferred image of corporate and bureaucratic conservatism, solidity and respectability (Wolfe 1982) provides an important example of the way in which the dominant social order is able to protect itself from opposing ideological forces. In this particular example, the energy of opposing ideological forces – idealist radicalism – has been neatly diverted into the defence of the *status quo*. The question is: how? One answer is that the professional ideology and career structure within which most practising architects (as opposed to the *avant garde*) operate is itself heavily oriented towards Establishment values and sensitively tuned to the existing institutional setting and economic order. Consequently, the meaning and symbolism of new architectural styles emanating from radical quarters tend to be modified as they are institutionalized and converted into commercialism; while the core movement itself, having forfeited its raw power in the process of 'commodification', passes quietly into the mythology of architectural education and the coffee-table books of the *cognoscenti*. There is a direct parallel here in the way that the liberal ideology of the town planning movement was transformed into a defensive arm of urbanized capital (Chapter 2), systematically working to the advantage of the middle-class community in general and the business community in particular (Knox and Cullen 1981a). According to this perspective, architects, like planners, can be seen as unwitting functionaries, part of a series of 'internal survival mechanisms' which have evolved to meet the imperatives of urbanized capital.

Another way in which architects serve these imperatives is in helping to stimulate consumption and extract surplus value. It is vital, if the capitalist economy is to be successfully maintained, for urbanization to facilitate the manipulation of effective demand in order not only to increase consumption but also to ensure the constant circulation of capital. The architect, by virtue of the prestige and mystique socially accorded to creativity, adds exchange value to a building through his or her decisions about 'design', 'so that the label "architect designed" confers a presumption of quality even though, like the emperor's clothes, this quality may not be apparent to the observer' (Darke and Darke 1981: 12). Moreover, as one of the key arbiters of style in modern society, the architect is in a powerful position to stimulate consumption merely by generating and/or endorsing changes in the nuances of building design.

The professional ideology and career structure that rewards innovation and the ability to feel the pulse of fashion also serves to promote the circulation of capital. Without a steady supply of new fashions in domestic architecture (reinforced by innovations in kitchen technology, heating systems, etc.), the filtering mechanisms on which the whole owner-occupier housing market is based would slow down to a level unacceptable not only to builders and developers but also to the 'exchange professionals' (surveyors, real estate agents, etc.) and the whole range of financial institutions involved in the housing market. The rich and the upper-middle classes, in short, must be encouraged to move from their comfortable homes to new dwellings with even more 'design' and 'convenience' features in order to help maintain a sufficient turnover in the housing market. One way in which they are enticed to move is through the cachet of fashionable design and state-of-the-art technology. Hence the rapid diffusion of innovations such as energy-conserving homes; and the desperate search for successful design themes to be revived and 're-released', just like the contrived revivals of *haute couture* and pop music. In parts of the United States, the process has advanced to the stage where many upper-middle class suburban developments resemble small chunks of Disneyland, with mock-Tudor, Spanish Colonial, mock-Georgian, Victorian gothic and log cabin *de luxe* standing together: style for style's sake, the *zeit* for sore eyes. And, in some cities, new housing for upper-income groups is now promoted through annual exhibitions of 'this year's' designs, much like the automobile industry's carefully-planned obsolescence in design.

But it is by no means only 'high' architecture and expensive housing which helps to sustain urbanized capital. Parkin (1971) has suggested that the maintenance of the entire social system is partly dependent on the way in which the everyday settings of workplace and neighbourhood function to reproduce and 'structurate' class relations. What has not been explored systematically, however, is the way in which architectural design contributes to the 'conditioning' of working-class populations in distinctive 'settings'. One of the more straightforward functions of architecture in this respect would seem to be the symbolic distancing of social groups. The aesthetic sterility of most British public housing, for example, serves to distance its inhabitants from other, neighbouring, social groups. At a further level, it can be argued that the scarcity of symbolic stimuli typical of many planned, post-war working-class environments may act as a kind of intellectual and emotional straitjacket, minimizing people's self-esteem and sense of potential while fostering attitudes of deference and defeatism (Cullen and Knox 1981). Although the process is at present very poorly understood, the role of the architect is clearly central to the eventual outcome not only in terms of the social order of the city but also in terms of the existential meaning of urban settings.

This brings us to a final but crucial consideration: the role of the self in the interaction between society and environment. At this point, the perspective offered by Marxian theory offers little help. It is fundamental to Marxian theory that the spirit and consciousness of men and women is determined by work and economic activity: human personality consequently becomes 'collectivized out of existence' (Barrett 1974). But, when we move down from high-level generalizations about social process and urban form, we find that people often endow their spatial environments with meaning in ways which are often highly individualistic and often independent of their class or power. This is where the experiential concepts described in Chapter 3 fit in. It follows that we must accept, in the short term at least, a multi-stranded approach to the social production of the built environment. One possible organizing framework for such an approach is shown in Fig. 4.6, which is loosely based on Appleyard's (1979a) 'communications model' of environmental action. Accepting architectural design as part of the superstructure of culture and ideas stemming from the basic socio-economic organization of society (whether as part of the prevailing ideology or as part of the counter-ideology), this framework focuses attention on

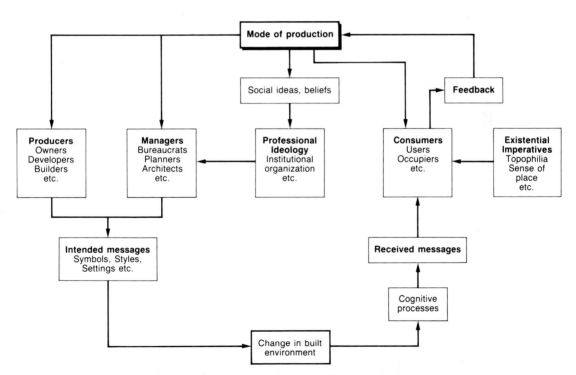

**Fig. 4.6**  Signs, symbolism and settings: a framework for analysis.
*Source*: Knox (1984), Fig. 1, p. 119.

(i) the intended messages emanating from particular owners/producers and mediated by professional 'managers' (architects, planners, etc.), and (ii) the received messages of environmental 'consumers' as seen through the prisms of cognitive processes and existential imperatives and the filter of the dominant ideology.

## Subjective descriptions

Identifying the underlying morphological regions produced by the inter-relationships among *all* the relevant characteristics of building style, layout and usage represents a massive task which, many would argue, can only be tackled with sophisticated multivariate statistical techniques. Yet, although such techniques have been widely available since the late 1960s, their application in morphological studies has been limited – in marked contrast to studies of the socio-economic structure of the city. This reticence is attributable in part to the difficulty of adequately quantifying all the components of townscape. As Burke (1976) observes, townscapes are not simply the sum of the attributes of style, layout and function: it is the form in which these morphological elements are set in relation to each other and to unbuilt spaces that creates the *genius loci* which lends distinctiveness to one morphological region in comparison with another. Indeed, a good case can be made for an entirely subjective approach, with morphological regions being articulated by written descriptions rather than statistical analysis

The strength of written description in conveying the flavour and character of particular parts of the city is illustrated in these brief extracts from Jonathan Raban's *Soft City*. Of Kentish Town, in London, he writes:

Most of the houses are survivals of the most notorious period of Victorian speculative jerry-building. They were erected in short terraces of what were accurately described by their builders as 'fourth-rate residences' . . . Their doors and windows are cheaply gabled and scalloped, and in line on the terrace they look like brick railway carriages, their decorations skimped, their narrow front strips of garden a long balding patch of tarry grass with motor scooters parked under flapping tarpaulins with holes in them (Raban 1975: 109)

And of Roxbury, in Boston:

Roxbury was the first and the sweetest of the nineteenth-century 'streetcar suburbs' of Boston . . . The churches, the houses, the tall trees on the streets, are there still. The paint is pocky, much of the wood is rotten, and slats of shingling have fallen away exposing the skeletal frames, but the basic lineaments of the old dream are clear enough even now. It takes a few minutes before you notice that the windows are mostly gone and only a few shutters are left. Each house stares blindly through eyes of cardboard and torn newspaper. Burn marks run in tongues up their sides, and on most blocks there is a gutted shell, sinking onto its knees in a flapping ruin of blackened lath and tar-paper. Our own century has added rows of single-storey brick shacks, where bail-bondsmen and pawnbrokers do their business. What were once front lawns are now oily patches of bare earth. The carcases of wrecked Buicks, Chevrolets and Fords are jacked up on bricks, their hoods open like mouths, their guts looted. No-one is white (Raban 1975: 215)

Reyner Banham is another writer who is able to capture the 'feel' of a townscape in this way. He provides an evocative description of the principal townscapes of a whole city in his exposition of the architecture of Los Angeles (Banham 1973). Unconstrained by the jargon and conventions of urban geography, Banham divides Los Angeles into three major morphological regions, or 'architectural ecologies' (Fig. 4.7).

1. *Surfurbia* – the coastal strip of Los Angeles stretching from Malibu to Balboa, and typified by the Beach Cities of Playa del Rey, El Segundo, Manhattan Beach, Redondo Beach and, further south, Huntingdon Beach. The townscape here consists of a narrow strip of four or five streets deep and draws its distinctive character from beach houses, fantasy architecture, surfboard art and beautified oil rigs.

2. *The Foothills* – stretching along the lower slopes of the Hollywood Hills and the Santa Monica Mountains between Pacific Palisades and Highland Park, with an exclave on the slopes of Palos Verdes, the morphology

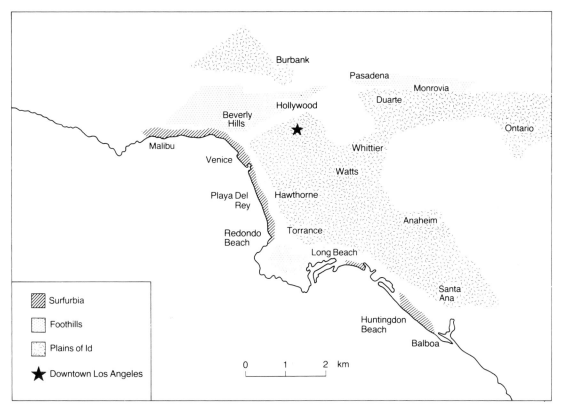

**Fig. 4.7** The architectural ecologies of Los Angeles.

of the Foothills reflects the marked correlation in Los Angeles between altitude and socio-economic status. It is characterized by:

narrow, tortuous residential roads serving precipitous house plots that often back up directly on unimproved wilderness . . . The fat life of the delectable mountains is well known around the world, wherever television re-runs old movies . . . it is the life, factual and fictional, of Hollywood's classic years . . . Where would the private eyes of the forties have been without laurel shrubberies to lurk in, sweeping front drives to turn the car in, terraces from which to observe the garden below, massive Spanish Colonial Revival doors at which to knock, . . . or rambling split-level ranch house plans in which to lose the opposition, . . . and the essential swimming pool for the bodies? (Banham 1973: 101).

3. *The Plains of Id* – the greater part of the Los Angeles metropolitan area, also familiar to television viewers and part of the popular image of the city:

an endless plain endlessly gridded with endless streets, peppered endlessly with ticky-tacky houses clustered in indistinguishable neighbourhoods, slashed across by endless freeways that have destroyed any community spirit that may once have existed, and so on . . . endlessly (Banham 1973: 161).

Although encompassing a wide variety of socio-economic neighbourhoods, the whole area, Banham suggests, is characterized by the 'dingbat' – a two-storey walk-up apartment block built of wood and stuccoed over, with simple rectangular forms and flush smooth surfaces to the sides and rear but with an eclectic façade containing all kinds of architectural styles and fantasies:

a statement about the culture of individualism . . . the true symptom of Los Angeles's urban Id trying to cope with . . . residential densities too high to be subsumed within the illusions of homestead living (Banham 1973: 175–7).

Superimposed on these three major morphological regions is a fourth 'ecology', *Autopia*: the built environment of the freeway system which, says Banham, is physically large enough and functionally important enough to amount to 'a single comprehensible place, a coherent state of mind, a complete way of life, the fourth ecology of the Angeleno' (Banham 1973: 213). Other distinctive morphological elements in the city include the downtown area – distinctive because of its relative lack of high density commercial development and historic 'centrality' – and various enclaves of West Coast architecture scattered around the city, from the pioneer architecture of Frank Lloyd Wright and Irving Gill to the fantasy architecture of restaurants, fast food outlets and shopping centres and residential indulgences like Venice – built complete with lagoon and canal bridges and now a hippy haven.

## Multivariate analysis

In contrast to Banham's individualistic treatment of urban morphology have been the attempts of a few analysts to apply multivariate statistical techniques to townscape analysis. These studies are designed to discover the actual association of physical features which distinguish morphological regions. As with all statistical analysis, of course, their utility is governed by the quality and selection of the data used; and it can be a particularly burdensome task to collect house-by-house (or even block-by-block) data for all the relevant characteristics of buildings for the whole of an urban area. Not surprisingly, some analysts have preferred to concentrate on samples or case studies. Corey (1966), for example, focused on one neighbourhood – Corryville – in his pioneer multivariate analysis of urban morphology in Cincinnati. Using a combination of principal components analysis and discriminant analysis, he analysed the relationship between 40 variables selected to represent different aspects of building age, type and size, building materials, roof type and porch type; and was able to produce an 'objective' classification of morphological regions within the study area.

One particularly useful application of such techniques was Openshaw's (1969) study of South Shields, in Durham, which went on to relate statistically-derived morphological regions to the socio-economic characteristics of their inhabitants. A close relationship between socio-economic status and morphological regions is implicit in much socio-geographical writing but, as Herbert has observed, 'the assumption that certain social and demographic characteristics are associated with . . . various types of housing . . . [are known] to be broadly accurate but they have not in fact been proved' (Herbert 1967b: 6). Openshaw, using canonical correlation techniques, was able to prove the association, at least as far as the evidence from a 10 per cent sample of households and houses in South Shields enumeration districts would allow. Although not all of the variation in his data could be explained, he found strong relationships between:

1. morphological elements associated with late Victorian byelaw terracing and low-status tenants renting unfurnished accommodation;
2. inter-war housing and high-status, car-owning owner-occupiers;
3. post-1963 public housing and population with a young age structure and a high fertility rate; and
4. high-status Edwardian housing and families in social class III (intermediate), indicating a subdivision of dwellings as they have 'filtered down' the social scale (see p. 192).

A similar analysis of Edmonton, Canada, concluded that the major constructs of residential morphology showed meaningful spatial relationships with the social dimensions of the city (McCann and Smith 1972), while Morgan (1971, 1973) has also demonstrated a broad fit between morphological regions and social areas in Exeter. Such relationships, however, are subject to considerable qualification. Important social and demographic variations, for example, often exist within morphologically homogeneous regions. Moreover, the *nature* of the link between morphological and social areas in a city – the particular socio-economic groups associated with particular morphological regions – does not appear to be very consistent from one city to another; although there is considerable scope for further research in this direction.

## Environmental quality

One other approach to the geography of the built environment which should be mentioned here is the analysis of spatial variations in environmental quality. This is a topic which extends beyond the immediate characteristics of urban morphology to include aspects of amenity provision and factors such as noise and air pollution which are not necessarily a function of the local built environment. The focus, however, is on the condition of streets and buildings, an aspect of the built environment which has been of increasing interest to town planners and community groups as well as to geographers. Indeed, much of the methodology appropriate to such studies has been developed by planning agencies in Europe and North America in preparing strategic plans and delimiting environmental 'action areas' of various sorts. In a majority of cases, the 'quality' of residential environments is evaluated by field survey and involves the allocation of points to buildings or groups of buildings according to the presence or absence of environmental *defects* of various sorts, and these points are subsequently summed to give an overall index score for the location. A good example of the technique is represented in Table 4.1.

Although such schedules are employed most frequently in detailed surveys of perhaps just a few city blocks, it is possible to employ sampling procedures in order to cover a much larger area, either to provide a background for more detailed investigations or simply to obtain a generalized picture of intra-urban patterns of environmental quality. Such an approach was employed by the author in a study of environmental quality in Sheffield, using a schedule designed to award up to 100 penalty points according to the relative degree of deficiency in a number of specific aspects of the environment, including the visual

**Table 4.1** Extract from an environmental quality assessment schedule

|  | Penalty points | Maximum |
|---|---|---|
| **Traffic:** | | |
| normal residential traffic | 0 | 6 |
| above normal residential traffic | 3 | |
| large amount ind. and through traffic | 6 | |
| **Visual quality:** | | |
| higher standard than environment | 0 | |
| same standard as environment | 1 | 3 |
| lower standard than environment | 3 | |
| **Access to Public Open Space:** | | |
| park/POS within 5 mins walk | 0 | 3 |
| no park/POS within 5 mins walk | 3 | |
| **Access to shops and primary schools:** | | |
| primary school and shops within 5 mins walk | 0 | |
| primary school but no shops in 5 mins walk | 2 | |
| shops but no primary school in 5 mins walk | 5 | |
| no primary school or shops in 5 mins walk | 7 | 7 |
| **Access to public transportation to major centres:** | | |
| less than 3 mins walk | 0 | 3 |
| more than 3 mins walk | 3 | |
| **Landscape quality:** | | |
| mature, good quality abundant landscape | 0 | |
| immature, insufficient amounts | 2 | |
| total or almost total lack of landscape | 5 | 5 |
| **Air pollution:** | | |
| negligible | 0 | |
| light | 3 | 9 |
| heavy | 9 | |
| **Privacy:** | | |
| no overlooking on either side | 0 | |
| overlooking on one side | 2 | 5 |
| overlooking on both sides | 5 | |
| **Noise:** | | |
| normal residential standard | 0 | |
| above residential but not ind./comm. std. | 2 | 5 |
| ind./comm. e.g. main street standard | 5 | |

*Source:* Duncan 1971: 60–1.

quality of houses, streets and gardens, the separation of pedestrians and traffic, access to public open space, and the presence of 'street furniture' such as bus shelters, post boxes, street lighting and telephone kiosks (Knox

1976; see also Moffat 1984). The resulting map and transects reveal a large variation in the quality of the environment (from less than 10 to nearly 90 defect points), with a clear spatial patterning (Fig. 4.8). Environmental quality is positively associated with distance from the city centre and with owner-occupied and local authority housing; and negatively associated with the occurrence of industrial land use and the age of the built environment. In terms of its spatial configuration, the index exhibits a markedly zonal pattern, with a steady improvement from the highly defective inner areas to the high quality suburban environments: a pattern which, it is worth noting, bears only a loose resemblance to the pattern of socio-economic status in the city. Deviations from the zonal pattern were found

**Fig. 4.8** Environmental quality in Sheffield. *Source*: Knox (1976), p. 105.

to be related principally to the effects of topography, local authority redevelopment schemes, and industrial location. To the west of the city centre, for example, the high quality environment of the suburbs intrudes markedly inwards, following the high-status housing associated with the Hallam Ridge. Conversely, the 'islands' of better environmental quality to the south-east and north-west of the city centre are associated with recent local authority developments. The areas which show up most clearly on the map are those in the Norfolk Park and Netherthorpe districts, although it is likely that a finer mesh of sampling points (only 100 were used in the survey) would have highlighted more such areas. Finally, the greatest distortion of the concentric pattern is represented by the extensive area of low-quality environment stretching north-eastwards from the cutlery quarter near the CBD, along the floor of the Don valley to Attercliffe and Carbrook. Here, the inhabitants of the terrace houses that were contemporary with and adjacent to the older cutlery factories and steelworks must live with the dereliction, noise, fumes and congestion associated with present concentrations of traffic and industry.

Again, it is difficult to generalize about intra-urban patterns because of the paucity of empirical research. Moreover, it should be acknowledged that the available measurement techniques are far from pefect. In particular, it would be fallacious to assume that assessment techniques carry any real degree of objectivity, since the choice of the aspects of 'quality' to be measured and the weightings assigned to different degrees of quality (or defectiveness) are always dependent on the subjectivity of those who design the schedule. We therefore have to rely to a great extent on the experience and expertise of those 'who know best' (or who think they do) about measuring environmental quality, and their decisions will always be debatable. Weightings, for example, can only be justified by assuming the researcher's awareness of the consensus of values amongst the people whose environment is being measured. As Southworth and Southworth (1973) have shown, however, there seems to be a considerable dissonance in the operational definitions of environmental quality used by planners – in the United States, at least. Because of this uncertainty, and because of the implications of basing important practical decisions (such as whether to schedule an area for demolition or to designate an area as eligible for home improvement grants) on the basis of index scores, there has been some opposition to the idea of quantifying environmental quality, at least as a planning tool (see for example, Dennis 1978).

What is really needed, of course, is some comprehensive attitudinal survey of what components of environmental quality people think are important, and how important they feel they are in relation to one another. In reality, however, people's opinions will differ widely, for environmental quality is highly income-elastic. The less well-off, with more urgent needs to satisfy, may well be relatively unconcerned about many aspects of environmental quality; whilst the rich, having satisfied their own material needs, may be particularly sensitive to environmental factors such as the appearance of houses, streets and gardens. This problem, together with the magnitude of the task involved in evaluating community preferences, must mean that such surveys will be regarded as impracticable for all but the most intensive of studies. Perhaps the solution is simply to ask the residents of each street or neighbourhood to rate their own level of satisfaction with the quality of their environment on some numerical or semantic scale. But here we should necessarily become involved in awkward questions of definition. Thus if two people each give a score of 9 out of 10 for environmental quality, how do we know that they are both evaluating the same concept? One may be thinking more of noise and pollution whilst the other sees the question in terms of the visual qualities of the built environment. If we try to standardize the response by offering a comprehensive definition of what environmental quality is, we are back to the problem subjective definitions on the part of the researcher.

Despite such problems, some researchers have attempted to analyse the determinants and patterns of environmental quality using questionnaire data. Pacione (1982, 1984), in a study of a low-status public housing district in Glasgow, concluded that residents' satisfaction with the quality of their neighbourhood was largely a product of their perceptions of (i) traffic problems, (ii) street cleanliness and maintenance, (iii) accessibility to open space, (iv) anti-social activity (e.g. vandalism, roving dogs), (v) accessibility within the city as a whole, (vi) social interaction, and (vii) landscaping. Dahmann (1985), in an analysis of data from the US Annual Housing Survey, has shown overall satisfaction with neighbourhood environmental quality to be inversely related to centrality and to city size, with low levels of satisfaction being a function, in particular, of the presence of rundown housing units, abandoned buildings, litter, street crime, air pollution, street noise and heavy traffic. These, of course, are aggregate findings: different *types* of household, with different backgrounds and values, react in different ways to the same kind of environment. Galster and Hester (1981), for example, have shown that certain people (younger, married female heads, blacks, those with many children) tend to express significantly lower levels of satisfaction in any residential context (Greer-Wootten and Velidis 1983).

# The socio-economic environment

## Social area analysis

Social area analysis, *sensu strictu*, provides a means of portraying the social geography of a city as part of a deductive model of social change based largely on Wirthian theory. Although the object of heated academic argument, it is undoubtedly the source of most modern social area studies. It was developed by Shevky, Williams and Bell (Shevky and Williams 1949; Shevky and Bell 1955) in an attempt to identify the 'community areas' of Los Angeles and San Francisco. Faced with the wide variety of social, demographic and economic data that were available for census tracts in American cities and suspecting that

single 'diagnostic' variables such as income or occupation were unlikely to provide an adequate means of portraying a complex phenomenon, Shevky and his co-workers decided to employ classifying criteria based on a series of postulates about social differentiation in the industrial society of postwar North America. Drawing heavily on Wirth's ideas, it was argued that urban social areas were the product of three major trends deriving from the *increasing scale* of society: (i) changes in the range and intensity of relations, (ii) an increasing functional differentiation, and (iii) an increasing complexity of social organization. These trends, it was suggested, were manifested respectively in terms of changes in the division of labour (with a shift towards clerical, supervisory and management functions), in the role of the household (with a movement of women into urban occupations and a spread of 'alternative' family patterns), and in the composition of local populations (with a tendency towards greater mobility and, consequently, greater spatial segregation).

In order to encompass these trends in a methodology capable of classifying social areas in terms of census data, Shevky *et al.* translated each one into a construct which could be measured by a composite index of census variables (Table 4.2). The three constructs were termed *social rank, urbanization* and *segregation* (although Bell preferred 'economic status', 'family status', and 'ethnic status' respectively), and the variables selected to represent them were as follows:

---

**Social Rank:** 1. percentage of manual workers
2. percentage of adults with less than 9 years schooling

**Urbanization:** 1. fertility rate
2. percentage of women in the labour force
3. percentage of housing stock consisting of single-family dwellings

**Segregation:** 1. the combined proportions of minority ethnic groups: blacks, other races, foreign-born whites from Eastern and Southern Europe, foreign-born persons from continents other than Europe.

---

**Table 4.2**  Social area analysis: steps in construct formation and index construction

| Postulates concerning industrial society (aspects of increasing scale) (1) | Statistics of trends (2) | Changes in the structure of a given social system (3) | Constructs (4) | Sample statistics (related to the constructs) (5) | Derived measures (from col. 5) (6) |
|---|---|---|---|---|---|
| Change in the range and intensity of relations | Changing distribution of skills: Lessening importance of manual productive operations – growing importance of clerical, supervisory, management operations | Changes in the arrangement of occupations based on function | **Social Rank** (economic status) | Years of schooling Employment status Class of worker Major occupation group Value of home Rent by dwelling unit Plumbing and repair Persons per room Heating and refrigeration | Occupation Schooling Rent } Index I |
| Differentiation of function  Complexity of organization | Changing structure of productive activity: Lessening importance of primary production – growing importance of relations centered in cities – lessening importance of the household as economic unit | Changes in the ways of living – movement of women into urban occupations – spread of alternative family patterns | **Urbanization** (family status) | Age and sex Owner or tenant House structure Persons in household | Fertility Women at work Single-family dwelling units } Index II |
|  | Changing composition of population: Increasing movement – alterations in age and sex distribution – increasing diversity | Redistribution in space – changes in the proportion of supporting and dependent population – isolation and segregation of groups | **Segregation** (ethnic status) | Race and nativity Country of birth Citizenship | Racial and national groups in relative isolation } Index III |

*Source:* Shevky and Bell 1955: 4

The index used to measure each construct was based on an unweighted average of standardized scores for each of these variables (for a full account of the method, see the reviews by Johnston (1976a) and Rees (1972)). With the resultant index scores it is possible to classify each census tract using a process of logical division. The most popular strategy is that proposed by Shevky and Bell in 1955, in which the social rank and urbanization indexes are plotted orthogonally, with the range of each index (0 to 100) divided into four equal parts. This yields 16 types, which can be further divided on the basis of above- or below-average scores on the segregation index. Figure 4.9 shows an example of the typology using data from Shevky and Bell's analysis of San Francisco. Such figures, sometimes referred to as social space diagrams, provide a useful summary of the socio-economic composition of a city's population. Locating the information on these diagrams in geographical space provides a map of the city's social areas which can then be used as the basis for further study. Shevky and Bell claimed that these social areas 'generally

contain persons having the same level of living, the same way of life, and the same ethnic background; and we hypothesize that persons living in a particular type of social area would systematically differ with respect to characteristic attitudes and behaviours from persons living in another type of social area' (Shevky and Bell 1955: 20).

Such properties make social area analysis an attractive basis for sample surveys in urban areas, since it can be used to inform researchers about the likely location of certain social groups and to show where a particular social environment will be found. Since they are purported to be sensitive measures of social differentiation, social area scores have also been employed in behavioural research as independent variables in attempts to explain the incidence of particular phenomena (see, for example, Polk's work (1957) on juvenile delinquency). In addition, of course, maps of social area scores provide a means of identifying the spatial relationships between social areas. Shevky and Bell's analysis of San Francisco (Fig. 4.10) revealed a marked area of low social rank and low urbanization

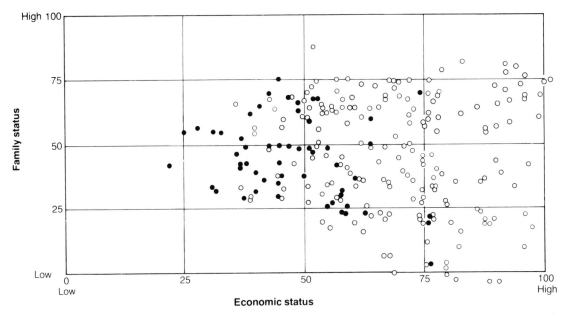

**Fig. 4.9** Distribution of census tracts in the social areas of the San Francisco Bay Region, 1950. *Source*: Murdie (1969), p. 22.

**Fig. 4.10** The social areas of San Francisco, 1950.
*Source*: Shevky and Bell (1949), Fig. V.14.

characteristics (i.e. high family status) in the south-east of the city around the industrial and commercial district facing the Bay, a large area characterized by high social rank and low urbanization in the south-west of the city, a small area of low social rank and high urbanization in the transitional zone between the CBD and the docks area; and a larger area of low social rank and low urbanization in the north of the city, with a particularly marked concentration of minority group members around the CBD in the north-east. This pattern, however, owes much to San Francisco's unique site and topography and it is therefore difficult to include in any generalizations about the spatial relationships of urban sub-areas. This question was pursued by Anderson and Egeland (1961), who selected four almost circular and topographi-

cally uniform US cities (Akron, Dayton, Indianapolis and Syracuse) with populations ranging from 200,000 to 500,000 and used analysis of variance techniques to establish whether the cities' social area scores exhibited zonal or sectoral patterns, or neither. They found a consistent pattern, with social rank scores in each city exhibiting a significant sectoral pattern while the urbanization scores conformed to a pattern of concentric zones. Similar analyses of other North American cities have produced parallel results (Curtis *et al*. 1967; Gagnon 1960; Herbert 1972). Evidence from cities outside North America has proved less conclusive, however. Apart from anything else, there are few studies upon which to base comparisons, partly because social area analysis had already been overtaken by factorial ecology methods (discussed below) by the time it had diffused to Europe and Australasia, and partly because of variations between countries in the composition and availability of the census data required for social area analysis. Thus McElrath (1962) had to substitute a literacy ratio for the education variable in his study of Rome, and could calculate neither the proportion of single-family dwellings nor the segregation construct. The spatial pattern revealed by his analysis did exhibit a sectoral-zonal configuration, although he also found a marked zone on the periphery of the city occupied by large families of low economic status. In Britain, Herbert (1967a) applied a similarly-modified social area analysis to Newcastle-under-Lyme, Staffordshire; but the small size and atypical economic structure of the town, together with doubts about the validity of the census data Herbert used (they were based on a 10 per cent sample of enumeration districts with very small populations) tend to weaken the value of the study as a basis for comparison.

Social area analysis has been criticized on a number of grounds, and the debate surrounding this criticism has also served to divert further exploration of the generalities of urban spatial structure. The whole rationale of the approach was attacked by Hawley and Duncan (1957) as an *ex post facto* rationalization of an *ad hoc* selection of census variables and indexes. Bell later admitted as much (Bell and Moskos 1964); and also accepted the suggestion by Anderson and Bean (1961) that the urbanization construct might in fact mask two quite separate social trends – 'familism' and 'urbanism'. Moreover, to the extent that Wirthian theory itself remains controversial, the whole conceptual basis of social area analysis must be open to doubt. This position was reinforced by the results of empirical tests by Udry (1964), who showed that the trends Shevky and Bell postulated were not typical of the United States over previous decades. Udry also went on to point out that there is in any case no basis for translating a theory of societal change into a typology of social areas: nowhere do the advocates of social area analysis suggest the mechanisms or processes by which homogeneous social groups end up in different territories. Other criticisms noted

by Timms (1971) in his extensive review of the schema include the charge that social change is represented in overly economic terms and that little attention is given to differences in people's value orientations or to the distribution of power. McElrath's reformulation of the schema (1968) represents an attempt to overcome these shortcomings. Greater attention is given to the relationships between structural change and social differentiation, with *industrialization* leading to differentiation in terms of occupational structure, educational achievement, family structure and female activity rates; and *urbanization* leading to differentiation in terms of geographical mobility, life-cycle characteristics and ethnic status. Little attempt, however, is made to spell out the key process of residential clustering.

These criticisms of social area analysis also prompted a good deal of empirical testing. Surprisingly, perhaps, the methodology stands up rather well to these tests, although certain shortcomings are revealed. One aspect of the methodology which has been widely tested is the relationship between the constructs postulated by Shevky and Bell. The indexes measuring each construct should be statistically independent of one another according to the logic of the procedure, and it also follows that the variables selected to represent each construct should be closely related to one another while having no significant association with variables representing other constructs. The predicted relationships between the variables is set out in Table 4.3, together with the correlation coefficients computed from the data used in social area analysis of several different cities. These results demonstrate a broad consistency, with the observed relationships matching the predicted relationships quite closely. The one significant exception is the unspecified correlation between occupation and fertility, thus lending some substance to the doubts expressed by Anderson and Bean about the soundness of the urbanization construct.

A more rigorous test of the inter-relationships between the variables (not just the pairwise relationships) is provided by factor analysis, a technique which enables the

**Table 4.3**  Social area analysis: predicted and actual relationships between variables

| Indicant | Single family dwellings | Women in workforce | Non-manual workers | Ethnicity |
|---|---|---|---|---|
| **Fertility** | | | | |
| Predicted | | | | |
| Correlation* | + | − | 0 | 0 |
| Auckland | 0.61 | −0.60 | −0.37 | 0.22 |
| Brisbane | 0.53 | −0.69 | −0.27 | −0.18 |
| Winnipeg | 0.45 | −0.53 | −0.53 | |
| San Francisco | 0.48 | −0.76 | −0.68 | 0.21 |
| Rome | | −0.69 | −0.68 | |
| Ten Cities † | 0.31 | −0.64 | −0.55 | −0.12 |
| **Single family dwellings** | | | | |
| Predicted | | | | |
| Correlation | | − | 0 | 0 |
| Auckland | | −0.89 | −0.03 | −0.24 |
| Brisbane | | −0.81 | −0.05 | −0.58 |
| Winnipeg | | −0.68 | 0.07 | |
| San Francisco | | −0.75 | 0.19 | −0.25 |
| Rome | | | | |
| Ten Cities | | −0.66 | 0.11 | −0.26 |
| **Women in workforce** | | | | |
| Predicted | | | | |
| Correlation | | | 0 | 0 |
| Auckland | | | 0.20 | 0.43 |
| Brisbane | | | 0.04 | 0.16 |
| Winnipeg | | | −0.03 | |
| San Francisco | | | 0.48 | 0.07 |
| Rome | | | 0.64 | |
| Ten Cities | | | 0.16 | 0.11 |
| **Non-manual workers** | | | | |
| Predicted | | | | |
| Correlation | | | | 0 |
| Auckland | | | | −0.66 |
| Brisbane | | | | −0.13 |
| Winnipeg | | | | |
| San Francisco | | | | −0.14 |
| Rome | | | | |
| Ten Cities | | | | −0.23 |

\* + denotes high positive correlation
 − denotes high negative correlation
 0 denotes insignificant correlation
† The ten cities analysed by Van Arsdol et al. (1958): Akron, Atlanta, Birmingham, Kansas City, Louisville, Minneapolis, Portland, Providence, Rochester, Seattle.

Source: Timms 1971: 164; Herbert 1972: 144

analyst to ascertain the major independent patterns of variation in a data matrix (see p. 126). Bell himself used this technique on data for San Francisco and found that the six constituent variables of the three constructs did in fact collapse to three independent dimensions representing, as hypothesized, social rank, urbanization and segregation. Van Arsdol et al. (1958) replicated this analysis in their ten-city study, with broadly similar conclusions; although in four Southern cities (Atlanta, Birmingham, Kansas City and Louisville) patterns of fertility were associated with social rank as well as urbanization and in Providence the pattern of single-family dwellings was evidently associated with social rank instead of urbanization. These observations were explained by the authors in terms of the unusual social composition of the cities concerned, but the uncertainty generated by their findings led others to question whether the inclusion of a wider variety of variables would still result in the same three principal dimensions of differentiation. This initiated an inductive research methodology which soon eclipsed social area analysis and which is discussed in detail below. One of the major contributions of social area analysis *sensu strictu*, therefore, has been to generate a new and widely-accepted research strategy. However, it should also be acknowledged as a classifying procedure with intrinsic empirical value. Furthermore, notwithstanding the details of the argument relating to the underlying theory of social change, the conceptual basis of the schema is useful in emphasizing the link between urban structure and the macro-processes of social change. As Timms concludes:

The most important contribution which Shevky and his colleagues have made . . . lies not so much in the details of their arguments as in the emphasis they place on the relationship between the city and the wider society of which it is a part. In sensitizing the student of the city to the reciprocal relations which exist between the characteristics of the urban community and those of the encompassing society Shevky and Bell have helped to bridge the gap which exists between urban and general sociologies (Timms 1971: 209–10).

These 'reciprocal relations' were to become somewhat obscured by the statistical sophistry associated with studies of factorial ecology and it is only recently that urban geographers have redirected their attention towards them.

## Studies of factorial ecology

Factor analysis, together with the associated family of multivariate statistical techniques which includes principal components analysis, has become one of the most widely used techniques in social research of all kinds; and it is now generally the preferred approach for dealing with the complex question (Fig. 4.11) of measuring urban socio-spatial differentiation. In this context, factor analysis is used primarily as an inductive device with which to analyse the relationships between a wide range of social, economic, demographic and housing characteristics, with the objective of establishing what common patterns, if any, exist in the data. This, of course, is in direct contrast to social area analysis, where these relationships are pre-determined by deductive 'theory'. As noted above, the approach stems directly from attempts to validate the hypotheses implicit in social area analysis. Following the factor analyses by Bell (1955) and van Arsdol *et al.* (1958) of the six standard social area analysis variables, Anderson and Bean (1961) extended the approach, seeking to establish whether the inclusion of other variables would still result in the three dimensions postulated by Shevky and Bell. Using data for 13 variables for census tracts in Toledo, Ohio, they in fact discovered four major independent patterns of association – 'dimensions' – in the data: one representing social rank, one representing segregation, and two representing separate parts of the urbanization construct. Their work prompted other studies, notably by sociologists such as Gittus (1964), Sweetser (1965a; 1965b) and Schmid and Tagashira (1965), and within a short time the techniques diffused to geographers and planners, helped by an increasing general interest in quantitative techniques. In addition, innovations in computer technology and programming encouraged the use of a larger selection of input variables and so led to a more explicitly inductive approach. Subsequently, the bandwagon effect generated by the 'quantitative revolution' in geography led to factorial ecology studies of a wide range of cities, thus forming the basis for reliable high-level generalizations about urban socio-spatial structure.

### The method

It is not within the scope of this book to discuss details of the methodology of factor analysis and related techniques. Useful outlines are provided by Johnston (1978) and Rummel (1967), while Johnston (1971; 1976a), Davies (1984) and Rees (1971; 1972) provide extended critiques of the methodology in the context of factorial ecology

**Fig. 4.11**   Social spaces and structures.   *Source*: Davies (1984), Fig. 9.4, p. 305.

studies. Essentially, they can be regarded as summarizing or synthesizing techniques which are able to identify groups of variables with similar patterns of variation. These are expressed in terms of new, hybrid variables called factors or components which account for measurable amounts of the variance in the input data and which, like 'ordinary' variables, can be mapped or used as input data for other statistical analysis. The relationships and spatial pattern which they describe are known collectively as a *factorial ecology*. The usual factoring procedure produces a series of hybrid variables, each statistically independent of one another and each successively accounting for a smaller proportion of the total variance in the input data. Since the objective of the technique is to identify only the major dimensions of co-variance in the data, it is usual to retain only those factors which account for a greater proportion of the total variance than could any one of the original variables. These are identifiable through the relevant *eigenvalues*, which should have a minimum value of 1.0 and whose magnitude is in direct proportion to the explanatory power of the factor to which it relates. The composition of the factors is reflected in another part of the output: the *loadings*, which are simply correlation coefficients computed between the new hybrid variables and each of the original input variables. The spatial expression of the factors is derived from the respective vectors of *scores*, computed as the sum of the products of the original (standardized) variables and the relevant loadings.

In addition to these basic outputs there are certain refinements which are frequently used. The most important of these is the *rotation* of the factor axes in an attempt to maximize their fit to patterns in the original data. The most frequently used method of rotation in factorial ecology studies is the Varimax procedure, which retains the orthogonality (i.e. the statistical independence) of the factors. It is possible, however, to relax the orthogonality constraint in order to search for separate yet related dimensions of co-variance in the data. Rotation procedures of this kind are referred to as *oblique* solutions, and are

regarded by many as being the most sensitive approach when factoring socio-economic data of any kind. Relatively few such solutions have been used in factorial ecology studies, however; partly because they require a series of intuitive decisions from the analyst and partly because the relevant computer software has in any case diffused relatively slowly (Johnston 1976a).

### An example

The typical approach is illustrated here using the example of the city of Baltimore in 1980 and employing the areal framework (census tracts) and data source (the census) most often used in factorial ecology studies. The 21 variables used in this example (Table 4.4) have also been selected to be representative of the 'typical' input of studies of North American cities, although the choice of certain variables relates to a preliminary inspection of census data. Thus the proportion of persons of Italian origin is included because such persons constitute a sizeable minority of the city's population; Mexican Americans, on the other hand, are numerically unimportant in Baltimore and so are excluded from the analysis. Using a Varimax rotation of a principal axes solution, the input variables collapse to four major dimensions which

**Table 4.4** Input variables for factorial ecology of Baltimore, 1980

| | |
|---|---|
| 1. | Per cent aged 19–30 |
| 2. | Per cent aged 65 or over |
| 3. | Per cent persons never married |
| 4. | Sex ratio |
| 5. | Per cent adults with a college degree |
| 6. | Per cent Italian origin |
| 7. | Per cent Spanish speaking |
| 8. | Per cent black |
| 9. | Per cent recent migrants |
| 10. | Per cent unemployed |
| 11. | Per cent managers, administrators and professionals |
| 12. | Per cent operatives |
| 13. | Median family income |
| 14. | Per cent families below poverty level |
| 15. | Per cent dwellings vacant |
| 16. | Per cent dwellings privately rented |
| 17. | Per cent dwellings with 2 or more bathrooms |
| 18. | Per cent dwellings with less than 2 bedrooms |
| 19. | Per cent dwellings without complete kitchen facilities |
| 20. | Per cent single-parent households. |

**Table 4.5** Baltimore city: factor structure in 1980

**(A) Explanatory power of each factor**

| Factor | Per cent variance explained | Cumulative (%) | Eigenvalue |
|--------|------|------|------|
| I | 32.5 | 32.5 | 6.8 |
| II | 18.2 | 50.7 | 3.8 |
| III | 14.4 | 65.1 | 3.0 |
| IV | 7.1 | 72.2 | 1.5 |

**(B) The nature of the factors**

| Factor | | Loadings | |
|--------|--|----------|--|
| I. | 'Underclass' | Rented housing | 0.88 |
| | | Extreme poverty | 0.79 |
| | | Vacant dwellings | 0.70 |
| | | Inadequate kitchens | 0.68 |
| | | Single persons | 0.68 |
| | | Unemployment | 0.65 |
| II. | 'Socio-economic status' | Two or more bathrooms | 0.85 |
| | | Family income | 0.84 |
| | | College degree | 0.78 |
| | | Managers, administrators and professionals | 0.75 |
| III. | 'Youth/migrants' | Migrants | 0.88 |
| | | Age 19–30 | 0.88 |
| | | Sex ratio | 0.84 |
| | | Spanish speaking | 0.57 |
| IV. | 'Black poverty' | Blacks | 0.82 |
| | | Italian origin | −0.68 |
| | | Single-parent families | 0.55 |
| | | Poverty | 0.54 |

together account for 72.2 per cent of the variance in the initial data set (Table 4.5). By far the most important of these is factor I, which alone accounts for over 30 per cent of the variance. An examination of the highest loadings on this factor (Table 4.5) suggests that it is strongly and positively associated with extreme poverty and disadvantage, rented accommodation, and single-person households (but, interestingly, not with the general population of black or working-class households). It thus appears to be differentiating an 'underclass' of impoverished neighbourhoods from the rest of the city. Factor II represents a combination of variables reflecting socio-economic status: income, education, occupation, and material possessions. This

differentiation between high- and low-status areas explains just over 18 per cent of the total variance. Factor III (which explains over 14 per cent of the variance) is equally distinctive, representing an ethnic/migrant dimension which identifies census tracts with high proportions of in-migrants, young people, Spanish-speaking people, and a predominance of males. Factor IV is associated with black households, families living in poverty (but not extreme poverty), and single-parent families, and accounts for just over seven per cent of the total variance.

Figure 4.12 shows the spatial expression of the two leading dimensions of residential differentiation in Baltimore. While a detailed examination of the social geography of Baltimore need not detain us here, it is worth noting the principal features of these maps, particularly the solid block of census tracts in the inner city that is associated with the 'underclass' dimension and the equally cohesive group of tracts in the northern and western suburbs that is associated with the socio-economic status dimension.

### The generality of factorial ecologies

The most striking feature of these results is that they are rather different from those reported in the great majority of studies of other North American cities and, indeed, of cities in Australia, New Zealand, and some other parts of the world, where the three leading factors usually bear a close resemblance to the Social Area Analysis constructs of social rank, urbanization and segregation. Not only does this lend empirical support to the constructs postulated by Shevky *et al.* (although this does not suggest any support for the associated theory of increasing scale); it also raises the possibility of building a more sensitive model of urban residential differentiation from comparative analyses of factorial ecologies. Several attempts have been made to review the relevant literature in search of generalizations about urban structure (Rees 1971, 1972, 1979; Timms 1971). By far the major finding is that residential differentiation in the great majority of cities is dominated by a socio-economic status dimension, with a second dimension characterized by family

FACTOR I

FACTOR II

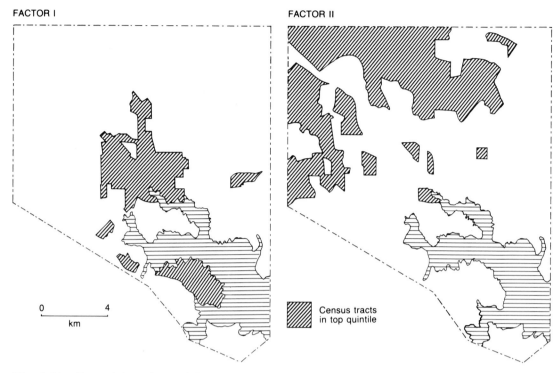

0        4
km

Census tracts
in top quintile

**Fig. 4.12**  Factorial ecology of Baltimore, 1980.

status/life-cycle characteristics and a third
dimension relating to segregation along ethnic
divisions. Moreover, these dimensions appear
to be consistent even in the face of variations
in input variables and in the statistical solution
employed; and evidence from the limited
number of studies of factorial ecology *change*
which have been undertaken shows that these
major dimensions tend to persist over periods
of two or three decades at least (Greer-
Wootten 1972; Hunter 1974; Johnston 1973a;
Murdie 1969). There also appears to be a
consistent pattern in the spatial expression of
these dimensions, both from city to city and
from one census year to the next. Salins, for
example, has shown how the socio-economic
status dimension of four US cities – Buffalo,
Indianapolis, Kansas City and Spokane – was
reflected in an essentially sectoral pattern in
1940, 1950 and 1960, while the family status
dimension exhibited a zonal gradient over the
same period (Fig. 4.13); patterns of ethnicity
were subject to greater change, although they

were consistent in exhibiting a clustered
pattern with a tendency to extend in a sectoral
fashion (Salins 1971). Cross-reference with
other studies confirms the generality of these
findings, and the significance of sectoral and
zonal configuration of the two leading dimensions has been further substantiated by
analysis of variance tests conducted on the
relevant sets of factor scores (Murdie 1969,
1976; Rees 1970).

Murdie has suggested that socio-economic
status, family status and ethnicity should be
regarded as representing major dimensions of
social space which, when superimposed on the
physical space of the city, serve to isolate
areas of social homogeneity 'in cells defined
by the spider's web of the sectoral-zonal
lattice' (Murdie 1969: 168). The resultant
idealized model of urban ecological structure
is shown in Figure 4.14. Yet, as Murdie
acknowledges, these sectors and zones are not
simply superimposed on the city's morphology:
they result from detailed interactions with it.

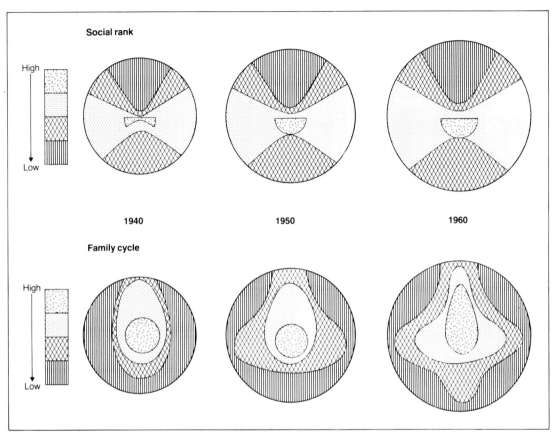

**Fig. 4.13**  Changing patterns of social rank and family status in American cities, 1940–1960. *Source*: Salins (1971), pp. 243 and 245.

Radial transport routes, for example, are likely to govern the positioning of sectors and to distort zonal patterns, as indicated in Chapter 2. Similarly, the configuration of both sectors and zones is likely to be influenced by specific patterns of land use and by patterns of urban growth. By introducing such features to the idealized model it should be possible to provide a closer approximation to the real world. One attempt to do this is represented in Figure 4.15, which is based on the example of Chicago (Berry and Rees 1969). In this model, the major dimensions of residential differentiation – socio-economic status (A), family status (B) and ethnicity (C) – are superimposed on each other to form a series of relatively homogeneous communities (D). These attributes are then integrated with a

number of other factors which tend to modify or distort the basic 'sectoral-zonal lattice'. First, it is suggested that the segregated ethnic areas will contain the entire range of life-cycle characteristics, but in a compressed form, so that zonal variation in family status will differ by direction about the city centre (E). A second distortion results from variations in the growth of the city (F), the effect of which is to create a star-shaped city, with 'tear faults' developing as zones cross sectoral boundaries, displacing zones outward in the early-growth sectors (G). Thirdly, the decentralization of industry is introduced (H), resulting in the formation of areas of relatively low socio-economic status around some of the peripheral industrial centres (I).

In addition to (and sometimes instead of)

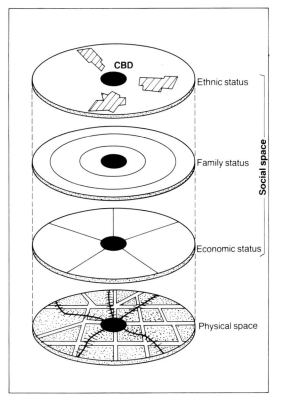

**Fig. 4.14** Idealized model of urban ecological structure. *Source*: Murdie (1969), p. 8.

the three 'classic' dimensions represented in these models, it is quite common for factor-ecological analyses to identify *other* dimensions of residential differentiation: as, for example, in our example of Baltimore. Often, these are related to particular local conditions, but the occurrence of some of them is quite widespread. Davies (1984) recognizes six: migration status, housing substandardness/skid row, pre-family, late/established family, tenure (public housing tenure, usually associated with family life-cycle characteristics), and urban fringe – each with a characteristic spatial pattern (Fig. 4.16).

It is important to emphasize that these observations represent a high level of generalization and that the results of many studies are ambiguous or even contradictory. In Montreal, for example, the socio-economic

status dimension is not 'pure', for it contains some 'ethnic' elements (Foggin and Polese 1977; Greer-Wootten 1972). Nevertheless, many geographers have suggested that the idealized 3-factor model has substantial generality throughout the Western culture area. This is certainly borne out by factorial ecologies of cities in Canada (Davies and Barrow 1973), Australia (Stimpson 1982) and New Zealand (Johnston 1973b, 1973c), but evidence from studies of European cities tends to be less conclusive. Overall, residential differentiation in continental European cities does tend to be dominated by a socio-economic status dimension, though it is often associated with housing status and the localization of self-employed workers. Continental cities also tend to conform to the 'classical' ecological model in that the second most important dimension generally relates to family status (though often in a complex manner). Ethnicity, however, does not generally occur as an independent dimension, partly because of the absence of substantial ethnic minorities, and partly because those which do exist appear to be more integrated – at census tract level – with the indigenous population (Burtenshaw, Bateman and Ashworth 1981; White 1984). British cities, however, do not conform so closely to the general Western model. Indeed, it has been suggested (Herbert 1968; D. Evans 1973) that British cities exhibit a distinctive ecological structure, with the principal dimensions of the classical model being modified by the construction and letting policies associated with the large public housing sector. Figure 4.17 shows the typical outcome.

### Factorial ecologies as a product of social structure

If there is such a thing as a general model of Western city structure, then these modifications must be viewed as the product of special conditions, or of the absence or attenuation of the basic conditions necessary for the classic dimensions to emerge. But what are these necessary conditions? Janet Abu-Lughod (1969) has attempted to answer this question in relation to the socio-economic status and family status dimensions. She suggests that

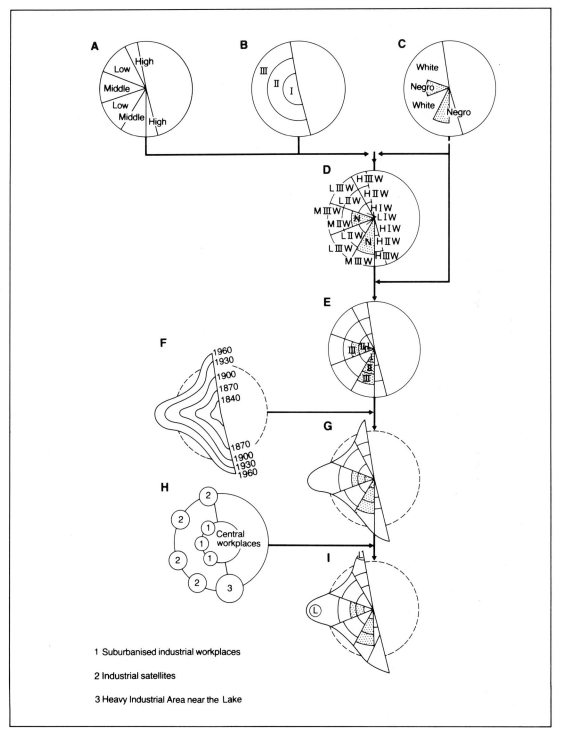

**Fig. 4.15**   An integrated spatial model of the metropolis.
*Source*: Berry and Rees (1969), Fig. 13.

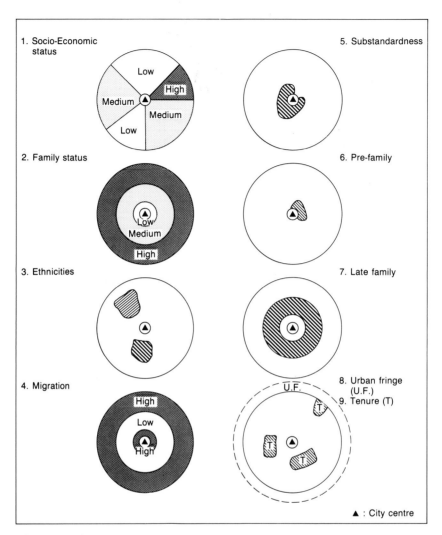

**Fig. 4.16**  Spatial patterns associated with major dimensions of urban structure.  *Source*: Davies (1984), Fig. 9.6, p. 323.

residential differentiation in terms of socio-economic status will only occur:

1. where there is an effective ranking system in society as a whole which differentiates population groups according to status or prestige; and

2. where this ranking system is matched by corresponding subdivisions of the housing market.

Similarly, she suggests that a family status dimension will occur where families at different stages of the family life-cycle exhibit different residential needs *and* where the nature and spatial arrangement of the housing stock is able to fulfil these needs. Implicit in these conditions is the important assumption that the population is sufficiently mobile to match up social status and life-cycle needs to existing housing opportunities. Abu-Lughod points out that these conditions are characteristic of contemporary North American society: a pre-welfare state in which people are geographically very mobile, and where social

**Fig. 4.17** A model of social regions for British cities.
*Source*: Davies (1984) Fig. 9.8, p. 341.

1. Central business district
   (retail, offices, wholesaling)

2. Inner city
a. Substandard, working class
b. Substandard, immigrant
c. Bedsit, transient
d. Aging status
e. Old council
f. Renewed: council
g. Renewed: gentrification

3. Middle city
   (late and established family)
a. High status
b. Middle income
c. Council housing

4. Outer city
a. High status
b. Middle income
c. Council housing
d. Undeveloped

5. Fringe
a. High status
b. Mixed status satellites
c. Older villages
d. Rural

status is ascribed principally by occupation and income.

Accepting the validity of these ideas, it is clearly possible to relate factorial ecologies to a wider view of society and to begin to build a body of theory around the generalized model of the Western city. Little attempt has been made to do this, however; researchers have been preoccupied more with the technical pros and cons of different aspects of factor analysis. Nevertheless, Abu-Lughod's work provides a useful framework against which deviations from the general model can be explained. In Montreal, for example, where the socio-economic status dimension overlaps with ethnicity, the explanation can be found in the unusually large minority popu-

lation of French-speakers which occupies most of the lower part of the social ladder with the result that ethnicity and social status are not independent phenomena (Foggin and Polese 1977). In Swedish cities, the existence of three separate family status dimensions can be attributed to the relative immobility of Swedes, compared to American norms (Janson 1971). The tendency for the ecology of English cities to be dominated by housing market characteristics can be seen as a reflection of the country's more highly developed public sector. The association between the family status dimension and measures of crowding found in most British studies, for example, can be related to the letting policies of local authority housing departments, many of which allocate public housing on the basis of family size, among other things, as an indicant of housing need (see also pages 217–222). Similarly, the use of economic criteria of housing need in determining people's eligibility for council houses ensures that there is a close association between socio-economic status and housing tenure.

Davies (1984), following Timms (1971), provides a different framework for explaining variations in urban structure. He suggests that, historically, four major dimensions of social differentiation have dominated cities everywhere – social rank, family status, ethnicity and migration status – and that these are *combined in different ways in different types of society* to produce varying urban structures (Fig. 4.18). In traditional or feudal societies, family-related considerations dominated the social structure, since prestige and status were based primarily on kinship. In the 'feudal' city, therefore, a single axis of differentiation can be expected, combining social rank and family status as well as the limited amount of ethnic and migrant variation. With economic specialization and the development of external economic linkages, division of labour intensifies, a merchant class is added to the political élite, and selective migration streams add to the social and ethnic complexity of cities. Davies postulates that these changes led to the creation of three very different types of urban structure, each composed of two dominant axes of differentiation that combined the four basic dimensions in different ways. In 'pre-industrial' cities, the perpetuation of family kinship patterns and the continued importance of the established élite combined to produce a single axis of differentiation (social rank/family status), while the arrival of migrant groups of different ethnic origins created a second major axis of differentiation. In 'colonial' cities that were located in previously-settled areas, immigrants would be politically and socially dominant, so that social rank, ethnicity and migration status would be collapsed into a single dimension. Meanwhile, family status characteristics would represent an independent dimension of differentiation. In 'immigrant' cities, the indigenous political élite

remained dominant, while the age-, ethnic- and sex-selective process of in-migration tended to overwhelm residential variations in family status. As a result, social rank and migration/ethnicity/family status emerge as the major dimensions of residential structure. The onset of industrialization brought a great increase in specialization, while income and wealth became more important as yardsticks of social prestige. As transport technologies made large-scale suburbanization possible, these changes produced a transformation in the characteristics of social prestige and in family organization, eventually leading to quite distinct patterns of differentiation in terms of social rank and family status. Similarly, processes of segregation led to the separation of various ethnic and migrant groups in different parts of cities, thus completing the 'classic' structure of the modern industrial city.

### Some unresolved difficulties

Notwithstanding the considerable potential of factorial ecologies, several important methodological issues remain as stumbling blocks in the pursuit of a more sophisticated theory of residential differentiation. These issues have been the subject of extensive debate, the details of which are summarized by Johnston (1976a). Among the chief limitations identified by Johnston is the fact that most analyses rely almost exclusively on decennial or quinquennial censuses for their data. This means that research is often constrained by a lack of data covering a full range of socio-economic characteristics, since many census authorities have been chary of demanding information on sensitive subjects such as religion and have been unwilling to expend limited resources collecting information on complex phenomena such as people's lifestyle or activity patterns.

This may help to explain Palm's interesting finding that the geography of 'communities of interest' in Minneapolis – St Paul, as reflected by patterns of newspaper and magazine readership, was quite different from the factorial ecology of the city (Palm 1973). Indeed, the generality of factorial ecology results may be partly attributable to similarities in the input

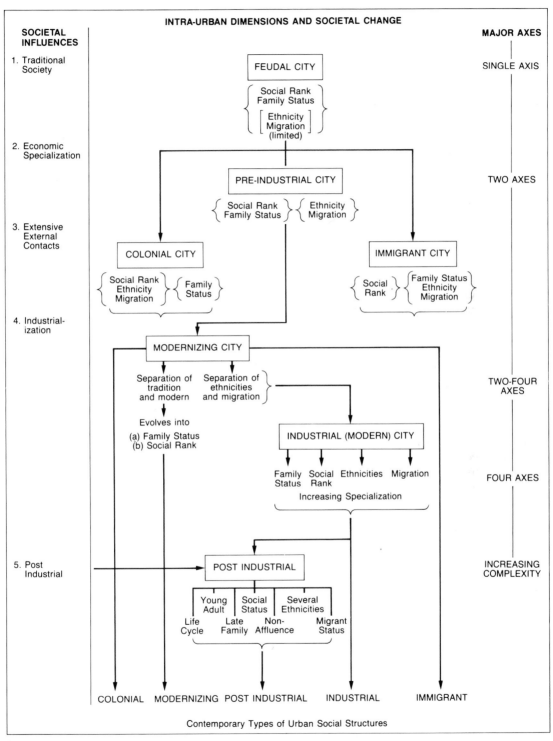

**Fig. 4.18**  A developmental sequence of social structures.
*Source*: Davies (1984) Fig. 9.5, p. 309.

variables used in different studies. The territorial units for which aggregate census data are published may also have a considerable effect upon the analysis. Despite the probability that the boundaries of census sub-areas will not match actual patterns of residential variation on the ground, the implicit assumption in the methodology is that these territories are homogeneous. Research by Newton and Johnston, however, has shown that not only do census sub-areas tend to be relatively heterogeneous, but that the incorporation of measures of homogeneity in the data matrix can suggest important qualifications to 'classical' factorial ecologies. In their analysis of Christchurch, New Zealand, they found that areas ranked highest on the socio-economic status dimension were also the least homogeneous in their population characteristics; while the suburban areas ranked highest on a 'life-style' dimension (associated with family status and housing quality variables) exhibited a fairly high level of homogeneity in their population characteristics (Newton and Johnston 1976). Another, more intractable problem arising from the boundary locations of census sub-areas is that of spatial autocorrelation, although the *extent* to which this distorts the results of factorial ecologies is a matter of debate (Cliff and Ord 1973). It should also be recognized that census sub-areas represent only one of the very large number of ways that a city can be sub-divided, thus raising the question as to whether the same factorial ecology would result from different spatial frameworks; and, if not, whether the difference is a product of scale-specific processes or merely an artefact of the data set.

A further issue, and one with particularly important implications for comparative studies, concerns the degree to which factorial ecologies cover functional, as opposed to administrative, urban areas. Most research has been conducted at the level of administratively-defined cities, as in our example of Baltimore. Yet it is clear that, as urbanization produces larger metropolitan areas, the scale of residential differentiation is likely to change. Expanding the factorial ecology of Baltimore to the metropolitan scale of the Standard Metropolitan Statistical Area (SMSA) brings into the analysis many of the city's upper-income suburbs, with the result that the dominant dimension of the ecological structure becomes socio-economic status, as in the classic model (Table 4.6). Much therefore depends on the researcher's definition of what constitutes the ecological 'universe'. Perle (1981) has suggested that central city and suburban ecologies can be viewed as separate phenomena, with central city ecological structure becoming more differentiated over time, and suburbia developing a more general ecology that is dominated by status dimensions.

**Table 4.6** Baltimore SMSA: factor structure in 1980

**(A) Explanatory power of each factor**

| Factor | Per cent variance explained | Cumulative (%) | Eigenvalue |
|---|---|---|---|
| I | 30.3 | 30.3 | 6.4 |
| II | 15.0 | 45.3 | 3.2 |
| III | 9.9 | 55.2 | 2.1 |
| IV | 7.6 | 62.8 | 1.6 |
| V | 6.1 | 68.9 | 1.3 |

**(B) The nature of the factors**

| Factor | | Loadings | |
|---|---|---|---|
| I. | 'Socio-economic status' | College degree | 0.91 |
| | | Managers, administrators and professionals | 0.89 |
| | | Two or more bathrooms | 0.86 |
| | | Median family income | 0.75 |
| II. | 'Poverty' | Unemployment | 0.87 |
| | | Single-parent families | 0.84 |
| | | Extreme poverty | 0.79 |
| | | Rented housing | 0.58 |
| III. | 'Elderly, inadequate housing' | Less than two bedrooms | 0.85 |
| | | Rented dwellings | 0.60 |
| | | Elderly | 0.52 |
| | | Inadequate kitchens | 0.52 |
| IV. | 'Black poverty' | Poverty | 0.74 |
| | | Blacks | 0.71 |
| | | Italian origin | −0.62 |
| | | Elderly | −0.50 |
| V. | 'Youth/migrants' | Age 19–30 | 0.79 |
| | | Migrants | 0.69 |
| | | Single persons | 0.56 |

Another important stumbling block concerns the interpretation of the results of factorial ecologies. In addition to the hazards of the ecological fallacy (see p. 88) which are by now well known to geographers, there are certain less well-known dangers involved in the substantive interpretation of the output of factor analyses. In particular Johnston (1976a) cites the danger of 'overinterpretation' in situations where, despite low inter-correlations between variables (suggesting that their distributions are more different than similar), high loadings may still be generated. Overinterpretation may also arise where the input includes several variables which between them define a 'closed system' of a particular phenomenon. Thus the inclusion of variables measuring the percentage of the population in each of an exhaustive series of occupational categories would almost certainly produce an 'occupation' dimension which, because of correlations with other variables, is likely to lead to a spurious result. Another problem of overinterpretation has been identified by Palm and Caruso (1972), who suggest that the tendency to interpret factors using only a few major loadings leads to a coarse labelling of factors which obscures important variations in variables with lower loadings.

In an attempt to sidestep some of these problems, analysts whose main interest is in the *overall* spatial pattern defined by the input variables rather than in the underlying dimensions of differentiation and their associated spatial expression have sometimes used grouping procedures such as cluster analysis and multiple discriminant analysis in order to achieve a multivariate classification of census sub-areas. Such techniques generally group sub-areas according to their proximity in $n$-dimensional space (where $n$ = the number of input variables), so that the result is a typology of sub-areas in which within-group variation is minimized and between-group variation is maximized. The number of groups or clusters of sub-areas produced depends, in part, upon subjective decisions by the analyst, although there is a clear relationship between the number of groups and the sensitivity of the classification: the fewer the groups the greater the loss of detail (for a full discussion of such techniques see Everitt (1974) and Johnston (1976b)). Planners, in particular, have been attracted to these techniques because of the relative ease with which the output can be understood by non-professionals. In detail, however, the methodology involved is not without pitfalls. Indeed, some cluster analysis procedures are based on an initial factoring of the data; and all multivariate grouping procedures, like factorial ecologies, are subject to the constraints imposed by the shortcomings of census data. Moreover, the nature of the technique makes inter-city comparisons of residential typologies very difficult so that, in relation to the search for high-level generalizations about urban residential structure, factor analysis is likely to remain the preferred technique.

## Urban social indicators

As we have seen, one of the major shortcomings of traditional factorial ecology studies is that the mix of input variables overlooks many important aspects of urban life, including environmental quality, accessibility to facilities like hospitals, shopping centres, libraries and parks, and the local incidence of social pathologies such as crime, delinquency and drug addiction. The emergence of 'quality of life' and 'territorial justice' as central concerns within human geography has meant that much more attention has been given to such issues, allowing the presentation of a rather different perspective on patterns of socio-economic differentiation.

It should be acknowledged at the outset that interest in patterns of social well-being and the quality of life (the two terms are used here synonymously) and the distribution of social *malaise* in cities is by no means new. Charles Booth used a set of six variables, including measures of poverty, crowding and mortality, to construct a composite index of 'social conditions' for the neighbourhoods of Victorian London (Booth 1893), and the description of the geography of personal and social pathologies has received a great deal of attention over the years in connection with the ecological theories outlined in Chapter 3.

Nevertheless, it is fair to say that within the last decade or so patterns of deprivation and variation in the quality of life have become a central concern within geography. The reasons for the rather sudden awakening of interest in what have collectively been called 'welfare' issues (Smith 1977, 1979a) can be traced to the events of the 1960s: the rioting and disorder in American cities associated with the blacks' struggle for civil rights, and the 'revolutionary' alliance between students and factory workers in parts of Europe associated with popular protest against the hegemony of Big Business and Big Government.

The scale of these events was impressive: in the Watts riots in Los Angeles in 1965, 34 people were killed, over 1,000 were badly injured, more than 500 buildings were looted and burnt down, and $100 m. of damage was sustained; in Berlin, Hamburg, Munich, Frankfurt and Hanover, five days of rioting followed the police shooting of student leader Rudi Dutschke; and at the height of the revolutionary movement in France in May 1968, over 800,000 people turned out to march in Paris, while over two-thirds of the country's workforce joined in a general strike. But the long term effects of these events were more significant, if less dramatic. Society in general became sensitized to a wide range of social and environmental issues; and geographers and other social scientists, in parallel with politicians and the media, began to examine these issues more closely. One major focus of interest was the question of the distribution of the 'bads' or 'ills' which were, apparently, the inevitable handmaidens of economic growth. Reinforced by a welter of mass media features, concern for those sections of the community who found themselves the victims rather than the beneficiaries of national economic growth helped to shift the objectives of national and local governments away from the promotion of economic growth to the improvement of the quality of life. This inevitably raised the question of how to recognize improvements to the quality of life when they did occur, for it was clear that traditional yardsticks of national and local performance were wholly insensitive to many of the qualitative aspects of life.

Part of the collective response of academics, administrators and policy-makers was manifested in the so-called 'social indicators movement'. Rather ironically, the initial impetus for the movement came from the North American Space Administration, which sought to develop quantitative measures of the 'social spin-off' of its activities (Bauer 1966). Within a short time, however, social indicators had established a firm footing in federal administrative thinking. Official interest was first declared in a document produced by the United States Department of Health, Education and Welfare, which went on to define a social indicator as:

a statistic of direct normative interest which facilitates concise, comprehensive and balanced judgements about the conditions of major aspects of a society. It is in all cases a direct measure of welfare and it is subject to the interpretation that, if it changes in the 'right' direction, while other things remain equal, things have got better, or people are 'better off' (USDHEW 1969: 97).

The task of developing such indicators has subsequently occupied a large number of scholars and policy-makers in the United States, Europe, Australasia and Japan, and there now exists an extensive literature on the construction and use of social indicators in a variety of contexts (see, for example, OECD 1977; Knox 1978c; Carley 1981). As David Smith has shown, *territorial* social indicators provide a very useful descriptive device in the context of geographical analysis. Smith has made a strong case for a 'welfare approach' to human geography, with the central concern being 'who gets what, where, and how?'. Following this approach, territorial social indicators are seen as fundamental to 'the major and immediate research task' of describing the geography of social well-being at different spatial scales. This, it is argued, will not only provide the context for empirical research concerned with *explaining* the mechanisms and processes which create and sustain territorial disparities in well-being but will also facilitate the *evaluation* of these disparities in the light of prevailing societal values and, if necessary, the *prescription* of remedial policies (Smith 1973b, 1974a, 1977). Since the early

1970s, something of a start has been made on the application of territorial social indicators at the intra-urban level. Two kinds of study are of particular interest here: those which attempt to describe variations in the overall level of local social well-being – 'quality of life' studies – and those which attempt to identify particular sub-areas whose residents are relatively disadvantaged – studies of 'deprivation'.

## The quality of urban life

Quality of life studies are of interest here because they offer the possibility of portraying the essential socio-geographical expression of urban communities on a conceptual scale which ranges along a continuum from 'good' to 'bad', thus providing a potent index with which to regionalize the city. The construction of such an index presents a number of difficulties, however. The first task is to set out a definition of social well-being which can be translated into a composite statistical measure: something which has taxed social scientists a great deal. The range of factors which potentially influence people's well-being for better or worse is enormous. Moreover, opinions about the importance of different contributory factors often vary between socio-geographical groups; and factors which might be important at one geographic scale can be completely irrelevant at another. Smith (1973b: 46) concludes that 'we are apparently faced with the problem of trying to measure something which is not directly observable, for which there is no generally accepted *numeraire*, and which theory tells us is some function of things which ultimately rest on societal values'. Any search for conclusive or universal definitions of social well-being is therefore futile. Nevertheless, as Smith himself argues, 'the imperative of empirical analysis in welfare geography means that we must be prepared to move in where the angels fear to tread' (Smith 1973b: 47). His analysis of Tampa, Florida, provides a good case study of intra-urban variations in the quality of life. Table 4.7 shows the 47 variables used to operationalize the seven criteria of social well-being and illustrates vividly the scope of quality of life

studies: measures of welfare dependency, air pollution, recreational facilities, drug offences, family stability and public participation in local affairs are all included, in marked contrast to the urban geographer's conventional view of the city. Smith acknowledged that his selection of variables was 'a compromise between the ideal and what was possible given the constraints of time and resources', but maintained that 'the data assembled provide a satisfactory reflection of the general concept of social well-being and embody many important conditions which have a bearing on the quality of individual life' (Smith 1973b: 125). An overal measure of social well-being was derived from these data using the relatively simple procedure of aggregating, for each census tract, the standardized scores on all the variables. The resultant index is mapped in Figure 4.19. Despite the rather peculiar shape of the city, with its CBD close to the bay and its southern suburbs surrounded on three sides by water, there is a clear pattern to the geography of well-being: a sink of ill-being occupies the inner city area, with relatively poor areas extending towards the city limits in a north-easterly direction. The best areas occupy the opposite sector of the city, although most suburban neighbourhoods enjoy a quality of life which is well above the average.

Similar results have emerged from other quality of life studies: they typically describe a sharply bi-polar society, in which the geography of social well-being exhibits both sectoral and zonal elements (see, for example, Stimpson 1982). In addition, most studies have revealed a close association between race and the quality of life.

One of the major potential weaknesses of this kind of approach is the implicit assumption that the aggregation of a series of measures of different aspects of social well-being will produce a meaningful statistic. Although this procedure may be an acceptable expedient in many circumstances, it is clear that social well-being should in fact be regarded as the product of a series of contributory factors which are *weighted* according to their relative importance to the people whose well-being is under consideration. It is evident, for

**Table 4.7** Criteria of social well-being and variables used in Smith's Tampa study

**Criteria and variables**

### I. Economic status
(i) Income
    1. Income per capita ($) of persons 14 and over, 1970
    2. Families with income less than $3000 (%) 1970
    3. Families with income over $10,000 (%) 1970
    4. Persons in families below poverty level (%) 1970
(ii) Employment
    5. Unemployed persons (% total workforce) 1970
    6. Persons aged 16–24 working less than 40 weeks (%) 1969
    7. White-collar workers (%) 1970
    8. Blue-collar workers (%) 1970
(iii) Welfare
    9. Families on AFDC program (%) October 1971
    10. Persons aged 65 and over on Old Age Assistance (%) Oct. 1971

### II. Environment
(i) Housing
    11. Average value of owner-occupied units ($) 1970
    12. Owner-occupied units valued less than $10,000 (%) 1970
    13. Average monthly rental of rented units ($) 1970
    14. Rented units with monthly rentals less than $60 (%) 1970
    15. Units with complete plumbing facilities (%) 1970
    16. Deteriorating and dilapidated houses (%) 1971
(ii) Streets and sewers
    17. Streets needing reconstruction (% of total length) 1971
    18. Streets needing scarification and resurfacing (% of total length) 1971
    19. Sanitary sewer deficiencies (% of total area) 1971
    20. Storm sewer deficiencies (% of total area) 1971
(iii) Air pollution
    21. Maximum monthly dustfall (tons/sq. mile) 1969
    22. Average suspended particulates 1969 ($\mu gm/m^3$/day) 1969
    23. Maximum monthly sulfation 1969 (mg/$SO_3$/100 cm$^2$/day) 1969
(iv) Open space
    24. Area lacking park and recreation facilities (%) 1971

### III. Health
(i) General mortality
    25. Infant deaths (per 1,000 live births) 1970
    26. Death rate (per 10,000 persons 65 or over) 1970
(ii) Chronic diseases
    27. Cancer deaths (per 100,000 population) 1970
    28. Stroke deaths (per 100,000 population) 1970
    29. Heart disease deaths (per 100,000 population) 1970
    30. New active tuberculosis cases (per 10,000 population) 1970

### IV. Education
(i) Duration
    31. Persons age 18–24 with 4 or more years high school or college (%) 1970
    32. Persons over 25 with 8 years or less school (%) 1970
    33. Persons over 25 with 4 years high school (%) 1970
    34. Persons over 25 with 4 years college (%) 1970

### V. Social disorganization
(i) Personal pathologies
    35. Narcotic violations arrests (per 10,000 residents) 1971
    36. Venereal disease cases (per 10,000 population) 1970
(ii) Family breakdown
    37. Families with children, having husband and wife present (%) 1970
    38. Persons separated or divorced (% never married) 1970
(iii) Overcrowding
    39. Dwellings with more than 1.0 persons per room (%) 1970
(iv) Public order and safety
    40. Criminal violation arrests (per 1,000 residents) 1971
    41. Juvenile delinquency arrests (per 10,000 residents) 1971
    42. Accidental deaths (per 1000,000 population) 1970
(v) Delinquency
    43. Juvenile delinquency arrests by residency (per 10,000 population, 1971)

### VI. Participation and equality
(i) Democratic participation
    44. Registered voters (% population 18 and over) 1971
    45. Eligible voters voting in mayoral election (%) 1971
(ii) Equality
    46. Racial distribution index 1970
    47. Income distribution index 1970

**Fig. 4.19** Standard scores on a general indicator of social well-being for Tampa, Florida. *Source*: Smith (1973), p. 126.

plenty of reasons for such variations. To begin with, some aspects of social well-being (leisure and material consumption, for example) are highly income-elastic, so that successive increases in expendable income will bring about marked increases in the intensity with which they are valued. This conforms conveniently with Maslow's (1970) suggestion that human motivation is related to a hierarchy of human needs, so that as people's basic needs – for nutrition, shelter and personal safety – are satisfied, motivation turns towards higher goals such as the attainment of social status, prestige, and self-expression. Accepting this model of behaviour, it follows that people with low levels of material well-being will attach more importance to materialistic than to aesthetic, spiritual or cultural aspects of life. People's values also vary according to their stage in the family life cycle, and to their membership of particular religious or cultural groups. Moreover, the social geography of the city is itself likely to generate or reinforce differences in values from one neighbourhood to another, for the socio-demographic composition of different neighbourhoods creates distinctive local reference groups which contribute significantly to people's attitudes to life (Eyles 1973).

The crucial issue for quality of life studies is whether these variations in people's values are great enough to blunt the effectiveness of unweighted bundles of statistics such as those used by Smith. Unfortunately, few studies have pursued this question in any detail, largely because of the difficulties involved in obtaining reliable data on people's values: the cost of properly-conducted surveys is simply too great for most research projects. Nevertheless, the available evidence suggests that weighting indicators of local well-being according to prevailing local values does not make a significant difference to overall patterns of the quality of life. The chief source of evidence for this conclusion is a study of the geography of social well-being in Dundee reported by Knox and MacLaran (1978). In this study, an overall index of 'level of living' was computed for each of 14 neighbourhood types using survey data on 50 variables

example, that British and American people do not regard housing conditions as being as important to their well-being as their health, whereas both factors are felt to be much more important than accessibility to recreational facilities (Abrams 1973; Campbell, Converse and Rodgers 1976). Moreover, these values tend to vary significantly between socio-geographical groups: Lovrich, for example, has described the very different priorities of Anglo, Black and Mexican-American voters in Denver (Lovrich 1974); and in Britain, intra-urban variations in attitudes to education have become part of the conventional wisdom of a whole generation of educationalists (Douglas 1964; Robson 1969). There are relating to eleven 'domains' of life: health, housing, employment opportunities, education, personal security, income and consumption, leisure, social and political participation, access to amenities, environmental quality, and social stability. According to this unweighted index, the owner-occupied neighbourhoods to the east and west of the city were by far the best-off, followed by more central neighbourhoods containing the most stable and sought-after of the city's older public housing estates. At the other end of the spectrum were most of the inner-city neighbourhoods, together with a few of the outlying suburbs of more recent public housing. Data on people's values collected in the same survey showed that there were statistically significant differences between the fourteen neighbourhood types in the importance attached to all but two of the domains (income/finance and leisure); but when these data were used to weight the level of living index it was found that 'The results of these calculations show that weighted description, although it is arguably more sensitive to variations in well-being . . . produces much the same picture, ecologically, as the conventional unweighted approach' (Knox and MacLaran 1978: 224). Interestingly, the survey results also showed that people tended to attach most value to the things they found themselves to be best at, or had most of – thus helping to explain the close relationship between the weighted and unweighted index values.

## Patterns of deprivation

Interest in welfare issues quickly spread from the pursuit of overall yardsticks of well-being to the construction of territorial indicators designed explicitly to identify 'problem areas' and areas of 'social stress' or 'social malaise', where urban deprivation was at its worst (Smith 1979b). Much of the impetus for this work came from professional planners and administrators wanting quantitative measures of the intensity of deprivation in order to be able to formulate spatial policies with which to rectify or ameliorate the problem. Many of the resultant policies have taken the form of

*positive discrimination*, directing resources into areas which have been identified as the locus of deprivation. It should be noted at once that the utility of such policies is open to some doubt: their effect on the social geography of the city is discussed in Chapter 8. In this chapter, however, interest is the indicators themselves and the spatial patterns which they describe.

The main reason for this interest is simply that patterns of deprivation represent an important facet of the geography of the city (Herbert 1975). In this context, it is useful to regard deprivation as multi-dimensional, directing attention to the spatial configuration and inter-relationships of different aspects of deprivation. The Norwegian geographer Asbjorn Aase (1978) has suggested that these patterns may be of three different kinds:

1. *random*, with no observable co-variance between different aspects of deprivation;
2. *compensatory*, where the local occurrence of particular aspects of deprivation is accompanied by above-average conditions in relation to other aspects of life;
3. *accumulative*, where there is a high degree of spatial overlap in the distribution of deprivations, resulting in areas of 'multiple deprivation'.

To these we must add a fourth possibility: that the distribution of deprivations may form distinctive constellations of problems, thus reflecting different *kinds* of deprived areas containing different combinations of deprivation. At this point it is necessary to emphasize that we are concerned here with *area* deprivations, expressed in terms of the average characteristics of spatially-defined groups of people. Once again, therefore, it is necessary to guard against the dangers of ecological fallacy: not everyone in a deprived area is necessarily deprived; and not every deprived person in an area of 'multiple deprivation' is necessarily multiply deprived.

Aase's own empirical research (with Britt Dale) suggested that the tendency within Norwegian cities is for the accumulative distribution of deprivations. In Trondheim, for example, low-status neighbourhoods tended to fare badly on most of the 19 indicators used

**Fig. 4.20** The localization of deprivation in Trondheim, Norway: rankings for 19 level-of-living indicators among 7 areas. *Source*: Aase and Dale (1978), p. 49.

to measure relative levels of deprivation and prosperity (Fig. 4.20). The same tendency for the accumulative distribution of deprivations is evident in Fig. 4.21, which shows the distribution of fourteen different aspects of deprivation in Liverpool, by wards. In every case, the worst levels of deprivation are to be found in the inner city, with certain suburban neighbourhoods consistently falling within the two next-worst categories. This tendency has encouraged the development of overall measures of deprivation: if the distribution of deprivations is accumulative, it seems fair to aggregate indicators to produce a single index of 'multiple deprivation' (Smith 1979c). A good example of this approach is provided by the work of the City of Glasgow Planning Department (Rae 1983). Working at enumeration district level, ten census indicators of deprivation – covering housing amenities, overcrowding, vacant dwellings, child density (children as a proportion of all persons living above ground floor level), low-income occupations, unemployment, handicapped/permanently sick persons, single-parent fami-

lies, and large households – were used to compute an overall index derived from the scores on the dominant dimension of a factor analysis of the data. Figure 4.22 shows that, in Glasgow, pockets of deprivation are found throughout the city, not only in central areas of older, private, tenemental housing, but also – and indeed predominantly – in some of the newer, peripheral public housing estates.

This kind of approach has been criticized on several grounds, however, including the desirability of aggregating indicators of several different aspects of deprivation and the validity of assigning them equal weight in the overall index (Craig and Driver 1972; Hatch and Sherrot 1973). Also important is the danger that aggregate measures may in fact mask distinctive combinations of deprivations in one part of the city or another. Although the examples outlined above suggest that the general trend is for an accumulative distribution of deprivations in inner city areas and (in Britain) in some peripheral public housing estates, detailed statistical analysis sometimes reveals significant localized constellations of particular aspects of deprivation. In Belfast, for example, Boal *et al.* (1978) found that a factor analysis of seven social malaise variables produced two major dimensions of deprivation: one characterized by unemployment, illegitimacy, high proportions of children in public care and high rates of mortality from bronchitis and associated with inner-city neighbourhoods; and the other characterized by high levels of unemployment overcrowding and delinquency and associated with a sectoral distribution westwards from the city centre.

Another study which demonstrates the existence of deprived areas of different kinds within cities is Coulter's (1978) analysis of 1 km-square census data for the seven largest British conurbations: Birmingham, Glasgow, Leeds, Liverpool, London, Manchester and Newcastle upon Tyne. According to Coulter, the most common syndrome of deprivation in these conurbations involves overcrowding, unemployment, low wages (reflected by high proportions of unskilled workers), low levels of car ownership and high levels of ill-health, and is typically located centrally within the

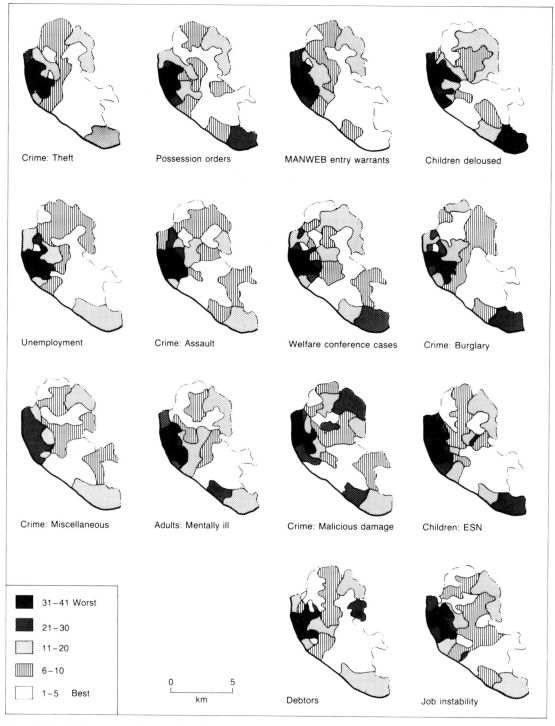

**Fig. 4.21** Patterns of deprivation in Liverpool. *Source*: Brooks (1977), p. 26.

**Fig. 4.22** Social deprivation in Glasgow, 1981. *Source:* Rae (1983) Map 1, p. 20.

Worst 0–10% of Enumeration Districts in Glasgow.

Worst 10–20% of Enumeration Districts in Glasgow.

District Council Priority Area Boundaries.

Easterhouse

Barlanark

Ruchazie

Blackhill

Barmulloch

Germiston

Parkhead

Bridgeton

Dalmarnock

Cambuslang

Castlemilk

Milton

Ruchill

Possilpark

Woodlands

East Pollockshields

Govan

Yoker

Drumchapel

Pollock

Priesthill/Nitshill

km

core of the conurbation. This, however, is by no means the only deprivation syndrome in evidence. Leeds, Liverpool, Glasgow and (to a lesser extent) Manchester all exhibit an additional syndrome of deprivation involving poor housing – mostly privately-rented, furnished accommodation – associated with inner-city areas containing high proportions of New Commonwealth immigrants. In addition, some conurbations have distinctive syndromes of deprivation which are associated with outer suburban areas. Some council estates within the outer zone of the Birmingham, Glasgow and Manchester conurbations, for example, suffer particularly from a syndrome involving low educational achievement, low wages and

**Table 4.8**  Social malaise in Liverpool

| | Neighbourhood performance* | | | | |
|---|---|---|---|---|---|
| | High status areas | Rooming house areas | Inner council estates | Outer council estates | Older terraced housing |
| Long term unemployment | 32 | 136 | 250 | 102 | 89 |
| Youth unemployment | 33 | 110 | 199 | 145 | 63 |
| Youth job instability | 17 | 151 | 302 | 112 | 68 |
| Free school meals | 29 | 81 | 201 | 147 | 74 |
| Educationally sub-normal | 42 | 91 | 212 | 127 | 79 |
| Absenteeism | 18 | 98 | 295 | 121 | 76 |
| Low reading ability | 30 | 91 | 210 | 131 | 86 |
| Higher education grants | 225 | 123 | 32 | 67 | 54 |
| Immunization | 96 | 89 | 37 | 77 | 156 |
| Infant mortality | 75 | 157 | 158 | 69 | 118 |
| Illegitimacy | 35 | 247 | 185 | 83 | 96 |
| Infectious diseases | 68 | 167 | 143 | 82 | 110 |
| Short-term care | 22 | 199 | 154 | 113 | 95 |
| Long-term care | 15 | 272 | 212 | 74 | 104 |
| Delinquency | 21 | 91 | 397 | 93 | 75 |
| Supervision orders | 22 | 108 | 313 | 111 | 75 |
| Repair notices | 52 | 191 | 58 | 22 | 215 |
| Disinfestation | 58 | 82 | 265 | 84 | 104 |
| Possession orders | 27 | 124 | 189 | 136 | 77 |
| Children born | 78 | 146 | 108 | 78 | 125 |

* Calculated as a percentage of the mean for the city as a whole.

*Source:* Webber 1975: 111

lack of a car.

Another illuminating piece of research is the analysis of deprivation and social pathology in Liverpool undertaken by the Planning Research Applications Groups as a follow-up to their pioneering Social Malaise Study (Webber 1975). Table 4.8 summarizes the distribution of a wide range of symptoms of deprivation, revealing a marked variation in the nature and intensity of deprivation between the five principal types of neighbourhood in the city. By far the worst off were the inner council estates, with four times the city-wide level of delinquency, three times the average levels of job instability among youths and of school absenteeism, and over twice the average levels of disinfestation, children in long-term care, low reading ability, educational subnormality, unemployment and family poverty (as reflected by childrens' eligibility for free school meals). Rooming-house areas also scored badly across a wide range of indicators, but were particularly characterized by high proportions of children in care, by large numbers of housing repair notices, and by a high incidence of infectious diseases. Finally, the nature of the symptoms of deprivation in the city's peripheral council estates was different again, centring on family poverty, youth unemployment and the incidence of possession orders.

It would be wise to be cautious about the findings of such studies, however. Several important conceptual and methodological issues remain unresolved, not least of which is the question of defining 'deprivation' more rigorously. As Edwards has observed, the rush for empirical results has effectively put the cart before the horse, with deprivation being 'defined' only in terms of the available indicators. 'To put it less charitably, it has been a hotch-potch approach in which any variable deemed by the researcher to be even vaguely relevant . . . has been thrown into the statistical melting pot' (Edwards 1975: 281). This is partly a result a the difficulty of obtaining data which are *direct* indicators of deprivation: the use of surrogate indicators and indicators of phenomena which are supposedly symptomatic of deprivation inevitably leads to ambiguity and obfuscation.

More important, however, is the uncertainty about the nature of deprivation itself. While there are several schools of thought on the matter (see pp. 309–312), we do not yet have a generally accepted model or theory of deprivation upon which to base empirical measurement (Bebington and Davies 1980). The paradox, of course, is that the development of the one is to a large extent dependent on the other.

## The perceived environment

Whereas traditional approaches to the analysis of urban spatial differentiation have been almost exclusively concerned with measuring, mapping and classifying objective characteristics, a new approach has recently emerged which is not merely different but in direct contrast. It is wholeheartedly subjective, with an emphasis on studying the world as it seems to be rather than as it is: not as physical reality but as perceived experience. The aim is to portray the city as it is seen through the prism of people's personal experience, coloured by their hopes and fears and distorted by prejudice and predilection.

Although this interest in the perceived environment can be traced back to Lewin (1983) – a psychologist, de Lauwe (1952) – a sociologist, and Boulding (1956) – an economist, it was not until the early 1960s and the publication of papers by Lowenthal (1961) and Kirk (1963) that the utility of perception studies became known widely to a geographical audience. Since then, however, a large number of geographers have become involved in the increasingly interdisciplinary field of environmental perception, and there now exists a significant body of scientific research on the perception of the urban environment by its inhabitants (Downs and Stea 1973; Gold 1979; Moore and Golledge 1976; Pocock and Hudson 1978). Furthermore, general interest in perception studies has been reinforced by the emergence within geography of a school of thought stemming from the phenomenological tradition of Husserl and giving a central position on the experiential 'sense of place' associated with different urban environments (Tuan 1974, 1978; Relph 1976). The net effect has been to provide geographers with a stimulating new dimension of study. As Herbert and Johnston observe (1976b: 13), 'It has been the arrival of this new dimension, perhaps more than any other, which has pulled up social geographers with a jolt.' Not only does it provide a powerful antidote to the impression that cities are populated by land uses and pathologies rather than people; it also provides an enlightening background to the behavioural patterns which contribute so much to the 'objective' geography of the city.

Central to the whole approach are the images, inner representations, mental maps and schemata derived from people's perception of the environment. These are the result of a process in which personal experience and values are used to filter the barrage of environmental stimuli to which the brain is subjected, thus producing a partial, simplified (and often distorted) version of reality. The same environmental stimuli may thus evoke different responses from different individuals, with each person effectively living in his or her 'own world'. Nevertheless, it is logical to assume that certain aspects of imagery will be held in common over quite large groups of people because of similarities in their socialization, past experience and present urban environment.

What are these images like? What urban geographies exist within the minds of urbanites, and how do they relate to the objective world? As yet it is possible to give only tentative answers to these questions, for the study of the perceived environment is still in its infancy, and most existing work has been produced in an *ad hoc*, atheoretical way. What is clear is that people do not have a single image or mental map which can be consulted or recalled at will. Rather, we appear to possess a series of latent images which are unconsciously operationalized in reponse to specific behavioural tasks. In this context, a useful distinction can be made between:

1. the *designative* aspects of people's imagery which relate to the mental or cog-nitive organization of space necessary to their orientation within the urban environment; and

2. the *appraisive* aspects of imagery which reflect people's feelings about the environment and which are related to decision-making within the urban environment.

## Designative aspects of urban imagery

The seminal work in this field was Kevin Lynch's book *The Image of the City*, published in 1960 and based on the results of lengthy interviews with (very) small samples of middle- and upper-class residents in three cities: Boston, Jersey City, and Los Angeles (see also Lynch 1984). In the course of these interviews, respondents were asked to describe the city, to indicate the location of features which were important to them, and to make outline sketches, the intention being to gently tease out a mental map from the subject's consciousness. From an examination of the resultant data, Lynch found that people apparently structure their mental image of the city in terms of five different kinds of *elements*. These are:

1. *Paths*: the channels along which the observer customarily, occasionally, or potentially moves. They may be streets, walkways, transit lines, canals, railroads. For many people, these are the predominant elements in their image. People observe the city while moving through it, and along these paths the other environmental elements are arranged and related.

2. *Edges*: Edges are the linear elements not used or considered as paths by the observer. They are the boundaries between two phases, linear breaks in continuity: shores, railroad cuts, edges of developments, walls. They may be barriers more or less penetrable, which close one region off from another; or they may be seams, lines along which two regions are related and joined together.

3. *Districts*: Districts are the medium-to-large sections of the city, conceived of as having two-dimesional extent, which the observer mentally enters . . . and which are recognizable as having some common, identifying character.

4. *Nodes*: are the strategic spots in a city into which an observer can enter, and which are the intensive foci to and from which he is travelling.

They may be primarily junctions, places of a break in transportation, a crossing or convergence of paths . . . Or the nodes may simply be concentrations which gain their importance from being the condensation of some use or physical character, as a street corner hangout or an enclosed square. Some of these concentration nodes are the focus and epitome of a district, over which their influence radiates and of which they stand as a symbol.

5. *Landmarks*: Landmarks are another type of point-reference, but in this case the observer does not enter them . . . They are usually a rather simply defined physical object: building, sign, store, or mountain. (Lynch 1960: 47–8).

As Lynch pointed out, none of these elements exist in isolation in people's minds. Districts are structured with nodes, defined by edges, penetrated by paths and sprinkled with landmarks. Elements thus overlap and pierce one another, and some may be psychologically more dominant than others.

Lynch also found that the residents of a given city tend to structure their mental map of the city with the same elements as one another, and he produced ingenious maps with which to demonstrate the collective image of Boston (Fig. 4.23), using symbols of different boldness to indicate the proportion of respondents who had mentioned each element. Another important finding was that, whereas the collective image of Boston was structured by a fairly dense combination of elements, those of Los Angeles and Jersey City were much less complex. Lynch suggested that this reflected a difference in the *legibility* or imageability of the cities resulting from differences in the 'form qualities' of the built environment. These, he argued, include the clarity and simplicity of visible form, the continuity and 'rhythm' of edges and surfaces, the dominance (whether in terms of size, intensity of interest) of one morphological unit over others, and the presence or absence of directional differentiation in terms of asymmetries, gradients and radial features.

Although Lynch's work has been criticized for its intuitive approach to the identification of image elements and the validity of attempting to aggregate the imagery of people with quite different backgrounds and experience has been questioned (Lee 1976), his

techniques have found wide application elsewhere (Harrison and Howard 1972: Milgram and Jodelet 1976; De Jonge 1962; Orleans 1973; Francescato and Mebane 1973; Goodey *et al.* 1971), and these studies provide an intriguing pool of information about the way different groups of people in different places structure their image of the city. Amsterdam, for example, was found to be much more legible to its inhabitants than were Rotterdam or The Hague to theirs, apparently because of its striking spider-web pattern of concentric canals and its strong linear core incorporating the Mint Square, the Central Station and The Dam – a great square containing the Royal Palace. The same study, however, found evidence to suggest that although environments with salient paths and nodes tend to be most legible, people also like *illegible* environments, possibly because of abstract qualities such as 'quaintness' (de Jonge 1962). A comparison of Milan and Rome found that both cities are highly legible, but in different ways: the mental maps of Milanese are structured by a clearly-connected set of paths relating to their city's radial street pattern, whereas Romans' mental maps exhibit a greater diversity of content and tend to be structured around the landmarks and edges associated with their city's historic buildings, its hills, and the course of the Tiber (Francescato and Mebane 1973).

The same study was also able to demonstrate the differences which exist between the social classes in their image of the city. Basically, middle-class residents held a more comprehensive image than lower-class residents, covering a much wider territory and including a larger number and greater variety of elements. A similar conclusion can be drawn from the maps compiled from respondents living in different neighbourhoods in Los Angeles, where ethnicity is closely associated with socio-economic status. The high-status, white residents of Westwood, (a 'foothills' neighbourhood situated between Beverly Hills and Santa Monica) have a well-formed, detailed and generalized image of the entire Los Angeles Basin (Fig. 4.24a), whereas the middle-class residents of Northridge (a suburb in the San Fernando Valley) have a less

**Fig. 4.23** Designative images of Boston: (A) as derived from verbal interviewing; (B) as derived from sketch maps. *Source*: Lynch (1960), p. 146.

**Fig. 4.24** Designative images of Los Angeles: (A) as seen by residents of Westwood; (B) as seen by residents of Northridge; (C) as seen by residents of Avalon; (D) as seen by residents of Boyle Heights.    *Source*: Orleans (1973), pp. 120–123.

comprehensive image which is oriented away from the city proper (Fig. 4.24b):

As a sign on the Ventura Freeway proclaims: 'Topanga Plaza (in the [San Fernando] Valley) is downtown for over a million people.' Thus, although they have a reasonably detailed image of the San Fernando Valley extension of the city, the Santa Monica mountain chain effectively segregates Northridge residents from the rest of this sprawling metropolis (Orleans 1973: 118–19).

At the other end of the socio-economic ladder, residents of the black ghetto neighbourhood of Avalon, near Watts, have a vaguer image of the city which, in contrast to the white images which are structured around the major east-west boulevards and freeways, is dominated by the grid-iron layout of streets between Watts and the city centre (Fig. 4.24c). Reasons for these differences are not hard to find. The greater wealth and extended education of higher-status whites confers a greater mobility, a greater propensity to visit other parts of the city, and a tendency to utilize a wider range of information sources. In contrast, the less mobile poor, with a shorter journey to work, and with less exposure to other sources of environmental information, will naturally tend to have a local rather than a metropolitan orientation: something which will be buttressed by racial or ethnic segregation. Where language barriers further reinforce this introversion, the likely outcome is an extremely restricted image of the city, as in the Spanish-speaking neighbourhood of Boyle Heights (Fig. 4.24d).

One aspect of Lynch's technique which has been pursued separately for its own sake is the use of sketch maps. Although they do not lend themselves to the compilation of a composite image, sketch maps do help to illuminate the way in which people perceive the city. The images of New York portrayed in Figures 4.25 and 4.26 show very clearly how each person structures the city quite differently, with the organization and content of their sketch reflecting their own life-style and emotional concerns. These two sketches are part of the sample of 332 derived from a questionnaire in *New York* magazine and organized by Milgram, who found that, in addition to the idiosyncratic aspects of the sketches,

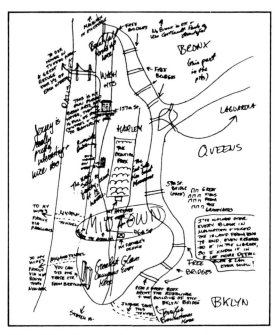

**Fig. 4.25** A mental map of New York City drawn by a 29-year-old writer from the West Side. *Source*: Duncan (1977), p. 53. c 1977, News Group Publications Inc.

many were drawn from the perspective of the individual's immediate neighbourhood (as in Fig. 4.26). On the other hand, many respondents made Manhattan the central feature, even though they lived and worked in one of the city's other boroughs (Duncan 1977).

Appleyard (1970) has suggested that the kinds of map people draw can be categorized according to their *accuracy* and the *type of element* emphasized, with a basic division between those who emphasize 'sequential' elements (such as roads and pathways) and those who emphasize 'spatial' elements (such as individual buildings, landmarks and districts). His eight-fold typology has been used in a number of studies (Goodchild 1974; Pocock 1975; Spencer and Lloyd 1974), and it appears that the overall tendency is for a sequential structuring, with working-class and female respondents tending to draw the least sophisticated maps. Most researchers have also noted, like Milgram, the tendency for people's mental maps to be oriented around the home

**Fig. 4.26** A mental map of New York City drawn by a teacher in her forties and living in Harlem. *Source*: Duncan (1977), p. 53. *c*. 1977, News Group Publications Inc.

neighbourhood or city centre, while Pocock (1976) has emphasized the tendency for people to 'better' the environment, recording a structure more uniform and less haphazard than the real world – a tendency which evidently increases with familiarity with the city concerned.

*Cognitive distance*

Underlying the organization of people's mental maps is the *cognitive distance* between image elements, and this is another aspect of imagery which has been shown to exhibit interesting and important regularities. Cognitive distance is the basis for the spatial information stored in cognitive representations of the environment. It is generated from a variety of mechanisms which includes the brain's perception of the distance between visible objects, the use-patterns and structure of the visible environment, and the impact of

symbolic representations of the environment such as maps and road signs (Briggs 1973). For the majority of people, intra-urban cognitive distance is generally greater than objective distance, regardless of city size and their usual means of transport (Canter and Tagg 1975; Gollege *et al.* 1969; Lee 1970), although there is evidence to suggest that this over-estimation declines with increasing physical distance. Thus in both London and Dundee distances were in fact reported as being shorter than they were in reality (Canter 1975; Pocock 1972). Interestingly, the break-point in the relationship was much greater in London than in Dundee, suggesting that the overall scale and layout of the environment is itself an important determinant of cognitive distance. Gollege and Zannaras have argued that people's images and cognitive distance estimates are a function of the number and type of environmental stimuli, or *cues*, they encounter along the paths, or *supports*, that they normally use, and that the actual form of the city is of greater importance in determining the cue selection process than any personal characteristics, including length of residence. They have also suggested that different types of urban structure will result in the selection of different cues, thus generating a different metric of cognitive distance and producing different kinds of mental maps. Residents of concentrically-zoned cities might be expected to respond more to changes in land use, for example, than residents of sectorally-structured cities, who might be expected to respond more to traffic-related cues along the typical path from suburb to city centre and back (Gollege and Zannaras 1970, 1973).

Another interesting feature of cognitive distance is that it appears to be dependent upon orientation in relation to the city centre. Lee, for example, drew the conclusion from a study of Cambridge housewives' imagery that the 'schema of the whole city includes a *focal orientation*, built up by the satisfactions of the centre. These satisfactions . . . have a dynamic effect on the perceptual process, causing a foreshortening of perceived distances in the inward direction' (Lee 1970: 41). To see if this tendency operated on a wider basis, Lee conducted an experiment in which 171 students from the University of Dundee were asked to estimate the walking distance from a fixed focal point to 22 well-known locations within the city. These were paired so as to be approximately the same distance inward to the centre or outward to the periphery; but the cognitive distances derived from the students for inward destinations were significantly shorter than those for outward destinations (Lee 1970). Pocock and Hudson (1978) point out that this tendency is consistent with research findings from other studies which have related cognitive distance to the characteristics of 'origins' and 'destinations' in mental maps: cognitive distance tends to shrink with the perceived utility or attractiveness of the 'destination'. Thus a general survey of neighbourhood characteristics in Baltimore, Maryland, revealed that desirable elements such as parks, post offices, and libraries were felt to be closer to respondents' homes than they actually were, while less desirable elements such as parking lots and expressway interchanges were thought to be further away than they actually were (Lowery 1973). Similarly, socially desirable neighbourhoods are often felt to be nearer than they really are (Eyles 1968; Watson 1972); and the attractions of shopping centres tend to foreshorten the real distance between the home and the shop (Brennan 1948; Klein 1967; Thompson 1963).

Given the distorting effect of the values attached to different 'origins' and 'destinations', it seems likely that people possess a basic image of the city consisting of the branching network of their 'action space' which undergoes topological deformation, perhaps hourly, as they move about the city from one major node – home, workplace, city centre – to another. 'Who, for instance, has not experienced a homeward trip to be shorter than the identical outward journey?' (Pocock and Hudson 1978: 57). The relationship of such a cognitive structure to the more general Lynch-type image of the city has not yet been properly explored, but it seems logical to expect that most people will possess an interlocking hierarchy of images which relates directly to the different geographical scales at which they act out different aspects of their lives.

## Appraisive aspects of urban imagery

In many circumstances it is not so much the structural aspects of people's imagery which are important so much as the meaning attached to, or evoked by, the different components of the urban environment in their mental map. Behaviour of all kinds obviously depends not only on *what* people perceive as being *where* but also on how they *feel* about these different elements. A specific node or district, for example, may be regarded as attractive or repellent, exciting or relaxing, fearsome or reassuring or, more likely, it may evoke a combination of such feelings. These reactions reflect what Pocock and Hudson (1978) have called the *appraisive* aspects of urban imagery.

In overall terms, the appraisive imagery of the city is reflected by the desirability or attractiveness of different neighbourhoods as residential locations. This is something which can be measured and aggregated to produce a map of the collective image of the city which can be regarded as a synthesis of all the feelings, positive and negative, which people have about different neighbourhoods. A good example of this approach is provided by Clark and Cadwallader's (1973) work on Los Angeles, in which respondents were asked to indicate the three neighbourhoods they would most like to live in, bearing in mind their family income. Fig. 4.27 shows their first-choice preferences, revealing an interesting geography which is by no means a simple reflection of the 'objective' socio-economic geography of the city. Thus, while the widespread popularity of communities such as Santa Monica, Westwood Village, Beverly Hills and Hollywood could be accounted for in terms of their physically attractive environment, the presence of several well-developed employment centres, and a wide variety of shopping and entertainment facilities, and the popularity of 'beach' communities such as Redondo Beach could be related to their lifestyle, Clark and Cadwallader point out that

**Fig. 4.27**  Residential desirability of Los Angeles neighbourhoods.    *Source*: Clark and Cadwallader (1973), p. 697.

the widespread preference for communities in the eastern portion of the Los Angeles basin – Pasadena, Monterey Park, Alhambra and Arcadia – is 'less easily understood'. The inclusion of large parts of the San Fernando Valley in the least-preferred category is also puzzling, since it has been one of the most rapidly-growing residential regions of the Los Angeles metropolitan area.

In a very different setting, Smith and Ford (1985) have examined the attractiveness of different public housing environments to public housing tenants in Birmingham, England. They found that people's preferences were highly influenced by their own designative imagery, with the result that most of the most-preferred and many of the least-preferred environments were selected from the sector of the city which people knew best – usually their 'home' sector. Beyond this, it seems, most people also tend to prefer well-established suburban environments that have a low incidence of Asian and West Indian immigrants.

### The cognitive dimensions of the urban environment

Given that people are able to make these overall evaluations of residential desirability, the question arises as to their derivation. In other words, what are the components of people's overall evaluation of a given place or neighbourhood, and how do they feel about these particular aspects of the environment? Johnston (1973d), in an attempt to explain the process of neighbourhood evaluation, has investigated the perceived attributes of eleven different suburbs in Christchurch, New Zealand. His analysis suggests that neighbourhood preferences are based on three underlying evaluative dimensions which are invariant with area of residence in the city:

1. the 'impersonal environment', composed mainly of the physical attributes of the neighbourhood;
2. the 'interpersonal environment', composed mainly of the social attributes of the neighbourhood;
3. the locational attributes of the neighbourhood.

Another recent analysis of the cognitive dimensions of the urban environment which asked respondents to consider the relevance of 100 different items to their *own* neighbourhood (in the San Francisco Bay area) found as many as 20 'meaningful' dimensions. These include:

1. aspects related to the *aesthetics* of the neighbourhood – its general appearance, tidiness, colourfulness, and level of maintenance, and the 'spaciousness' and general level of service provision in the area;
2. aspects related to *neighbours* – their friendliness, helpfulness, or snobbishness; and the feelings of contentment, happiness, pride, power, loneliness and safety which stem from living among them;
3. aspects related to *noise* – these include noise from the immediate environment (neighbours' children or lawnmowers, for example) as well as noise from aircraft and trains;
4. aspects related to *safety* – these centred on two distinctive dimensions, one related to danger from traffic and the other to the safety and security of people and property;
5. aspects related to *accessibility* and mobility – these include accessibility to freeways, neighbourhood parking conditions, and accessibility to public transport;
6. aspects regarded as *annoyances*, such

as the lack of privacy, the incidence of door-to-door salesmen, and the presence of animal nuisances (Carp *et al.* 1976).

Generalizations such as these should be treated with caution, however. Both the Christchurch and San Francisco studies were based on analyses of data which were aggregated across different neighbourhoods. Cadwallader (1979), using a methodology similar to Johnston's in an analysis of Madison, Wisconsin, found that the evaluative dimensions associated with different neighbourhoods were in fact 'far from identical', although there was some evidence that similar neighbourhoods evoked similar cognitive responses and that Johnston's three main evaluative dimensions were 'generally identifiable' in people's feelings about different neighbourhoods. There clearly remains a good deal of investigation to be undertaken before the composition of appraisive imagery in cities can be fully understood. Moreover, it must be recognized that there are some important aspects of appraisive imagery which extend beyond the context of residential desirability, having been derived from people's evaluations of the urban environment in less specific circumstances. This is illustrated by the results of a survey of residents of Bath, Somerset (Harrison and Sarre 1971). Using a methodology based on the repertory grid, an interview technique which ensures a minimum of interference from the researcher's ideas, Harrison and Sarre found that people's appraisive imagery tended simply to contrast places which were liked and beautiful (especially the Georgian areas of the city) with those which were disliked and ugly (mainly the working-class, industrialized areas of the lower Avon valley). A second dimension was found to contrast places in which respondents were involved (the city centre and the middle-class residential areas) with places where they felt out of place (notably the Georgian areas); while a third dimension contrasted places with a wide significance and which had been known for a long time with recently-discovered places of only local significance.

Other, more specific aspects of appraisive imagery have been elicited by researchers pursuing particular themes. Ley (1974), for instance, has illustrated the local geography of perceived danger in an inner-city neighbour-hood in Philadelphia, showing how most people recognized – and avoided – the danger points near gang hang-outs, abandoned build-ings, and places where drugs are peddled. On a larger scale, Milgram has compiled a 'fear map' from a survey of New Yorkers (Fig. 4.28), which highlights the rather different kinds of urban environment – Harlem, Times Square, Wall Street, and Central Park – which generate feelings of fear or oppression among a city's inhabitants (Duncan 1977). Tranter and Parkes (1979) have pointed out that such imagery is often time-dependent: public parks, for example, may be felt to be tranquil and safe places by day but might induce quite different feelings at night. This points to an area of research which has yet to be fully explored; and there are still other aspects of appraisive imagery which have barely been touched upon by geographic research. One of these is the way in which some areas of some large cities (Glasgow and Liverpool, for example) become stigmatized, with their inhabitants being labelled as 'work-shy', 'unreliable', or 'trouble-some', thus making it difficult for them to compete in local housing and job-markets (McGregor 1977). Another concerns the role of clothes and personal objects (rather than buildings and social characteristics) in contri-buting towards our feelings about different parts of the city. As Raban (1975) observes, many of our clothes and personal possessions are used, consciously or not, to communicate what we like or believe in: the pair of shoes, the book, the wall poster and the cut of a pair of jeans become 'briefly exhibited signs and badges' which not only help their owners to say something about themselves but which also help others to attach meaning and signifi-cance to their owners and to *their owners' environment*. Raban (1975: 168) gives his own reaction to the people he associates with different Underground routes in London:

People who live on the Northern Line I take to be sensitive citizens; it is a friendly communication route where one notes commuters reading proper books and, when they talk,

finishing their sentences. But the Piccadilly Line is full of fly-by-nights and stripe-shirted young men who run dubious agencies, and I go to elaborate lengths to avoid travelling on it. It is an entirely irrational way of imposing order on the city, but it does give it a shape in the mind, takes whole chunks of experience out of the realm of choice and deliberation, and places them in the less strenuous context of habit and prejudice.

Yet another under-investigated area concerns the way in which perception of the city in influenced by symbolism which has been culturally developed and which appears to exist collectively on a sub-cognitive level (Lasswell 1979). Obvious examples include the symbolic and emotional potency of special historic districts, the authoritarian symbolism of administrative sub-districts, and the senti-mental symbolism of the area lived in during childhood. Thus, just as individual personality is reflected in home and possessions, so collec-tive personality and values are translated into the wider environment of 'cultural landscapes' (Lowenthal and Prince 1964). The existence of such relationships between places and people leads to the idea of a 'sense of place', which incorporates aspects of imageability, the symbolic meaning of places, and 'topo-philia' – the affective *bond* between man and place (Tuan 1974; Relph 1976).

### Images of the home area

In the general context of urban geography, the most important aspect of this sense of place is probably the attachment people feel to their *home area*. There is no doubt that the immediate physical and social environment is crucially important in the early psychological and social development of the individual, and it seems that this generates a strong bond – often amounting almost to reverence – for the territorial homeland: a phenomenon which Tuan (1976) calls 'geopiety'. Such feelings are clearly related to the idea of territoriality (see p. 83), and there is plenty of evidence to suggest that they exist as a kind of latent 'neighbourhood attachment' in most people who have lived in a particular area for any length of time. The most striking evidence of such feelings emerges after people have been forced to leave their home neighbourhood in

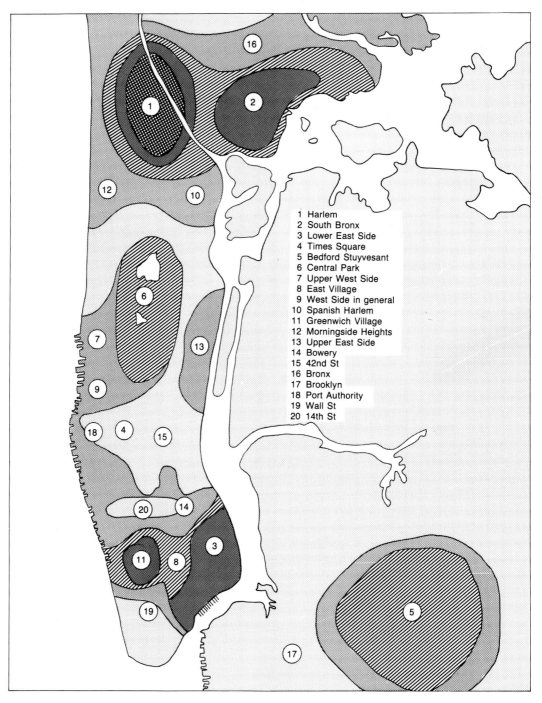

1 Harlem
2 South Bronx
3 Lower East Side
4 Times Square
5 Bedford Stuyvesant
6 Central Park
7 Upper West Side
8 East Village
9 West Side in general
10 Spanish Harlem
11 Greenwich Village
12 Morningside Heights
13 Upper East Side
14 Bowery
15 42nd St
16 Bronx
17 Brooklyn
18 Port Authority
19 Wall St
20 14th St

**Fig. 4.28** The topography of fear in New York, 1977. The darker the shading, the more widespread the fear among New Yorkers of that particular part of town. The numbered locations list, in rank order, the 20 'most fearsome' neighbourhoods in the city.
*Source*: Duncan (1977), p. 57. c. 1977, News Group Publications Inc.

the cause of redevelopment or renewal schemes, when many report feelings of grief at the loss of their old neighbourhood (Fried 1963). This is because, as Pocock and Hudson (1978: 85) observe: 'It is not only the built environment that is razed but also the contextual environment, the symbol of life's experience: part of people's roots, part of *themselves* is lost.'

Most people seem to have an attachment to a home area which they mentally 'recognize' and identify with. Evidence for this comes from the Royal Commission on Local Government in England (1969), which contracted Research Services Ltd to carry out a survey of a carefully stratified sample of 2,000 in order to ascertain the most appropriate size of local government units. One of the questions asked in the study was: 'Is there an area around here, where you are now living, which you would say you belonged to, and where you feel "at home"?' Approximately 80 per cent of the respondents claimed to possess some feelings of attachment to a 'home' community area, and this tendency tended to increase with length of residence. Similar findings have emerged from a survey of Los Angeles residents (Everitt and Cadwallader 1972, 1977), where it was also found that the size and orientation of husbands' and wives' home areas tended to differ, largely as a result of their differential use of space around the home. In addition, it seems that subjectively-defined local areas exhibit a high degree of stability over time (Pacione 1983).

The home area thus seems to exist and to be closely related to people's 'activity space' around the home. Jonathan Raban (1975: 166–7) gives us this graphic description of his own 'home area':

The Greater London Council is responsible for a sprawl shaped like a rugby ball about twenty-five miles long and twenty miles wide; my city is a concise kidney-shaped patch within that space, in which no point is more than about seven miles from any other. On the south, it is bounded by the river, on the north by the fat tongue of Hampstead Heath and Highgate Village, on the west by Brompton cemetery and on the east by Liverpool Street station. I hardly ever trespass beyond those limits and when I do I feel I'm in foreign territory, a landscape of hazard and

rumour. Kilburn, on the far side of my northern and western boundaries, I imagine to be inhabited by vicious drunken Irishmen; Hackney and Dalston by crooked car dealers with pencil moustaches and goldfilled teeth; London south of the Thames still seems impossibly illogical and contingent, a territory of meaningless circles, incomprehensible one-way systems, warehouses and cage-bird shops. Like any tribesman hedging himself in a stockade of taboos, I mark my boundaries with graveyards, terminal transportation points and wildernesses. Beyond them, nothing is to be trusted and anything might happen.

The constrictedness of this private city-within-a-city has the character of a self-fulfilling prophecy. Its boundaries, originally arrived at by chance and usage, grow more not less real the longer I live in London. I have friends who live in Clapham, only three miles away, but to visit them is a definite journey, for it involves crossing the river. I can, though, drop in on friends in Islington, twice as far away as Clapham, since it is within what I feel to be my own territory.

But how typical is this imagery, and how might it relate to people's social behaviour? Terence Lee, a psychologist, has made a major contribution to this issue (Lee 1968). He suggests that people build up a mental model, or *schema*, of the area in which their daily lives are played out – their home area. In order to elaborate this idea, Lee developed a technique in which respondents were asked to 'please draw a line around the point which you consider acts as your neighbourhood or district', and applied it to a representative sample of the residential areas of Cambridge, England. While it can be argued that such instructions predispose an obliging respondent to construe his or her world in a way that may be alien or unnatural, it should be emphasized that the technique was used only after a large number of pilot interviews had suggested that some kind of neighbourhood structuring of the city was widespread, and that people described their area mainly by delineating its boundaries in a variety of ways. As in the Royal Commission survey, Lee found that about 80 per cent of the people could delineate a home area. What is interesting, however, is that these turned out to be highly personal and idiosyncratic, with a map of superimposed home areas resembling 'a plate of spaghetti'. Nevertheless, there were also several interesting and significant regularities in the data. Firstly, the *area* covered by people's schemata tended to be fairly consistent: about 100 acres (40 ha.). Secondly, it was found that this size was quite unrelated to changes in population density, so that the home areas or schemata of suburban residents tend to extend over the same amount of territory as the home areas of inner-city residents. Lee suggests that this is probably because the home area is dependent on an action space based on walking distance and argues that this is of special significance to urban planning, since his findings suggest that it is possible to achieve the necessary number of consumers to support basic neighbourhood services and facilities within the kind of territory that appears to correspond with people's perception of a meaningful home area. From a closer examination of the 165 schemata produced by his respondents, Lee has also proposed a typology of neighbourhoods:

1. *The social acquaintance neighbourhood*: a small area in which people 'keep themselves to themselves' and where the main support in times of trouble is from kin rather than neighbours. This kind of neighbourhood is much more a function of people than locality. That is, it could be found in a variety of localities but only amongst a certain kind of person.

2. *The homogeneous neighbourhood*: here the schema includes greater awareness of physical aspects of the environment as well as people. An underlying principle is that the neighbourhood is comprised not only of 'people like us' but also of 'people who live in houses like ours'.

3. *The unit neighbourhood*: a territory which approximates to planners' conceptions of 'neighbourhood' – larger, with a heterogeneous population and a balanced range of amenities.

Further analysis of people's schemata was achieved by computing a 'neighbourhood quotient' which measured the size and complexity (in terms of the content of houses, shops and amenities) of neighbourhoods while holding constant the physical area in which they were drawn. The mean value of these quotients for a particular social or spatial group thus reflects its overall level of 'sociophysical involvement' in the locality, while the range of values serves as a measure of that group's agreement or, as Lee calls it, 'consentaneity'. Using this technique, Lee found evidence to support the classic planning axiom that a neighbourhood with well-defined boundaries will have an associated high level of social participation; and he also found that participation tends to increase with the social heterogeneity of an area's population: something which also has relevance to planning practice (see also Bardo 1984).

The very existence of these schemata, of course, is highly relevant to the debate on communities and neighbourhoods outlined in Chapter 3, and several researchers have attempted to relate functional neighbourhoods (based on patterns of social interaction and economic behaviour) to the perceived neighbourhood or home area. Buttimer (1972), for example, has demonstrated the rather variable relationship between the size and orientation of people's 'micro-service' activity spaces, 'macro-service' activity spaces, 'social participation' spaces and perceived home areas in different parts of Glasgow; while Everitt (1976) has demonstrated the broad congruence between the perceived home areas of a sample of Los Angeles residents and their activity patterns in relation to workplace, friends' residences, and clubs. Perhaps the most useful work in this context is the re-analysis by Berry and Kasarda (1977) of the Royal Commission data. They found that community sentiments, including the ability to identify a 'home area', are primarily influenced by participation in local social networks, and that this participation, in turn, is influenced mainly by length of residence in the area. This relationship held true even when population size, density, socio-economic status and life-cycle factors were held constant, suggesting that the 'systemic model' of community organization – based on length of residence and the strength of local social networks – is more appropriate than the 'linear development' model based on population size and density and stemming from the ideas of Tönnies and Wirth.

# 5 Housing demand, residential mobility and urban residential structure

Although there are several important aspects of urban social geography which are concerned with people's behaviour outside the home, the mosaic of residential neighbourhoods is clearly the central concern of the subject. Having outlined the social dimensions of urban life and described the spatial configuration of the residential mosaic from several perspectives, attention is now turned towards the mechanisms and processes which produce these patterns.

As will already be apparent, it is possible to identify a large number of different influences on the residential structure of the city. What is more difficult, however, is to establish an overall perspective of their relative importance and the way in which they interact in shaping the residential environment. Several theoretical perspectives have been developed to complement or challenge the conventional wisdom of Wirthian and ecological theories and their derivations; and each tends to embrace several different schools of thought. Neo-classical economic theory, behaviouralist models, 'managerialist' approaches and structuralist analyses derived from Marxist theory all merit attention, since the central concern of all of them is the interpretation of the workings of urban land and housing markets. In this chapter, the focus of attention is on *demand-based* explanations of residential differentiation, following the 'mainstream' tradition of research which has highlighted the behaviour of households in competing for land, a dwelling and an 'address' within the city. An introductory consideration of neoclassical economic land-use theory is followed by a detailed examination of the determinants of housing demand and a summary of the behavioural aspects of residential mobility, leading to an evaluation of the cumulative effects of mobility processes on residential differentiation and the socio-spatial structure of the city.

## The neoclassical economic approach

Models of urban structure based on neoclassical micro-economic theory stand with Burgess's ecological model as the most widely-known approaches to explaining the internal structure of cities. Originally developed to illuminate intra-urban patterns of land values and the relative location of different urban land-uses, these models are essentially elaborations of the von Thünen agricultural land-use model. They stem from a tradition of land economics which can be traced to Haig (1962). Hurd (1903) and Ratcliff (1949), but their full exposition dates from the more recent work of Alonso (1960, 1964), Wingo (1961), Mills (1967), Kain (1962), Muth (1969) and A. Evans (1973). The cornerstone of the approach is an attempt to determine the pattern of land consumption through an analysis of the pricing mechanism, with a central role being given to the relationship between location, ground rent and transport costs. It describes a process through which households and firms compete for space in a way that maximizes satisfaction, within budget constraints, for every competitor; thus also maximizing the 'efficiency' of the urban spatial economy. The end result is a static equilibrium which simultaneously explains the aggregate pattern of land uses, house prices (or rents) and population densities.

## Assumptions

Such analysis is subject to a number of initial assumptions. Most models assume an urban area located within a uniform plain, so that all sites are homogeneous apart from their relative distances from one another. The CBD is assumed to be located centrally within this area and is therefore the single most accessible point. It is also assumed to be the only employment centre in the whole city. Transport is assumed to be ubiquitous, with transport costs being a direct function of the linear distance between places. The city is assumed to be inhabited by 'economic man': a rational being whose behaviour is geared to maximizing profits, utility and satisfaction. Competition between firms and households is assumed to be perfect, with no restrictions on land or buildings and no buyers or sellers with sufficient resources to affect the state of the market by their own activities.

## The theory

Given these conditions, the argument is basically as follows: the most central sites will be more attractive than others for all types of land users; they are most desirable for shops because their accessibility enables retailers to tap the largest possible potential market; they are most desirable for manufacturers because their centrality minimizes the aggregate costs of assembling raw materials and distributing finished products; and they are most desirable for householders because their proximity to jobs minimizes the costs of commuting. However, the geometry of the city means that there are relatively few central sites in relation to the total space available. As a result, competition for central sites will be intense,

and the prices offered for them will be higher than those offered for more peripheral sites. The ground rent accruing to each site may thus be seen simply as a charge for the utility of accessibility.

Nevertheless, it is recognized that different types of land users will place different financial evaluations on the utility of centrality, depending upon their particular budget constraints. It is, for example, logical to expect shops to be both able and willing to outbid households for central sites because the extra income accruing to a centrally-located shop through increased custom is likely to outweigh the savings in commuting costs obtained at the same site by a household – or even by several households living in the same dwelling. Similarly, it is recognized that the utility of progressively less central sites will decline at different rates for different land users, with the marginal losses from decreased accessibility being greater for retailing and commercial users than for residential users. Because of this, Alonso (1960) suggested, each type of land user can be thought of as having a characterisitc *bid-rent curve*, reflecting the prices they are prepared to pay for sites at different distances from the CBD (Fig. 5.1). These curves are similar to the indifference curves of neoclassical economics in that each point on the curve represents a location of equal utility for that particular type of land user. Thus, for retailing, lower sales further out are offset by lower rents; and for households the lower rents of peripheral locations are balanced by the higher costs of commuting. In theory, therefore, each land user should be indifferent to locating anywhere along its bid-rent curve.

What does this mean in terms of the structure of the city? Juxtaposing the bid-rent curves of different users (Fig. 5.2) reveals that those with steeper curves – retailing and commercial activities – capture the more central sites while those with shallower curves – residential users – are left with peripheral sites. This locational equilibrium is reflected in a simple pattern of concentric zones: a 'doughnut city' consisting of a CBD surrounded by a residential ring. As Ratcliff (1949: 375) concluded: 'in summary one might say that

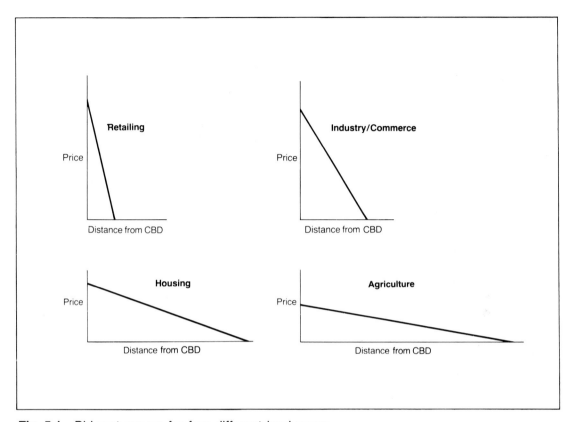

**Fig. 5.1** Bid-rent curves for four different land users.

the structure of the city is determined through the dollar evaluation of the importance of convenience.'

A more detailed breakdown of land-use types would provide a more detailed picture of urban spatial structure, with more zones. It might be determined, for example, that under conditions of perfect competition the outer reaches of the CBD would consist of successive zones of offices, food stores and warehouses. This, however, does not tell us a great deal about *residential* differentiation. In fact, further assumptions about household behaviour must be made in order to predict the locational equilibrium of different kinds of household. The usual assumption, following Alonso (1960; 1964), is that different house-holds will bid for different-sized sites in different locations according to their relative preferences for living space and accessibility, subject to their overall budget constraints.

Assuming also that expenditure on other goods and services remains (proportionally) constant for every household, the issue becomes one of balancing 'the costs and bother of commuting against the advantages of cheaper land with increasing distance from the center of the city and the satisfaction of more space for living' (Alonso 1960: 154). In other words, residential locations represent a *trade-off* between land and commuting costs. For this reason, neoclassical economic models of the sort described here are commonly referred to as 'trade-off' models.

Given two types of household, 'rich' and 'poor', most trade-off models proceed on the assumption that the rich have a preference for living space and that they can, moreover, afford to pay the recurring costs of commuting. It follows from this that rich households will tend to live in the suburbs, consuming rela-tively large amounts of cheaper land, while

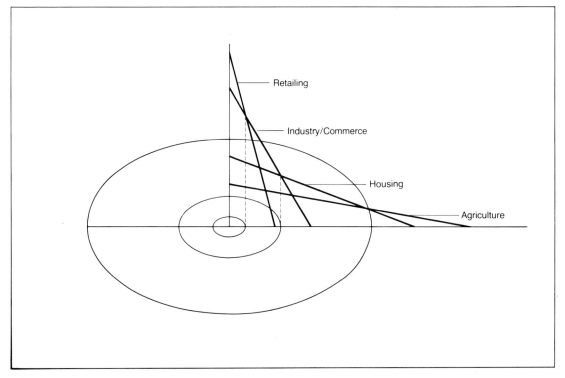

**Fig. 5.2** The zonal urban structure suggested by the basic trade-off model.

poor households are confined to more expensive inner-city sites. This apparent paradox is resolved by the fact that poor households adapt to the high cost of inner-city land by consuming less of it, and so living at higher densities. In spatial terms then, trade-off models project a locational equilibrium in which higher socio-economic groups occupy successively more peripheral zones of the basic 'doughnut' city. At the same time, it is possible to show that population densities decrease regularly with distance from the city centre while residential lot sizes increase steadily with distance in the same direction. In morphological terms, one might therefore expect to find a succession of:

1. large multi-family dwelling-units (which spread the high cost of central sites over as large as possible a number of purchasers or renters);
2. low- rise apartment buildings;
3. terrace housing and/or single-storey apartment blocks;
4. semi-detached single-family dwellings; and
5. detached single-family dwellings standing in large lots;

with each type of housing being occupied by different socio-economic groups.

## Extensions of the trade-off model

Such prognoses have sufficient resemblance to the reality of many cities to have encouraged researchers to extend the basic model, relaxing some of the more restrictive assumptions and introducing new variables. By allowing for secondary centres of employment and shopping and introducing the influence of major routeways, for example, it is possible to obtain a much more 'realistic' model of urban structure (Fig. 5.3). De Leeuw (1972),

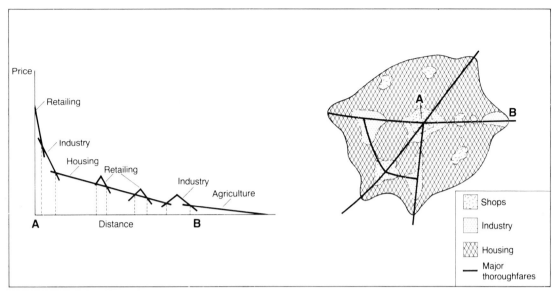

**Fig. 5.3**   The trade-off model modified to take into account the effects of major thoroughfares and additional nodes of shops and industry.

Papageorgiou (1976) and Romanos (1976) have elaborated the idea of multicentric urban areas in some detail, while others have extended the model in other ways. Among these are attempts to incorporate a choice of housing tenure (Doling 1973; Straszheim 1975), to include a fuller range of housing services (Olson 1969; Isler 1970), and to account for the effects of variations in environmental quality (Kain and Quigley 1972; Berry and Bednarz 1975), of different types of transport (Lave 1970), of local variations in housing taxes and subsidies (Beckmann 1973), and of racial discrimination (Kain and Quigley 1975). Moreover, the basic trade-off model has also been used to underpin the 'New Urban Economics', which attempts to integrate urban economics and welfare economics within a general equilibrium framework, using mathematical methods to derive generalized, qualitative results (Mills and MacKinnon 1973; Richardson 1977).

One of the most comprehensive attempts to extend the trade-off model is represented in the work of Evans (1973). Having set out the basic model in some detail, Evans introduces the assumption that households in a given socio-economic group will prefer to locate in the same neighbourhood as others of the same status, with the result that the model takes on a *sectoral* dimension in relation to socio-economic residential differentiation. Subsequently, Evans extends the model further. First, allowance is made for the phenomenon of 'gentrification', whereby higher-status people – from teaching, architecture or similar professions but not, usually, from the business world – invade inner-city areas, upgrading and renovating housing previously occupied by low-income households. Second, the effect of variations in economic activity rates is introduced, with the result that households with non-working wives and children of school age or less are shown to be more likely to live further from the CBD than households with no children, where the wife is likely to be in paid employment and the demand for space is likely to be less. Third, the effect of transport improvements is evaluated, and it is demonstrated that among the likely effects are: (a) a 'flight to the suburbs' by high-income households, and (b) the emergence of an inner-city ring of old, high-density housing which it is unprofitable to demolish. Finally, the effects of relaxing the assumption of a monocentric city are examined and it is shown that, among other things, the existence of employment sub-centres is likely to reinforce the sectoral dimension of urban structure. These elaborations illustrate what Evans clearly regards as the potency and flexibility of the trade-off approach, not only as a positive theory of residential location but also as a normative model with which to evaluate the effects of public policy on urban spatial structure.

## Criticisms of trade-off models

In contrast, many observers view such extensions merely as further wrinkles and twists to an analytical framework which is basically unsatisfactory. At the root of much criticism is the argument that the conditions of perfect competition assumed by neoclassical models are not even approached in the real world. Richardson (1971) has vigorously attacked trade-off models on these grounds, detailing the inconsistencies between their assumptions and the way people actually behave in the housing market. As he stressed, and as will be illustrated in subsequent sections of this chapter, people do not behave like 'economic man', always minimizing financial costs, travelling the shortest distance, possessing perfect knowledge, and choosing freely between different locations. Rather, their behaviour is conditioned by habit, convention, experience, deference, ignorance and, sometimes, downright irrationality; and their search for a place to live is constrained by limited time and money, imperfect information and the fact that only a relatively small proportion of residential sites are available for changes in occupancy in the short term. Moreover, the increasing dominance of large, powerful corporations, together with the influence of urban governments and their bureaucracies has led many to regard the 'free market' in land as something of a myth; and the housing market is clearly partitioned into distinct submarkets – all of which are imperfect (Bourne 1976; Ball 1979).

More specific criticism of neoclassical

models includes the charge that they rest too heavily on the assertion that people's preference for increased space rather than for the convenience of short journeys will lead them to purchase more space as they grow richer (Wheaton 1977). In fact, very little is known in a systematic, quantitative way about the way in which households make the complex trade-offs between housing expenditures, travel expenditure and the many other household budget items – holidays, clothing and so on – which loom large in many people's lives but which tend to be overlooked in most trade-off models. What empirical evidence there is, however, suggests that accessibility to workplaces is of minor importance in the household location decision (Short 1978a). In contrast, other less tangible environmental qualities and externalities (which would be difficult to build in to trade-off models) have been shown to be important determinants of the choice of residential environment (Michelson 1977).

Another weakness of the trade-off model to which Kirby (1976) has drawn attention is that whereas the analysis is based on the clearly established phenomenon of negative *land* price gradients, very few households do in fact purchase land. Most purchase (or rent) a *dwelling* from the existing stock and, because of the typical nature of this stock, the suburban dweller *must* purchase a large amount of surplus land in order to gain a roof over his head. As Kirby points out, 'This space, although perhaps cheaper per square foot than in the city proper, will *in toto* cost more than the flats or terraced housing more typically found in the inner city. . . . Therefore, despite the existence of certain negative price gradients, emphasis must rest upon the presence of a positive house price/distance relationship throughout the bulk of the city' (Kirby 1976: 3). Accepting Kirby's point, of course, means that it is no longer possible to think in terms of a trade-off between travel costs and housing costs, thus undermining a fundamental part of the model.

A related objection is that the existence of a given stock of housing of different kinds (as opposed to the homogeneous surface assumed by neoclassical theory) tends to confound the instantaneous equilibrium implied in most models. As Richardson (1971) points out, such a concept is difficult to introduce into an established city since the theoretically most desirable sites may already be occupied by users whose inertia has left them in a sub-optimal location. These observations draw attention to a more general objection to neoclassical models: their ahistorical nature. Apart from overlooking the legacy of the past which is represented in the contemporary housing stock, neoclassical models, as Walker (1978: 167) observes, 'provide no insight into the process of historical change of the qualitative, rather than quantitative, sort and thus help not at all in developing an understanding of how we came to our present urban condition, whether it need be as it is, and from what direction change is likely to spring'.

A final and most damaging criticism concerns the failure of neoclassical models to deal adequately with the supply of land and housing. Under the assumptions of profit maximization and perfect competition, supply follows automatically from the structure of demand. In reality, however, the supply of urban land and housing is constrained by national and even international economic fluctuations, by planning regulations and fiscal controls, by the intervention of special interest groups such as conservationists and tenants' associations, and by the actions of key professionals and power-holders such as building society (i.e. savings and loan) managers, real estate agents and developers (Bourne 1981). The influence of such factors is examined in detail in subsequent chapters, and it is sufficient to note here that their combined effect on residential location is, to say the least, considerable.

In spite of these criticisms, it is generally accepted that trade-off models do offer some valuable insights into the pattern of urban structure, albeit as descriptive rather than explanatory models. Empirical tests of the model and its various extensions have provided a certain amount of support for the postulates of the approach, but the explanatory power of the model, in statistical terms, has been weak; and the nature of the results has varied from study to study (see, for example, Ball 1973; Evans 1973; Kain and Quigley 1972; Muth 1969). The fact is that even the most elaborate models must lead to an impasse because of the number of unknown parameters relating to household preferences and market behaviour. Nevertheless, the approach does provide a useful starting-point for the the analysis of residential location, and in this respect its main value has been in stimulating alternative avenues of research. Among these are the 'New Urban Economics', urban development models (Chapin and Weiss 1968; Wilson 1974) and residential location models (Cripps and Foot 1969; Wilson 1970), all of which – like Alonso's model – concentrate upon the interactions between residences and workplaces, giving prominence to accessibility. The most fruitful area of research for urban geographers, however, has been the exploration of the cumulative effects of residential mobility on the overall structure of the city, and it is this field of enquiry to which attention is now turned.

## Housing demand and residential mobility

Although it is widely accepted that the movement of households from one residence to another plays an important part in shaping and reshaping urban social areas, the relationship between residential structure and patterns of residential mobility are only imperfectly understood. In part, this is because intra-urban mobility, despite accounting for some two-thirds of all migration in most western countries, was, until recently, a neglected topic. But it is also a reflection of the complexity of these relationships. While migration creates and remodels the social and demographic structure of city neighbourhoods, it is also conditioned by the existing ecology of the city. Moreover, the process in undergoing constant modification, as each household's decision to move (or not to move) has repercussions for the rest of the system. Chain reactions of vacancies and moves are set off as dwellings become newly available, and this movement may itself trigger further mobility as households react to changes in neighbourhood status and tone.

The basic relationship between residential mobility and urban structure is outlined in Fig. 5.4, which emphasizes the circular and cumulative effects of housing demand and urban structure on each other. Mobility is seen as a product of *housing opportunities* – the new and vacant dwellings resulting from suburban expansion, inner-city renewal and rehabilitation, etc, – and the housing *needs* and *expectations* of households, which are

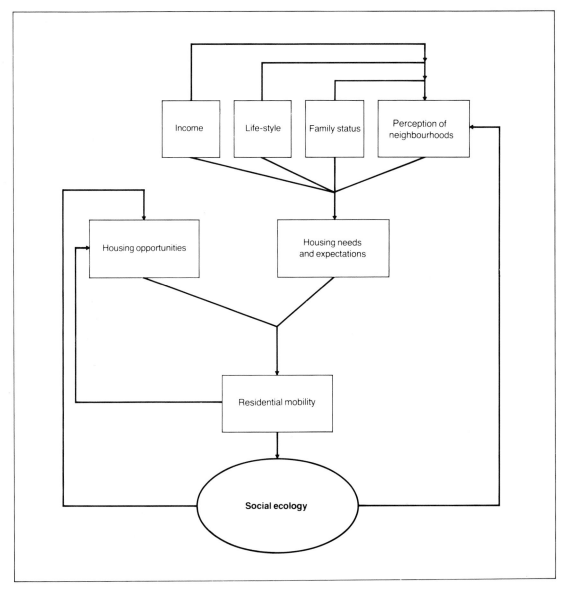

**Fig. 5.4** Relationships between housing demand, residential mobility and the social ecology of the city.

themselves a product of income, family size and lifestyle. Given a sufficient amount of mobility, the residential structure of the city will be substantively altered, resulting in changes both to the 'objective' social ecology and to the associated neighbourhood images which help to attract or deter further potential movers. Households, then, may be seen as decision-making units whose aggregate response to housing opportunities is central to ecological change. It therefore seems logical to begin the task of disentangling the relationship between movement and urban structure by seeking to establish the fundamental parameters of household mobility. How many households do actually move in a given period? Do particular types of household have a greater propensity to move than others? And are there any spatial regularities in the pattern of migration?

## Patterns of household mobility

In fact, the amount of movement by households in Western cities is considerable. In Australia, New Zealand and North America, about 20 per cent of all urban households move in any one year. Having said this, it is of course important to recognize that some cities experience much higher levels of mobility than others. Adams and Gilder (1976), for example, point out that cities in the fast-growing West, South and Gulf Coast of the United States – Reno, Colorado Springs, Las Vegas and Anaheim/Santa Ana/Garden Grove, for instance – have an annual turnover of population which is double that of the likes of Scranton, Johnstown and Wilkes-Barre/Hazleton in the more stable North East. In Western Europe, rates of mobility also vary a good deal, but in general they range between 5 and 10 per cent (Table 5.1). It is also important to recognize that the magnitude of this movement stems partly from economic and social forces which extend well beyond the housing markets of individual cities. One of the most important determinants of the overall level of residential mobility is the business cycle which is endemic to capitalist economies. During economic upswings the increase in employment opportunities and wages leads to an increase in the effective demand for new housing which, when completed, allows whole chains of households to change homes. Changes in social organization – particularly those involving changes in family structure and the rate of household formation, dissolution and fusion – also effect the overall level of mobility by exerting a direct influence on the demand for accommodation. Long-term changes in the structure of the housing market itself are also important. In many European countries, for example, the expansion of owner-occupied

**Table 5.1** Intra-urban migration rates, 1980 (or latest available year), selected European cities

| | Movers per 1000 population | | Movers per 1000 population |
|---|---|---|---|
| Aberdeen | 73.8 | Lisbon | 39.9 |
| Amsterdam | 93.3 | Lyons | 71.9 |
| Berlin (West) | 116.3 | Manchester | 66.4 |
| Brussels | 57.0 | Munich | 72.9 |
| Copenhagen | 116.0 | Newcastle | 70.9 |
| Cork | 21.3 | Oporto | 39.9 |
| Dijon | 70.3 | Paris | 59.9 |
| Dublin | 20.3 | Rome | 70.5 |
| Geneva | 100.6 | Tampere | 120.7 |
| Gothenburg | 97.1 | Turku | 113.5 |
| Hamburg | 85.9 | Sheffield | 70.5 |
| Helsinki | 119.4 | Stockholm | 57.5 |
| Köln | 83.0 | Vienna | 48.8 |
| Lausanne | 109.4 | Zurich | 103.1 |
| London | 76.2 | | |

*Source:* Derived from White (1985), Table 2.

and public housing at the expense of the privately rented sector has led to a general decrease in mobility because of the higher costs and longer delays involved in moving (Short 1978a). An analysis by White (1985) of the factors affecting mobility rates in nine West European cities found that, in addition to the composition of housing markets, mobility was chiefly related to the local balance between housing construction and population growth, the presence of foreign workers, and population density. White also noted that since the onset of the international economic depression in the mid-1970s, levels of intra-urban mobility have fallen everywhere. In Munich, for example, the rate had fallen, by 1982, by 23 per cent from its level in the early 1970s; while in Köln the fall was 18 per cent and in Copenhagen it was 15 per cent.

Notwithstanding these general factors, it is clear that residential mobility is a selective process. Households of different types are not equally mobile. Some have a propensity to move quite often; others, having once gained entry to the housing system, never move at all, thus lending a degree of stability to the residential mosaic. This basic dichotomy between 'movers' and 'stayers' (Wolpert 1966) has been identified in a number of studies, and it has been found that the composition of each group tends to be related to the lifestyle and tenure characteristics of households. In particular, younger households have been found to move more frequently than older households; and private renters have been found to be more mobile than households in other tenure categories. People can also be conceptualized as 'locals' or 'cosmopolitans', depending on the type and intensity of their attachments to their immediate social environments, and this distinction has been shown to have a significant bearing on intra-urban mobility (Dahmann 1982). In addition, there appears to be an independent duration-of-residence effect whereby the longer a household remains in a dwelling the less likely it is to move. This has been termed the principle of 'cumulative inertia', and is usually explained in terms of the emotional attachments which develop towards the dwelling and immediate

neighbourhood and the reluctance to sever increasingly strong and complex social networks in favour of the 'unknown quantity' of the pattern of daily life elsewhere (Moore 1972). In contrast, the actual experience of moving home probably reinforces the propensity to move. As Van Arsdol *et al.* found, movers 'are more oriented to future mobility than are persons who have not moved in the past and are better able to actualize a moving plan and choice' (Van Arsdol, Sabagh and Butler 1968: 266).

Spatial regularities in the migration patterns of movers have proved difficult to establish, partly because of the problems involved in obtaining and analyzing migration data. Census data, although reliable, rarely include sufficient information about the origin of migrants; and few countries outside the Netherlands and Scandinavia have registers of households which can be used to plot household movements. Questionnaire surveys provide an obvious alternative, but they involve the expenditure of a large amount of time and money in order to obtain a sufficiently large sample of migrants. In North America, many researchers have resorted to data based on changes of address worked out from telephone directories; but European researchers, faced with large numbers of households who do not have telephones, have often had to rely on town directories and electoral lists, both of which are known to be rather incomplete sources of information. Difficulties have also been experienced in analyzing migration data. In addition to the pitfalls of the ecological fallacy, these include the statistical problem of multi-collinearity and the practical problems involved in handling the large, complex data sets associated with migration studies (Clark and Moore 1978).

## Patterns of in-migration

Nevertheless, it is possible to suggest a number of important regularities in people's migration behaviour. At this stage it is useful to distinguish between the spatial behaviour of intra-urban movers and that of in-migrants from other cities, regions and countries. Furthermore, in-migrants can be usefully divided into high-and low-status movers. The latter, as seen in Chapter 2, were particularly influential in shaping the residential structure of cities earlier this century. There are some cities, however, where low-status in-migrants continue to represent a significant component of migration patterns. Johnston's study of population movements in London, for example, showed that in-migrants from foreign countries and from Scotland and Ireland (the majority of whom can safely be assumed to have been of low socio-economic status) were still making a significant contribution to the city's residential structure, with large numbers moving to cheap housing in the western sector of the inner city (Johnston 1969b). Substantial flows of low-status in-migrants have also been shown to be directed to fairly narrowly defined inner-city districts in other cities: Cincinnati, for example, where the in-migrants are mainly poor whites from Appalachia (Hyland 1970); Australian cities such as Melbourne and Sydney, where the in-migrants are mainly foreign born (Burnley 1976; Stimpson 1970); and some West European cities, where the in-migrants are *gastarbeiter* ('guest workers'), chiefly from the less prosperous regions of the Mediterranean (Lichtenberger 1984; Mik 1983; O'Loughlin 1980). It should be noted, however, that the impact of these in-migrants on urban social ecology is often finely tuned in relation to the national and regional origins, religion and ethnic status of the migrants involved: a process which is explored in detail in Chapter 7.

High-status in-migrants are similar to low-status in-migrants in that the majority are drawn into the city in response to its economic opportunities. Their locational behaviour, however, is quite different. The majority constitutes part of a highly mobile group of the better-educated middle classes whose members move from one city to another in search of better jobs or career advancement. Some of these moves are voluntary and some are made in response to the administrative fiat of large companies and government departments. The vast majority, though, follow the same basic pattern, moving to a rather narrowly defined kind of neighbourhood: newly-established suburban developments containing housing towards the top end of the price range. Such areas are particularly attractive to the mobile élite because the lack of an established neighbourhood character and social network minimizes the risk of settling amongst neighbours who are unfriendly, too friendly, 'snobbish' or 'common': something which may otherwise happen very easily, since out-of-town households must usually search the property market and make a housing selection in a matter of days. Moreover, housing in such areas tends to conform to 'conventional' floor and window shapes and sizes, so that there is a good chance that furnishings from the previous residence will fit the new one. Nevertheless, once established in the new city, it is common for such households to make one or more follow-up or 'corrective' moves in response to their increasing awareness of the social ambience of different neighbourhoods and the quality of their schools and shops.

## Intra-urban moves

This brings us conveniently to the general category of intra-urban moves which makes up the bulk of all residential mobility and which therefore merits rather closer consideration. Indeed, a good deal of research effort has been devoted to the task of searching for regularities in intra-urban movement in the belief that such regularities, if they exist, might help to illuminate the relationships between residential mobility and urban ecology.

One of the most consistent findings of this research concerns the *distance moved*. In virtually every study, the majority of moves has been found to be relatively short, although the distances involved clearly depend to a certain extent on the overall size of the city concerned. In a national sample of United States movers, almost 45 per cent had moved within the same central city, with half of these moves taking place within the same neighbourhood (Butler *et al.* 1969). Results from studies of individual cities, including Minneapolis (Adams 1969), Philadelphia (Rossi

1980), Providence, Rhode Island (Speare *et al.* 1975), Melbourne (Johnston 1969c), Glasgow (Forbes and Robertson 1978), Swansea (Herbert 1973b) and Duisburg and Düsseldorf (O'Loughlin and Glebe 1984), are consistent with these findings. Within Minneapolis, for example, the longest moves made by relocating households in 1970–71 were over 20 miles (32 km); but the modal distance moved was nearer to one mile (1.6 km) and about 30 per cent of all the moves involved distances of less than one mile (Nordstrand 1973). This tendency for short moves notwithstanding, variability in distance moved is generally explained best by income, race and previous tenure, with higher-income white owner-occupier households tending to move furthest.

*Directional* bias has also been investigated in a number of migration studies, but with rather less consistent results. While it is widely recognized that there is a general tendency for migration to push outward from inner-city neighbourhoods towards the suburbs, reverse flows and cross-currents always exist to complicate the issue. Adams (1969) has suggested that the strong orientation of the urban system towards the jobs and shops of the CBD tends to suppress lateral flows, leaving a mixture of inward and outward moves to dominate the pattern of intra-urban mobility. Johnston's (1969c) analysis of Melbourne lends some support to this idea, although he found that little of the short-distance movement originating in the inner city exhibited any strong directional bias. However, of the moves terminating in the suburbs, 54 per cent were found to stay within the sector of origin, and moves from residences in outer zones were found to be even more likely to end within the same sector than those from inner zones, suggesting that once households have lived in one segment of suburbia they are reluctant to leave it for another. A broadly similar directional bias is reported by Clark (1971), who found that households from suburban neighbourhoods relocating within Christchurch, New Zealand, tended to move towards the CBD, while inner-city movements, like those in Melbourne, were essentially random.

The most significant regularities in intra-urban movement patterns, however, relate to the relative *socio-economic status* of origin and destination areas. As Simmons (1968) noted in his review of intra-urban mobility, a vast majority of moves – about 80 per cent in the USA – take place within census tracts of similar socio-economic characteristics. A parallel and related tendency is for a very high proportion of moves to take place within tenure categories (Murie, Niner and Watson 1976). In other words, relocation within 'community space' and 'housing space' usually involves only short distances. These tendencies were first documented for the Providence, Rhode Island, metropolitan area (Goldstein and Mayer 1961), and have since been observed in sufficient cities to suggest that the phenomenon is universal (Brown and Longbrake 1970; Clark 1976; Short 1978b; Speare, Goldstein and Frey 1975). It follows from these observations that, while intra-urban mobility may have a significant impact on the spatial expression of social and economic cleavages, the overall degree of residential segregation tends to be maintained or even reinforced by relocation processes.

Putting together these empirical regularities in an overall spatial context, we are presented with a three-fold zonal division of the city. The innermost zone is characterized by high levels of mobility, which are swollen by the arrival of low-status in-migrants. Similarly, high levels of mobility in the outermost zone are supplemented by the arrival and subsequent follow-up mobility of higher-status in-migrants. Between the two is a zone of relative stability containing households whose housing needs are evidently satisfied. Here, turnover is low simply because few housing opportunities arise, either through vacancies or through new construction. It is probably the existence of such a zone which accounts for longer-distance moves and which helps to explain the sectoral 'leap-frogging' of lower-middle class and working class households to new suburban estates and dormitory towns. In an attempt to throw further light on these patterns, several researchers have undertaken analyses of the spatial correlates of mobility rates. Moore (1969; 1971), for example, has investigated the ecological correlates of population turnover in Brisbane, and Herbert (1973a) has analyzed the ecological correlates of residential mobility in Swansea. In general, however, the results of such studies have been inconclusive. Herbert was able to demonstrate that in-migration had a much greater impact on Swansea's affluent suburbs than on inner-city areas, but he found no statistically significant correlations between intra-urban mobility and urban structure. Moore, on the other hand, did establish significant associations between population turnover and several socio-economic variables, but he was not satisfied that these justified any causal inferences, largely because of the well-known fallibilities of ecological analysis. The most rigorous and systematic analysis of the ecological relationships exhibited by rates of residential mobility is that undertaken by Cadwallader (1981). In a study of Canton, Des Moines, Knoxville and Portland, he was able to establish that housing type (i.e. tenure and size characteristics) is consistently the single most important determinant of residential mobility, with the lowest rates being associated with neighbourhoods dominated by owner-occupied and single-family dwelling units.

Finally, it should be emphasized that the generalizations made here must be qualified by a measure of caution. In particular, patterns of movement within many European cities are complicated by the presence of significant amounts of public sector housing for which the entry and transfer rules are completely different from the rest of the housing market (see pp. 217–224). In general this does not distort the overall pattern of household movement, although it is likely that different elements of the pattern will be linked to particular sectors of the housing market. In Glasgow, for example, where the privately-rented and owner-occupied sectors are truncated by a massive public sector (in 1983, 63.3 per cent of the city's households lived in publicly-owned dwellings), the overall pattern of residential mobility still exhibits the 'typical' components of short-distance relocation within the neighbourhood of origin and of outward sectoral movement

over larger distances. But a closer examination of migration flows reveals that these components are derived in composite fashion from the various flows within and between the main tenure categories. Thus, while short-distance moves dominate both the owner-occupied and public sector (see Figs. 5.5 and 5.6), longer-distance sectoral movements stem from:

1. outward flows of owner-occupiers and council tenants from first-tier suburban neighbourhoods toward peripheral locations outside the city boundary;
2. outward flows of households from inner-city slum-clearance areas to suburban public housing estates; and
3. a smaller, inward flow of households moving from public housing to older, owner-occupier tenement property nearer the centre of the city (Forbes and Robertson 1978).

## The determinants of residential mobility

If the outward configuration of intra-urban mobility is difficult to pin down, its internal dynamics are even more obscure. The flows of mobility which shape urban structure derive from aggregate patterns of demand for accommodation which in turn spring from the complex deliberations of individual households. An understanding of how these deliberations are structured is thus likely to provide some insight into the relocation process, and a considerable amount of attention has therefore been given by geographers to two important aspects of household behaviour:

1. the decision to seek a new residence;
2. the search for and selection of a new residence.

This two-stage approach is adopted here. First, attention is focused on the personal, residential and environmental circumstances which appear to precipitate the decision to move, and a conceptual model of the decision to move is outlined. Subsequently, attention is focused on how this decision is acted upon,

**Fig. 5.5** Moves within the owner-occupied sector of Glasgow District involving three or more households, 1974. Numbers represent the number of internal moves in each grid square. *Source*: Forbes and Robertson (1978).

highlighting the bias imposed on locational behaviour by differential access to, and use of, information.

### Reasons for moving

In any consideration of migration it is important to make a distinction between *voluntary* and *involuntary* moves. As Rossi (1980) showed in his classic study of migration in Philadelphia, involuntary moves make up a significant proportion of the total. In Philadelphia, almost a quarter of the moves were involuntary, and the majority of these were precipitated by property demolitions and evictions. Similar findings have been reported from studies of other cities, but remarkably little is known about the locational behaviour of affected households. In addition to these purely involuntary moves is a further category of 'forced' moves (Moore 1972) arising from marriage, divorce, retirement, ill-health, death in the family, and long-distance job changes. These frequently account for a further 15 per cent of all moves, leaving around 60 per cent as voluntary moves.

Survey data show that the decision to move home voluntarily is attributed to a number of quite different factors. It must be acknowl-

**Fig. 5.6**  Moves into and within local authority and Scottish Special Housing Association housing in Glasgow District involving 15 or more households, 1974. Numbers represent the number of internal moves in each grid square.

edged, however, that the reasons given for moving in the course of household interviews are not always entirely reliable. Some people have a tendency to rationalize and justify their own decisions, others may not be able to recollect past motivations; and most will inevitably articulate reasons which are simpler and more clear-cut than the complex of factors under consideration at the time of the move. Nevertheless, survey data are useful in indicating the major elements which need to be taken into consideration in explaining movement behaviour. Table 5.2 presents the reasons given for moving – both voluntarily and involuntarily – by a large sample of

recently-moved British households, revealing a mixture of housing, environmental and personal factors. Among the more frequently-cited housing factors associated with voluntary moves are complaints about dwelling and garden space, about housing and repair costs and about style obsolescence. Environmental factors encompass complaints about the presence of noxious activities such as factories, about noisy children, and about the incidence of litter, garbage and pet dogs. Personal factors are mostly associated with forced moves, but some voluntary moves are attributed to personal factors, such as a negative reaction to new neighbours. These generali-

**Table 5.2** Reasons for wishing to move: British households, 1976

| | % |
|---|---|
| **Housing reasons** | |
| Too large | 6 |
| Too small | 16 |
| Poor amenities or standard/poor repair | 8 |
| Condemned/due for demolition | 3 |
| Too expensive | 4 |
| Other | 10 |
| Total | 47 |
| **Environmental reasons** | |
| Job/study reasons (change of job, etc.) | 21 |
| Other | 7 |
| **Personal reasons** | |
| Ill health | 3 |
| To join relatives/friends | 5 |
| Retirement and other | 4 |
| Total | 12 |
| **Other reasons** | |
| To be nearer work † | 3 |
| Been asked to leave (by landlord) | 2 |
| To buy a house/flat | 4 |
| Other | 3 |
| Total | 12 |
| Base (= 100%) | 1040 |

* Excluding members of the Armed Forces, full-time students, and those who have never worked
† Excluding a change of job
*Source*: Office of Population Censuses and Surveys 1978: 164.

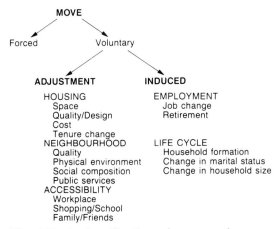

**Fig. 5.7** A classification of reasons for household relocation. *Source*: Clark and Onaka (1983), Fig. 2, p. 50.

zations hold true for sample populations in North America, Australia and New Zealand, as well as Britain (Barrett 1973; Butler *et al.* 1969; Clark and Onaka 1983; Rossi 1980; Stimpson 1982.) Figure 5.7 illustrates a general classification of the reasons for household relocation.

Important variations do exist, however, between population sub-groups, with equally important implications for the social ecology of the city. The General Household Survey, for example, shows that only 36 per cent of British professionals, employers and managers who moved house in 1976 did so for 'housing' reasons, compared to 55 per cent of skilled manual workers and 50 per cent of semi-skilled and unskilled manual and personal service workers (Office of Population Censuses and Surveys 1978.) Not surprisingly, therefore, moves from different types of neighbourhood tend to be prompted differentially by different factors. In Swansea, for instance, Herbert (1973a) found that the high-status district of Derwen Fawr was distinctive in that a much larger proportion of movers than elsewhere gave employment as their main reason for having moved; and a comparison of four different neighbourhoods in Bristol shows clearly the differential importance of factors such as troublesome neighbours, housing costs and the physical condition of housing (Table 5.3).

### Residential mobility and the family life-cycle

Of the more frequently cited reasons for moving, it is generally agreed that the most important and widespread is related to the household's need for dwelling space. More than half of the movers in Rossi's study cited complaints about too much or too little living space as contributing to their desire to move (with 44 per cent giving it as a primary reason). Subsequent surveys have confirmed the decisive importance of living-space in the decision to move and, furthermore, have established that the crucial factor is not so much space *per se* but the relationship between the size and composition of a household and its *perceived* space requirements.

**Table 5.3**  Reasons for moving house, by neighbourhood, in Bristol

| | Percentage of households in each sample | Reason given |
|---|---|---|
| **Bedminster** (19th-century terraced dwellings, manual household, owner-occupied) | 70 | Marriage/to own a house |
| | 13 | Change in household size |
| **St George** (Cheaper new owner-occupied housing) | 66 | Marriage/to own a house |
| | 12 | Change in household size |
| | 12 | Troublesome neighbours |
| **Westburg** (High status owner-occupied housing) | 28 | Change in household size |
| | 23 | To own a house |
| | 10 | Previous residence was only temporary |
| **St Pauls** (Mixed, run-down inner-city) | 21 | Forced to move |
| | 21 | Setting up new household |
| | 20 | Changing space requirement |
| | 12 | Last place too expensive |
| | 10 | Poor physical condition of previous dwelling |

*Source:* Short 1978: 538.

Because both of these are closely related to the family life-cycle, it is widely believed that life-cycle changes provide the foundation for much of the residential relocation within cities. Moreover, the attractions of the family life-cycle as an explanatory variable are considerably reinforced by its relationships with several other frequently cited reasons for moving, such as the desire to own (rather than rent) a home and the desire for a change of environmental setting. Abu-Lughod and Foley (1960) have proposed a model which links all these factors together rather succinctly (Table 5.4)

According to their scheme, the typical family life-cycle begins with a brief stage living alone or with friends after leaving home to study or find work. The first year or two of marriage, when wives generally remain at work, may be regarded as a continuation of this phase. Whereas the physical size of the dwelling is unlikely to be important, accessibility to jobs and social amenities is often a major consideration in choosing a home, so that central locations are favoured. With the birth of a child, the household's real and perceived needs change considerably, reversing the relative importance of dwelling-space and accessibility and placing a premium on safe, quiet residential environments. However, the loss of one income during this 'child-bearing'

**Table 5.4**  Simplified representation of Abu-Lughod and Foley's family-cycle model

| Stage | Access | Space | Median tenure | Housing age | Mobility | Locational Preference |
|---|---|---|---|---|---|---|
| Pre-child | Important | Unimportant | Rented flat | | 1 move to own home | Centre city |
| Child-bearing | Less important | Increasingly important | Rented house Old | | High 2–3 moves | Middle and outer rings of centre city |
| Child-rearing | Not important | Important | Owned | Relatively new | 1 move to owned house | Periphery of city or suburbs |
| Child-launching | Not important | Very important | Owned | New | 1 move to second home | |
| Post-child | Not important | Unimportant | Owned | New when first bought | Unlikely to move | |
| Later life | Not important | Unimportant | | Widow leaves owned house to live with grown child | | |

*Source:* Morgan 1976: 86.

stage tends to prevent an immediate move to the suburban ideal. Instead, it is more likely that a series of adjusting moves will be made as household income increases and the space requirements of the growing family increase. By the time the children are of secondary school age, access to neighbourhood facilities – especially social facilities and schools – becomes increasingly significant. Meanwhile, the earning power of the household is likely to be at a peak, so that – for middle-class families at least – it is common to move to a larger new suburban home. Later, when the children have left home, the space requirements of the household decrease considerably. At this stage, however, it is recognized that neighbourhood ties and sentimental attachments will prevent many couples from moving to smaller accommodation. The final residential change for many people, therefore, comes at the 'later life' stage, with a move to live with a son or daughter, to institutionalized accommodation, or to specialist retirement communities.

Evidence from Michelson's comprehensive analysis of housing in Toronto lends some general support to this process, showing a significant movement of childless families into the downtown area, with larger families moving to suburban areas from more central locations and from out of town (Table 5.5). Only families of six or more persons were not tending to move towards the suburbs, but this was because they were there already (Michelson 1977). A recent study of *intending* migrants in the inner London borough of Lambeth also provides some support for life-cycle related mobility. Over half of those who wanted to move out from Lambeth to the

suburbs were families with children, whereas of those wanting to stay in inner London only a third were families with children and over a quarter were single people (Department of the Environment 1978).

It follows from these observations that a marked residential segregation will emerge as households at similar stages in the family life-cycle respond in similar ways to their changing circumstances. This, of course, fits conveniently with the results of the many descriptive studies (including factorial ecology studies) which have demonstrated a zonal pattern of family status. The generally accepted sequence to these zones runs from a youthful inner-city zone through successive zones of older and middle-aged family types to a zone of late youth/early middle-age on the periphery (Morgan 1976). It must be acknowledged, however, that such a pattern may be the result of factors other than those associated directly with the dynamic of the family life cycle. As Adams and Gilder (1976: 165) observe: 'Households often undergo changes in their family status at the same time as they experience changes in income and social status,' so it is dangerous to explain mobility exclusively in terms of one or the other. Quite different factors may also be at work. North American and Scandinavian developers, for example, knowing that many households prefer to live among families similar to their own in age and composition as well as socio-economic status, have reinforced family status segregation by building apartment complexes and housing estates for specific household types, with exclusionary covenants and contracts designed to keep out 'non-conforming' residents. It is thus quite common for entire condominiums

**Table 5.5** Residential relocation in Toronto
Location change (%)

| Number in Household | Downtown to downtown | Centralizing and outside Toronto to downtown | Suburbs to suburbs | Decentralizing and outside to suburbs |
|---|---|---|---|---|
| 2 | 27.9 | 26.0 | 10.6 | 35.6 |
| 3 | 11.5 | 7.7 | 17.3 | 63.5 |
| 4 | 7.4 | 5.2 | 28.7 | 58.7 |
| 5 | 6.9 | 11.9 | 36.6 | 44.6 |
| 6 or more | 10.8 | 9.2 | 46.2 | 33.8 |

*Source:* Michelson 1977: 140.

to be inhabited by single people or by childless couples. The extreme form of this phenomenon is represented by Sun City, a satellite suburb of Phoenix, Arizona, where no resident under the age of 50 is allowed, and where the whole townscape is dominated by the design needs of the so-called 'grey panthers', who whir along the quiet streets in golf caddy-cars, travelling from one social engagement to the next. In contrast, much of the family status segregation in British cities with large amounts of public housing can be attributed to the letting policies of local authorities, since eligibility for public housing is partly a product of household size (see pp. 241–244).

It should also be stressed that the correlation between the family life-cycle and family status segregation is in any case by no means perfect or universal. The relevance of the life-cycle model to British cities has been questioned by Morgan (1976), whose study of family status segregation in Exeter showed that progression through the family life-cycle was not significantly associated with relative location or changes in housing tenure. Rather, households were found to be asssociated with housing built at the time of, soon after, their formation. In other words, the segregation of family status groups in Exeter is best understood in terms of the inertia of ageing cohorts of households. Even in North American cities, where the higher overall levels of mobility seem more closely aligned to the life-cycle model, much of the movement postulated by the model is suppressed by a series of intervening factors. For one thing, by no means every household is 'typical'. Many, including an increasing number of voluntarily childless couples, experience a life-cycle whose major stages and associated housing needs bear only a loose resemblance to those in the Abu-Lughod/Foley model. More important is the fact that many of the households which do want to relocate because of housing needs related to the idealized life-cycle are prevented from doing so either because suitable accommodation is not available or because they cannot afford it. In relation to the question of affordability, it is clear that, for families living near or below the poverty line, the relationships between family life-cycle, tenure and residential mobility are critical (Fig. 5.8). As a result, households at different stages of the family life-cycle have to adopt different *coping strategies* in order to resolve the pressures that are brought to bear on them (Kemeny 1980).

# A conceptual framework:
# 1. The decision to move

An alternative approach to residential mobility is provided by behaviouralist work which, rather than invoking specific processes such as the family life-cycle to explain the relocation process, emphasize the individual decision to move within a general conceptual framework. Brown and Moore (1970) have outlined the basis of a widely accepted scheme (Fig. 5.9) in which the first major decision – whether or not to move home – is viewed as a product of the *stress* generated by discordance between the household's needs, expectations and aspirations on the one hand and its actual housing conditions and environmental setting on the other.

While the nature of the stresses associated with housing and environmental conditions should be clear, it is necessary at this point to elaborate upon the idea of people's housing *expectations* and *aspirations*. Basically, these are thought by behaviouralists to stem from the different frames of reference which people adopt in making sense of their lives and, in particular, in interpreting their housing situation. These frames of reference are the product of a wide range of factors which includes age, class background, religion, ethnic origin, and past experience of all aspects of urban life. What they amount to is a series of *life-styles* – privatized, familistic, cosmopolitan, and so on – each with a distinctive set of orientations in relation to housing and residential location. Bell (1958; 1968) suggested that there are in fact three main life-styles, whose adherents may be termed familists, careerists and consumerists.

*Family-oriented* people are also home-centred and tend to spend much of their spare time with their children. As a result, their housing orientations are dominated by their

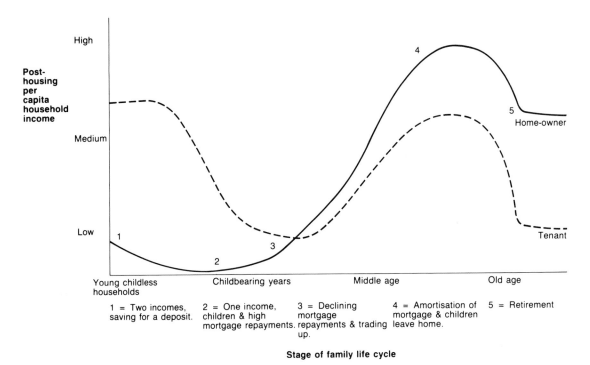

**Fig. 5.8** Schematic representation of housing tenure and the cycle of poverty.
*Source*: Kemeny (1980) Fig. 1, p. 20.

perceptions of their children's needs for play space, a clean, safe environment, proximity to child clinics and school, and so on. Bell found that 83 per cent of the households in his sample who had moved to suburban locations in Chicago had done so 'for the sake of the children'.

*Careerists* have a life-style centred on career advancement. Since movement is often a necessary part of this process, careerists tend to be highly mobile; and since they are, by definition, status conscious, their housing orientations tend to be focused on prestige neighbourhoods appropriate to their jobs, their salary and their self-image.

*Consumerists* are strongly oriented towards enjoying the material benefits and amenities of modern urban society, and their housing preferences are therefore dominated by a desire to live in downtown areas, close to clubs, theatres, art galleries, discotheques, restaurants, and so on.

To these, Moore (1972) added *community*

*seekers*, who stress a life-style which is centred on social interaction with other people with the same kind of group-oriented values. Examples include members of 'alternative' life-styles and cultures, who tend to gather in cheaper inner-city areas; and some of the more affluent elderly population, who seek the companionship of suburban retirement communities.

Bell's typology can be criticized for its middle-class tenor, since it overlooks the 'life-style' of the large number of households whose economic position reduces their housing aspirations to the level of survival. As Rainwater (1966) has shown, many working-class households view their homes as havens from the outside world rather than as platforms for the enactment of a favoured life-style. This limitation, however, is allowed for by the behaviouralist model outlined in Fig. 5.9. Quite simply, households with more modest incomes are expected to aspire only to housing which meets their minimum absolute

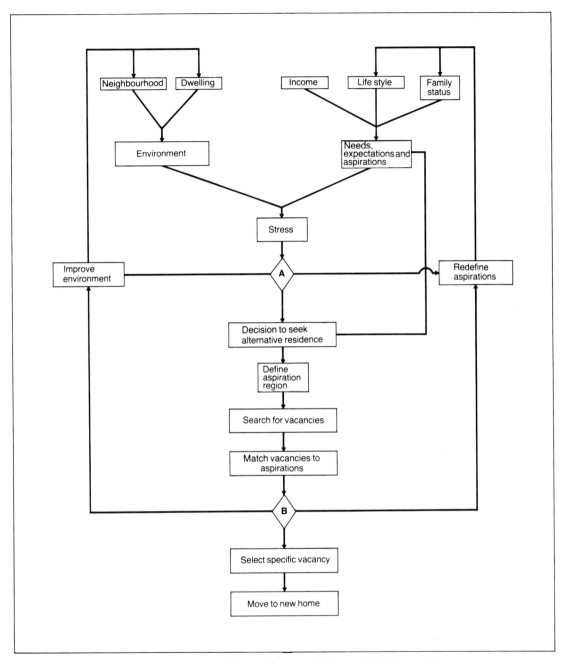

**Fig. 5.9** A model of residential mobility.  *Source*: Robson (1975), p. 33.

needs. The latter are generally held to be a function of family size, so that the idea of life-cycle related mobility plugs in conveniently to the behaviouralist model without equating stress automatically with mobility.

Whatever the household's expectations and aspirations may be, the crucial determinant of the decision to move is the intensity of the stress (if any) generated as a result of the difference between these and its actual circumstances. The point where tolerable stress becomes intolerable strain will be different for each household (Wolpert 1966) but, once it is reached (at point 'A' on Fig. 5.9) the household must decide between three avenues of behaviour:

i. *Environmental improvement*. This embraces a wide range of activities, depending on the nature of the stressors involved. Small dwellings can be enlarged with an extension, cold dwellings can have central heating, double glazing and wall cavity insulation installed, dilapidated dwellings can be rewired and redecorated, and over-large dwellings can be filled by taking in lodgers. Neighbourhood or 'situational' stressors can also be countered in various ways: inaccessibility to shops and amenities, for example, can be tackled through the purchase of a car or by petitioning the local authority to provide better bus services. Environmental degradation and intrusive land-users can be tackled through residents' associations and action committees; and undesirable neighbours can be harassed or ostracized. As with other aspects of residential behaviour, these strategies vary in their appeal according to household circumstances. Owner-occupiers, for example, are much more likely to opt for neighbourhood activism than renters (Cox 1983).

ii. *Lowering aspirations*. This is an alternative means of coming to terms with existing housing conditions. It appears to be a common strategy, since survey data show that for every household that moves there are two or three more who report that they would like to move if they could. Lowering aspirations may involve a change in life-style or a reformulation of plans: the decision to have children may be deferred, for example. More commonly it is simply a psychological matter of 'dissonance reduction' – learning to like what one has and to become indifferent to what one knows one cannot get. Not surprisingly, the older people get, the more proficient they become at dissonance reduction (Campbell, Converse and Rodgers 1976).

iii. *Residential relocation*. This, as we have

seen, is the course chosen by a large minority of households. The decision to move, however, leads to a second important area of locational behaviour: the search for and selection of a new residence.

## 2. The search for a new residence

Whether the decision to move is voluntary or involuntary, all relocating households must go through the procedure of searching for suitable vacancies and then deciding upon the most appropriate new home. The chief interest of geographers in this procedure lies in the question of whether it is spatially biased and, if so, whether it is biased in different ways for different groups of households (Clark and Flowerdew 1982). In other words, do spatially biased search procedures contribute to the changing social ecology? Although information on the way people behave in looking for a new home is rather fragmentary, the general process is conveniently encompassed within the decision-making framework of Brown and Moore's behavioural model (Fig. 5.9). Accordingly, it is useful to break household behaviour down into three stages:

1. the specification of criteria for evaluating vacancies;
2. the search for dwellings which satisfy these criteria;
3. the final choice of a new dwelling.

### Specifying the desiderata of a new home

In behaviouralist terms, the household's first step in coping with the problem of acquiring and organizing information about potential new dwelling is to define, consciously or subconsciously, its *aspiration region*. Quite simply, this is a conception of the limits of acceptability which a household is prepared to entertain as an alternative to its current accommodation. These limits may be defined in terms of the desired *site* characteristics – attributes of the dwelling itself – and/or the desired *situational* characteristics – the physical and social environment of the neighbourhood, its proximity to schools, shops, etc. The lower limits of the aspiration region are commonly defined by the characteristics of the dwelling the household is leaving, while the upper limits are set by the standards to which the household can reasonably aspire. In many cases these will be determined by income constraints, but there are important exceptions: some householders, for example, may not want to take on a large garden, regardless of house price; others may rule out affordable dwellings in certain high status areas because the neighbourhood does not conform with their desired life-style.

In general, the criteria used by households in specifying their aspiration region reflect their motivations in deciding to move. We can thus expect living-space, tenure, dwelling amenities, environmental quality and social composition to be amongst the more frequently used criteria. This is confirmed by Table 5.6, which compares the reasons given for moving with those given for selecting a new residence by a sample of Toronto households. But, in addition to the broad correspondence between the two, it is worth noting that some of the criteria used in evaluating the new residence are largely unrelated to the problems encountered in the previous residence. Interior aspects of the dwelling, the social character-

istics of the neighbourhood and accessibility to various facilities are more important in attracting people to a new home than in propelling them away, for example. It also appears that movers of different types tend to differ quite a lot in the criteria they use. In Toronto, households moving to houses are evidently more likely to be concerned with situational characteristics than those moving to apartments. Furthermore, those moving to suburban houses tend to be particularly concerned with the layout of the dwelling and its potential as an investment, whereas for those moving to downtown houses the aesthetics of dwelling style and the neighbourhood environment tends to be a more important criterion (Michelson 1977). The existence of differently conceived aspiration regions is, of course, a function of the different needs and aspirations which prompt households to move in the first place. Their significance to the relocation process lies not only in the consequent variability in the evaluation of particular housing opportunities, but also in the fact that households set out from the very start to look for vacancies with quite different housing goals in mind.

### Searching for vacancies

The general objective of the search procedure is to find the right kind of dwelling, at the right price, in the time available. It must be acknowledged that there are some households that do not have to search deliberately because their decision to move has come after accidentally discovering an attractive vacancy. Rossi (1980), who termed these 'windfall' moves, found that as many as 25 per cent of the movers in his sample had done so in this way. The majority of movers, though, must somehow organize themselves into finding a suitable home within a limited period of deciding to relocate. According to Brown and Moore (1970), most households organize the search procedure in locational terms, focusing attention on particular neighbourhoods which are selected on the basis of (a) their perceived *situational* characteristics and (b) the household's evaluation of the probability of finding vacancies satisfying their *site* criteria. Moreover, faced with the problem of searching

**Table 5.6** Motivations associated with intra-urban mobility, Toronto

| Reasons* | For move away from current home (%) | For a choice of a new residence (%) |
|---|---|---|
| Unit interior size and layout | 17.0 | 23.7 |
| Unit interior features | 3.1 | 4.7 |
| Exterior setting | 16.8 | 17.3 |
| Dwelling unit | 20.2 | 10.2 |
| Neighbourhood | 12.4 | 19.0 |
| Access | 7.1 | 17.4 |
| Family composition | 15.0 | 1.3 |
| Interaction with people | 1.1 | 0.2 |
| Leisure activities | 0.6 | 0.4 |
| Fiscal considerations | 8.0 | 6.0 |
| Other | 0.8 | 0.1 |
| Total reasons | 2,658 | 4,019 |

* Up to but not necessarily four reasons per person

*Source:* Michelson 1977: 115 and 122.

even a limited amount of space, it is natural that households will attempt to further reduce both effort and uncertainty by concentrating their search in areas which are best-known and most accessible to them (Silk 1971).

The upshot is that households concentrate their house-hunting activities within a limited *search space* which is spatially biased by their familiarity with different districts. In behaviouralist terminology, this search space is a subset of a more general *awareness space*, which is usually regarded as a product of (a) people's *activity space* or *action space* (the sum of all the places with which people have regular contact as a result of their normal activites) and (b) information from secondary sources such as radio, television, newspapers, and even word-of-mouth. Both elements, as we have seen (pp. 149–162) are subject to a mental filtering and coding which produces a set of imagery which constitutes the operational part of the individual's awareness space. The subset of this space which constitutes the search space is simply the area (or areas) which a household feels to be relevant to its aspiration region, and it is spatially biased because of the inherent bias in both activity spaces and mental maps. It follows that different sub-groups of households, with distinctive activity spaces and mental maps, will tend to exhibit an equally distinctive spatial bias in their search behaviour. In particular, we may expect the more limited activity spaces and more localized and intensive images of the home area to limit the search space of low-income households to a relatively small area centred on the previous home, while more mobile, higher-income households will have a search space which is more extensive but focused on the most familiar sector of the city between home and workplace. What empirical evidence there is tends to support this proposition. Brown and Holmes (1971), for example, have demonstrated that patterns of social contacts and vacancies visited in the search for a new home were much more compact and localized around the former residence for low-income, inner-city residents (of Cedar Rapids, Iowa) than for higher-income suburban dwellers, who searched over a wider area and displayed

both directional bias, towards the CBD, and sectoral bias, towards the sector of their previous residence. This, it will be observed, ties in neatly with the regularities in actual migration patterns outlined above.

The *information sources* used to find vacant dwellings within the search space can also exert a significant spatial bias. Moreover, since different types of households tend to rely on different sequences and combinations of sources, there results a further process of socio-spatial sorting. Overall, the most frequently used sources of information about housing vacancies are newspaper advertisements, real estate agents, friends and relatives, and personal observation of 'for sale' signs, although their relative importance and effectiveness seems to vary somewhat from one city to another (see, for example, Clark and Smith 1979; Talarchek 1982). Although little research has been done on these information sources, it is clear that each tends to be biased in a different way. Personal observation, for example, will be closely determined by personal activity space, while the quantity and quality of information from friends and relatives will depend a lot on social class and the structure of the searcher's social networks. Estate agents also exert a considerable spatial bias in their role as mediators of information. Risa Palm (1976a; 1976b) has shown that this operates in two ways: first, each business tends to specialize in limited portions of the housing market in terms of both price and area; second, while most estate agents were found to have a fairly accurate knowledge of the city-wide housing market, they tended to over-recommend dwellings in the area in which they were most experienced in selling and listing accommodation and with which they were most familiar. As a result, 'households which are dependent on realty salesman for information . . . are making use of a highly structured and spatially limited information source' (Palm 1976b: 28).

The critical issue in the present context, however, is the relative importance and effectiveness of different information sources for different households. Again, empirical evidence is rather patchy, but survey data from

Swansea and Toronto do show a marked variation in the emphasis that different movers put on different sources. In Swansea, migrants from a high-cost housing area used estate agents and newspaper advertisements much more than migrants from a low-cost area, though informal sources of information were dominant for both groups (Herbert 1973b). In Toronto, where Michelson (1977) used a more detailed breakdown of movers, several sharp differences emerged. Newspaper advertisements were a much more effective source of information for households searching for an apartment than for those searching for a house. Conversely, estate agents were consulted mainly about houses, proving a very effective source (in the sense that a high proportion of movers eventually found their new homes as a result of information obtained from estate agents rather than from other sources), particularly for housing in the downtown area. Personal observation (in the form of 'driving around'), on the other hand, was a more popular and effective source of information for suburban house-hunters.

Accessibility to information channels is also related to another important issue affecting residential behaviour: the problem of *search barriers*. Weisbrod and Vidal (1981) discuss two aspects of this problem: barriers that raise the costs of searching or gathering information, and barriers that explicitly limit the choice of housing units or locations available to households. Factors related to search costs include, for example, lack of transportation for searching and lack of child care facilities while searching, as well as lack of knowledge about specific information channels. Factors that limit housing choice include financial constraints, discrimination in the housing market, and the housing quality standards of rent assistance programmes.

This differential use and effectiveness clearly serves to increase the degree of socio-spatial sorting arising from the migration process, while at the same time making it more complex. Another important compounding factor in this sense is the constraint of *time* in the search procedure. Both search space and search procedures are likely to alter as households spend increasing amounts of time and money looking for a new home. When time starts to run out, the search strategy must change to ensure that a home will be found. Anxiety produced by a lack of success may result in a modification of the household's aspiration region, a restriction of their search space, and a shift in their use of information sources; and the pressure of time may lead people to make poor choices. On the other hand, the longer the search goes on, the greater the household's knowledge of the housing market. Each household therefore has to balance the advantages of searching and learning against the costs – real and psychological – of doing so. This dilemma is analogous to the so-called 'marriage problem', which has been stated by Lindley (1961: 47), from a male point of view, as follows:

A known number, $n$, of ladies are presented to you one at a time in random order. After inspecting any number $r$ ($1 \leq r \leq n$) of them you are able to rank them from best to worst and this order will not be changed if the $(r + 1)$th lady is inspected; she will merely be inserted into the order. At any stage of the 'game' you may either propose to lady *then being inspected* (there is no going back!), when the game stops, or inspect the next lady; however, if you reach the last lady you have to propose. All proposals are accepted. What is the optimum strategy?

Statistical probability models have been developed in order to devise the optimal 'stopping rule' for this type of problem. Evidently the optimal strategy in the marriage problem is to pass by all opportunities (of marriage!) until the age of 26, and then propose to the first 'lady' who compares favourably with the best of those encountered before. The probability of marrying the 'best' possible partner in this way is, rather dauntingly, estimated at just over 36 per cent (Lindley 1961). No such bold conclusions have yet been derived for house-hunting, although Flowerdew (1976; 1978) has outlined the bases of a relatively sophisticated stopping-rule model for house-hunting (see also Clark 1982). One of the difficulties in operationalizing such models, however, is the variability of personality and psychological factors in decision-making. Conservative households, for example, may tend to take an acceptable vacancy instead of pushing on to find a better deal. Survey data in fact show a consistent tendency for the majority of households to seriously consider only a few vacancies (usually, only two or three) before selecting a new home, an observation which may appear to undermine the utility of developing elaborate models and theories of search behaviour. Nevertheless, this phenomenon can itself be explained with a behaviouralist framework. As Barrett (1973) points out, households are able to reduce the element of uncertainty in their decision-making by restricting serious consideration to only a few vacancies. Moreover, as Short (1978a) observes, most households begin with an aspiration region which is quite narrowly defined (either because of income constraints or locational requirements), so that what appears to be an inhibited search pattern is in fact a logical extension of the decisions formulated in the preceding stage of the search procedure.

A useful example of the aggregate patterns of searching arising from these influences is provided by Barrett's (1973) work on Toronto. Using an index of the 'temporal intensity' of the search for housing calculated from the number of vacancies examined divided by the time spent searching, Barrett found a generally low intensity, with few vacancies searched within a short period, and a random spatial distribution of vacancies. It was found that households with a temporally intensive search pattern were mainly associated with the central city area, where keen competition for accommodation had created a sellers' market. Households taking time to view more vacancies tended to be those searching the suburban house market. A second index was use to measure the 'spatial intensity' of household search patterns. This was calculated as the mean distance to all searched vacancies from the mean centre of their locations. For over 90 per cent of the households, this turned out to be three miles (4.8 km) or less, compared to an urban area radius of 13 miles (20.8 km). The lowest values of all were found amongst households of below-average socio-economic status. Dividing the first index by the second gave an index of the concentration of search. High

values, suggesting casual and erratic search patterns, were found to be associated with central-city searchers; while low values, suggesting more intensive and thorough search behaviour, were common in newer suburban housing estates.

## Choosing a new home

Those households which do find two or more vacancies which fall within their aspiration region must eventually make a choice. Theoretically, this kind of choice is made on the basis of household *utility functions* which are used to give a subjective rating to each vacancy. In other words, vacancies are evaluated in terms of the weighted sum of the attributes used to delineate the aspiration region. These weights reflect the relative importance of the criteria used to specify the aspiration region, and so they will vary according to the preferences and predilections of the household concerned. Difficulties arise, however, in attempting to operationalize the theory for more than one household at a time, when non-transitive preferences and the 'paradox of majority rule' (Arrow 1951) wreak havoc with the theoretical elegance of utility functions.

Nevertheless, it is clear that some criteria are given greater weight than others. The national survey of United States movers, for example, discovered an overall tendency for people to value neighbourhood quality more than housing quality and accessibility, to value interior style and appearance more than the exterior style and appearance of a dwelling, and to prefer neighbourhoods with better-than-average schools and relatively high local taxes to those with lower taxes but poorer schools (Butler *et al.* 1969). What is not yet known, though, is whether there are consistent differences in the housing preferences of different demographic and socio-economic groups. Without this kind of information, few inferences can be made about the nature of socio-spatial outcomes, if any, associated with the choice of housing. Lyon and Wood (1977) have suggested that the constraints of time, coupled with the limitations of human information-processing abilities and a general lack of motivation, mean that a real choice of the kind implied in behaviouralist theory is seldom made: people are happy to take any reasonable vacancy, so long as it does not involve a great deal of inconvenience. The fact that their sample was drawn from a modern housing estate in south London goes some way towards explaining their conclusions, however, for there certainly seems little to choose between amongst the cautious architectural variations which are typical of post-war British housing. Nevertheless, it remains for behaviouralists to suggest the exact nature of spatial bias resulting from the actual choice between alternative vacancies.

Finally, it should be noted that the basic behavioural model allows for those households which are unable to find vacancies within their aspiration region in the time available to them (point 'B' on Fig. 5.9) to change their strategy to one of the two options open to them at point 'A' on the diagram: environmental improvement or a redefinition of aspirations. Although the basic model stops at this point, it is a simple matter to extend the behaviouralist perspective to treat mobility as a continual process. Kennedy (1975), for example, has outlined a model involving:

1. a comparison of the new dwelling with the household's prior expectations of it; and
2. a comparison of the new dwelling with the household's previous dwelling.

In the light of this reflection, Kennedy points out, some households will experience satisfaction and decide to stay, while others, dissatisfied with their new dwelling, will find themselves once more at the equivalent of point 'A' on Figure 5.9.

Finally, we must recognize that there are many households in every city whose residential location is constrained to the point where behavioural approaches are of marginal significance. The most obvious sub-group here are low-income households. Bourne suggests that at least one-third of all households in most cities have little or no choice in their housing. 'These people may be the real working poor, the elderly, the very young, the unemployed, or the transient. In any case,

their numbers are large' (Bourne 1981: 143). Other sub-groups whose residential choice is heavily constrained include households who have special needs (e.g. large families, single-parent families, non-married couples, former inmates of institutions, and 'problem' families), households who cannot relocate because of personal handicaps, family situations or medical needs; and households who are unwilling to move because of the psychological stress of moving from familiar environments.

## Residential mobility and neighbourhood change

Although the behavioural approach provides important insights into the spatial implications of mobility, the emphasis on individual decision-making tends to divert attention from the aggregate patterns of neighbourhood change which result 'as like individuals make like choices' (Rees 1970: 313). In this section, therefore, some consideration is given to the macro-scale generalizations which have been advanced about processes of mobility and neighbourhood change.

One scheme which has already been introduced and discussed is the zonal pattern of family status associated with moves arising from family life-cycle changes (see above, pp. 180–183). Another is the zonal patterning of socio-economic status associated with the sequence of invasion-succession-dominance postulated by Burgess in his model of ecological change (see pp. 59–65). The dynamic of this model, it will be recalled, was based on the pressure of low-status in-migrants arriving in inner-city areas. As this pressure increases, some families penetrate surrounding neighbourhoods, thus initiating a chain reaction whereby the residents of each successively higher status zone are forced to move further out from the centre in order to counter the lowering of neighbourhood status. Notwithstanding the criticisms of ecological theory *per se*, with its heavy reliance on biotic analogy, the concept of invasion–succession–dominance provides a useful explanatory framework for the observed sequence of neighbourhood change in cities where rapid urban growth is fuelled by large-scale in-migration of low-status famililes. The classic example, of course, is Chicago during the 1920s and 1930s, although many of the industrial cities in Britain had undergone a similar process of neighbourhood change during the nineteenth century. More recently, the postwar flow of overseas immigrants to London, Paris and larger Australian cities such as Melbourne and Sydney and the flow of *gastarbeiter* to the industrial cities of north-western Europe has generated a sequence of change in some neighbourhoods which also fits the invasion/succession model. Nevertheless, this model is of limited relevance to most modern cities, since its driving force – the inflow of low-status migrants – is of diminishing importance; the bulk of in-migrants is now accounted for by middle-income families moving from a suburb in one city to a similar suburb in another.

### High status movement, filtering and vacancy chains

An alternative view of neighbourhood change and residential mobility stems from Hoyt's (1939) model of urban growth and socio-economic structure. Hoyt's ideas were derived from a detailed study of rental values in 142 US cities which was undertaken in order to classify neighbourhood types according to their mortgage lending risk. This study led him to believe that the key to urban residential structure is to be found in the behaviour of high status households. These, he argued, pre-empt the most desirable land in the emerging city away from industrial activity. With urban growth, the high-status area expands axially along natural routeways, in response to the desire amongst the well-off to combine accessibility with suburban living. This sectoral movement is reinforced by a tendency amongst 'community leaders' to favour non-industrial waterside sites and higher ground; and for the rest of the higher-income groups to seek the social cachet of living in the same neighbourhood as these *prominenti*. Further sectoral development occurs when dissatisfaction with their existing

housing prompts a move outwards to new housing in order to maintain standards of exclusivity. In the wake of this continual outward movement of high-status households, the housing they vacate is occupied by middle-status households whose own housing is in turn occupied by lower-status households. At the end of this chain of movement, the vacancies created by the lowest-status groups are either demolished or occupied by low-status in-migrants. Subsequently, as other residential areas also expand outwards, the sectoral structure of the city will be preserved, with zonal components emerging as a secondary element because of variations in the age and condition of the housing stock.

The validity of Hoyt's sectoral model has been much debated. Empirical studies of the emerging pattern of élite residential areas and tests of the existence of sectoral gradients in socio-economic status have provided a good deal of general support for the spatial configuration of Hoyt's model (see, for example, Johnston 1970, 1971; Murdie 1976), although the relative dominance of sectoral over zonal components in urban structure is evidently by no means a simple or universal phenomenon. In particular, emphasis has been given to the persistence of élite neighbourhoods in the innermost zone of many cities (Johnston 1966, 1969d), a phenomenon to which Firey first drew attention in 1945.

It is the *mechanism* of neighbourhood change implied in Hoyt's model which is of interest here, however. The basis of this mechanism is the chain of moves initiated by the construction of new dwellings for the wealthy, resulting in their older properties *filtering down* the social scale while individual households *filter up* the housing scale. In order for this filtering process to operate at a sufficient level to have any real impact on urban structure, there has to be more new construction than that required simply to replace the deteriorating housing of the élite. According to Hoyt, this will be ensured by the *obsolescence* of housing as well as its physical deterioration. For the rich, there are several kinds of obsolescence which may trigger a desire for new housing. Advances in kitchen technology and heating systems and the innovation of new luxury features such as swimming pools, saunas and solaria may cause 'functional obsolescence', while more general social and economic changes may cause obsolescence of a different kind: the trend away from large families combined with relative increase in the cost of domestic labour, for example, has made large free-standing dwellings something of a white elephant. Changes in design trends may also cause obsolescence – 'style obsolescence' – in the eyes of those who can afford to be sensitive to architectural fads and fashions. Finally, given a tax structure which allows mortgage repayments to be offset against taxable income (as in Britain and many other Western countries), dwellings may become 'financially obsolescent' as increases in household income and/or inflation reduce the relative size of mortgage repayments (and therefore of tax relief). Driven on to new housing by one or more of these factors, the wealthy will thus create a significant number of vacancies which the next-richest group will be impelled to fill through a desire for a greater quantity and/or quality of housing. This desire can be seen not only as the manifestation of a general preference for better housing but also as a result of the influence of changing housing needs associated with the family life-cycle. In addition, Harvey (1973) has suggested that the social and economic pressures resulting from proximity to the poorest groups in society may prompt those immediately above them to move as soon as the opportunity presents itself, either by moving into vacancies created by the construction of new housing for others or by moving out into new subdivisions specially constructed for the lower-middle classes. Harvey calls this the 'blow-out' theory and suggests that 'the dynamics of the housing market can probably best be viewed as a combination of "blow-out" and "filter down" (Harvey 1973: 173)

In practice, however, the dynamics of the housing market are rather more complex than this. To begin with, vacancy chains may start in other ways than the construction of new housing, whether for the rich (as in Hoyt's model) or for middle-income families (as in Harvey's blow-out theory). A substantial proportion of vacancies arise through the subdivision of dwelling units into flats and the conversion of non-residential property to residential uses. Even more occur through the death of a household, through the move of an existing household to share accommodation with another, and through emigration outside the city. Similarly, vacancy chains may be ended in several ways other than the demolition of the worst dwellings or their occupation by poor in-migrants. Some vacancies are rendered ineffective through conversion to commercial use, while others may be cancelled out by rehabilitation or conversion schemes which involve knocking two or more dwellings into one. Vacancy chains will also end if the household which moves into a vacant dwelling is a 'new' one and so leaves no vacancy behind for others to fill. This may arise through the marriage of a couple who had both previously been living with friends or parents, through divorced people setting up separate homes, or through the splitting of an existing household with, for example, a son or daughter moving out to their own flat.

A closer examination of the filtering process between the start and finish of vacancy chains also reveals a certain amount of complexity. This is not helped by the lack of agreement on how to measure the process, despite a lengthy and often bitter debate in the literature. Conceptions of filtering have involved notions of change in price and housing quality as well as changes in occupancy. Ratcliff (1949) described the filtering process as the changing of occupancy as the housing that is occupied by one income group becomes available to the next lower income group as a result of a decline in price. Smith (1964) also regarded filtering as a change in the occupancy of dwellings by different income groups. Others, notably Fisher and Winnick (1951) and Lowry (1960), have proposed definitions based solely on changes in the price of housing, although the issue is further complicated by the several ways in which price changes can be measured – against changes in the prices and rentals of all dwellings, for example; or against consumer prices. Amongst the narrower definitions of filtering is that proposed by Grigsby, who suggests that 'filtering only occurs when value declines more rapidly than quality so that families can obtain either higher quality and more space at the same price or the same quality and space at a lower price than formerly' (Grigsby 1963: 97). This clearly comes close to the conception of filtering in Hoyt's model. It is also useful in emphasizing the role of filtering not just as a mechanism of intra-urban mobility but also as a means of facilitating a general improvement of housing conditions as new houses filter down the social scale.

This aspect of filtering has attracted more attention than any other because of its policy implications, since it can be argued that facilitating new housebuilding for higher income groups will result in an eventual improvement in the housing conditions of the poor through the natural process of filtering, without recourse to public intervention in the housing market. This argument has a long history, dating to the paternalistic logic of the nine-teenth-century housing reformers who used it to justify the construction of model housing for the 'industrious' and 'respectable' working classes rather than the poorest sections of society to whom their efforts were ostensibly directed (Tarn 1973). Subsequently, it became the central plank of government housing policy in many countries. Up to the 1930s, Britain relied almost entirely on the filtering process to improve the housing conditions of the working classes, while it still remains the basis of US housing strategy (Gray and Boddy 1979; Kirby 1979).

### Empirical studies of vacancy chains

The general validity of the filtering concept is not disputed, apart from the obvious exception of movement into and within the public sector. Many of the once-fashionable quarters of the rich, now sub-divided into flats and bedsitters, can be seen to be occupied by distinctly less prosperous families, students, single-person households and the aged. What is not clear, however, is the impact of this process on different social groups and different neighbourhoods. Relatively few studies have been able to furnish detailed

empirical evidence, and their results are rather inconclusive. One of the most compre-hensive analyses of vacancy chains so far undertaken is that by Lansing, Clifton and Morgan in the United States. They sought to answer a series of questions, including 'what is the economic level of people who move into new housing? If rich people who move into new housing, do poor people benefit directly by moving into vacancies further along in the sequence? Or do the sequences stop before they reach low income people?' (Lansing, Clifton and Morgan 1969: 111). An examin-ation of over 1,100 vacancy chains generated by the construction of new dwellings showed that while the average sequence of moves thus initiated was 3.5, those resulting from the construction of more expensive houses ($30,000 or more) were roughly twice as long as those resulting from the construction of cheaper houses (less than $15,000) and rental units costing less than $150 per month. It was also found that a majority of the families moving into a dwelling had a lower income and socio-economic status than the previous occupants. At the same time, almost two-thirds of the moves resulted in an increase in dwelling space. It is also interesting to note in relation to both Hoyt's model and the family life-cycle model that the average distance from the centre of the city was found to decrease with each successive link in the chain, and that whereas over 40 per cent of the households moving into a house were at an 'earlier' stage in the life-cycle than families moving out, only 28 per cent were at a later stage.

These results seem to suggest that an upward filtering of households does arise from the construction of few homes for the wealthy. Nevertheless, closer inspection of the results shows that the benefits to poor families (in terms of vacant housing opportunities) are not in proportion to their numbers, suggesting that filtering is unlikely to be an important agent of neighbourhood change in poor areas. Moreover, the fact that a large proportion of the vacancy chains ended through the forma-tion of 'new' households while only a small proportion ended through demolitions also suggests that the filtering mechanism rarely penetrates the lower spectrum of the housing

market to any great extent. We must therefore set aside the idea of a general upward
filtering of social classes in favour of a more
selective process of movement. This is also the
conclusion of a recent study of moves arising
from the construction of single-family dwellings in Windsor, Ontario (Dzus and Romsa
1977). The general pattern of vacancy chains
in Windsor is evidently very much the same
as in other cities (see, for example Jones 1978;
Sharpe 1978; Watson 1974), with higher-priced
homes generating rather larger chains of
movement and the bulk of all terminations
being caused by the formation of new households. However, a close examination of the
individual moves revealed a complex and
highly segmented pattern of movement arising
from the new construction. In particular, the
spatial distribution and directional flow of
moves was found to be highly localized, with
little upward filtering originating from poorer
inner-city neighbourhoods or the city's southern
suburbs. The conclusion drawn from this is
that the construction of new single-family
housing 'will only affect the urban structure
of middle class areas' (Dzus and Romsa
1977: 232).

In summary then, filtering offers a useful
but nevertheless partial explanation of patterns
of neighbourhood change. Amongst the
factors which can be identified as inhibiting
the hypothesized sequence of movement
arising from new high status housing are:

1.  the failure of high income housing
    construction to keep pace with the
    overall rate of new household forma-
    tion and in-migration;
2.  the structure of income distribution
    which, since higher-income groups
    constitute a relatively small class,
    means that the houses they vacate in
    preference for new homes are demanded
    by a much larger group, thus main-
    taining high prices and suppressing the
    process of filtering;
3.  the inertia and non-economic behav-
    iour of some households. This includes
    many of the behavioural patterns
    discussed above (see pp. 177–191),
    although the most striking barrier to
    the filtering process is the persistence

of élite neighbourhoods in symboli-
cally prestigious inner-city locations;
4.  the existence of other processes of
    neighbourhood change whose dynamic
    is unrelated to the construction of new,
    high-income housing. Reference has
    already been made to the process of
    invasion/succession, the 'blow-out'
    process identified by Harvey (1973),
    and the process of neighbourhood
    change associated with changes in the
    family life-cycle. In addition, two other
    processes merit consideration: the aban-
    donment of slum housing and the
    'gentrification' of more solid inner-city
    neighbourhoods.

### Abandonment and contagion

It should be stressed at the outset that the
abandonment of housing is a much less widespread phenomenon than any of the other
processes of neighbourhood change so far
discussed. It is mainly encountered in the
worst-off neighbourhoods in the largest cities,
and it is much more common in North American cities than elsewhere. Nevertheless, it
must be recognized as an increasingly
important agent of neighbourhood change.
Large-scale localized abandonment is a
phenomenon which emerged during the 1960s
in most of the larger American cities of the
eastern seaboard and midwest. Kristoff (1970)
calculated that about 100,000 housing units
had been withdrawn from the market in New
York City alone between 1965 and 1968,
displacing as many as 275,000 persons; while
Grigsby and several associates indicated that
Baltimore was losing up to 4,000 units per
year during the 1960s (Grigsby et al. 1970). By
the end of the decade, concern over this trend
led the United States Department of Housing
and Urban Development (HUD) to commission
a study of abandonment in Chicago, New
Orleans, Oakland and St Louis. At the same
time, the National Urban League undertook
a survey of housing abandonment encompassing seven more cities. From the resultant
reports (Linton, Mields and Coston 1971;
National Urban League 1971) it became clear
that not only was the incidence of abandonment increasing but also that its increasing

localization was triggering marked changes in the social, economic and demographic composition of whole neighbourhoods.

There appear to be several contributing factors to this process. The reduction in the flow of low-income in-migrants to inner-city areas has inevitably meant the abandonment of a certain amount of housing as the lowest income groups get the opportunity to filter up the housing scale, leaving unwanted and difficult-to-let dwellings behind. But this alone is not a sufficient explanation of the intensity of abandonment in cities like Chicago, Detroit and Newark: it has already been shown that relatively few inner-city households get the chance to filter out of slum housing in this way. What seems to have been behind the particularly high levels of abandonment in parts of these cities is a combination of factors related to the general decline of the inner city within metropolitan areas. The loss of much of the employment base traditionally associated with these areas, combined with a steady deterioration of property, has taken the heart out of the private market for low-income housing. Landlords, faced with escalating maintenance costs and unable to increase revenue because of rent controls and the depressed state of the inner-city housing market, have simply written off their least attractive property by abandoning it to long-term vacancy. In desperation, some New York 'slumlords' have reportedly resorted to arson in an attempt to at least salvage insurance moneys.

Given this general propensity for abandonment in the inner city, the localization of abandonment in particular neighbourhoods and the consequent change in neighbourhood character seems to be best explained in terms of a *contagion* effect. This, at least, is the conclusion drawn from a recent study of abandonment in the Tioga district of central Philadelphia, where the incidence of abandoned residential structures increased from 3.7 per cent to 4.6 per cent between 1969 and 1971 (Dear 1976). An examination of the spatial distribution of these structures led Dear to suggest that abandonment can be viewed as a contagious process having at least two distinct stages. Initially there emerges a broad scatter of loosely-defined clusters of abandoned structures, each consisting of several 'microgroups' of two or three abandoned units. 'With the passage of time, the pattern is intensified: the broad scatter is maintained, although the small groups now contain a greater number of structures' (Dear 1976: 65). The reasons for this intensification through contagion are closely related to the depressing effects of long-term vacancy on the value and desirability of adjacent property. The fact that abandoned structures make good sites for crime and vandalism provides a further stimulus for the abandonment of nearby property, and this downward spiral is reinforced by what Dear calls the 'psychological abandonment' of the wider area by estate agents, financiers, landlords and urban governments who, having seen the writing on the wall (*sic*), accelerate the decline of the area through disinvestment and cutting back on maintenance and municipal services. The effect of this process on the structure of the city is a polarization of neighbourhood status and environmental quality within the inner city. Where abandonment takes hold, decay accelerates to the point where a residual population of the city's losers is left in an environment downgraded beyong rehabilitation. (Glazer 1979; D. Morgan 1980). Elsewhere, the remainder of the shrinking inner-city population regroups and consolidates in neighbourhoods where the physical fabric has not yet reached the critical point at which both residents and owners lose confidence in the neighbourhood's capacity for self-regeneration.

## Gentrification

In contrast, gentrification involves a sequence of residential mobility the end result of which is an improvement of the socio-economic status and environmental quality of inner-city neighbourhoods. Put simply, gentrification is 'the invasion of traditionally working class areas by middle and upper income groups' (Hamnett 1973: 252). This process usually begins with the movement of young couples from the arts, design and teaching professions into older, run-down working-class areas. By renovating such property, these 'pioneer' middle classes are able to obtain proximity to the city centre at a reasonable cost. In addition, they are likely to be given credit with their friends for going to live among the working classes, thus generating a 'trendiness' which soon ensures that the pioneers acquire a substantial number of middle-class neighbours of similarly adventurous and liberal outlook to themselves. Meanwhile, of course, their initial investment in the house will have reassuringly risen in value. As this invasion continues, the status of the area also rises and it becomes socially acceptable for young businesss executives and lawyers to move in, thereby escalating rents and property values even further and edging out the working-class families who had previously occupied the neighbourhood. This process effectively narrows the 'rent gap' produced in inner city neighbourhoods by the twin processes of capital depreciation and urban expansion:

Gentrification occurs when the gap is wide enough that developers can purchase shells cheaply, can pay the builders' costs and profit for rehabilitation, can pay interest on mortgage and construction loans, and can then sell the product for a sale price that leaves satisfactory return to the developer. The entire ground rent, or a large portion of it, is now capitalized; the neighbourhood has been 'recycled' and begins a new cycle of use (N. Smith 1975: 545).

Gentrification, then, must be seen as a movement of capital as much as a movement of people. This is a theme which is taken up in Chapter 9.

The areas which have been most intensively gentrified are those which are near both the city centre and acknowledged areas of high social status within the inner city. As Hamnett observes, many of these areas were originally built for the middle classes and have subsequently undergone invasion and succession in an almost classical ecological fashion. They are now experiencing a reversal of this sequence as the excess of demand over supply in adjacent high-status neighbourhoods creates a 'price shadow' which makes rehabilitation and renovation a worthwhile undertaking. The success of the middle classes in wresting these areas from the working classes stems largely from their ability to operate and

manipulate the mechanisms of the housing market and to satisfy the requirements of the financiers of house purchase and rehabilitation. Williams (1976a), for example, has written of the reluctance of building societies to lend funds for house purchase and/or improvement in Islington (London) until the feasibility of 'reclaiming' old property had been demonstrated by the financially reliable middle classes. Similarly, the middle classes have been shown to be better able to exploit the availability of government grants for the improvement and conversion of property (Hamnett 1973; Pearson and Henney 1972,) even though these grants are ostensibly designed to facilitate the self-regeneration of declining working-class neighbourhoods. Overall, the gentrifying middle classes can be seen as an example of human agency initiating urban change within a specific structural context. This is demonstrated very clearly in a study of Society Hill, Philadelphia, and False Creek, Vancouver, where the lineaments of neighbourhood change are shown to be a product of the evolving interplay of key individual and interest groups, shifting finance and property markets, imperfectly orchestrated consumer demands, unpredictable electoral responses, and changing priorities and intervention strategies on the part of government at different levels (Cybriwsky, Ley and Western 1986).

Examples of gentrified neighbourhoods can be found in most large cities (Smith and Williams 1986). The best-known examples include Barnsbury and Canonbury in Islington and Georgetown in Washington, DC, sought out early on for their attractive Georgian and Victorian terraced town houses. Gentrification has now spilled over into neighbourhoods where the original housing was built for artisans rather than the middle classes but which nevertheless offers scope for internal redesign and renovation, with a potential environmental and aesthetic appeal – a 'raffish chic' – which attracts the inverted snobbery of the pioneering young professionals. In London for example, gentrification has penetrated to Clapham. As Angela Carter observes, 'You can't walk home from the tube, these days, without seeing somebody moving their Swiss-cheese plants into a white-painted room, probably with a chrome and glass coffee table and maybe spotlight fittings' (Carter 1977: 189). Apart from the changing social status of the affected areas, the manifestations of neighbourhood change resulting from this movement are striking, although they do not always lend themselves to the protocol of 'scientific' investigation. In Clapham, the 'seedy respectability of soiled net curtains', the 'well-attended dancing classes, classical and tap, held in bay-windowed front rooms', and the 'jellied eels and mashed potatoes consumed in white-tile eel-and-pie shops' have been joined, if not entirely replaced, by the trappings of life necessary to young professional couples:

A health food shop has opened to sell them black beans. The bookshop has display cases of Picador Books, the publications of Pluto Press, *Spare Rib*, and God knows what else besides . . . Kids called Gareth and Emma [play] with their Galt toys on the floor of the bank while – *at the same time* – down the road, an old lady in the pub removes her teeth in order to sing *Some of these days* with passion and vibrancy, to tumultuous applause (Carter 1977: 189).

One study which has documented the neighbourhood changes associated with gentrification in a more systematic way is that by Cybriwsky (1978) of the Fairmount area of central Philadelphia. Cybriwsky points out that the gentrified part of Fairmount is adjacent to a district of townhouses and high-rise flats occupied by upper-and middle-income whites and buffered from the declining property values, urban decay and hostility of black working-class neighbourhoods of northern Philadelphia by a 'defended neighbourhood' occupied by working-class whites. Between 15 and 20 per cent of the residents of this gentrified area moved in during the 1970s They are mostly young 'singles' and childless couples in their twenties and thirties earning 'comfortable' salaries. Unlike the host population, they are politically liberal and home- rather than neighbourhood-oriented; and they have brought a radically different lifestyle, commercial structure and social organization to the neighbourhood. Renovation has contrived an ambience of 'Colonial Philadelphia', together with a proliferation of roof gardens and patios. Changes in the neighbourhood's commercial structure include the replacement of several 'Ma and Pa' stores with an art gallery, an antique shop and two house-plant shops, and the arrival of a film studio and the headquarters of the Pennsylvania Ballet in former industrial premises. Not surprisingly, Cybriwsky found that the social networks of the newcomers seldom extended to the host population, in spite of their having moved in 'to be amongst the people'. They find themselves rejected by Fairmounters, a rejection which is sometimes expressed in terms of petty vandalism of newcomers' property by the neighbourhood youth and which has brought about the emergence of increased policing and formal residents' 'block associations', replacing the close-knit social networks an informal social controls of the 'urban village' of pre-gentrification Fairmount.

## Typologies of neighbourhood change

Recognizing that there is no single mechanism linking residential mobility to ecological change, several attempts have been made to set out a typology of the neighbourhood changes associated with the various ebbs and flows of residential mobility. Moore (1972), for example, has set out a four-fold typology which is intended to be 'illustrative rather than exhaustive' of the relationships between the mobility characteristics of neighbourhoods and their socio-economic and demographic characteristics (Fig. 5.10). Moore points out that Type II situations, with stable characteristics yet high levels of mobility, are probably more common than Type I situations (high mobility and rapid change), an observation which is clearly related to the tendency for most moves to take place within the same 'community-space'. *Type I* situations include the classic invasion/succession sequence which is probably most frequently encountered where an ethnic or racial minority is invading the territory of another group. Other Type I situations include both the gentrification and the abandonment of inner-city neighbourhoods, as well as the high mobility and rapid social change associated with the intrusion into middle-class neighbourhoods of undesir-

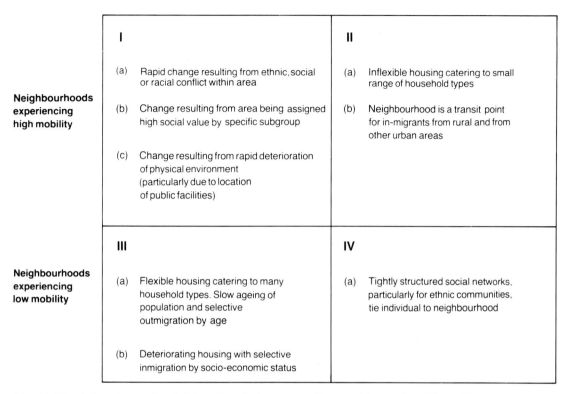

**Fig. 5.10**  A typology of neighbourhood change.  *Source*: Moore (1972), p. 33.

able features such as motorways, factories and residential homes for juvenile delinquents.

*Type II* situations are typified by neighbourhoods which specifically cater for a transient population, such as the districts of small rented flats close to the CBD occupied by young single persons or newly married couples as a stepping stone to home ownership in the suburbs. Other examples of this type of situation include the slum district which serves as a receiving area for low-income in-migrants and the newer suburbs which serve as ports of entry for successive waves of middle-class in migrants. *Type III* situations, where neighbourhood change is associated with low levels of mobility, are generally the product of steady selective in- or out-migration. This includes a large selection of middle-class neighbourhoods whose socio-economic composition steadily changes as the housing stock filters down the social ladder. In addition, neighbourhoods which experience a

gradual demographic change as a cohort of 'stayers' ages together also fall into this category. *Type IV* situations, where low rates of mobility are accompanied by stability of neighbourhood characteristics, find their strongest expression in the tightly-knit ethnic neighbourhoods and urban villages of the inner city, together with some of the most affluent white suburbs. All such areas derive their stability from the lack of incentive for members of their distinctive communities to move elsewhere in the city, to 'alien' and potentially hostile environments.

A more comprehensive typology is represented by Bourne's (1976) attempt to link both physical and socio-economic changes to residential mobility within the concept of a *neighbourhood life-cycle* (Table 5.6). This provides a useful descriptive summary although, as Bourne points out, it would be very difficult to test its validity empirically, let alone extend the typology into a model or theory of

**Table 5.7**   Summary of neighbourhood life-cycles

| Stage | Physical changes | | |
| --- | --- | --- | --- |
| | Dwelling type (predominate additions) | Level of construction | Population density |
| 1. Suburbanization (new growth) 'homogeneity' | Single-family (low-density multiple) | High | Low (but increasing) |
| 2. In-filling (on vacant land) | Multi-family | Low, decreasing | Medium (increasing slowly or stable) |
| 3. Downgrading (stability and decline) | Conversions of existing dwellings to multi-family | Very low | Medium (increasing slowly), population total down |
| 4. Thinning out | Non-residential construction-demolitions of existing units | Low | Declining (net densities may be increasing) |
| 5. Renewal | (a) Public housing | High | Increasing (net) |
| | (b) Luxury high-rise apartment | Medium | Increasing (net) |
| | Townhouse conversions | Low | Decreasing (net) |

*Source:* Bourne 1976: 139.

residential mobility and neighbourhood change. Nevertheless, the idea of neighbourhood life-cycles can provide a useful explanation of urban residential structure, as Webber (1975) has shown in his analysis of social areas in Liverpool. Webber emphasizes the point that large new housing subdivisions tend to be located at the edge of the currently built-up area, to contain dwellings of a similar type or size, to be designed to meet the requirements of a specific and relatively homogeneous socio-economic group, and to be populated by families at an early stage of the family life-cycle. With the passage of time, Webber recognizes three major aspects of change:

1.  the gradual ageing of the original colonizing cohort;
2.  the structural obsolescence of buildings; and
3.  the technical obsolescence of dwellings.

He also points out that periodicity of the ageing cycle is shorter than that of structural obsolescence, so that the period between the dying-off of the original colonizing cohort and the eventual abandonment or demolition of housing may take up to 50 years, during which time the social composition of neighbourhood will change through invasion and filtering. Meanwhile, the effects of technical obsolescence will result in some neighbourhoods being more vulnerable to change than others: 'Large villas, of the type which characterize the rooming house area for instance, are clearly less adaptable in an age without service than the Victorian artisan terraces. This type of housing reponds to technical change by attracting a different household type as well as a different socio-economic class' (Webber 1975: 95).

The residential structure of Liverpool lends itself easily to an interpretation based on this conception of neighbourhood life-cycles. Thus the inner-city public housing estates correspond to those areas which have already experienced one cycle of structural obsolescence and which have now been redeveloped. Where the original inner-city housing was built to a higher standard – to house prosperous Victorian merchants – the cycle of

| Social changes | | | Other changes |
|---|---|---|---|
| Family structure | Social status income | Migration mobility | Other characteristics |
| Young families, small children, large households | High (increasing) | High net in-migration, high mobility turnover | Initial development stage; cluster development; large-scale projects, usually on virgin land |
| Ageing families, older children, more mixing | High (stable) | Low net in-migration, low mobility turnover | First transition stage-less homogeneity in age, class, housing first apartments; some replacements |
| Older families, fewer children | Medium (declining) | Low net out-migration, high turnover | Long period of depreciation and stagnation; some non-residential succession |
| Older families, few children, non-family households | Declining | Higher net out-migration, high turnover | Selective non-residential succession |
| Young families, many children | Declining | High net in-migration, high turnover | The second transition stage-may take either of two forms depending on conditions |
| Mixed Few children | Increasing Increasing | Medium Low | |

structural obsolescence is somewhat longer, and these dwellings remain as a residual neighbourhood which has now filtered down the social scale to become a rooming-house area, with the technical obsolescence of large units being resolved by subdivision and multi-occupation. Beyond these areas are neighbourhoods of older terrace housing whose colonizing cohort has died off and which have become technically obsolescent for most families because of their lack of basic amenities like inside lavatories. As a result, successive zones of terrace housing have been invaded by the very lowest socio-economic group, producing local concentrations of the unskilled, the unemployed, and New Commonwealth immigrants.

Further out still are the city's middle-class neighbourhoods which, since they date from the interwar period, have not yet suffered particularly from either structural or technical obsolescence. Moreover, most still contain a large proportion of the original colonizing population. The exceptions are the oldest, innermost middle-class neighbourhoods – which have reached the stage at which a large number of young families are moving in – and the newest, outermost neighbourhoods – which are still under development and colonization. Similarly, most of the suburban public housing estates have pronounced concentrations of particular age groups, reflecting the period of their original development.

# 6 Housing supply: opportunities and constraints

Although the analyses of housing demand and residential mobility discussed in the previous chapter provide some understanding of the process of residential differentiation, their emphasis on choice rather than constraint has tended to divert attention away from the effects of housing supply agencies. It is now recognized that the supply of housing is at best only indirectly responsive to demand, and a good deal of attention has been given to the social stratification and residential differentiation arising from the regulation and manipulation of housing supply by various institutions, interest groups and individuals. Indeed, the prominence given to constraints on housing opportunities in contemporary urban research has reached the point where 'The rising tide of interest in residential mobility may well be sweeping onto a deserted beach' (Short 1978a: 421).

It will be clear to the reader by now that the supply of housing is derived from several sources, including the creation of vacancies through the dissolution or migration of households, the subdivision or conversion of dwellings, and the construction of new dwellings – which is, of course, the chief source of supply in the long run. None of these sources of supply, however, is directly responsive to demand in the way that most other goods are. In part, this is due to the special nature of housing as a commodity. As Harvey (1972: 16) has observed, 'It is fixed in geographic space, it changes hands infrequently, it is a commodity which we cannot do without, and it is a form of stored wealth which is subject to speculative activities in the market . . . In

addition, the house has various forms of value to the user and above all it is the point from which the user relates to every other aspect of the urban scene.' These qualities make for a highly complex housing market in which the needs and aspirations of different socio-economic groups are matched to particular types of housing by a series of different market arrangements. In short, there exists in each city a series of distinctive sub-markets for housing. To the extent that these sub-markets are localized, they have a direct expression in the residential structure of the city. Moreover, it is now evident that the spatial outcome of each sub-market is significantly influenced by the actions of key decision-makers and mediators such as landowners, developers, estate agents and housing managers, whose motivation and behaviour effectively structures the supply of housing from which relocating households make their choice. Before going on to examine the ramifications of this behaviour in detail, however, it is essential to expand upon the nature of the major sub-markets for housing in contemporary cities.

## Housing sub-markets and the housing stock

It is important to bear in mind that the 'housing' available in any particular sub-market is a complex package of goods and services which extends well beyond the shelter provided by the dwelling itself. Housing is a primary determinant of personal security, autonomy, comfort, well-being and status, and the ownership of housing itself structures access to other scarce resources, such as educational, medical and leisure facilities. Harvey (1972: 15) has listed the services a person obtains by renting or purchasing a house or flat as follows:

1. Shelter.
2. A quantity of space for the exclusive use of the purchaser or renter . . .
3. A relative location which is:
   (a) Accessible to –
       (i) workplace;
       (ii) retail opportunities;
       (iii) social services (schools, hospitals, etc.);
       (iv) entertainment and recreational facilities;
       (v) family and friends (people you like);
   (b) Proximate to:
       (i) sources of pollution (noxious facilities);
       (ii) areas of congestion;
       (iii) sources of crime, fire hazard, noise, etc.;
       (iv) people you don't like.
4. A neighbourhood which is characterized by:
       (i) people of a certain sort;
       (ii) a physical environment of a certain sort;
       (iii) an address which indicates prestige or social status
5. An absolute location with respect to:
       (i) other absolute locations around you;
       (ii) the total transport network as it exists around you at a given point in time.

The net utility of these services is generally referred to as the *use value* of housing. As Harvey points out, this value is not fixed by the attributes of housing alone, for utility is very much in the eyes of the beholder and will vary a good deal according to life-cycle, lifestyle, social class, and so on. The use value of housing will be a major determinant of its *exchange value* in the market place, although

the special properties of housing as a commodity tend to distort the relationship. In particular, the role of housing as a form of stored wealth means that its exchange value will be influenced by its potential for reaping unearned income and for increasing capital.

This complexity in the nature of housing services is compounded by differences in tenure, type of accommodation (detached house, terrace house, maisonette, etc.), physical condition, location, price range and method of financing which make the precise identification of sub-markets a rather tricky undertaking. It is also evident that the structure and composition of housing sub-markets will vary from one city to another according to differences in the attributes of the local housing stock and the characteristics of the local population. At the inter-regional and international scale, these differences are sharpened by varying cultural attitudes to housing, by differences in methods of financing housing and by different housing policies. Moreover, variations in the spatial scale at which buyers and sellers operate defy any neat categorization of housing sub-markets. Thus, while the market for most households and some suppliers is limited to a single city, or part of it, some households and many construction firms and investment companies see their market in regional or national terms. These complexities are reflected in the difficulties encountered in empirical analyses of intra-urban variations in house prices (Ball and Kirwan 1977; Palm 1978; Straszheim 1975) and in the variety of criteria used by geographers and economists to classify housing sub-markets in different cities (Bourne 1976; 1981).

In general it is useful to think in terms of housing markets as the focus of a variety of 'actors' operating within the various constraints of political and institutional contexts, the result of which are spatial outcomes that can be identified in terms of land use changes, occupancy patterns, social area changes, housing prices, and housing quality (Fig. 6.1). Traditional definitions of housing sub-markets have been couched in terms of the attributes of housing stock (type of dwelling, type of tenancy, and price), household type (family

**Fig. 6.1**   Actors and institutions in the housing market.
*Source*: Bourne (1981) Fig. 4.8, p. 85.

status, economic status, and ethnicity), or location (Fig. 6.2). But it is unusual for housing sub-markets to form such neat, discrete compartments within any given city. Two examples illustrate the point well.

The first of the two examples taken here is drawn from David Harvey's work on the city of Baltimore, in which the major housing markets are identified in terms of the nature of housing finance available to different population sub-groups (Harvey 1974; Harvey and Chatterjee 1974). For Harvey and Chatterjee, the major feature of the Baltimore housing system is the highly structured relationship between household characteristics (particularly income) and the availability of mortgage funds. This relationship is identified in terms of 13 sub-markets, each having a distinctive mix of financing sources (Table 6.1). The main features of these sub-markets are:

1. An inner-city area consisting of low-priced rented dwellings, occupied mainly by low-income black families, where property sales are dominated by cash and private transactions.
2. White 'ethnic areas' dominated by home ownership which is chiefly financed by small, community-based savings and loan associations (the

North American equivalent of building societies).
3. Black residential areas (particularly West Baltimore) where a large proportion of home ownership has been financed by costly 'land-instalment contracts' – the only way in which low- or moderate-income blacks could become home owners in the early 1960s.
4. Areas of high turnover and racial change where house purchase is serviced by a combination of mortgage banker finance and Federal Housing Administration (FHA) guarantees (often requiring no down payment) as a result of government policies aimed at creating a socially stable class of home owners amongst blacks and the poor.
5. White middle class areas which were originally financed by earlier FHA programmes (i.e. in the 1930s) and where house purchase is now financed through federal savings and loan associations, together with some FHA guarantees.
6. Affluent areas where house purchase is achieved by way of savings banks and commercial banks, without the assistance of FHA guarantees.

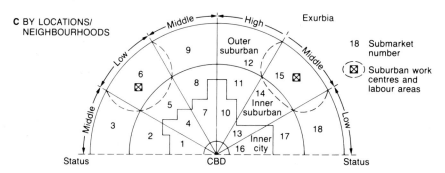

**Fig. 6.2** Intra-urban housing sub-markets: traditional definitions.
*Source*: Bourne (1981) Fig. 4.9, p. 89.

As Harvey and Chatterjee observe, this geographical structure of sub-markets forms a 'decision environment' in the context of which individual households make housing choices. Most of these choices, they suggest, are likely to conform to the structure and to reinforce it. But in the long term the geographic structure 'is continuously being transformed by the ebb and flow of market forces, the operations of speculators and realtors, the changing potential for homeownership, the changing profitability of landlordism, the pressures emanating from community action, the interventions and disruptions brought about by changing governmental and institutional policies, and the like' (Harvey and Chatterjee 1974: 25). Furthermore, they suggest that this process of transformation 'must be the focus for understanding residential differentiation' (Harvey and Chatterjee 1974: 25).

Research undertaken in the London Borough of Southwark provides a rather different perspective on the nature of sub-markets which exist within inner London. Here, the interaction between a series of *housing groups* and a number of *housing agencies* is seen as the chief determinant of the structure of housing supply. Table 6.2 shows the six major housing groups identified within Southwark classified according to income, socio-economic status and national origin – variables which are used jointly as proxy measures of housing needs and aspirations and of the 'capacity' to realize these needs and aspirations. The latter, in turn, is regarded as a product of employment status, income, capital, intelligence, education, knowledge about housing, and social acceptability (London Borough of Southwark 1973). As indicated in Table 6.2, these characteristics led different housing groups to seek accommodation of different kinds (distinguished chiefly by tenure) within varying geographical limits. Thus, for example, the housing opportunities of indigenous lower-income households encompassed both furnished and unfurnished privately-rented accommodation, publicly-rented accommodation and owner-occupation; although they were rather limited geographically. Table 6.3 shows the major housing supply agencies operating in Southwark; and an indication of their relationship with the main housing groups is given in Fig. 6.3, which is effectively a summary of the housing sub-markets within the borough. It can be seen that each housing group enjoyed access to a different range of housing opportunities through different combinations of supply agencies offering different degrees of security of tenure. Much of the potential choice implied in Fig. 6.3, however, is negated by competition for accommodation between

| Agencies ▶<br>Housing groups ▼ | Owner occupation purchase | Local authority | Housing association | Estate | Small estate landlord | New landlord |
|---|---|---|---|---|---|---|
| Upper income | ✓ | | | | | ✓ |
| Indigenous middle income | ✓ | ✓ | ✓ | ✓ | ✓ | ✓ |
| Indigenous lower income | | ✓ | ✓ | ✓ | ✓ | |
| Immigrant middle income coloured | ✓ | ✓ | ✓ | | | ✓ |
| Immigrant middle income non-coloured | | ✓ | ✓ | | ✓ | ✓ |
| Immigrant lower income | | ✓ | | | | ✓ |

**Fig. 6.3**   Housing supply agencies in inner London. *Source*: London Borough of Southwark (1973), p. 40.

housing groups and by competition between housing supply agencies for the acquisition and management of property. A more sensitive portrayal of the submarkets within this part of London therefore requires recognition of the effects of this competition. This is attempted in Figs. 6.4 and 6.5, which show the major areas of effective competition between housing groups and supply agencies respectively. A more detailed investigation of these areas of conflict revealed several important consequences, including:

1.  The loss of privately rented accommodation to owner-occupation and local authority redevelopment, resulting in fierce competition for the remaining privately-rented stock amongst the worst-off housing groups;
2.  The increasing reliance of lower income groups on housing supplied by housing associations and the local authority; and
3.  The precipitation of a residuum of homeless families as a result of an overall deficiency of housing (London Borough of Southwark 1973).

**Table 6.1**   Housing sub-markets in Baltimore City

| | Total houses sold | Sales per 100 properties | Cash | pvt | % Transactions by source of funds | | |
|---|---|---|---|---|---|---|---|
| | | | | | Federal S. & L. | State S. & L. | Mortgage Bank |
| **Inner city** | 1,199 | 1.86 | 65.7 | 15.0 | 3.0 | 12.0 | 2.2 |
| 1. East | 646 | 2.33 | 64.7 | 15.0 | 2.2 | 14.3 | 2.2 |
| 2. West | 553 | 1.51 | 67.0 | 15.1 | 4.0 | 9.2 | 2.3 |
| **Ethnic** | 760 | 3.34 | 39.9 | 5.5 | 6.1 | 43.2 | 2.0 |
| 1. East Baltimore | 579 | 3.40 | 39.7 | 4.8 | 5.5 | 43.7 | 2.4 |
| 2. South Baltimore | 181 | 3.20 | 40.3 | 7.7 | 7.7 | 41.4 | 0.6 |
| **Hampden** | 99 | 2.40 | 40.4 | 8.1 | 18.2 | 26.3 | 4.0 |
| **West Baltimore** | 497 | 2.32 | 30.6 | 12.5 | 12.1 | 11.7 | 22.3 |
| **South Baltimore** | 322 | 3.16 | 28.3 | 7.4 | 22.7 | 13.4 | 13.4 |
| **High turnover** | 2,072 | 5.28 | 19.1 | 6.1 | 13.6 | 14.9 | 32.8 |
| 1. North-west | 1,071 | 5.42 | 20.0 | 7.2 | 9.7 | 13.8 | 40.9 |
| 2. North-east | 693 | 5.07 | 20.6 | 6.4 | 14.4 | 16.5 | 29.0 |
| 3. North | 308 | 5.35 | 12.7 | 1.4 | 25.3 | 18.1 | 13.3 |
| **Middle income** | 1,077 | 3.15 | 20.8 | 4.4 | 29.8 | 17.0 | 8.6 |
| 1. South-west | 212 | 3.46 | 17.0 | 6.6 | 29.2 | 8.5 | 15.1 |
| 2. North-east | 865 | 3.09 | 21.7 | 3.8 | 30.0 | 19.2 | 7.0 |
| **Upper income** | 361 | 3.84 | 19.4 | 6.9 | 23.5 | 10.5 | 8.6 |

\* Assumed mortgages and subject to mortgage
† Ground rent is sometimes included in the sale price and this distorts the averages in certain respects. The relative differentials between the sub-markets are of the right order, however

**Table 6.2**   Housing groups in Southwark

| Housing groups | Socio-economic groups | Housing opportunities in terms of tenure | Location |
|---|---|---|---|
| 1 Upper income | Primarily professional, managerial and self-employed | Permanent: owner occupation, (high cost unfurnished) Temporary: furnished preceding ownership | Degree of flexibility in location, throughout London |
| 2 Indigenous, middle income | Skilled and semi-skilled | Permanent: owner occupation unfurnished, local authority | Owner occupied throughout London, tenants mainly Inner London and locally |
| 3 Indigenous, lower income | Semi-skilled and unskilled | Permanent: unfurnished, local authority, long-standing owner occupation. Temporary: furnished | Mainly Inner London, emphasis on Southwark |
| 4 Immigrant, middle income, coloured, (West Indian, Pakistani, (Greek etc.) | Skilled and semi-skilled | Permanent: furnished, owner occupation. Temporary: furnished | London area, often in immigrant community, may be temporary UK resident |
| 5 Immigrant, middle income non-coloured (mainly Irish) | Skilled, semi-skilled and unskilled | Permanent: unfurnished, local authority furnished. Temporary: furnished | Mainly Inner London for jobs, may be temporary UK residents |
| 6 Immigrant, lower income coloured and non-coloured. | Semi-skilled and unskilled | Permanent: furnished, local authority, temporary: furnished | Mainly Inner London, many with their own communities |

*Note*: (a) Location preference is noted to indicate the degree to which Southwark might be substituted for any other housing location, assuming jobs, schools etc. to be satisfactory
(b) Only the main housing groups and their housing opportunities are noted

*Source: London Borough of Southwark 1973: 29–30.*

| Community Bank | Savings Bank | Other* | % Sales insured | | Average sale price ($)† |
|---|---|---|---|---|---|
| | | | FHA | VA | |
| 0.5 | 0.2 | 1.7 | 2.9 | 1.1 | 3,498 |
| 0.5 | 0.1 | 1.2 | 3.4 | 1.4 | 3,437 |
| 0.4 | 0.4 | 2.2 | 2.3 | 0.6 | 3,568 |
| 0.8 | 0.9 | 2.2 | 2.6 | 0.7 | 6.372 |
| 1.0 | 1.2 | 2.2 | 3.2 | 0.07 | 6,769 |
| – | – | 2.2 | 0.6 | 0.6 | 5,102 |
| – | 3.0 | – | 14.1 | 2.0 | 7,059 |
| 1.6 | 3.1 | 6.0 | 25.8 | 4.2 | 8,664 |
| 1.9 | 4.0 | 9.0 | 22.7 | 10.6 | 8,751 |
| 1.2 | 5.7 | 6.2 | 38.2 | 9.5 | 992 |
| 1.1 | 2.9 | 4.5 | 46.8 | 7.4 | 9,312 |
| 1.4 | 5.6 | 5.9 | 34.5 | 10.2 | 9,779 |
| 0.7 | 15.9 | 12.7 | 31.5 | 15.5 | 12,330 |
| 1.9 | 8.7 | 9.0 | 17.7 | 11.1 | 12,760 |
| 1.0 | 10.8 | 11.7 | 30.2 | 17.0 | 12,848 |
| 2.0 | 8.2 | 8.2 | 14.7 | 9.7 | 12,751 |
| 7.2 | 21.1 | 2.8 | 11.9 | 3.6 | 27,413 |

**Table 6.3**  Provision and goals of housing agencies

| Agency | Provision | Goal |
|---|---|---|
| Developers | Providing mainly new houses and flats for sale, little new renting is provided | Profit from the development process is capitalized |
| Landlords | Providing unfurnished and furnished lettings on a small scale, lettings often controlled or regulated | May be to retain interest, may wish to sell |
| Large established (estate) landlords | Providing large numbers of unfurnished lettings, concentrated in certain areas | Tradition and responsibility to community, limited profit |
| Small and large new landlords | Providing mainly furnished renting; (quality variable, better with larger landlords) | Profit, perhaps service to particular groups |
| Local authorities | Providing unfurnished lettings in new buildings or conversions | Service to the community, better environment |
| Housing associations | Providing unfurnished lettings | Service to the community, and professional fees |
| Housing societies | Providing co-ownership 'renting' | Provision of a transition tenure between renting and ownership; and professional fees |
| Owner occupiers | Householders seeking owner occupation are their own agency | Accommodation that is an investment |

*Source: London Borough of Southwark 1973: 33.*

| Housing groups ▶ | Upper income | Indigenous middle income | Indigenous lower income | Immigrant middle income coloured | Immigrant middle income non-coloured | Immigrant lower income |
|---|---|---|---|---|---|---|
| Upper income | | AB | B | A | B | |
| Indigenous middle income | A | | ABC | AB | AB | B |
| Indigenous lower income | | C | | C | C | C |
| Immigrant middle income coloured | A | AB | BC | | BC | BC |
| Immigrant middle income | C | C | | C | | C |
| Owner occupier | | C | C | C | C | |

**Fig. 6.4** Competition between different groups for housing in inner London. A = competition for owner occupation of similar property, B = rented property bought for owner-occupation, C = competition for the same rented property. *Source*: London Borough of Southwark (1973), p. 42.

| Agencies ▶ | Developer | Small landlord | Estate landlord | New landlord | Local authority | Housing association | Owner occupier |
|---|---|---|---|---|---|---|---|
| Developer | | B | | | | A | AB |
| Small landlord | C | | | C | C | C | C |
| Estate landlord | | | | C | C | | |
| New landlord | | B | | | A | A | A |
| Local authority | | B | B | A | | A | AB |
| Housing association | | B | | A | A | | AB |
| Owner occupier | B | B | | | | C | |

**Fig. 6.5** Competition between different housing supply agencies in inner London. A = competition to buy and redevelop or convert the same property, B = one agency seeking to buy property from another, C = one agency under pressure to sell to another.

In Harvey and Chatterjee's terms, these outcomes were part of the transformation process which they maintain is crucial to the understanding of residential differentiation. As we shall see, Southwark's experience in this respect is fairly typical of many central city areas throughout the Western world. In the remainder of this chapter, detailed consideration is given to the implications of the dynamics of housing supply, beginning with a summary and explanation of the major trends in the transformation of the urban housing stock: the increase in the construction of dwellings for home ownership, the decrease in the availability of cheaper privately-rented dwellings, and the increase (in many countries) in the construction and letting of dwellings by public authorities. In doing so, we shall see that the dynamics of housing supply are socially constructed: they are, ultimately, a product of the inter-relationships of political, economic, and ideological factors. Most of these factors recur throughout the Western world; but their precise composition and their inter-relationships make for significant variability between individual cities and nations (Harloe and Martens 1984; Dickens *et al.* 1985).

## The growth of home ownership

The growth of home ownership is characteristic of all Western countries and it has had a marked effect not only on residential differentiation but also on the whole space-economy of urbanized societies. In the United States, the overall proportion of owner-occupied dwellings rose from 20 per cent in 1920 to 44 per cent in 1940 and 66 per cent in 1980; in Britain, the proportion of owner-occupied dwellings rose steadily from 10.6 per cent in 1914 to 28 per cent in 1953, accelerated to reach 52 per cent by 1973, and stood at 56 per cent in 1983. Other countries exhibit compar-

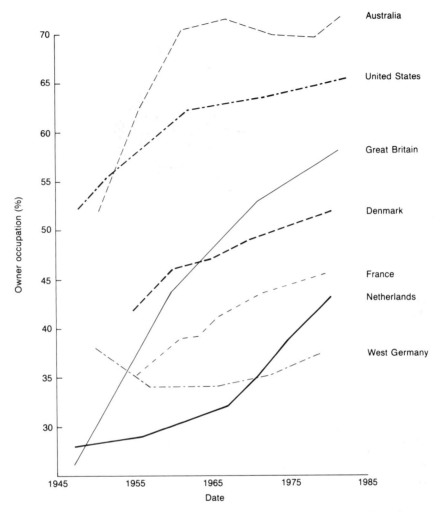

**Fig. 6.6**  The rise of owner-occupation. Based on Martens (1985) Fig. 1., p. 607.

able trends (Fig. 6.6). As shown in Chapter 2, the socio-spatial manifestations of this trend include the development of extensive tracts of low-density suburban sprawl, with an associated increase in residential differentiation according to households' ability to pay for different grades of housing and for transport between home and work. It is not necessary to reiterate these developments in detail; nor should it be necessary to emphasize the relationship between suburban home ownership and the imperatives of the family life-cycle, the filtering process, and the general

residential preferences of a majority of households. The point which must be made here, however, is that the growth in home ownership has not been entirely the result of increasing affluence among a progressively wider section of society. In other words, supply has not simply followed demand.

What has happened in most countries is that the supply of owner-occupier housing has been deliberately stimulated by government policies. No doubt part of the motivation for these policies can be attributed to the notion of giving the electorate what it wants. But it is more likely that political and social stabiliz-ation has been the major motive for govern-ment intervention. One of the principal areas of state intervention has been the fostering of the institutions – building societies, savings and loan associations, and the like – which finance the purchase (and ultimately, there-fore, the supply) of private housing. These institutions originated in Britain in the late eighteenth century as savings clubs and friendly societies which used the proceeds of their efforts to build houses for members. The first such organization to appear in the United States was the Oxford Provident Building Association, set up in Philadelphia in 1831. By the early twentieth century, organizations in both countries had proliferated and grown into substantial institutions controlling large amounts of capital. Because of their role in financing home ownership amongst the middle and upper-working classes, they soon came to be regarded as an essential mechanism in the promotion of a property-owning democracy. This objective assumed considerable import-ance to Western governments in the light of the political unrest of the time, and so home ownership was actively fostered as a 'Bulwark against Bolshevism' (Forrest, Murie and Williams 1985). In other words, government sought to defend the property system by giving as many people as possible a stake in it. Financing this ownership by way of long-term loans from organizations such as building societies provided a further source of social and political stability, since the widespread debt encumbrance represented by mortgage repayments committed home 'owners' to oppose any changes to the social and econ-omic structure of society which might endanger the value of their property or make it more difficult for them to pay off their debt (Boddy 1976a; Stone 1978).

One of the first significant steps towards promoting home ownership in Britain came soon after the First World War with the estab-lishment of concessionary tax rates – a quarter of the standard rate – on interest received from investments in building societies. This rapidly swelled the resources of the societies and, together with low interest rates and the relatively low costs of labour and materials in

the 1930s, facilitated the housebuilding boom which spawned the extensive interwar sprawl and ribbon development which revolutionized the social geography of British cities. Although this boom was interrupted by the Second World War and, briefly, by the postwar Labour government's strong committment to cheap working-class housing for rent, the promotion of home ownership was again pursued vigorously from the 1950s onwards with the return of a Conservative government, under the Labour administrations of Wilson and Callaghan, and under the Thatcher government of the 1980s (Ball 1983; Merrett and Gray 1982; Short 1982). Among the various policy instruments which have been used to encourage home ownership are:

1.  Grants to building societies in order to keep interest rates below market rates and to encourage the purchase of pre-1919 dwellings which were formerly rented;
2.  The abolition of taxation on the imputed income from property while preserving the tax payer's right to deduct mortgage interest repayments from gross taxable income;
3.  The exemption of homes from capital gains taxes;
4.  The provision of mortgages by local authorities;
5.  The sale of local authority dwellings to 'sitting tenants' or newly-married couples at a substantial discount from the market price;
6.  The introduction of the 'option mort-gage' scheme to provide cheap loans for first-time housebuyers from lower income groups;
7.  The utilization of public powers of compulsory purchase to acquire devel-opment land on which owner-occupier houses could be built;
8.  The underwriting of the 'voluntary sector' of housebuilding for home ownership through housing associ-ations; and
9.  The discount sale of the stock of public housing (see p. 218).

During the 1970s, tax relief subsidies grew

fivefold in real terms, and by the early 1980s state subsidies to owner-occupation were 30 per cent higher than to public-sector housing (Ball 1983).

Similar developments have occurred in other countries, though the policy instruments have sometimes been different. In many West European countries, for example, direct subsidies to owner-occupation have played a major role in the expansion of home ownership, with subsidized loans being made available to lower-income households (Martens 1985; Wynn 1984). In the United States, the growth of home ownership has been encouraged by a variety of mortgage guarantees and subsidies. One of the earliest programmes was the Federal National Home Loan Bank System, set up in the 1930s to insure savings accounts in the wake of the uncertainty created by the Depression. After the Second World War, further assistance was given to private house financing, partly in response to the mounting disorder in larger cities. As the US National Committee on Urban Problems (1968: 401) observed, 'Home ownership encourages social stability and financial responsibility. It gives the home owner a financial stake in society . . . It helps eliminate the "alienated tenant" psychology.' Among the major programmes which have been initiated are the Federal Housing Administration and Veterans Administration mortgage guarantee schemes, together with the Government National Mortgage Association, the Federal Home Loan Mortgage Corporation and various state housing finance agencies created to channel more funds into the owner-occupied sector.

In spite of all this state protection and subsidization, it has become increasingly difficult for many households to afford to buy their own home. The reason is inflation. Since the early 1970s, house prices have tended to rise faster than the overall rate of economic inflation, largely because of rapidly rising construction and finance costs. In the United States, for example, home owners in 1983 were on average using 18 per cent more of their incomes to pay for their homes than in 1973; and similar trends have been reported throughout the Western world. Such figures,

of course, obscure some very large variations as the dynamics of urban change are reflected on neighbourhood price levels. The differential escalation of prices clearly has important implications in relation to variations in, among other things, the capital gains that can be obtained from exchange values in different neighbourhoods. In Sydney, Australia, neighbourhood price changes in 1978/9 fell into four categories (Fig. 6.7):

First, there are the areas where *big money* was earned, these being a mixture of north shore suburbs such as Mosman, Neutral Bay, Hornsby and Gordon, eastern suburbs such as Randwick, Paddington and Centennial Park, and a few inner western suburbs such as Strathfield and Belmore. Second, there were a few suburbs categorised as earning *smart money*, such as the inner western suburbs of Ashfield, Hurstville and Revesby, where the property boom was about to take off in 1978. Thirdly, there are the suburbs mainly in the inner city such as Leichhardt, and the outer western and south-western areas, stretching through Parramatta, Penrith, Bankstown, Blacktown to Liverpool, where *no money* was made. Finally, there are the isolated examples, such as Mona Vale, which were *bad money* suburbs, where prices actually fell (Stimpson 1982: 136).

However, it is important to stress that, these local effects notwithstanding, the overall effect of house-price inflation has *not* been to dampen demand. On the contrary, inflation has underscored the urgency of many households to participate in the long-term benefits of home ownership and the possibility of capturing large capital gains. The growth of home ownership has been sustained at the expense of households' consumption in other fields, and by the increasing tendency for women to re-enter the labour market after having, or raising, children, and by moves among developers to build smaller houses at higher densities in order to reduce construction costs.

Nevertheless, there is at the same time an increasing number of households for whom house-price inflation has put home ownership clearly out of reach. Indeed, there is strong evidence that social *polarization* has been taking place between housing tenure cat-

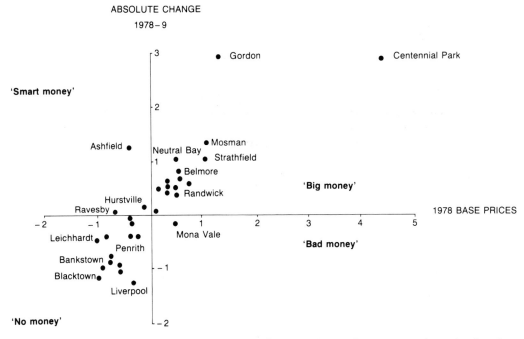

**Fig. 6.7** Change in private dwelling prices in Sydney, Australia, 1978–9 (standardized values: zero mean, units in standard deviations).
*Source*: Stimpson (1982), Fig. 5.2, p. 136.

egories. In Britain, for example, the rate of increase in home ownership among lower-status groups (unskilled manual) in the 1970s was less than 4 per cent, compared to growth rates of nearly 7 per cent among professionals/managers/employers and over 11 per cent among intermediate and junior non-manual workers. Conversely, unskilled and semi-skilled manual households were increasingly localized in public housing (Hamnett 1984). This clearly has important implications for urban social geography. In addition to the implications for socio-ecological patterns, the polarization of socio-economic groups by housing tenure raises some critical issues in relation to patterns of income and wealth, class structure, and social conflict. As more and more households become outright owners (having paid off mortgages), so an important new mechanism for the *transfer of wealth* is being created. And, as more and more of these owners are drawn from the higher socio-economic groups, communities will become increasingly polarized economically (Murie and Forrest 1980). As Hamnett puts it (1984: 404), 'Disraeli's Two Nations are being perpetually recreated on a tenurial basis.' The relationships between owner-occupation and *class structure and class-consciousness* are less clear (Agnew 1981; Forrest and Williams 1980; Thorns 1981). As we have seen, there is a case for regarding home ownership as an instrument through which sections of the working class have been incorporated within the conservatism of a property-owning democracy. On the other hand, it has been argued that home ownership has generated specific economic interests which have fractured the traditional divisions of class (Saunders 1978). But class structure and class-consciousness are forged from the totality of life experience at both home *and* work. There are owner-occupiers and owner-occupiers: 'If you are screwed at work, the likelihood is that you are screwed in your housing construction. And being an owner-occupier does not compensate for living in a shoddily-built, high-density box in the middle of a housing estate, with the dim prospects of a real gain at the end of your housing career' (Short 1982: 150). Moreover, as different groups of owner-occupiers seek to protect and enhance the exchange value of their property, so they will inevitably come into *conflict* with one another and with other interest groups. The resolution of this conflict is part of the constant redefinition and recreation of urban structure, both physical and social.

## The decline of the privately rented sector

The corollary of the growth in home ownership has been the decline of privately rented housing. In cities everywhere as recently as the 1920s, between 80 and 90 per cent of all households lived in privately-rented accommodation, whereas the equivalent figure now stands at between 25 and 35 per cent in North American cities and between 10 and 20 per cent in most European and Australian cities. (West German cities are an exception here, with around 45 per cent of all households living in privately rented accommodation, including 15–20 per cent living in accommodation rented from employers). Nowhere has this decline been more marked than in Britain, where only 12 per cent of the housing stock is now rented from private landlords, compared to around 60 per cent in 1947 and 90 per cent in 1914. In general terms, this decline reflects the response by landlords to changes in the relative rates of return provided by the ownership of rental accommodation and by households to the artificial financial advantages associated with home ownership and (in Europe) public tenure. Put another way, it is not related to any decline in the demand for privately-rented accommodation as such: it is the product of wider economic and political changes (Downs 1983; Harloe 1985; Paris 1984).

It is not difficult to understand the landlord's desire to disinvest in rental accommodation. Before 1914, investment in rented property produced an income which was almost double the return of gilt-edged securities, even allowing for maintenance and management costs; but by 1970 landlords in Britain could only obtain around 6 per cent on their investment, compared to the 9 per cent obtainable from long-dated government securities (Eversley 1975). Moreover, investments in rental accommodation compare unfavourably with other forms of property investment, particularly in industrial, commercial and retail property. Ambrose (1976) has suggested that the average annual revenue derived from privately rented housing is exceeded by a factor of 2.5 by the average revenue derived from a similar-sized parcel of land given over to factories or warehouses, by a factor of 7.5 for shops, and by a factor of 40 for offices in provincial cities.

One of the major factors influencing the relatively low returns on investment in rental housing (thus impeding its supply) has been the existence of *rent controls*. These were introduced in many countries to curtail profiteering by landlords in the wake of housing shortages created by the lack of housebuilding during the First World War. Once introduced, however, rent controls have tended to persist because of government fears of unpopularity with urban electorates. The effect of such controls has been to restrict the ability of landlords to cover loan charges, maintenance and management costs as well as extracting an adequate profit. This situation has been exacerbated by taxation policies which do not allow landlords to deduct depreciation costs from taxes and by the introduction and enforcement of more rigorous building standards and housing codes (Hirsch and Law 1979). Another compounding factor has been the fact that the incomes of tenants in the privately rented sector have, in general, risen more slowly than the average. With inflation increasing landlords' costs sharply from the 1960s onwards, landlords responded by selling their property, either to owner-occupiers or to developers interested in site redevelopment. In some neighbourhoods, as we have seen, the deterioration of the housing stock has reached the stage where landlords can find no buyers and so are forced to abandon their property (Palm 1979). In other areas, where there is a high level of demand for accommodation, specialist agencies have moved in to expedite disinvestment. This has been especially noticeable in London, where large numbers of purpose-built flats in interwar suburbs like Ealing, Chiswick and Streatham and in some central areas – Kensington, Clelsea and Westminster – have been sold by specialist 'breakup' companies on behalf of large landlords such as property companies and insurance companies (Hamnett 1979a; Hamnett and Randolph 1984).

Overall, 2.6 m. dwellings were sold by landlords to owner-occupiers in Britain between 1938 and 1975 (Short 1982). Moreover, little new property has been built for private renting in the last 50 years, so that what is left of the privately rented sector is old (about 70 per cent of the existing stock in England and Wales was built before 1914) and, because of a succession of rent controls, most of it has deteriorated badly. This deterioration has itself led to a further depletion of the privately rented stock in many inner-city areas, as urban renewal schemes have demolished large tracts of housing. It is also worth noting that many European cities suffered a considerable loss of privately-rented housing through bomb damage during the Second World War. (It should also be noted that the exceptionally high levels of privately rented housing in West German cities are largely the product of the massive housing shortage that resulted from war damage, combined with rapid rates of economic growth, urbanization, household formation and immigration in the postwar period that led governments to provide generous production subsidies for apartments.)

This decline in the quantity and quality of privately-rented accommodation has affected the social geography of the city in several ways. In general terms, it has clearly hastened the decay of inner-city areas whilst reinforcing the shift of a large proportion of the lower-middle and more prosperous working classes to owner-occupied housing in the suburbs. It has also led to a resorting and realignment of inner-city neighbourhoods and populations as the various groups requiring cheap rented accommodation are squeezed into a smaller and smaller pool of housing. These groups encompass a variety of 'short stay' households, including young single persons and young couples for whom private rental accommodation is a temporary but essential stepping-stone to either owner-occupied or public housing. In addition there are the more permanent residents who have little chance of obtaining a mortgage, saving for a house or being allocated a house in the public sector. These include some indigenous low-income households, low-income migrants, transient individuals, single-parent families, and elderly households on fixed incomes. Fierce competition for the diminishing supply of cheap rental housing between these economically similar but socially and racially very different groups inevitably results in an increase in social conflict which in turn leads to territorial segregation and the development of 'defended neighbourhoods'.

In Britain, it appears that the evolution of the privately rented sector has produced four main subdivisions, each containing tenants with differing requirements and landlords with varying objectives and constraints (Bovaird *et al.* 1985). The biggest subdivision, accounting for around 50 per cent of the privately rented stock, is the *traditional* sub-sector, which includes households who have always regarded private renting as their normal lifetime tenure, and now contains mainly the elderly and younger single-person households. Most landlords are individuals who have been in business a long time or who have inherited property. The sub-sector providing for *young and mobile* households is next largest (25–30 per cent of the total), and supply here is dominated by large-scale landlords of furnished accommodation letting units in multiple occupation, and by individuals letting parts of their own homes. Accommodation *rented with job or business* is for households of working age (most of them with children) and accounts for a further 20 per cent of the total. Finally, there is a small *residual* sub-sector made up mainly of lower-income non-family households, of recent migrants and those who have been forced to move from their previous accommodation. Supply is dominated by landlords of furnished, multi-occupancy units of poor quality. Given these distinctive sub-sectors, it is clear that future outcomes will depend very much on the types of household that will continue to demand privately rented accommodation, the types of landlord that will be prepared to continue to let, and the *match between the requirements of the two groups* (Whitehead *et al.* 1985).

Finally, it should be noted that the shrinkage of the privately-rented sector has been selective. In larger cities, the demand for centrally-situated luxury flats has been sufficient to encourage investment in this type of property. Thus, in cities like London, Paris, Brussels and Zurich, the more expensive element of the privately-rented sector has been preserved intact, if not enhanced, by the dominance of pure rent over housing and tax legislation. It must also be recognized that in some of the larger and more affluent cities of Australia and North America the privately-rented sector has maintained its overall share of the housing stock though the expansion of high-income rental apartments, even though low-income rental accommodation has been rapidly disappearing. Bourne, for instance, has drawn attention to the occurrence of this sub-market in Toronto during the 1960s in response to the interplay of several supply factors. These included the rising costs of purchasing suburban land and providing the infra-structure of roads, drains and other services, the consequent increase in the costs of home ownership, and the structure of local tax and education costs (Bourne 1968). Combined with a shift in personal attitudes towards living in flats, these factors have led to an increase in the proportion of flats in the city's housing stock from 42 per cent in 1958 to 73 per cent in 1967, altering both the structure and location of the city's housing stock away from 'traditional' patterns. A similar boom in apartment construction in Sydney, Australia, is described by Stimpson (1982).

More recently, continuing shortages in the supply of land and capital in the faster-growing cities of North America has further restored the position of rental housing. Basically, what has happened is that the cost of financing low density owner-occupier housing has risen beyond the pocket of many potential housebuyers. Indeed, the proportion of US households buying homes decreased between 1980 and 1982 for the first time since the Great Depression as the total costs of home ownership rose to consume over 40 per cent of median incomes. The result has been that the development and construction industry has turned to the production of multiple-unit structures for sale or rent. In 1984, two-thirds of all housing starts were multi-family units. This apartment boom has begun to ring the edges of American cities with apartment complexes and terrace houses for the middle classes: a development which completely flies in the face of traditional land-use patterns (Vance 1976).

## The development of public housing

Like the other major changes in the long-term pattern of housing supply, the emergence of public housing is a product of wider economic and political factors rather than the result of secular changes in the underlying pattern of housing need or demand. Public housing is supplied in a variety of ways. In Britain, the bulk of all public housing is purpose-built by local authorities; in the Netherlands, Denmark and Sweden much public housing is supplied by way of co-operatives; while in West Germany the public housing programme is dominated by *Neue Heimat*, an adjunct of the trades union movement (Wynn 1984). But, whatever the organizational framework, the quality and extent of public housing supply is ultimately dependent upon the resources and disposition of central and local governments and public institutions. For this reason, it is difficult to make sense of trends in the provision of public housing without recourse to specific examples. Here, attention is focused on the two very different histories of public housing in Britain and the United States.

### Britain

As we have seen, public sector housing accounts for a large proportion of the housing stock in British cities: 25 to 30 per cent on average, rising to over 50 per cent in Scottish cities. The provision of low-rent public housing dates from the late nineteenth century, when it emerged as part of the reformist public health and town planning movements (see Chapter 2). Nevertheless, public housing was slow to develop. The nineteenth century legislation was permissive: local authorities could build housing for the poor but were under no obligation to do so, and there was no question of financial support from the central government. Not surprisingly, most local authorities did nothing, preferring to rely on the activities of philanthropic and charitable housing trusts. The first major step towards large-scale public housing provision came in 1919, when the acute housing shortage which had developed because of the virtual cessation of building during the war years was made even more pressing by Lloyd George's highly publicized promise of 'Homes fit for Heroes'. As Bowley (1945: 9) observed 'It was politically necessary to make some effort to control and organize the supply of new houses, particularly of working class houses to let.' The response was to give local authorities the responsibility and the funding to provide such housing. Subsequently, although public housing became something of a political football, the level of exchequer subsidies was steadily raised, and a succession of legislation gave local authorities increasing powers and responsibility to build public housing for a wider section of the community (Melling 1980).

After the Second World War there was again a backlog of housing, this time exacerbated by war damage. Moreover, the incoming Labour government was heavily committed to the public sector and in 1949 passed a Housing Act which removed the limitation restricting local authorities to the provision of housing for the 'working classes'. From this date, local authorities were free to gear the supply of public housing to the more general needs of the community. The immediate result was a surge in housebuilding to make up the postwar backlog – the so-called 'pack 'em in' phase. Later, with the return of the Conservatives to power, the supply of public housing was more closely tied to slum clearance programmes and the needs of specific groups such as the elderly and the poor. By the mid-1960s, however, it had become evident that there was a continuing 'housing problem' of considerable proportions, and the Labour government which took office in 1964 initiated a new phase of 'general needs' housebuilding with a target of 500,000 houses a year. While this target was never reached (the peak was reached in 1967 when 204,000 dwellings were completed), the housing stock of every British city was substantially altered during the 1960s by the addition of large amounts of public housing (Dunleavy 1981). During the 1970s the supply of public housing continued to increase, albeit at a somewhat diminished rate in response to changing political and economic circumstances. The unusual combinaton of inflation and economic recession which followed the rise in petroleum prices in Western countries in the mid-1970s, together with the cut-backs in public expenditure imposed by the 1979 Thatcher government, have considerably reduced the supply of new public housing. Moreover, the stock of existing public housing is now being eroded by the Conservatives' policy of encouraging the sale of local authority housing to sitting tenants at a discount of up to 60 per cent of the assessed value of the property. This retreat from public housing is part of a general 'recapitalization' of capital, aided by the emergence of a 'New Right' in politics whose response to the widespread collapse of profits has been to pursue cutbacks in public expenditure, reductions in taxation, and reductions in wages, to 'privatize' (or 'decollectivize') public services, and to tolerate high levels of unemployment (Harloe 1981; see also Eisinger 1982; Fincher 1984; Hoggart 1985; Roistacher 1984). In practice, the cuts in Britain have been imposed disproportionately on local government expenditures, and on housing in particular. Thus, whereas central government expenditure increased by 8 per cent between 1975/6 and 1981/2, local government expenditure decreased by some 21 per cent and expenditure on housing was reduced by 52 per cent during the same period. As Harloe and Paris (1984) observe, the reason for this lopsidedness is that it would have been much more difficult to implement similar cuts in social security, defence, education or health: they would have directly undermined the political constituency of the governing party. Nevertheless, the political dimensions of the retreat from public housing are complex (Bassett 1980). The Labour party as well as the Conservative party, for example, has long supported the extension of owner-occupation, and sales of public housing rose steadily under the Callaghan administration to reach more than 41,000 in 1979. Moreover, surveys have shown that as many as 60 per cent of the tenants of public housing would prefer owner-occupation.

Yet a significantly lower proportion (around 20 per cent) would actually want to purchase their existing dwelling (Murie 1982). In addition, it is clear that it is the better-paid, economically active tenants with at least 20 years of earning (and mortgage repayments) ahead of them who are the main customers. For the unemployed, the elderly, and the single-parent family, the 'opportunity' of home ownership is likely to prove more illusory than real. Such cleavages cut across traditional party lines, clouding the politics of public housing. What is clear, however, is that public housing is increasingly regarded as – and is increasingly becoming – a *residual service* for disadvantaged households (English 1982; Forrest and Murie 1983, 1986; McDowell 1983a).

The legacy of these public housing policies has had a profound effect on the morphology and social geography of British cities. Tracts of public housing are to be found throughout the urban fabric, with a particular concentration in suburban locations. In general terms, and certainly in comparison with the location of public housing in North American cities, the location of public housing in British cities is remarkable for its integration with owner-occupied housing and for its occupation by a wide band of the socio-economic spectrum (Cox and Agnew 1974). The former is partly explained by the extensive planning powers of British local authorities; and the latter by standards of construction which compare favourably with those found in the lower end of the private market – a factor which is especially important when the costs of renting public housing and buying private housing are compared. This broad social and spatial integration fits conveniently with Sopher's (1972) proposition that societies with a high degree of social stratification (like Britain) require only a symbolic distancing of social groups, in contrast to the more overt territorial segregation of social groups required in more 'open' societies like the United States. It is interesting to speculate on the role of architecture in this respect for, as Nevitt (1978) points out, the aesthetic sterility of much local authority housing seems far in excess of any limitations on design imposed by financial constraints alone.

This image of spatial and social integration should not be exaggerated, however. Public housing developments do not find a ready welcome near established owner-occupier neighbourhoods because the general perception of their morphological and social characteristics leads to fears among owner-occupiers of a fall in their existing quality of life and (perhaps more significantly) in the future exchange value of their houses. Vigorous opposition is therefore common, as exemplified by the episode of the Cutteslowe Walls (see p. 76); and despite the legislative power of urban governments to override such opposition, it is usually deemed to be politically wiser to seek out the least contentious locations for public housing. Moreover, financial pressures on local authorities tend to encourage the purchase of cheaper land whenever possible (Ambrose 1977b). For these reasons, many public housing developments tend to be located on extremely peripheral sites, thus effectively isolating their residents from the rest of the city, at least until residential infill and the general socio-economic infra-structure catch up with the initial housing construction.

It must also be recognized that a considerable amount of differentiation exists *within* the stock of public housing. As English (1976) observes, public housing in Britain is highly stratified, providing accommodation and environments which range from excellent to appalling. Much of this differentiation can be explained in the context of the chronology of the supply of public housing. Thus whereas most of the early public housing estates (i.e. those built during the 1920s) were 'cottage-style' semi-detached dwellings, the succeeding generation of council estates built in the 1930s was dominated by 3- and 4-storey walk-up flats built for slum clearance families. These acquired a social character quite different from the earlier estates and have subsequently developed a poor reputation in the popular imagination, even if not always justified in practice (Niner and Watson 1978). A different character again was produced by the postwar boom in public housing construction. The accommodation provided at this time – in the face of waiting lists of tens of thousands in every city and in the context of strict financial constraints and a severe shortage of conventional building materials – created vast tracts of functional but austere housing on the outskirts of cities, much of it in the form of low-rise multi-occupation units. Moreover, because these peripheral estates were catering for those at the top of the waiting list (and who were therefore deemed to be most needy), there developed a sequential segregation along socio-economic lines. The first estates to be completed were thus dominated by the unskilled and semi-skilled who were the least able to compete in the private sector, and with large families whose previous accommodation was overcrowded. As these families were siphoned from the top of the waiting list, later estates were given over to relatively smaller and more prosperous families.

After the backlog had been cleared, architectural and planning experiments provided further differentiation of the public housing stock, leading specific housing schemes to acquire varying levels of popularity and, therefore, of status. The public housing boom of the 1960s brought yet another set of distinctive housing environments, this time dominated by maisonettes and high-rise blocks of flats, most of which were located in inner-city areas on slum-clearance sites. As Ambrose (1977b) has pointed out, the heavy emphasis on high-rise developments in the 1960s was the product of several factors in addition to the infatuation of architects and planners with the 'modern movement' in architectural

design and the doctrine of high-rise solutions to urban sprawl (Malpass 1975). Ambrose specifically mentions:

1. the pattern of government subsidies, which favoured the construction of high-density, high-rise housing schemes; and
2. the tendering policies of large construction and civil engineering companies, who were anxious to obtain contracts for high-rise buildings in order to recoup the considerable investment they had made in 'system' building.

To these we should add a third factor: the feeling on many city councils that large high-rise buildings were 'prestige' developments with which to display civic pride and achievement – another example of the interaction of 'spirit and matter'. Since 1968 there has been a rapid retreat from this kind of development, partly as a result of the publicity given to the damaging effects of high-rise living on family and social life, partly because of shortcomings in the design and construction of high-rise buildings (the partial collapse of the Ronan Point flats in east London were crucial in this respect), and partly because the big construction firms began to turn their attention to the 'office boom' which began in the late 1960s. Having experienced the consequences of low-cost, high-rise, high-density living, the current trend is towards the development of low-rise, small-scale housing schemes with 'vernacular' architectural touches and the provision of at least some 'defensible space' There is, therefore, a considerable stratification of the public housing stock which is reflected in the morphology of the city as a whole. In Newcastle upon Tyne, for example, the distribution of flats and maisonettes reflects the large-scale building schemes undertaken from the late 1950s through the early 1970s in the city's outer fringes and in inner city redevelopment schemes (Fig. 6.8). Morphological patterns such as these are also reflected in social patterns. Within Aberdeen, for example, there are distinctive and significant patterns of social segregation within the public sector (though they are not as marked as in the private sector), with particular concentrations

**Fig. 6.8**  Distribution of Council flats and maisonettes in Newcastle upon Tyne.
*Source*: Taylor and Hadfield (1982) Fig. 12.2, p. 248.

of deprived, unskilled and semi-skilled manual households in the estates built under slum clearance and crowding legislation in the 1930s (Twine and Williams 1983). Such patterns form the basis for further segregation as a result of the actions of housing managers and other local authority officials (see below, pp. 241–244).

The sale of public housing can also be seen to have differential effects on urban structure. In England as a whole over 400,000 applications to buy had been received within two years of the passing of the Housing Act 1980. This represents 9 per cent of all tenants. In Scotland, where public housing is much more prevalent, around 6 per cent of all tenants had applied. Both demand and the actual level of sales varied a good deal from city to city in response to variations in the profile of local housing sub-markets and the enthusiasm of local authorities to sell their property. In Scotland, for example, sales to June 1982 ranged from 0.8 per cent in Dundee and 1.3 per cent in Glasgow to 3.1 per cent in Aberdeen, 4.9

per cent in Edinburgh, 10.1 per cent in Cumbernauld New Town and 12.4 per cent in East Kilbride. In every case (and in the cities of England and Wales), these sales have been dominated by self-contained family houses. In Glasgow, for example, 74.9 per cent of all sales were detached, semi-detached or terrace dwellings, and these represented a loss of over 15 per cent of the city's stock of such dwellings in two years (City of Glasgow 1983); in Aberdeen, the equivalent figures were 86.1 per cent and 6.6 per cent (Sewel *et al.* 1984); and in Newcastle upon Tyne 99 per cent of sales were houses or bungalows, representing a loss of some 7 per cent of the total stock of this category (Barke 1983). The spatial pattern of sales, reflecting the distribution of estates containing more desirable self-contained family dwellings, has been very uneven. Sales in some neighbourhoods had already amounted to between 25 and 35 per cent by mid 1982, whereas sales in many less attractive neighbourhoods dominated by flats and maisonettes had been nil. These patterns have important implications for the social geography of British cities, not least in the fact that both the residualization and the privatization of the public sector are clearly being intensified at the neighbourhood level. It remains to be seen whether the depletion of cities' most sought-after stock will continue, but it is already evident that local authorities are not receiving enough cash from sales to enable replacement properties to be built. In Glasgow, the average selling price of the first 1,000 properties sold was £9,469, whereas their average valuation was £17,728 and the average replacement cost was £32,000 (City of Glasgow 1983). All this at a time when the city had over 80,000 applicants on file for public sector lets. As a result of such arithmetic, it will be increasingly difficult for the public sector to meet the needs of those who want or need public housing. This, in turn, will inevitably induce change in other components of urban ecology as other housing sub-markets respond to the situation.

### The United States

The history of public housing in the United States represents the polar opposite to that of Britain. Although public housing programmes have been operating for over 40 years, and although a succession of studies have established that about one-third of all families in American cities require basic housing which they cannot afford (Fuerst 1974; Montgomery and Mandelker 1979), the supply of public housing units has been restricted to a very narrow clientele. This is the obverse of a national housing policy which is orientated towards the encouragement of owner-occupation on the premise that the process of filtering will eliminate the housing problem at the lower end of the market. Vance (1976) has suggested that this approach can be attributed to the 'geographical' characteristics of US cities: the widespread availability of low-cost development land coupled with cheap and flexible intra-urban transport, which facilitates the free-market provision of housing via suburban expansion. While this may be so, it does not take into account the failure of filtering mechanisms to provide housing for

the poor. We must, therefore, look to wider economic and political forces in explaining the failure of US public housing programmes to match the expansion experienced in most Western European countries.

The initial public housing legislation (1937) was a product of the Depression and the political climate created by the New Deal, and much of the rationale for the first low-rent public housing was couched in terms of its utility as an employment programme. But although it was significant in establishing a federal presence in the housing market its effects were curtailed by the Second World War. Afterwards, the supply of public housing was invigorated by the Housing Act of 1949 which linked construction with slum clearance programmes and expressed a committment to subsidized housing for the poor. Bollens and Schmandt (1975: 173) suggest that the Act managed to get past strong opposition because the various interested parties, 'like the blind men feeling the elephant, made entirely different assumptions about the purpose of the legislation.' While liberals saw it as a means of eliminating slums and rehousing the poor, businessmen saw it as a means of bolstering waning property values in and around CBDs; and fiscally-oriented administrators looked upon it as a means of bolstering the tax base and luring back some of the more affluent consumers and taxpayers who had moved to the suburbs. The Act authorized the construction of 810,000 low-rent units over six years, and has since been amended and re-inforced by a series of programmes (Aaron 1972). The conventional method of supplying this housing has been for the federal government to underwrite the bonds issued by local public housing authorities to finance land and construction costs; but in 1965, in an attempt to provide a wider range of housing opportunities, provision was made for housing authorities to lease dwellings from private owners for rent at low rates to families who are eligible for public housing. The private owner receives market rental rates, with federal contributions covering the difference. More recently, the emphasis has been on the construction of multi-unit projects to house the lower-middle and low-income elderly by providing cheap loans to local authorities, non-profit organizations and consumer co-operatives.

The success of these programmes has been derisory. The 810,000 units called for in the 1949 legislation took 25 years to materialize, and although the pace of subsidized housing construction has increased since Lyndon Johnson's Housing and Redevelopment Act of 1968 (itself a response to the riots and civil disorder of the 1960s), the net contribution of public housing programmes to the low-rent housing stock of most cities has been insignificant (Downs 1973). Several reasons may be advanced for this poor record. Above all, it must be recognized that the aggressively free-enterprise social and political climate of the United States makes a poor environment for housing reform (Marcuse 1980). In addition to widespread public antipathy towards any form of 'creeping socialism', the political clout of vested interests within the urban business lobby has effectively retarded the fruition of public housing programmes. Spearheading the opposition to the generosity and coerciveness of national legislation have been the National Association of Real Estate Boards, the National Association of Home Builders and the United States Savings and Loan League, backed up by the powerful support of the US Chamber of Commerce, the Mortgage Bankers Association of America and the American Bankers Association. It is also significant that the major postwar debate about public housing took place during the McCarthy era, with the inevitable charges of communist infiltration (Cox and Agnew 1974). The effectiveness of this opposition is reflected in the poverty of US public housing programmes. Moreover, even where public funds have been appropriated for housing construction, the organization and tactics of local business interests and the corruption of key housing officials and FHA inspectors has ensured that 'free enterprise' has emerged as the winner, with most of the benefit of federal subsidies being siphoned off by the local construction industry, its professionalized handmaidens – the so-called 'exchange professionals' such as mortgage brokers and estate agents – and the somewhat less professional 'quick buck artists'

(Boyer 1973; Fried 1971).

It should also be borne in mind that he imperative for housing reform has been less pressing in the United States than in most Western European countries. The housing stock of most cities is much younger, and none were subject to war damage. In addition, levels of investment in private housing have traditionally been higher in the United States than in Europe (Vance 1976). Nevertheless, there has for a long time been a chronic housing problem for a large minority of the American urban poor. The decisive factor in the continued rejection of public housing as a solution to this problem has probably been the failure of existing public housing projects to effect a substantial improvement of the urban housing problem, just as its opponents predicted. To a large extent this has been a self-fulfilling prophecy, because most of the shortcomings of public housing can be traced to restrictions on the financing and allocation of public housing built into the relevant legislative framework by its opponents (Lazin 1980). The most important factor in this respect has been the existence of strict means-testing for households wishing to rent public housing. This has taken the form of an established maximum income which has varied locally but which has generally been only marginally above the officially-defined poverty line. Only families with incomes below this level were admitted and, more important, as soon as their incomes rose 25 per cent above it they were required to leave. Thus public housing has effectively been treated as a receptacle for the economically incompetent. The residents themselves, with no security of tenure, have no reason to care for their homes and no reason to expect to be able to develop local ties. Not surprisingly, such an environment is conducive to the intensification of a wide range of social problems; a situation exacerbated by the low quality of the dwelling units themselves. Between 1949 and 1965 a dollar limit on construction costs (it was $2,400) meant that many homes were handed over to tenants without doors on the lavatory, without seats on the toilet, and without either a bath or a shower. As a result, many large public housing projects rapidly deteriorated to the point where they were more of a liability to the community than a solution to its housing problems, and a number have gone the way of the celebrated Pruitt-Igoe project in St Louis: dynamited by the housing authority to forestall further increases in the incidence of murder, arson, robbery and vandalism.

Restrictions on location have also contributed to the poor reputation of public housing. Local housing authorities have no powers of compulsory purchase, and the process of site selection is frequently decided by default. A study of site selection processes in Chicago, San Francisco and Oakland came to the conclusion that middle-class communities were able to intervene so successfully that there was effectively little chance for public housing outside existing slum areas (Peel *et al.* 1971). Thus, to the extent that public housing can be said to have any real impact on the spatial structure of the American city, its effect is to reinforce economic and racial segregation, compounding social problems by localizing them. In Chicago, the housing authority's various projects fan outwards from the CBD in three linear belts (Fig. 6.9). Almost all the conventional housing projects (92 per cent) are situated within low-income black neighbourhoods. One project alone – Taylor Homes – contains over 4,300 units, with 75 per cent of its residents officially classed as 'broken families' and many of its 25,250 inhabitants being the perpetrators or the victims of crime, vandalism and alcoholism (Mercer and Hultquist 1976). Attempts to disperse public housing and thereby reduce the intensity of such problems through the federally-sponsored leased housing programme have met with limited success, since only in a few neighbourhoods are private landlords willing to enter into such an arrangement. Consequently, leased housing units are concentrated in areas such as Woodlawn–Englewood, a black neighbourhood on Chicago's south side (Mercer and Hultquist 1976). Mercer and Hultquist also point out that litigation has also been unsuccessful, so far, in achieving a less segregated distribution of public housing. In response to a court action by the American Civil Liberties Union

in 1969, the Chicago Housing Authority was ordered to build 700 public housing units in white residential areas immediately and thereafter to build three units in white neighbourhoods for every one in non-white areas. When the Authority's proposals were presented to the city council two years later they were found to be politically unacceptable, and a much smaller and less dispersed list of sites was re-submitted as a result of the ensuing political uproar. Not surprisingly, progress in the actual construction of these dwellings was slow, with no prospect of any real expansion, territorially or numerically, in the city's supply of public housing.

## Managerialism and social gatekeepers

The consideration of housing sub-markets and the changing structure of housing supply suggests that any search for universal laws and straightforward economic determinants of housing supply is unlikely to succeed. What does seem to offer considerable potential, however, is the exploration of the housing circumstances of particular groups within the major sub-systems of the housing market. This involves the identification, first, of groups of households in the same kind of situation in relation to housing opportunities and, second, the investigation of the way these opportunities are shaped and constrained by the various agencies and professional mediators of housing supply. Such an approach stems largely from the view of class relations and social differentiation developed by Max Weber, whose writings have been very influential in shaping the nature of conventional sociological inquiry. Weberian analysis centres on an 'action frame of reference' which puts 'man as the actor' on the centre of the stage and seeks to explain social systems in terms of the people who make and sustain them. The focus of this approach is the conflict of interests arising from the variety of orientations, aspirations and motivations which people have, and it describes a society 'where interest groups

CBD

Elderly-only project

Other public housing projects

0                                  8
                   km

**Fig. 6.9**  Chicago Housing Authority public housing projects, 1972.
*Source*: Mercer and Hultquist (1976), p. 126.

collide, collude and cohere in the control of institutions, where privilege and status are negotiated, where, in short, power becomes the crucial variable' (Lambert, Paris and Blackaby 1978: 6). Institutional arrangements and key 'actors' are therefore studied in order to explain the outcome of competition between conflicting social groups.

The development of this approach in relation to housing can be traced to the work of Rex and Moore (1967) in their study of the inner-city districts of Birmingham. Dissatisfied with the explanatory powers of ecological orthodoxy, they turned to a consideration of the underlying pattern of social relations in order to explain, rather than merely describe, the nature of residential differentiation. In doing so, they explicitly followed Weber, 'who saw that class struggle was apt to emerge whenever people in a market situation enjoyed differential access to property' (Rex and Moore 1967: 273). According to Rex and Moore, this struggle over the use of housing is the central process of the city as a social unit. Moreover, they suggest that it is *not necessarily linked to economic power*, for 'men in the same labour market may come to have differential degrees of access to housing' (Rex and Moore 1967: 273). There thus emerges the idea of *housing classes* as the basis of conflict: groups of households with common housing opportunities structured by bureaucratic and political forces as well as economic ones. The housing classes identified by Rex and Moore each had a territorial distribution and were ranked according to their power to achieve access to scarce and desired housing resources. Two criteria were identified as governing these housing opportunities. The first was the size and stability of household income, since this is crucial in obtaining mortgage finance; the second was the ability to meet the 'need' and length-of-residence qualifications laid down by the local authority as entry rules for the public housing sector. Rex (1968) has described the housing classes as:

1. the outright owners of large houses in desirable areas;
2. mortgage payers who 'own' whole houses in desirable areas;
3. local authority tenants in houses built by the local authority;
4. local authority tenants in slum houses awaiting demolition;
5. tenants of private house owners;
6. house owners who must take lodgers to meet repayments;
7. lodgers in rooms.

It should be remembered that these housing classes are specific to central Birmingham. Indeed, they should not be thought of as definitive in any way. The problems of identifying groups of people in a similar 'market situation' are considerable, and Rex and Moore themselves were by no means dogmatic as to the classification. Their objective was merely to suggest a classification which might 'pose questions' and 'point the way' towards a more precise delineation of the social structure and conflicts of the city. The central focus of their research was not so much the refinement of the concept of housing classes as the exploration of the opportunities and constraints facing one particular group (low-income immigrants) who enjoyed neither high incomes and secure employment nor could fulfill the eligibility rules of the local authority and who were therefore obliged to seek shelter in the declining and decaying private rented accommodation located in the inner city 'zone of transition'.

Nevertheless, the concept of housing classes and its emphasis on housing opportunities has stimulated widespread interest which has in turn triggered some important contributions to the analysis of residential differentiation. Haddon's (1970) critique of Rex and Moore's work has been influential in this context. He drew attention to the problem of defining housing classes according to *current* housing situations: it does not follow that those who share a common housing situation at any one time also share a common capacity to obtain better housing in the future. It thus becomes necessary to distinguish between those who are trapped in a given housing situation and cannot move out, those who choose to live in a particular area and type of housing but who could move out if they wished, and those who, in time, will move up the housing ladder once they have satisfied the requirements of the housing institutions, whether in the private or the public sector. As Haddon put it, 'The emphasis of the analysis ought to be on the *means and criteria of access* to desirable housing, and the ability of different people to negotiate the rules of eligibility' (Haddon 1970: 129). This brings us to a focus on the relationships between different households and the key actors in the various institutions and agencies concerned with housing supply.

This approach was developed in a wider context by Ray Pahl. In a provocative and influential essay (Pahl 1969) he argued that the proper focus or urban research should be the interplay of spatial and social constraints which determine opportunities of access to urban resources and facilities – transport, education and so on, as well as housing. Furthermore, he suggested, the key to understanding the social constraints could be found in the activities, policies and ideologies of the managers or controllers of the urban system. Very broadly, this is the basis of what has become known as the 'managerialist thesis'. In the context of housing, the managers of scarce resources (or the 'middle dogs' or 'social gatekeepers' as they are sometimes called) include key personnel from the spheres of:

1. *finance capital*, e.g. building society and savings and loan association managers and others engaged in lending money for house purchase, housing development and housing improvements;

2. *industrial capital*, e.g. developers and builders;

3. *commercial capital*, e.g. exchange professionals such as estate agents, lawyers and surveyors engaged in the market distribution of housing;

4. *landed capital*, e.g. landowners and *rentiers* such as private landlords;

5. *state agencies*, e.g. social security offices; and

6. *agencies of the local state* (local government). The most directly influential managers to be found within the public sector are housing managers *per se* and their related staff of lettings officers and housing visitors. To the extent that city planners control certain aspects of the housing environment they may also be regarded as 'managers' within the housing system.

As Norman (1975) observes, what these groups have in common is a job at the interface between available resources and a client (or supplicant) population. 'It is in terms of the day-to-day decision-making of these groups that individual access to resources is determined' (Norman 1975: 76). And it is in terms of their cumulative day-to-day decision-making that socio-spatial differentiation takes place.

It should be made clear at this point that urban managerialism is not a theory nor even an agreed perspective (Leonard 1982). Indeed, Pahl himself has reformulated his own position more than once and now seems unsure of the utility of managerialist analyses in the wider context of urban political economy (see p. 244). It is instead a framework for study, and at this level it offers 'a useful way of penetrating into the complex of relationships that structure urban areas' (Williams 1978: 240). A succession of empirical studies has left no doubt that there are managers in every sphere of housing supply whose activities exert a considerable impact on urban residential differentiation, particularly in Western Europe, where the expansion of welfare capitalism has produced a powerful and easily-identifiable bureaucratic influence on the housing scene. (Moreover, their influence can be shown to extend beyond day-to-day decision-making, for such is the power of the institutions of housing supply that they not only shape people's actual opportunities but also their *sense* of possibilities). The following sections illustrate the effects of particular types of managers and social gatekeepers on residential structure. The managerial role of city planners, which spans the whole housing system, is considered in Chapter 8, where a broader view is taken of their part in mediating conflict between different social groups.

## Landowners

Landowners stand at the beginning of a chain of key actors and decision-makers whose activities, like the households they ultimately supply, are governed by a variety of objectives and orientations, not all of which are framed in 'rational' economic terms. As Kaiser and Weiss and their associates at the University of North Carolina have shown, it is possible to construct a behavioural model of the process of residential development and redevelopment in much the same way as others have built models of households' residential location decision process (Kaiser and Weiss 1970; Weiss *et al.* 1966). Landowners exert a significant influence on the outcome of this process, though it must be acknowledged that this influence is less now than it was, largely because of the lattice of public policy constraints on the use of urban land and housing. Following Robson (1975) it is possible to recognize two main ways in which land ownership can influence the course of residential development. First, the pattern of land ownership, particularly in relation to the *size* of the parcels of land held by different owners, can influence the *nature* of development. We have already seen (Chapter 2), for instance, how the pattern of land holdings helped to guide the location of railway infrastructure as well as that of the larger and more comprehensively planned residential developments in nineteenth-century cities. More recently, the location of interwar local authority housing estates was guided by the availability of large parcels of land (Mortimore 1969; Ward 1962); and the pattern of speculative suburban development in Los Angeles has been shown to have followed the layout of the old *ranchos* and mission lands (Banham 1973). In contrast, small and fragmented parcels of land, which do not allow developers to benefit from economies of scale, give rise to haphazard and piecemeal development whose quality depends a great deal on their relative location.

Equally important is the influence which landowners can exert through imposing their wishes as to the *type* of development which takes place and, indeed, whether it takes place at all. Some owners hold on to their land for purely speculative reasons, releasing the land for urban development as soon as the chance of substantial profit is presented. This can have a considerable effect on the morphology of cities, not least in the way that plots tied up in speculation schemes act as barriers to development (Sargent 1976) and in the sequence that land is released. In addition, a study of suburban development by Harvey and Clark found that the manipulation of the tax system by landowners was having a distinct effect on the nature of the development. Since owners were taxed less if they sold their land in small parcels over a period than if they sold it all at once, they favoured the operation of 'instalment contracts' with developers, who took up agreed portions of land at convenient intervals. This forced other developers to find land in other neighbourhoods, thus increasing what appeared to be 'random' urban sprawl (Harvey and Clark 1965). However, because of the special properties of land as a commodity, many landowners are reluctant to sell unless they need to raise capital. Moreover, for many of the 'traditional' large landholders, land ownership is steeped in social and political significance which makes its disposal a matter of some concern. Spring (1951), for instance, detailed the determination of the landed gentry of the nineteenth century to hold on to their land even when considerable financial gains could be achieved by selling. The reason, of course, was to maintain the status and political influence deriving from land ownership.

When landowners do sell, they sometimes limit the nature of subsequent development through restrictive covenants, either for idealistic reasons, or, more likely, to protect the exchange value of land they still hold. Such covenants usually discriminate in favour of high-status groups, although they are generally framed in a rather oblique way: by stipulating certain minimum plot sizes, for example, or by forbidding the construction of public houses (as in Dundee's Edwardian exurb of Wormit) in the hope that this will ensure development for a 'better' class of person. Robson (1975) cites the contrasting examples of, on the one hand, middle-class suburbs in North London which resulted from the insistence on high standards of construction and layout by the landowners (Eton College) and, on the other, the slums in Sheffield built on land whose owner (the Duke of Norfolk) allowed building to take place without restriction. Other, well-documented examples include the close control exerted by the Fitzwilliam family on the quality and extent of residential development on their Bierlow estate in Sheffield (Rowley 1975) and the differential residential and commercial development within Scunthorpe resulting from the various policies of the major landowners in the town (Pocock 1970). The use of restrictive convenants is less common nowadays, partly because of an increase in land-use regulations, and partly because some have been successfully challenged in the courts.

In conclusion, it should be emphasized that there are clearly different types of landowners, each with rather different priorities and time horizons. Massey and Catalano (1978) identify three main types in Britain. The biggest single group, which they term 'former landed property', includes the Church, the Crown Estates, the landed aristocracy, and the landed gentry. For this group profitability is important but is strongly mediated by social and historical ties, and strategic decisions are made with an eye to the very long term. The second type, 'industrial land ownership', is dominated by owner-occupier farmers, a group which is of crucial importance to the land conversion process at the urban fringe. Their decision-making typically has to balance short-term financial considerations against longer-term social ones. The third type, 'financial land ownership', consists of financial institutions (such as insurance companies, pension funds and banks) and property companies. The importance of the former grew very rapidly in the postwar period as they channelled savings and profits into long-term investments, often involving city centre land. The property companies, on the other hand, are less concerned with the long-term appreciation of assets and more with the exploitation of urban land markets for short- and medium-term profits.

## Builders and developers

Considering the very important role of private-sector builders and developers, surprisingly little is known about the way decisions are made in individual firms or the effect these may have on the pattern of housing opportunities within the city. Some research has been conducted into the process of site selection and housing type: see, for example, Baerwald (1981), Bather (1976), Craven (1975), Hepner (1983), Neutze (1971) and Nicholls *et al.* 1982). What emerges from these studies is a fairly consistent pattern of activity in response to the search for profitability. Prime amongst the economic considerations facing builders and developers is the cost of urban land and its sheer scarcity, as well as the need for speed of operation (because they have to finance land preparation and construction long before receiving income from the sale of completed dwellings). On the other hand, the market for new housing tends to be a sellers' market in which the builder has a reasonable latitude in what he produces, knowing that it is likely to be sold quickly. Together, these factors shape the rather distinctive patterns of operation pursued by builders and developers. In Craven's words, the developer becomes 'a catalyst who interprets, albeit inaccurately, major forces in the urban environment; an initiator of action based on this interpretation and a challenger of public policies which obstruct such action' (Craven 1975: 124).

To begin with, builders and developers may play an important part in shaping the pattern and direction of residential growth; and since they are catering mainly for a middle-class market, this really means that they exert an important influence on the location of middle-class neighbourhoods. Larger companies, with an urgent need to acquire land at a rapid rate in order to keep their organization fully employed, search out and bid for suitable land even before it has been put on the market: a strategy known as 'bird-dogging' in the United States. The outcome of this activity, of course, does not always coincide with the ideas of planners as to the most desirable location for new residential development, so that developers should not be regarded as completely independent actors in this context. Nevertheless, the profits to be made from land speculation give developers a strong incentive to proceed, and the size of the larger companies enables them to exert strong economic and political pressure on local governments. Harvey (1972) cites the example of developers in Baltimore who, having had proposals turned down by the city Planning Board, found that their applications were approved by councilmen whose political campaign had previously been supported by large donations from the developers. Other, more subtle strategies on the part of British developers have been reported by Craven (1975) and Harloe, Isacharoff and Minns (1974).

It is worth noting here that large builders and developers have come to represent a powerful lobby: so powerful, in fact, that they

have been able to shape the nature of many of the government programmes affecting housing and urban development (Checkoway 1980; Smyth 1985).

The general process of site selection by *suburban* builders and developers is illustrated in Fig. 6.10. The first stage is a determination of the general nature and scale of the project, the second is an evaluation of relatively large areas aimed at identifying areas likely to offer suitable sites, and the third is an evaluation of specific sites in the areas highlighted in the second state. During each stage, a variety of site selection criteria are involved (Fig 6.11), but an overarching criterion is that of price:

Builders constructing lower-priced units are concerned primarily with minimizing costs. They seek to supply basic housing without frills; flat terrain with few trees is ideal. By contrast, builders of higher-priced houses look for sites

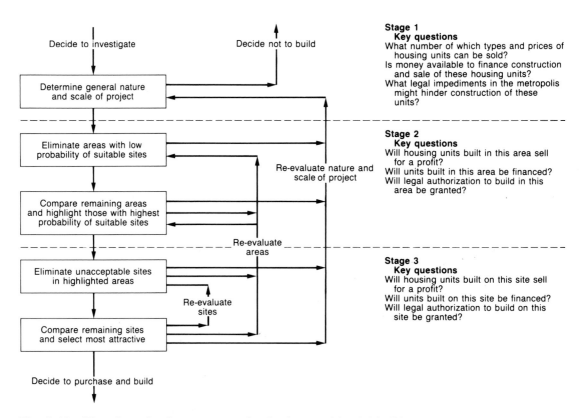

**Fig. 6.10** The site selection process of suburban residential builders. *Source*: Baerwald (1981) Fig. 2, p. 345.

|  | Stage 1 | Stage 2 | Stage 3 |
|---|---|---|---|
| **Goals** | Determine general nature and scale of project | Eliminate areas with low probability of suitable sites, highlight areas with highest probabilities of having suitable sites | Eliminate sites judged unacceptable, compare sites that remain and select most attractive |
| **Limiting factors** |  |  | Governmental regulations (zoning, subdivision regulations) Private property agreements (covenants, deeds) |
| **Limiting factors or trade-off characteristics** (Depending on the nature of the project and the builder) | General economic conditions Availability and costs of financing Builder's organization, interests, capabilities, and existing work load and financial situation | Availability of land or improved parcels Cost of land Access to paved roads Public and private utilities Public service systems Terrain Drainage Ground water Neighbouring land uses Reputation and 'social location' of neighbourhoods Governmental policies and regulations Attitudes and efficiency of local governments Builder's experience and predilections | Size, shape, and availability of land or lots Cost of land or lots Roads Public and private utilities Soils Terrain Drainage Ground water Vegetation Reputation and 'social location' or neighbourhood Neighbouring land uses Builder's experience and predilections |
| **Trade-off characteristics** | Style, size, and design demands of households Construction costs and trends Policies of competitors Governmental policies | General accessibility Soils Vegetation Surface water Scenic attractiveness Schools and other public services | General accessibility Surface water Scenic attractiveness Schools and other public services |

**Fig. 6.11** Site selection criteria of suburban residential builders.
*Source*: Baerwald (1981) Fig. 3, p. 350.

with natural or social amenities. The costs of building on more rugged terrain and in denser vegetation are higher, but builders invariably find that the value of the completed house is increased by an even greater amount. When units will be sold for a higher price, builders and subdividers may create ponds out of marshes or add to the relief of an otherwise flat area by cutting streets lower and piling excess dirt up on the building sites. Characteristics that are limiting factors to the builder of lower-priced houses therefore are considered in a positive light in the trade-off calculations of the builders of higher-priced houses. (Baerwald 1981: 351)

In contrast, the overarching criterion for residential development in *inner city* areas appears to be the availability of land (Nicholls *et al.* 1982).

Having secured the land they need, developers are able to exert a considerable influence on the physical and social character of the housing they build. Because they are operating in a sellers' market they are able to build what they think the public wants, and what is easiest and safest to produce. Given their need for plentiful supplies of cheap land and for speed of construction, together with the advantages to be derived from economies of scale and standardization, the net result is a propensity to build large, uniform housing estates on peripheral sites. Moreover, the imperatives of profitability ensure that the housing is built at relatively high densities and to relatively low standards: the resultant stereotype being epitomized in Pete Seeger's song about 'little boxes made of ticky-tacky . . .

(that) all look just the same'. In Britain, houses at the lower end of the private market have for some time been of poorer quality and less generous space standards than the statutory minima governing public housing, but attempts by the National House Builders Registration Council to upgrade the minimum standards of private house construction have been resisted 'in the interests of the consumer', who would have to bear the extra cost. Housing opportunities for the broad spectrum of middle classes thus tend to be rather limited in scope. In North America, the well-tried norm of detached, single-storey, single-family dwellings has now been joined, because of the rising costs of suburban land, by suburban apartment blocks. Variety is provided through deviations in façades and architectural detail: mock-Georgian doors and porticoes, mock-Tudor leaded windows and brick chimneys, and mock-Spanish Colonial stucco and wrought iron. Thrown together on a single housing development, these 'personalized' features can sometimes create an unfortunate Disneyland effect. In contrast, British estates tend to be uniform down to the styling of doors, windows and garden furniture.

More important from the point of view of housing opportunities, however, is the uniformity of size of house. In Britain, the norm is a 3-bedroom, 2-storey, semi-detached or terraced house, while the lower end of the market is dominated by two-bedroom maisonettes and flats (Murie, Niner and Watson 1976). Whole estates are built to this tried-and-trusted formula, with perhaps a sprinkling of larger houses in order to increase sales through raising the potential social status of the estate. Consequently, substantial numbers of 'atypical' middle-class families – single persons and large families – are effectively denied access to the new owner-occupier sub-market and so must seek accommodation either in the older owner-occupier stock or in the privately rented sector. On the other hand, 'typical' families become increasingly localized – and isolated – in suburban estates.

Finally, it should be noted that the nature of building companies' activities has been found to be related to their size and internal organization. The typical large builder reduces costs through direct purchasing of materials by the wagonload, the maintenance of large inventories, the development of efficient subcontracting relationships, the use of a specialized labour force, the use of government financial aid and housing research, and the use of mass production methods on large tracts of land (Checkoway 1980). In order to achieve this, large builders are inevitably concerned almost exclusively with mass-market suburban development. Medium-sized companies cannot afford to take risks on land for which they might not secure permission to build, or to pay the interest on large parcels of land which take a long time to develop. When they do get sites of suitable size, they therefore seek to maximize profits either by building blocks of flats at high densities or by catering for the top end of the market, building low-density detached houses in 'exclusive' subdivisions. This leaves small firms to use their more detailed local knowledge to scavenge for smaller infill sites, where they will assemble the necessary materials and manpower and seek to build as quickly as possible, usually aiming at the market for larger, higher-quality dwellings in neighbourhoods with an established social reputation. In this context it is significant for the future pattern of housing opportunities that although the building industry in most countries tends to be dominated by small firms, the tendency everywhere is for an increasing proportion of output to be accounted for by a few large companies with regional or national operations.

## Mortgage financiers

The allocative decisions of mortgage finance companies – building societies, banks, savings and loan companies, etc. – represent one of the more striking examples of social gatekeeping in the housing system, and there is now a small body of literature documenting the outcome of mortgage financiers' activities. Much of the empirical research has been conducted in Britain and directed towards the role of the branch managers of building societies, who are responsible for financing the bulk of all house purchasing by private households. Nevertheless, what evidence there is from elsewhere suggests that it is safe to assume that the managers of mortgage finance companies in other countries exert a broadly similar influence on the social geography of the city in similar ways to their British counterparts. It should be stressed at the outset that mortgage-finance managers are not independent decision-makers. Much of their activity is closely circumscribed by head office policy, while many of their day-to-day decisions are dependent upon the activities of lawyers, estate agents, surveyors, bank managers and the like. Nevertheless, building society managers enjoy a pivotal position in this 'magic-circle' of exchange professionals, and although the self-image of the trade is that of a passive broker in the supply of housing, the mortgage allocation system 'exerts a decisive influence over who lives where, how much new housing gets built, and whether neighbourhoods survive' (Stone 1978: 190).

In order to be properly understood, the activity of building society managers must be seen against the general background of their commercial objectives. Although building societies are non-profit making organizations, their success depends upon financial growth and security and the maintenance of large reserve funds. Their chief allegiance, therefore, is to the investor rather than the borrower. Not surprisingly, societies operate a fairly rigid system of rules to protect their operations and encourage an ethos of conservative paternalism among their staff (Boddy 1980). Indeed, there is some evidence to support the idea of building society managers as a rather narrowly-defined breed: an 'ideal type' with a uniformity of attitudes resulting from the recruitment of a certain group (white Anglo-Saxon Protestant moderately-educated family men) and the absorption of society traditions and lending policies through a career structure with a high degree of internal promotion which rewards personnel with a 'clean' record of lending decisions (Ford 1975; Harloe, Isacharoff and Minns 1974). As a group, then, building society managers tend to have good reason to be

cautious, investment-oriented, and suspicious of unconventional behaviour in others. Likewise, the ground rules of society lending policy are cautious, devised to ensure financial security both in terms of the 'paying ability' of potential borrowers and the future exchange value of dwellings they are willing to finance.

In operating these ground rules, building society managers effectively act as social gatekeepers – wittingly or unwittingly – in a number of ways. It is normal practice for societies to lend only 80 to 90 per cent of the total cost or valuation of a house (whichever is the less), and for the maximum loan to be computed as a multiple of the household's main income (although some societies also take into consideration a proportion of a second income, if there is one). This means that people need to raise a certain amount of capital in order to qualify for a mortgage in the first place, and it has been suggested (Robson 1975) that this might discriminate against people with lower earnings who may be less able or less predisposed to accumulate the necessary savings. While this may be so, it is in the evaluation of potential borrowers' ability to maintain the flow of repayments that the first major stratification by building society managers takes place. Because of their desire for risk-minimization, branch managers give a lot of weight to the general creditworthiness of applicants. Credit register searches are used to reveal previous financial delinquency, which normally results in the refusal to advance a loan. Having passed this test, applicants are then judged principally in terms of the *stability* of their income and their future *expectations*. This, of course, tends to favour white-collar workers since their pay structure commonly has a built-in annual increment and is not subject to the ups and downs of overtime and short-time working. Conversely, several groups will find that their chances of obtaining a mortgage are marginal, including the self-employed, the lowly-paid and single women. The importance of this factor has been borne out by the findings of a study of new private housing in outer London, where clerical workers were able to obtain higher mortgages, and buy more expensive houses, than skilled manual workers *whose average earnings were higher* (Barbolet 1969).

Further allocation procedures operate to the disadvantage of the marginally qualified in situations where building society funds are oversubscribed. Many societies give priority to existing clients who are selling their houses in order to buy another; and for first-time buyers it is often essential to have saved with the society for some time before getting a loan. In addition, quotas of finance may be allocated to estate agents, solicitors and brokers, so that the chance of getting a loan may depend on the applicant's connections with these other professionals. It is also important for 'marginal' households to choose the right building society to approach for a loan, since lending policies, although broadly similar, tend to vary in the way that marginal cases are dealt with. In Lambeth, for example, Harloe, Isacharoft and Minns (1974) found that one particular society prided itself in attempts to encourage a wide spectrum of the community to become owner-occupiers and was one of the first societies to introduce 35-year mortgages. In Dudley, Williams (1982) found that different building societies operated distinctively different lending profiles, with the result that particular sub-groups received substantially different treatment between different societies.

There is also evidence that purely subjective factors influence managers' decisions. Managers appear to categorize applicants in terms of a set of operational stereotypes ranging from bad risks to good ones, although it has proved difficult to pin down these operational stereotypes in detail and to establish their generality within the profession. As Ford (1975) found, it is difficult even for the managers themselves to articulate something which is an unconscious activity. Nevertheless, the criteria they employ in making subjective judgements about people seem to be closely related to their values of financial caution and social conventionality. Harloe, Isacharoff and Minns (1974) quote one manager who was impressed by people who had 'worked things out', suggesting that the prospective buyer who did not display this ability might be at a disadvantage in securing a loan; and Ford

quotes managers as saying 'I always try and assess the ability and willingness of the wife to work' and 'Those people who do not perceive that they must live an English way of life would be treated with caution' (Ford 1975: 298). This last quote is an oblique reference to coloured immigrants, who seem to be particularly disadvantaged by managers' subjective judgements (see also Leahy 1985; Ryker, Pol and Guy 1984). Duncan (1976: 310) quotes one manager in Huddersfield as saying that 'From a building society point of view, they [blacks] do not have satisfactory status' and another who observed that 'whether we like it or not, the coloured people are here, and we have to be very careful. There's no doubt coloured gentlemen are good savers, but we're very careful.'

Socio-spatial sorting also takes place through managers' evaluation of the *property* for which funds are sought. With any loan, the manager's first concern is with the liquidity of the asset, so that if the borrower defaults and the society is forced to foreclose, the sale of the property will at least cover the amount advanced. The assessment of this liquidity ultimately rests with professional surveyors, but building societies tend to have clear ideas as to the 'safest' property in terms of price range, size and location, and surveyors tend to anticipate these criteria in formulating their survey reports (Lambert 1976). Many managers evidently assume that market demand for properties which deviate from their ideal (a postwar, suburban house with three or four bedrooms) is very limited, and therefore regard them as greater risks and are more cautious about advancing funds for them (Williams 1976b). Managers tend to be particularly concerned with the *size* of dwellings because of the possibility of multiple occupation and the consequent problem of reposession if the borrower defaults. Their concern with *age* is related to the possibility that the property will deteriorate before the mortgage is fully redeemed; and their concern with *location* is related to the possibility of property values being undermined by changes in neighbourhood racial or social composition. Their concern with *price* reflects their anxiety that applicants should not overstretch themselves financially (Doling and Williams 1983).

Managers thus effectively decide not only who gets loans but also what kinds of property they can aspire to. Households with more modest financial status, for example, will find it more difficult to buy older property even though the overall price may not be beyond their means, since loans for older property generally have to be repaid over a shorter period, thus increasing the monthly repayments.

The spatial outcome is often a dramatic contrast in lending levels for different neighbourhoods. In Sacramento, for example, the steep gradient in the pattern of mortgage loans for single-family dwellings reveals a clearly sectoral pattern (Fig. 6.12) which correlates closely with the social ecology of the city: high-status neighbourhoods attract the most loans (Dingemans 1979; see also Grime and Smith 1982; Kantor and Nystuen

**Fig. 6.12** Single family mortgage loans in Sacramento. The number of mortgages for structures with one-to-four units is given as percentage of units in one-to-four unit structures in the tract in 1975.
*Source*: Dingemans (1979), Fig. 1, p. 229.

1982). The most striking aspect of the gate-keeping activities of building society managers in this context is their practice of refusing to advance funds on any property within neighbourhoods which they perceive to be bad risks – usually inner-city areas, as in Birmingham (Fig. 6.13). This practice is known as *redlining* and has been well documented in a number of studies even though managers are usually reluctant to admit to redlining policies. In their survey of building society managers in Bristol, Bassett and Short (1980: 286–7) found that:

All the managers had heard of redlining, . . . and said they did not practise it. One manager stated categorically 'we do not redline'. Later in the discussion he pointed to the St Paul's area on the map and said that 'there are certain areas in the city in which we won't lend'!

In British cities, the key indicators of 'risky' neighbourhood status seem to be the presence of black people and students (Boddy 1976a; Duncan 1976). Weir (1976: 113) quotes the example of a library assistant in Leeds who was informed by the Northern Rock building society that 'it was doubtful if a mortgage would be available' on a Headingley property 'owing to the nearness of the "blue zone", i.e. high proportion of students and immigrants'. Another company operating in the same city, London Life, explained to a lecturer that they could not make a loan because 'immigrants were moving into the area . . . with the probable effect of depressing the value of property there'. The lecturer objected that eminent people such as Lord Boyle lived in one of these areas. The London Life man replied: 'One swallow doesn't make a summer.'

In the United States, some states have passed anti-redlining laws, and federal law requires lenders to disclose their policies and lending profiles in an attempt to discourage redlining. Nevertheless, redlining continues to exist, largely through covert means: discouraging would-be borrowers with higher interest rates, higher down payments, lower loan-to-value rates and shorter loan maturity terms for property in redlined areas (Darden 1980; Kantor and Nystuen 1982; Bradford and Marino 1977).

Although redlining may be an understandable and (in most countries) legitimate business practice, it has important consequences for the social geography of the city. Following Darden (1980), we can summarize the consequences of the redlining process as follows:

*Stage 1*  Covert redlining means higher down-payments on mortgages, higher interest rates on loans, and shorter loan maturities, effectively putting much cheaper housing beyond the reach of many low-income households.

*Stage 2*  Older houses are denied mortgage loans altogether. As housing deteriorates, the rest of the neighbourhood follows in a self-perpetuating cycle of decay.

*Stage 3*  Home improvement loans are denied in the area, often leading to poor maintenance and, in extreme cases, to housing abandonment. It also undermines the effectiveness of government-sponsored neighbourhood improvement schemes (Boddy 1976a; Lambert 1976).

*Stage 4*  As conditions worsen, property insurance becomes exorbitant or is denied altogether. Neighbourhood businesses begin to fail, taking essential services and important sources of cash flow out of the neighbourhood.

*Stage 5*  Property values decrease at an accelerated rate and property loans of any kind become even more difficult to obtain. Selective outmigration leaves behind a residual population of the disadvantaged and the elderly.

*Stage 6*  The declining property values in the redlined neighbourhood are financially felt by the entire city as revenues decline while the demand for social services increases. Redlining spreads to other neighbourhoods.

*Stage 7*  The entire city is drained of so much revenue because of redlining that the quality and quantity of public services have to be reduced and/or tax rates have to be increased.

**Fig. 6.13** The 'red line' district in Birmingham in relation to the city's inner area improvement programme. *Source*: Weir (1976), p. 111.

The practice of redlining thus 'guarantees that property values will decline and generally leads to neighbourhood deterioration, destruction and abandonment. This process makes more credit available for the resale and financing of homes in other neighbourhoods, thus perpetuating differential neighbourhood quality, growth, decline and home ownership' (Darden 1980: 98). This flow of capital to the suburbs, it should be noted, is closely tied to the wider operations of mortgage finance companies; they are often heavily involved in financing and controlling the suburban activities of large construction companies. Boddy (1976b) points out that such involvement is commonly reinforced by organizational connections. Thus, in the north of England, Boddy found that the Northern Rock building society had directors in common with Bellway Holdings, a major house-building company, while William Leech (Builders) Ltd had directors in common with both Northern Rock and Bellway Holdings. It should also be noted that a substantial proportion of the capital used to finance suburban house construction and purchase is derived from small investors in inner-city areas, so that the net effect of building society policies is to redistribute a scarce resource (investment capital) from a relatively deprived area to a relatively affluent one (Harvey 1977). In a study of Boston, for example, it was found that levels of reinvestment of savings deposits in inner-city communities were between 3 and 33 per cent, compared with levels of between 108 and 543 per cent in the outermost suburbs (Taggart and Smith 1981).

## Estate agents

Estate agents are responsible for a wide range of activities connected with the exchange and management of residential property. They find houses and sometimes arrange finance for buyers; they attract purchasers and transact paperwork for sellers. In addition, they may also be involved in surveying, auctioneering, valuation, property management and insurance. They have close links with mortgage financiers, collecting mortgage repayments for

companies and channelling investment funds to them. The mortgage financiers reciprocate by apportioning a quota of mortgage funds to be allocated by the estate agent and by paying a small commission on investment funds received through the agent. Estate agents then use their quota of mortgage funds to expedite the sale of properties on their books. Since estate agents' profits are derived from percentage commissions on the purchase price of houses, one of their chief concerns is to maintain a high level of prices in the market whilst encouraging a high turnover of sales.

In many countries of Western Europe and North America, estates agents account for between 50 and 70 per cent of all house sales; in Australia, the sale of houses is almost entirely in the hands of estate agents (Kemeny 1983). They are not simply passive brokers in these transactions, however, for they influence their social and spatial outcome in several ways. In addition to the bias introduced in their role as mediators of information (Palm 1976a, 1976b; see also p. 188). estate agents sometimes introduce a deliberate bias by channelling households into, or away from, specific neighbourhoods in order to maintain what they regard as optimal market conditions (Palm 1979). Williams (1976b) explains this activity as follows: existing residents in a given neighbourhood represent potential clients for an agent, and if an agent is seen to be acting against their interests by introducing 'undesirable' purchasers to the area, he may suffer both by being denied any further custom and through any fall in prices which might result from panic selling. 'Thus the safest response is to keep like with like and to deter persons from moving to areas occupied by persons "unlike" themselves' (Williams 1976b: 58). This process was demonstrated over 30 years ago by Palmer (1955), who seems to have coined the term 'social gatekeeper'. His study of estate agents in New Haven, Connecticut, showed that they clearly saw their role as controllers of residential opportunities. As one put it:

People often try to get in higher class areas than they'll be accepted in. We just don't show them any houses in those areas. If they insist, we try and talk them out of it in one way or another.

I've purposely lost many a sale doing just that. It pays in the long run. People in the community respect you for it and they put business your way (Palmer 1955: 77)

Palmer found that agents carefully evaluated clients' status in terms of race, ethnic origin, religion, occupation, income, education and personal appearance. Failure to satisfy the agent's notions of appropriate social attributes for a specific neighbourhood nearly always resulted in diversionary tactics, either by lying – 'it's sold' – or by warnings of unhappiness – 'you won't fit in'. Even small social handicaps could (in the 1950s) apparently disbar a person from high-status neighbourhoods. Palmer quotes one agent as saying of a person seeking a house in a high-status neighbourhood:

What does he do for a living. Maybe he's on the road and sells – well let's call them rubber goods for the prevention of disease . . . like a fellow who drove up here a few months ago. He didn't tell me that but I checked around and found out . . . well a man who'd fit into a top area around here just wouldn't be in that kind of business (Palmer 1955: 79).

But the most widespread discrimination undertaken by estate agents is based on race and ethnicity. The segregation in US cities resulting from this activity has been well documented (Brown 1972; Forman 1971; Helper 1969), and Burney (1967) and Hatch (1973) have shown that a similar process also operates on a significant scale in British cities. Burney (1967: 39) quotes one agent as saying:

I would do my best to head off black buyers from a good suburban or new estate. In fact it would be my duty to do so in the interests of the community and for the sake of people who have bought houses in good faith.

On the other hand, estate agents sometimes introduce black families to a white neighbourhood in the hope that whites will sell up quickly at deflated prices, allowing the agents to buy houses and then resell them to incoming black families at a much higher price: a practice known as *block busting*.

Edmondson Village, Baltimore, houses which were purchased from departing white families for an average price of $7,500 were sold to incoming blacks for $12,500 (Harvey 1972). Because the white residents of targeted neighbourhoods can and do distinguish between middle- and lower-class blacks, blockbusters have sometimes resorted to a variety of tactics in order to give the impression that the incoming blacks represent a 'bad element': telephone calls, door-to-door solicitations, and the posting of bogus For Sale signs on front lawns; even, in extreme cases, hiring outsiders to commit petty acts of vandalism or to pose as indolent 'welfare cases'. A similar process involves the purchase of older properties in prime development sites. These properties are subsequently given over to low-income apartments or rooming houses and promptly neglected. As other residents see the neighbourhood beginning to deteriorate, more and more sell up to estate agents, who allow the properties to deteriorate along with the original 'seed' properties. 'As deterioration continues, the area becomes a fire risk, and as fire insurance companies refuse to renew insurance policies, more owners are persuaded to sell out' (Holmes 1976: 411). When a sufficient number of dwellings have been acquired, the agents themselves are able to sell out at a considerable profit to developers seeking large plots of land for redevelopment schemes.

This kind of opportunism has also been shown to have been involved in the process of *gentrification*. Williams (1976a) suggests that gentrification in parts of Islington, London, can be attributed as much to the activities of estate agents as to the incomers themselves. He found that it was often estate agents who persuaded mortgage financiers to give loans for the purchase and renovation of old working-class dwellings. In addition, some agents purchased and renovated property themselves before selling to incoming young professionals. The role of estate agents in manipulating housing supply and shaping social geography in this context is well illustrated by these quotes from the *London Property Letter*, which is written by cells of estate agents:

The fascinating thing about London is that it throws up an endless supply of new possibilities for the property pioneer and Brixton is about as near to the Klondike as you can get without actually digging.

Nestling down at the bottom of the Archway area is a distinctly working class area which presents possibilities for reclamation.

Grubby Kennington has been providing rich killings for sharp hunters. But the best parts of the carcass are disappearing fast leaving late comers only the bones to pick over. Where next will the South Bank hunt turn? Our money goes on the Stockwell Vauxhall sector where prices are at last starting to skip in anticipation of the Victoria Line's arrival.

(quoted in Williams 1976b: 60.)

Finally, it should be noted that estate agents also operate as gatekeepers in the privately rented sector. Estate agents act as property managers for both large and small property owners, collecting rents, attending to paperwork, and overseeing the maintenance of property. In order to minimize management problems many agents are selective in their choice of tenants, discriminating quite subjectively against people they feel will cause problems in one way or another, whether through rent arrears, maltreatment of property, or anti-social behaviour. it is also worth noting that in university towns it is common for university accommodation officers to take upon themselves the role of gatekeepers in a similar way, 'shutting out' students they perceive to be somehow undesirable in order to preserve good relations with landlords in the longer term (McDowell 1978).

## Private landlords

On the face of it, there are few formal 'qualifications' for access to privately-rented housing: all that is needed – in theory, at least – is an ability to pay the rent and to respond quickly to vacancies in a sub-market where housing is usually in short supply. In practice, however, access to privately-rented housing is often constrained by the gatekeeping activities of landlords. 'Through their ability to select or reject tenants, through their ability . . . to set the conditions of letting, they have power over those who rent and their many individual decisions combine to produce obvious and

well-established differences in the social composition of neighbourhoods' (Elliot and McCrone 1975: 541).

This sorting of households can take several forms. Some landlords deliberately set out to manage their stock of accommodation in a 'socially responsible' way. Thus, for example, two of the large institutional landlords operating in Southwark – Alleyn's College Estate and the Church Commissioners – allocate vacancies in favour of Southwark residents, with preference being given to friends and relatives of existing tenants (London Borough of Southwark 1973). Similarly, institutional landlords (the Duchy of Cornwall and the Church Commissioners) operating in Lambeth were found to be maintaining a proportion of low-income housing in their stock as a gesture of 'social concern' rather than for economic reasons, with priority again being given to relatives of existing tenants (Harloe, Isacharoff and Minns 1974). More often, letting policies are formulated for the benefit of the landlord. Given the strength of demand compared with supply in the private rented sector, landlords – even the small landlord with poor quality property in the inner city – are in a position to deny access to 'unsuitable' individuals or families. It is quite common for landlords to demand character references and to scrutinize rent books for evidence of financial instability. In Bristol, Short (1979) found that most of the small-scale landlords were concerned to select 'good' tenants: those who do not make undue noise, who pay the rent regularly and who generally give the landlord a trouble-free source of income. In contrast, most of the larger individual and corporate landlords were attempting to allocate vacancies to short-stay tenants. According to Short, there were three reasons for this narrow letting policy. First, some landlords felt that short-stay tenants were unlikely to apply to the city Rent Officer to get the rent fixed at a 'fair' level. Secondly, a continual turnover of tenants allows rent increases to be made more easily; and, if the rent has previously been fixed, a high turnover will allow the full fixed rent to be charged to new incoming tenants irrespective of any previous phasing arrangements. Thirdly, having short-stay tenants has the advantage that obtaining vacant possession for subsequent sale is relatively easy. Without vacant possession, it is impossible to sell to owner-occupiers, and the price received from selling to another landlord may be depressed by as much as a half. As Short points out, the net result of this discrimination in favour of short-stay tenants is that households with children find it particularly difficult to gain access to privately-rented accommodation. 'They are seen as the type of tenants who want long term accommodation and are felt to be likely to go to the Rent Officer to get the rent level fixed.' As one landlord put it: 'My policy is to let to under-30s, students, single people and young married couples with no children – I steer clear of couples over thirty with children; by this age they should have a house of their own' (Short 1979: 71).

Elliot and McCrone (1975) emphasize that the nature of landlordism tends to vary from one neighbourhood to another according to the dominance of different types of landlord. One important contrast is between the activities of individual landlords (whether large or small) and corporate landlords: allocation by the former may involve more subtle, non-economic elements of personal judgement; while the latter tend to operate in a more formal, bureaucratic way. There are, however, several other categories of landlord, each with rather different motivations and letting policies. In Edinburgh, for instance, Elliot and McCrone identified six main types of landlords: individuals, property companies, trusts, welfare organizations, commercial firms such as brewery companies which had diversified into property, and institutions such as churches and universities. Relatively little, however, is known about the particular effects of these specific types of landlord on the structure of residential opportunities.

## Public housing managers

Within the public sector the principal gate-keepers are the housing managers and their staff who operate the housing authority's admissions and allocation policies. In Britain, the discretion given to local authorities in formulating and operating such policies is very broad and is encumbered by the minimum of legal regulation. There is a requirement to rehouse families displaced by clearance or other public action as well as those officially classed as overcrowded, but otherwise it is only necessary to give 'reasonable preference' to households in 'unsatisfactory' housing conditions. Since demand for public housing often exceeds supply, housing managers in most cities are in a position of considerable power and importance in relation to the spatial outcome of public housing programmes.

The rationing of available housing is carried out through a wide variety of eligibility rules and priority systems (Niner 1975; Welsh Consumer Council 1976). Most local authorities operate waiting lists, although these vary in practice from a simple first-come first-served basis to sophisticated queueing systems using 'points schemes' to evaluate need for a specific type of dwelling: points may be awarded, for example, for overcrowding, ill-health or disability, sub-standard accommodation, marital status, length of time on the waiting list and so on, together (in some authorities) with discretionary points awarded by housing managers to enable priority to be given to 'special cases' (Housing Advisory Group 1978). A general representation of the allocation process in public sector housing is shown in Fig. 6.14.

Not surprisingly, different schemes have different outcomes, and families in identical circumstances may find themselves with quite different degrees of access to council housing, depending on the local authority within whose jurisdiction they live (Murie, Niner and Watson 1976). In general, those households with least access to public housing in British cities include young single people without dependents, newcomers to the area, and former owner-occupiers. Conversely, the letting policies of most authorities tend to favour households from slum clearance and redevelopment areas, households living in overcrowded conditions, small elderly households, new households who lack their own accommodations and are living with parents or in-laws, and households with young children (Niner and Watson 1978).

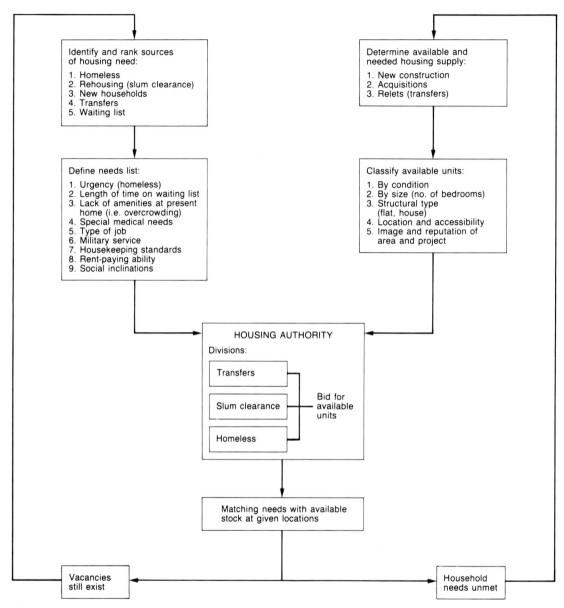

**Fig. 6.14**  The allocation process for public sector housing.
*Source*: Bourne (1981), Fig. 10.2, p. 222.

But in addition to the question of whether or not a household is offered accommodation there is the question of *what sort* of accommodation is offered, and in *what area* (Dieleman 1983). For housing managers it makes sense not only to allocate households to dwellings according to size characteristics but also to match 'good' tenants to their best housing in order to minimize maintenance costs, to ensure that the aged and 'problem families' are easily supervised, and (some would argue: see Byrne 1974) to punish unsatisfactory tenants (those with records of rent arrears and unsociable behaviour in their previous accommodation) by sending them to 'dump' estates. In this situation, problem families are often doubly disadvantaged by living in low-grade property while having to pay rent at comparable levels to families in more attractive housing schemes. The isolation of problem families in this way can be traced to the policy of housing 'socially weak' families in specially-designed austere and durable public housing schemes in France and the Netherlands in the 1930s (Scobie 1975; Vance 1976). After 1945, many local authorities in Britain pursued similar, if less well publicized, policies using obsolescent housing stock rather than purpose-built developments. By the 1960s, the segregation and localization of 'problem families' as well as grading of other tenants according to their worthiness for particular housing vacancies was commonplace, exciting little or no attention (Lewis 1976). In 1969, however, the 'moralistic' attitudes of local authorities were condemned (in suitably diplomatic language) by the Central Housing Advisory Committee:

the underlying philosophy seemed to be that council tenancies were to be given only to those who 'deserved' them and that the 'most deserving' should get the best houses. Thus, unmarried mothers, cohabitees, 'dirty' families and 'transients' tended to be grouped together as 'undesirable'. Moral rectitude, social conformity, clean living and a 'clean' rent book . . . seemed to be essential qualifications for eligibility – at least for new housing
(Central Housing Advisory Committee 1969, para 96.)

The process of screening tenants and allocating them to vacancies according to their 'suitability' has been described by several writers (Byrne 1974; Corina 1976; Damer and Madigan 1974; English 1979; Gray 1976a; Henderson and Karn 1984; Means 1977; Skellington 1981). Central to the whole procedure is the housing visitor's report, and it is here that the temptation to succumb to value judgements derived from impressionistic grounds is strongest, as illustrated by the following excerpts from housing investigators' reports in Hull and Bedford:

'Fairly good type – suitable for post-war re-let or pre-war property'
'Poor type, will need supervision – suitable for old property . . . seems to have taken over the tenancy of this house and sat back until rehoused'
'A good type of applicant – this is not a long-haired person. Suitable for a post-war re-let' (Gray 1976a: 41).
'Poor, untidy and grubby: rats on premises. Even allowing for the poorness of the accommodation and his health, I would have thought he could have achieved more to make the place habitable. They have no kitchen, sink is pulled away from the wall. His effects consisted of the cot, three-piece suite (poor) and *colour TV*'.
'Flat is very overcrowded. This was self-inflicted as they knew what problems would arise before they moved in. Would make poor tenants'.
'Poor standard. A few furnishings in very poor condition. No bathroom. Children wash at school. Family sleep on floor'.
'If Buckingham Palace became available she might accept' (Skellington 1981: 188)

Similarly, Damer and Madigan (1974) found that the grading of tenants in Glasgow was 'arbitrary and subjective'. At the time of their research, the Glasgow housing department classified its stock of housing into eight groups, ranked roughly in order of physical attractiveness, desirability to the public, and rent. At the top end were two kinds of estate: older developments which had withstood the test of desirability over time 'and now exhibit an air of embourgoisement – mature trees, well-manicured lawns, and beautifully-appointed houses' (Damer and Madigan 1974: 226), and newly-constructed housing (usually multi-storey flats) which remains in the top grade until such time as popular demand falls off. At the other end of the scale, Group 8 accommodation tended 'to have a blitzed, semi-derelict and thoroughly depressing appearance' (Damer and Madigan 1974: 226) and to be 'difficult to let' because of its image. In order to match tenants to these carefully graded housing estates, Glasgow corporation employed seven housing visitors – all middle-aged married women – to search council records and electricity and gas board records for evidence of debt on the part of tenants and to interview them in their homes in order to inspect the house and its occupants and, subsequently, grade them. The official grading was arrived at by way of three fivefold classifications of 'cleanliness', 'furniture', and 'type of person'. According to Damer and Madigan, households faring best on this grading system were those who were most articulate, grateful and deferential. Those who fared worst were debtors, the 'wilfully' unemployed, and previous tenants who had either done 'moonlight flits' leaving rent arrears or who had been evicted. The result, of course, is that the Group 8 estates rapidly became 'ghettos' of socially unacceptable (by middle-class standards) families. Damer and Madigan found that such families included many single-parent households and families with a husband/father who was either chronically unemployed, in prison, or suffering from an incapacitating illness.

It should also be noted that the socio-spatial segregation resulting from allocation policies is constantly reinforced by applications by existing tenants for *transfers* from one dwelling to another. This provides further opportunities for screening and grading, allowing 'deserving' and 'respectable' households to maintain or improve their housing status rather than having to remain in accommodation which may be ageing (Niner 1980; Hughes and Jones 1979).

It is now recognized that the localization of families in dump estates sets in motion a labelling process which results in the stigmatization of both the estate and its residents (Damer 1974; Taylor 1978). Because of this stigmatization, accommodation in such areas becomes difficult to let, and housing officials eventually tend to admit households who would normally be ineligible for public housing but who are desperate for any vacancy, thus reinforcing the initial grading process (English 1976). Means (1977), following Cohen's (1973) model of deviancy amplification, suggests that the problem is further exacerbated by societal reaction to dump estates, with media coverage helping to dramatize the situation and to reinforce 'moral panic' through the creation of sensational and sometimes distorted stereotypes. This, in turn, polarizes attitudes and behaviour both inside and outside dump estates, leading to an increase in anti-social behaviour on the part of the inhabitants, and therefore to a confirmation of the stereotypes and a further reinforcement of the area's undesirable character.

It is important to bear in mind, as Taylor and Hadfield (1982) emphasize, that housing managers do not have the power to determine the structure, form and quantity of the resources they distribute, even though they can control allocation procedures: 'No housing manager would *plan* to have problem estates but they have become endemic in British cities. Both tenants and managers are ultimately pawns of the system they operate in' (Taylor and Hadfield 1982: 259). Thus, while the basic operating principle in the public sector is 'need', families with the greatest need tend to end up in the least desirable accommodation (Ineichen 1983). 'The end result is a hierarchy of council house estates in a manner not unlike the ranking of private estates by market mechanisms' (Taylor and Hadfield 1982: 258; see also Twine and Williams 1983). Figure 6.15 illustrates the geography of this hierarchy in Newcastle upon Tyne.

## A final comment: managerialism in perspective

In concluding this chapter it is important to set managerialist research against the wider perspective of the urban system. Pahl (1975, 1977, 1979) has warned of the dangers of ascribing too much power to the managers of the system (and too little to political power-holders), and Norman has suggested that the managerialist approach lacks a theory of the distribution of power 'which would solve the problem of which groups are the most significant gatekeepers in given localities' (Norman 1975: 66). This question of the relative power of gatekeepers is important, and it is essential to recognize that 'managerial' decisions, as we have seen in the case of public housing managers, are themselves subject to constraints determined by the wider economic, political and ideological structure of society and that there are forces completely beyond the

**Fig. 6.15**  Estate quality in Newcastle upon Tyne as defined by consumers.
*Source*: Taylor and Hadfield (1982), Fig. 12.7, p. 256.

control of the managers which exert a signifi- cant influence on urban patterns (Leonard 1982).

In his earlier writings, Pahl (1969, 1970a) recognized the importance of spatial constraints and ecological limitations but, as Saunders (1981) has observed, he failed to explain how these factors are articulated with the activities of urban managers to produce what he called the 'socio-ecological system' as a whole; and he under-emphasized the significance of other factors such as the control exercised by central government and the constraints imposed on urban managers by the reliance of the system on continued capital accumulation. Thus the managerial approach 'in concentrating on studying the allocation and distribution of "scarce resources", fails to ask why resources are in scarce supply' (Gray 1976b: 81). Urban managers, then, should be seen as actors of significant but limited importance in the context of an urban system in which econ- omic, social and political processes set the

limits for their activities whilst their professional *modus operandi* determines the detail of the resulting patterns (Johnston 1979a). They are not, as Saunders (1981) puts it, independent variables so much as intervening variables mediating between, on the one hand, the contradictory pressures of private sector prof- itability and social needs, and, on the other, the demands of central government and the needs and preferences of the local population. In other words, the managerialist thesis has been pronounced dead, but the managers themselves nevertheless need not lie down. In this context, Williams (1982) has stressed the importance of exploring and understanding the *institutional and organizational settings* in which the managers operate. In the remaining chapters of this book, attention is turned towards the relationships between urban structure and the forces – spatial, social, political and economic – which determine the context and framework for both urban managers and their operational settings.

# 7 Spatial organization and locational conflict

Urban residential structure is not merely the result of the interplay of housing demand and supply. As we saw in Chapter six, housing provides a relative location which confers access to a package of neighbourhood and community attributes including health services, educational facilities, recreational amenities and environmental quality as well as a social and cultural milieu. Competition in the housing market, of course, has much to do with gaining access to these geographically-restricted packages of facilities, but the spatial structure of the city cannot be fully understood without reference to the *group* competition and *group* conflict which occurs over the organization of city neighbourhoods and the location and allocation of services and amenities.

The 'groups' involved in such conflict are themselves a product of the differential wealth, power and prestige derived from people's position in the occupational structure – a position which is in part determined by ethnic status.

## Externalities

Much of the conflict between these socio-economic and ethnic groups is set in a spatial framework and derives from their desire to maximize the net *externalities* of urban life. Externalities, sometimes called 'spillover' or 'third-party' effects, are unpriced by-products of the production or consumption of goods and services of all kinds. An externality effect exists if the activity of one person, group or institution impinges on the welfare of others.

The classic example is the factory which pollutes local air and water supplies in the course of its operations, bringing *negative* externalities to nearby residents. In contrast, well-kept public parks produce *positive* externalities for most nearby residents. The behaviour of private individuals also gives rise to externality effects. These can be divided into 'public behaviour' externalities and 'status' externalities. The former include people's behaviour in relation to public comportment (e.g. quiet, sobriety, and tidiness), the upkeep of property and the upbringing of children. Status externalities relate to the 'reflected glory' (or otherwise) of living in a socially or ethnically distinctive neighbourhood. Externality effects therefore can take a variety of forms. They are, moreover, very complex in operation. Consider, for example, the behaviour of a householder in adding an imitation stone façade to the exterior of his house, adding new coach lamps as finishing touches to his work. For one neighbour this activity may generate a positive externality in the form of improved environmental quality; but for another, with different tastes in design, it may produce an equally strong negative externality effect.

For the geographer, much of the significance of externality effects stems from the fact that their intensity is usually a function of relative location. In other words, externalities may be regarded as having a spatially limited 'field'. Figure 7.1 shows the example of two types of externality fields surrounding a sports stadium located in the middle of a residential area. Note that the noise nuisance is much

**The Dell** ■
**Non-residential areas**
**Main routes** - - -
**City centre** C
**Station** S
Spillover is not present □
Spillover is present but no nuisance
Spillover is a nuisance
Spillover is a severe nuisance

The spatial extent and intensity of the parked cars nuisance field.

The spatial extent and intensity of the noise nuisance field.

**Fig. 7.1** Negative externality fields around a soccer stadium ('The Dell', Southampton). *Source*: Humphreys, Mason and Pinch (1983), Figs. 4 and 5, pp. 405.

more localized than the nuisance of parked cars, and that the latter does not exhibit a simple distance gradient from the stadium. Harvey (1973) makes a useful distinction between the *price of accessibility* to desirable urban amenities and the *costs of proximity* to the unwanted aspects of urban life. Both, however, are a product of relative location, and it is clear that the spatial organization of social groups in relation to one another and to the urban infrastructure therefore determines the net intensity of the externality effects which they enjoy. As a general rule, of course, those with the greatest wealth, the most power and the best knowledge will be best placed to reap the benefits of positive externalities and to fend off activities which generate negative externalities. As Pahl put it, 'The unequal distribution of power, wealth and prestige created by the occupational structure may be simply reinforced in a given locality – so that the less privileged are made even more "less privileged" by differential access to facilities' (Pahl 1970a: 113). The

location of public facilities such as transport routes, hospitals, and sports centres is often intended to ameliorate the regressive nature of locational advantage resulting from private competition but, as Harvey (1973) has shown, the 'hidden mechanisms' of group conflict tend to ensure that the inhabitants of the richest and most powerful neighbourhoods enjoy a large net benefit as a result of decisions affecting the location of public goods and the organization of public services.

### Community conflict

It is clear, then, that the pattern of externality fields can exert a powerful influence on people's welfare. Because of this, many commentators regard the social geography of the city as the outcome of conflicts which are worked out in society as a whole between unequally endowed groups seeking to obtain more or less exclusive access to positive externalities and to deflect negative externality fields elsewhere. As Harvey puts it, 'much of what goes on in a city . . . can be interpreted as an attempt to organize the distribution of externality effects to gain income advantages' (Harvey 1973: 58). Harvey is particularly concerned to show that the form, location and focus of such conflict depends, ultimately, on long-term urban structure changes and broader class conflicts, a point which is also emphasized by Johnston:

Because changes to the urban fabric introduce new sources of positive and negative externalities, they are potential generators of local conflicts. In the face of such proposed changes, the main protestors are usually those with most to lose: property owners, who perceive possible falls in land values, and parents, who identify potential deterioration in an area's schools. In general, it is the more affluent property owners who have the most to lose, and who, because of their ability to purchase legal and technical advice and their greater knowledge of, and links to, the political systems within which such conflicts are adjudicated, are most likely to prevent changes likely to injure their interests. Such conflicts are usually played out locally, but *their existence is part of the dynamic of capitalist cities*. Alterations in land use are needed if investors are to achieve profits, and if the losers in the conflicts over changes are the less affluent, then the price paid for those changes is substantially carried by them. *Local conflicts are part of the general contest between classes within capitalist society* (Johnston 1984a: 171, emphases added).

In the long run, one of the principal outcomes of the resolution of locational conflicts is the creation of a set of *de facto* territories on the basis of income and ethnicity as people respond by relocating to neighbourhoods where they can share their positive externalities with one another and are able to avoid, as much possible, those who impose negative externalities. The residents of such territories also attempt to improve and preserve their quality of life through collective action: competing through formal and informal neighbourhood groups and local political institutions to attract the utility-enhancing and keep out the utility-detracting. One of the most common community strategies in this context is that of *voicing* claims over a particular issue (Johnston 1982a; Orbell and Uno 1972), whether by organizing petitions, lobbying politicians and bureaucrats, writing

to newspapers, forming local resident groups, picketing, or distributing handbills and posters. As Dear and Long (1978) point out, this sometimes extends to *illegal activities*, such as personal violence, damage to property, sit-ins and deliberate violations of anti-discrimination laws. Alternatively, some communities are able to use formal channels of *participation* as a profitable strategy when they find themselves in conflict with other communities or institutions (Lake 1986). Another 'strategy' available to communities is that of *resignation* to the imposition of negative externalities. This is especially common where communities feel that voicing strategies are regularly ignored or overruled and that participation is ineffective. Many people who disapprove of city plans, for example, simply resign themselves to the 'inevitable' because they feel unable, individually or collectively, to exert any real influence on policy-makers. The final strategy is that of re-location, or *exit*, which is a household rather than a community strategy, and brings us back to the idea of a continually evolving geography of *de facto* territories.

### Spatial partitioning and community conflicts

Not all intra-metropolitan conflict is acted out at the level of *de facto* territories, however. A good deal of inter-group conflict is associated with the *de jure* organization of space which determines many aspects of the quality of neighbourhood life (Coates, Johnston and Knox 1977; Massam 1975). Much of the intra-metropolitan variation in levels of community welfare stems from variations in the overall level of public service provision in different jurisdictions and on the particular packages of public services available for a given level of taxation. It follows that each social group will tend to seek out the jurisdiction which maximizes its *fiscal surplus* and, once established, will compete with residents of other jurisdictions to attract the fiscally desirable – those whose demands for public services are small relative to the tax revenues they contribute – and to exclude the fiscally undesirable. In this way, inter-group conflict becomes institutionalized and is resolved through the activities of local governments and their representatives. One of the most important strategies in this context, for example, is the use of local authority controls over land use through zoning regulations which, if they are carefully drawn up, can effectively exclude specific social, ethnic or demographic groups from an entire jurisdiction.

The geometry of specialized *de jure* territories also serves to accentuate intra-metropolitan variations in community well-being and to provide the basis for further inter-community conflict. School catchment areas, for example, are often designed to maximize the homogeneity of school pupil compositions with respect to social class, thus accentuating local variations in 'public behaviour' externalities (Cox 1973). Where such districts have their own powers to raise revenues – as American school districts do – there is a direct relationship between the location of district boundaries and the relative welfare of communities on either side of the boundary line (Herbert 1976c). Conflict over resources and the use of space is also reflected in the way that space is organized into electoral subdivisions, and there is now a good deal of evidence documenting the manipulation of political boundaries by particular groups seeking to enhance their political power and, therefore, their ability to influence the intra-urban distribution of public resources (Johnston 1979b; Taylor and Johnston 1979).

The social geography of the city can thus be seen as the product of inter-group conflict over the organization and use of urban space and resources. In the remainder of this chapter, attention is focused on three important aspects of this conflict: the organization of ethnic minority groups into distinctive *de facto* territories, the organization and manipulation of *de jure* political and administrative boundaries, and the location and accessibility of urban services.

## The spatial segregation of ethnic groups

The residential behaviour of ethnic groups in Western cities provides a useful example of the way in which group conflict is resolved through the housing market. The utility of a 'conflict' interpretation of ethnic residential segregation has been stressed by Boal (1976; 1981), whose analysis of the field provides the framework for this section. Following the work of Duncan and Lieberson (1959) and Lazarus (1969), Boal suggests that ethnic segregation is inversely related to the process of assimilation with the host society, a process which is itself governed by different forms of group behaviour designed to minimize real or perceived threats to the group from outsiders. But before going on to examine this behaviour and its spatial consequences in detail, it is first necessary to clarify the meaning of terms such as 'ethnic group', 'host society', 'segregation' and 'assimilation'.

Quite simply, the term 'ethnic group' is used to mean any group which is defined or characterized by race, religion, nationality or culture. Implicit in its use is the idea that ethnic groups are minority groups whose presence in the city stems from a past or continuing stream of in-migration. Ethnic groups in this sense therefore include blacks, Puerto Ricans, Italians, Jews, Mexicans, Vietnamese, and (Asian) Indians in American cities; West Indians, Asians and Irish in British cities; Algerians and Spaniards in French cities; Turks and Yugoslavs in West German cities; and so on. While the host society may not be ethnically homogeneous, it always contains a *charter group* which represents the dominant matrix into which new ethnic groups are inserted. In North America, Australasia and Britain the charter group in most cities is white, with an 'Anglo-Saxon' culture. The degree to which ethnic groups are spatially segregated from the charter group varies a good deal from city to city according to the group involved. *Segregation* is taken here to refer to situations where members of an ethnic group are not distributed absolutely uniformly in relation to the rest of the population. This clearly covers a wide range of circumstances, and it is useful to be able to quantify the overall degree of segregation in some way. Several indexes of segregation are available (see, for example, Duncan and Duncan 1955a; Lieberson 1981; Taeuber and Taeuber 1965), although the sensitivity of all of them depends on the scale of the areal units employed (Jones and McEvoy 1978; Wood 1976).

One of the most widely used methods of quantifying the degree to which an ethnic group is residentially segregated is the index of dissimilarity, which is analogous to the Gini index of inequality and which produces a theoretical range of values from 0 (no segregation) to 100 (complete segregation). Index values calculated from census tract data in US cities show that blacks are generally the most segregated of the ethnic minorities in America. A study by Taeuber (1965) found the median index value to be 88, while Van Valey *et al.* (1977) found that over half of the 237 cities they examined had index values of 70 or more, with Chicago, Dallas, Fort Lauderdale, Las Vegas, Monroe (La.), Oklahoma City, Orlando (Fla.) and West Palm Beach having index values of over 90. Puerto Ricans and Cubans have also been found to be very highly segregated in American cities, with index values at the tract level commonly exceeding 60; as have the new immigrant groups of the 1970s and 1980s – Mexicans and Asians (Garcia 1985).

By comparison, ethnic residential segregation in European cities is relatively low. In Britain, for example, index values calculated for major coloured immigrant groups – West Indians, Pakistanis, Bangladeshis, Indians and Africans – at the enumeration district level range between 40 and 70 (Baboolal 1981; Jones 1979; Peach 1984; Robinson 1984). The *Gastarbeiter* (guest worker) population of continental European cities is even less segregated: index values for Turks, Greeks, Yugoslavs and Italians in West German cities, for example, range between 20 and 45 (O'Loughlin 1980). At more detailed levels of analysis the degree of segregation can be much higher. Jones and McEvoy (1978), for example, computed an index value of 81.6 for Asians in Huddersfield at the scale of individual streets, while O'Loughlin computed index values of between 50 and 70 at a similar scale of analysis for Turks, Greeks, Yugoslavs, Italians and Spaniards in Düsseldorf; and values of between 80 and 100 for the same groups at the scale of apartment buildings. This empha-

sizes the vulnerability of statistical indexes, and makes inter-city comparisons difficult. Another practical difficulty in making precise statements about the degree of residential segregation is that ethnic groupings may subsume important internal differences. Statements about the segregation of Asians in British cities, for instance, overlook the tendency for Indians, Pakistanis and Bangladeshis to exist in quite separate communities, even though these communities may appear to outsiders to be part and parcel of the same community. Muslims are separated from Hindus, Gujerati speakers from Punjabi speakers, and East African Asians from all other Asians; and these segregations are preserved even within public-sector housing (Robinson 1981). Similarly, the distinctive island communities of the West Indies can be identified on the map of London:

There is an archipelago of Windward and
Leeward islanders north of the Thames;
Dominicans and St Lucians have their core areas
in Notting Hill; Grenadians are found in the west
in Hammersmith and Ealing; Montserratians are
concentrated around Stoke Newington, Hackney
and Finsbury Park; Antiguans spill over to the
east in Hackney, Waltham Forest and Newham;
south of the river is Jamaica (Peach 1984: 224)

What is clear enough from the available evidence, however, is that most ethnic minorities tend to be highly segregated from the charter group. Moreover, this segregation has been shown to be greater than might be anticipated from the socio-economic status of the groups concerned. In other words, the low socio-economic status of ethnic groups can only partially explain their high levels of residential segregation (Berry 1972; Lee 1977; Taeuber 1965). The maintenance of the ethnic in-migrant group 'as a distinctive social and spatial entity' will depend, as Boal (1976: 43) observes, 'on the degree to which assimilation occurs'. This process can take place at different speeds for different groups, depending on the perceived social distance between them and the charter group. Moreover, behavioural assimilation – the acquisition by the ethnic group of a cultural life in common with the charter group – may take place faster than structural assimilation – the diffusion of members of the ethnic group through the social and occupational strata of the charter group society. In general, the rate and degree of assimilation of an ethnic minority group will depend on two sets of factors: (1) external factors, including charter group attitudes and 'fabric' effects, and (2) internal group cohesiveness. Between them, these factors determine not only the degree and nature of conflict between ethnic groups and the charter group, but also the spatial pattern of residential segregation.

## External factors

Ethnic groups which are perceived by members of the charter group to be socially undesirable will find themselves spatially isolated through a variety of mechanisms. One of the most obvious and straightforward of these is the 'blocking' strategy by existing occupants of city neighbourhoods in order to resist the 'invasion' of ethnic groups. Established tightly-knit ethnic clusters tend to be the most resistant to invasion, actively defending their own territory in a variety of ways (ranging from social hostility and the refusal to sell or rent homes to petty violence and deliberate vandalism) against intruding members of ethnic groups of inferior status. Perhaps the best-known example of this is the resistance by residents of the 'Polish Principality' of Hamtramck in Detroit to the residential expansion of blacks (Clark 1964). Where this strategy of 'voicing' opposition is unsuccessful, or where the territory in question is occupied by socially and geographically more mobile households, the charter group strategy commonly becomes one of 'exit'. The invasion of charter group territory generally precipitates an outflow of charter group residents which continues steadily until the critical point is reached where the proportion of households from the invading ethnic group precipitates a much faster exodus. This is known as the 'tipping point'. The precise level of the tipping point is difficult to establish, although Rose (1970) suggested that for whites facing 'invasion' by blacks the tipping

point may be expected to occur when black occupancy reaches a level of about 30 per cent. The subsequent withdrawal of charter group residents to other neighbourhoods effectively resolves the territorial conflict between the two groups, leaving the ethnic group spatially isolated until its next phase of territorial expansion.

The spatial isolation of ethnic groups is also contrived through discrimination in the housing market, thus limiting ethnic groups to small niches within the urban fabric. Although formal discriminatory barriers are illegal, ethnic minorities are systematically excluded from charter group neighbourhoods in a variety of ways. As we have seen (pp. 232–240), the role of estate agents and mortgage financiers in the owner-occupied sector is particularly important, while the general gatekeeping role of private landlords also tends to perpetuate ethnically segregated local sub-markets (Daniel 1968). There is also a considerable weight of evidence to suggest that immigrants and ethnic minorities are discriminated against in the public sector. In Britain, racial minorities have found themselves disadvantaged within the public sector in three respects. First, they have had more difficulty in gaining access to any public housing at all; second, they have often been allocated to poor-quality property, particularly older flats; and, third, they have been disproportionately allocated to unpopular inner-city housing estates, thus intensifying the localization of the non-white population in the inner city. These disadvantages are partly the result of unintentional discrimination (such as the residential requirements associated with eligibility rules), and partly the result of more deliberate discrimination through the personal prejudices, for example, of housing visitors, who may have little or no understanding of the cultural background and family life of immigrant households (Henderson and Karn 1984; Parker and Dugmore 1976; Peach and Shah 1980). This type of discrimination is exacerbated by the discriminatory policies of city planners. Again, some of this discrimination is unintentional, as in the omission of ethnic neighbourhoods from urban renewal and rehabilitation schemes (Rex and

Moore 1967), but much is deliberate, as in the manipulation of land-use plans and zoning regulations in order to exclude non-whites from suburban residential areas of US cities.

The net effect of this discrimination is to render much of the housing stock unavailable to members of ethnic groups, thus trapping them in privately-rented accommodation and allowing landlords to charge inflated rents while providing little security of tenure. In an attempt to escape from this situation, some householders reluctantly become landlords, buying large deteriorating houses and sub-letting part of the house in order to maintain mortgage repayments and/or repair costs. Others manage to purchase smaller dwellings which are shared with another family or a lodger, but many can only finance the purchase through burdensome and unorthodox means. Asians, in particular, have been found to exhibit a strong propensity towards home ownership in preference to tenancy, notwithstanding the extra financial costs (Dahya 1974). The localized nature of cheaper accommodation (whether for sale or rent) is another important 'fabric' effect which serves to segregate ethnic minority groups from the rest of the population by channelling them into a limited niche. Moreover, since many ethnic groups have an atypical demographic structure, with a predominance of young adult males and/or large, extended families, their housing needs – single-room accommodation and large dwellings respectively – can be met only in very specific locations. In many cities, therefore, the distribution of ethnic clusters is closely related to the geography of the housing stock.

Underlying both charter group discrimination and the localization of ethnic groups in particular pockets of low-cost housing is their position in the overall social and economic structure of society. Rex and Moore, for example, suggested that while some of the discriminatory behaviour they found in Sparkbrook, Birmingham, may have been due to innate tendencies or personality disturbances, a great deal of it could be explained by Birmingham's social structure and by conflicts of interests and roles which were built into Birmingham society (Rex and Moore 1967). This approaches the Marxist analysis of race

relations in Britain, which holds that 'the position of immigrants in society is not one of an "outgroup" cut off from society by the "factor of colour"; rather it recognizes that the subordinate, oppressed position of such groups is conditioned by their racial distinctiveness and *reinforced by their concentration in the working class*, leading to their super-exploitation in society' (Doherty 1973: 50, emphasis added). In this context, discrimination by working-class members of the charter group is related to the role attributed to ethnic groups in job and housing markets as competitors whose presence serves to depress wages and erode the quality of life. In short, ethnic groups are treated as the scapegoats for the shortcomings of the economic system.

But it is the concentration of ethnic groups at the lower end of the occupational structure which is the more fundamental factor in their localization in poor housing. Because of their lack of skills and educational qualifications, members of ethnic minority groups tend to be concentrated in occupations which are unattractive to members of the charter group, which are often unpleasant or degrading in one way or another, and which are usually associated with low wages (Unit for Manpower Studies 1976). The majority of such occupations are associated with the CBD and its immediate surrounds, and the dependence of ethnic groups on centralized job opportunities is widely cited as a prime determinant in the location of ethnic residential clusters (Lee 1977; O'Loughlin 1980). This factor, in turn, is reinforced by the location of suitably cheap accommodation in inner-city neighbourhoods surrounding the CBD. Moreover, the isolation of ethnic groups in this sector of the housing and labour markets is increasingly exacerbated by the suburbanization of job opportunities which effectively become inaccessible to the inner-city poor because of their inability to meet the necessary transportation costs (Bederman and Adams 1974; de Vise 1976).

## Internal group cohesiveness

While charter group attitudes, fabric effects and occupational status go a long way towards explaining residential segregation, they do not satisfactorily explain the clustering of ethnic groups into discrete, ethnically homogeneous territories. According to Boal (1976), such clusters are basically defensive and conservative in function, partly in response to the external pressures outlined above. As he puts it:

Conflict situations in cities lead people to feel threatened. This will particularly apply to recent in-migrants, who may vary culturally and indeed racially from the 'host' population . . . The perceived threat may materialize in the form of physical violence or remain as a psychological threat. At the same time, and indeed sometimes because of the threat, the ethnic group may have a strong urge to internal cohesion, so that the cultural 'heritage' of the group may be retained (Boal 1976: 45).

Boal suggests that the clustering of ethnic groups serves four principal functions: defence, support, preservation and attack.

The *defensive* role of ethnic clusters is most prominent when charter group discrimination is extremely widespread and intense, so that the existence of a territorial heartland enables member of the ethnic groups to withdraw from the hostility of the wider society. Jewish ghettos in medieval European cities functioned in this way, and Boal himself has vividly demonstrated the way in which working-class Catholic and Protestant communities in Belfast have become increasingly segregated from one another in response to their need for physical safety (Boal 1974; 1978). Nowhere has this phenomenon been more marked than on the Shankhill–Falls 'Divide' between the Protestant neighbourhood of Shankhill and the Catholic neighbourhood of Clonard–Springfield. Transitional between the two, and marking the Divide between the two ethnic groups, is the Cupar Street area, which had acquired a mixed residential pattern in the years up to 1968. When the 'troubles' broke out in 1969, however, the territorial boundary between the two groups took on a much sharper definition. Sixty-five households moved to the relative safety of their own religious heartland from Cupar Street alone during August/September 1969 in response to the mounting incidence of

physical attacks in the district. It is estimated that within the following seven years between 35,000 and 60,000 people from the Belfast area relocated for similar reasons, thus reinforcing the segregation of Protestants and Catholics into what have become known in army circles as 'tribal areas' (Boal 1978).

It should be emphasized, then, that the defensive role of ethnic clusters is really as much an involuntary product of external pressure (or perceived pressure) as it is a voluntary product of internal cohesiveness. As Shah (1979) concluded from a study of the Bangladeshi community in the East End of London:

There is certain evidence . . . that one of the determinants of residential concentration of the Bangladeshi is the lack of confidence the community has in the police's ability to protect them from racial attacks which have been a dominant feature in London's East End. Certainly this is 'voluntary segregation' but inasmuch as the distinction between voluntary and involuntary segregation is related to freely determined choice, segregation as a defensive act lies more in the realm of imposed rather than self-imposed segregation (Shah 1979: 450, cited in Smith 1981: 51).

Closely related to the defensive functions of ethnic clusters is their role as a haven, providing *support* for members of the group in a variety of ways. These range from formal ethnic-oriented institutions and businesses to informal friendship and kinship ties. Clustered together in a mutually supportive haven, members of the group are able to avoid the hostility and rejection of the charter group, exchanging insecurity and anxiety for familiarity and strength. This 'buffer' function of ethnic clusters has been documented in a number of studies, including Raveau's (1970) description of the segregation of black Africans in Paris, Deakin's (1970) analysis of coloured groups in British cities, and Kramer's (1970) discussion of ethnic minorities in American cities. The existence of ethnic institutions within the territorial cluster is one of the most important factors in protecting group members from unwanted contact with the host community. Hiro (1973), for example, describes how Sikh temples and Moslem mosques in British cities have become the focus of Sikh and Pakistani local welfare systems, offering a source of food, shelter, recreation and education as well as being a cultural and religious focus.

More generally, most ethnic immigrant groups develop informal self-help networks and welfare organizations in order to provide both material and social support for group members. At the same time, the desire to avoid outside contact and the existence of a local concentration of an ethnic population with distinctive, culturally-based needs serve to provide what Hannerz (1974) calls 'protected niches' for ethnic enterprise, both legitimate and illegitimate. One example given by Hannerz is the success of the Cosa Nostra in Italian-American communities; but it is clear that ethnic enterprise is an important component of community cohesion in ethnic neighbourhoods everywhere, providing an expression of group solidarity as well as a means of economic and social advancement for successful entrepreneurs and an alternative route by which ethnic workers can bypass the white-controlled labour market (Freedman 1985). In their classic study of the black community in Chicago, Drake and Cayton (1962) describe the doctrine of the 'double-duty dollar', according to which members of the community should use their money not only to satisfy their personal needs but also to 'advance the race' by making their purchases in black-owned businesses. In Britain, the most distinctive manifestations of ethnic enterprise are the clusters of banks, butchers, grocery stores, travel agencies, cinemas and clothing shops which have developed in response to the food taboos, specialized clothing styles and general cultural aloofness of Asian communities, combined with the economic repression of British society (Aldrich *et al.* 1981; Cater and Jones 1978).

This brings us to a third major function of ethnic residential clustering: that of *preserving* and promoting a distinctive cultural heritage. Ethnic group consciousness sometimes results from external pressure, as in the use of Jamaican Creole by young blacks in London as a private language to shut out the oppress-

ive elements of the white world (Sutcliffe 1982). But for many groups there exists an inherent desire to maintain a distinctive cultural identity rather than to become completely assimilated within the charter group. Residential clustering helps to achieve this not only through the operation of ethnic institutions and businesses but also through the effects of residential propinquity on marriage patterns. Several writers have emphasized the self-segregating tendencies of Asian communities in British cities in this context (Dahya 1974; Kearsley and Srivastava 1974), while Rosenthal (1961) suggested that the persistence of Jewish residential clusters in Chicago was closely related to the knowledge among Jewish parents that residence in a Jewish neighbourhood conferred a very high probability of their children marrying a Jewish person. Other examples include Cypriots in British cities (Peach 1975) and Greeks in Australian cities (Peach 1974). The residential clustering of some ethnic groups is also directly related to the demands of their religious precepts relating to dietary laws, the preparation of food, and attendance for prayer and religious ceremony. Where such *mores* form an important part of the group's culture, they are clearly followed more easily where the group is territorially clustered. On the other hand, where group consciousness is weak and the group culture is not especially distinctive, ties between group members tend to be superficial – sentimental rather than functional – with the result that residential clustering as well as group solidarity is steadily eroded: a process which Dench (1975) has tellingly documented in relation to the Maltese in London.

The fourth major function of ethnic spatial concentration is the provision of a 'base' for action in the struggle of its members with society in general. This *attack* function, as Boal calls it, is usually both peaceful and legitimate. Spatial concentrations of group members represent considerable electoral power and often enable ethnic groups to gain official representation within the institutional framework of urban politics. This has been an important factor in the political power base of blacks in the United States, where the Black

Power movement has been able to exploit the electoral power of the ghetto with considerable success – to the extent that black politicians now constitute an important (and sometimes decisive) voice in the urban political arena (Brunn 1974). Ethnic clusters also provide a convenient base for illegitimate attacks on the charter group. Insurrectionary groups and urban guerrillas with ethnic affiliations are able to 'disappear' in their own group's territory, camouflaged by a relative anonymity within their own cultural milieu and protected by a silence resulting from a mixture of sympathy and intimidation. An obvious example of this is the way in which the IRA and Loyalist para-military organizations have taken advantage of their respective territorial heartlands in Belfast; and, indeed, the way in which the IRA has used Irish communities in Birmingham, Liverpool, London and Southampton as bases for terrorist attacks.

## Spatial outcomes

The spatial expression of ethnic group/charter group conflict is determined by the interplay of charter group attitudes, fabric effects, and the strength of internal group cohesion. Where the perceived social distance between the ethnic group and the charter group is relatively small, the effects of both charter group discrimination and internal cohesion are likely to be minimized and so ethnic residental clusters are likely to be only a temporary stage in the assimilation of the group into the wider urban socio-spatial fabric. Such clusters may be termed *colonies*. They essentially serve as a port-of-entry for members of the ethnic group concerned, providing a base from which group members are culturally assimilated and spatially dispersed. Their persistence over time is thus dependent on the continuing input of new ethnic group members. Examples of this type of pattern include the distribution of European ethnic groups in North American cities during the 1920s and 1930s, of similar groups in Australasian cities during the 1950s and 1960s, and of the Maltese in London during the 1950s (Duncan and Lieberson

1959; Burnley 1972; Dench 1975).

Ethnic clusters which persist over the longer term are usually a product of the interaction between discrimination and internal cohesion. Where the latter is the more dominant of the forces, the resultant residential clusters may be termed *enclaves*; and where external factors are more dominant, the residential clusters are generally referred to as *ghettos*. In reality, of course, it is often difficult to ascertain the degree to which segregation is voluntary or involuntary, and it is more realistic to think in terms of a continuum rather than a twofold classification. Boal (1976) has identified several distinctive spatial patterns in relation to this enclave/ghetto continuum. The first of these is exemplifed by Jewish residential areas in many cities, where an initial residential clustering in inner-city areas has formed the base for the subseqent formation of new suburban residential clusters (Fig. 7.2; see also Newman 1985). The fact that this suburbanization represents a general upward shift in socio-economic status and that it is usually accompanied by the transferral of Jewish cultural and religious institutions to the suburbs suggests that this type of pattern is largely the result of voluntary segregation.

The second distinctive expression of the enclave/ghetto takes the form of a concentric zone of ethnic neighbourhoods which has spread from an initial cluster to encircle the CBD. Such zones are often patchy, the discontinuities reflecting variations in the urban fabric in terms of house types and resistant social groups. The growth of black areas in many American cities tends to conform to this pattern, while other examples include the distribution of Asians, Irish and West Indians in Birmingham (Jones 1979), of Asians in Glasgow (Kearsley and Srivastava 1974), of West Indians in London (Lee 1977; Peach 1984) and of Asians in Leicester (Fig. 7.3: see Phillips 1981). It should be noted, however, that the same pattern may occur in different places for different reasons. In the case of the Glasgow Asians, for example, Kearsley and Srivastava suggest that the concentric pattern derives from a process of 'uncontested filtering' into tenement housing which has been made available by the

**Fig. 7.2**   Changing distribution of Jews in Winnipeg, Manitoba, 1941–1961.
*Source*: Driedger and Church (1974), p. 38 and 40.

out-migration of indigenous Glaswegians. In contrast, the concentric pattern of black neighbourhoods in certain American cities seems to be related more to twin effects of occupational status and racial discrimination (Rose 1971). It should also be noted that the individual clusters within such patterns may also exhibit a distinctive morphology. Baboolal (1981), for example, has typified black residential clusters in south London as an aureole-nebula configuration (Fig. 7.4), with successive zones of decreasing concentrations of black households. This latter feature, it seems, is the result of the black clusters being focused on sub-centres where older housing had been redeveloped and replaced by local authority housing or non-residential land uses.

Where an ethnic group continues to grow numerically, and provided that a sufficient number of its population are able to afford better housing, residential segregation is likely to result in a sectoral spatial pattern. The distribution of blacks in many of the more prosperous and rapidly expanding cities of the United States tends towards this model although, as Boal (1976) points out, sectoral development is often truncated because of economic constraints operating at the suburban

margin. The distribution of the black population in Oklahoma City provides a good example of this type of pattern. As Fig. 7.5 shows, the city's black population has been almost entirely confined to the north-eastern sector: few census tracts outside this area contain even 1 per cent of black persons. Other examples of this sort of spatial pattern include the distribution of blacks in Grand Rapids, Michigan (Boal 1976) and of Catholics in Belfast (Poole and Boal 1973). Finally, it should be noted that, whatever the overall spatial pattern, most ethnic groups display an internal differentiation on a social class basis. Gordon (1964) has suggested that a series of sub-societies is created by the intersection of the vertical stratification of ethnicity with the horizontal stratification of social class. These sub-societies – what Gordon calls 'ethclasses' – are explicit in the integrated model of urban factorial ecology put forward by Berry and Rees (1969), where ethnic social stratification is associated with a zonal spatial pattern (Fig. 4.15). Such a pattern was also demonstrated by Frazier (1967) in his study of black residential patterns in Chicago. As Table 7.1 shows, almost all the indices of family life, social organization and economic and family

**Fig. 7.3**  Distribution of Hindu households in Leicester, 1978.
*Source*: Phillips (1981), Fig. 3, p. 107.

status display clear zonal trends. It must be emphasized, however, that this pattern of zonal ethclass segregation is relevant only to ethnic groups whose overall residential pattern is sectoral. Where concentric patterns or nodal enclaves form the overall spatial framework, other patterns will emerge. In New York City, for example, darker-skinned and less-affluent Puerto Ricans are becoming more concentrated in a near black neighbourhoods, while lighter-skinned and more affluent Puerto Ricans are becoming increasingly dispersed (Jackson 1981).

It will be clear by now that most large cities contain a variety of ethnic minorities, each responding to a different mix of internal and external factors, each exhibiting rather different spatial outcomes, and each changing in different rates and in different ways. A recent study of Detroit's minority populations between 1940 and 1970 illustrates the point well (Agócs 1981). On the basis of three key measures – suburbanization, clustering and segregation – for each of ten ethnic groups in 1940 and 1970, Agócs has demonstrated how the black population, together with Hispanics,

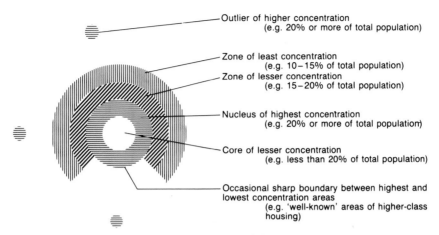

Outlier of higher concentration
(e.g. 20% or more of total population)

Zone of least concentration
(e.g. 10–15% of total population)

Zone of lesser concentration
(e.g. 15–20% of total population)

Nucleus of highest concentration
(e.g. 20% or more of total population)

Core of lesser concentration
(e.g. less than 20% of total population)

Occasional sharp boundary between highest and
lowest concentration areas
(e.g. 'well-known' areas of higher-class
housing)

**Fig. 7.4** Diagrammatic representation of the morphology of black
residential clusters in south London: an aureole-nebula spatial pattern.
*Source*: Baboolal (1981), Fig. 6, p. 75.

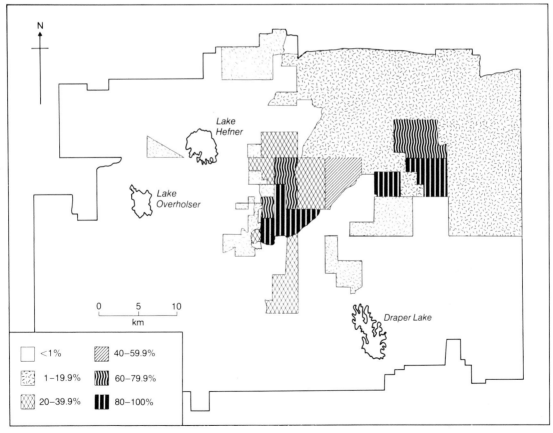

**Fig. 7.5** The distribution of the black population in Oklahoma City, 1970.

was characterized by centralization, clustering and segregation. Jews, Hungarians and Italians, on the other hand, were characterized by suburbanization, clustering and segregation. British and German households were characterized by suburbanization, dispersal and integration; while Polish, Irish and Russian households were characterized by the centralization of the immigrant generation and suburbanization of their descendants. Further investigation resulted in a sevenfold typology of ethnic communities (Table 7.1):

**Table 7.1** A typology of ethnic communities

| Ethnic population distribution | Clustered and segregated | Dispersed and integrated |
|---|---|---|
| Centralized | 1. Ghetto<br>2. Immigrant reception center<br>3. Urban village | 4. Residual community |
| Suburbanized | 5. Transplanted community<br>6. New suburban settlement | 7. Community without neighbourhood |

*Source:* Agócs (1981), Fig. 2, p. 132.

1. *The ghetto*: a single compact concentration of black households with clear boundaries, almost entirely confined to the older, deteriorating zones of the metropolitan area.
2. *Recent immigrant reception centres*: some located in inner-city districts (e.g. Detroit's Mexican neighbourhood); others, as a result of the chain migration process, in generationally mixed neighbourhoods in the suburbs, near industrial districts.
3. *Urban villages*: stable concentrations dominated by second generation immigrants, each containing a variety of supporting ethnic institutions: schools, churches, social, cultural and political organizations, and businesses. The major urban villages in Detroit were Polish (in the middle zone of older suburbs) and Hispanic (in inner-city neighbourhoods).

4. *Residual communities*: islands of ethnic concentration in inner-city and middle-zone neighbourhoods that had largely passed to other groups
5. *Transplanted communities*: highly clustered and segregated, but located in a new setting far from earlier locations – the typical outcome of the residential dynamics of Jewish populations in American cities
6. *New suburban settlements*: less compact, less dense and less well-bounded than transplanted communities, and generally a product of sectoral migration streams. Best exemplified in Detroit by Hungarians, Italians and Poles.
7. *Communities without neighbourhoods*: dispersed and suburbanized populations – chiefly German and British – for whom ethnic community life is based less on residential propinquity than on the communication, interaction and shared activities of widely dispersed social networks and the continued (though less frequent) use of ethnic institutions in old central city neighbourhoods.

*An illustrative example: migrant workers in European cities*

During the postwar period, an important new dimension has been added to the social geography of continental European cities with the arrival of tens of thousands of migrant workers, most of them from the poorer regions of the Mediterranean. Although estimates vary a good deal, there were at the beginning of the 1980s some 14 million aliens living in Western European countries. About half of these were young adult males who had emigrated in order to seek work, originally, at least, on a temporary basis. The rest were wives and families who had joined them. At the heart of this influx of foreign-born workers were the labour needs of the more developed regions, coupled with the demographic 'echo effect' of low birth rates in the 1930s and 1940s: a sluggish rate of growth in the indigenous labour force. As the demand for labour in more developed countries expanded, so indigenous workers found themselves able to shun low-wage, unpleasant and menial occupations; immigrant labour filled the vacuum (Castles and Kosack 1985). At the same time, the more prosperous countries perceived that foreign workers might provide a buffer for the indigenous labour force against the effects of economic cycles – the so-called *konjunkturpuffer* philosophy. The peak of these streams of immigrants occurred in the mid-1960s and early 1970s. The onset of deep economic recession in 1973, however, brought a dramatic check to the flows. Restrictions on the admission of non-EEC immigrants began in West Germany in November 1973, and within twelve months France, Belgium, and the Netherlands had followed with new restrictions. By this time there were nearly two million foreign workers in West Germany, over 1.5 million in France, half a million in Switzerland, and around a quarter of a million in Belgium and Sweden. Within each of these countries the impact of migrant labour has been localized in larger urban areas, reflecting the immigrants' role as replacement labour for the low-paid, assembly-line and service sector jobs vacated in inner-city areas by the upward socio-economic mobility and outward geographical mobility of the indigenous population. Thus, for example, more than one-third of the 4.1 million aliens living in France in 1975 lived in the Paris region, representing 14.5 per cent of its population. Other French cities where aliens account for more than 10 per cent of the population include Lyon, Marseille, Nice and St Etienne. In West Germany the increasing concentrations of foreign workers in large cities (except Berlin) led to the imposition in April 1975 of quotas which limit the numbers of aliens living in city centres.

The arrival of these migrant workers in established urban settings which had hitherto not contained any significant ethnic dimension has provided some very graphic examples of socio-spatial conflict, though it should be noted at the outset that this conflict has been somewhat muted by the initial expectation (by both charter groups and ethnic minorities) that the guest workers would eventually return to their countries of origin. In the event, the idea of an early return has turned out to be something of a myth – just as it did for the West Indian and Asian migrant workforce that had earlier been drawn into British cities.

The key to the conflicts and issues surrounding the presence of migrant labour in European cities lies in the type of work they were recruited to do. Since nearly all of the jobs have involved low-skill, low-wage occupations, immigrants have inevitably been channelled towards the cheapest housing and the most run-down neighbourhoods. The position of immigrants in the labour market is of course partly self-inflicted: for many the objective has been to earn as much as possible as quickly as possible, the easiest strategy being to take on employment with an hourly wage where overtime and even a second job can be pursued. As Castles and Kosack point out, however, most immigrants tend to be *kept* at the foot of the economic ladder by a combination of official restrictions and social discrimination. The net result is reflected by the statistics for West Germany in the mid-1970s: only 1 per cent of migrant workers held non-manual jobs (King 1976).

Similarly, immigrants' position in housing markets is partly self-inflicted: cheapness is of the essence. But the localization of immigrants in camps, factory hostels, *hôtels meublés* (immigrant hostels), *bidonvilles* (suburban shanty towns) and inner-city tenements is also reinforced by restrictions and discrimination. Concentrated in such housing, immigrants find themselves in an environment which creates problems both for themselves and for the indigenous population. Trapped in limited niches of the housing stock, they are vulnerable to exploitation. A survey of housing conditions in the Ruhr, for example, found that immigrant workers were paying an average of 30 per cent more rent than German nationals, even though the latter had better accommodation (Böhning 1972). One response has been the notorious 'hotbed' arrangement, whereby two or even three workers on different shifts take turns at sleeping in the same bed. In France a more common response has been to retreat to the cardboard and corrugated iron bidonvilles, where although there may be no sanitary facilities immigrants can at least live inexpensively among their own countrymen. In such circumstances, health and welfare-related problems proliferate, further polarizing the immigrant community in terms of social well-being. Yet most foreign workers do not have the same civil rights as the indigenous population, nor are local social services geared to deal with their problems. Educational problems have become particularly acute as a second generation of immigrants makes its presence felt. Already there are over one million foreign children in the educational systems of both France and West Germany and more than 300,000 in Switzerland. In some cities, such children represent over 20 per cent of the total school population; in some school catchment areas they represent an overwhelming majority. Educational systems and educational resources have so far proved unable to deal with the special problems of language and culture faced by immigrant children. Moreover, educational issues have become a common focus for the mistrust and resentment felt by local residents towards immigrant communities. Social conflict of this sort serves in turn to reinforce the separateness and isolation of immigrant communities, accentuating cultural and religious differences and preventing assimilation.

In terms of spatial outcomes, a fairly consistent pattern has emerged, despite the very different minority populations involved in different cities – Yugoslavs and Turks in Duisburg, Frankfurt, Köln and Vienna; Algerians, Italians and Tunisians in Paris; and Surinamese and Turks in Rotterdam, for example. In short, just as the migrants are replacing the lower echelons of the indigenous population in the labour market, so they are acting as a partial replacement for the rapidly declining indigenous population in the older neighbourhoods of privately rented housing near to sources of service employment and factory jobs (Leitner 1983; Lichtenberger 1984; White 1984). This produces the kind of spatial patterns depicted in Fig. 7.6 for Greeks, Yugoslavs, Spaniards, Turks and Italians in central Nürnberg. The overlap of these groups has produced three major ethnic clus-

ters or 'pressure points' (*Schwerpunkte*): the nineteenth-century industrial axis of the Fürtherstrasse that extends westwards from the edge of the Altstadt, the slum area of the Südstadt to the south of the Hauptbanhof (railway station), and the inner-city tenement district of St Leonhard (Jones 1983). Quite simply, the overriding priority for migrant workers is to live close to their jobs in cheap accommodation. This applies to all national groups, so that similar spatial patterns have persisted even as the culturally more alien Turkish, Yugoslavian and North African populations have replaced older and more familiar groups such as Greeks and Spaniards.

# Spatial organization, community conflict and the quality of life

The geo-political organization of metropolitan areas has become an important determinant of the quality of neighbourhood life. To a large extent, the magnitude and composition of the 'social wage' – the benefits derived from public expenditure – is decided by the policies of local governments and their administrative bureaucracies. Moreover, the *de jure* territories in which these institutions operate can be seen to serve as a framework for the resolution of inter-community conflict over the resources which constitute the social wage. In this section, therefore, we examine the evolution of *de jure* spaces at the intra-metropolitan level and discuss some of the major implications of the way in which space has been partitioned for political and administrative purposes.

## Metropolitan fragmentation and the evolution of special districts

Modern metropolitan areas are characterized by a complex partitioning of space into multi-purpose local government jurisdictions and a wide variety of special administrative districts responsible for single functions such as the provision of schools, hospitals, water and

**Fig. 7.6**  Inner Nuremberg: population changes 1974–1980 by national groups.
*Source*: Jones (1983), Fig. 4, p. 129.

sewage facilities. This complexity is greatest in Australia and North America, where the ethic of local autonomy is stronger, and it reaches a peak in the United States, where in 1977 the 35 largest metropolitan areas each had an average of 293 separate jurisdictions (Bollens and Schmandt 1982; Johnston 1981a). While never reaching these levels of complexity, the same phenomenon can be found in Europe. In Britain, for example, the Birmingham, Manchester, Merseyside and Tyneside conurbations were all under the control of at least four major multi-purpose local authorities until the whole system of local government was reorganized in the mid-1970s; the government of the London conurbation is still fragmented between 32 boroughs, which until recently had the Greater London Council presiding over them all as an extra tier of government; and in every city there are special district authorities which are responsible for the provision of health services and water supplies.

Much of this complexity can be seen as the response of political and administrative systems to the changing economic and social structure of the metropolis. In short, the decentralization of jobs and residences from the urban core has brought about a corresponding decentralization and proliferation of local jurisdictions. New local governments have been created to service the populations of new suburban and exurban dormitory communities, resulting in the 'balkanization' of metropolitan areas into competing jurisdictions. In the United States, this process has been accelerated by policies which, guided by the principle of local autonomy, made the annexation of territory by existing cities more difficult while keeping incorporation procedures 'outlandishly easy' (Bollens and Schmandt 1982). New single-function special districts, on the other hand, have proliferated throughout metropolitan areas, largely in response to the failure of existing political and administrative systems to cope with the changing needs and demands of the population. Between 1942 and 1972, the number of non-school special districts in the US increased from 6,299 to 23,885) (Coates, Johnston and Knox 1977). As Stetzer (1975) points out, new spatial districts are an attractive solution to a wide range of problems because they are able to avoid the statutory limitations on financial and legal powers which apply to local governments. In particular, a community can increase its debt or tax revenue by creating an additional layer of government for a specific purpose. Special districts also have the advantage of corresponding more closely to functional areas and, therefore, of being more finely tuned to local social organization and participation. Another reason for their proliferation has been the influence of special interest groups, including (a) citizen groups concerned with a particular function or issue and (b) business enterprises which stand to benefit economically from the creation of a special district.

Although fragmentation can be defended on the grounds of fostering the sensitivity of politicians and administrators to local preferences, it can also be shown to have spawned administrative complexity, political disorganization, fiscal imbalance and an inefficient distribution of public goods and services. Not least of these problems is the sheer confusion resulting from the functional and spatial overlapping of different jurisdictions. Decentralized decision-making leads to the burgeoning of costly bureaucracies, the duplication of services and the pursuit of conflicting policies. Of course, not all public services require metropolitan-wide organization: some urban problems are of a purely local nature. But for many services – such as water supply, planning, transport, health care, housing and welfare – economies of scale make large areal units with large populations a more efficient and equitable base.

Problems of policy co-ordination and economic efficiency notwithstanding, Yeates and Garner (1976) suggest that the proliferation of special districts has in fact led to an attenuation of public control over public policy. Their argument is that the public is simply not aware of the numbers of different units of local government which influence their daily lives and that this lack of awareness leaves the control of most authorities to a self-selected knot of individuals and special interest groups. The balkanization of general-purpose government in the United States has also led to the suppression of political conflict between social groups. As Newton (1978: 84) observes:

Social groups can confront each other when they are in the same political arena, but this possibility is reduced when they are separated into different arenas. Political differences are easier to express when groups occupy the same political system and share the same political institutions, but this is more difficult when the groups are divided by political boundaries and do not contest the same elections, do not fight for control of the same elected offices, do not contest public policies for the same political units, or do not argue about the same municipal budgets.

This erosion of democracy means in turn that community politics tend to be low-key affairs, while the politics of the whole metropolitan area are often notable for their absence. The balkanization of the city means that it is difficult to make, or even think about, area-wide decisions for area-wide problems. 'The result is a series of parish-pump and parochial politics in which small issues rule the day for want of a political structure which could handle anything larger' (Newton 1978: 86). More specifically, Hoch (1984) has argued that the proliferation of suburban jurisdictions has provided 'a form of territorial political cohesion for small employers and members of the middle class, while simultaneously fragmenting the capacity for such cohesion among members of either the working or the capitalist classes at the local level' (p. 102).

### Fiscal mercantilism

One particularly unfortunate aspect of metropolitan political fragmentation arises from the competition between neighbouring governments seeking to increase revenue by attracting lucrative taxable land users. Cox and Dear (1975), who call this competition *fiscal mercantilism*, point out that its outcome has important implications for residential segregation as well as the geography of public service provision. In a fiscal context, desirable households include those owning large amounts of taxable capital (in the form of housing) relative to the size of the household and the extent of its need for public services. Low-

income households are seen as imposing a fiscal burden, since they not only possess relatively little taxable capital but also tend to be in greatest need of public services. Moreover, their presence in an area inevitably lowers the social status of the community, thus making it less attractive to high-income households. In competing for desirable residents, therefore, jurisdictions must offer low tax rates while providing good schools, high levels of public safety and environmental quality and pursuing policies which keep out the socially and fiscally undesirable.

Tiebout (1956), noting the different 'bundles' of public goods provided by different metropolitan jurisdictions, suggested that households will tend to sort themselves naturally along municipal lines according to their preferences for particular services and their ability to pay for them. It is now increasingly recognized, however, that a good deal of sociospatial sorting is deliberately engineered by local governments pursuing mercantilist policies (Herr 1982; Kasarda 1972; Newton 1975; Young and Kramer 1977). The most widespread strategy in the US involves the manipulation of land-use zoning powers, which can be employed to exclude the fiscally undesirable in several ways. Perhaps the most common is 'large lot zoning', whereby land within a jurisdiction is set aside for housing standing on individual plots of a minimum size – usually at least half an acre (0.2 ha.) – which precludes all but the most expensive housing developments and so keeps out the fiscally and socially undesirable. More than two-thirds of suburban Philadelphia, for example, is zoned for occupation at not less than one acre per dwelling (Johnston 1979b). Other exclusionary tactics include zoning out apartments, the imposition of moratoria on sewage hookups, and the introduction of building codes calling for expensive construction techniques (Babcock and Bosselman 1973; Danielson 1976). As Cox and Dear (1975) observe, the existence of large tracts of undeveloped land within a jurisdiction represents a major asset, since it can be zoned to keep out the poor and attract either rich households or fiscally lucrative commercial activities such as offices and shopping centres. Inner metropolitan jurisdictions, lacking developable land, have to turn to other, more expensive strategies in order to enhance their tax base. These include urban renewal projects designed to replace low-yielding slum dwellings with high-yielding office developments – projects which also have the effect of displacing low-income families to other parts of the city, often to other jurisdictions.

The net effect is that central city populations are left the privilege of voting to impose disproportionate costs of social maintenance and control upon themselves. Markusen (1984), pursuing a Marxist analysis, goes further:

> . . . the salient function of suburban governments is to insulate class consumption and capital from the costs of social accumulation and social expenses in the central city, thereby forcing the poor to finance their own oppressive police force and welfare system. The suburban government actually constructs its own public-service market by employing policy tools such as zoning in which class aims for levels and types of social consumption and class reproduction can be achieved by excluding high-cost residents and attracting those with ample resources. At the same time, the independence of the suburban government allows it to use these same exclusionary tools to *enhance the private-sector functions of suburbia* – the class assimilation of children by restricting their playmates and experience, the removal of class conflict from living situations, and the preservation of asset value of housing (Markusen 1984: 93, emphasis added).

In short, and in crude terms, different social sub-classes reproduce themselves in different types of juridical areas. This is a point to which we shall return in the discussion of urban services.

Finally, it should be noted that the mercantilism and protectionism of the suburbs has not gone unchallenged. In the United States, the major challenges have taken place in the Supreme Court, invoking the equal protection clause of the Fourteenth Amendment. For the most part, however, judicial interpretations of the Federal Constitution have not supported challenges to suburban protectionism (Johnston 1981b, 1981c, 1982, 1983).

## Fiscal imbalance

One of the most detrimental consequences of metropolitan fragmentation and fiscal mercantilism in the *fiscal imbalance* which leaves central city governments with insufficient funds and resources relative to the demands for the services for which they are responsible. The decentralization of jobs and homes, the inevitable ageing of inner-city environments and the concentration of low-income households in inner-city neighbourhoods has led to a narrowing tax base accompanied by rising demands for public services (Nathan and Adams 1976; Oakland 1979). The ageing, high-density housing typical of inner-city areas, for example, requires high levels of fire protection; high crime rates mean higher policing costs; and high levels of unemployment and ill-health mean high levels of need for welfare services and health care facilities. As a result of these pressures, many central cities in the United States have experienced a *fiscal squeeze* of the type which led to the near-bankruptcy of New York City in 1975 (Tabb 1984). Some have suggested that such problems are aggravated by additional demands for public services in central city areas which stem from suburbanites working or shopping there. This is the so-called 'suburban exploitation' thesis (Neenan 1972), although its validity remains in some doubt. There is no question that the presence of suburban commuters and shoppers precipitates higher expenditures on roads, parking space, public utilities, policing, and so on; on the other hand, it is equally clear that the patronage of downtown businesses by suburbanites enhances the central city tax base while their own suburban governments have to bear the costs of educating their children. The extent to which these costs and benefits balance out has not yet been conclusively demonstrated.

A more compelling argument has been put forward by Friedland (1981), who has interpreted fiscal squeeze as a product of the nature of economic change. In particular, he suggests, it has been the growth of new kinds of *private* economic activity that has imposed high costs on the *public* sector. In general, the growth of new kinds of urban economic activity has been expensive because (1) it has failed to provide employment and income for central city residents, and (2) it has made demands on the public sector for infrastructure expenditures which were not self-financing:

On the one hand, new economic growth in the central cities did not provide sufficient employment and income benefits to the central city's residents. Industrial jobs were taken by suburbanized union workers. Construction work was dominated by restrictive craft unions. And the new office economy was drawing on the better educated, better heeled, suburban workforce. Industrial investments were now part of vast multilocational networks of plants, thus weakening the local multipliers from local plant investments. This export of the income benefits of local economic growth meant a continuous reservoir of poor, structurally unemployed people who turned to city governments for jobs and services.

On the other hand, the rising office economy of the central city required a restructuring of urban space to move people and information most efficiently. This required a massive investment in public capital for mass transit, parking, urban renewal, and the more traditional forms of infrastructure (Friedland 1981: 370–371)

These infrastructural investments were insulated from conflict, Friedland argues, through the exploitation of new forms of administration and financing: autonomous special districts, banker committees, and new forms of revenue and tax increment bonding. As a result there emerged two worlds of local expenditure: one oriented to providing services and public employment for the city's residents, the other to constructing the infrastructure necessary to profitable private development. 'These two worlds – of social wage and social capital – were structurally segregated. The former was governed by electoral politics and the excesses of patronage. The latter was housed in bureaucratic agencies, dominated by men of business who survived by their efficiency' (Friedland 1981: 371).

Fiscal crises of the sort epitomized by the plight of New York City in the mid-1970s are seen by Hill (1984) as an important catalyst for change in the political economy of central cities. He is not, however, optimistic as to the eventual outcome. One particularly gloomy

scenario, which Hill suggests can be recognized in the central areas of cities like Newark and St Louis, is the emergence of what he calls a 'pariah city', a form of 'geographical and political apartheid – a "reservation" for the economically disenfranchised labour force' (Hill 1984: 311). Those left behind in the 'pariah city', he suggests, will be the poor, the deviant, and the unwanted, together with those who make a business or career of managing them for the rest of society.

## Reform

Scenarios such as this have prompted widespread interest in local government reform. The problem facing reformists, of course, is to reconcile demands for local self-determination and equity of service provision while ensuring that jurisdictions are large enough to realize the advantages of economies of scale. This problem is difficult enough to resolve without the resistance of existing jurisdictions to change: as Soja (1971) observes, the reaction of many to the prospect of consolidation or reform resembles that of nineteenth-century nation states encountering a challenge to their sovereignty. This attitude of 'sacred inviolability', fostered by bureaucrats and politicians with vested interests in the *status quo*, has been one of the biggest stumbling-blocks to local government reform. In England and Wales, for example, the administrative reforms carried out in 1974 did not embody the full recommendations of the preceding Royal Commission (the Redcliffe-Maud Commission) because of the political pressure exerted by those who had most to lose from the revision of geographical boundaries. Thus, for example, much of suburban north–eastern Cheshire, which is functionally part of the Manchester conurbation, was kept separate from Manchester as much on the grounds of tradition as anything else. Similarly, when Scottish local government was reformed in the mid-1970s, the Dundee area was denied its fiscally lucrative exurbs on the southern bank of the Tay estuary on the grounds that they were part of the ancient 'Kingdom' of Fife.

In the United States, local government

reform has been more piecemeal, lacking the coherence of a nationally formulated framework. Honey (1976) lists a wide range of approaches to metropolitan governance which have been advanced as solutions to the problems of fragmentation and decentralization. These include: (1) the acquisition of extra-territorial powers; (2) the transfer of functions to a higher tier of government; (3) the institution of inter-governmental agreements whereby one sells a service to another or they jointly perform a function; (4) the creation of councils of governments; (5) the federation of governments within a clearly structured hierarchy; and (6) the consolidation of two or more jurisdictions into a unitary, multi-function authority. In addition, there are purely fiscal strategies which do not involve any territorial or administrative reorganization. The best-known of these is the 'revenue sharing' programme introduced by the Nixon administration in 1972, which provided for the allocation of $30.2 billions of federal funds over a 5-year period to state and local governments in an attempt to alleviate the worst consequences of metropolitan fiscal imbalance. Many observers, however, are sceptical of the effectiveness of these strategies. To date, spatial and administrative reforms have been rather tentative (Honey 1976; Reynolds 1976), and there have been fears that fiscal programmes such as the revenue sharing scheme will be abused by local officials spending the money to satisfy their most influential constituencies rather than in the pursuit of a more equitable distribution of public services.

## Malapportionment and gerrymandering

Much of the conflict over the distribution of public services is of course mediated by the electoral process. As the same time, the spatial organization of the electoral process is itself both a source and an outcome of conflict. Electoral results, in other words, are influenced by the size and shape of electoral districts in relation to the distribution of the electorate. Put another way, a vote can be regarded as a resource whose value varies according to the degree to which it permits the voter to secure preferred policies. This value tends to vary from one neighbourhood to another according to the individual voter's relative numerical importance within his own constituency. At the same time, it is a function of the marginality of his constituency in terms of the balance between the major conflicting social groups and political parties.

Evaluating the effects of geo-political organization on community power and well-being in this context is not easy, since systems of electoral representation and their associated spatial frameworks can be very complex. This complexity is compounded by the existence, in most countries, of a hierarchy of governments responsible for a variety of different functions. The Greater London boroughs discussed above, for example, have been both independent multi-purpose jurisdictions and constituencies for the Greater London Council, which was responsible for certain aspects of strategic planning, housing management and slum clearance. They also happen to be constituencies for the House of Commons and they are themselves divided into wards for the election of their own political office-holders. A person may therefore find his vote much more effective in influencing policy at one level of government than at another. A further complicating factor is the electoral system itself which, for any given set of constituencies may operate on the basis of: (1) a single-member plurality system; (2) a multi-member plurality system; (3) a weighted plurality system; (4) preferential voting in single-member constituencies; (5) preferential voting in multi-member constituencies; or (6) a list system in multi-member constituencies (Taylor and Johnston 1979). It is not possible to do justice here to the potential effect of each of these systems on the geography of social well-being, nor to deal with their effectiveness in providing a democratic and equitable resolution of inter-group conflict (see, however, Johnston 1979b). Rather, attention is directed towards two of the more widespread ways in which the spatial organization of electoral districts has been engineered in favour of particular communities, social groups and political parties: malapportionment and gerrymandering.

*Malapportionment* refers to the unequal population sizes of electoral subdivisions. Quite simply, the electorate in smaller constituencies will be over-represented in most electoral systems, while voters in larger-than-average constitutencies will be under-represented. Deliberate malapportionment involves creating larger-than-average constituencies in the areas where opposing groups have an electoral majority. Some of the best-known examples of malapportionment have been at the expense of metropolitan areas and in favour of rural-based interest groups in Australia and the United States (Johnston 1979b). In the United States, malapportionment of congressional, state senatorial and state assembly districts was ended by the Supreme Court in a series of decisions between 1962 and 1965 which began the so-called 'reapportionment revolution'. But malapportionment continues to exist at the city council level, and deviations in constituency size as large as 30 per cent are common in Chicago, Philadelphia, Atlanta and St Louis (O'Loughlin 1976). Deviations of this magnitude also exist at the intra-metropolitan level in Britain, effectively disenfranchising large numbers of citizens. If, as is often the case, the malapportioned group involves the inner-city poor, 'the problem assumes an even more serious nature. Policies such as rent control and garbage collection, and questions such as the location of noxious facilities or the imposition of a commuter tax will be decided in favour of the outer city' (O'Loughlin 1976: 540).

*Gerrymandering* occurs where a specific group or political party gains an electoral advantage through the spatial configuration of constituency boundaries. Not all gerrymanders are deliberate, however: some groups may suffer as a result of any system of spatial partitioning because of their geographical concentration or dispersal. Gerrymandering by a party for its own ends is usually termed 'partisan gerrymandering' and it occurs most frequently where – as in the United States – the power to redraw constituency boundaries

lies in the hands of incumbent political parties. According to Orr (1969), partisan gerrymandering can be undertaken in four main ways;

1. creating *stacked districts* which usually have a grotesque shape designed to encompass pockets of support for the gerrymandering party;
2. creating *packed districts*, in which the opposition party's voters are concentrated into a few very safe seats;
3. creating *cracked districts*, in which opposition voting strength is fragmented, leaving them as a minority in a large number of seats;
4. operating a *silent gerrymander*, which involves the preservation of constituency boundaries over a long period, thereby creating malapportionment as the distribution of population changes.

It is very difficult to prove that gerrymandering has taken place: all that is usually possible is to produce strong circumstantial evidence. The curious boundaries used in Cleveland for the 1960 congressional elections, for example (Fig. 7.7) seem to be a deliberate attempt by Cleveland Democrats to concentrate Republican strength in district 23 (Busteed 1975). There is also considerable evidence of gerrymandering against blacks in US cities. O'Loughlin (1976; 1982) suggests that in cities with relatively small black neighbourhoods the most common type of racial gerrymander involves the creation of cracked districts, while in cities with black neighbourhoods large enough to warrant two or more elected representatives it is common for the electoral map to include only one black majority district, with the rest of the black area subdivided into white majority districts. Examples of the latter given by O'Loughlin include the US congressional districts of New York City and Chicago, the state senatorial districts of Philadelphia and Milwaukee, and the city council districts of Atlanta. Finally, it should be noted that although the definition of constituency boundaries is left to non-partisan Boundary Commissions in Britain and some other countries, their efforts often result in an unintentional gerrymander which

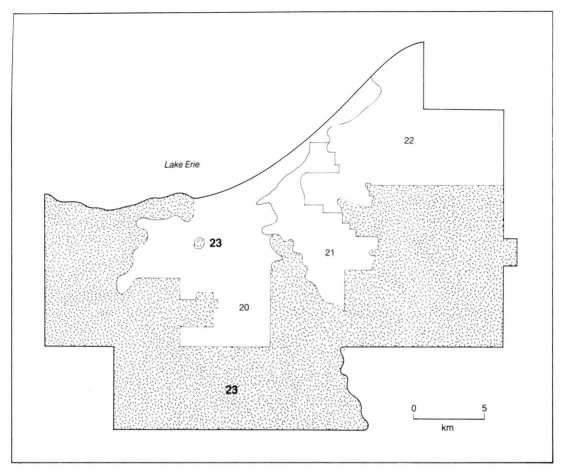

**Fig. 7.7** Gerrymandered congressional districts in Cleveland, Ohio.
*Source*: Busteed (1975), p. 10.

favours the majority party, thus reinforcing its dominance in the electoral assembly. Taylor and Gudgin (1976), for example, have shown how the application of the rules for the creation of parliamentary constituencies from an amalgamation of city wards by the fiercely neutral English Boundary Commission tends to produce a packed gerrymander in favour of the majority party simply because of the marked spatial segregation of the social classes which provide the support for the principal political parties.

## Urban services: conflicts and outcomes

### Metropolitan fragmentation and territorial justice

The conflicts over resources that are embodied in the issues surrounding fiscal mercantilism, fiscal imbalance and the spatial organization of administrative and electoral systems are at once the cause and the effect of significant inter-jurisdictional disparities in public service provision. The extent of these disparities in a fragmented metropolitan area can be illustrated with reference to the example of social services for the elderly in Greater London. From a geographical point of view, the 'ideal' distribution of such resources might be one that is in direct proportion to the levels of need in each of the 32 Greater London boroughs: a situation which represents what Davies (1968) has called 'territorial justice'. An examination by Pinch (1979) of the provision of home helps, meals-on-wheels, home nurses and residential accommodation for the elderly, however, found evidence of considerable variability in the extent to which territorial justice has been achieved. In order to quantify local levels of need for social services for the elderly, Pinch used an index of social conditions based on a mixture of variables measuring local levels of health, housing conditions, unemployment and socio-economic status, as well as the incidence of pensioners living alone. Levels of provision were measured both in terms of the *financial input* committed to each service by the local authorities and in terms of the *extensiveness* and *intensity* of the services provided by this expenditure. The extensiveness of service provision is taken to be the proportion of those eligible for a service who actually receive it (e.g. the percentage of the elderly who receive home helps or meals-on-wheels), while the intensity of service provision is evaluated in terms of the average amount of monetary or physical resources provided per recipient of the service.

Correlations between the index of need and a series of measures of service provision (Table 7.2) show that although the overall trend is for a positive relationship between need and provision, the situation falls a long way short of the criterion of territorial justice. Indeed, there are some aspects of the home nursing and health visiting services for the elderly for which the overall spatial distribution is regressive, as shown by the negative correlation coefficients in Table 7.2. Most of the domiciliary services for the aged are distributed more equitably, although the correlation between needs and provision is far from perfect. This is illustrated by Fig. 7.8, which shows the relationship between Pinch's index of social conditions and the average net

expenditures on residential accommodation for the elderly. Not surprisingly, several of the boroughs with poor social conditions (i.e. high levels of need) and relatively low levels of provision are inner-city jurisdictions – the likes of Islington, Lambeth and Lewisham, where the fiscal squeeze has been most severe. On the other hand, there are several needy inner-city boroughs which provide a relatively high standard of service – Camden, Hammersmith and Southwark, for example. The explanation for this seem to be rooted in local political disparities which, like the local resource base, are very closely influenced by the spatial configuration of local government boundaries.

## The location and accessibility of services and amenities

Not all urban services are publicly provided, and not all disparities in service provision operate at the scale of municipal jurisdictions. In this section, we examine the conflicts that are attached to the location of particular urban services and amenities – both public and private – within urban settings as a whole. emphasizing how the cumulative, net effects of variations in service provision are related to established patterns of power and social well-being within cities.

At this level, then, we are concerned not with the conflicts that occur over positive or negative 'spillovers' from one municipality to another but with conflicts over positive and negative externalities and the 'tapering' of these externalities through the effects of relative location. It will be clear by now that in every city there is a large number and a great variety of services and amenities that are tied to specific locations and which therefore exhibit externalities with tapering effects: parks, schools, restaurants, theatres, libraries, fire stations, shops, doctors' clinics, hospitals, day care centres, post offices, riverside walks, and so on. To these we must add certain place-specific disamenities and the noxious activities associated with some services: refuse dumps and crematoria, for example; and we must recognize that what constitutes an

**Table 7.2**  Correlations between Social Conditions Index and indices of provision of social services for the elderly in Greater London boroughs

| | Correlations with Social Conditions Index | | Correlations with Social Conditions Index |
|---|---|---|---|
| **(A) Residential accommodation** | | **(D). Home nursing** | |
| 1. Average net expenditure on residential accommodation for the elderly and disabled provided directly by London boroughs and registered voluntary and private agencies on their behalf between 1965 and 1968 (per 1,000 population) | 0.45 | 8. Average net expenditure on home nursing by London boroughs between 1965 and 1968 per 1,000 population | 0.15 |
| | | 9. Number of home nurses employed by London boroughs in 1969 per 1,000 population aged 65 and over | −0.03 |
| 2. Number of persons (excluding staff) in residential accommodation for the elderly and disabled provided directly by London boroughs and registered voluntary and private agencies on their behalf on 31 December 1971 per 1,000 population of pensionable age in 1971 | 0.65 | 10. Number of persons aged 65 and over first visited by a home nurse during the year 1971 per 1,000 population aged 65 and over | −0.25 |
| **(B). Home-helps service** | | **(E). Health visiting** | |
| 3. Average net expenditure by London boroughs on home helps between 1971 to 1972 per 1,000 population | 0.76 | 11. Average net expenditure on health visiting by London boroughs between 1965 and 1968 per 1,000 population | 0.65 |
| 4. Number of home helps employed by London boroughs per 1,000 population of pensionable age in 1971 | 0.68 | 12. Number of persons aged 65 and over first visited by a health visitor in 1971 per 1,000 population aged 55 and over | −0.44 |
| 5. Number of persons aged 65 or over on first visit by a home-help during 1971 per 1,000 population aged 65 and over | 0.81 | | |
| **(C). Meals-on-wheels service** | | | |
| 6. Number of persons aged 65 and over served with meals-on-wheels by London boroughs and voluntary agencies in a one week period in 1970 per 1,000 population aged 65 and over | 0.67 | | |
| 7 Number of meals-on-wheels served to persons aged 65 and over by London boroughs and voluntary agencies in a one week period in 1970 per 1,000 population aged 65 and over | 0.72 | | |

*Source:* Pinch 1979: 213–18.

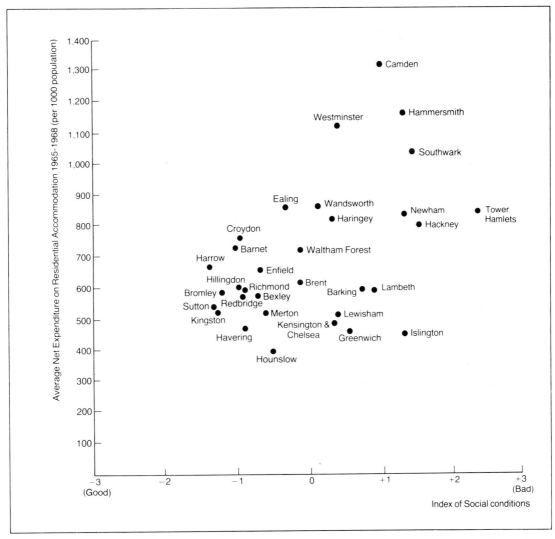

**Fig. 7.8** The relationship between social conditions and local expenditure on residential accommodation for the elderly in Greater London. *Source*: Pinch (1979), p. 214.

amenity to some (a school, or a soccer stadium, for example) may represent a disamenity to others. From another perspective, it is clear that some externalities apply only to users while others apply to whole neighbourhoods (Dear 1976b). In addition, we must recognize that each individual service or amenity may generate several different types of externality effect, as in the example of the soccer stadium (Fig. 7.1). Finally, we must

recognize that the *intensity* of the externality effects will also vary according to people's preferred distance from particular services or amenities (Fig. 7.9). We are thus faced with a very complex set of phenomena (Pinch 1985).

The externalities associated with physical proximity to services, amenities and disamenities not only prompt competition and conflict between households within different housing

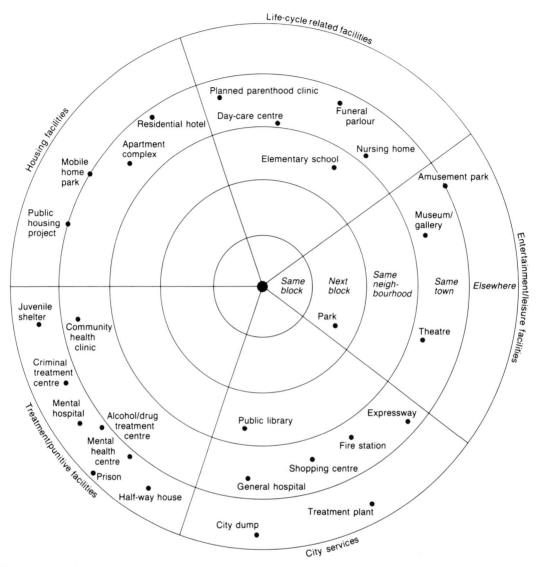

**Fig. 7.9** Preferred residential distance from different public facilities.
*Source*: Smith (1980).

markets but also precipitate collective political strategies, including the formation of coalitions between different institutions and organizations and the propagation of distinctive *de facto* communities whose mutuality involves life-styles which are dependent to some extent on accessibility to specific amenities. These coalitions and communities represent the major protagonists in much of the conflict over the preservation and fortification of the relative quality of life in different urban settings. It should be noted, however, that overt conflicts associated with neighbourhood activism have become more frequent with the extension of owner-occupation and as larger-scale housing and construction projects have replaced smaller-scale activities as the dominant aspect of urban development (Cox and McCarthy

1980). It follows that a good deal of neighbourhood activism is directly associated with construction and development activity around the urban fringe. A study of Columbus, Ohio, suggested that it is those with the greatest stakes in a particular local setting, or 'turf' (i.e. owner-occupiers and parents of school-age children), who are most likely to become involved in neighbourhood activism, and that the dominant types of conflicts tend to be associated with the public regulation of privately-initiated patterns of urban development, with publicly-initiated construction projects (e.g. new highways, street widenings, and urban renewal projects), and with the quality of public services (Cox and McCarthy 1982). More generally, neighbourhood activism has been categorized in terms of four types, according to the aims and strategies of the neighbourhood groups involved: defensive and exclusionary, demand-aggregating and articulation, resource allocation, and concession-seeking and supportive (Rich 1979b;

Burnett and Hill 1982). It must be recognized, however, that conflict occurs over different issues in different urban settings in response to different kinds of environmental change. Figure 7.10 illustrates the variety of locational conflicts which might be expected within a city exhibiting the classic concentric pattern of land uses and socio-demographic characteristics and in which the development process is dominated by a combination of outward expansion and internal reorganization. Conflict over transportation, for example, is expected to exhibit a bimodal distribution, with peaks of conflict intensity in areas of peripheral expansion and in the region immediately surrounding the reorganizing city centre. On the other hand, conflict over 'cultural' issues – such as the encroachment of one ethnic group upon the territory of another – are expected to decline in number and intensity with increasing distance from the city core, reflecting the lower residential densities and increased ethnic homogeneity of the suburbs.

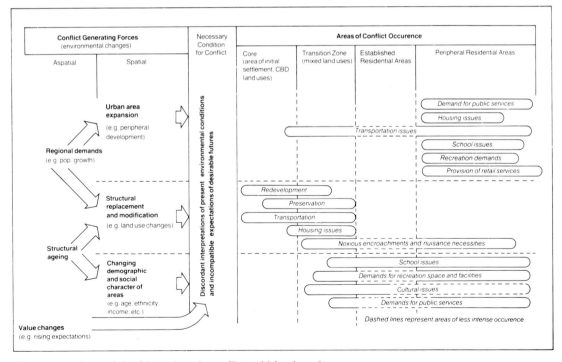

**Fig. 7.10**  A model of locational conflict within the city.
*Source*: Janelle and Millward (1976), p. 103.

Finally, we must acknowledge that understanding patterns of service delivery and amenity location is not simply a matter of competition and conflict over which households win proximity to the most desirable services and amenities and which communities are able to 'capture' new services and amenities. The geography of many services and amenities is also a product of other factors; the 'fabric' effects of the urban environment, the internal organization and politics of particular professions and service-delivery agencies, and the functional linkages that exist between certain services and other activities, for example. This, of course, means that aggregate patterns of service and amenity provision rarely exhibit clear or unambiguous relationships with urban social ecology. Nevertheless, it is clear that the general tendency is for the most affluent, most powerful and most active communities to capture a disproportionate share of the positive externalities associated with urban services and amenities. In the following sections, this tendency is illustrated, first in terms of patterns of medical care in cities generally, and then in terms of a spectrum of services and amenities in one particular city. Attention is then turned to the implications of such patterns for the political economy of cities.

### An illustrative example: accessibility to medical care

Patterns of accessibility to health care facilities provide a particularly good example of the way in which the location of amenities can affect the quality of neighbourhood life and so serve as the focus for competition and conflict between households and communities. In countries like the United States and Australia, where health care delivery systems are essentially run on *laissez-faire* principles, wide variations have come to exist between neighbourhoods in the availability and quality of medical care. In the United States, the best-documented city in this respect is Chicago, where geographers such as Earickson, Morrill, Pyle and Rees were involved in the lavish Chicago Regional Hospital Study (see de Vise 1973). Working papers from the Study described Chicago's hospital system as 'apartheid', discriminating on the basis of race, residence and age not only in terms of the relative location of hospitals but also in terms of waiting time, quality of care, and cost. In general, the spatial arrangement of hospital services tends to follow the intra-urban commercial hierarchy, except that there is rarely the same degree of suburbanization of facilities. As a result, there tends to be an excess of capacity in the central city and a shortage in the suburbs, especially the less prosperous black and working-class suburbs. Such a pattern has been demonstrated by Megee (1976), and Shannon and Dever (1974) in other North American cities, and by Morris (1976), Cleland *et al.* (1977), and Stimpson (1978) in Australian cities. In relation to Adelaide, South Australia, for example, Cleland *et al.* (1977: 50) conclude that:

the overall pattern is one of a marked hierarchical system of hospital provision . . . with high concentration of facilities in the inner city locations . . . with lower order facilities, almost always of the private type, located in the higher status areas or at locations that are old settlement nodes . . . As a result, patients and the friends and relatives visiting them will have relatively long journeys to make to gain access to a hospital.

The spatial organization of primary care in cities also tends to be regressive. In addition to the important limitations on people's accessibility to primary care imposed by income constraints and socio-psychological barriers, home-to-surgery distance is especially important because of its repercussions on local patterns of health and well-being, due to the deterrent effect of distance in relation to 'therapeutic behaviour' – the seeking of medical advice. In cities where large sectors of the population are still without private transport, the actual distance from home to the family doctor's surgery is particularly critical. About 0.75 kilometres – 'pram-pushing distance' – is often regarded as the upper limit for mothers with pre-school children and for the elderly; and travelling much more than this by public transport may involve a long wait or a change of bus unless both home and surgery lie conveniently near a bus route. Class differences in car ownership are also exacerbated by the time constraints of the working classes, who are normally subject to much more inflexible working hours than the middle classes. The disutility of travelling to the surgery can thus act as a substantial barrier to proper care, influencing therapeutic behaviour just as educational, religious and class-related barriers do (Mechanic 1968; Phillips 1979). Patients living further away will tend to make light of symptoms and put up with discomfort, gambling that their condition is not serious rather than making the effort to travel to their doctor. Distance has been shown to have a marked negative effect on consultation rates, and it seems reasonable to suppose that this will eventually exercise a direct effect on local patterns of morbidity and mortality. It is also worth noting that blue-collar workers are, in general, less inclined to consult family doctors and much less concerned than white-collar workers with preventive medicine, with the likely result that distance will affect the delivery of medical care differentially by social class, notwithstanding class differences in personal mobility. Moreover, such effects do not appear to be attenuated by increased requests for home visits: Hopkins *et al.* (1968), for example, found that patients living further away from the surgery not only had lower utilization rates than others, but were more reluctant to call out their doctor for home visits. (For a thorough review of the relationships between accessibility and the utilization of health care facilities, see Joseph and Phillips 1984).

In this context, intra-urban variations in the provision of primary care are alarming. Where primary care is provided on a competitive fee-for-service basis – as in Australia and North America – the locational behaviour of general practitioners is influenced primarily by local effective demand and the propensity for people to want (rather than need) medical care. Other factors which have been identified as influencing the location of surgeries include neighbourhood ethnicity, the availability of office space, the proximity of specialist hospital facilities, the availability of manpower to cover illness and vacations, the approval of the neighbourhood by the doctor's spouse,

and the pull of local family ties (see, for example, Diseker and Chappel 1976; Rosenberg 1984). The result is a gross imbalance between medical needs and resources, with physicians tending to be clustered around hospitals and nodes of commercial activity and in affluent white suburbs (Rosenberg 1983; Gober and Gordon 1980). These outcomes are rooted in the pattern of service delivery that evolved during the urban transition of the late nineteenth century, when the professional specialization of orthodox medicine coincided with the socio-spatial realignment of cities, with the result that medical care ceased to be a ubiquitous, neighbourhood oriented service (Knox, Bohland and Shumsky 1983, 1984).

Recent studies of the distribution of general practitioners (GPs) in Sydney, Australia, have established a positive correlation between neighbourhood status and the incidence of primary care facilities, although the dominant spatial pattern is one of declining access to facilities with distance from the city centre (Freestone 1975; Donald 1978). This maldistribution is also typical of Adelaide (Cleland, Stimpson and Goldsworthy 1977), and Melbourne (Morris 1976). Similar patterns are evident in North American cities, although the most striking feature of the distribution of GPs in many US cities is the lack of primary care resources in black neighbourhoods. In Chicago, the aversion of private physicians to poor black neighbourhoods meant that the ratio of physicians to population in the city's ten poorest comunities – which were mostly black – deteriorated from 0.99 per 1,000 in 1950 to 0.26 per 1,000 in 1970, whilst in the ten most affluent communities the ratio improved from 1.78 to 2.10 per 1,000 (de Vise and Dewey 1972). This left welfare physicians to serve an average of 7,000 people rather than 700, to see 80 patients a day rather than 80 a week and to cease home visits altogether (de Vise 1968).

Even in countries such as the United Kingdom and New Zealand, where nationalized health services make adequate health care a legitimate expectation for all, the maldistribution of GPs within cities has given cause for concern (Barnett 1978; Barnett and Sheerin 1977; Drury 1983; Knox 1978b,

1979a, 1979b, 1980b). In Britain, the locational inertia of GPs has meant that their distribution is much as it was at the inception of the NHS in 1948, with a polarized, localized pattern that had emerged, as in the United States, during the urban transition in response to the interactions of professional realignment and urban restructuring (Knox 1982a). This pattern has been characterized by a concentration of surgeries in the older and more central neighbourhoods, particularly those of higher socio-economic status where large dwellings can be used to incorporate both surgery and residence. Although controls and incentives have been introduced under the NHS in order to regulate the spatial distribution of GPs, these policies have rarely operated at a scale below that of whole towns or cities, so that these intra-urban disparities have been reinforced by the natural tendency for family doctors to live and work in well-established high-status areas where there often exists the possibility of earning extra income with fees from private patients (Knox and Pacione 1980). At the same time, the structure and ideology of the medical profession in Britain has discouraged the location of GPs in working-class areas, since not only is working in blue-collar neighbourhoods held to be unglamorous and unsatisfactory, but time spent in general practice in such areas is regarded as almost certain disqualification for any further career advancement. Having said this, however, it is important to point out that the locational behaviour of GPs has also been influenced by 'fabric' effects, which have tended to reinforce the relative advantages enjoyed by older middle-class neighbourhoods. There is, for instance, an almost complete lack of accommodation suitable for use as doctors' surgeries in the large housing estates – both public and speculatively built – which have encircled most British cities since 1945. The net result is maldistribution of medical resources which is part of what Hart (1971) has called the *inverse care law*: the tendency for medical care to vary inversely with the need of the population served.

This tendency is evident in the distribution of primary care resources in Edinburgh (Fig. 7.11), although the pattern does not conform exactly with the notion of an inverse care law, the localization of surgeries in the older central areas of the city tending to favour several of the more deprived inner-city neighbourhoods as well as the prestigious Georgian neighbourhoods of the city centre.

At the other extreme are neighbourhoods consisting of public housing estates which, between them, house over two-thirds of the city's population. These neighbourhoods, containing many of the city's most notorious 'problem estates', have very few local surgeries at all. In addition, levels of personal mobility are very low (typically, over three-quarters of the households in these neighbourhoods do not have a car); and bus services to other parts of the city are infrequent and expensive. Large numbers of people have to face long return journeys in order to see their GP, and the problem is particularly acute for families rehoused from substandard tenement dwellings in the inner city, since the shortage of surgeries in peripheral estates often means that they have no alternative but to remain on the list of their inner-city GP, thus facing even longer return journeys.

The regressive nature of these patterns is rather more apparent when local variations in car ownership are taken into account. Fig. 7.12 shows the results of an index which takes into account the relative size and location of general practitioner services, local levels of car ownership, and the relative speed of public and private transport (Knox 1980a). Scores of more than 100 on the index indicate that a neighbourhood has more than its fair 'share' of accessibility to the city's primary care facilities. In general, accessibility corresponds systematically and inversely to the social geography of the city. There is a Y-shaped area of 'over-doctored' neighbourhoods, which are all middle-class, owner-occupied neighbourhoods, the best-served of which – Morningside–Merchiston, Murrayfield, the New Town and Clermiston – also contain some of the most prestigious districts in terms of income and social status. Conversely, the city's worst-served areas correspond depressingly with 'deprived' local

**Fig. 7.11**   The distribution of general practitioners in Edinburgh, 1973.

authority estates: Granton–Pilton–Drylaw in the south, Sighthill–Stenhouse in the west, and a large uninterrupted tract in the east stretching from Lochend through Duddingston, Craigmillar, Ferniehill and Gilmerton to Liberton.

This relationship between accessibility and urban ecology has also been demonstrated in Reading, a very different type of city (Jones and Kirby 1982). Figure 7.13 shows neighbourhoods with poor accessibility to both family doctors and dental practitioners, with each neighbourhood differentiated according to a national typology devised by Webber (1977). It emerges that, as in Edinburgh, the worst-off neighbourhoods are peripheral areas, dominated by newer owner-occupier housing (families 2 and 3) and public housing estates (family 5).

Physical inaccessibility to GPs, however, is only one aspect of medical deprivation in urban areas, and other aspects of the geography of primary care lend still more support to the idea of an inverse care law, with the deprived areas of the inner-city emerging as the worst off in terms of the quality, if not the availability, of primary care facilities. A good example is provided by Glasgow's East End, one of the harshest and most brutalized urban environments in Britain, with a population of over 150,000 and where the extent and intensity of unemployment, housing stress, environ-

**Fig. 7.12** Accessibility to primary medical care in Edinburgh.

mental deprivation and social pathology is practically unrivalled in north-west Europe (Knox 1979a). It has a large and increasingly elderly population and contains high proportions of vagrants, in-migrants, one-parent families, students and other indigent and vulnerable groups with special medical needs; but it has not attracted medical manpower in proportion to these needs. In 1978, almost 75 per cent of the East End's GPs were aged over 45, and 17 per cent over 65, reflecting the persistent unattractiveness of the area since the late 1940s, when a post-war glut of newly qualified doctors forced many of them to take jobs in depressed areas like the East End. Moreover, the organization of the area's doctors has remained static, with a lack of teamwork and group practices: over 40 per cent of East End practices are single-handed. Equally disturbing is the condition of many of the surgeries, for many of the lock-up premises have deteriorated at a rate which matches that of the East End as a whole. In addition to the damage these poorly equipped, damp and grubby premises inflict on the morale of both doctors and patients there is also a perceived threat to people's health (local conventional wisdom holds that 'you go in with the flu and come out with pneumonia'), which probably acts as a further barrier to proper health care.

The situation in other large cities is little different. Melanie Phillips (1978) has described the reality of primary care in the Vauxhall area of Liverpool in these terms:

There are no chairs [in the waiting room]. From the ceiling a large piece of wallpaper hangs down limply. Unshaded light bulbs, coated in grime, hang among drooping coils of lighting flex. Nearby, three GPs hold their surgeries in a converted pair of shops. The windows are boarded up and one of the few panes of glass is smashed. The waiting area smells damp. It contains chairs – red plush, former cinema seats, torn and losing their stuffing, and wooden benches arrayed around the walls.

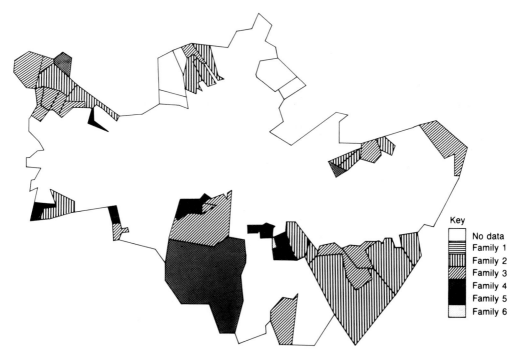

**Fig. 7.13**   Enumeration districts more than 1 km from both a family doctor and a dental practitioner, Reading, 1980, by 'family' type. Unshaded districts are within the distance threshold.   *Source*: Jones and Kirby (1982), Fig. 4, p. 307.

Complaints by patients of cursory and unsympathetic treatment by doctors are rife. In such areas it is the conditions in which primary care is presented – what Dutton (1978) describes as a 'dehumanising ambience' – which constitute the major barrier to therapeutic behaviour, and not distance between home and surgery. Nevertheless, there are many patients who are subject to both deterrents. As in Glasgow, patients who move out – or are moved – to suburbs such as Speke and Netherley as part of urban renewal schemes are often forced to remain on the list of the GP in the area from which they were rehoused. As a result, many patients must face journeys of over 30 minutes by car each way; or a total of at least four bus journeys.

In London, a detailed survey of primary care in Thornhill – a deprived inner-city area between Kings Cross and Barnsbury – provides an equally depressing story (Thornhill Neighbourhood Project 1978; see also DHSS 1981). Thornhill has above average

levels of infant mortality, malnutrition and tuberculosis in a population which contains above average numbers of young children, pensioners, members of ethnic minority groups, alcoholics, vagrants, and physically and mentally handicapped people. The health care needs of the area are also swollen by the local workforce, many of whom register with a Thornhill GP even though they live outside the neighbourhood. As in Glasgow's East End, physical accessibility to primary care is high: there are 21 GPs practising from 13 surgeries in the 1.5 square mile area, and the average number of patients per doctor in this part of London is 2,162, a low enough figure for the Medical Practices Committee to restrict the area to all new practitioners on the grounds of over-doctoring. But Thornhill is medically deprived. Like their counterparts in Liverpool and Glasgow, Thornhill people must attend poorly-equipped surgeries to consult doctors who are mostly working single-handedly and who therefore find it difficult to employ a nurse or receptionist, to attend in-service courses, and to find a deputy familiar with their patients and their needs. One in three of the area's doctors in 1978 were over 70, and this included two practitioners of over 80 years of age: whose training took place ten years before the discovery of penicillin. Whatever the value of experience, it must be doubtful whether people of this age can effectively tackle a full workload in an area whose medical needs are as intense and specialized as Thornhill's. In fact, many of the older GPs have deliberately restricted their catchment areas and pruned their lists. Thus, what appears to be a local abundance of manpower turns out to be a rather depleted group of GPs working in an uncoordinated way from under-equipped surgeries.

### Aggregate patterns of accessibility: the example of Oklahoma City

When we examine a wider range of services and amenities, do we find that there are certain neighbourhoods which suffer from poor accessibility on the whole spectrum of facilities? Or are there, for example, distinctive constellations of facilities which give rise to different 'packages' of accessibility/inaccessibility in different parts of a city? An analysis of accessibility to seventeen different services and amenities (including the location of job opportunities) in Oklahoma City suggests that there are in fact distinctive variations in the type as well as the level of accessibility enjoyed by different communities (Knox 1982b). Patterns of accessibility to each of the facilities (ambulance services, banks, community centres, day nurseries, dentists, elementary schools, family doctors, fire stations, golf courses, hospitals, libraries, managerial jobs, post offices, public parks, service jobs, unemployment offices and variety stores) were factor analysed, resulting in the identification of four major dimensions of differentiation which between them accounted for over 87 per cent of the total variance (Table 7.3). The first factor alone accounts for more than 50 per cent of the total variance. As shown by the factor loadings in Table 7.3, it is strongly associated with patterns of accessibility to jobs (both man-

**Table 7.3** Factor structure of accessibility variables

| Factor I: | 'central city/suburbs' (variance explained = 56.1%) | |
|---|---|---|
| | Variable | Loading |
| | Managerial jobs | −0.98 |
| | Service jobs | −0.91 |
| | Public parks | −0.74 |
| | Hospitals | 0.68 |
| | Department stores/variety stores | −0.51 |
| Factor II: | 'public services' (variance explained = 17.8%) | |
| | Variable | Loading |
| | Libraries | 0.74 |
| | Post offices | 0.73 |
| | Elementary schools | 0.69 |
| | Ambulance services | 0.68 |
| | Community centres | 0.64 |
| | Fire stations | 0.51 |
| Factor III: | 'personal services' (variance explained = 10.9%) | |
| | Variable | Loading |
| | Banks | 0.95 |
| | Day nurseries | 0.93 |
| | Dentists | 0.87 |
| | General medical practitioners | 0.61 |
| Factor IV: | 'outdoor amenities' (variance explained = 6.2%) | |
| | Variable | Loading |
| | Golf courses | 0.56 |
| | Public parks | 0.54 |

*Source:* Knox (1982b) Table 8.3, p. 76.

agerial and service-sector), shopping opportunities, parks and hospitals. Essentially, this factor has identified a dichotomy between the *central city* – with high levels of accessibility to concentrations of employment, shops and parks – and *suburban* districts, which have poor accessibility to these facilities but rather better accessibility to hospitals. The individual accessibility surfaces for service-sector jobs (Fig. 7.14) and department stores (Fig. 7.14), for example, both exhibit a basic central city/suburban contrast, although they differ somewhat in local detail.

The remaining three factors are each associated with distinctive types of facilities. Factor II is strongly associated with patterns of accessibility to *public services*, with particularly high loadings on variables measuring accessibility to libraries, post offices (Fig. 7.14), elementary schools, community centres (Fig. 7.14) and fire stations, as well as to the

**Fig. 7.14**   Accessibility surfaces in Oklahoma City.   *Source*: Knox (1982), Fig. 4.3, p. 78.

(privately organized) ambulance services. The third factor is equally distinctive in that it is clearly associated with a specific group of facilities relating to *personal services* of various kinds, including banks, day nurseries (Fig. 7.14) and the offices of dentists and general practitioners. Finally, factor IV suggests a distinctive dimension of accessibility associated with *outdoor amenities* such as public parks (Fig. 7.14) and golf courses.

Given these distinctive dimensions, the question arises as to how they relate to the social ecology of the city. Figure 7.15 represents an attempt to answer this question. It is a regionalization of the city's census tracts based on a cluster analysis of the 17 accessibility variables together with 25 socio-economic variables. As might be expected from an analysis including so many distance-based variables, there is a good deal of coherence and contiguity to the map. Located in the centre of the inner city are *type 1* census tracts. These represent a core area of deprivation on socio-economic indicators, and they are characterized by high levels of accessibility to concentrations of employment and to public parks but very poor accessibility to community centres, libraries, hospitals and ambulance services. To the north and south

of this district are extensive areas of *type 2* census tracts, which exhibit similar (though less extreme) characteristics of poverty and deprivation and which are similarly deficient in accessibility to health care facilities and community centres. To the east of the CBD and adjacent to these neighbourhoods is a relatively compact district of *type 3* census tracts. This coincides with the heart of the city's black ghetto. In addition, it is characterized by a high incidence of poverty, of single males and single-parent families, and of people employed in service-sector jobs. Although the area enjoys relatively high levels of accessibility to public parks, it is particularly deficient in accessibility to elementary schools, community centres, and health care facilities.

Forming an almost continuous zone around these three inner city community types is a large number of *type 4* census tracts. While these neighbourhoods are of average prosperity, they do not enjoy particularly good accessibility. Indeed, they are significantly deficient in physical accessibility to several public services, including elementary schools, post offices, libraries and community centres. To the northwest of the city is a small enclave of *type 5* census tracts containing an affluent

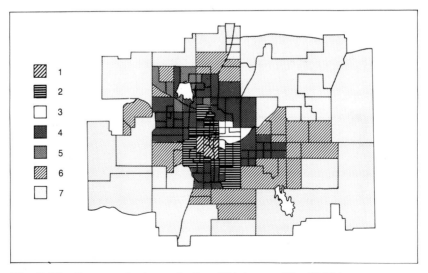

**Fig. 7.15** Community types in the Oklahoma City SMSA.
*Source*: Knox (1982), Fig. 4.4, p. 79.

and high status population which, in terms of accessibility to facilities, is particularly well placed in relation to parks, golf courses and general practitioners' offices. *Type 6* census tracts, located in a series of neighbourhoods in the northern, western and south-eastern suburbs of the city, are also relatively affluent. As a group, they tend to be occupied by large households with a young age structure and to have experienced a high level of population turnover. Although they enjoy better-than-average accessibility to hospitals and ambulance services, they are poorly served by the location of the city's jobs, parks and shopping opportunities. Finally, there are the peripheral *type 7* census tracts. Although fairly prosperous, these outlying areas contain a high proportion of crowded dwellings and large numbers of people with relatively low levels of educational achievement. They are also characterized by low levels of accessibility to jobs, public parks, shopping opportunities and hospitals. Such patterns provide an essential backcloth for the understanding of *past* conflict and competition between communities and households; they also help to illuminate the major dimensions of accessibility which are likely to form the basis of *future* conflict as different groups attempt to improve or enhance the net benefits conferred by the present accessibility structure of the city.

## The aggregate effects of aggregate patterns

We have seen that much of what takes place within the urban arena involves the resolution of conflicts over spatial organization and the relative location of certain 'goods' and 'bads'. The question remains, however, as to the relationships between, on the one hand, the outcome of these conflicts (segregated communities, *de facto* and *de jure*, with access to different 'packages' of services and externalities) and, on the other, the overall process of urban differentiation and change.

At the beginning of this chapter it was suggested that the richest and most powerful neighbourhoods will enjoy a cumulative net benefit as a result of the outcome of conflict and competition over the organization and location of services and amenities. The impli-

cation of this is that urban development is dominated by marginal adjustments in social ecology as new developments are made to fit the mould of the *status quo*. Many of the examples we have examined can be interpreted as supporting this proposition; but it is also clear that it is a crude generalization. Indeed, it is legitimate to ask why there is not a closer correspondence between community status and the geography of externality effects. Several studies of the intra-urban distribution of services and amenities have in fact stressed the 'unpatterned' nature of the disparities that exist (see, for example, Lineberry 1977; Mladenka and Hill 1977, 1978; Rich 1982a, 1982b), attributing the lack of correspondence between community status and the spatial organization of services and amenities to a combination of idiosyncratic events and bureaucratic decision rules (Lineberry 1977) or to the typical spatial structure of Western cities, whose geometry is such that low-income groups are inevitably favoured, notwithstanding the ability of more affluent communities to exert a disproportionate influence on the outcome of conflict and competition (McLafferty 1982).

Other studies point not so much to the idea of unpatterned inequality as to patterns which are a little more complex than we might expect, given the inequalities of income and power implicit in the social ecology of cities. A study of municipal expenditures in New York City, for example, found that expenditures on some services (fire, sanitation) did match socio-economic gradients while others (health, welfare, education) did not (Boyle and Jacobs 1982). Similarly, a study of the distribution of 16 different kinds of facilities in a cross-section of 12 West German cities found that some facilities (secondary schools, health facilities, public open space, nursery schools) favoured middle-class neighbourhoods, some (leisure centres, sports facilities, sheltered housing) were evenly distributed, and some (day care centres, day centres for the elderly, playgrounds) favoured working-class neighbourhoods. At the same time, there were some working-class neighbourhoods in inner-city or extreme peripheral locations that were very poorly served in relation to most facilities (Göschel *et al.* 1982). It thus seems that what may appear to be 'unpatterned' or 'complex' distributions of services and amenities are in fact likely to be the aggregate of two very different sets of patterns – the essentially regressive patterns of property-related services and amenities and the more regressive patterns of 'compensatory', welfare-related services – both of which may, in detail, be conditioned by idiosyncratic effects, bureaucratic decision rules and the constraints imposed by the geometry of the city. In this context, we should note the work of Wolch (1980, 1981, 1982), who has illuminated the spatial linkages which underpin the progressive patterns of many compensatory services. She attributes the localization of the service-dependent poor *and* their support services in the inner city to: (1) the dominance of housing and transportation-to-services costs in the locational decisions of service-dependent households, (2) the desire of service facility administrators to minimize clients' transportation costs, and (3) the budgetary constraints of both clients and services, which dictate low-rent, inner-city locations.

Finally, we must consider the implications of aggregate patterns of service and amenity location not just in relation to the way that they intensify or ameliorate socio-economic differentiation but also in relation to the dynamics of urban development. What is at issue here is the way that the economic and class relationships inherent to capitalism are perpetuated in cities through ecological processes. According to Marxian interpretations, the ecology of cities provides some of the conditions necessary for the *reproduction* of the necessary relationships between labour and capital and for the *stabilization* of the associated social formation. Thus we find 'a white collar labour force being "reproduced" in a white collar neighbourhood, a blue collar labour force being reproduced in a blue collar neighbourhood, and so on' (Harvey 1975: 363). An essential factor in this reproduction, Harvey suggests, is the differential access to scarce resources – especially educational resources – between neighbourhoods, since it helps preserve class and neighbourhood differences in 'market capacity' (the ability to undertake certain functions within the economic order) from one generation to another. At the same time, the location of 'compensatory' services and amenities not only helps to reproduce and maintain a ready population of workers (at the expense of taxpayers rather than employers) but also helps to defuse the discontent that their position might otherwise foster. Patterns of service and amenity provision, then, are at once the product of the social formation and an element in its continuing survival (Preteceille 1986). (For an illustration and extension of this argument in relation to specific examples, see Dear 1981 and Pinch 1984.)

# 8 Politics, planning and society

Consideration of inter-group conflict over the location and allocation of urban goods and the spatial organization of the city leads inevitably to an examination of the wider political context. Indeed, a large number of geographers now accept that there is virtually no aspect of urban change or development which can be properly understood without reference to the nature and operation or urban power structures and political processes. For the most part, urban political systems are based on agreed sets of rules and procedures which effectively reduce inter-group conflict and confrontation to the routine and unspectacular ritual of the ballot box and council chamber. This routinization of the political process, however, should not be allowed to obscure the fundamental importance of local power structures to the social geography of the city. In this chapter, attention is focused on the relationships between different interest groups, paying particular attention to the links between the political process, the planning process and the structure of the city – both physical and social. We begin, however, with a consideration of the motivation and relative influence of the principal protagonists in the urban political process: voters, office holders, bureaucrats, business élites, organized labour, citizen organizations and special interest groups.

## The democratic base and the para political structure

In all Western cities, the political framework is structured around the democratic idea of power resting, ultimately, with an electorate in which all citizens have equal status. The outstanding feature of urban politics in practice, however, is the low turnout of voters at election time. Seldom do more than 50 per cent of the registered voters go to the polls in municipal elections: the more likely figure is 30 per cent, and it is not uncommon for the vote to drop to less than 25 per cent of the electorate. Moreover, although data on voting behaviour at municipal elections is rather fragmentary, it seems probable that about a fifth of the electorate never vote at all. This passivity can be attributed to two very different perspectives on life. On the one hand there are those who feel that their interests are well-served by the existing power structure and who therefore do not feel the need to act; and on the other there are those who feel that their interests are consistently neglected or sacrificed by government but who feel they can do little about it. Such passivity is clearly undesirable from the standpoint of civic vitality; even more serious is the consequent lack of sensitivity of the political system to the interests of all sectors of society, since non-voters are by no means distributed randomly throughout the population. People living in rented accommodation tend to vote less than home owners; women tend to vote less than men; young people and retired people are less likely to go to the polls than are people in intervening age groups; people with lower incomes and lower educational qualifications tend to vote less than the rich and the well-educated; and recent in-migrants are less inclined to vote than long-term residents (Wolfinger and Rosenstone 1980). This amounts to a distortion of the democratic base which inevitably leads to a bias in the political complexion of elected representatives; and, given the overall composition of voters compared with non-voters, it is logical to expect that this bias will find expression in municipal policies which are conservative rather than radical.

In addition to this bias, the formal democracy of urban politics is also subject to imperfections in the behaviour of the elected holders of political office. Although city councillors are ostensibly representative of their local communities, there are several reasons for doubting their effectiveness in pursuing their constituents' interests within the corridors of power. Apart from anything else, councillors are by no means representative in the sense that their personal attributes, characteristics and attitudes reflect those of the electorate at large. Even in large cities the number of people who engage actively in local politics is small and, as Hampton has observed in relation to Sheffield, they tend to form a community of interest of their own: 'they meet each other regularly, share common interests, and denounce public apathy towards their activities with a vehemence only matched by the suspicion they sometimes evidence towards those who seek to contest their authority' (Hampton 1970: 49). Moreover, those who end up as councillors tend to be markedly more middle-class and older than the electorate as a whole, and a large majority are men.

Notwithstanding these differences between councillors and their constituents, it is in any case doubtful whether many councillors are able – or, indeed, willing – to act in the best interests of their constituents all the time. Councillors with party political affiliations, for example, may sometimes find that official party policy conflicts with constituency feelings. Alternatively, some councillors' behaviour may be influenced by the urge for personal gain or political glory. A graphic though perhaps extreme example of this is provided by the politicians of the Democratic 'machine' in Chicago described by Rakove (1975). Their approach to politics and public office, coloured heavily by economic self-interest and the desire for power, leaves little room for the broader considerations of community well-being:

They have little concept of broad social problems and social movements. They deal with each other, and with the problems of the community, on a person-to-person, individual basis. They shrink from striking out in new directions, have no interest in blazing new trails, abhor radical solutions to problems, and, in general, resist activism of any sort about anything. 'I got two rules', 29th Ward Committeeman Bernard Neistein confided when asked how he operated so successfully in politics in Chicago for most of his adult life. 'The first one is "Don't make no waves". The second one is "Don't back no losers"' (Rakove 1975: 11).

Another doubt about the effectiveness of councillors as local representatives stems from the conflicting demands of public office. In particular, it is evident that many councillors soon come to view their public role mainly in terms of responsibility for the city as a whole or in terms of their duties as committee members rather than as general spokespersons for specific communities (Batley 1972; Newton 1976). Moreover, after election, 'a councillor's perceptions become increasingly socialized into ways of looking at things dominated by other councillors, and his views become more similar to others in his stratum of the political élite' (Davies 1976: 352). It is therefore not surprising to find that empirical evidence suggests that there is a marked discrepancy between the priorities and preoccupations of local electorates and those of their representatives (Table 8.1; see also Bryant 1975). At least part of this gap between councillors' perceptions and those of their constituents must be attributable to the dearth of mutual contact: one survey of 1,235 local councillors in England and Wales found that almost half of them had contact with less than nine elec-

**Table 8.1**  Assessment by councillors and electors of the importance of local issues in Sheffield

| Issue: | Proportion placing issue 1st, 2nd, or 3rd in importance | | | | | | | |
|---|---|---|---|---|---|---|---|---|
| | | Total | | Cons. supporters | | Lab. supporters | | Others |
| | Base | Cllrs. 108 | Electors 584 | Cllrs. 48 | Electors 198 | Cllrs. 59 | Electors 300 | Electors 86 |
| | | % | % | % | % | % | % | % |
| Provision of housing | | 62 | 49 | 46 | 55 | 76 | 45 | 52 |
| Comprehensive education | | 52 | 25 | 35 | 22 | 66 | 26 | 29 |
| Rent rebate scheme | | 43 | 37 | 54 | 30 | 34 | 43 | 31 |
| Provision of education | | 35 | 27 | 38 | 29 | 34 | 24 | 31 |
| Redevelopment | | 32 | 42 | 31 | 38 | 34 | 44 | 49 |
| Roads and Traffic | | 19 | 53 | 31 | 56 | 10 | 53 | 50 |
| Recreation and social facilities | | 15 | 13 | 2 | 11 | 25 | 14 | 12 |
| Utility services | | 11 | 21 | 15 | 26 | 8 | 18 | 21 |
| Closed shop for council employees | | 11 | 4 | 23 | 4 | 2 | 5 | 5 |
| Local airport | | 7 | 16 | 17 | 21 | 0 | 13 | 12 |
| Local radio station | | 1 | 6 | 2 | 6 | 0 | 6 | 3 |

*Source:* Hampton 1970: 207.

tors over a four-week period (Committee on the Management of Local Government 1967). Moreover, the bulk of this contact tends to take place in the rather uneasy atmosphere of councillors' advice bureaux and clinics, where discussion is focused almost exclusively on personal grievances of one sort of another – usually connected with housing (Helco 1969: Newton 1976). Personal links within the constituency also appear to be weak. In Hampton's (1970) survey of Sheffield councillors for instance, only one-third were found to live within their own constituency, while less than one-sixth reported that a majority of their friends lived in their constituency. In short, it seems that the 'communion' with a district often claimed by councillors is more mystical than actual.

## Bureaucrats Rule OK

Some writers have also questioned the effectiveness of councillors inside the city hall, especially in relation to committee work. Harrison, for example, has suggested that many councillors overlook the wider implications of policy and resource allocation whilst devoting undue amounts of time to detail; and quotes an experienced development control planner as saying:

You get an old lady saying something . . . and everyone looks round and grins. They will spend half an hour discussing the extension to the back of a house and then an application worth a million pounds goes straight through! (Harrison 1972: 265).

It is, however, the nature of the relationship between councillors and professional officers – city planners and the like – which concerns most commentators. Because of the increasing complexity and sophistication of urban administration, councillors have to feed on professional appraisal and know-how in a wide range of areas, thus placing the professional officers in an influential position. In theory, the expert professional is 'on tap' but not 'on top', but there are many who believe, like Max Weber (1947), that the sheer complexity of governmental procedure has brought about a 'dictatorship of the official'. Lineberry (1977), for instance, has argued that the influence of professional personnel and the decision rules by which they operate is so great as to effectively remove the allocation of most public services from the control of even the strongest political power groups. The crucial point here is that the objectives and motivations of professional officers are not always coincident with the best interests of the public nor in accordance with the views of their elected representatives. Although it would be unfair to suggest that bureaucrats do not have the 'public good' at heart, it is clear that they are all subject to distinctive professional ideologies and conventions; and their success in conforming to these may be more valuable to them in career terms than how they accomplish their tasks as defined by their clientele. The professional ideology of city planners, for example, centred on the trinity of Beauty, Health and Efficiency and with a veneer of technical sophistication, has encouraged some practitioners to become zealots, as if they believed they were in possession of The Truth about urban systems; and it has given many more an evangelistic attitude towards the implementation of policies which emanate from the ideological fountainhead.

Some of the 'bureaucratic offensives' pursued in this way by professional planners are examined in the second half of this chapter. For the moment, however, the point at issue is the extent to which the democratic process is subverted by bureaucratic intervention and manipulation. Few would deny that a certain amount of essentially 'political' decision-making must be undertaken by professional officers because of the complexity and immediacy of urban administrative problems, but there is a growing body of opinion in support of the idea that the power of bureaucracy consistently outweighs that of the elected representatives. Dennis (1972), for example, concluded that the planners in Sunderland were quite out of control over most policy issues, while Kravitz (1970) and Ravetz (1980) have written at length about the increased influence of professional planners, particularly the 'mandarinism' of senior planners. There are several techniques which bureaucrats are able to use in getting their own way. Amongst the more widely recognized are: (1) 'swamping' councillors with a large number of long reports; (2) 'blinding councillors with science' – mainly by writing reports which are full of technicalities and statistics; (3) presenting reports which make only one conclusion possible; (4) withholding information or bringing it forward too late to affect decisions; (5) rewriting but not changing

a rejected plan, and submitting it after a decent interval; and (6) introducing deliberate errors in the first few paragraphs of a report in the hope that councillors will be so pleased at finding them that they let the rest go through. In the graphic words of one councillor in Birmingham:

It's a subtle blend of bullshit and flannel and making sure things go their way. And writing reports. Report writing, I would say, is the most important part of their job. They put out so many reports that you get swamped by it all . . . Just look at this lot. That's for one committee. It's – what – about two inches thick. Well this thing may cost £200, and the other lot may cost three million. It may all be on the same size paper. Same size print. You've got to be on the watch for what's going on . . . It's all protective confetti to the officers (Newton 1976: 156–7).

The idea of politicians as part-time dilettantes, powerless to control ever growing regiments of highly-trained, technically expert and crafty officials is of course very close to the spirit of the 'managerialist thesis' outlined in Chapter six. But there is by no means common agreement as to the degree of autonomy enjoyed by professional officers. As pointed out in relation to housing managers, there are broad economic and social forces which are completely beyond the control of any urban 'manager' as well as strong constraints on their activities which derive from central government directives (Blowers 1980). In addition, it has been argued that the highest stakes in urban politics are won and lost in the budgetary process to which few professional officers are privy. Thus, 'having set the rules of the game', politicians 'can leave the calling of the plays to the bureaucratic referees' (Rich 1979: 148).

## The para-political structure

Bureaucrats as well as politicians may in turn be influenced by elements of what Greer and Orleans (1962) called the *parapolitical structure* – informal groups which serve as mediating agencies between the individual household and the machinery of institutional politics. These include business organizations, trade unions and voluntary groups of all kinds, such as tenants' associations and conservation societies. Although relatively few such organizations are explicitly 'political' in nature, many of them are 'politicized' inasmuch as they occasionally pursue group activities through the medium of government. Indeed, there is a school of thought among political scientists which argues that, in American cities at least, private groups are highly influential in raising and defining issues for public debate (see for example, Banfield and Wilson 1963; Kaplan 1967). According to this school of thought, politicians and officials tend to back off until it is clear what the alignment of groups on any particular issue will be and whether any official decision-making will be required. In essence, this gives urban government the role of umpiring the struggle among private and partial interests, leaving these outsiders to decide the outcome of major issues in all but a formal sense. The idea of a strong para-political structure is also central to the school of thought which subscribes to what Gale and Moore (1975) call the 'manipulated city' hypothesis. Here, the city is regarded as a distributive system in which coalitions of major private interests are able to operate the legal and institutional framework in order to obtain favourable resource allocations.

## Business

Businessmen and business organizations have of course long been active in civic affairs. One of the more active and influential business organizations in most towns is the Chamber of Commerce, but it is by no means the only vehicle for private business interests. Business itself typically engages in *coalition building*. Business executives take a leading part in forming and guiding a number of civic organizations, they often play a major role in fund raising for cultural and charitable activities, and they hold many of the board positions of educational, medical and religious institutions. Lynda Ewen (1978), for example, has shown how the leading business families of Detroit are able to influence policy-makers and exer-

cise social control through their presence on university, hospital and library committees, and as prominent members of civic organizations such as the Detroit Urban League and New Detroit Inc. Because of its contribution to the city's economic health in the form of employment and tax revenues, the business community is in an extremely strong bargaining position and, as a result, its interests are often not so much directly expressed as *anticipated* by politicians and senior bureaucrats, many of whom seek the prestige, legitimacy and patronage which the business élite is able to confer.

The basic reason for business organizations' interest in urban politics is clearly related to their desire to influence the allocation of public resources in favour of their localized investments. In general, the most influential nexus of interests occurs in what Cox (1973) calls the 'downtown business élite': directors of insurance companies, department stores and banks, together with the owners and directors of local newspapers who rely heavily on central city business fortunes for the maintenance of their advertising revenue. The policies for which this group lobbies are those which can be expected to sustain and increase the commercial vitality of the central city. Given the widespread trend towards the decentralization of jobs and residences, one of their chief objectives has been to increase the accessibility and attractiveness of the CBD as a place in which to work and shop, and this has led business interests to support urban motorway programmes, improvements to public transport systems, urban renewal schemes and the construction of major amenities such as convention centres and theatres from public funds. In Washington DC, for example, merchants have formed a Downtown Retail Merchants Association to fight for what they describe as the 'survival of small retailers'.

## Labour

Organized labour, in the form of trade unions, represents the obvious counterbalance to the influence of the business élite in urban affairs. But, while organized labour is a major component of the para-political structure at the national level, it has traditionally exercised little influence on the allocation of resources at the intra-urban level. It is true that union representation on civic organizations has been widespread, and many union officials have been actively engaged in local party political activities; but organized labour in general has been unwilling to use its *power* (the withdrawal of labour) over issues which are not directly related to members' wages and conditions. In Britain, Trades Councils have provided a more community-based forum for trade unionists and have taken a direct interest in housing and broader social problems, but they are concerned primarily with bread-and-butter industrial issues rather than those related to the size and allocation of the 'social wage'. The point is that organized labour in most countries (France and Italy being the obvious exceptions) is essentially and inherently reformist. It has never posed a direct challenge to the interests of capital and the likelihood is that it never will. Ocassionally, however, union activity does have direct repercussions on the urban environment. In Australia, for example, the Builders' Labourers Federation has organized 'Green Bans' since the 1970s which have held up development projects on the grounds that they were environmentally undesirable; and, on a rather different level, construction unions in the United States have resisted changes to building regulations which threatened to reduce the job potential of their members (Lowe and Goyder 1983).

More recently, however, the pressures of local government fiscal retrenchment have drawn public-employee unions directly into the local political arena. Strikes by teachers have become especially prevalent. Where strikes by public employees are illegal (as with the police and fire services), 'sick outs' have provided one alternative. Another has been the work-to-rule. Maryland State Police, for example, recently proposed to write fewer traffic tickets and thereby cut state revenues by nearly $4 million; and officers in one county created a work slowdown by writing detailed reports on such matters as stolen bicycles, displaced manhole covers and accidentally-triggered security alarms.

### Citizen organizations and special interest groups

It has commonly been claimed in the literature of political sociology that voluntary associations are an essential component of the democratic infrastructure, helping to articulate and direct the feelings of individuals into the relevant government channel (Almond and Verba 1965; Dahl 1967; Rich 1979b). There is plenty of evidence that the outcomes of the planning process and public service delivery processes, in particular, have been heavily influenced by the mobilization of attitudes by public pressure groups. The most graphic examples can be seen where grand plans for urban change have failed to take account of the complexity of local feelings. Ravetz (1980), for example, recounts the case of Chesterfield market, where local opposition was mounted against the local authority's scheme to demolish listed buildings and an open air market to make way for a speculative developer's shopping complex. Between 1956 and 1973 the proposal successfully found its way through the various statutory stages, only to be shelved in 1974 after a protest march of several thousand citizens and a petition signed by over 30,000 persons. A similar example is provided by the proposed redevelopment of Covent Garden in London (Christensen 1982). But relatively little is actually known about the number of citizen organizations of different kinds in cities, whose interests they represent, and how many of them are ever politically active. There have been numerous case studies of pressure group activity over controversial issues such as urban renewal, transportation and school organization (Susskind and Elliot 1983), but these represent, as Newton (1976) puts it, only the tip of the pressure-group iceberg, leaving the remaining nine-tenths unexplored. This other nine-tenths encompasses a vast range of organizations, including work-based clubs and associations, church clubs, welfare organizations, community groups such as tenants' associations and parents' associations, sports clubs, social clubs, cause-oriented groups such as Shelter, Help the Aged, and the Child Poverty Action Group, groups which emerge over particular local issues (e.g. the 'Save Covent Garden' campaign) as well as political organizations *per se*.

Given the nature of local government decision-making, many of these are able to influence policy and resource allocation on the 'squeaky wheel' principle. This need not necessarily involve vociferous and demonstrative campaigns. The Los Angeles system of landscaped parkways, for example, is widely recognized as the result of steady lobbying by *Sunset* magazine, the official organ of obsessive gardening and planting in Southern California (Banham 1973). But not all organizations are politically active in any sense of the word. In his study of Birmingham, Newton (1976) found over 4,000 formally organized voluntary associations, from the local branch of Alcoholics Anonymous to the Zoroastrian society. Of these, only 30 per cent were considered to have been at all politically active, with social welfare, youth- and health-related organizations and trades unions being most active of all. It appears, therefore, that the bulk of the 'pressure-group iceberg' is in fact fairly passive. A typical example is provided by working-men's clubs, one of the most popular types of local voluntary organization in British industrial cities (Batley, 1972; Hampton, 1970). In Newcastle, Batley found that working-men's clubs firmly rejected the idea of involvement in community issues: 'It's not our job to get involved in politics. The members wouldn't stand for it.' Club committees were therefore expected, as Batley found, 'not so much to provide leadership as to manage the existing and traditional activities of the clubs. Even members' often-asserted pride in the co-operative self-government of their clubs seemed to carry with it a rejection of the outside world in which they were not masters.' Thus, 'In spite of their important social role in the local community, the workingmen's clubs were peculiarly defenceless' (Batley 1972: 103). Such passivity is of course a reflection of the passivity of the community at large. It should

not be confused with neutrality, however, since passivity is effectively conservative, serving to reinforce the *status quo* of urban affairs. Moreover, this conservatism is not balanced by any real radicalism amongst the minority of citizens who are politically active. On the contrary, there is evidence to suggest that activists, like decision-makers, are generally more conservative than non-activists (Verba and Nie 1972).

## Community power structures and the role of the local state

How are the relationships between these various groups and decision-makers structured? Who really runs the community and what difference does it make to the local quality of life? These are questions which have concerned political scientists and urban sociologists for some time and which have now caught the attention of urban geographers because of their implications for the socio-spatial structure of the city. There are two 'classic' types of urban power structure – monolithic and pluralistic – each of which has been identified in a wide range of cities since their 'discovery' by Hunter (1953) and Dahl (1961) respectively. In his study of 'Regional City' (Atlanta), Hunter found that nearly all decisions were made by a handful of individuals who stood at the top of a stable power hierarchy. These people, drawn largely from business and industrial circles, constituted a strongly entrenched and select group: with their blessing, projects could move ahead, but without their express or tacit consent little of significance was ever accomplished.

In contrast, the pluralistic model of community power advanced by Dahl in the light of his analysis of decision-making in New Haven, Connecticut, holds that power tends to be dispersed, with different élites dominant at different times over different issues. Thus, if the issue involves public housing, one set of participants will control the outcome; if it involves the construction of a new health centre, a different coalition of leaders will dominate. In Dahl's model, therefore, business élites of the kind Hunter found to be in control of Atlanta are only one among many influential 'power clusters'. As Dahl puts it, 'The Economic Notables, far from being a ruling group, are simply one of many groups out of which individuals sporadically emerge to influence the politics and acts of city officials. Almost anything one might say about the influence of the Economic Notables could be said with equal justice about half a dozen other groups in the New Haven community' (Dahl 1961: 72). Dahl argued that the system as a whole is democratic, drawing on a wide spectrum of the para-political structure and ensuring political freedom through the competition of élites for mass loyalty. When the policies and activities of existing power structures depart from the values of the electorate, he suggested, people will be motivated to voice their concerns and a new power cluster will emerge. According to the pluralist model, therefore, we may expect the interplay of views and interests within a city to produce, in the long run, an allocation of resources which satisfies, to a degree, the needs of all interest groups and neighbourhoods (Kirby 1979a): problems such as area deprivation are seen merely as short-term failures of participation in the political process (Eyles 1978). On the other hand, we might expect monolithic power structures to lead to polarization of well-being, with few concessions to the long-term interests of the controlling élite.

More recently, it has been suggested that US urban politics should be seen not in terms of monolithic versus pluralistic power structures but in terms of the evolution and succession of a series of regimes, each of which is dominated by 'pro-growth coalitions' put together by political entrepreneurs in order to achieve concrete solutions to particular problems (Elkin 1985; Mollenkopf 1983).

While the validity of both classic models has been widely debated, the central issue of 'who governs?' has been somewhat obscured by a lack of comparability in the techniques used to establish the nature of community power structures (Burt 1981). Basically, studies using the 'reputational' type of analysis employed by Hunter have tended to conclude that community power resides in the hands of a business élite, whereas those using the 'power-in-action' analysis favoured by Dahl have tended to support the pluralist model (Curtis and Petras 1970). Moreover, a major weakness of all three models is their failure to adequately deal with the relationship between the controlling élite(s) and the rest of the population. The crucial question here is whether the legitimacy of the élite(s) is in fact voluntarily ceded from below or imposed in some way from above. Both the classic models assume, implicitly or explicitly, that the passivity of the bulk of the population is a reflection of their voluntary acceptance of a relationship in which they follow the decisions of the leadership in return for the latter's pursuit of the 'common good', with the electoral system providing redress for any serious abuse of power. A number of observers, however, have rejected the view that political inaction is necessarily indicative of a consensus of interests between the controlling élite and society in general. Rather, it is suggested, this passivity is the net result of the suffocation of opposition within the political system. According to Bachrach and Baratz (1970), it is possible to recognize three main ways in which opposition to the policies of powerful élites may be defused:

1. the failure of disgruntled groups to press their demands, either because they *anticipate* a retaliatory response or because they believe it would be futile to do so;

2. the failure of those in powerful positions to respond to the articulation of political demands by less powerful groups. This may be achieved, for example, by establishing committees or inquiries which fail to report until years later;

3. the 'mobilization of bias'. This involves the manipulation by the powerful of the values, beliefs and opinions of the general public. Thus, for example, demands for change may be denied legitimacy by being branded 'commu-

nistic' or 'a threat to the freedom of the individual'. In this context, control over resources such as the mass media is particularly important. Given such control, the élite is able to restrict public consideration to those matters considered 'safe' and, as a result, the demands or grievances of some segments of the community may never be heard.

According to this view, therefore, the issues debated in local politics are no more than 'political crumbs strewn carelessly about by an élite with its hands clasped firmly round the cake' (Saunders 1979: 30–1). Such an interpretation suggests that we must look beyond the immediate apparatus of community power structures to the wider relationships within the organization of society itself in order to understand cities.

## Marxist views of urban political economy

In recent years an increasing number of scholars have turned to Marxist theories of political economy in response to the need to relate urban structure to the wider organization of society. This has led to the emergence of a 'New Urban Sociology', a 'New Urban Politics' and a 'radical' urban geography; although it should be acknowledged at the outset that the literature on the subject contains an eclectic mixture of views which sometimes disguises fundamentally opposed theoretical positions. This possibly derives from the fact that Marx himself was not especially sensitive to urbanism or spatial issues, and so it has been left to others to interpret and elaborate his work in the context of the modern city. It is, however, possible to outline those strands of Marxist theory and its derivatives which are more widely accepted as relevant to an understanding of the urban 'problematic'.

At its most fundamental level, Marxist theory turns on the contention that all social phenomena are linked to the prevailing mode of production. This is the material economic *base* from which everything else – the social

*superstructure* – derives, In historical terms, the economic base is the product of a dialectical process in which the prevailing ideology, or 'thesis', of successive modes of production is overthrown by contradictory forces (the 'antithesis'), thus bringing about a *transformation* of society to a higher stage of development: from subsistence tribalism through feudalism and capitalism to socialism. Based in Western society is of course the capitalist mode of production and, like other bases, it is characterized by conflict between opposing social classes inherent in the economic order. The superstructure of capitalism encompasses everything which stems from and relates to this economic order, including tangible features such as the morphology of the city as well as more nebulous phenomena like legal and political institutions, the ideology of capitalism, and the counter-ideology of its antithesis.

As part of this superstructure, one of the major functions of the city is to fulfil the imperatives of capitalism, the most important of which is the circulation and accumulation of capital. Thus the spatial form of the city, by reducing indirect costs of production and costs of circulation and consumption, speeds up the rotation of capital, leading to its greater accumulation. Another important role of the city, according to Marxist theory, is to provide the conditions necessary for the perpetuation of the economic base. In short, this entails the reproduction of the relationship between labour and capital and, therefore, the stabilization of the associated social structure. One aspect of this is the perpetuation of the economic class relationships through ecological processes, particularly the development of a variety of suburban settings with differential access to different kinds of services, amenities and resources (Harris 1984; Levenstein 1981; see also pp. 27 and 286). The role of government is particularly important in this respect because of its control over the patterns and conditions of provision of schools, housing, shopping, leisure facilities, and the whole spectrum of 'collective consumption' (Castells 1977). Moreover, it can also be argued that urban neighbourhoods provide distinctive milieux from which individuals derive many of their consumption habits, moral codes, values and expectations. The resulting homogenization of life-experiences within different neighbourhoods 'reinforces the tendency for relatively permanent social groupings to emerge within a relatively permanent structure of residential differentiation' (Harvey 1975: 364). The division of the proletariat into distinctive, locality-based communities through the process of residential differentiation also serves to fragment class consciousness and solidarity whilst reinforcing the traditional authority of élite groups (Bell and Newby 1976), something which is also strengthened, as we have seen (Chapter 2), by the symbolic power of the built environment. In short, the city is at once an expression of capitalism and a means of its perpetuation.

At the same time, however, it is recognized that the structure of the city reflects and incorporates many of the contradictions in capitalist society, thus leading to local friction and conflict. This is intensified as the city's economic landscape is continually altered in response to capital's drive towards the accumulation of profit. Residential neighbourhoods are cleared to make way for new office developments; disinvestment in privately-rented accommodation leads to the dissolution of inner-city communities; while the switch of capital to more profitable investment in private housing leads to an expansion of the suburbs; and so on. This continual tearing down, re-creation and transformation of spatial arrangements brings about locational conflict in several ways. Big capital, as Cox (1977) observes, comes into conflict with small capital in the form of retailers, property developers and small businesses in general. Meanwhile, conflict also arises locally between, on the one hand, capitalists (both large and small) and, on the other, those obtaining important use – and exchange-values from existing spatial arrangements. This includes conflict over the nature and location of new urban development, over urban renewal, road construction, conservation, land-use zoning, and so on: over the whole spectrum, in fact, of urban activity. Much of this conflict, of course, is formalized and routinized within the structure of institutional politics, but some writers have argued that crises in the provision and allocation by the state of various components of collective consumption precipitate the development of 'urban social movements', or popular alliances (e.g. between tenants and shopkeepers) which operate outside orthodox political channels and which therefore, it is suggested, offer one of the principal sources of real social change in advanced capitalist society (Pickvance 1976a).

Underlying most Marxist analyses of the city is the additional hypothesis involving the role of the state as a legitimating agent, helping to fulfil the imperatives of capitalism in a number of ways (Johnston 1984b). These include defusing discontent through the pursuit of welfare policies, the provision of a stable and predictable environment for business through the legal and judicial system, and the propagation of an ideology conducive to the operation and maintenance of the economic base through its control and penetration of socializing agencies such as the educational system, the armed forces and the civil service.

From these various strands of Marxist theory there has emerged a corpus of research which has collectively been termed the 'New Urban Sociology' (or, depending on disciplinary predilections, the 'New Urban Politics' or 'radical' geography). The principal contributors to this movement include David Harvey (1973; 1982; 1985) as well as members of the French 'school' of urban sociology such as Manuel Castells (1977; 1978), Jean Lojkine (1974) and Edmund Preteceille (1973), whose work was introduced to the English-speaking world by Chris Pickvance (1976b) and Michael Harloe (1977) (see also Huxley and McLoughlin 1985). Some of this work has justifiably been criticized for its epistemological self-righteousness and a predilection for cryptic literary styles which all but an inner circle of *cognoscenti* find difficult to understand.

A much more important criticism is that Marxist theory does not give sufficient recognition to the influence of human agency: the actions of individuals are seen in Marxist theory as a direct function of economic and socio-political structures. It has been argued, however, that there are elemental and universal human drives and behavioural responses which give life and structure to the city and that people are capable of generating, independently, important ideas and behaviours. Furthermore, it is argued that these products of the human spirit can sometimes contribute to the economic and socio-political structures that Marxist theory attributes exclusively to the material economic base (Cullen and Knox 1982; Duncan and Ley 1982; Ellison 1983; Eyles 1981).

But the overall contribution of Marxist theory is clearly significant. It provides a clear break with earlier, narrower conceptions of urban socio-spatial relationships and a flexible theoretical framework for a wide range of phenomena. Much of this new work reflects national intellectual traditions as well as differences in the nature of national policies and urban development. A good deal of recent French, Italian and Spanish work has been concerned with the emergence of urban social movements (Castells *et al.* 1977; Ceccarelli 1982; Marcelloni 1979; Olives 1976), whereas American research has tended to be concerned more with analyses of the fiscal crises of cities (Tabb and Sawers 1984) and British research has focused on questions of collective consumption at the local level, and on the role of the 'local state' (Forrest, Henderson and Williams 1982; Lambert, Paris and Blackaby 1978; Rees and Lambert 1985).

## Politics, planning and the local state

Despite the clear importance of local government – even simply in terms of the magnitude of expenditure on public services – there is no properly developed and generally accepted theory of the behaviour and objectives of local government, or the 'local state'. Within the debate on this question, however, three principal positions have emerged:

1. that the local state is controlled by officials, and that their goals and values are crucial in determining policy outcomes (the 'managerialist' view);
2. that the local state is an adjunct of the national state, with both acting in response to the prevailing balance of class forces within society (the 'structuralist' view);
3. that the local state is an instrument of the business élite (the 'instrumentalist' view).

The first of these has, as we have seen (pp. 224–245) generated widespread interest and support, and it is clear that a focus on the activities and ideologies of professional decision-makers can contribute a lot to the understanding of urban socio-spatial processes. We have also seen, however, that the managerialist approach does not give adequate recognition either to the influence of local élites and pressure groups or to the economic and political constraints stemming from the national level.

Because of such shortcomings, attention has recently been focused on the structuralist and instrumentalist positions, both of which stem directly from Marxist theory. Although the flavour of discussion has been somewhat abstract and rarefied, it is possible to make some general statements about the putative role of the local state. Saunders (1979), following O'Connor (1973) and Cockburn (1977), suggests that the key functions of the local state are as follows:

*1. The sustenance of private production and capital accumulation*
   (a) through the provision of an urban infrastructure of roads, sewage disposal, water supply, etc.;
   (b) by easing spatial aspects of the reorganization of production through the planning process and the initiation of urban renewal programmes, etc.;
   (c) by investment in 'human capital' through the provision of educational facilities in general and technical education in particular;
   (d) through 'demand orchestration' which, through public works contracts etc., brings stability and security to markets which might otherwise be volatile and unpredictable.
*2. The reproduction of labour power through collective consumption*
   (a) by means of the material conditions of existence (e.g. low-rent public housing);

(b) by means of the cultural conditions of existence (e.g. libraries, art galleries, parks).

3. *The maintenance of order and social cohesion*

(a) through agents of coercion (e.g. the police);

(b) through the provision of welfare programmes and social services to support the 'surplus population';

(c) through the support of 'agencies of legitimation' such as schools, the social work system and public participation schemes.

Although this taxonomy of the functions of the local state draws heavily on Marxist analysis, it does not imply the acceptance of any particular theoretical position. Where the structuralist view differs from the instrumentalist view is not so much in the identification of the functions of the state as in the question of for whom or for what the functions operate, whether they are class-biased, and the extent to which they reflect external political forces (Duncan and Goodwin 1982).

One of the first detailed empirical analyses of the local state in this context was Cockburn's (1977) study of Lambeth, in London. She identified two dominant trends within the borough – corporate management and community development – and interpreted these as a reflection of the position of the local state in relation both to the national state and to business interests. As she points out, the trend towards corporate management was initiated by the central government in an attempt to replace the fragmented administrative structure of local authorities with a corporate approach borrowed from business. This meant the establishment of an integrated senior management team and a shift of power away from junior administrators and backbench councillors. But, while municipal efficiency was increased, the concentration of power at the top meant a decrease in contact between the local population and the powerholders. Apart from anything else, this reduced the feedback of information essential to the effective management of the corporate-style system. Moreover, the erosion of democracy, both real and perceived, tended to

undermine the legitimacy of the local authority and encourage 'the managed' to seek sources of power outside the orthodox system of representative democracy. It was in order to remedy this situation, it is argued, that 'community development' (i.e. public participation) was encouraged, with the intiative again coming from central government. Meanwhile, the onset of the economic crisis in the mid-1970s revealed that the power of the corporate decision-makers in the town hall was strictly limited, especially in comparison with the power of local property speculators and industrialists. Cockburn's interpretation of events thus generally supports the structuralist view that the local state, as a relatively autonomous adjunct of the national state, tends to safeguard the long-term interests of the dominant class (in this case, monopoly capital) while 'buying off' the working class through reformist strategies (Poulantzas 1973: Castells 1977).

The instrumentalist view of the local state derives from Miliband's work (1969, 1977), in which he emphasizes the significance of the class backgrounds of top decision-makers, presenting evidence to show that the social composition of senior positions in government, the civil service, the judiciary, the police, legislative assemblies and local governments is such as generally to ensure that the interests of capital will receive a sympathetic hearing. He also argues that the state itself is dependent upon continued capitalist accumulation, which it is therefore constrained to support. This, in turn, serves to enhance the leverage of the already powerful business élite which represents the interests of capital. These ideas have found some support in a study of community power in the London borough of Croydon, where 'the local authority's commitment to private profitability is mediated by an interpersonal "community of interest and sentiment" which exists between leading politicians and top business leaders in the town' (Saunders 1979: 207).

In short, it seems that each of the three models of the local state – managerialist, structuralist and instrumentalist – contain useful insights which are relevant in some areas of explanation but less so in others. Put another way, none of the three models can be completely dismissed on the rather limited evidence available at present. Not surprisingly, some theorists have attempted to reconcile elements of the different models. One example of this is the work of Offe (1974; 1976), whose theorizing about the state in advanced capitalist economies contains elements of both instrumentalist and managerialist perspectives; but perhaps more relevant to the role of the local state is Pahl's later work on urban managerialism, which has led him to set managerialism within a general theory of the state. Pahl now distinguishes between local 'managers' in the private sector and those in the public sector, with the former being seen as gatekeepers in a very general sense, while bureaucrats in the local state are seen as performing crucial mediating roles both between the state and the private sector and between the state and various special interest groups (Pahl 1977). This, however, returns us to the knotty question of central–local relationships and the degree of autonomy of the local state (Boddy 1983). In Britain, these relationships have been thrown into focus by the central–local conflicts resulting from the Thatcher government's drive to curb local government spending (see, for example, the accounts by Elliot and McCrone (1984) of the resistance of Dundee District to the privatization of housing and of Lothian Region to the imposition of budget cuts). The details of these arguments need not detain us here, but it will be appreciated that the reconciliation of different theoretical perspectives is a difficult task. For the present, therefore, it seems reasonable to follow Kirby (1979a) and Saunders (1979) in suggesting that 'theoretical pluralism and epistemological tolerance' offer the most useful approach to the study of the city. It is in this spirit that we now turn to an examination of the implications and spatial outcomes of the relationships between the urban planning machine, the urban power structure and the community at large.

## Planners, the city, and society

As Ruth Glass observed, cities are 'a mirror . . . of history, class structure and culture' (Glass 1968: 48). The fact that cities are dominated by the huge buildings of commercial and state bureaucracies says something about the power of those bureacracies; just as barracks-like public housing schemes say something about the relationship between those who put them up and those who live in them; and the range of facilities available in a neighbourhood says something about the economic and political importance of its inhabitants. At the heart of the relationship between power, society and the built environment in modern cities is the city planning profession which, through a mixture of default and intent, finds itself the arbiter between the interests of different classes and communities.

The crucial feature of this role is that it has never been (and, indeed, cannot ever be) neutral. Although concerned mainly with improving the physical environment, city planning has for a long time been oriented towards certain people, even if only indirectly and implicitly. According to Gans (1969), these people have been the planning profession itself, its political supporters, and the middle-class citizen in general. Thus, he argues, just as architects often seem to design buildings with an eye more to professional acclaim than to the effects of their buildings on users, so planners have sought to create the kind of city they wanted. At the same time, the planners' ideal city reflects their own class-culture, leaning towards the promotion of solid, single-family dwellings and the creation of facilities catering to middle-class tastes. Finally, since planners have to work with an eye to the businessmen and civic leaders who sit on planning committees, they tend to work towards an 'efficient' city which is good for business. But

The planner did not realise he was planning for himself, his supporters and people of his class, however; he thought that by focusing on what he thought were desirable types of housing, business and industry, he was planning for everybody. As a professional he thought he knew what was best for the community and for people . . . Because he was a descendant of a missionary reform cause, he never questioned his aims or his activities (Gans 1969: 36).

As a result, the planning profession has tended to proceed on the assumption of a value consensus when in reality society is made up of groups who stand to gain or lose differentially by different plans. A good example of this is the British green belt policy. Although it commands widespread public acceptance because of its conservationist aims, it has had a number of important side-effects conferring capital gains on property owners in or near green belts, increasing the need for long-distance commuter travel, increasing the housing costs of inner-city residents who are unable to commute, and so on. This, however, is not an isolated example. There are convincing arguments that many aspects of planning activity are, ultimately, regressive in their effects (Kirk 1980; Simmie 1974, 1981).

## Planning ideology and planning praxis

It follows from all this that, whatever the degree of autonomy ascribed to the profession as a whole (and this of course depends on the theoretical perspective one adopts), the key to the relationship between planning, society and urban structure is likely to be found in the motivation, ideology and *modus operandi*, or praxis, of professional planners. As we saw in Chapter two, the town planning movement in Britain grew from a coalition of sanitary reformers, garden city idealists, would-be conservers of Britain's countryside and architectural heritage, and farmers and politicians who were worried about the loss of agricultural land. Together they had a bold and progressive vision which has subsequently been translated into a huge, powerful and professionalized machine. For all its progressivism, however, it was an essentially reactionary movement, in the sense that it aimed at containing the city and preserving the countryside from contamination by it. Patrick Geddes, the visionary inspiration of the emerging planning movement, saw cities as 'sprawling man-reefs', expanding like 'ink-stains and grease-spots' over the 'natural' environment, creating nothing but 'slum, semi-slum and super-slum' with social

environments that 'stunt the mind' (Geddes 1915). Cities, therefore, were to be thinned out, tidied up, penned in by green belts, fragmented into 'neighbourhood units' and generally made as like villages as possible. In other countries, too, urban planning became a vehicle for the utopian and prophylactic strains of Western liberal thought, nurtured by a coalition of anti-urban interests (Boyer 1983; Chaline 1984; Cherry 1980; Hajdu 1983). In the struggle to establish itself as a profession with intellectual standing as well as statutory powers, it developed a 'great tradition', with heroes to match: Howard and Geddes were joined by Abercrombie, Unwin, Perry, Soria y Mata and, borrowed from architecture, Frank Lloyd Wright and Le Corbusier (Donnison and Soto 1980; Hall 1974; Krueckeberg 1983). The assumptions which governed their approach to town planning and the arguments they employed in order to justify its practice have entered into the ideology of the profession, and their postulates form part of the mythology of planning to which all new recruits are introduced. *Ideology* in this context refers to the ideas derived from previous experience which are brought to bear on a situation in order to identify the 'correct' strategy in professional situations. The trainee is socialized into these ideas through formal education, meetings, journals and general day-to-day contact with fellow professionals. In relation to planning, for example, the descriptions of the trials, tribulations and final vindication of Geddes, Abercrombie, Unwin *et al.* given to planning students are not mere academic exercises in the history of the subject: they are the moral equipment of the professional planner, teaching him what to expect – which groups have been hostile to the growth of his profession in the past, why they were hostile, and what responses were successful in disarming them (Baum 1983; Davies 1972).

In overall terms, the ideology of the profession constitutes the basic operating rationale by which the planner feels able to justify his own activities and to judge the claims of others for his sympathetic attention. It is also reflected in conventional planning praxis – the routine, day-to-day procedure for dealing with the problems which are considered to be within their sphere of competence. It is important, therefore, to identify the major strands of thought which contribute to planning ideology. Although these strands are closely intertwined, it is possible to identify five themes which have had a major influence on planning praxis everywhere: environmentalism, aesthetics, spatial determinism, the systems approach and futurism.

The theme of *environmentalism* in planning ideology can be traced back to the sanitary reformers, philanthropists and utopianists of the Victorian era. A brief outline of their background has been given in Chapter two and need not be reiterated here. Their major contribution to planning ideology has been the rather naive assumption that the key to improvements in physical, moral and social welfare is to be found in the provision of facilities and the upgrading of the physical environment. As Gans rather disparagingly puts it, the belief is that

if poor people were provided with a set of properly designed facilities, ranging from model tenements to better work places and parks and playgrounds, they would not only give up their slum abodes but also change themselves in the process . . . The founders of the playground movement believed that if the poor could be provided with playgrounds and community centres, they would stop frequenting the taverns, cafes, brothels and later the movie houses in which they spent their leisure time, and would desert the street corner gangs and clubs which they had created for social life (Gans 1969: 34).

Although crude environmental determinism no longer dominates planning ideology to the extent that it did in the early days of the profession, it remains a strong influence on planning praxis, not least in the prescription of all kinds of formulae and standards for achieving a satisfactory environment, both in the home and outside.

The concern with *aesthetics* also has a long history, stemming from the links between planning, civic design and architecture (Wilson 1980). Considerations of 'scale', 'harmony', 'townscape' and 'visual order' predominate here, together with a predilection for erasing blots on the urban landscape. Little emphasis is given to the economic or social implications of such objectives, however. An extreme example of the viewpoint is provided by Harrison, who quotes an exchange at one of the annual British Town and Country Planning Summer Schools. A speaker was asked if a planning application for a new factory in a stone-built village said to be dying for lack of employment should be turned down if it was not to be built in stone. The reply was that 'it was a question of the greatest good for the greatest number, and that particular village might have to forgo its industry if there were a greater number of people for whom the landscape provided something of eternal value' (Harrison 1975: 262). As with the environmentalist perspective, such attitudes are underlain by more than a little moral righteousness and professional paternalism. Opposition to the aesthetic judgement of the planner is derided as irrational or ill-informed, although how or why the planner himself should be superior is never explained, save for the invocation of professional experience. This, of course, is a flimsy and vulnerable qualification, since the criteria of quality in the built environment require constant redefinition. The 'ugly' may survive to become 'interesting' or 'significant'; what was once deemed to be 'harmonious and orderly' may later be seen as 'monotonous and mechanical', while the 'excessively vulgar' may become 'imaginative and vital'. Nevertheless, the aesthetic strand of planning ideology has entered everyday planning practice in a variety of forms including controls over building height, the alignment of buildings and outhouses on residential streets, and even the colour of pigeon lofts and garages; while on a different scale it has undoubtedly influenced the way in which planners have approached slum clearance, redevelopment schemes and environmental improvement programmes. Perhaps more than anything else, however, it is reflected in the way in which the profession has embraced the *zeitgeist* of successive architectural messiahs such as Mies van der Rohe, Walter Gropius, Frank Lloyd Wright and Le Corbusier, allowing architectural fads and fashions to influence civic design at the expense of human use and scale. As Inglis puts it: 'Style for style's sake: the *zeit* for sore eyes' (Inglis 1975: 182).

*Spatial determinism* encompasses a wide range of planning wisdom whose common feature is an assumption that the imposition of spatial order brings social and economic benefits. This attitude is associated with a belief that one of planning's chief concerns should be with the 'best use' of the limited supply of land: hence the preoccupation with zoning, separating different kinds of land uses. A closely related theme is the concern with traffic and transport which, at least in Britain, was greatly fostered by the appointment of engineers to senior planning positions during the formative years of the profession. The logic here is that efficient traffic systems are fundamental to the welfare of all city users: businesses become more profitable, commuters become less frustrated and residents and pedestrians become less vulnerable to traffic hazards. Spatial determinism is also implicit in the concept of 'neighbourhood units' pioneered by Clarence Perry. The underlying assumption – and here there are clear links with environmentalism – was that the careful layout of roads, dwellings, precincts and amenities would lead to social interaction, the stimulation of feelings of security and stability, and the development of 'community'. Through this rudimentary social engineering, it was believed, the threats to social order implied by urbanization could be subverted by the creation of local social structures similar to those of traditional society (Bell and Newby 1976). Although the concept of the neighbourhood unit is now less fashionable, spatial determinism in general stil remains a major component of planning ideology, partly because of the influx of geography graduates to the profession during the 1960s and early 1970s, bringing with them a whole kitbag of techniques of locational analysis and an academic tradition of concern with spatial oganization.

Geographers have also been closely associated with the propagation of the *systems approach* in planning. According to this school of thought, the role of the planner lies in optimizing the performance of the city system, and the task is to be approached through the empirical analysis of inter-relationships and interactions (McLoughlin 1969). Stemming largely from the American planning vanguard, systems planning attempts to bring together the all-round vision of the traditional planner and the techniques of operational research, systems analysis and cybernetics. Stimulated by the availability of new statistical techniques and computer hardware, the modelling and monitoring of urban economic, demographic and social systems have become objectives in their own right. Town planning is thus redefined as a distinctive method, a process of arriving at decisions rather than as a responsibility for a delimited field or as a substantive body of theory. It is an abstract process, which 'may be applied to many sets of circumstances, and is characterized by its analytical technique, its synoptic concern for the total environment, and its orientation towards problem-solving action' (Amos 1972: 305). Like spatial determinism, the systems approach has an aura of being rational, uncontroversial and 'scientific'. In reality, of course, it involves some of the biggest political questions of all, since it is concerned with the allocation of resources and opportunities.

An orientation towards the future is implicit in the very idea of planning, but the *futurism* of planning ideology involves something more than far-sightedness. It extends to a vision of a life-style based on planners' own class-culture and on an overly optimistic view of social and economic trends. Typically, this vision is dominated by the pursuits and concerns of the present-day rich, whose life-style is assumed to be aspired to – and attainable – by all. The resulting planning praxis is what Gladstone (1976) refers to as 'dream planning'. It is manifested in planning documents which are generously sprinkled with references to yachting marinas, golf courses, shopping malls and leisure centres, to the needs of households with second homes and second cars, to the problems of providing retailing complexes to cater for mass consumption on unprecedented scales, and to the urgency of remodelling the environment to match the spirit of the bright new future. Planning based on these conceptions is an expensive commodity, since it is the taxpayer of today who must pay for the planners' vision of the future. It can also be expensive in the wider sense for, in the urge to adapt society to its future rather than vice versa, planning has been seduced by newness, modernism, and technology *per se*. As a result, planning praxis tends to favour futuristic designs and schemes which exploit all the possibilities of the latest building and transport technology: as witnessed by the concrete slabs, girder grids and curtain facing of many of the city centres redeveloped during the 1960s and 1970s. Closely linked to this aspect of futurism is the profession's vulnerability to being 'captured' by one fashion after another: low densities; high rise apartments; urban motorways; no urban motorways; no high-rise apartments; renewal; rehabilitation; 'community'; public participation; high densities; defensible space; low densities again; and so on.

Overlying all five major ideological strands is the mantle of what Davies (1972) dubbed the 'Evangelistic Bureaucrat'. According to Davies, this mantle has been acquired by the profession in order to immunize itself against the persistent criticisms levelled against its members as a result of the conflicts which inevitably arise from the pursuit of their trade. It is related to a self-image of imaginative far-sightedness, selflessness, fairness and humanitarianism, 'beset by the carping criticisms of narrow-minded rate payers, greedy speculators, parochial councillors, apathetic citizenry, calculated vested interests . . . irresponsible young people, jealous rival professionals, reluctant legislators and twittering academics' (Davies 1972: 94–5). The mantle of evangelism allows the planner to turn a deaf ear to these criticisms. But it can also lead to what Cox (1976) called 'bureaucratic aggression' – the relentless pursuit of their policies at the expense of 'defenceless citizens'. Such behaviour is compounded by the fact that once an idea or strategy has been floated it tends to acquire an almost autonomous life of its own. As Cox points out, once some actor in a situation decides to support an idea, he has in effect made an investment in it: an investment

of his own prestige which he will be reluctant to see lost. At the same time, others will tend to judge the idea in the light of the support it has gathered as much as by its intrinsic merits, thus bolstering the momentum of potentially faulty policies.

The cumulative result of this evangelism and aggression, according to some, has been to transform planning from an 'enabling' to a 'disabling' profession (Ravetz 1980). It should always be borne in mind, however, that the idea of a professional ideology represents a high-level generalization, so that, in practice, we can expect to find some planners with quite different emphases in terms of their role and attitudes (see, for example, Knox and Cullen 1981b). Furthermore, we must recognize that planners with particular personalities, working in particular settings, often develop distinctive (and sometimes innovative) styles and purposes (Catanese 1984): a good example of the interplay between structure and human agency referred to above.

## Bureaucratic offensives: land use and urban renewal

Doctors, according to the old adage, bury their mistakes, while lawyers hang theirs. Those at the receiving end of the mistaken prescriptions and unanticipated side-effects of the bureaucratic offensives launched by planners suffer a variety of maladies. Urban motorways are a case in point. As Simmie observed, they penalize low-income groups in several ways:

In the first place they tend to destroy more poor homes than rich ones while at the same time employing funds which, among other things, means the forgoing of other opportunities such as the building of more local authority housing. After they are built, they do not serve the poor unless they possess private transport. Such is not often the case among the unemployed, the low paid, the chronically sick, the old, and children (Simmie 1974: 146).

It would be naïve and misleading to suggest that the net effect of town planning is consistently regressive, or that the sole explanation of those policies which are regressive is to be found in the inexorable machinations of a bureaucracy guided inflexibly by its professional ideology. Town planning can justifiably claim to have advanced liberal reform on a broad front, the results of which have been expressed in a variety of ways in the changing face of the city. Space does not permit even a brief catalogue of these changes; but it is important to illustrate the way in which planning ideology can be translated into policies which have quite different effects on the fortunes of different neighbourhoods, and this is most readily apparent where evagelical zeal has been converted into strategic policies whose momentum has been sufficient to support the notion of 'bureaucratic offensives'.

One example is the practice of *zoning* parcels of land for specific uses, which stems directly from the strand of spatial determinism in the professional ideology. In essence, land-use planning, zoning and development control constitute police powers which have been designed to rationalize the urban system, maximizing efficiency and minimizing the incidence of public nuisances by separating each of the four major urban functions – commercial, industrial, residential and recreational. These powers have been acquired by planners in most countries and have been vigorously exercised by the 'getting things done' school of postwar planners. As a result, cities everywhere have become tidier: nonconforming land uses have been weeded out and order and stability imposed in their place. The benefits that this has brought, however, have been differentially distributed. Apart from the general reduction in the incidence of negative externalities arising from the juxtaposition of different land uses, the main benefits of land-use control have been enjoyed by the owners and developers of property. For the former, land-use regulations serve to secure and enhance the exchange value of property by reducing the uncertainty that new development nearby might be of the kind which would depress property values. For the latter, land-use regulations – especially the existence of an 'official map' of permissible land uses – serve to reduce the uncertainty involved in property investment.

As Rees and Lambert conclude in relation to the British system (1985: 78):

by far and away the most dramatic gains were made by those who had a substantial stake in the land and property markets. Those owners whose land was granted permission to develop reaped the reward of 'unearned increment'; although, of course, simply granting permission did not ensure actual development and the realization of the enhanced value. Equally, those with interests in the development process gained large profits, part of which derived from the context for development created by the planning system

On the other hand, the casualties of the planners' land-use 'offensive' have been the propertyless poor, the indigent, and inner-city residents in general. The excision of the traditional mixture of industry, warehousing and working-class residences in inner-city areas, for example, had hastened the decentralization of jobs, depriving inner-city neighbourhoods of their local employment base. The rigidity of land-use planning has also been criticized because of the consequent discouragement of imaginative development, the suppression of social interaction associated with uncontrolled 'organic' development, and the loss of the richness that is brought to urban living by the backstreet workshops, junk shops, embryo publishing firms, secondhand furniture shops, design studios and scrap metal merchants which are typical of inner-city neighbourhoods. The most regressive effects of land-use planning are associated with the American zoning system, in which qualitative standards as well as the broad category of land use may be stipulated. This has resulted in the use of zoning regulations as an instrument for reinforcing racial and class segregation (Danielson 1976). As we have seen (p. 265), many suburban municipalities stipulate large plot sizes or minimum floor space requirements to keep out low-income families as part of their strategy of fiscal mercantilism. But, while the motivation may be fiscal, the exclusionary effect is discriminatory in terms of race and social class, serving to impact low-income families, the elderly, large families, welfare families (particularly those with a female head of household) and racial minorities in the inner city (Harvey 1972). Contrasting the fortunes of different groups in relation to land-use planning, Constance Perin suggests that zoning practices are a straight reflection of the social order: 'a shorthand of the unstated rules governing what are widely regarded as correct social categories and relationships – that is, not only how land uses should be arranged but how land users, as social categories, are to be related to one another' (Perin 1977: 3). She also goes on to point out that the adoption of complex zoning legislation by so many conservative city councils in the United States could never have come about if zoning were not so advantageous to powerful property interests – a significant point in relation to the competing theories outlined above.

*Urban renewal* can be reckoned to have been the focus of the biggest 'offensive' ever launched by the planning profession. It is not surprising, therefore, that the objectives of urban renewal conform very closely with several of the major strands of professional ideology. The dislike of the 'impure' associated with environmentalism has its expression in the first phase of urban renewal – slum clearance. It is the abhorrence of slum conditions and their effects on people's well-being that has given urgency to slum clearance programmes, thereby justifying a certain amount of evangelical aggression on the part of planners as they attempt to sweep the housing problem away in one fell plan, for the benefit of everyone. The second phase of urban renewal – redevelopment – serves to satisfy several more ideological urges. The removal of deteriorating housing from highly desirable inner-city locations allows the land to be given over to a 'higher and better use' (Rothenberg 1967), thus helping to fulfil the imperatives of spatial determinism. And the concern with aesthetics and futurism finds expression in the redevelopment schemes themselves – architecturally adventurous, technologically advanced and visually and functionally integrated.

As with land-use planning, however, the benefits of urban renewal have been rather unevenly distributed. In excising the worst slums from city centres, urban renewal has undoubtedly contributed significantly to the 'common good' in terms of environmental quality and public health. But in rehousing the residents of clearance areas and replacing the built environment, planners have presided over some spectacular débâcles. The principal charge against them in this context is the dismantling of whole communities, scattering their members across the city in order to make room for luxury housing, office developments (including, in many instances, new accommodation for the urban bureaucracy), shopping areas, conference centres and libraries (Gans 1975). A secondary charge – urban blight – stems from the discrepancy between the ambitions of planners and what can actually be achieved within a reasonable future. During the intervening period, neighbourhoods scheduled for renewal are allowed to slide inexorably down a social and economic spiral. No landlord will repair a condemned house if he can help it; tenants who can afford it will move out; shopkeepers will close and drift away; and the city council, waiting for comprehensive redevelopment, will meanwhile defer any 'unnecessary' expenditure on maintenance. Schools, public buildings, roads and open space become rundown, matching the condition of the remaining population of the poor and the elderly (Daly 1982; Ravetz 1980). This dereliction has been extensive in many cities. Combined with the actual demolition of condemned property, the effect has been to empty large tracts of the inner city, turning its inhabitants into refugees. As Smith (1977) observes in relation to Liverpool, Lord Haw-Haw could never have envisaged, when making his dire predictions about the fate of the city in 1941, that the mantle of the Luftwaffe would be inherited by the city's own bureaucracy. Although this analogy is somewhat forced, it is not altogether misplaced. Large areas have been laid waste and thousands of families have been displaced. Moreover, the problem has been compounded since, as the worst parts of the cities' housing stock has been cleared, the bureaucratic offensive has gone on to condemn housing which is relatively sound, turning slum clearance from a beneficent if blunt instrument into a bureaucratic juggernaut. As Norman Dennis described in his book on *People and Planning*

(1970), the criteria for deciding which areas to include in second- and third-generation clearance schemes can be arbitrary, with the result that a substantial number of the houses scheduled for demolition are neither insanitary nor unsafe; and are consequently regarded by their inhabitants as providing a satisfactory environment.

These families have been the biggest losers in the crusade for urban renewal. By removing the structure of social and emotional support provided by the neighbourhood, and by forcing people to rebuild their lives separately amid strangers elsewhere, slum clearance has often imposed a serious psychological cost upon its supposed beneficiaries (Fried 1963). At the same time, relocatees typically face a steep increase in rents because of their forced move 'upmarket': the median rent of the families in Hartman's early study (1964) of Boston's West End rose by over 70 per cent. In Britain, most slum clearance families are rehoused in the public sector, but this also brings disadvantages which may outweigh the attractions of more modern accommodation at subsidized rents. Slum clearance families must face the vicissitudes of a housing bureaucracy whose scale and split responsibilities tend to make it insensitive to their needs (English, Madigan and Norman 1976). Since they are 'slum dwellers', the new accommodation which is offered to them is likely to be in low-status estates. Even the offer of accommodation in new maisonettes or high-rise apartments may compare unfavourably with the tried-and-tested environment of old inner-city neighbourhoods. The open spaces, pedestrian pathways and community centres regarded as major advantages by planners may seem of minor importance to their users; while some such 'amenities' serve only as focal points of vandalism, souring the whole social atmosphere. Moreover, because much new residential planning has been guided by the objective of fostering 'community' feelings, problems of a different nature can be precipitated by the lack of privacy on new estates. Apartments and maisonettes tend to be worst in this respect, since common stairways, lifts and deck access mean that interaction with uncongenial neighbours is unavoidable (Dennis

1970). On the other hand, the planned and regulated environment of new estates has little of the richness of opportunity associated with older neighbourhoods. As Gladstone puts it (1976: 22), 'The death of pigeon fancying is spelt by the death of a place to keep the pigeons.' Finally, it is worth noting that not everyone from clearance areas ends up being relocated in sound accommodation, let alone satisfactory or desirable housing. Hartman's study of rehousing in Boston, for example, found that over 25 per cent of families displaced from slum clearance areas were not properly rehoused. Furthermore, it transpires that renewal sometimes creates new slums (especially in North American cities where the public housing stock is so small) by pushing relocatees into areas and buildings which become overcrowded and therefore deteriorate rapidly. This has principally been the case with black families who, for both economic and racial reasons, have been forced to double up in other ghettos (Hartman 1964; Anderson 1964).

The chief beneficiaries of urban renewal, apart from the planners themselves (who get the kind of city they want to see) are the dominant political and economic élites of the city. The former benefit from the existence of a much more lucrative tax base with which to finance public services, as well as the feelings of civic pride generated by redevelopment schemes and the symbolization of power they represent. One particularly well-documented example of this is Newcastle upon Tyne, where a unique Victorian townscape, as well as the less appealing housing of the terraced streets off the Scotswood Road, has been replaced by a city centre which earned the leader of the council the title of 'man of the year' from the *Architect's Journal* and led the city's politicians proudly to boast of the city as the 'Brasilia of the North' (Davies 1972). The dominant business élite, meanwhile, benefits in much more tangible ways. In his book on *The Rape and Plunder of the Shankhill*, for example, Wiener (1976) has shown how the redevelopment of Belfast city centre has served to benefit monopoly capital by wiping out small retailers, thus giving the big stores and large supermarkets the market they require. But it is the speculative developers of property whose interests have been best served by urban renewal (Hartman and Kessler 1978). Obtaining sites which have been cleared at public expense, they have been encouraged by planners to develop them for 'higher' uses – offices, hotels, conference centres and shopping precincts. The planners' 'Reconquest of Paris', for example, has resulted in the replacement of deteriorating housing (but not the worst housing, which did not happen to occupy prime sites), public facilities and public open space with large-scale commercial installations and office blocks (Castells 1978). Such developments have been highly lucrative, and it is therefore not surprising to find that, in many cities, developers have 'worked' the planning system in order to secure ever greater profits (Ambrose and Colenutt 1975; Daly 1982; MacLaran, Malone and Beamish 1985; Sandercock 1976).

## Planning and social welfare: area-based positive discrimination

In recent years a concern with social welfare has emerged as an additional strand of planning ideology in response to the changing climate of opinion within society in general and within the social sciences in particular (Robson 1981; Diamond 1975; Healey and Underwood 1978). In terms of planning praxis, this concern has found expression in area-based policies of positive discrimination. Much of the impetus for this stems from the 'rediscovery' of poverty in the social sciences which was itself precipitated by the civil unrest of the 1960s (see p. 140). The existence of localized pockets of severe deprivation in large cities was recognized in a series of influential government reports in the latter part of the same decade. In the United States, these included the President's Committee on Juvenile Delinquency, the Report of the Advisory Commission on Civil Disorder, and the President's Committee on Urban Housing; and in Britain problems of urban deprivation were given prominence in publications such as

the Plowden Report (on primary education), the Milner Holland Report (on housing in London), and the Seebohm Report (on social welfare services). Area-based programmes of positive discrimination, whose antecedents can be traced to Ford Foundation demonstration projects in the 1950s (Eyles 1979), were introduced on a large scale soon afterwards in order to complement existing welfare policies which, it was believed, were failing to reach the most deprived. There developed, as Donnison (1974) pointed out, a three-pronged anti-poverty strategy in most Western countries, aimed at: (1) *structural* effects (with policies designed to provide cheaper and better education, health service, housing, etc.); (ii) effects related to the *lifetime cycle of incomes* (with the provision of family allowances, old age pensions, etc.); (iii) *area effects* whereby the spatial concentration of deprivation serves to compound and reinforce individual deprivations – the 'treatment' of which is undertaken through area-based positive discrimination. The latter is especially attractive to politicians and administrators, since it secures the major advantage of selective welfare systems (concentrating resources where they are most needed) whilst avoiding the major disadvantages (means testing and limited take-up). Furthermore, it also offers a means of staving off local unrest and discontent, combining maximum political effect with minimum public expenditure (Coates, Johnston and Knox 1977).

For these reasons, area-based policies of positive discrimination became widely adopted. Following the Ford Foundation initiatives, the War on Poverty declared by the Kennedy administration gave rise to Community Action Programs (Kramer 1969); these were subsequently supplemented by other area-based programmes in the form of Project Headstart (an educational programme) and the Model Cities Program (involving localized demonstration projects encompassing renewal, rehabilitation, health and educational facilities, and job opportunities). The ideas involved in these schemes did not take long to diffuse across the Atlantic, albeit in slightly modified form (Carley 1981; Edwards and Batley 1978). In Britain, several important programmes had been established by the mid-1970s, including the Educational Priority Area scheme (Halsey 1974), the General Improvement Area scheme (Roberts 1976), the Housing Action Area scheme (Kirby 1977), the Urban Programme, and the Community Development Project scheme (Edwards and Batley 1978; CDP 1974). These programmes, and others like them organized on an *ad hoc* basis by individual city planning departments, represented an important new agent of socio-spatial change. As such, they came to merit attention in their own right. Indeed, it was found that they were operating to the advantage of certain groups and to the disadvantage of others even within their 'target' areas (Bassett and Hauser 1975; Duncan 1974; Kilroy 1972).

But, as the 'offensive' of positive discrimination got under way, driven by planners' renewed concern over social welfare, doubts were being expressed in some quarters as to its real value in tackling urban deprivation. As we have seen (pp. 140–149), there are important methodological difficulties associated with the social indicators commonly used to identify target areas. In particular, there is widespread disagreement and confusion about the concept of multiple deprivation itself (Edwards 1975). This confusion is critical, in that the model or theory of deprivation held by policy-makers determines the way in which deprivation is viewed, the causes thought to

be operative, and the type of aid deemed most appropriate (Hamnett 1976). In fact, there are several explanations of deprivation, ranging from the concept of a 'culture of poverty' – which sees urban deprivation as pathological condition – to the theoretical formulations which interpret deprivation as a product of structural class conflict. Currently, there are five major themes within the social sciences; these are set out in Table 8.2.

The idea of a *culture of poverty* was first advanced by Oscar Lewis (1966) in the context of Mexico, but it has had a strong influence on the development of anti-poverty programmes in the more advanced economies on both sides of the Atlantic. Lewis himself described the culture of poverty as being both an adaption and a reaction of the poor to their marginal position in society, representing an effort to cope with the feelings of helplessness and despair which develop from the realization of the improbability of achieving success within a capitalist system. In short, it results in a vicious cycle of lack of opportunity and lack of aspiration. There is, however, considerable room for debate as to whether culture is more of an effect than a cause of poverty and, indeed, whether the values, aspirations and cultural attributes of the poor in Western cities really are significantly different from those of the rest of society.

The idea of *transmitted deprivation* has also been influential in policy-making circles,

**Table 8.2** Differing explanations of urban deprivation

| Theoretical model | Explanation | Location of the problems |
|---|---|---|
| 1. Culture of poverty | Problems arising from the internal pathology of deviant groups | Internal dynamics of deviant behaviour |
| 2. Transmitted deprivation (cycle of deprivation) | Problems arising from individual psychological handicaps and inadequacies transmitted from one generation to the next | Relationships between individuals, families and groups |
| 3. Institutional malfunctioning | Problems arising from failures of planning, management or administration | Relationship between the 'disadvantaged' and the bureaucracy |
| 4. Maldistribution of resources and opportunities | Problems arising from an inequitable distribution of resources | Relationship between the underprivileged and the formal political machine |
| 5. Structural class conflict | Problems arising from the divisions necessary to maintain an economic system based on private profit | Relationship between the working class and the political and economic structure |

*Source: Community Development Project 1975.*

having been adopted, for example, by Sir Keith Joseph when he was Britain's Secretary of State for Health and Social Security during 1972–3. It is really concerned with explaining why, despite long periods of full employment and the introduction of improved welfare services, problems of deprivation persist. According to this model, the answer lies in a cyclical process of transmission of social maladjustment from one generation to another. Thus, while it is acknowledged that low wages, poor housing and lack of opportunity are important factors, the emphasis is on the inadequacies of the home background and the upbringing of children (Bowlby 1965; Rutter and Madge 1976).

The three other models outlined in Table 8.2 all take a wider perspective, and each can be related to theoretical stances discussed earlier in this chapter. The idea of *institutional malfunctioning* shares some common ground with the managerialist school of thought, since the behaviour of bureaucrats is given a central role in explaining the persistence of deprivation. Here, however, it is not so much the 'gatekeeping' role of bureaucrats which is emphasized as the administrative structure within which they work. Thus, it is argued, the formulation of public policy in separate departments concerned with housing, education, welfare, planning and so on is inevitably ineffective in dealing with the interlocking problems of deprivation. Moreover, such organizational structures are vulnerable to inter-departmental rivalries and power struggles which can only reduce their overall effectiveness.

The idea of a *maldistribution of opportunities and resources* can be accommodated within pluralist political theory, with deprivation being seen as the result of failures of participation and representation of certain interests in the political process (Eyles 1978). Finally, the model based on *structural class conflict* clearly stems from Marxist theory, in which problems of deprivation are seen as an inevitable result of the overall economic order (Bor 1973; Miliband 1974).

While they are not mutually exclusive, these five models of deprivation do tend to point towards very different solutions. Those subscribing to the 'culture of poverty' model, for example, tend to regard expenditure on housing, slum clearance, income maintenance and so on as superfluous, advocating instead a concentration of resources on social education (Banfield 1974). Adherents to the idea of transmitted deprivation, although accepting the necessity for a broad range of anti-poverty programmes, emphasize the importance of the provision of facilities and services such as playgrounds and health visitors which help parents in the upbringing of children; while the solution to institutional malfunctioning is seen in terms of corporate management. Policies of positive discrimination are favoured mostly by those who see deprivation as the result of a maldistribution of resources and opportunities, whereas they make little sense at all in terms of the 'structural class conflict' model.

Interestingly, this last view came to be supported by those involved in the British Community Development Project initiative, which was established with the objective of tackling localized pockets of deprivation through 'action teams' and 'research teams' whose job was to co-ordinate personal social services in the field and mobilize self-help and mutual aid in the community. This kind of involvement, however, led the teams to conclude that

The problems of the 12 CDP areas are not reducible to problems of employment, housing, income and education. They are not isolated pockets suffering an unfortunate combination of circumstances. They are a central part of the dynamics of the urban system and as such represent those who have lost out in the competition for jobs, housing and educational opportunity . . . The problems in these areas are not going to be solved by marginal re-arrangements to take account of their special minority needs' (CDP 1974: 52).

This view, of course, made the original role of the project teams somewhat superfluous, and eventually the Home Office, embarassed by the teams' activities, phased the whole programme out.

The CDP teams are not alone in doubting the utility of area-based programmes, however. There is a growing feeling amongst geographers (if not planners) that it is not possible to abstract the problems of particular areas from the wider societal context. Thus Lawless (1979), Lee (1976), Hamnett (1979a) and others have criticized the 'fetishism of space', whereby relations between social groups are viewed as relations between areas, and spatial causes are inferred from spatial manifestations. In addition, area-based projects have been criticized on the grounds that they are the product of a covert system of discretionary bureaucracy – with social indicators being used as 'vindicators' for planners' preferred policies (Brand 1975; Dennis 1978); and that they are merely cosmetic, serving only to 'gild the ghetto' and 'paper over the cracks' without touching the underlying causes of deprivation (Higgins *et al*. 1983; Loney 1983). Meanwhile, uncertainty as to the proportion of deprived households covered by area-based policies has further eroded confidence in such policies (MacLaran 1981; Taylor 1980); though research using micro-data from the British census suggests that *most* deprived households *are* localized in cities' worst-off neighbourhoods, though not overwhelmingly so (Knox 1986a).

## Planning, public participation and urban social movements

Given the generally regressive nature of much urban planning and the incidence of unforeseen and unfortunate side effects, it is not surprising to find one commentator observing that 'the contemporary city is cast from a split mould of which one side is avarice and the other systems analysis. Human values appear to have little or no influence . . .' (Smith 1977: 12). Nevertheless some attempts have been made to incorporate the values of the 'man in the street' within the planning process. Indeed, the idea of 'citizen participation' in planning can be traced back to the early 1960s: the Ford Foundation projects in the US laid considerable emphasis on the idea of local citizen involvement, and the idea of public participation was written into the Community Action Program section of the 1964 Economic Opportunity Act and the Model Cities Program section of the 1966 Demonstration Cities and Metropolitan Development Act. In Britain, public participation was introduced on the recommendation of the Skeffington Report (1969), and planning authorities now have a statutory obligation to ascertain public reaction to major planning proposals before proceeding with them. In Scotland, an additional framework for public participation has been set up in the form of Community Councils – neighbourhood-based 'consumer panels' intended to ascertain, co-ordinate and express the views of residents to relevant public bodies (SDD 1974).

The official rationale for the introduction of public participation is that it is a mechanism for transferring power from government and the bureaucracy to the people. At the same time, it is suggested, the planning profession will benefit from an increased flow of information, thus making for more rational decision-making. It is also possible to argue, however, that the formal recognition of participation merely helps to legitimize the activity of planners, reinforcing the myth of a civic democracy while in reality providing the means by which the public can be 'managed' more effectively. Whatever the theoretical standpoint on this issue, it is now clear that public participation has not really been successful in accommodating the values and priorities of the public within the planning process. Although people seem keen on the idea of 'having a say', they do not seem so keen on getting up and saying it. Levels of turnout for the election of neighbourhood representatives for the Community Action Programs in the US for example, were desperately low: only 4.2 per cent in Boston, and 0.7 per cent in Los Angeles (Rubin 1967). In Britain also the 'silent majority' has remained silent even after having been assailed by expensive displays, broadsheets, newspapers (in 'popular' tabloid format), comic strips and door-to-door interviewing. A national survey of over 1,600 adults in 1974 found 70 per cent knew nothing about participation in planning. Only 7 per cent had been to public meetings, 9 per cent to exhibitions, 3 per cent had completed questionnaires and 1 per cent had been interviewed by planning officials (Jones and Eyles 1977). Moreover, the socio-economic composition of those who do become involved in participation exercises suggests that any influence that might be brought to bear on the decision-making process is likely to favour the interests of the propertied middle classes. Professionals, businessmen and owner-occupiers are nearly always over-represented, partly because they are better able to operate within the legal and adminis-trative framework that exists for participation, and partly because working-class people are simply reluctant to join in this form of social activity (Redburn *et al.* 1980; Stringer and Taylor 1974). It has also been suggested that certain sections of the community lack the economic resources to sustain an effective contribution to participatory programmes; that some local political cultures are unrecep-tive to group activity of any kind; and that the effectiveness of middle-class amenity groups tends to deter the emergence of other groups with different social compositions. The net effect of all this, of course, is to 'accentuate existing disparities between the favoured environments of the powerful and wealthy and the degraded environments of the deprived' (Lowe 1977: 35).

For their part, planners have been less than wholehearted in their commitment to partici-pation exercises. Although such exercises have now become a conventional part of the planning process, they are often regarded as a way of educating the public into the plan-ners' ways of thinking and not vice versa. As one British chief officer said in an interview, the objective is 'to tell the people what you are going to do . . . so as to carry them along with you' (Batley 1972: 107). The assumption, therefore, is that plans would be well advanced before being exposed to public comment. Verba (1961: 220) described this concept of participation as referring 'not to a technique of decision but to a technique of persuasion'; and it is not difficult to find examples where the limits of debate are set by planners before 'participation' begins by the simple strategy of restricting consideration to clearcut alternatives (Stringer *et al.* 1980. In this context, participation merely serves to

legitimize the planners' own ideas. Thus Peter Hall, reviewing the West Central Scotland Plan, wrote that it was 'an élitist plan, in which a perfunctory consultation exercise is used to support professional prejudice wher-ever convenient' (Hall 1975: 344). The reasons for planners' reluctance to enter into the spirit of participation are twofold. First, there exists within every bureaucracy an imperative not to waste resources of time, money and manpower, which results in a tendency to (i) consider a minimum number of alternatives, (ii) favour those strategies prepared in advance and 'ready to go', and (iii) restrict participation to as small a number of actors as possible (Downs 1964). Second, many planners believe that participation is an extravagance of democracy which undervalues their professional expertise. England (1973), for example, suggests that basing planning decisions on public opinion would be like a blindfolded man 'picking his football pool selection with a pin'. Others, such as Powell (1973), argue that the preference of different groups will cancel each other out or, at best, produce only a broad and indecisive picture which can only be resolved by the planner's expertise.

The complacent vanity of these sentiments fits well with Davies's (1972) image of the evangelistic bureaucrat, while the perfunctory nature of some participation exercises lends support to Scott Greer's description of plan-ning as 'sympathetic magic and public ritual' (Greer 1971: 261). Moreover, the idea of participation itself has been criticized on a number of grounds. Apart from the bias towards middle-class interests which results from their over-representation and the bias towards planners' predilections ensured by the restriction of discussion, the main charge is that participation programmes simply serve to co-opt and disarm opposition to the ruling élite. In relation to citizen involvement in the United States Community Action Program, for example, it has been suggested that the result has been to skim off the local leadership of deprived communities, to divert 'trouble-makers', and to encourage compromise and conciliation in return for minimal concessions (Coit 1978). Similarly, the role of the Scottish and Italian community council systems have been questioned on the grounds of their potential as a locus for a small community élite, as an intelligence system for more effective evangelism, bureaucratic aggression and obstruction, and as part of the planners' ideology of localism, in which the place-oriented organization of society helps to maintain an inegalitarian social structure (Dente and Regonini 1980; Knox 1978a). 'In this context, community councils would be seen as internal survival mechanisms of local government, helping an élite oligarchy to preserve power by internalizing opposing forces (such as action groups, squatters and tenants' associations) which would otherwise exist outside orthodox political structures and therefore pose a volatile, less manageable and more dangerous threat to the *status quo*' (Knox 1978a: 391).

### Advocacy planning, bureaucratic guerrillas and urban social movements

One of the intrinsic weaknesses of the idea of citizen involvement in the planning process is that the very groups who are most disadvantaged by the traditional system find themselves least able to communicate with people who insist on speaking the language of statistics, diagrams, maps and computers. An awareness of this situation, together with a recognition of the regressive effects of planning in general has prompted the introduction of *advocacy planning*: the use of experts by neighbourhood organizations and special interest groups to articulate their needs and make their case in the technical language of professional planners (Davidoff 1965: Peattie 1968). In practice, two kinds of advocacy planning emerged. One is where experts are retained by individual groups to prepare plans for them and to argue for their adoption much as a lawyer pleads for his client. The other is where a 'clientless' professional activates a group because he or she feels that an important community issue is not being properly dealt with (Kasperson and Breitbart 1974). Both kinds rely on individuals whose ideology is very different from that of the mainstream, 'traditional' planners. In particular, they question the objectivity of many evalu-

ative planning techniques, reject the idea that the existing political system can accommodate all the conflicting interest groups which exist in the city, and deny the planner's role as a neutral mediator.

A good deal of advocacy planning focused on specific issues involving urban renewal schemes and plans for the construction of motorways through low-income neighbourhoods (Blecher 1971; Corey 1972), although there have also been attempts to broaden the scope of advocacy activities. These include the work of the Suburban Action Institute in New York (Davidoff, Davidoff and Gold 1970) and the Detroit Geographical Expedition. The latter, under the leadership of William Bunge in the late 1960s and early 1970s, attempted to train 'folk geographers' from local black and poor-white communities to control their own research and come up with their own planning proposals as part of a broad attempt to expand the power base of such communities (Bunge 1971; Colenutt 1971). In general, however, advocacy planning achieved only limited success. While it can be seen to have been reasonably effective in blocking the implementation of official plans it has not been particularly successful in winning acceptance for alternative proposals drawn from community groups. This has brought about a certain amount of disillusionment with advocacy. Goodman, for example, having been a supporter of advocacy as a means of ensuring that the inarticulate poor obtain their legal, welfare and planning rights, soon came to feel that it simply promulgates the myth that only professional knowledge can solve the problems of the poor (Goodman 1972). Such feelings led some to abandon the role of advocate in favour of that of the *bureaucratic guerrilla*, working covertly in the interests of deprived communities whilst in the employment of the city bureaucracy. One example of such activity given by Hartnett (1975) is of a local authority employee in London who was sympathetic to the aims of the Southwark Family Squatting Association, which had been protesting against the policy of Southwark Borough Council of acquiring property for redevelopment and keeping it vacant for periods of up to five years prior to demolition, all in the context of an acute local shortage of housing. The borough refused to negotiate with the Squatting Association and adopted the policy of gutting most of its short-life housing, blocking drains and sewers and pulling up floorboards. In addition, public statements systematically understated the number of council-owned properties that were kept empty. The 'bureaucratic guerrilla', feeling that these policies were aggravating the housing crisis, supplied information to the squatters on the number and location of suitable empty properties acquired by the borough. After an unsuccessful witch-hunt the borough, finding its position undermined, signed an agreement with the Squatting Association whereby the Association would rehabilitate, with volunteer labour, properties the borough considered uneconomic to let.

As with advocacy planning, however, the achievements of bureaucratic guerrillas have been modest. Quite simply, it is difficult to work effectively within the system when the cause of the problem is often the system itself. Furthermore, crisis of both advocacy planning and the idea of guerrilla tactics have stressed the limitations of their 'fire-fighting' role in reacting to issues raised by official policy. This, it is argued, has limited change to palliative adjustments within the existing social, economic and political system, at the same time serving to divert the poor from more effective forms of gaining power. A second general criticism concerns the lack of involvement of the disadvantaged themselves in deciding upon the strategies with which to counter the policies of the bureaucracy, thereby placing the advocate planner/guerrilla in a position of undue power and leaving powerless communities just as vulnerable to manipulation after their departure as they had been originally. This leads, in turn, to a third criticism: the danger of group opinion being moulded to fit the advocate's own conception of what the community's desires should be (Kasperson and Breitbart 1974; Marris and Rein 1973).

These criticisms inevitably raise the question of whether it is possible for disadvantaged groups to achieve greater power in the modern city and, if so, how. Piven and Cloward (1977), reviewing the activities of 'poor people's movements', observe that most attempts to achieve greater power are based on the conviction that formal organization is the key to success. This conviction, they suggest, is based on the assumption that formal organization facilitates the co-ordination of the economic and political resources of large numbers of people who separately have few such resources. Formal organization also permits the strategic use of these resources in political conflict and helps to ensure the continuity of lower-class mobilization over time. Their conclusion, however, is that this concern for organization serves only to blunt and curb the disruptive force which lower-class communities are sometimes able to mobilize, and that 'leaders and organizers of the lower classes act in the end to facilitate the efforts of the élite to channel the insurgent masses into normal politics, believing all the while that they are taking the long and arduous but certain road to power' (Piven and Cloward 1977: 12). In contrast, Castells (1983a) regards organization as crucial to the success of urban social movements; although he does not regard it as sufficient in itself. According to Castells, the vital rupture to the political status quo will result from crises in the provision of the means of collective consumption, whose effects will injure the middle as well as working classes. Thus, it is argued, the middle class needs hospitals, uses public transport (especially commuter rail links), sends its children to state schools, and so on just as the working class does; and conflict over the provision of such facilities provides the opportunity for a new kind of class struggle, with urban social movements being based on a broad alliance of anti-capitalistic classes rather than on the proletariat alone. The significance of such movements is therefore twofold: they open up new fronts in the class struggle as well as creating new alliances.

Supporters of this argument found encouragement in a series of events during the 1970s in continental Europe. In Paris, lower-class groups have mobilized against evictions and the commercial redevelopment of their neighbourhoods (Olives 1976; Castells 1977); in

Copenhagen, citizens have organized to force the city authorities to increase facilities and initiate improvements (Gamst-Nielsen 1974); in Amsterdam, a spate of social movements centred on housing issues (Andereisen 1981; Draaisma and Hoogstraten 1983; Priemus 1983); and in the major industrial cities of Italy there has been widespread occupation of newly built public housing as well as the 'autoreduction' of public utility rates by users – that is, the refusal to pay more than a proportion of the price of public transport, telephones, rents, etc. (Coit 1978; Marcelloni 1979).

Relatively little research has been undertaken on the emergence of urban social movements in Britain, North America or Australasia, although Castells's ideas have found a receptive audience in many quarters (Gendrot 1982). Nevertheless, there are several reasons for doubting the relevance of his analysis to the situation within cities of the English-speaking world. The evidence to hand for these cities suggests that most urban struggles, including squatting movements, rent strikes and campaigns against disruptive planning proposals, are generally sporadic and isolated both from each other and the working-class movement. Indeed, the most successful struggles have usually been those of the middle class, which have resulted in a redistribution of resources away from more disadvantaged areas. Moreover, even the momentum of social movements in continental European cities has not been sustained into the 1980s, and it has proved difficult to establish whether they really do represent the prospect of a significant dimension of urban change (Cox 1984; Pickvance 1985).

# 9 Change in the late 20th-century city

In previous chapters we have examined systematically the various dimensions of the social geography of modern Western cities and we have explored the major processes that have contributed – and are contributing – to these patterns. In this chapter, we shall outline the implications of the intersection of economic, technological, demographic, cultural and political trends for urban change in the late twentieth century; and speculate a little on the likely nature of urban development and restructuring in the first decade or two of the twenty-first century. One reason for pursuing this theme is that it draws together in a dynamic context many of the ideas discussed in earlier chapters, thus providing a convenient note of synthesis on which to conclude our review of urban social geography. Another, more important, reason is that it is clear that Western societies have recently entered a new phase – or, at least, begun a distinctive transitional phase – with important implications for the trajectory of urbanization and the nature of urban development. This new phase has its roots in the dynamics of capitalism and, in particular, the increasing internationalization of the capitalist economy, the increasing dominance of big conglomerate corporations, and the steady shift within the world's core economies away from manufacturing industries towards service activities – hence the labels 'advanced capitalism', 'corporate capitalism', 'monopoly capitalism' and 'late capitalism'. Yet, as this fundamental economic transition has been gathering momentum, other shifts – in technology, in demographic composition, and in cultural and political life

– have also begun to crystalize. In many ways, the catalyst for this crystallization was the economic system-shock precipitated by the dramatic increase in energy prices in the early 1970s – hence the label 'post affluent' (Gappert 1979). According to Gappert, the transition to post-affluent societies is characterized by:

1. The overarching demographic influence of the 'baby boomers': the product of the postwar population bulge that has now begun to crowd housing and labour markets.
2. The economic polarization of society.
3. Uncertainty and indecision within major economic and political institutions.
4. The emergence and recognition of a 'post-affluent consciousness' in which expectations – particularly those of the middle classes – have been much reduced.
5. Changing relationships within – and between – workplaces and households.
6. The gradual development of synergistic lifestyles within an increasingly 'androgynous' culture (i.e. a culture that does not discriminate against women).

Because they are deep-rooted and often mutually reinforcing, these (and other) elements of change are not likely to disappear within the next 10 or 15 years which take us into the twenty-first century. The immediate future is thus likely to look significantly different from the immediate past. The ques-

**Fig. 9.1** Perspectives on societal futures. *Source*: Gappert (1982), Fig. 1.1, p. 18.

tion is, how will it be different? Gappert himself, following Ouichi (1981), postulates three possible scenarios (Fig. 9.1). The first, 'System X', is based on the assumption that issues of economic productivity and efficiency will lead to both fiercer competition and greater disappointment unless the economic vitality of the core economies improve. In this perspective, we should anticipate increased outbreaks of social conflict. The second, 'System Y', is based on the assumption that although economic growth rates may decline, the underlying strength of the core economies relative to those of the less developed world will ensure high overall levels of prosperity, even though individual gains may take longer to achieve. In this scenario, people's pursuit of purely economic objectives will tend to be postponed, deflected or sublimated by activities associated with quality-of-life concerns. It will be evident that substantial elements of both of these scenarios already exist as part of the constrained, post-affluent economy. Support can also be found for the third scenario, 'System Z', though it is much less well developed and represents a longer-term prospect as the template for socio-economic change. The assumption of this scenario is that a new kind of industrial progress will emerge, based on new technologies that are knowledge-intensive, resource-conserving and environmentally benign.

With such divergent scenarios (and there are still more in the futures literature), the question of how cities will be affected by the socio-economic changes of the post-affluent era seems to be wide open. The danger here is that it can be easy to get carried away with exotic visions of the urban future. Dickey (1985), for example, envisages a future urban society that is much more attuned to self-gratification, sensualism and sensationalism, with suburbs containing 'erotic zones' of entertainment and recreation catering to these 'higher-order' needs. Others have predicted the rapid demise of cities in their present form in response to new communications technologies that will be central to the increasingly dominant service sector of Western economies. In their place, it is suggested, there will be highly dispersed 'virtual cities' at regional, national and international scales: 'wired cities' in which people live, work and shop in 'electronic cottages' (Abler 1975; Lehman-Wilzig 1981; Toffler 1981). We should be cautious of this kind of futurism in which grains of truth are expanded and elaborated to the point where little else can be seen. The idea of the decentralized, 'wired' city, for example, involves several fundamental assumptions, none of which are realistic. First is the idea that isolated living with good communications will satisfy most people; second is the idea that the information (or disinformation or misinformation) transmitted by new telecommunications technologies will be adequate to sustain most people's work or leisure needs; third is the idea that the quality, discipline and availability of labour resource could be maintained by remote control; fourth is the idea that the energy and materials required to maintain the 'wired city' would not be too costly (not to mention the costs of junking the capital investments that are tied up in the bricks and mortar of existing cities); and finally there is the idea that most people have no reason for being in traditional urban settings other than those associated with their efficiency as workers (Gottman 1977, 1983). It follows that evaluations of urban change in the post-affluent era must be undertaken against the background of a broad review of economic, technological, demographic, cultural and political trends.

## Economic change

Since the 1960s, the world's core economies have entered a substantially different phase in terms of *what* they produce, *how* they produce it, and *where* they produce it.

In terms of *what* they produce, the dominant trend has been a shift away from agriculture and manufacturing industries towards service activities. This sectoral shift stems from the cumulative interaction of several processes. One of the origins of the expanded role of the service sector can be traced to the specialization inherent to industrialization, the result of which was not only to stimulate trade but also to generate new opportunities for employment and investment in trade-related services – transportation, communications, utilities, and wholesaling (distribution services) – and services which enable firms to maintain their specialized roles: marketing, advertising, administration, finance and insurance (producer services). On the other hand, the increased productivity of agriculture and manufacturing which resulted from mechanization, automation and improved business organization has meant that fewer people are required to produce a given amount of goods. Meanwhile, the market for some basic goods and commodities has become saturated, leaving consumers free to spend a larger proportion of their incomes on various personal services (consumer services). Market saturation in the manufacturing sector has also encouraged firms to seek ways of making existing products

more cheaply or, better still, of developing new products to market, thus creating another kind of producer service: scientific research and development (R & D). Finally, a large number of jobs has been created in the public sector as central and local governments have expanded their range of activities and responsibilities in response to the increasing complexity of economic and social organization.

Thus it emerges that in the US, for example, the manufacturing sector accounted for less than one quarter of all employment in 1980, compared with almost one third in 1947. The service sector increased its share of total employment by about 12 per cent over the same period. In Britain, the service sector had come to account for nearly 65 per cent of all employment by the mid-1980s; and with almost one third of all jobs in the manufacturing sector actually involving clerical, technical or administrative work, this meant that four out of every five workers were effectively in service jobs (Marshall 1985). There have been, however, substantial differences in the performance of different *types* of services. Contrary to the popular view of retail and consumer services as a driving force in advanced economies, they have not in fact grown very rapidly. Rather, it has been producer services, public sector services and non-profit services (mainly higher education and certain aspects of health care) that have contributed most to the expansion in service-sector employment.

In terms of *how* production is organized, the major trend has been towards oligopoly as larger and more efficient corporations have driven out their competitors and sought to diversify their activities. In the US there were over 3,000 mergers per annum at the peak in the late 1960s. As a result, the 50 largest companies increased their share of the total value added in manufacturing from 17 per cent to 24 per cent in the 30 years to 1977; and the largest 200 increased their share from 30 per cent to 44 per cent. Within the service sector, the control of retailing and producer services has become particularly concentrated and centralized.

In terms of *where* production takes place, the major trend has been a redeployment of activity at metropolitan, national and international scales – largely in response to the restructuring of the big conglomerates. As the big new conglomerates have evolved, they have rationalized their operations in a variety of ways, eliminating the duplication of activities between operations in different regions and nations, moving routine production and assembly operations to regions with lower labour costs, moving 'back office' operations to suburbs with lower rents and taxes, and consolidating head-office functions and R & D laboratories in key settings. As a result, a complex and contradictory set of processes has begun to recast many of the world's economic landscapes. One of the major outcomes in relation to urban social geography has been the *deindustrialization* of many of the cities and urban regions of the industrial heartlands in Europe and North America. Another has been the accelerated *decentralization* of both manufacturing and service employment within metropolitan regions. And a third has been the transformation of a few of the largest cities into 'global cities' specializing in the production, processing and trading of specialized information and intelligence.

### Crisis and restructuring

While these structural transformations were taking place, the international economic system experienced a prolonged crisis during the decade 1973–82. This crisis was the result of the conjunction of several factors: slowed economic growth, rising inflation, increased international monetary instability, suddenly increased energy prices, increased international competition, a resurgence of political volatility, and intensified problems of indebtedness among less developed nations (Castells 1980; Hamilton 1984). According to Carnoy and Castells (1984), the advanced (or post-affluent) capitalist economies are emerging from this crisis by means of setting up a new model of economic accumulation, social organization and political legitimation. Under this new scheme of things, new relationships between capital and labour are being forged, with capital recapturing the initiative over wages and regulations. New roles for the public sector are also being forged, not merely in reducing levels of government intervention and support but also in shifting the emphasis from collective consumption to capital accumulation and from legitimation to domination. The new international, regional and metropolitan division of labour resulting from sectoral shifts and corporate reorganization is central to these processes: the variable geometry of capital, labour, production, markets and management allowing new relationships to be established.

Quite clearly, changes this fundamental are likely to precipitate major changes in the social geography of every city, affecting everything from class structure and community organization to urban service delivery and the structure of urban politics. Meanwhile, economic crisis and transition has already produced some important changes in the composition of urban labour markets. One obvious outcome has been the massive increase in unemployment. In Western Europe, unemployment rose from a level of three million in 1971 (when one of the major concerns of an International Labour Office report was the increasing difficulty of filling unpopular jobs), to more than ten million at the end of 1981, with unemployment in the UK alone standing at over three million. In the US, unemployment rose from just over four million in 1970 to over 10.7 million in 1983, with 40 per cent of this number consisting of the long-term unemployed. Another important outcome has been that the shift away from manufacturing has resulted in a substantial decrease in blue-collar employment and a commensurate increase in white-collar employment. Moreover, it seems that white-collar employment itself has been increasingly dichotomized between professional and managerial jobs on the one hand and routine clerical jobs on the other (Noyelle 1983). Within the manufacturing sector, meanwhile, advances in technology and automation have begun to polarize employment opportunities between those for engineers/technicians and those for unskilled/semi-skilled operatives. Within the service sector, retailing and consumer services have come to be dominated by part-time jobs and 'secondary' jobs (jobs in small firms or in the small shops or offices of large firms, where few skills are required, levels of pay are low, and there is little opportunity for advancement: Gordon 1979). Government services, on the other hand, tend to have increased the pool of 'primary' jobs (jobs with higher levels of pay and security).

The aggregate effect of all these changes, according to some observers, is a tendency towards the erosion of the intermediate segment of the labour market, with increased numbers of higher-qualified and higher-paid employees on the one hand and of employees in 'secondary' jobs on the other (Edwards, Reich and Gordon 1975; Stanback and Noyelle 1982). The evidence on earnings seems to support this, though it should be borne in mind that the data also reflect changes in inflation and the age- and sex-structure of the available labour force at different times (Sternlieb and Hughes 1984). Between 1960 and 1975, 54 per cent of the jobs created in the US were in the lower-earning (<80 per cent of the average for all workers) segment and 35 per cent were in the upper-earning (>120 per cent of the average) segment. As a result, the proportion of low-paid workers rose from 32 to 38 per cent of the workforce, the proportion of high-paid workers rose from 32 to 34 per cent, while the intermediate earnings segment fell from 36 to 28 per cent.

One important consequence of these changes, from our point of view, is that the idea of a 'living wage' can no longer be taken for granted. In other words, a growing proportion of both working- and middle-class families find it increasingly difficult to achieve what they regard as an acceptable level of living on only one income (Bird 1979; Blumberg 1980). One response to this has been the expansion of the two-paycheck household; another has been the growth and sophistication of the 'black' or informal economy; which in turn has begun to create new kinds of household organization, new divisions of domestic and urban space, and new forms of communal relations (Pahl 1981).

Finally, it is important to bear in mind that many of the changes emanating from economic transformation are taking place simul-taneously within most large cities. Thus we see, side by side, the growth of advanced corporate services and the development of sweatshops operated by undocumented workers, the emergence of newly-affluent groups of manager-technocrats and the marginalization of newly disadvantaged groups. As a result, the emerging geography of larger cities is complex. It is creating distinct new social spheres, yet it has to link these spheres within the same functional unit. As Castells puts it:

This trend is different from the old phenomenon of social inequality and spatial segregation in the big city. There is something else than the distinction between rich and poor or white and non-white. It is the formation of different systems of production and social organization, which are equally dynamic and equally new, yet profoundly different in the wealth, power and prestige that they accumulate . . . Yet these different worlds (the high tech world, the advanced services world, the auxiliary services world, the various immigrant worlds, the traditional black ghettoes, the protected middle-class suburbs, etc.) develop along separate lines in terms of their own dynamics, while still contributing altogether to the complex picture of the new supercity. The new labor market is at the basis of this newly polarized sociospatial structure. We witness the rise of dualized supercities that segregate internally their activities, social groups and cultures while reconnecting them in terms of their structural interdependency. These metropolises are magnets on a world level, attracting people, capital, minds, information, materials and energy while keeping separate the channels of operation for all these elements in the actual fabric of the metropolis. . . . We are witnessing the rise of urban schizophrenia. Or, in other words, the contradictory coexistence of different social, cultural and economic logics within the same spatial structure (1985: 24).

## Technological change

Intimately related to these economic changes and to their implications for urban and regional reorganization are the technological advances that are transforming our ways of producing, consuming, interacting, living and dying. According to many observers, the advanced economies of the world are on the threshold of a major upswing – the fifth Kondratieff cycle – which will be led by the widespread commercial development of new technologies that emerged during the 1970s and early 1980s: the downswing phase of the previous cycle. These include high-speed computing, advanced telecommunications, software synthesis, robotics, biotechnology and new energy-related technologies such as heat pumps and solar energy systems. In addition, we must recognize the impact of improvements to existing technologies: computerized business systems, wide-bodied cargo jets, high-speed urban transit systems, and the like; and the impact of technological responses to the increased awareness of the finiteness of energy resources and to the sharp rise in energy costs: smaller, more efficient automobiles and new forms and standards of residential design, for example (Burchell and Listokin 1982).

As with each previous technological era, the locational logic of the cluster of these leading technologies is different from their predecessors, so that only some cities and some urban settings will experience directly the economic benefits of their development; the experience of others, meanwhile, will be dominated by the consequences of the relative decline of superseded technologies. A major characteristic of contemporary economic and technological change is locational freedom. Developments in office automation, data transmission, on-line information services, electronic funds transfer systems, 'teleshopping' and telecommunications generally offer the possibility for a generalized decentralization of both workplace and home (Table 9.1): hence the widely accepted prospect of metropolitan decentralization and various scenarios for the 'paperless office', the 'wired city', the 'transactional city' and the 'virtual city' (Coates 1982; Kellerman 1984; Stern 1983). Nevertheless, the increasing footlooseness of more and more activities is not likely to result, as some have suggested (Nicol 1983), in the disappearance of the spatial dimension of economic and social organization. Rather, it seems likely that the internal logic of economic, social and political organizations will tend to overlay the logic of factors associated with specific places. We will still be confronted by spatial differentiation, but it will increasingly be a space of *flows*. In other words, a hierarchy of functions will structure metro-

**Table 9.1** Potential impacts of new technologies on urban form

| Telematics devices and systems | Probable impacts (1980–2001) |
| --- | --- |
| Microcomputers; Large-scale integrated circuits; New memory systems; solid state laser, bubble, backend processes; Morpheme generator | Movement away from centralized office space to suburban locations, homes and small work sites. Home work-study centre and around-the-clock focus of the household used for entertainment and socialising with the outside world. |
| **Software and significant systems** Information utilities – The Source, Lockheed, Prestel Teletext Videotext Pattern recognition – voice, signature Encryption | Large cohorts of population in voice-to-voice, face-to-face, or data communication at any place at any time. Decentralization of offices, work-at-home, electronic cottages. Estimate that, by 2000, the average household will have an investment in telematics roughly equivalent to its present investment in the automobile. Greater public participation and influence in the actions taken by governments. Computer-console shopping for durable goods. Rush-hour (peak commuting) a thing of the past as many work routines are integrated with work-at-home and flextime schedules. |

*Source:* Pressman (1985), pp. 352–3

politan, national and international space, separating units of production, distribution and management in order to locate each one in the most favourable setting, yet articulating all of them through a communications network (Webber 1980). But with constant changes in communications technology and organizational logic, and with a multiplicity of large-scale organizations, the role and meaning of individual places is then likely to be redefined constantly (Castells 1985).

It should also be emphasized that the acceleration of decentralization at the metropolitan scale is likely to be selective. Employment in financial services provides a good example. Most jobs in insurance are likely to decentralize to the metropolitan periphery because the daily decisions in the insurance business are very largely dependent on documents (or electronically-filed information). On the other hand, only some banking jobs are likely to decentralize because many of its important transactions depend on the kind of trust and quick responses that can only be derived from face-to-face interaction (Meier 1985). Moreover, the continued expansion of commerce and retailing in the suburbs need not spell the end of the central business district so much as its modification, with the headquarters of major transactional companies, together with broadcasting, publishing, tourism and convention-related activities expanding as some of the 'traditional' CBD activities move out.

What is less well recognized is that some of the new technologies will also bring new opportunities for urban 'gatekeeping' and new conflicts over collective consumption. Telecommunications technology, for example, has traditionally been treated as a 'natural monopoly', because of the fact that equipment and software has to be compatible across large areas. But the volatility resulting from rapid technological change has prompted some governments (notably those of the UK and the US) to opt for a certain amount of deregulation and privatization. This has opened up significant roles for managers/gatekeepers of various kinds at the local level (determining, for example, which neighbourhoods are hooked into new cable systems, and what programming to provide on them). Mean-

while, as sophisticated telecommunications technologies become increasingly important in all spheres of private and community life, those which do remain under public control will inevitably come to represent a correspondingly important component of collective consumption.

## Demographic change

In the past 15 or so years, some important demographic changes have occurred which have already begun to be translated into the social geography of the late twentieth-century city. The storybook family in Dick-and-Jane readers (with an aproned mother baking cakes for the two children as they await father's return from a day of breadwinning) has by no means disappeared, but it is fast being outnumbered by other kinds of families. In the United States, for instance, most people live in households where there are two wage-earners. The single-parent family is the fastest-growing of all household types, and one in every four households consists of a person living alone (Table 9.2). Similar changes are occurring in most other Western societies in response to the same complex of factors (Westoff 1983).

Central to all these changes is the experience of the generation born after the Second World War (the baby boomers), partly in response to the catching-up process of births delayed by the war and partly as a result of a sharp decrease in the average age at marriage. The peak birth rate of this population boom occurred in the mid-1960s, creating a 'disadvantaged cohort' of population which has entered the labour market at a time of economic recession and which seems likely to experience much greater competition not only in the labour market but also in housing markets and many other spheres of life for the next 20 years at least. This is already beginning to show up in aggregate statistics. In the United States, for example, after-tax income for families headed by a person aged 25–34 was 2.3 per cent lower, in real terms, in 1982 than it had been in 1961. This fall is actually worse than it seems at face value, since many

**Table 9.2**  Household composition: 1950–1980 (percentages)

| | Married couples | | Headed by women | Primary individuals[c] | Other[d] | Total |
|---|---|---|---|---|---|---|
| | Home-making wife[a] | Working wife[b] | | | | |
| 1950 | 59.4 | 19.6 | 8.4 | 10.8 | 1.8 | 100 |
| 1955 | 54.2 | 21.7 | 8.8 | 12.8 | 2.5 | 100 |
| 1960 | 51.2 | 23.2 | 8.5 | 14.9 | 2.5 | 100 |
| 1965 | 47.0 | 25.6 | 8.7 | 16.7 | 2.0 | 100 |
| 1970 | 41.6 | 28.9 | 8.8 | 18.8 | 1.9 | 100 |
| 1975 | 36.6 | 29.2 | 10.0 | 21.9 | 2.3 | 100 |
| 1980 | 30.3 | 30.6 | 10.8 | 26.1 | 2.2 | 100 |

a. Husband-wife families with wife outside the labor force (breakdown by presence of children not available).
b. Husband-wife families with wife in labor force.
c. Single adult living alone or with unrelated persons.
d. Primarily male-headed families with no wife present.

*Sources*: Hirschhorn (1977); U.S. Bureau of the Census (1981a).
*Source*: Gerson (1983), Table 1, p. 140.

more of the households in 1982 were two-paycheck households. In the mid-1960s, however, fertility levels fell significantly, so that, with fairly stable death rates, rates of population growth slowed dramatically. In some cases this resulted in net decreases of population. This was most pronounced in West Germany, where a natural increase of over 420,000 a year in the mid-1960s had been converted to a natural decrease of 150,000 a year by 1975. The reasons for this shift are several. There appears to have been a wide-spread change in lifestyle preferences away from familism towards consumerism. Young and Willmott (1973) wrote of the 'mid-century alliance of family and technology' and suggested that the family should now be regarded not so much as a unit of production as a unit of consumption. The advent of reliable methods of birth control also fostered the growth of consumerism and the postponement of childbearing. Meanwhile, the demise of the 'living wage', noted above, prompted still more women to take up full-time employment and to postpone childbearing or to return to work soon after childbirth. These trends will have some important consequences for urban social geography. In addition to the impli-cations of an increasingly consumerist urban lifestyle, the effects of reduced birth rates on many aspects of collective consumption

(school enrolments, for example), and the effects of higher proportions of working women on the demand for child care facilities, there are the implications of the changes in social attitudes that have occurred. It has been established, for example, that dual-career couples in the United States are less religious than other couples, less concerned about their own relatives, more inclined to change jobs and/or move house, and less concerned about making or keeping friends (Spain and Nock 1984). Thus we seem to be witnessing a significant change in urbanism as a way of life. Perhaps most important of all is the general, if gradual and incomplete, change in attitudes towards women that has accompanied consumerism, birth control and increased female participation in the labour market (Gerson 1983; Holcomb 1984).

Already, changing attitudes about the status of women have come to be reflected in improved educational opportunities and a wider choice of employment (though by no means yet commensurate with Gappert's idea of an androgynous society), both of which have fostered the development of non-traditional family structures and lifestyles. In addition, once the proposition that sex need not be aimed primarily or solely at procreation had become generally accepted, further trends were set in motion. The social value of marriage decreased, with a consequent decline in the rate of marriage, an increase in the average age at marriage, an increase in divorce, and an increase in cohabitation without marriage – all conspiring to depress the fertility rate still further and to create large numbers of 'unconventional' households (single-parent households, in particular) with unconventional housing needs, unconventional residential behaviour, and unconventional demands on urban services. Meanwhile, the increased number of female-headed households, coupled with the generally inferior role allocated to women in the labour market, has precipitated yet another phenomenon with important implications for urban social geography: the 'feminization of poverty' (Holcomb 1984; McDowell 1983b; Women and Geography Study Group 1984).

Finally, we should note that the slowing of population growth caused by fertility decline will also have some important implications for urban change because of the longer-term effects of the ageing of the baby-boomers. This, incidentally, seems likely to be accentuated by the effects of technological change: redundancy, 'burnout' and early retirement. Perhaps the single most important issue relating to ageing is the burden of dependency that will be imposed on the post-1965 generation. The elderly cost twice as much as children in terms of public expenditure *per capita*, requiring sheltered housing, specialized health care facilities, domiciliary services and specialized transportation and environmental design as well as pensions (Amman 1981; Millas 1980).

## Cultural change

As we have seen, the rise of consumerism and the propagation of materialistic values has been one of the dominant cultural trends. Like many of the other trends enumerated in this chapter, it has its roots in the evolution of capitalist economies. In crude terms, people have been made more materialistic as capitalism has had to turn, in its search for profits, away from the increasingly regulated realm of production towards the more easily exploited

realm of consumption (Gartner and Reissman 1974). Meanwhile, the relative affluence of the postwar period allowed many households to be more attentive to consumerism, and people soon came to be schooled in the sophistry of conspicuous consumption. One of the pivotal aspects of this trend, from the point of view of urban social geography, has been the demand for home ownership and the consequent emphasis on the home as an expression of self and status.

Against the background of this overall trend towards consumerism there emerged in the 1960s a distinctive middle-class youth counterculture based on a reaction against materialism, scale, and high technology. These ideas have found widespread acceptance, to the point where Peter Hall (1984b) has identified them as a major influence on urban change. Their influence can be seen, for example, in the politicization of liberal/ecological values in relation to urban development and collective consumption (Ley 1980), and in the realm of 'spirit and matter': their architectural expression taking the form of post-modernist, neo-romantic styles. It should be noted, however, that the spread of these values has not, for the most part, displaced materialism. Rather, they have grown up alongside. The middle classes have come to have their cake and eat it too, facilitated by the commercial development of products and services geared to liberal/ecological tastes. Yet, at the same time, the energy crisis and economic recession of the early 1970s brought a further modification in values: 'in 1973–5 the expectations of the American middle class were shattered. Within those two years the purchasing power of the dollar shrank by nearly 20 per cent, the volume of household savings and other wealth and assets declined about 12 per cent, and the size of household debts rose by over 18 per cent' (Gappert 1979: 46). This has brought about the emergence of what Gappert has called a 'post-affluent consciousness' which has in turn led to a re-evaluation of people's needs and wants. Gappert suggests that the downsizing of the American automobile, the downsizing of suburban homes and the trend towards living in apartment complexes are all signs of this, though it is not yet clear whether 'post-affluent consciousness' is simply the enforced product of changed circumstances or the beginning of a more radical and widespread shift in attitudes that will see conspicuous consumption replaced by 'conspicuous frugality' and 'voluntary austerity'.

Meanwhile, economic and technological change has induced a certain amount of cultural change which is likely to feed back, in turn, to social behaviour and community organization (Fischer 1985). Studies of the effects of mass communications, for example, have found that a homogenized cultural mainstream is emerging, rebuilding the collective conscience that Durkheim and the Chicago School felt would be eliminated by urbanization. Given what we have seen of economic transformation and technological change, one consequence of this trend may be the attenuation of the meaning of place in people's lives. 'The outer experience is cut off from the inner experience. The new attempted urban meaning is the spatial and cultural separation of people from their product and from their history. It is the space of collective alienation and of individual violence. . . . Life is transformed into abstraction, cities into shadows' (Castells 1983b: 7). The corollary of *this*, in turn, is an increased concern with conserving and developing the urban sense of place (Appleyard 1979b): another aspect of change which is related to the liberal/ecological values of the 1960s counter culture.

## Political change

The complex and intertwined trends outlined above are pregnant with problems and predicaments that will inevitably figure among the dominant political issues of the late 1980s and 1990s. The new spatial division of labour is forging a realignment of class relations which are being drawn increasingly along geographical (as well as structural) lines, with the polarization of social well-being in large metropolitan areas creating the preconditions for incendiary urban disturbances (Scott 1985). In addition, the unfinished restructuring of the space-economy will continue to provoke a constant stream of political tensions as labour markets become more segmented, as differential processes of growth and decline work themselves out, and as shifts in the balance of economic and social power reshape the political landscape (Hill 1984).

Meanwhile, a fundamental political change has occurred in response to the general economic recession of the post-affluent period, in that the appeal of a 'new conservatism' has set in motion some substantial changes in the role and orientation of the public sector. Electoral victories by right-of-centre parties in Australia, the Netherlands, New Zealand, the United Kingdom and the United States have been associated with an ideological stance based on the belief that the welfare state had not only generated unreasonably high levels of taxation, budget deficits, disincentives to work and save, and a bloated class of unproductive workers, but also that it may have fostered 'soft' attitudes towards 'problem' groups in society. Ironically, the electoral appeal of this ideology can be attributed to the very success of welfare states in erasing from the minds of the electorate the immediate spectre of material deprivation. Consequently, the priority accorded to welfare expenditures has receded (though the logic and, critically, the costs of maintaining them have not: Navarro 1982). The retrenchment of the public sector has already brought some important changes to the urban scene, as we saw, for example, in relation to the 'decollectivization' of housing (Chapter 6) and public services (Chapter 8). In broader perspective, these changes can be interpreted as part of the shift in emphasis from collective consumption to capital accumulation that is in turn one of the mechanisms through which the lead economies of the world-system have attempted to steer themselves out of the 'crisis' of capitalism (Castells 1985). In this context, the decollectivization of housing and public services may only be a prelude to much more far-reaching changes in urban politics and urban outcomes (Knox 1986b).

Meanwhile, deindustrialization and economic recession mean that socio-spatial disparities have been reinforced. Even the US President's *Commission for a National Agenda for the Eighties* accepted the inevitability of a 'nearly permanent' urban underclass. If, as seems likely, this underclass gets larger and even worse off, it is logical to expect a political response. Here again there is evidence of change, with 'traditional' working-class politics, having lost much of its momentum and even more of its appeal, being displaced by a 'new wave' of socialist politics. The vanguard of this new wave is to be found among middle-class civil servants (Piven and Cloward 1984), middle-class career politicians (Elliott and McCrone 1984) and middle-class intellectuals (Lojkine 1984).

# Urban restructuring

With all this change at hand, it is clear that many cities are likely to change a good deal over the next couple of decades. The question is, just *how* will they change and *how much* will they change; or might the inertia of existing urban form and residential differentiation prevail over change? In this section, we review existing ideas about changing urban form, evaluate the nature of contemporary changes in the social mosaic of cities, and highlight some of the key issues that are emerging as a result of change.

## Changing urban form

Although there are many forces influencing the morphological evolution of cities, they can be thought, in general terms, as tending towards one of two different outcomes: dispersal and concentration. Pressman (1985) suggests that the following trends will tend to work towards a more *dispersed* urban pattern:

1. The increasing capacity and sophistication of electronic communications.
2. Increasing freedom from the locational constraints affecting all kinds of economic activities.
3. The suburbanization of 'back-office' white-collar jobs.

4. Increasing preferences for lower-density, rural-character environments.
5. Increasing congestion and rising operating costs of older public transport systems.
6. The internationalization of the economy.

On the other hand, there are several trends whose outcomes tend toward a *concentrated* urban structure:

1. continuing needs for face-to-face interaction in certain economic activities;
2. increasing energy costs and uncertain energy supplies;
3. the emergence of an anti-technology attitude;
4. the persistence of an impoverished urban underclass;
5. the increasing attractiveness of revitalized inner urban settings to some elements of the young middle classes;
6. the inaccessibility of sophisticated (and expensive) telecommunications to the less-affluent.

The net outcome will of course depend on the relative strength and balance of these forces, and will vary from place to place according to economic circumstances and historical antecedents. We must also recognize that, whatever the outcome in terms of these two sets of forces, the scale of urbanization has already begun to increase to the point where it is often not relevant to think in terms of the concentration or decentralization of free-standing, nuclear cities. Rather, it is increasingly necessary to think in terms of complex, polynuclear metropolitan settings. As Gibson (1977) points out, such settings can take on any one of a number of different configurations, depending on, among other things, planning and transportation strategies (Fig. 9.2).

The consensus of opinion suggests that we should anticipate the emergence of metropolitan settings that contain constellations of relatively diversified yet integrated nodal centres, covering larger areas than present forms but also providing more concentration through a high degree of sub-metropolitan integration (Pressman 1985; van Til 1980). According to

1. Dispersed sheet (Orthogonal Gridiron)

Spread of generally undifferentiated growth,
without significant, major focal centres,
e.g. Los Angeles, Tokyo.

2. Spider web (Radio-concentric) or (Ring Radial)

One of the most common urban forms. A
high-density, exhibiting vital centrality,
with surrounding development is the
distinguishing characteristic, e.g. Paris,
Vienna, Dallas.

3. Star (Finger)

Basically a 'spider web' form with linear
radials usually defining some type of
open space, e.g. Copenhagen,
Washington, D.C.

4. Satellite (Cluster)

Variation of the 'galaxy' but with a
predominant central core or city
centre, e.g. Stockholm, London.

5. Linear

Development is organised along a
dominant 'corridor' (a single 'finger'
variation of the 'star' shape),
e.g. Cumbernauld, Ciudad Lineal
(Madrid), Megalopolis.

6. Ring

Linear form which closes upon
itself. It has a large open space
at the centre, e.g. San Francisco
Bay Area, Principal cities of the
Netherlands.

Note: Types 1 through 3 are normally produced by short-run,
small-scale individual entrepreneurial decision, whereas
4 through 6 forms require advance planning and careful
control.

7. Galaxy

A series of linked 'cores' appropriated
in the landscape at functional distances
from each other, e.g. large urban regions,
cities of Northern Germany.

8. Polycentred net

Diversely spread urban organisation with
differentiated foci, dominant and minor
arteries, built-up and open spaces – an
articulated distribution, e.g. Detroit.

Levan (1979), these new metropolitan forms will be determined mainly by the spatial logic of consumption, rather than production. The increased scale of metropolitan settings (Leven asserts that in the United States there will be a convergence towards populations of two to ten million, spread across 100–300 miles), it is argued, will allow people to live at different scales simultaneously: smaller, more concentrated communities centred on most work, shopping and leisure activities, but much larger functional groupings to sustain higher-order jobs, services and amenities. It follows that metropolitan settings of this scale will be settled *discontinuously*, with metropolitan-wide linkages being dominated by telecommunications rather than transport flows, which would operate more at the scale of local commuting. Leven suggests that, in the transition to such settings, the present core areas of larger metropolitan areas will prosper, along with smaller towns and exurbs in the metropolitan hinterland, while second- and third-tier suburbs are likely to struggle to maintain present levels of population and affluence.

Peter Hall (1984c) sees this kind of scenario as the fifth and final stage of urban evolution (Fig. 9.3). The first stage of this model corresponds to the urban experience of the core economies of the nineteenth century, where the central areas of dominant, primate-city regions grew rapidly at the expense of almost everywhere else, while other urban regions began to concentrate around nodal centres. In the second stage, industrialization has spread from the major city to a number of provincial cities which now provide additional magnets for the labour which continues to pour off the land. These cities now join the primate city in a state of *absolute centralization*: their cores are gaining at the expense of their still-rural 'rings', while urban regions generally are gaining at the expense of purely rural areas. 'Meanwhile, in all probability, the primate city system has kept a step ahead by entering a third state of urban evolution: its growth is such that it washes out into the suburban ring, so that core and ring are both growing, though the core's growth is still faster than the ring's' (Hall 1984c: 247–9). This third stage is one of

*relative centralization*, and is followed by *relative decentralization*, in which urban cores still grow, but not as fast as their surrounding rings. By the time provincial cities are experiencing this, however, primate cities have begun to lose population from their core while still adding to their suburban ring population. This is the stage of *absolute decentralization* associated with the automobile era and which has characterized the cities of most of the world's core economies for most of the postwar period. In the fifth and final stage (though Hall does not suggest why it should be the final rather than the latest stage), there is further evolution, already in evidence in Britain and the United States and which, if fully developed, would provide the foundations for the kind of urban/metropolitan scenario described above.

Now, the cores of the other city systems begin to empty out and to decline absolutely, while their suburbs continue to grow; they too have reached the stage of absolute decentralization. As ever though, the first city system is one step ahead: the loss of population from its core is now so great that the continuing weak gain of the suburban ring – if indeed it continues at all – cannot compensate, so we have a situation of *decentralization during loss*. As this happens, naturally, there is a marked fall in the primacy index. However, by this stage the primacy index has generally been falling for some time, and a more general phenomenon starts to take its place: that of negative returns to urban scale, whereby smaller city systems tend to gain people while larger ones, not merely the largest of all, stagnate or decline. This in turn is associated with a spread of the decentralization-during-loss pattern from the rest of the system to perhaps half-a-dozen or more of the leading second-order urban systems in the country. At this stage, for the first time, the growth of non-metropolitan areas is faster than that of metropolitan areas: the 'clean break' has taken place (Hall 1984c: 249, emphsis added)

It should be noted, however, that the idea of a 'clean break' is by no means clearly established. Already, there are signs that the influx of population to non-metropolitan settings has slowed, and there have been claims for a 'back to the city' movement. It should also be borne in mind that the inertia of the built

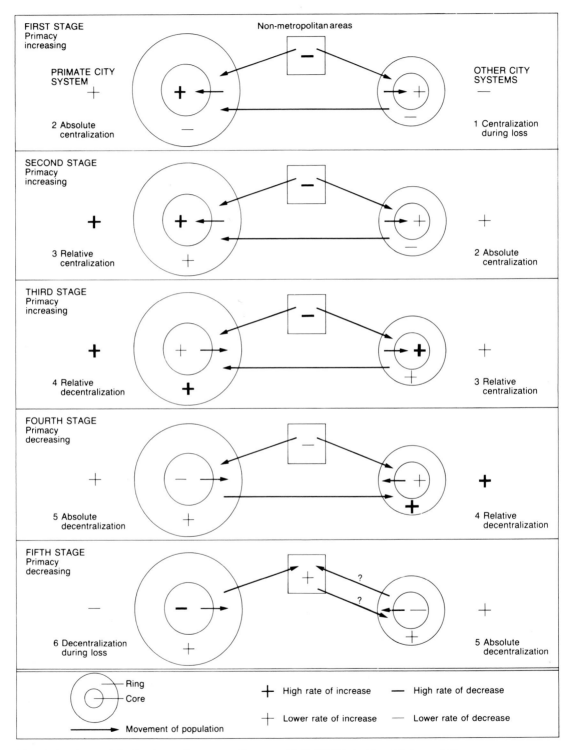

**Fig. 9.3** A model of urban change. *Source*: Hall (1984c), Fig. 10.3, p. 248.

environment and of existing institutional structures are likely to present formidable barriers to radical changes in urban form, so that *change will occur slowly and in piecemeal fashion*.

## The homogenization of urban space?

Within the changing framework of urban form, other forces, more complex still, are modifying patterns of residential differentiation. As a result, it is very likely that the classical model of urban structure, as identified by studies of factorial ecology (Chapter 4), will soon be overwritten. At the same time, advances in telecommunications have already begun to remove many of the traditional frictions of space for households as well as for economic activities, so that there is a strong possibility of a homogenization of urban space. This is not to suggest that residential differentiation and segregation will disappear, but that it will be manifest in more complex ways and at a finer level of resolution than the sectors, zones and clusters that have been associated with socio-economic status, family status and ethnicity.

Davies (1984), reviewing the implications of economic, technological, demographic and social change for ecological structure, concludes that 'the increasing complexity of society means that there are likely to be many more axes of differentiation, some of which are derived from the fission of the . . . constructs identified in previous societies' (p. 311). Among these are:

1. The emergence of *migrant* status as a potent source of differentiation.
2. The reinforcement of *ethnic* differentiation with the arrival of new immigrant groups.
3. The emergence of new dimensions of *occupational differentiation* related to the expansion of service jobs.
4. The appearance of significant distinctions in the degree of *welfare dependency*.
5. A relative increase in the importance of *poverty* and *substandard housing* as a result of the consolidation of the urban underclass.

6. The increased socio-spatial differentiation of *young adults* and of the *elderly* as a result of changes in household organization.
7. The emergence of a distinctive *urban fringe* milieux.

There is already some evidence that the ecological structure of central city areas in America is becoming more finely differentiated into specialized dimensions which were formerly part of more general constructs, while suburban space is becoming homogenized around more general constructs (Perle 1981). At the same time, longstanding differences between suburban and central city areas have begun to disappear as the suburbs have taken over the role of economic 'growth machine' (Erickson 1983; Schwartz 1976) and become not only the 'hub of daily activity' (Sly and Tayman 1980) but also host to some of the characteristics traditionally associated with central city areas (Masotti and Hadden 1973); while sections of most central cities have been renewed, upgraded or gentrified, bringing some 'suburban' socio-economic and demographic profiles to some inner-city neighbourhoods. As a result, it is only ethnicity that effectively differentiates between American central cities and their suburbs (Gober and Behr 1982). In short, while the white middle classes seem to be successful in extending and differentiating their suburban realm and in invading and 'revitalizing' inner-city neighbourhoods, blacks, hispanics and other ethnic groups seem to be much less successful in extending their realm.

### The changing social mosaic: the example of central city revitalization

In detail, the social mosaic of cities shows that these broad outcomes are the product of complex interactions between, on the one hand, the major economic, demographic, technological, cultural and political trends outlined at the beginning of this chapter and, on the other, local socio-economic and political circumstances. The revitalization of central city neighbourhoods provides a good example of this. 'Revitalization' here includes the effects of commercial redevelopment, incumbent upgrading (the improvement of residential neighbourhoods by existing residents), and gentrification (see p. 196). While none of these are new aspects of urban change, all three seemed to increase considerably in importance during the 1970s. In North America,

Baltimore's Inner Harbor was rebuilt, and previously dilapidated houses on Federal Hill and in Fells Point were renovated for middle class residents. In St. Paul, the Lowertown area, once a warehousing, manufacturing and transportation center, is being converted to a commercial and residential 'village'. New commercial investment focused upon historic market structures in Boston, while nearby warehouses on harbor wharves were being transformed into residences. Neighbourhoods in Washington were upgraded ('gentrified') to upper-middle-class respectability; in Vancouver the former industrial area of False Creek became the site of new, amenity-rich housing. Charleston's historic preservation continued to capture public enthusiasm, and in Los Angeles major redevelopment is occurring in the Bunker Hill area (Holcomb and Beauregard 1981: 1).

In Europe, some of the better-known examples include the redevelopment of some of London's docklands, the restoration of the Marais district of Paris, the construction of the Thistle Centre and St. James's Centre in Edinburgh, and the gentrification of many of London's first-tier Victorian suburbs.

The antecedents of these recent examples of revitalization can be found in the urban renewal 'offensives' of the 1950s and 1960s (see p. 307), which we can now see as part of the wider transformation of the economic functions and character of the city (Kleniewski 1984). As Mollenkopf puts it: 'renewal played midwife to the emerging corporate economy that now characterizes the major cities' (1981: 16). The recent surge of revitalization is a product of the same logic; it has been a means of capturing increases in locational values brought about by economic, demographic, social and cultural change, and a means of eliminating barriers to the continued accumulation of wealth.

Though they have usually involved only a small residential component, downtown commercial redevelopment projects have been central to changes in the urban social mosaic because of their 'shadow effects' in terms of property values and because of their critical role in changing the pattern of employment opportunities. The recent surge of downtown commercial redevelopment can be seen as an attempt to reinvest in valuable assets that had been severely threatened by urban decentralization. This reinvestment has involved similar strategies in many different cities: bold physical forms – waterfront developments, plazas, and pedestrian mall complexes – containing new shops and new offices, together with, perhaps, convention centres, sports arenas, museums and concert halls. In line with the corporate and political trends associated with the post-affluent era, it has also been characterized by the formation of 'public-private partnerships' which have brought major developers, financial institutions and community leaders together with city councils and their bureaucratic officers (Holcomb and Beauregard 1981; Rees and Lambert 1985). The initiative has thus shifted away from urban renewal agencies to the business community; and there are signs that the shift will continue, with corporations taking the initiative in identifying blighted areas, conceptualizing renewal or rehabilitation projects, organizing the projects, working out the necessary arrangements with the city, and carrying out the work. One example is provided by the Franklin Town project in Philadelphia, where local industrialists felt that the area's deterioration had come to threaten their operations. The result was the creation of a major new commercial and residential complex, along with street improvements and landscaped public open space. Similar projects have been initiated by General Motors in Detroit and by Pfitzer Inc. in Brooklyn, each attempting to revitalize the area around its own corporate complex.

Residential revitalization has also exhibited a recent surge. It has, moreover, been more widespread; though it should be acknowledged at the outset that it accounts for only a fraction of the *total* change in the social mosaic of central city areas (despite the disproportionate amount of attention it has been given in the literature). Surveys of US cities have found evidence of residential revitalization in about half of all urban areas, with the larger, older cities of the East, not surprisingly, providing the bulk of the reported cases (Black 1980; Clay 1979). In *absolute* terms these cases represent a substantial phenomenon. In New York City, for example, over 10,000 industrial lofts have been converted to residential use (Zukin 1982); while it has been estimated that in the US as a whole gentrification has been displacing about 900,000 households a year (Le Gates and Hartman 1981). But in *relative* terms revitalization has to be seen as piecemeal and uneven. Within individual cities, revitalization typically involves less than 5 per cent (and often less than 1 per cent) of the population (Schill and Nathan 1983). Within 'revitalizing' neighbourhoods, the proportion of rehabilitated properties appears to vary between 5 and 30 per cent (De Giovanni 1984). The significance of residential revitalization really lies, however, in its qualitative, symbolic and ideological implications for urban change. While other kinds of neighbourhood change tend to be slow and incremental, revitalization tends to be relatively rapid, involving a marked change of neighbourhood character, a good chance of conflict, and the probability of substantial externality effects, both positive and negative (Henig, 1981, 1982; Holcomb and Beauregard 1981; Tournier 1984). Because it results in improvements to the built environment, encourages new retail activity, and expands the local tax base using a minimum of public funds, it has become an important symbol and prospect for urban change for the 'new right' of urban politics (Thomas 1986). Because it fosters capital accumulation, the reproduction of the middle classes and the restructuring of urban space to accommodate the economic transformation of cities, it has become an important symbol and portent of urban change for the 'new wave' of socialist urban politics.

Not surprisingly, research on revitalization tends to reflect these different perspectives (Beauregard 1985; London *et al.* 1981; Williams 1984). How, then, should we conceptualize the process of revitalization in relation to urban change? Perhaps the most useful suggestion is to view residential revitalization as the product of two sets of forces: preconditions that are the product of *structural*, economic trends, and *contingent* factors that are the locally and temporally specific product of human agency in seeking to manipulate or resist these preconditions (Clark 1985; Jackson 1985b). The preconditions for residential revitalization include the need for capital to reinvest in neighbourhoods affected by deindustrialization and decentralization (in order to protect the massive investments of capital that are tied up in the built environment: Harvey 1975; Smith 1982), the expansion of new forms of skilled service employment in inner-city locations, the emergence of new household types with new values, and the existence of a pliant public sector willing to respond to the service requirements of newcomers in gentrifying neighbourhoods. Because these preconditions stem from the pervasive structural trends outlined at the beginning of this chapter, they result in a certain amount of *convergence* in terms of urban change. On the other hand, we can recognize that the detailed outcomes of residential revitalization are complex and varied as a result of local variations such as regional economic conditions, local political, demographic and cultural characteristics, and the stage in the neighbourhood life cycle reached by different parts of the city.

## Urban issues for the 1990s

It follows from the nature of the trends described above that some new issues will emerge in the next decade or two, and some old ones will be accentuated. This is not the place to attempt to deal with all of these issues systematically. Instead, we must be content with an examination of two of the major issue areas that relate to themes developed earlier in this book: issues of accessibility that arise from continued urban decentralization, and issues related to planning and managing the post-affluent city.

## Decentralization and accessibility issues

The ascendancy of the automobile as the dominant means of transportation, together with the consequent spread of low-density suburban development, has brought to an end the traditional notion that jobs, shops, schools, health services and community facilities will be within ready walking distance of homes. Even by 1960, over 90 per cent of the households in the most recently developed parts of metropolitan California had at least one car, and between 40 and 45 per cent had two or more. By 1970, comparable levels of car ownership had been achieved in most other metropolitan areas of the United States (Foley 1975), while in Europe the spread of car ownership was at last beginning to accelerate rapidly. One result of this trend has been that employers, retailers and planners have tended to make their location decisions on the assumption of perfect personal mobility. A prime example of this is the proliferation of suburban shopping centres and shopping malls around freeway intersections and access points in many North American cities. These suburban shopping malls have brought downtown sophistication to the suburbs and elevated the old highway culture from 'hamburger and coke' to 'lobster and Lowenbrau' in a single location situated conveniently (for some) just off arterial highways in enormous parking lots. In these malls it is possible to buy anything from Gucci shoes to canned beans; and in some it is possible to go to church, register to vote, bet, give blood, and run on special indoor jogging tracks. Their magnetic power has rearranged not only the commercial geography of urban areas but also the whole social life of the suburbs. Malls have become *the* most popular gathering places for suburban teenagers, and adults use them to stroll and promenade, much as continental Europeans have used their city centres on Sundays. Americans now spend more time at shopping malls than anywhere outside their homes and workplaces (Kowinski 1978).

The benefits of increased personal mobility are enjoyed disproportionately by the middle-class, the middle-aged and the male population, however. In the United States, for example, although the overall ratio of motor vehicles to households increased from 1.3 to nearly 2.0 between 1960 and 1983, only the more affluent households actually had an increase in car ownership. Less affluent households, as a group, were worse off in 1983 than in 1960. Indeed, surveys have shown that, despite the advent of the 'automobile age', around three out of ten urban residents lack direct personal access to a motor vehicle. Many of these individuals are old, poor or black, and a good many are inner-city residents (Foley 1975; Koutsopoulos and Schmidt 1976; Paaswell and Berechman 1976). Women are also significantly deficient in access to motor vehicles for, although their household unit may own a car, its use by other members of the household is likely to render it unavailable for much of the time (Coutras and Fagnani 1978; Fox 1983; Pickup 1984). In Foley's study of San Francisco households, six or seven out of every ten women were unable to claim direct personal access to a motor vehicle. And, where this gender constraint was compounded by age and low household income, levels of car availability dropped to only two in every ten women. In contrast, nine out of every ten males in moderately affluent households did have direct access to a car. Furthermore, the urban form which the automobile has triggered – low-density development spread over a wide area – has made it very difficult to provide public transport systems which are able to meet the needs of carless suburban women, the elderly, and the poor.

One aspect of this whole trend which has received some attention from geographers is the residential location of the poor and the unemployed in relation to job opportunities. Many jobs have moved out to the suburbs along with the general trend towards urban decentralization. The city of Chicago, for example, lost 435,000 jobs between 1960 and 1975 while its suburbs gained 445,000. Meanwhile, the poor – especially the black poor – tend to remain trapped in the inner city, separated from the suburbanized job opportunities by distances of between 15 and 45 kilometres. In Chicago, jobs have been suburbanizing twice as fast as the labour force, so that, as in cities elsewhere, a large number of workers have become involved in 'reverse commuting'. It has also meant that car-less job-seekers have been at a considerable disadvantage, being forced to find employment either within walking distance of their homes or along the routes of public transport systems. Given the decreasing employment base of the inner city and the tendency for urban bus services to operate along radial routes with few crosstown connections, the net effect is an intensification of the problems of unemployment and deprivation in the inner city (Falcocchio *et al.* 1972; Stutz 1976). Even the new jobs that are brought into the inner city are generally inappropriate to the local labour force. In Britain, Ambrose (1977a) and others have drawn attention to the effects of inner city redevelopment schemes which replace unskilled manual and service jobs with office jobs. Without the qualifications to secure these new job opportunities, inner-city residents are left to search elsewhere for employment while their position in the local employment market is taken by suburban commuters.

In most American cities the situation has been exacerbated by the lack of an open housing market for the black population. De Vise (1976) has calculated that the number of blacks working in Chicago suburbs is less than half the number that would be expected from their occupational, industrial and earning characteristics. Although this can be partially explained by the paucity of information about suburban housing and job opportunities reaching black inner-city neighbourhoods (Bernstein 1973), the chief reasons for their exclusion from suburban areas seem to be associated with racial discrimination and the residential segregation of blacks. Transport-based solutions to this particular accessibility problem are therefore of doubtful value. One scheme designed to link the ghetto with outlying suburban trading estates in St. Louis, for example, failed because the industrialists were reluctant to employ blacks and because many of the ghetto residents were unwilling to work in white suburbia (Muller 1976b).

### Time budgets and effective accessibility

Recent work by geographers such as Carlstein, Parkes and Thrift (1978) has emphasized that questions of accessibility to jobs, services and amenities must be carefully qualified in terms of people's time budgets. Since most people's daily lives follow a variety of closely constrained and well-worn paths through time and space, it follows that *effective accessibility* to particular locations will depend not only on their physical proximity but also on whether they are free to make the journey in the first place. Hagerstrand (1970) has outlined a framework for the study of *time geography* which is based on the environment of resources and opportunities (including jobs, goods, services and social contacts) which surrounds each individual. According to Hagerstrand, the individual's capacity to move from one place or activity to another within this environment is defined by three different sorts of constraint:

1.  *Capability constraints* – which include the need for a minimum amount of sleep (which limits the time that can be spent travelling) and the kind of transportation that is available (which will determine the radius of the territory which can be included in the daily life path).
2.  *Authority constraints* – which include laws, rules and customs which limit accessibility to certain places and curtail participation in certain activities. Some restaurants, for example, require women to have a male escort.
3.  *Coupling constraints* – which stem from the limited periods during which particular opportunities are available for access. As Hagerstrand points out, people's daily activities are highly dependent on the opening hours of shops and offices, the scheduling of public transport, and the timing and duration of 'rush hours'.

The *time budget* of any indiviudal within his or her environment can be depicted graphically by representing distance along a horizontal axis, and time along a vertical axis: the

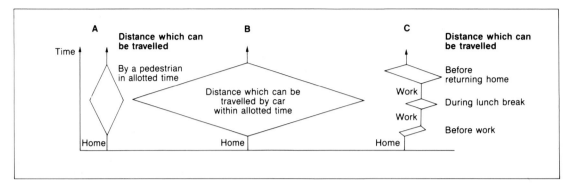

**Fig. 9.4** Time budgets and daily prisms. *Source*: Pred and Palm (1978), p. 103.

effective range of a person is then described by a 'prism'. As Fig. 9.4 shows, the shape of the prism depends on the available mode of transport. It may also vary from day to day, depending on the places and activities involved. Moreover, every stop, for whatever reason, causes the range of the prism (or subprisms) to shrink in proportion to the length of stay ((c) on Fig. 9.4).

The time budgets of some population sub-groups will clearly make for more effective accessibility to the city's opportunities than will those of others. One group which is particularly vulnerable to time-related constraints on locational accessibility is women (Hanson and Hanson 1980; Marston 1985). Pred and Palm (1974, 1978) have argued that even the suburban housewife *with* access to a car is limited in her opportunities because of the limits of the subprisms that are sandwiched between her fixed 'duties' as a housewife: providing breakfast for the family and driving the children to school, preparing lunch, picking up the children from school, chauffeuring them to sporting or social engagements, and preparing dinner. In addition, she may have to be home to accept deliveries, supervise repair workers or care for a sick child. This fragmentation of time gives rise to coupling constraints which limit her quality of life by effectively barring her from much of her environment. Women without cars, of course, suffer much greater restrictions on their quality of life. As we have seen, women do not, in general, enjoy very good levels of accessibility to cars, even in the

United States. As Pred and Palm put it, the daily prism of the car-less suburban housewife:

is restricted to those opportunities which can be reached on foot or by the use of a bus service (which in many suburbs is inconvenient and in some non-existent). . . . Even routine shopping becomes a chore. Socializing is limited to the neighbourhood in which she lives. . . . With children under school age she is virtually locked into a world of very limited physical space because of coupling constraints and societal expectations concerning her family role. Viewed from a time-geographic perspective, she has the greatest number of leisure hours and yet little opportunity to invest leisure time in personal fulfilment (Pred and Palm 1978: 108).

Some of the most severe accessibility problems arising from urban decentralization are experienced by suburban single parents. As Robertson (1984: 198) points out:

lone parents must inevitably have lifestyles which differ from those of two-parent families. They have much less flexibility in employment and in recreation, for example, having to dovetail their activities to the time schedules of their children. Those parents with school-age children may find full-time employment impossible without after-school and holiday care facilities, while those with pre-school children are dependent on crèches and day nurseries. In both cases the proximity of relatives and friends is often critical. Late opening of commercial and other enterprises is also vital if a single parent is to incorporate visits to shops, banks, libraries and offices in the weekly activity pattern.

Among single-parent households, those living in the deprived, peripheral public housing estates of British cities must have a strong claim to the worst problems of all. In Glasgow, where Robertson has investigated the time-geographic aspects of single-parent lifestyles, one in six of the households allocated to peripheral estates is a single-parent family, In parts of one neighbourhood (Drumchapel) studied by Robertson, the time requirements for fundamental activity sequences common to single parents were extremely high. For some, the return journey (on foot, for lack of any alternatives) to the nearest day care centre takes over an hour and a half. A visit to the nearest unemployment office also takes an hour and a half from some parts of Drumchapel; and so on. Moreover, Robertson found that most of the single-parent households are located in the very districts with the worst locations in terms of 19 different activity sequences typical of single-parent households.

As McDowell (1983b) and others have pointed out, the predicament of suburban women is not simply a consequence of urban decentralization. It is intimately related to a whole nexus of the trends outlined at the beginning of this chapter. The intersection of economic, demographic, social and cultural trends, for example, has allocated to women a pivotal role in the consumption-oriented suburban lifestyles that dominate the logic of contemporary urbanism. In short, women are trapped economically, socially and culturally, as well as ecologically. Meanwhile, the suburban environment has evolved in ways that reinforce inequality between the sexes, contributing, among other things, to emotional strain and the erosion of 'community' (Allport 1983; Fava 1980; Hayden 1984).

## Managing the post-affluent city

The issues precipitated by urban change will in turn precipitate changes in urban policy and planning which, mediated by a changing political climate, will eventually bring about still further modifications to the urban environment. The problems of suburban womens' isolation, for example, call for changes in the design of suburban homes (Graff 1982; Hayden 1984), and, in the case of public housing estates, alterations in housing allocation policies and patterns of public service provision (Robertson 1984).

At the top of the list for many people concerned with urban planning and management is the question of how to respond to the economic trends that are resulting in the closure of manufacturing plants and the loss of 'traditional' blue-collar jobs from urban areas, particularly the inner areas of industrial cities. Given the shift in the political climate towards conservative, free-market orientations, the implication is that the issue is likely to be 'managed' by treating the prospects of deindustrialized urban economies as a lost cause, with public policy geared towards encouraging people to move into new settings – metropolitan or non-metropolitan – wherever jobs are being created (Norton 1983). As Badcock puts it, 'with the global reshuffling of industrial capital the reality of the "throwaway" region is upon us' (1984: 366). A compromise position, directed at ameliorating the predicament of deindustrializing urban cores while re-orienting policy towards 'liberating' free enterprise has been the espousal of 'enterprise zones': portions of the inner-urban environment where planning restrictions would be relaxed and tax incentives offered to employers in the hope of promoting private-sector job creation and, in particular, incubating new firms. But we have already learnt (even if politicians such as Britain's Norman Tebbitt have not) from the experience of earlier economic transitions that it is incorrect to assume that redundant workers are free to move to areas that offer better prospects. Housing may be impossible to sell (or transfer), there may be other workers in the household to consider, the redundant worker may have insufficient skills, or, in the case of unemployed school leavers, may not be able to sustain an effective job search away from the home base. The compromise of enterprise zones seems to offer few prospects of success, however. On the one hand, there is little reason to believe that the planning restrictions and taxes that have been removed from enterprise zones ever contributed in a major way to the deindustrialization of urban areas

(Anderson 1983). On the other, there is little evidence of the kind of job creation that might counter the momentum of spatially decentralizing industrial systems. Many of the firms locating in enterprise zones have simply transferred over short distances in order to take advantage of tax incentives, or have been new firms that were already intending to open new branches or start from scratch in inner-urban settings (Tym and Partners 1982; Shutt 1984).

Closely related to the issue of economic decline is that of deprivation and poverty. The shift towards free-enterprise orientations has of course downplayed the relative importance of the problem even as the retreat from the liberal welfare state has intensified the absolute severity of the problem. Meanwhile, changes in urban structure, combined with economic, demographic and policy changes, have begun to alter the spatial distribution of disadvantaged and service-dependent households. The distribution of deprived households in Glasgow (Fig. 4.22), for example, reflects a striking change from the situation in the early 1970s, when pockets of severe deprivation were much more localized in inner-city neighbourhoods such as Maryhill and the East End (Rae 1983). In Glasgow, the major reason for change in the spatial distribution of deprivation seems to have been urban renewal, combined with the interaction of socio-economic change and the housing allocation process. In American cities, the dissolution of 'service-dependent ghettos' of the poor and disadvantaged seems to be the product of rather more complex interactions between local economic development patterns, local land use policies that have limited housing opportunities for the poor and disadvantaged, and reductions in funds for welfare programmes (Wolch and Gabriel 1984, 1985). These changes, in turn, are posing new problems for policymakers and planners: forcing some dependent clients back into institutional settings, into inappropriate service settings, or onto the streets. At the same time, economic, demographic and technological change is marginalizing new groups. Nowotny (1981) suggests that this kind of marginalization will particularly affect (i) women, (ii) computer illiterates (i.e. the less educated and the educationally less-qualified), and (iii) 'misfits' who do not or cannot conform to the new standards of behaviour associated with the changing social and economic milieux of the post-affluent city.

Amidst all this change it seems reasonable to anticipate that conservation will continue to be a high priority, at least for the more affluent groups in society. With the arrival of the post-affluent era in the 1970s, new building work began to decline and attitudes to the existing building stock were reassessed:

The inevitable pause, in what had been a breathless era, allowed the developing conservation strategies to mature. What had been a plea by a thoughtful minority became a much more broadly based cause which fitted a new mood. . . . The popular view of architecture became more critical, or rather the criticisms were increasingly articulate, particularly of work done in the recent past. Conservation as a concept relevant to whole areas rather than just to individual buildings caught the popular imagination and became the thread of an ideal which ran through much of the thinking about a wide range of urban issues (Tarn 1985: 258).

Yet we can also see the conservation movement as part of a more general shift away from the idea of creating 'modern' cities in favour of the idea of stressing sense of place and historic continuity that was fostered by the 1960s counterculture. And we should also acknowledge that the conservation movement, once under way, was buttressed by the successes of retail-oriented schemes such as the pedestrianization of central Norwich; and of residentially-oriented schemes such as the conservation of the Marais in Paris. The finding that trade expanded in upgraded historic environments and that residential conservation could lead to profits via gentrification converted private capital to the cause. Meanwhile, as conservation increases in importance, new issues are beginning to emerge: questions of social justice arising from localized gains in exchange values, and questions relating to behavioural responses to conserved environments (Kain 1981).

Colouring all these issues will be the overarching 'austerity politics' (Hill 1984) that now dominate urban affairs as a result of the conjunction of fiscal stress, international economic recession, and the rise of the 'new conservatism'. This political milieux has brought with it some important implications for several aspects of urban development. Not least is the threat to the maintenance of urban infrastructure, particularly in older cities where economic and fiscal problems are most acute and where roads, bridges, school buildings and transit systems are in the most critical state of decay. Public service provision is another area, as we have seen, where austerity politics brings an immediate impact on urban social geography.

*Yet, just as all of these changes are poised to leave their imprint on the city, the prospect of managing them in a coherent way has receded.* Along with the general retreat of the liberal welfare state, urban planning has lost much of its power and resources, lost some of its status, and lost its way. With the economic crisis of the mid-1970s, the policy environment everywhere changed dramatically. No longer was controlling urban growth perceived as the dominant problem; no longer was unemployment and poverty limited to traditional groups and neighbourhoods, and no longer was there a broad consensus on the goals of urban planning. The idea of urban management and future-oriented planning against a background of economic growth quickly evaporated. Likewise, the accompanying methodological toolkit no longer appeared relevant. At the same time, urban planning and its associated bureaucracy did not sit well with the ideology of new conservatism, and public disillusionment with the bureaucratic offensives of the preceding 20 years had matured. In the face of these changes, 'professional architects and planners have virtually ceased to work on questions relating to the future city, other than with regard to the immediate future. With the tone of academic work being mainly critical of error rather than forward-looking, there is little appearing that serves to make any impact on the current vacuum in our knowledge about the future city' (Gold 1984: 380). In short, the 'urban vision' that has guided planners since Geddes, Howard and Abercrombie has faded rapidly, almost to the point of extinction. This, of course, opens up the whole question of the nature and orientation of urban management in the future. Much will depend on whether, in Gappert's terminology, Western societies move towards 'System X', 'System Y' or 'System Z' (Fig. 9.1). The first of these offers the prospect of a hardening of the dominant, polarizing tendencies of corporate capitalism and authoritarian control by central governments, unmitigated by local planning or management. The second offers the possibility of defending collective consumption, rescuing community identity and enhancing political self-management (Castells 1983b). The third, and most optimistic, scenario, requires the articulation and application of entirely *new* styles of management and forms of policy development to match the new technologies, new forms of social organization and new social values that will be required to sustain more prosperous, egalitarian and humane urban environments (Gappert 1982).

# References and Bibliography

**Aaron, H. J.** (1972) *Shelter and subsidies*, The Brookings Institution, Washington, DC.

**Aase, A.** (1978) Interregional and interurban variations in levels of living, paper delivered to the joint seminar of the Committee for Space Economy and Planning at Polska Akademia Nauk and the Norden Section of the Regional Science Association, Kazimierz, Poland.

**Abler, R.** (1975) Effects of space-adjusting technologies on the human geography of the future, pp. 35–56 in R. Abler, D. Janelle, A. Philbrick and J. Sommer (eds) *Human Geography in a Shrinking World*, Duxbury Press, North Scituate, Mass.

**Abler, R., Janelle, D., Philbrick, A.** and **Sommer, J.** (eds) (1975) *Human Geography in a Shrinking World*, Duxbury Press, North Scituate, Mass.

**Abrams, M.** (1973) Subjective social indicators, *Social Trends*, **4**, 35–50.

**Abrams, P.** and **Wrigley, E. A.** (eds) (1978) *Towns in Societies*, Cambridge University Press, Cambridge.

**Abrams, R. H.** (1943) Residential propinquity as a factor in marriage selection, *American Sociological Review*, **8**, 288–94.

**Abu-Lughod, J. L.** (1969) Testing the theory of social area analysis: the ecology of Cairo, Egypt, *American Sociological Review*, **34**, 198–212.

**Abu-Lughod, J. L.** and **Foley, M. M.** (1960) Consumer strategies, pp. 387–447 in Foote, N., Abu-Lughod, J. L., Foley, M. M. and Winnick, L. (eds), *Housing Choices and Constraints*, McGraw-Hill, New York.

**Adams, J. S.** (1969) Directional bias in intra-urban migration, *Economic Geography*, **45**, 302–23.

**Adams, J. S.** (1970) Residential structure of Midwestern cities, *Annals, Association of American Geographers*, **60**, 37–62.

**Adams, J. S.** (1973) *New homes, vacancy chains and housing sub-markets in the Twin City Area*, Center for Urban and Regional Affairs, University of Minnesota, Minneapolis.

**Adams, J. S.** (ed.) (1976) *Urban Policymaking and Metropolitan Dynamics*, Ballinger, Cambridge, Mass.

**Adams, J. S.** and **Gilder, K.** (1976) Household location and intra-urban migration, pp. 159–93 in Herbert, D. and Johnston, R. J. (eds) *Social Areas in Cities*, Vol. 1, Spatial Processes and Form, Wiley, Chichester.

**Agnew, J. A.** (1981) Homeownership and the capitalist social order, in M. Dear and A. J. Scott (eds). *Urbanization and Urban Planning in Capitalist Society*, Methuen, London, 457–80.

**Agnew, J. A.** (1982) Homeownership and identity in capitalist societies, pp. 60–98 in J. S. Duncan (ed.) *Housing and Identity*, Holmes and Meier, New York.

**Agocs, C.** (1981) Ethnic settlement in a metropolitan area: a typology of communities, *Ethnicity*, **8**, 127–48.

**Ahlbrandt, R. S. Jr.** (1984) Ideology and the Reagan administration's First National Urban Policy Report, *Journal of the*

*American Planning Association*, **50**, 497–84.

**Aiken, M.** and **Alford, R. R.** (1970) Community structure and innovation: the case of public housing, *American Political Science Review*, **64**, 843–64.

**Aldrich, H. E., Cater, J. C., Jones, T. P.** and **McEvoy, D.** (1981) Business development and self-segregation: Asian enterprise in three British cities, pp. 170–90 in C. Peach, V. Robinson and S. Smith (eds) *Ethnic Segregation in Cities*, Croom Helm, London.

**Alexander, C.** (1967) The city as a mechanism for sustaining human contact, pp. 60–602. in W. R. Edward (ed.) *Environment for Man*, Indiana University Press, Bloomington, Indiana.

**Alihan, M. M.** (1938) *Social Ecology: A Critical Analysis*, Columbia University Press, New York.

**Allan, C. M.** (1965) The genesis of British urban redevelopment with special reference to Glasgow, *Economic History Review*, **18**, 598–613.

**Allport, C.** (1983) Women and suburban housing: postwar planning in Sydney 1943–61, in P. Williams (ed.), *Social Process and the City*, Allen and Unwin, Sydney.

**Almond, G. A.** and **Verba, S.** (1965) *The Civic Culture*, Little, Brown, Boston.

**Alonso, W.** (1960) A theory of the urban land market, *Papers and Proceedings of the Regional Science Association*, **6**, 149–58.

**Alonso, W.** (1964) The historic and structural theories of urban form: their implications for urban renewal, *Land Economics*, **40**, 227–31.

**Ambrose, P.** (1976) *The Land Market and the Housing System*, Working Paper No. 3, Department of Urban and Regional Studies, University of Sussex, Brighton.

**Ambrose, P.** (1977a) Access and spatial inequality, pp. 91–123, in *Values Relevance and Policy*, Units 22–24, Course D204, Open University Press, Milton Keynes.

**Ambrose, P.** (1977b) The determinants of urban land use change, *Values, Relevance and Policy*, Section III, Unit 26, Open University Press, Milton Keynes.

**Ambrose, P.** and **Colenutt, R.** (1975) *The Property Machine*, Penguin, Harmondsworth.

**Amman, A.** (1981) The status and prospects of aging in Western Europe, *Eurosocial Occasional Papers*, 8, Vienna.

**Amos, F. J. C.** (1972) The development of the planning process, *Journal of the Royal Town Planning Institute*, **58**, 341–3.

**Andereisen, G.** (1981) Tanks in the streets: the growing conflict over housing in Amsterdam, *International Journal of Urban and Regional Research*, **5**, 83–95.

**Anderson, J.** (1977) *Engels' Manchester: Industrialization, Workers' Housing and Urban Ideologies*, Architectural Association, Political Economy of Cities and Regions, No. 1.

**Anderson, J.** (1983) Geography as ideology and the politics of crisis – the enterprise zone experiment, pp. 313–50 in J. Anderson, S. Duncan, and R. Hudson (eds) *Redundant Spaces? Industrial decline and social change in cities and regions*, Academic Press, London.

**Anderson, M.** (1964) *The Federal Bulldozer*, M.I.T. Press, Cambridge, Mass.

**Anderson, T. R.** and **Bean, L. L.** (1961) The Shevky-Bell social areas: confirmation of results and a reinterpretation, *Social Forces*, **40**, 119–24.

**Anderson, T. R.** and **Egeland, J. A.** (1961) spatial aspects of social area analysis, *American Sociological Review*, **36**, 392–9.

**Antunes, G. E.** and **Plumlee, J. P.** (1977) The distribution of an urban public service: ethnicity, socio-economic status and bureaucracy as determinants of the quality of neighbourhood streets, *Urban Affairs Quarterly*, **12**, 312–32

**Appleyard, D.** (1970) Styles and methods of structuring a city, *Environment and Behaviour*, **2**, 100–117.

**Appleyard, D.** (1979a) The environment as a social symbol, *Journal of the American Planning Association*, **45**, 143–53.

**Appleyard, D.** (1979b) *The Conservation of European Cities*, MIT Press, Cambridge, Mass.

**Arbuthnot, J.** (1977) The roles of attitudinal and personality variables in the prediction of environmental behaviour and knowledge, *Environment and Behaviour*, **9**, 217–32.

**Ardrey, R.** (1966) *The Territorial Imperative*, Atheneum, New York.

**Ardrey, R.** (1970) *The Social Contract*, Delta, New York.

**Arensberg, C. M.** (1937) *The Irish Countryman*, Macmillan, London.

**Arrow, K. J.** (1951) *Social Choice and Individual Values*, Wiley, New York.

**Ashton, P. J.** (1984) Urbanization and the dynamics of suburban development under capitalism, pp. 54–81 in W. K. Tabb and L. Sawers (eds.) *Marxism and the Metropolis*, 2nd edition, Oxford University Press, New York.

**Ashworth, W.** (1954) *The Genesis of Modern British Town Planning*, Routledge & Kegan Paul, London.

**Babcock, R. F.** and **Bosselman, F. P.** (1973) *Exclusionary Zoning*, Praeger, New York.

**Baboolal, E.** (1981) Black residential distribution in South London, pp. 59–80 in P. Jackson and S. Smith (eds) *Social Interaction and Ethnic Segregation*, Institute of British Geographers Special Publication, No. 12, Academic press, London.

**Bachrach, P.** and **Baratz, M.** (1970) *Power and Poverty*, Oxford University Press, London.

**Badcock, B.** (1984) *Unfairly Structured Cities*, Blackwell, Oxford.

**Baerwald, T.** (1981) The site selection process of suburban residential builders, *Urban Geography*, **2**, 339–57.

**Baerwald, T.** (1983) Transportation and the Decentralization of Activity in North American Metropolises, *Proceedings*, International Geographical Union Working Group on the Geography of Transport, Department of Geography, University of Georgia, Athens, Georgia, pp. 1–20.

**Baerwald, T.** (1984) The geographic structure of modern North American metropolises, paper presented to the 25th International Geographical Congress, Paris.

**Bailey, P.** (1983) Sport and the Victorian City, *Urban History Review*, **12**, 71–6.

**Baldassare, M.** and **Fischer, C. S.** (1975) Suburban life: powerlessness and need for affiliation, *Urban Affairs Quarterly*, (March), 314–26.

**Baldassare, M.** and **Fischer, C. S.** (1976) The relevance of crowding experiments to urban studies, pp. 85–99 in Stokols, D. (ed.), *Psychological Perspectives on Environment and Behaviour*, Plenum Press, New York.

**Balwin, J.** (1975) Urban criminality and the problem estate, *Local Government Studies*, **1**, 12–20.

**Baldwin, J., Bottoms, A. E.** and **Walker, M. A.** (1976) *The Urban Criminal*, Tavistock, London.

**Ball, M.** (1979) A critique of urban economics, *International Journal of Urban and Regional Research*, **3**, 309–332.

**Ball, M.** (1983) *Housing Policy and Economic Power*, Methuen, London.

**Ball, M. J.** (1973) Recent empirical work on the determination of relative house prices, *Urban Studies*, **10**, 213–23.

**Ball, M. J.** and **Kirwan, R. M.** (1977) Accessibility and supply constraints in the urban housing market, *Urban Studies*, **14**, 11–32.

**Banfield, E. C.** (1974) *The Unheavenly City Revisited*, Little, Brown, Boston.

**Banfield, E. C.** and **Wilson, J. Q.** (1963) *City Politics*, Harvard University Press and M.I.T. Press, Cambridge, Mass.

**Banham, R.** (1973) *Los Angeles: The Architecture of Four Ecologies*, Penguin, Harmondsworth.

**Barbolet, R. H.** (1969) *Housing classes and the socio-ecological system*, University Working Paper No. 4, Centre for Environmental Studies, London.

**Bardo, J. W.** (1984) A re-examination of the neighborhood as a socio-spatial schema, *Sociological Inquiry*, **54**, 346–58.

**Barke, M.** (1983) The sale of council houses in Newcastle upon Tyne: Some early results, *Northern Economic Review*, **8**, 2–12.

**Barnes, J. A.** (1954) Class and community in a Norwegian island parish, *Human Relations*, **7**, 39–58.

**Barnett, J. R.** (1978) Race and physician location: trends in two New Zealand urban areas, *New Zealand Geographer*, **34**, 2–12.

**Barnett, J. R.** and **Sheerin, I. G.** (1977) Public policy and urban health: a review of selected programmes designed to influence the spatial distribution of physicians in New Zealand, *Proceedings, Ninth New Zealand Geography Conference*, Christchurch.

**Barrett, F. A.** (1973) *Residential Search Behaviour: A study of Intra-Urban Relocation in Toronto*, Geographical Monographs No. 1, York University, Atkinson College, Toronto.

**Barrett, W.** (1974) *Irrational Man: a study in existential philosophy*, Heinemann, London.

**Barth, G.** (1980) City People: *The Rise of Modern City Culture in Nineteenth Century America*, Oxford University Press, New York.

**Bassett, K.** and **Hauser, D.** (1975) Public policy and spatial structure: housing improvement in Bristol, pp. 20–66 in Peel, R., Chisholm, M. and Haggett, P. (eds) *Processes in Physical and Human Geography*, Heinemann, London.

**Bassett, K. A.** (1980) The sale of council houses as a political issue, *Policy and Politics*, **8**, 290–307.

**Bassett, K. A.** and **Short, J. R.** (1980) Patterns of building society and local authority mortgage lending in the 1970s, *Environment and Planning*, A, **12**, 279–300.

**Bather, N. J.** (1976) *The speculative residential developer and urban growth*, Geographical Paper No. 47, Department of Geography, University of Reading.

**Batley, R.** (1972) An explanation of non-participation in planning, *Policy and Politics*, **1**, 95–114.

**Bauer, R. A.** (ed.) (1966) *Social Indicators*, M.I.T. Press, Cambridge, Mass.

**Baum, A.** and **Epstein, Y.** (eds) (1979) *Human Response to Crowding*, Wiley, Chichester.

**Baum, H. S.** (1983) *Planners and Public Expectations*, Schenkman, Cambridge, Mass.

**Beauregard, R. A.** (1985) Politics, ideology and theories of gentrification, *Journal of Urban Affairs*, **7**, 51–62.

**Bebington, A. C.** and **Davies, B.** (1980) Territorial need indicators: a new approach, Part I *Journal of Social Policy*, **9**, 145–68.

**Beckmann, M. J.** (1973) Equilibrium models of residential location, *Regional and Urban Economics*, **3**, 361–8.

**Bederman, S.** (1974) The stratification of 'Quality of Life' in the black community of Atlanta, Georgia, *Southeastern Geographer*, **14**, 26–37.

**Bederman, S.** and **Adams J. S.** (1974) Job accessibility and underemployment, *Annals, Association of American Geographers*, **64**, 378–86.

**Bell, C.** and **Bell, R.** (1972) *City Fathers*, Penguin, Harmondsworth.

**Bell, C. R.** and **Newby, H.** (1971) *Community Studies*, Allen & Unwin, London.

**Bell, C. R.** and **Newby, H.** (1976) Community, Communion, Class and community action: the social sources of the new urban politics, pp. 189–208 in Herbert, D. and Johnston, R. J. (eds), *Social Areas in Cities*, Vol. 2, *Spatial Perspectives on Problems and Policies*, Wiley, Chichester.

**Bell, W.** (1955) Economic, family and ethnic status: an empirical test, *American Sociological Review*, **20**, 45–52.

**Bell, W.** (1958) Social choice, life styles and suburban residence, pp. 225–47 in Dobriner, W. (ed.), *The Suburban Community*, Putnam, New York.

**Bell, W.** (1968) The city, suburb and a theory of social choice, pp. 132–68 in Greer, S. *et al.* (eds), *The New Urbanization*, St. Martin's Press, New York.

**Bell, W.** and **Moskos, I.** (1964) A comment on Udry's increasing scale and spatial differentiation, *Social Forces*, **42**, 414–17.

**Bengston, S. F.** (1974) Housing and planning

in Sweden, pp. 99–109 in Fuerst, J. S. (ed.), *Public Housing in Europe and America*, Croom Helm, London.

**Berger, B.** (1960) *Working Class Suburb*, University of California Press, Berkeley.

**Berger, B. M.** (1971) *Looking for America: Essays on Youth, Suburbia and Other American Obsessions*, Prentice-Hall, Englewood Cliffs, New Jersey.

**Berger, P., Berger, B.** and **Kelliner H.** (1973) *The Homeless Mind*, Vintage, New York.

**Berkowitz, L.** and **McCauly, B.** (1972) *Altruism and Helping Behaviour*, Academic Press, New York.

**Bernstein, S. J.** (1973) Mass transit and the urban ghetto, *Traffic Quarterly*, **27**, 431–49.

**Berry, B. J. L.** (1959) Ribbon developments in the urban business pattern, *Annals, Association of American Geographers*, **49**, 145–55.

**Berry, B. J. L.** (ed.) (1972) *City Classification Handbook: Methods and Applications*, Wiley, New York.

**Berry, B. J. L.** (1973) *The Human Consequences of Urbanization*, St. Martin's Press, New York.

**Berry, B. J. L.** and **Bednarz, R.** (1975) A hedonic model of prices and assessments for single-family homes, *Land Economics*, **51**, 21–40.

**Berry, B. J. L.** and **Horton, F. E.** (eds), (1970) *Geographical Perspectives on Urban Systems*, Prentice-Hall, Englewood Cliffs, New Jersey.

**Berry, B. J. L.** and **Kasarda, J. D.** (1977) *Contemporary Urban Sociology*, Macmillan, New York.

**Berry, B. J. L.** and **Rees, P. H.** (1969) The factorial ecology of Calcutta, *American Journal of Sociology*, **74**, 455–91.

**Berthoud, R.** (1976) Where are London's poor? *Greater London Intelligence Quarterly*, **36**, 5–12.

**Beshers, J. M.** (1962) *Urban Social Structure*, Free Press, New York.

**Bird, C.** (1979) *The two-paycheck marriage*, Pocket Books, N.Y.

**Black, J. T.** (1980) The changing economic role of central cities and suburbs, pp. 80–123 in A. P. Solomon (ed.) *The Prospective City*, MIT Press, Cambridge, Mass.

**Blecher, E.** (1971) *Advocacy Planning for Urban Development*, Praeger, New York.

**Bloch, P. B.** (1974) *Equality of distribution of police services*, The Urban Institute, Washington, D.C.

**Blowers, A.** (1973) The neighbourhood: exploration of a concept, pp. 49–90 in *The City As A Social System*, Open University, Milton Keynes.

**Blowers, A.** (1980) *The Limits of Power: The Politics of Local Planning Policy*, Pergamon, Oxford.

**Blumberg, P.** (1980) *Inequality in an Age of Decline*, Oxford University Press, New York.

**Boaden, N.** (1971) *Urban Policy Making*, Cambridge University Press, Cambridge.

**Boal, F. W.** (1974) Territoriality in Belfast, pp. 192–212 in Bell, C. and Newby, H. (eds). *The Sociology of Community*, Cass, London.

**Boal, F. W.** (1976) Ethnic residential segregation, pp. 411–79 in D. Herbert and R. Johnston (eds), *Social Areas in Cities*, Vol. 1, Wiley, Chichester.

**Boal, F. W.** (1978) Territoriality on the Shankhill-Falls Divide, Belfast: the perspective from 1976, pp. 58–77 in Lanegran, D. and Palm, R. (eds), *An Invitation to Geography*, (2nd ed.), McGraw-Hill, New York.

**Boal, F. W.** (1981) Ethnic residential segregation, ethnic mixing and resource conflict: a study in Belfast, Northern Ireland, pp. 235–51 in C. Peach, V. Robinson and S. Smith (eds) *Ethnic Segregation in Cities*, Croom Helm, London.

**Boal, F. W., Doherty, P.** and **Pringle D. G.** (1978) *Social Problems in the Belfast Urban Area: An Exploratory Analysis*, Occasional Paper No. 12, Department of Geography, Queen Mary College, London.

**Boddy, M.** (1976a) The structure of mortgage finance: building societies and the British social formation, *Transactions, Institute of British Geographers*, New Series, **1**, 58–71.

**Boddy, M.** (1980) *The building societies*, Macmillan, London.

**Boddy, M.** (1983) Central-local government relations: Theory and practice, *Political Geography Quarterly*, **2**, 119–38.

**Boddy, N.** (1976b) Political economy of housing: mortgage-financed owner-occupation in Britain, *Antipode*, **8**, 15–24.

**Bogardus, E.** (1962) Social distance in the city, pp. 48–54 in Burgess, E. (ed.), *The Urban Community*, University of Chicago Press, Chicago.

**Boggs, S. L.** (1965) Urban crime patterns, *American Sociological Review*, **30**, 899–908.

**Böhning, W. R.** (1972) *The Migration of workers in the United Kingdom and the European Community*, Oxford University Press, London.

**Boissevain, J.** (1974) *Friends of Friends: Networks, Manipulators and Coalitions*, St. Martin's Press, New York.

**Bollens, J. C.** and **Schmandt, H. J.** (1975) *The Metropolis: Its People, Politics and Economic Life*, Harper and Row, New York.

**Bollens, J. C.** and **Schmandt, H. J.** (1982) *The Metropolis*, 4th ed., Harper & Row, New York.

**Bollerey, F.** and **Hartmann, K.** (1980) A Patriarchal Utopia: the garden city and housing reform in Germany at the turn of the century, pp. 135–65 in A. Sutcliffe (ed.) *The Rise of Modern Urban Planning*, Mansell, London.

**Booth, A.** (1976) *Human Crowding and Its Consequences*, Praeger, New York.

**Booth, C.** (1893) Life and labour of the people of London. *Journal of the Royal Statistical Society*, **55**, 557–91.

**Booth, C.** (1903) *Life and Labour of the People of London*, Macmillan, London.

**Boots, A.** *et al.* (1972) *Inequality in Local Government Services*, The Urban Institute, Washington, D.C.

**Boots, B. N.** (1979) Population density, crowding and human behaviour, *Progress in Human Geography*, **3**, 13–64.

**Bor, W.** (1973) Problems of inner city areas, with special reference to the Birmingham study, *Housing Review*, Sept./Oct., 156–63.

**Borchert, J. R.** (1967) American metropolitan evolution, *Geographical Review*, **57**, 301–32.

**Bott, E.** (1957) *Family and Social Networks*, Tavistock, London.

**Bottomore, T.** (1954) Social stratification in voluntary organisations, pp. 193–215 in Glass D. V. (ed.), *Social Mobility in Britain*, Routledge, London.

**Boulding, K. E.** (1956) *The Image*, University of Michigan Press, Ann Arbor.

**Bourne, L. S.** (1968) Market, location and site selection in apartment construction, *Canadian Geographer*, **12**, 211–26.

**Bourne, L. S.** (1976) Housing supply and housing market behaviour in residential development, pp. 111–58 in Herbert, D. T. and Johnston, R. J. (eds), *Social Areas in Cities*, Vol. 1, *Spatial Processes and Form*, Wiley, Chichester.

**Bourne, L. S.** (1981) *The Geography of Housing*, Arnold, London.

**Bovaird, A., Harloe, M.** and **Whitehead, C. M. E.** (1985) Private rented housing: its current role, *Journal of Social Policy*, **14**, 1–23.

**Bowlby, J.** (1965) *Child Care and the Growth of Love*, Penguin, Harmondsworth.

**Bowley, M.** (1945) *Housing and the State 1919–1944*, George Allen & Unwin, London.

**Boyer, B. D.** (1973) *Cities Destroyed for Cash: The FHA Scandal at HUD*, Follett, Chicago.

**Boyer, M. C.** (1983) *Dreaming the Rational City: The Myth of American City Planning*, MIT Press, Cambridge, Mass.

**Boyer, P.** (1978) *Urban Masses and Moral Order in America, 1820–1920*, Harvard University Press, Cambridge, Mass.

**Boyle, J.** and **Jacobs, D.** (1982) The intra-city distribution of services: a multivariate analysis, *American Political Science Review*, **76**, 371–9.

**Bradford, C.** and **Marino, D.** (1977) *Redlining and Disinvestment Association: a discriminatory practice in residential mortgage loans*, USGPO, Washington, D. C.

**Bradley, J. E., Kirby, A. M.** and **Taylor, P. J.** (1978) Distance decay and dental decay: a study of dental health among primary school children in Newcastle upon Tyne, *Regional Studies*, **12**, 529–40.

**Brand, J.** (1975) The politics of social indicators, *British Journal of Sociology*, **26**, 78–90.

**Brantingham, P. L.** and **Brantingham, J.** (1975) Residential burglary and urban form, *Urban Studies*, **12**, 273–84.

**Breitbart, M.** and **Peet, R.** (1974) A critique of advocacy planning, pp. 97–108, in Ley, D. (ed.), *Community Participation and the Spatial Order of the City*, Tantalus Research, Vancouver.

**Brennan, T.** (1948) *Midland City*, Dobson, London.

**Briggs, A.** (1968) *Victorian Cities*, Penguin, Harmondsworth.

**Briggs, R.** (1973) Urban cognitive distance, pp. 361–88 in Downs, R. and Stea, D. (eds), *Image and Environment*, Aldine, Chicago.

**Broadbent, G.** (1980) The deep structures of architecture, pp. 189–208 in G. Broadbent, R. Bont and C. Jencks, (eds) *Signs, Symbols and Architecture*, Wiley, Chichester.

**Brooks, E.** (1977) Geography and public policy, pp. 1–40 in *Values, Relevance and Policy*, Open University Course D204, Unit 30, Open University Press, Milton Keynes.

**Brown, L. A.** and **Holmes, J.** (1971) Search behaviour in an intra-urban migration context: a spatial perspective, *Environment and Planning*, **3**, 307–26.

**Brown, L. A.** and **Longbrake, D. B.** (1970) Migration flows in intra-urban space: place utility considerations, *Annals, Association of American Geographers*, **60**, 368–87.

**Brown, L. A.** and **Moore, E. G.** (1970) The intra-urban migration process: a perspective, *Geografiska Annaler*, **52B**, 1–13.

**Brown, M. A.** (1982) Modelling the spatial distribution of suburban crime, *Economic Geography.*, **58**, 247–61.

**Brown, W. H., Jr.** (1972) Access to housing: the role of the real estate industry, *Economic Geography*, **48**, 66–78.

**Brunn, S. D.** (1974) *Geography and Politics in America*, Harper & Row, New York.

**Bryant, B.** (1975) Citizen – official perceptions of metropolitan problems: a four-city study, pp. 5–24 in Wells, T. L. (ed.), *Urban Problems in a Metropolitan Setting*, Old Dominion University, Norfolk, Virginia.

**Bunge, W.** (1971) *Fitzgerald: Geography of a Revolution*, Schlenkman, Cambridge, Mass.

**Bunge, W.** (1975) Detroit humanly viewed: the American urban present, pp. 147–182 in Abler, R., Janelle, D., Philbrick, A. and Sommer, J. (eds) *Human Geography in a Shrinking World*, Duxbury Press, North Scituate, Mass.

**Burchell, R. W.** and **Listokin, D.** (eds) (1982) *Energy and Land Use*, Center for Urban Policy Research, Rutgers University, New Brunswick, N. J.

**Burgess, E. W.** (1924) The Growth of the City: An introduction to a research project, *Publications, American Sociological Society*, **18**, 85–97.

**Burgess, E. W.** (1925) The growth of the city: an introduction to a research project, pp. 47–62 in Park, R. E., Burgess, E. W. and McKenzie, R. D. (eds), *The City*, University of Chicago Press, Chicago.

**Burgess, E. W.** (ed.) (1926) *The Urban Community*, University of Chicago Press, Chicago.

**Burgess, E. W.** (1964) Natural area, p. 458 in Gould, J. and Kolb, W. L. (eds) *A Dictionary of the Social Sciences*, Free Press, New York.

**Burke, G.** (1976) *Townscapes*, Penguin, Harmondsworth.

**Burnett, A. D.** and **Hill, D.** (1982) Neighbourhood organizations and the distribution of public-service outputs in Britain, pp. 189–206 in R. C. Rich (ed.) *The Politics of Urban Public Services*, Lexington Books, Lexington, Mass.

**Burney, E.** (1967) *Housing on Trial*, Oxford University Press, Oxford.

**Burnley, I. H.** (1972) European immigration and settlement patterns in metropolitan

Sydney 1947–1966, *Australian Geographical studies*, **10**, 61–78.

Burnley, I. H. (1976) Southern European populations in the residential structure of Melbourne, *Australian Geographical Studies*, **14**, 116–32.

Burrell, F. A. (1865) *Report of the Council of Hygiene and Public Health upon the Sanitary Conditions of the City*, Citizens' Association of New York, New York.

Burstein, A. M. (1981) Immigrants and residential mobility: the Irish and Germans in Philadelphia, 1850–1880, pp. 174–203 in T. Hershberg (ed.) *Philadelphia*, Oxford University Press, New York.

Burt, R. S. (1981) Comparative power structures in American communities, *Social Science Research*, **10**, 115–76.

Burtenshaw, D, Bateman, M. and G. J. Ashworth (1981) *The City in West Europe*, Wiley, Chichester.

Busteed, M. A. (1975) *Geography and Voting Behaviour*, Oxford University Press, Oxford.

Butler, E. W., Chapin, F. S., Hemmens, G. C., Kaiser, E. J., Stegman, M. A. and Weiss, S. F. (1969) *Moving Behaviour and Residential Choice: A National Survey*, National Co-operative Highway Research Program Report No. 81, Highway Research Board, Washington, D.C.

Buttimer, A. (1972) Social space and the planning of residential areas, *Environment and Behaviour*, **4**, 279–318.

Buttimer, A. (1976) Grasping the dynamism of the life-world, *Annals, Association of American Geographers*, **66**, 227–92.

Buttimer, A. (1979) Reason, rationality and human creativity, *Geografiska Annaler*, B16 43–49.

Byrne, D. S. (1974) *'Problem Families': A Housing Lumpenproletariat*, Working Paper No. 5, Department of Sociology and Social Administration, University of Durham.

Cadwallader, M. T. (1979) Neighbourhood evaluation in residential mobility, *Environment and Planning*, **11A**, 393–401.

Cadwallader, M. T. (1981) A Unified Model of Urban Housing Patterns, Social Patterns and Residential Mobility, *Urban Geography*, **2**, 115–130.

Calabi, D. (1980) The genesis and special characteristics of town planning instruments in Italy 1880–1911, pp. 55–70 in A. Sutcliffe (ed.) *The Rise of Modern Urban Planning 1800–1914* Mansell, London.

Calhoun, J. B. (1962) Population density and social pathology, *Scientific American*, **206**, 139–48.

Callow, A. B., Jr. (ed). (1976) *The City Boss in America: An Interpretative Reader*, Oxford University Press, New York.

Campbell, R., Converse, P. and Rodgers, W. L. (1976) *The Quality of American Life: Perceptions, Evaluations and Satisfactions*, Russell Sage, New York.

Cannadine, D. (1977) Victorian cities: how different? *Social History*, **4**, 457–82.

Cannadine, D. (1982) Residential differentiation in nineteenth-century towns: from shapes on the ground to shapes in society, pp. 235–252 in J. J. Johnson and C. F. Pooley (eds.) *The Structure of Nineteenth Century Cities*, Croom Helm, London.

Canter, D. V. (1975) Distance estimation in Greater London, SSRC Final Report, University of Surrey.

Canter, D. V. and Tagg, S. K. (1975) Distance estimation in cities, *Environment and Behaviour*, **7**, 59–80.

Carey, L. and Mapes, R. (1972) *The Sociology of Planning*, Batsford, London.

Carley, M. (1981) *Social measurement and social indicators*, Allen and Unwin, London.

Carp, F. M. (1975) Life-style and location within the city, *The Gerontologist*, **75**, 27–33.

Carp, F. M., Zawadski, R. T., and Shokrkon, H. (1976) Dimensions of urban environmental quality, *Environment and Behaviour*, **8** 239–64.

Carlstein, T., Parkes, D. and Thrift, N. (eds) (1978) *Human Activity and Time Geography*, Arnold, London.

Carney, J. and Taylor, C. (1974)

Community development projects: review and comment, *Area*, **6**, 226–31.

**Carnoy, M.** and **Castells, M.** (1984) After the Crisis? *World Policy Journal*, Spring, 495–516.

**Carstairs, G. M.** (1966) Overcrowding and human aggression, pp. 751–64 in H. D. and Gurr, T. R. (eds) *Violence in America*, Bantam, New York.

**Carr, M. C.** (1982) The development and character of a metropolitan suburb: Bexley, Kent, pp. 211–268 in F. M. L. Thompson (ed.) *The Rise of Suburbia*, Lancaster University Press, Lancaster.

**Carter, A.** (1977) D'you mean south? *New society*, 28 July, 188–9.

**Carter, E.** (1979) Politics and architecture: an observer looks back at the 30s, *Architectural Review*, November, 324–325.

**Carter, H** (1975) *The Study of Urban Geography*, Arnold, London.

**Carter, H.** (1983) *An Introduction to Urban Historical Geography*, Arnold, London.

**Carter, H.** (1984) *Social Areas in Cities: Past and Future*, University of Maryland, Institute for Urban Studies, College Park, Maryland.

**Carter, R. L.** and **Hill, K. Q.** (1976) The criminal's image of the city and urban crime patterns, *Social Science Quarterly*, **57**, 597–607.

**Cassel, J.** (1972) Health consequences of population density and crowding, pp. 149–63, in Guttman, R. (ed.) *People and Buildings*, Basic Books, New York.

**Castells, M.** (1977) *The Urban Question*, Arnold, London.

**Castells, M.** (1978) *City, Class and Power*, Macmillan, London.

**Castells, M.** (1980) *The Economic Crisis and American Society*, Princeton University Press, Princeton, N. J.

**Castells, M.** (1983a) *The City and the Grassroots*, Arnold, London.

**Castells, M.** (1983b) Crisis, planning and the quality of life, *Environment & Planning D: Society and Space*, **1**, 3–21.

**Castells, M.** (1985) High technology, economic restructuring, and the urban-regional process in the United States, pp. 11–40 in M. Castells (ed.), *High Technology, Space and Society*, Sage, Beverly Hills.

**Castells, M., Cherki, E., Godard, F.** and **Mehl, D.** (1977) *Crise du logement et mouvements sociaux. Enquête sur la région Parisienne*, Mouton, Paris.

**Castle, I** and **Gittus, E.** (1957) The distribution of social defects in Liverpool, *Sociological Review*, **5**, 43–64.

**Castles, S.** and **Kosack, G.** (1985) *Immigrant Workers and Class Structure in Western Europe*, Oxford University Press, New York, 2nd edition.

**Catanese, A. J.** (1984) *The Politics of Planning and Development*, Sage Library of Social Research, No. 156, Sage, Beverly Hills.

**Cater, J.** and **Jones, T.** (1978) Asians in Bradford, *New Society*, **44**, 13 April, 81–2.

**Ceccarelli, P.** (1982) Politics, Parties and Urban Movements: Western Europe, pp. 261–76 in N. Fainstein and S. Fainstein (eds) *Urban Policy Under Capitalism*, Sage, Beverly Hills.

**Central Housing Advisory Committee** (1969) *Council Housing: Purposes, Procedures and Priorities*, Ninth Report of the Housing Management Subcommittee, H.M.S.O., London.

**Chaline, C. H.** (1984) Contemporary trends and policies in French city planning: a chronicle of successive urban policies 1950–1983, *Urban Geography*, **5**, 326–36.

**Chapin, F. S.** and **Weiss S. F.** (1968) A Probabilistic model for residential growth, *Transportation Research*, **2**, 375–90.

**Chapman, S. D.** (1971) *The History of Working Class Housing*, David & Charles, Newton Abbot.

**Chapple, E. D.** (1942) The measurement of interpersonal behaviour, *Transactions, New York Academy of Sciences*, **4**, 222–32.

**Checkoway, B.** (1980) Large builders, federal housing programmes, and postwar suburbanization, *International Journal of Urban and Regional Research*, **4**, 21–45.

**Cherry, G. (ed.)** (1980) *Shaping an Urban World*, Mansell, London.

**Cherry, G. E.** (1979) The town planning

movement and the late Victorian city, *Transactions, Institute of British Geographers*, NS4, 306–19.

Choldin, H. (1978) Urban density and pathology, *Annual Review of Sociology*, 4, 91–115.

Christensen, J. (1982) The politics of redevelopment: Covent Garden, pp. 129–51 in D. T. Herbert and R. J. Johnston (eds), *Geography and the Urban Environment*, vol. 4, Wiley, Chichester.

City of Glasgow (1983) *Annual Housing Review 1983*, City of Glasgow District Council Housing Department, Glasgow.

Clark, D. (1964) Immigrant enclaves in our cities pp. 205–218 in Elias, C. E., Jnr., Gillies, J. and Riemer, S. (eds), *Metropolis: Values in Conflict*, Wadsworth, Belmont, California.

Clark, W. A. V. (1970) Measurement and explanation in intra-urban residential mobility, *Tijdschrift voor Economische en Sociale Geografie*, 61, 49–57.

Clark, W. A. V. (1971) A test for directional bias in residential mobility, pp. 71–83, in McConnell, H. and Yasheen, D. W. (eds) *Models of Spatial Variation*, Illinois University Press, Illinois.

Clark, W. A. V. (1976) Migration in Milwaukee, *Economic Geography*, 52, 48–60.

Clark, W. A. V. (ed.) (1982) *Modelling Housing Market Search*, St Martin's, New York.

Clark, W. A. V. and Cadwallader, M. T. (1973) Residential preferences: an alternate view of intra-urban space, *Environment and Planning*, 5A, 693–703.

Clark, W. A. V. and Flowerdew, R. (1982) A review of search models and their application to search in the housing market, pp. 4–29 in W. A. V. Clark (ed.) *Modelling Housing Market Search*, St Martins, New York.

Clark, W. A. V. and Moore, E. G. (1978) *Population Mobility and Residential Change*, Northwestern University Studies in Geography, No. 25, Evanston, Illinois.

Clark, W. A. V. and Onaka, J. L. (1983) Life cycle and housing adjustment as explanations of residential mobility,

*Urban Studies*, 20, 47–57.

Clark, W. A. V. and Smith, T. R. (1979) Modelling information use in a spatial context, *Annals, Association of American Geographers*, 69, 575–88.

Clark, T. A. (1985) The interdependence among gentrifying neighbourhoods: central Denver since 1970, *Urban Geography*, 6, 246–73.

Clay, P L. (1979) *Neighbourhood Renewal, Middle-class Settlement and Incumbent Upgrading in American Neighbourhoods*, Lexington Books, Lexington, Mass.

Cleland, E. A., Stimpson, R. J., and Goldsworthy, A. J. (1977) *Suburban Health Care Behaviour in Adelaide*, Centre for Applied Social and Survey Research Monography Series No. 2, Flinders University, Adelaide.

Cliff, A. D. and Ord, J. K. (1973) *Spatial Autocorrelation*, Pion, London.

Coates, B., Johnston, R. J., and Knox, P. L. (1977) *Geography and Inequality*, Oxford University Press, London.

Coates, J. F. (1982) New technologies and their urban impact, pp. 177–195 in G. Gappert and R. V. Knight (eds) *Cities in the 21st Century*, Sage, Beverly Hills.

Coates, K. and Silburn, R. (1970) *Poverty: the Forgotten Englishmen*, Penguin, Harmondsworth.

Cockburn, C. (1977) *The Local State*, Pluto Press, London.

Cohen, A. K. (1955) *Delinquent Boys*, Free Press, Chicago.

Cohen, A. P. (1985) *The Symbolic Construction of Community*, Ellis Horwood, Chichester.

Cohen, S. (1973) *Folk Devils and Moral Panics*, Paladin, London.

Coit, K. (1978) Local action, not citizen participation, pp. 297–311 in Tabb, W. and Sawers, L. (eds) *Marxism and the Metropolis*, Oxford University Press, New York.

Coleman, R. P. (1978) Attitudes toward neighborhoods: how Americans choose to live, Working Paper No. 49, Joint Center for Urban Studies, Harvard/MIT, Cambridge, Mass.

Colenutt, R. (1971) Postscript on the Detroit

Geographical Expedition, *Antipode*, **3**, 85.

**Collins, A. H.** and **Pancoast, D. L.** (1976) *Natural Helping Networks: a strategy for prevention*, National Association of Social Workers, Washington, D.C.

**Collinson, P.** (1963) *The Cutteslowe Walls*, Faber & Faber, London.

**Committee on the Management of Local Government** (1967) *The Local Government Councillor*, H.M.S.O., London.

**Community Development Project** (1974) *Inter-Project Report*, C.D.P. Information and Intelligence Unit, H.M.S.O., London.

**Community Development Project** (1975) *Final Report, Part I: Coventry and Hillfields: Prosperity and the persistence of Inequality*, C. D. P. Information and Intelligence Unit, H.M.S.O., London.

**Community Development Project** (1976) *Whatever Happened to Council Housing?* CDP Information and Intelligence Unit, H.M.S.O., London.

**Connell, J.** (1973) Social networks in urban society, pp. 41–52 in Clark, B. and Gleave, M. (eds) *Social Patterns in Cities*, Institute of British Geographers, London.

**Connerly, C. E.** (1985) The community question: an extension of Wellman and Leighton, *Urban Affairs Quarterly*, **20**, 537–56.

**Conzen, M. P.** (1980) The morphology of nineteenth century cities in the United States, pp. 119–42 in W. Borah, J. Hardoy and G. A. Stelter (eds) *Urbanization in the Americas: The background in comparative perspective*, National Museum of Man, Ottawa.

**Conzen, M. P.** (1983) Historical geography: Changing spatial structure and social patterns of Western cities, *Progress in Human Geography*, **7**, 88–108.

**Conzen, M. R. G.** (1960) Alnwick: a study in town plan analysis, *Transactions, Institute of British Geographers*, **27**, 1–122.

**Cooper, C.** (1976) The house as symbol of the self, pp. 435–48 in Proshansky, H., Ittelson, W. and Rivlin, L. (eds) *Environmental Psychology: People and their Physical Settings*, Holt, Rinehart &

Winston, New York.

**Coppock, J. T.** and **Prince, H. C.** (1964) *The Geography of Greater London*, Faber, London.

**Corey, K. E.** (1966) *Urban house types: a methodological experiment in urban settlement geography*, Discussion Paper No. 3, Department of Geography, University of Cincinnati.

**Corey, K.** (1972) Advocacy in planning: a reflective analysis, *Antipode*, **4**, 46–63.

**Corina, L.** (1976) *Housing Allocation Policy and its Effects*, Department of Social Administration, University of York.

**Corsi, T. M.** and **Harvey, M. E.** (1975) The socio-economic determinants of crime in the city of Cleveland, *Tijdschrift Voor Economische en Sociale Geografie*, **66** 323–36.

**Costelloe, B. F. C.** (1899) *The Housing Problem*, J. Heywood, Manchester.

**Coutler, J.** (1978) *Grid-square census data as a source for the study of deprivation in British conurbations*, Working Paper No. 13, Census Research Unit, Department of Geography, University of Durham.

**Coutras, J.** and **Fagnani, J.** (1978) Femmes et transports en milieu urbain, *International Journal of Urban and Regional Research*. **2**, 432–9.

**Cowland, K.** (1979) The identification of social (class) areas and their place in nineteenth-century urban development, *Transactions, Institute of British Geographers*, **4**, 239–57.

**Cox, K. R.** (1969) The voting decision in a spatial context, *Progress in Geography*, **1**, 81–117.

**Cox, K. R.** (1973) *Conflict, Power and Politics in the City: A Geographic View*, McGraw-Hill, New York.

**Cox, K. R.** (1977) *Location and State in Market Societies*, Discussion Paper No. 61, Department of Geography, Ohio State University, Columbus.

**Cox, K. R.** (ed.), (1978) *Urbanization and Conflict in Market Societies*, Methuen, London.

**Cox, K. R.** (1983) Residential mobility, neighborhood activism and neighborhood problems, *Political Geography Quarterly*, **2**, 99–117.

Cox, K. R. (1984) Progress report: neighborhood conflict and urban social movements, *Urban Geography*, **5**, 343–55.

Cox, K. R. and Agnew, J. (1974) *The location of public housing: towards a comparative analysis*, Discussion Paper No. 45, Department of Geography, Ohio State University, Columbus.

Cox, K. R. and Dear, M. J. (1975) *Jurisdictional Organization and Urban Welfare*, Discussion Paper No. 47, Department of Geography, Ohio State University, Columbus.

Cox, K. R. and Reynolds, D. R. (1974) Locational approaches to power and conflict, pp. 19–14 in Cox, K. R., Reynolds, D. R. and Rokkan, S. (eds), *Locational Approaches to Power and Conflict*, Halstead Press, New York.

Cox, K. R. and McCarthy, J. J. (1980) Neighborhood Activism in the American city: behavioral relationships and evaluation, *Urban Geography*, **1**, 22–38.

Cox, K. R. and McCarthy, J. J. (1982) Neighborhood activism as a politics of turf: a critical analysis, pp. 196–219 in K. R. Cox and R. J. Johnston (eds) *Conflict, Politics and the Urban Scene*, Longman, London.

Cox, W. H. (1976) *Cities: The Public Dimension*, Penguin, Harmondsworth.

Craig, J. and Driver, A. (1972) The identification and comparison of small areas of adverse social conditions, *Journal of the Royal Statistical Society*, Series C, **21**, 25–35.

Craig, L. A. (1978) *The Federal Presence: Architecture, Politics and Symbols in US Government Building*, MIT Press, Cambridge, Mass.

Craven, E. (1975) Private residential expansion in Kent, pp. 124–44 in Pahl, R. E., *Whose City?*, Penguin Harmondsworth.

Cripps, E. L. and Foot, D. H. S. (1969) A land-use model for sub-regional planning, *Regional Studies*, **3**, 243–68.

Cullen, J. D. and Knox, P. L. (1981) The Triumph of the Eunuch, *Urban Affairs Quarterly*, **16**, 149–72.

Cullen, J. D. and Knox, P. L. (1982) The City, the Self and Urban Society, *Transactions, Institute of British Geographers*, **7**, 276–29.

Curl, J. S. (1970) *European Cities and Society*, Leonard Hill, London.

Curtis, J. E. and Petras, J. W. (1970) Community Power, Power Studies, and the Sociology of Knowledge, *Human Organization*, **29**, 204–18.

Curtis, J. H., Avesing, F. and Klosek, I. (1967) Urban Parishes as Social Areas, *The American Catholic Sociological Review*, **18**, 319–25.

Cybriwsky, R. A. (1978) Social aspects of neighbourhood change, *Annals, Association of American Geographers*, **68**, 17–33.

Cybriwsky, R. A., Ley, D., and Western, J. (1986) The political and social construction of revitalization in Society Hill, Philadelphia and False Creek, Vancouver, pp. 92–120 in N. Smith and P. Williams (eds) *Gentrification, Housing and the Restructuring of Urban Space*, Allen and Unwin, London.

Dahl, R. (1961) *Who Governs?* Yale University Press, New Haven.

Dahl, R. (1967) *Pluralist Democracy in the United States*, Rand-McNally, Chicago.

Dahmann, D. C. (1982) *Locals and Cosmopolitans, patterns of Spatial Mobility during the transition from Youth to Early Adulthood*, Department of Geography, University of Chicago, Research Paper 204.

Dahmann, D. C. (1983) Subjective assessments of neighbourhood quality by size of place, *Urban Studies*, **20**, 31–45.

Dahmann, D. C. (1985) Assessments of neighborhood quality in metropolitan America, *Urban Affairs Quarterly*, **20**, 511–36.

Dahya, B. (1974) The nature of Pakistani ethnicity in industrial cities in Britain, pp. 77–118 in Cohen, A. (ed.) *Urban Ethnicity*, Tavistock, London.

Daly, M. T. (1982) *Sydney Boom Sydney Bust. The City and its Property Market*

*1850–1981*, Allen and Unwin, Sydney.

**Damer, S.** (1974) Wine Alley: the sociology of a dreadful enclosure, *Sociological Review*, **22**, 221–48.

**Damer, S.** and **Madigan, R.** (1974) The housing investigator, *New Society*, **29**, 226–7.

**Daniel, W. W.** (1968) *Racial Discrimination in England*, Penguin, Harmondsworth.

**Danielson, M. N.** (1976) *The Politics of Exclusion*, Columbia University Press, New York.

**Darden, J.** (1980) Lending practices and policies affecting the American Metropolitan System, pp. 93–110 in S. D. Brunn and J. O. Wheeler (eds) *The American Metropolitan System: Present and Future*, Winston, New York.

**Darke, R.** and **Darke, J.** (1981) Towards a sociology of the built environment, *Architectural Psychology Newsletter*, **11**, 1–2.

**Daunton, M. J.** (1977) *Coal Metropolis: Cardiff, 1870–1914*, Leicester University Press, Leicester.

**Daunton M. J.** (1983) Public space and private space: the Victorian city and the working-class household, pp. 212–33 in D. Fraser and A. Sutcliffe (eds) *The Pursuit of Urban History*, Arnold, London.

**Davidoff, L.** (1979) The separation of home and work? Landladies and lodgers in nineteenth and twentieth-century England, pp. 64–97 in S. Burman (ed.) *Fit Work for Women*, Croom Helm, London.

**Davidoff, L.** and **Hall, C.** (1983) The architecture of public and private life: English middle-class society in a provincial town, 1780–1850, pp. 326–46. in D. Fraser and A. Sutcliffe (eds) *The Pursuit of Urban History*, Arnold, London.

**Davidoff, P.** (1965) Advocacy and pluralism in planning, *Journal of the American Institute of Planners*, **31**, 331–8.

**Davidoff, P., Davidoff, L** and **Gold, N.** (1970) Suburban action: advocate planning for an open society, *Journal of the American Institute of Planners*, **36**, 12–21.

**Davidson, R. N.** (1981) *Crime and*

*Environment*, Croom Helm, London.

**Davie, M. R.** (1937) The pattern of urban growth, pp. 133–61 in Murdock, G. (ed.), *Studies in the Science of Society*, Yale University Press, New Haven.

**Davies, B.** (1968) *Social Needs and Resources in Local Services*, Michael Joseph, London.

**Davies, B.** (1976) Territorial injustice, *New Society*, **36**, 352–54.

**Davies, J. G.** (1972) *The Evangelistic Bureaucrat*, Tavistock, London.

**Davies, J. L.** (1965) *The Elevated System and the Growth of Northern Chicago*, Studies in Geography, **10**, Northwestern University Press, Evanston, Illinois.

**Davies, S.** and **Albaum, H.** (1973) The mobility problems of the poor in Indianapolis, pp. 106–25 in Albaum, M. (ed.), *Geography and Contemporary Issues*, Wiley, New York.

**Davies, W.** and **Barrow, G.** (1973) Factorial ecology of three prairie cities, *Canadian Geographer*, **17**, 327–53.

**Davies, W. K. D.** (1984) *Factorial Ecology*, Grower, Aldershot.

**Deakin, N.** (1970) Race and human rights in the city, pp. 107–29 in Cowan, P. (ed.), *Developing Patterns of Urbanization*, Oliver & Boyd, Edinburgh.

**Dear, M. J.** (1976) Abandoned housing, pp. 59–99 in Adams, J. S. (ed.), *Urban Policymaking and Metropolitan Dynamics*, Ballinger, Cambridge, Mass.

**Dear, M. J.** (1976b) Spatial externalities and locational conflict, pp. 152–67 in D. Massey and P. Batey (eds) *London Papers in Regional Science: Alternative Frameworks for Analysis*, Pion, London.

**Dear, M. J.** (1981) Social and spatial reproduction of the mentally ill, pp. 481–500 in M. J. Dear and A. J. Scott (eds) *Urbanization and Urban Planning in Capitalist Society*, Methuen, London.

**Dear, M. J.** and **Long, J.** (1978) community strategies in locational conflict, pp. 113–27 in Cox, K. R. (ed.), *Urbanization and Conflict in Market Societies*, Methuen, London.

**De Giovanni, F. F.** (1984) An examination

of selected consequences of revitalization in six US cities, *Urban Studies*, **21**, 245–60.

Dench, G. (1975) *Maltese in London: A Case study in the Erosion of Ethnic Consciousness*, Routledge & Kegan Paul, London.

Dennis, N. (1970) *People and Planning*, Faber and Faber, London.

Dennis, N. (1972) *Public Participation and Planning Blight*, Faber and Faber, London.

Dennis, N. (1978) Housing policy areas: criteria and indicators in principle and practice, *Transactions, Institute of British Geographers*, N. S. **3**, 2–22.

Dennis, R. (1984) *English Industrial Cities of the Nineteenth Century: A Social Geography*, Cambridge University Press, Cambridge.

Dennis, R. and Daniels, S. J. (1981) 'Community' and the social geography of Victorian cities, *Urban History Yearbook 1981*, 7–23.

Dente, B. and Regonini, G. (1980) Urban policy and political legitimation: the case of Italian neighborhood councils, *International Political Science Review*, **1**, 14–27.

Department of the Environment (1978) *Study of Intending Migrants*, Department of the Environment, London.

DHSS (1981) *Primary Health Care in Inner London*, Department of Health and Social Services, London.

Diamond, D. (1975) Planning and the urban environment, *Geography*, **60**, 189–93.

Dickens, P. (1979) Marxism and architectural theory: a critique of recent work, *Environment and Planning B*, **6**, 105–17.

Dickens, P. (1980) Social Science of Design Theory, *Environment and Planning B*, **7**, 353–60.

Dickens, P., Duncan, S., Goodwin, M and Gray, F. (1986) *Housing, States and Localities*, Methuen, London.

Dickey, J. (1985) Urban impacts of information technology, pp. 175–87 in J. Brotchie *et al.* (eds) *The Future of Urban Form*, Croom Helm, London.

Dickinson, J. C., Gray, R. J. and Smith,

D. M. (1972) The quality of life in Gainesville, Florida: An application of territorial social indicators, *Southeastern Geographer*, **12**, 121–32.

Dieleman, F. M. (1983) Tenure and allocation policy in the Tilburg housing market, *Tijdschrift voor Economische on Sociale Geografie*, **74**, 162–74.

Dillon, T. (1973) The Irish in Leeds, 1851–1861, *Publications of the Thoresby Society*, **54**, 1–28.

Dingemans, D. (1979) Redlining and mortgage lending in Sacramento, *Annals, Association of American Geographers*, **69**, 225–239.

Diseker, R. A. and Chappell, J. A. (1976) Relative importance of variables in determination of practice location: a pilot study, *Social Science and Medicine*, **10**, 559–64.

Dodgshon, W. and Butlin, R. A. (eds) (1978) *An Historical Geography of England and Wales*, Academic Press, London.

Doherty, J. (1973) Race, class and residential segregation in Britain, *Antipode*, **3**, 45–51.

Doling, J. F. (1973) A two-stage model of tenure choice in the housing market, *Urban Studies*, **10**, 199–211.

Doling, J. F. and Williams, P. (1983) Building societies and local lending behaviour, *Environment and Planning*, A, **15**, 663–73.

Donald, O. D. (1978) *Access to Medical Care in Sydney*, Paper presented to the Regional Science Association, Australian and New Zealand Section, Third Annual Meeting, Monash University, Melbourne (mimeo).

Donaldson, S. (1969) *The Suburban Myth*, Columbia University Press, New York.

Donnison, D. (1974) Policies for priority areas, *Journal of Social Policy*, **3**, 127–35.

Donnison, D. and Soto, P. (1980) *The Good City*, Heinemann Educational, London.

Douglas, J. W. B. (1964) *The Home and the School*, McGibbon, St Albans.

Downs, A. (1964) *Inside Bureaucracy*, Rand, Chicago.

Downs, A. (1973) *Federal Housing Subsidies: How are they working?* D. C. Heath,

Lexington, Mass.

**Downs, A.** (1981) *Neighborhoods and Urban Development*, Brookings Institution Washington, D.C.

**Downs, A.** (1983) *Rental Housing in the 1980s*, Brookings Institution, Washington, D.C.

**Downs, R.** and **Stea, D.** (eds) (1973) *Image and Environment*, Aldine, Chicago.

**Draaisma, J.** and **Hoogstraten, P.** (1983) The squatter movement in Amsterdam, *International Journal of Urban and Regional Research*, **7**, 406–16.

**Drake, S.** and **Cayton, H. R.** (1962) *Black Metropolis: A Study of Negro life in a Northern City*, New York, Harper & Row.

**Drewnowski, J.** (1974) *On Measuring and Planning the Quality of Life*, Mouton, The Hague.

**Drury, P.** (1983) Some spatial aspects of health service developments: the British experience, *Progress in Human Geography*, **7**, 60–77.

**Duffy, F.** (1980) Office buildings and organizational change, pp. 255–281 in A. D. King (ed.) *Buildings and Society*, Routledge and Kegan Paul, London.

**Duncan, J. S.** (ed.) (1982) *Housing and Identity*, Holmes and Meier, New York.

**Duncan, J. S.** and **Duncan, N. G.** (1976) Housing as presentation of self and the structure of social networks, pp. 247–53 in G. T. Moore and R. G. Golledge (eds) *Environmental Knowing*, Dowden, Hutchinson and Ross, Stroudsburg, Penn.

**Duncan, J. S** and **Ley, D.** (1982) Structural Marxism and Human Geography: A Critical Assessment, *Annals, Association of American Geographers*, **72**, 30–59.

**Duncan, O. D.** and **Duncan, B.** (1955a) A methodological analysis of segregation indexes, *American Sociological Review*, **20**, 210–17.

**Duncan, O. D.** and **Duncan, B,** (1955b) Occupational stratification and residential distribution, *American Journal of Sociology*, **50**, 493–503.

**Duncan, O. D.** and **Lieberson, S.** (1959) Ethnic segregation and assimilation, *American Journal of Sociology*, **64**, 364–74.

**Duncan, O. D.** and **Schnore, L. F.** (1959) Cultural, behavioural and ecological perspectives in the study of social organization, *American Journal of Sociology*, **65**, 132–46.

**Duncan, S.** (1977) Mental maps of New York, *New York Magazine*, December 19, pp. 51–72.

**Duncan, S. S.** (1974) Cosmetic planning or social engineering? Improvement grants and improvement areas in Huddersfield, *Area*, **6**, 259–71.

**Duncan, S. S.** (1976) Self-help: the allocation of mortgages and the formation of housing sub-markets, *Area*, **8**, 307–16.

**Duncan, S. S.** and **Goodwin, M.** (1982) The local state: functionalism, autonomy and class relations in Cockburn and Saunders, *Political Geography Quarterly*, **1**, 77–96.

**Duncan, T. L. C.** (1971) *Measuring Housing Quality*, Occasional Paper No. 20, Centre for Urban and Regional Studies, University of Birmingham.

**Dunleavy, P. J.** (1981) *The Politics of Mass Housing in Britain 1945–1975*, Clarendon Press, Oxford.

**Dunstan, J. A. P.** and **Roberts, S. F.** (1980) Ecology, delinquency and socioeconomic status, *British Journal of Criminology*, **20**, 329–43.

**Durant, R.** (1959) *Watling: A Survey of Social Life on a New Housing Estate*, King, London.

**Durkheim, E.** (1893) *De La Division du Travail Social*, Alcan, Paris.

**Dutton, D.** (1978) Explaining the low use of health services by the poor: costs, attitudes or delivery systems? *American Sociological Review*, **43**, 348–68.

**Dyos, H. J.** (1968a) The speculative builders and developers of Victorian London, *Victorian Studies*, **11**, 641–90.

**Dyos, H. J.** (1968b) *The Study of Urban History*, Arnold, London.

**Dyos, H. J.** and **Wolff, M.** (eds.) (1973) *The Victorian City: Images and Realities*, Vol. 2, Routledge & Kegan Paul, London.

**Dzus, R.** and **Romsa, G.** (1977) Housing

construction, vacancy chains and residential mobility in Windsor, *Canadian Geographer*, **21**, 223–36.

Eagland, R. M. (1973) Evaluation and practise, pp. 197–213. in *Urban and Regional Models*, PTRC Seminar Proceedings, Planning and Tranport Research and Computation, London.

Eco, U. (1980) *Function and sign: the semiotics of architecture*, pp. 11–69 in G. Broadbent, R. Bont, and C. Jencks (eds) *Signs, Symbols and Architecture*, Wiley, Chichester.

Edney, J. J. (1976) The psychological role of property rights in human behaviour, *Environment and Planning*, **8A**, 811–22.

Edwards, A. M. (1981) *The Design of Suburbia*, Pembridge Press, London.

Edwards, J. (1975) Social indicators, urban deprivation and positive discrimination, *Journal of Sociology Policy*, **4**, 275–87.

Edwards, J. and Batley, R. (1978) *The Politics of Positive Discrimination*, Tavistock, London.

Edwards, R. C., Reich, M. and Gordon, D. (eds.) (1975) *Labor Market Segmentation*, Lexington Books, Lexington, Mass.

Eisinger, P. (1982) French urban housing and the mixed economy: the privatization of the public sector, *American Political Science Review*, **459**, 134–47.

Elkin, S. L. (1985) Twentieth century urban regimes, *Journal of Urban Affairs*, **7**, 11–28.

Elliot, B. and McCrone, D. (1975) Landlords in Edinburgh: some preliminary findings, *Sociological Review*, **23**, 539–62.

Elliott, B and McCrone, D. (1982) *The City: Patterns of Domination and Conflict*, Macmillan, London.

Elliot, B. and McCrone, D. (1984) Austerity and the politics of resistance, pp. 192–216 in I. Szelyeni (ed.) *Cities in Recession*, Sage, Beverly Hills.

Ellison, C. E. (1983) Marx and the modern city: public life and the problem of personality, *Review of Politics*, **45**, 393–420.

Engels, F. (1844) *The Condition of the Working class in England*, Panther,

London (reprint 1969).

English, J. (1976) Housing allocation and a deprived Scottish estate, *Urban Studies*, **13**, 319–23.

English, J. (1979) Access and deprivation in Local Authority housing, pp. 113–35 in Jones, C. (ed.), *Urban Deprivation and the Inner City*, Croom Helm, London.

English, J. (1982) *The Future of Council Housing*, Croom Helm, London.

English, J., Madigan, R. and Norman, P. (1976) *Slum Clearance*, Croom Helm, London.

Entrikin, J. N. (1980) Robert Park's Human Ecology and Human Geography, *Annals, Association of American Geographers*, **70**, 43–58.

Erickson, R. A. (1983) The evolution of the suburban space economy, *Urban Geography*, **4**, 95–121.

Esser, A. H. (ed.) (1971) *Behaviour and Environment*, Plenum, New York.

Evans, A. W. (1973) *The Economics of Residential Location*, Macmillan, London.

Evans, D J. (1973) A comparative study of urban social structures in South Wales, *Institute of British Geographers, Special Publication*, **5**, 87–102.

Evans, D. J. (1980) *Geographical Perspectives on Juvenile Delinquency*, Gower Westmead, Farnborough.

Evans, D. J. and Oulds, G. (1984) Geographical aspects of the incidence of residential burglary in Newcastle-under Lyme, UK, *Tijdschift-Voor Economische en Sociale Geographia*, **75**, 344–55.

Everitt, B. (1974) *Cluster Analysis*, SSRC Reviews of Current Research, No. 11, Heinemann, London.

Everitt, J. C. (1976) Community and propinquity in a city, *Annals, Association of American Geographers*, **66**, 104–16.

Everitt, J. C. and Cadwallader, M. T. (1972) The home area concept in urban analysis: the use of cognitive mapping and computer procedures as methodological tools, pp. 1.2.1.–1.2.10 in Mitchell, W. J. (ed.), *Environmental Design: Research and Practice*, University of California Press, Los Angeles.

Everitt, J. C. and Cadwallader, M. T. (1977)

Local area definition revisited, *Area*, **9**, 175–6.

**Eversley, D.** (1973) *The Planner in Society: The Changing Role of a Profession*, Faber & Faber, London.

**Eversley, D.** (1975) The landlords' slow farewell, *New Society*, **31**, 119–21.

**Ewen, L. A.** (1978) *Corporate Power and Urban Crisis in Detroit*, Princeton University Press, Princeton, N. J.

**Eyer, J.** (1977) Prosperity as a cause of death, *International Journal of Health Services*, **7**, 125–50.

**Eyles, J.** (1968) *Inhabitants' images of Highgate Village (London)*, Discussion Paper 15, Graduate School of Geography, London School of Economics.

**Eyles, J.** (1973) Spatial opportunity and the concept of the reference group, *Professional Geographer*, **25**, 121–3.

**Eyles, J.** (1978) Social geography and the study of the capitalist city: a review, *Tijdschrift voor Economische en Sociale Geografie*, **69**, 296–305.

**Eyles, J.** (1979) Area-based policies for the inner city: context, problems and prospects, pp. 226–43 in D. Herbert and D. M. Smith (eds), *Social Problems and The City*, Oxford University Press, Oxford.

**Eyles, J.** (1981) Why geography cannot be Marxist: towards an understanding of lived experience, *Environment and Planning*, A, **13**, 1371–88.

**Eyles, J.** (1986) The examination of social relationships in space: its territorial, empirical and practical parameters, *Geo Journal*, **9**, 247–253.

**Falcocchio, J., Pignataro, L.** and **Cantilli, E.** (1972) Modal choices and travel attributes of the inner-city poor, *Highway Research Record*, **403**, Highway Research Board, Washington, D. C.

**Faris, R. E. L.** and **Dunham, H. W.** (1939) *Mental Disorders in Urban Areas*, University of Chicago Press, Chicago.

**Fava, S.** (1980) Womens' place in the new suburbia, pp. 129–49. in G. Wekerle, R. Peterson and D. Morley (eds) *New Space for Women*, Westview Press, Boulder, CO.

**Feiffer, J.** (1968) *Little Murders*, Random House, New York.

**Feldman, S. D.** and **Thielbar, G. W.** (eds) (1975) *Life Styles: Diversity in American Society*, Little, Brown, Boston.

**Festinger, L., Schacter, S.** and **Back, K.** (1950) *Social Pressures in Informal Groups*, Harper, New York.

**Fincher, R.** (1984) The state apparatus and the commodification of Quebec's housing cooperatives, *Political Geography Quarterly*, **3**, 127–143.

**Fine, J., Glenn, N. D.** and **Monts, J. J.** (1971) The residential segregation of occupational groups in central cities and suburbs, *Demography*, **8** 91–102.

**Firey, W.** (1945) Sentiment and symbolism as ecological variables, *American Sociological Review*, 10, 140–148.

**Firey, W.** (1947) *Land Use in Central Boston*, Harvard University Press, Cambridge, Mass.

**Fischer, C. S.** (1973) On urban alienation and anomie, *American Sociological Review*, **38**, 311–26.

**Fischer, C. S.** (1975) Toward a subcultural theory of urbanism, *American Journal of Sociology*, **80**, 1319–41.

**Fischer, C. S.** (1976) *The Urban Experience*, Harcourt, Brace Jovanovich, New York.

**Fischer, C. S.** (1981) The public and private worlds of city life, *American Sociological Review*, **46**, 306–16.

**Fischer, C. S.** (1985) Studying technology and social life, pp. 284–300 in M. Castells (ed.) *High Technology, Space and Society*, Sage, Beverly Hills.

**Fischer, C. S.** and **Jackson, R M.** (1976) Suburbs networks and attitudes, pp. 279–306 in Schwartz, B. (ed.), *The Changing Face of the Suburbs*, University of Chicago Press, Chicago.

**Fischer, E. M.** and **Winnick, L.** (1951) A reformulation of the filtering concept, *Journal of Social Issues*, **1**, 47–58.

**Fischer, R. M.** (ed.) (1955) *The Metropolis in Modern Life*, Doubleday, New York.

**Flowerdew, R.** (1976) Search strategies and stopping rules in residential mobility, *Transactions, Institute of British Geographers*, New Series, **1**, 47–57.

**Flowerdew, R.** (1978) The role of time models in residential choice, pp. 99–121 in T. Carlstein, D. N. Parkes and N. J. Thrift (eds) *Human Activity and Time Geography*, Arnold, London.

**Foggin, P.** and **Polese, M.** (1977) *The Social Geography of Montreal in 1971*, University of Toronto, Centre for Urban and Community Studies, Research Paper No. 88, Toronto.

**Foley, D. L.** (1973) Institutional and contextual factors affecting the housing choice of minority residents, pp. 85–147 in Hawley, A. H. and Rock, V. P. (eds) *Segregation in Residential Areas*, National Academy of Sciences, Washington, D.C.

**Foley, D. L.** (1975) Accessibility for residents in the metropolitan environment, pp. 157–200 in Hawley, A. H. and Rock, V. P. (eds), *Metropolitan America in Contemporary Perspective*, Halstead Press, New York.

**Forbes, J.** and **Robertson, I. M. L.** (1978) Intra-urban migration in Greater Glasgow, paper given to the Population Studies Group of the Institute of British Geographers, Glasgow, September 1978.

**Ford, J. R.** (1975) The role of the building society manager in the urban stratification system: autonomy versus constraint, *Urban Studies*, **12**, 295–302.

**Ford, L. R.** (1973) Individual decisions in the creation of the American Downtown, *Geography*, **58**, 324–7.

**Forman, R.** (1971) *Black Ghettos, White Ghettos and Slums*, Prentice-Hall, Englewood Cliffs, New Jersey.

**Forrest, R., Henderson, J.** and **Williams, P, (eds.)** (1982) *Urban Political Economy and Social Theory*, Gower, Aldershot.

**Forrest, R.** and **Murie, A.** (1983) Residualization and council housing: aspects of the changing social relations of housing tenure, *Journal of Social Policy*, **12**, 453–468.

**Forrest, R., Murie,, A.** and **Williams, P.** (1985) *Bulwarks against Bolshevism*, Hutchinson, London.

**Forrest, R.** and **Murie. A.** (1986) Marginalization and subsidized individualism: the sale of council houses in the restructuring of the British welfare state, *International Journal of Urban and Regional Research*, 10, 46–66.

**Forrest, R.** and **Williams, P.** (1980) *The Commodification of Housing: emerging issues and contradictions*, Working Paper No. 73, Centre for Urban and Regional Studies University of Birmingham, England.

**Foster, J.** (1974) *Class Struggle and the Industrial Revolution*, Weidenfeld & Nicolson, London.

**Foster, J.** (1979) How Imperial London preserved its slums, *International Journal of Urban and Regional Research*, **3**, 94–114.

**Foster, M. S.** (1981) *From Streetcar to Superhighway: American City Planners and Urban Transportation, 1900–1940*, Temple University Press, Philadelphia.

**Foucault, M.** (1977) *Discipline and Punish: the birth of the prison*, Allen Lane, London.

**Fox, M.** (1983) Working women and travel, *Journal of the American Planning Association*, **49**, 156–170.

**Francescato, D.** and **Mebane, W.** (1973) How citizens view two great cities: Milan and Rome, pp. 131–47 in Downs, R. and Stea, D. (eds), *Image and Environment*, Aldine, Chicago.

**Fraser, D.** (1976) Urban Politics in Victorian England, Leicester University Press, Leicester.

**Fraser, D.** (1979) Politics and the Victorian City, *Urban History Yearbook 1979*, 2, 32–45.

**Frazier, E. F.** (1967) The Negro family in Chicago, pp. 224–38 in Burgess, E. W. and Bogue, D. J. (eds), *Urban Sociology*, University of Chicago Press, Chicago.

**Freedman, J. L.** (1975) *Crowding and Behaviour*, Freeman, San Francisco.

**Freedman, M.** (1985) Urban labor Markets and Ethnicity: segments and shelters re-examined, pp. 145–166 in L, Maldonado and J. Moore (eds) *Urban Ethnicity in the United States*, Sage, Beverly Hills.

**Freestone, R.** (1975) On Urban resource allocation: the distribution of medical practitioners in Sydney, *Geographical*

*Bulletin*, New South Wales Geographical Society, **7**, 14–25.

**Fried, J. P.** (1971) *Housing Crisis U.S.A.*, Praeger, New York.

**Fried, M.** (1963) Grieving for a lost home, pp. 151–71 in Duhl, L. J. (ed.) *The Urban Condition*, Basic Books, New York.

**Friedland, R.** (1981) Central city fiscal stress: the public costs of private growth, *International Journal of Urban and Regional Research*, **5**, 356–75.

**Friedrichs, C. R.** (1978) Capitalism, mobility and class formation in the Early Modern German city, pp. 187–214 in Abrams, P. and Wrigley, E. A. (eds) *Towns in Societies*, Cambridge University Press, Cambridge.

**Frisch, M. H.** (1969) The community élite and the emergence of urban politics: Springfield, Massachusetts, 1840–1880, pp. 277–96 in Thernstrom, S. and Sennett, R. (eds) *Nineteenth Century Cities*, Yale University Press, New Haven.

**Fuerst, J. S.** (ed.) (1974) *Public Housing in Europe and America*, Croom Helm, London.

**Gagnon, G.** (1960) Les zones sociales de l'Agglomeration de Quebec, *Recherches Sociographiques*, **1**, 255–67.

**Gale, S.** and **Moore, E. G.** (eds) (1975) *The Manipulated City*, Maaroufa Press, Chicago.

**Galle, O. R.** and **Gove, W. R.** (1983) Overcrowding, Isolation and Human Behaviour: exploring the extremes in population distribution, pp. 215–42 in M. Baldassare (ed.) *Cities and Urban Living*, Columbia University Press, New York.

**Galster, G. C.** and **Hester, G. W.** (1981) Residential Satisfaction: compositional and contextual correlates, *Environment and Behavior*, **13**, 735–58.

**Gamst-Nielsen, K.** (1974) Resistance from below – against exploitation of housing conditions, unpublished paper, University of Copenhagen.

**Gans, H. J.** (1961) Planning and social life: friendship and neighbour relations in suburban communities, *Journal of the*

*American Institute of Planners*, **27**, 134–40.

**Gans, H. J.** (1962) *The Urban Villagers*, Free Press, New York.

**Gans, H. J.** (1967) *The Levittowners*, Allen Lane, London.

**Gans, H. J.** (1969) Planning for people, not buildings, *Environment and Planning*, **1A**, 33–46.

**Gans, H. J.** (1972) *People and Plans*, Penguin, Harmondsworth.

**Gans, H. J.** (1975) The failure of urban renewal: a critique and proposals, pp. 199–212 in Gale, S. and Moore, E. G. (eds), *The Manipulated City*, Maaroufa Press, Chicago.

**Gappert, G.** (1979) *Post-Affluent America*, Franklin Watts, New York.

**Gappert, G.** (1982) future urban America: post-affluent or advanced industrial society, pp. 99–34 in G. Gappert and R. Knight (eds) *Cities in the 21st Century*, Sage, Beverly Hills.

**Garcia, P.** (1985) Immigration issues in urban ecology: the case of Los Angeles, pp. 73–100 in L. Maldonado and J. Moore (eds) *Urban Ethnicity in the United States*, Sage, Beverly Hills.

**Gardiner, J. A.** and **Olson, D. J.** (eds) (1974) *Theft of the City: Readings on Corruption in Urban America*, Indiana University Press, Bloomington, Indiana.

**Gartner, A.** and **Riessman, F.** (1974) *The service society and the consumer vanguard*, Harper & Row, New York.

**Gartner, A.** and **Reissman, F.** (1980) *Self-Help in Human Services*, Jossey-Bass, San Francisco.

**Gatrell, V. A. C.** (1982) Incorporation and the pursuit of Liberal hegemony in Manchester 1790–1839, pp. 15–60 in D. Fraser (ed). *Municipal Reform and the Industrial City*, Leicester University Press, Leicester.

**Gauldie, E.** (1974) *Cruel Habitations*, Allen & Unwin, London.

**Geddes, P.** (1915) *Cities in Evolution*, reprinted in 1947, J.Tyrwhitt, (ed.) Williams & Norgate, London.

**Gendrot, S. N.** (1982) governmental responses to popular movements: France and the United States, pp 277–300 in

N. I. Fainstein and S. S. Fainstein (eds) *Urban Policy Under Capitalism*, Sage, Beverly Hills.

Gerson, K. (1983) Changing family structure and the position of women, *Journal of the American Planning Association*, **49**, 138–148.

Gettys, W. E. (1940) Human ecology and social theory, Social Forces, **18**, 469–76.

Gibson, J. E. (1977) *Designing the New City*, Wiley-Interscience, New York.

Gittus, E. (1964) The structure of urban areas, *Town Planning review*, **35**, 5–20.

Gittus, E. and Stephens, C. J. (1973) Some problems in the use of canonical analysis, unpublished discussion paper, University of Newcastle Upon Tyne.

Glaab, C. N. and Brown, A. T. (1967) *A History of Urban America*, Macmillan, New York.

Gladstone, F. (1976) *The Politics of Planning*, Temple Smith, London.

Glass, D. V. (ed.) (1954) *Social Mobility in Britain*, Routledge & Kegan Paul, London.

Glass, R. *et. al.* (1964) *London: Aspects of Change*, MacGibbon & Kee, London.

Glass, R. (1968) Urban sociology in Great Britain, pp. 21–46 in Pahl, R. E. (ed.), *Readings in Urban Sociology*, Pergamon, Oxford.

Glazer, N. (1979) The urban dilemma: New York, *Ekistics*, **46**, 72–6.

Glennerster, H., and Hatch, S. (1974) *Positive Discrimination and Inequality*, Fabian Research Series no. 314, Fabian Society, London.

Gloag, J. (1979) Nazi Interlude, *Architectural Review*, **166**, 326–8.

Gober, P. and Behr, M. (1982) Central cities as distinct place types: Myth or fact? *Economic Geography*, **58**, 371–85.

Gober, P. and Gordon, R. J. (1980) Intraurban physician location: a case study of Phoenix, *Social Science and Medicine*, 14D, 407–17.

Goffman, E. (1959) *The presentation of self in everyday life*, Doubleday, New York.

Goffman, E. (1971) *Relations in Public*, Basic Books, New York.

Goheen, P. (1970) *Victorian Toronto, 1850 to 1900*, Research Paper No. 127, Department of Geography, University of Chicago.

Gold, J. R. (1979) *An Introduction to Behavioural Geography*, Oxford University Press, London.

Gold, J. R. (1982) Territoriality and Human spatial behaviour, *Progress in Human Geography*, **6**, 44–67.

Gold, J. R. (1984) The death of the urban vision? *Futures*, **16**, 372–81.

Goldberg, M. A. and Mercer, J. (1986) *The Myth of the North American City*, University of British Columbia Press, Vancouver.

Goldin, C. (1981) Family strategies and the family economy in the late nineteenth century, pp. 277–310 in T. Hershberg (ed.) *Philadelphia: Work, Space, Family and Group Experience in the Nineteenth Century*, Oxford University Press, New York.

Goldstein, S. and Mayer, K. B. (1961) *Metropolitanization and Population Change in Rhode Island*, Rhode island Development Council, Rhode Island.

Goldthorpe, J. H. *et al* (1967) The affluent worker and the thesis of embourgoisement: some preliminary research findings, *Sociology*, **1**, 11–31.

Goldthorpe, J. H., Lockwood, D., Bechhofer, F. and Platt, J. (1968) *The Affluent Worker*, Cambridge University Press, Cambrige.

Gollege, R. G., Briggs, R. and Demko, D. (1969) The configuration of distances in intra-urban space, *Proceedings, Association of American Geographers*, **1**, 60–8.

Gollege, R. G. and Zannaras, G. (1970) The perception of urban structure: an experimental approach, pp. 56–67 in Archea, J. and Eastman, C. (eds), *EDRA 2, Proceedings of Second Annual Conference*, Carnegie Press, Pittsburgh.

Gollege, R. G. and Zannaras, G. (1973) Cognitive approaches to the analysis of human spatial behaviour, pp. 59–94 in Ittleson, W. H. (ed.) *Environmental Cognition*, Seminar Press, New York.

Goodchild, B. (1974) Class differences in

environmental perception, *Urban Studies*, **11**, 157–69.

**Goodey, B., Duffet, A., Gold, J.** and **Spencer, D.** (1971) *The City Scene: An Exploration into the Image of Central Birmingham as seen by Area residents*, Research Memorandum No. 10, Centre for Urban and Regional Studies, University of Birmingham.

**Goodman, R.** (1972) *After the Planners*, Penguin Harmondsworth.

**Gordon, D. M.** (1979) *The working poor: towards a state agenda*, The Council of State Planning Agencies, Washington, D.C.

**Gordon, D. M.** (1984) Capitalist development and the history of American cities, pp. 21–53 in W. K. Tabb and L. Sawers (eds) *Marxism and the Metropolis*, Oxford University Press, New York, 2nd edition.

**Gordon, G.** (1979) The status areas of early to mid-Victorian Edinburgh, *Transactions, Institute of British Geographers*, New Series, **4**, 168–91.

**Gordon, G.** (1983) The status areas of Edinburgh in 1914, pp. 168–96 in G. Gordon and B. Dicks (eds) *Scottish Urban History*, Aberdeen University Press, Aberdeen.

**Gordon, M. M.** (1964) *Assimilation in American Life*, Oxford University Press, New York.

**Goschel, A., Herlyn, V., Kramer, J. Schardt, T.** and **Wendt, G.** (1982) Infrastructural inequality and segregation, *International Journal of Urban and Regional Research*, **6**, 503–31.

**Gottlieb, B. H. (ed.)** (1981) *Social Networks and Social Support*, Sage Beverly Hills.

**Gottlieb, M.** (1976) *Long Swings in Urban Development*, Schenckman, New York.

**Gottman, J.** (1961) *Megalopolis*, Twentieth Century Fund, New York.

**Gottman, J.** (1977) Megalopolis and Antipolis: the telephone and the structure of the city, pp. 303–17 in I. de S. Pool (ed.) *The Social Impact of the Telephone*, MIT Press, Cambridge, Mass.

**Gottman, J.** (1983) *The Coming of the Transactional City*, University of Maryland Institute for Urban Studies, College Park, MD.

**Graff, C. L.** (1982) Employment of women, suburbanization, and house styles, *Housing and Society*, **9**, 111–17.

**Graham, H. D.** and **Gurr, T. R.** (eds) (1969) *Violence in America*, Bantam, New York.

**Granovetter, M. S.** (1976) Network sampling: some first steps, *American Journal of Sociology*, **81**, 1287–303.

**Gray, F.** (1976a) Selection and allocation in council housing, *Transactions, Institute of British Geographers*, New Series, **1**, 34–46.

**Gray, F.** (1976b) The management of local authority housing, pp. 81–102, in *Housing and class in Britain*, Political Economy of Housing workshop, Conference of Socialist Economists, London.

**Gray, F.** and **Boddy, M.** (1979) The origins and use of theory in urban geography: household mobility and filtering theory, *Geoforum*, **10**, 117–27.

**Greenberg, S.** (1981) Industrial location and ethnic residential patterns in an industrializing city: Philadelphia, 1880, pp. 204–229 in T. Hershberg (ed.) *Philadelphia: Work, Space, Family and Group Experience in the Nineteenth Century*, Oxford University Press, New York.

**Greenwood, W.** (1933) *Love on the Dole*, Jonathan Cape, London.

**Greer, S.** (1971) Policy and the urban future, pp. 256–68 in Bell, W. and Mau, J. (eds), *Sociology of the Future*, Russell Sage Foundation, New York.

**Greer, S.** *et. al.* (eds) (1968) *The New Urbanization*, St. Martin's Press, New York.

**Greer, S.** and **Orleans, P.** (1962) The mass society and the parapolitical structure, *American Sociological Review*, **27**, 634–46.

**Greer-Wootten, B.** (1972) Changing social areas and the intra-urban migration process, *Review de geographie de Montreal*, **26**, 271–92.

**Greer-Wootten, B.** and **Velidis, S.** (1983) *The Relationships Between Objective and Subjective Indicators of the Quality of*

*Residential Environments, Toronto CMA, 1981*, Department of Geography. University of Toronto, Toronto.

**Gregory, D.** (1978) *Ideology, Science and Human Geography*, Hutchinson, London.

**Grigsby, W. G.,** (1963) *Housing Markets and Public Policy*, University of Pennsylvania Press, Philadelphia.

**Grigsby, W. G., Rosenburg, L., Stegman, M.** and **Taylor, J.** (1970) *Housing and Poverty: An Abstract*, Institute for Environmental Studies, University of Pennsylvania, Philadelphia.

**Grime, E. D.** and **Smith, A. G.** (1982) Mortgage allocation in Salford and Manchester, *Area*, **14**, 305–12

**Guest, A.** and **Lee, B. A.** (1983) The social organization of Local areas, *Urban Affairs Quarterly*, **19**, 217–240

**Gutman, R.** (ed.) (1972)) *People and Buildings*, Basic Books, New York.

**Haddon, R.** (1970) A minority in a welfare state: Location of West Indians in the London housing market, *New Atlantis*, **2**, 80–123.

**Hagerstrand, T.** (1970) What about people in regional science?, *Papers, Regional Science Association*, **24** 7–21

**Haggett, P.** and **Chorley, R. J.** (1969) *Network Analysis in Geography*, Arnold, London.

**Haig, R. M.** (1962) Toward an understanding of the metropolis, *Quarterly Journal of Economics*, **40**, 179–208, and 351–6.

**Hajdu, J. G.** (1983) Phases in the post-war German urban experience. *Town Planning Review*, **54** 267–86.

**Hall, P.** (1974) *Urban and Regional Planning*, Penguin, Harmondsworth.

**Hall, P.** (1975) Book review, *Urban Studies*, **12**, 343–4

**Hall, P., Thomas, R., Gracey, H.** and **Drewett, R.** (1973) *The Containment of Urban England*, Allen & Unwin, London.

**Hall, P.** (1984a) Metropolis 1890–1940: challenges and responses, pp. 19–66 in A. Sutcliffe (ed.), *Metropolis, 1890–1940*, University of Chicago Press, Chicago.

**Hall, P.** (1984b) The urban culture and suburban culture: a new look at an old paper, pp. 120–33 in J. Agnew, J. Mercer and D. E. Sopher (eds), *The City in Cultural Context*, Allen and Unwin, Boston

**Hall, P.** (1984c) *The World Cities*, 3rd edition, Weidenfeld and Nicolson, London.

**Hallman, H. W.** (1984) *Neighborhoods: Their Place in Urban Life*, Sage, Beverly Hills.

**Halsey, A. H.** (1974) Government against poverty in school and community, pp. 121–46 in Wedderburn, D. (ed.) *Poverty, Inequality and Class Structure*, Cambridge University Press, Cambridge.

**Hamilton, F. E. I.** (1984) Industrial restructuring: an international problem, *Geoforum*, **15**, 349–64.

**Hamnett, C.** (1973) Improvement grants as an indicator of gentrification in Inner London, *Area*, **5**, 252–61.

**Hamnett, C.** (1976) Multiple deprivation and the inner city, Unit 15, Course D302, *Patterns of Inequality*, Open University Press, Milton Keynes.

**Hamnett, C.** (1979a) The flat break-up market in London: a case study of large-scale disinvestment – its causes and consequences, pp. 35–55 in Boddy, M. (ed.), *Land, Property and Finance*, Working Paper No. 2, School for Advanced Urban Studies, University of Bristol.

**Hamnett, C.** (1979b) Area-based explanations: a critical appraisal, pp. 244–60 in D. Herbert and D. M. Smith (eds) *Social Problems and the City*, Oxford University Press, Oxford.

**Hamnett, C.** (1984) Housing the two nations, *Urban Studies*, **43**, 389–405.

**Hamnett, C.** and **Randolph, W.** (1984) The role of landlord disinvestment in housing market transformation: an analysis of the flat break-up market in central London, *Transactions, Institute of British Geographers*, **9**, 259–79.

**Hampton, W.** (1970) *Democracy and Community*, Oxford University Press, London.

**Hancock, J.** (1980) The apartment house in

urban America, pp. 151–290 in A. King (ed.) *Buildings and Society*, Routledge and Kegan Paul, London.

**Hannerz, U.** (1974) Ethnicity and opportunity in urban America, pp. 37–76 in Cohen, A. (ed.), *Urban Ethnicity*, Tavistock, London.

**Hanson, S.** and **Hanson, P.** (1980) Gender and urban activity patterns in Uppsala, Sweden, *Geographical Review*, **70**, 291–9.

**Harloe, M.** (ed.) (1977) *Captive Cities*, Wiley, London.

**Harloe, M.** (1981) The recommodification of housing, pp. 17–50 in M. Harloe and E. Lebas (eds) *City, Class and Capital: New developments in the political economy of cities and regions*, Arnold, London.

**Harloe, M.** (1985) *Private Rented Housing in the United States and Europe*, Croom Helm, Beckenham

**Harloe, M., Isacharoff, R.** and **Minns, R.** (1974) *The Organization of Housing*, Heinemann, London.

**Harloe, M.** and **Martens, M.** (1984) Comparative housing research, *Journal of Social Policy*, **13**, 255–77.

**Harloe, M.** and **Paris, C.** (1984) The decollectivization of consumption: housing and local government finance in England and Wales, 1979–81, pp. 70–98 in I. Szelyeni (ed.) *Cities in Recession: Critical Responses to the Urban Policies of the New Right*, Sage, London.

**Harries, K. D.** (1981) Crime rates and environmental denominators, *Journal of Environmental Systems*, **11**, 3–15.

**Harris, R.** (1984) Residential segregation and class formation in the capitalist city: a review and directions for research, *Progress in Human Geography*, **8**, 26–49.

**Harrison, J.** and **Howard, W.** (1972) The role of meaning in the urban image, *Environment and Behaviour*, **4**, 389–411.

**Harrison, J. A.** and **Sarre, P.** (1971) Personal construct theory in the measurement of environmental images: problems and methods, *Environment and Behaviour*, **3** 351–74.

**Harrison, M. L.** (1972) Development control: the influence of political, legal and ideological factors, *Town Planning Review*, **43**, 254–74.

**Harrison, M. L.** (1975) British town planning ideology and the welfare state, *Journal of Social Policy*, **4** 259–74.

**Harrison, P.** (1974) The life of cities, *New Society*, **30**, 5 December, 559–604.

**Hart, J. T.** (1971) The inverse care law, *Lancet*, **i**, 405–12.

**Hartman, C.** (1964) The housing of relocated families, *Journal of the American Institute of Planners*, **30**, 266–86.

**Hartman, C.** and **Kessler, R.** (1978) The illusion and reality of urban renewal: San Francisco's Yerba Buena Center, pp. 153–78 in Tabb, W. and Sawers, L. (eds), *Marxism and the Metropolis*, Oxford University Press, New York.

**Hartnett, B.** (1975) Advocacy planning and bureaucratic guerrillas, *Journal of the Royal Australian Planning Institute*, **13**, 46–9.

**Harvey, D. W.** (1972) *Society, The City and the Space-Economy of Urbanism*, Resource Paper No. 18, Commission on College Geography, Association of American Geographers, Washington, D.C.

**Harvey, D. W.** (1973) *Social Justice and the City*, Arnold, London.

**Harvey, D. W.** (1974) Class-monopoly rent, finance capital and the urban revolution, *Regional Studies*, **8**, 239–55.

**Harvey, D. W.** (1975) Class structure in a capitalist society and the theory of residential differentiation, pp. 354–69 in Peel, R., Chisholm, M. and Haggett, P. (eds) *Processes in Physical and Human Geography: Bristol Essays*, Heinemann, London.

**Harvey, D. W.** (1977) Government policies, financial institutions and neighbourhood change in U.S. cities, pp. 123–140 in Harloe, M. (ed.) *Captive Cities*, Wiley, London.

**Harvey, D. W.** (1978) Labor, capital and class struggle around the Built Environment pp. 9–37 in K. Cox (ed.) *Urbanization and Conflict in Market Societies*, Methuen, London.

**Harvey, D. W.** (1979) Monument and Myth,

*Annals*, Association of American Geographers, **69**, 362–81.

**Harvey, D. W.** (1982) *The Limits to Capital*, Blackwell, Oxford.

**Harvey, D. W.** (1985) *The urbanization of capital*, Blackwell, Oxford.

**Harvey, D. W.** and **Chatterjee, L.** (1974) Absolute rent and the structuring of space by governmental and financial institutions, *Antipode*, **6**, 22–36.

**Harvey, R. O.** and **Clark, W. A. V.** (1965) The nature and economics of urban sprawl, *Land Economics*, **41**, 1–9.

**Hatch, S.** (1973) Estate agents as urban gatekeepers, paper presented to British Sociological Association Stirling.

**Hatch, S,** and **Sherrott, R.** (1973) Positive discrimination and the distribution of deprivations, *Policy and Politics*, **1**, 223–40

**Hatt, P,** (1946) The concept of Natural Area, *American Sociological Review*, **11**, 423–7.

**Hawley, A. H.** (1950) *Human Ecology: A Theory of Community Structure*, Ronald Press, New York.

**Hawley, A. H.** and **Duncan, O. D.** (1957) Social area analysis: a critical appraisal, *Land Economics*, **33**, 227–45.

**Hawley, A. H.** and **Rock, V. P.** (eds) (1975) *Metropolitan America in Contemporary Perspective*, Halstead Press, New York.

**Hay, A.** (1979) Positivism in Human Geography: response to critics, pp. 1–26 in Herbert, D. and Johnston, R. J. (eds) *Geography and the Urban Environment*, Vol. 2, Wiley, Chichester.

**Hayden, D.** (1984) *Redesigning the urban dream: the future of housing, work and family life*, W. W. Norton & Co., New York.

**Healey, P.** and **Underwood, J.** (1978) Professional ideals and planning practice, *Progress in Planning*, **9**, 73–127.

**Heclo, H. A.** (1969) The Councillor's job, *Public Administration*, **43**, 185–202.

**Helper, R.** (1969) *Racial policies and practices of real estate brokers*, Minneapolis University Press, Minneapolis.

**Henderson, J.** and **Karn, V.** (1984) Race,

class and the allocation of public housing in Britain, *Urban Studies*, **21**, 115–128.

**Henig, J. R.** (1981) Gentrification and displacement of the elderly: an empirical analysis, *The Gerontologist*, **21**, 67–75.

**Henig, J. R.** (1982) *Neighborhood mobilization: redevelopment and response*, Rutgers University Press, New Brunswick, NJ.

**Hennock, E. P.** (1973) *Fit and Proper Persons*, Arnold London.

**Hepner, G. F.** (1983) An analysis of residential development location factors in a fast growth urban region, *Urban Geography*, **4**, 355–63.

**Herbert, D. T.** (1976a) Social area analysis: a British study, *Urban Studies*, **4**, 41–60.

**Herbert, D. T.** (1967b) The use of diagnostic variables in the analysis of urban structure, *Tijdschrift voor Economische en Sociale Geografie*, **58**, 5–10.

**Herbert, D. T.** (1968) Principal components analysis and British studies of urban-social structure, *Professional Geographer*, **20**, 280–3.

**Herbert, D. T.** (1972) *Urban Geography: A social Perspective*, David & Charles, Newton Abbot.

**Herbert, D. T.** (1973a) Residential mobility and preference: a study of Swansea, pp. 103–21 in Clark, B. D. and Gleave, M. B., (eds), *Social Patterns in Cities*, Institute of British Geographers, Special Publication No. 5, London.

**Herbert, D. T.** (1973b) The residential mobility process: some empirical observations, *Area*, **5**, 44–8.

**Herbert, D. T.** (1975) Urban deprivation: definition, measurement and spatial qualities, *Geographical Journal*, **141**, 362–72.

**Herbert, D. T.** (1976a) Social deviancy in the city: a spatial perspective, pp. 89–121 in Herbert D. and Johnston R. J. (eds), *Social Areas in Cities*, Vol. 2, Wiley, London.

**Herbert, D. T.** (1976b) The study of delinquency areas: a social geographical approach, *Transactions, Institute of British Geographers*, N.S. **1**, 472–492.

**Herbert, D. T.** (1976c) Urban education:

problems and policies, pp. 123–58 in Herbert, D. and Johnston, R. J. (eds), *Social Areas in Cities*, Vol. 2, Wiley, London.

Herbert, D. T. (1977a) Crime, delinquency and the urban environment, *Progress in Human Geography*, **1**, 208–39.

Herbert, D. T. (1977b) An areal and ecological analysis of delinquency residence: Cardiff 1966 and 1971, *Tijdschrift voor Economische en Sociale Geografie*, **68**, 83–99.

Herbert, D. T. (1979) Urban crime: a geographical perspective, pp. 117–38 in D. Herbert and D. M. Smith (eds), *Social Problems in the City*, Oxford University Press, Oxford.

Herbert, D. T. (1982) *The Geography of Urban Crime*, Longman, London.

Herbert, D. T. and Hyde, S. W. (1985) Environmental criminology: testing some area hypotheses, *Transactions, Institute of British Geographers*, **10**, 259–74.

Herbert, D. T. and Johnston, R. J. (1976a) *Social Areas in Cities*, Vol. 1, *Spatial Processes and Form*, Wiley, London.

Herbert, D. T. and Johnston, R. J. (1976b) *Social Areas in Cities*, Vol. 2, *Spatial Perspectives on Problems and Policies*, Wiley, London.

Herbert, D. T. and Johnston, R. J. (eds) (1978) *Geography and the Urban Environment: Progress in Research and Applications*, Vol. 1, Wiley, Chichester.

Herbert, D. T. and Raine, J. W. (1976) Defining communities within urban areas. *Town Planning Review*, **47**, 325–38.

Herr, J. P. (1982) Metropolitan political fragmentation and conflict in the location of commercial facilities: South Bend vs Mishawaka, pp. 28–44 in K. Cox and R. J. Johnston (eds) *Conflict, Politics and the Urban Scene*, Longman, London.

Hershberg, T. (ed.) (1981) *Philadelphia; Work, Space, Family and Group Experience in the Nineteenth Century*, Oxford University Press, New York.

Hershberg, T., Light, D., Cox, H. and Greenfield, R. R. (1981) The 'Journey to Work': An empirical investigation of work, residence and transportation, Philadelphia, 1850 and 1880, 128–73 in T. Hershberg (ed.) *Philadelphia; Work, Space, Family and Group Experience in the Nineteenth Century*, Oxford University Press, New York.

Higgins, J., Deakin, N., Edwards, J. and Wicks, M. (1983) *Government and Urban Policy: Inside the Policy-Making Process*, Blackwell Oxford.

Hill, D. (1970) *Participating in Local Affairs*, Penguin, Harmondsworth.

Hill, R. (1980) Architecture: the past fights back, *Marxism Today*, **24**, 21–5.

Hill, R. C. (1984) Fiscal crisis, austerity politics and alternative urban policies, pp. 298–322 in W. K. Tabb and L. Sawers (eds.) *Marxism and the Metropolis*, 2nd edition, Oxford University Press, New York.

Hillery, G. A. (1955) Definition of Community: Areas of Agreement, *Rural Sociology*, **20**, 111–23.

Hillier, B. *et al.* (1981) *Social Logic and Space*, Cambridge University Press, Cambridge.

Hiorns, F. R. (1965) *Town Building in History*, Arnold, London.

Hiro, D. (1973) *Black British, White British*, Penguin, Harmondsworth.

Hirsch, W. Z. and Law, C. K. (1979) Habitability laws and the shrinkage of substandard rental housing stock. *Urban Studies*, **16**, 19–28.

Hirschman, A. O. (1970) *Exit, Voice and Loyalty*, Harvard University Press, Cambridge, Mass.

Hoch, C. (1984) City Limits: Municipal Boundary Formation and Class Segregation, pp. 101–19 in W. K. Tabb and L. Sawers (eds.) *Marxism and the Metropolis*, 2nd edition, Oxford University Press, New York.

Hofstadter, R. (1955) *The Age of Reform*, Knopf, New York.

Hoggart, K. (1985) Political Party Control and the sale of local authority dwellings 1974–1983, *Environment & Planning C: Policy and Politics*, **3**, 463–74.

Hoggart, R. (1958) *The Uses of Literacy*, Penguin, Harmondsworth.

Hoivik, T. (1973) *Norvege 1990, Analyse et*

*Prèvision, Etudes Futuribles*, O.E.C.D., Paris.

**Hojnacki, W. P.** (1979) What is a neighbourhood? *Social Policy*, **10**, 47–52.

**Holcomb, B.** (1984) Women in the City, *Urban Geography*, **5**, 247–54.

**Holcomb, B.** (forthcoming) Metropolitan America, in P, Knox *et al. The United States: A contemporary human geography*, Longman, Harlow.

**Holcomb, B.** and **Beauregard, R. A.** (1981) *Revitalizing Cities*, Association of American Geographers, Washington, D.C.

**Holmes, J.** (1976) Urban housing problems and public policy, pp. 400–20 in Yeates, M. and Garner, B. *The North American City*, (2nd ed.), Harper & Row, New York.

**Homans, G. C.** (1950) *The Human Group*, Harcourt Brace, New York.

**Homans, G. C.** (1961) *Social Behaviour: Its Elementary Forms*, Routledge & Kegan Paul, London.

**Honey, R. D.** (1976) Metropolitan governance, pp. 425–62 in Adams, J. S. (ed.) *Urban Policymaking and Metropolitan Dynamics*, Ballinger, Mass.

**Hopkins, E. J., Pye A. M., Soloman, M.** and **Soloman, S.** (1968) The relation of patients' age, sex and distance from surgery to the demand on the family doctor, *Journal of the Royal College of General Practitioners*, **16**, 368–78.

**Housing Services Advisory Group** (1978) *Allocation of Council Housing*, Department of the Environment, London.

**Howard, E.** (1902) *Garden cities of Tomorrow*, reprinted by Faber & Faber, London (1946).

**Hoyt, H.** (1939) *The Structure and Growth of Residential Neighbourhoods in American cities*, Federal Housing Administration, Washington, D.C.

**Hughes, D. J.** and **Jones, S. R.** (1979) Bias in the allocation and transfer of local authority housing. *Journal of Social Welfare Law*, July, 273–95.

**Hughes, R.** (1980) *The Shock of the New*, British Broadcasting Corporation, London.

**Hume, J. R.** (1983) Transport and towns in Victorian Scotland, pp. 197–232 in G. Gordon and B. Dicks (eds) *Scottish Urban History*, Aberdeen University Press, Aberdeen.

**Humphrys, Mason,** and **Pinch, S.** (1983) The externality fields of football grounds: a case study of The Dell, Southampton, *Geoforum*, **14**, 401–12.

**Hunter, A. A.** (1974) Community change: a stochastic analysis of Chicago's local communities, 1930–1960, *American Journal of Sociology*, **79** 923–47.

**Hunter, A. A.** (1979) The urban neighborhood: its analytical and social contexts, *Urban Affairs Quarterly*, **14**, 267–88.

**Hunter, F.** (1953) *Community Power Structure: A Study of Decision Makers*, University of North Carolina Press, Chapel Hill.

**Hurd, R. M.** (1903) *Principles of city land values*, The Record and Guide, New York.

**Huxley, M.** and **McLoughlin, J. B.** (1985) *The New Urban Studies Literature: A Review with Special Reference to Australia*, Progress in Planning, P **24**, 161–245.

**Hyland, G.** (1970) Social interaction and urban opportunity: the Appalachian in-migrant in the Cincinnati Central City, *Antipode*, **2**, 68–83.

**Ignatieff, M.** (1978) *A Just Measure Of Pain: the penitentiary in the industrial revolution*, Macmillan, London.

**Ineichen, B.** (1983) Council housing and disadvantage: the allocation of council housing and its relation to social stratification, pp. 153–71 in M. Brown (ed.) *The Structure of Disadvantage*, Heinemann, London.

**Inglis, F.** (1975) Roads, office blocks and the new misery, pp. 168–88 in Abbs, P. (ed.), *The Black Rainbow*, Heinemann, London.

**Isard, W.** (1942) A neglected cycle: the transport building cycle, *Review of Economic Statistics*, **24**, 149–58.

**Irving, H.** (1978) Space and environment in

interpersonal relations, pp. 249–84 in Herbert, D. and Johnston, R. J. (eds), *Geography and the Urban Environment, Vol. 1, Wiley, Chichester.*

**Isler, M.** (1970) *Thinking About Housing*, Urban Institute, Washington.

**Jackson, B.** (1968) *Working Class Community*, Routledge & Kegan Paul, London.

**Jackson, P.** (1981) Paradoxes of Puerto Ricans Segregation in New York, pp. 109–26 in C. Peach, V. Robinson, and S. Smith (eds) *Ethnic Segregation in Cities*, Croom Helm, London.

**Jackson, P.** (1984) Social disorganization and moral order in the city, *Transactions, Institute of British Geographers*, **9**, 168–80.

**Jackson, P.** (1985a) Urban ethnography, *Progress in Human geography*, **9**, 157–76.

**Jackson, P.** (1985b) Neighbourhood change in New York: the loft conversion process, *Tijdscharift voor Economische en Sociale Geografie*, **76**, 216–22.

**Jackson, P.** and **Smith, S. J. (eds)** (1981) *Social Interaction and Ethnic Segregation*, Academic Press, London.

**Jacobs, J.** (1961) *The Death and Life of Great American Cities*, Vintage, New York.

**Jahn, M.** (1982) Suburban development in outer West London 1850–1900, pp. 93–156 in F. M. L. Thompson (ed.) *The Rise of Suburbia*, Lancaster University Press, Lancaster.

**Janelle, D. G.** and **Millward, H. A.** (1976) Locational conflict patterns and urban ecological structure, *Tijdschrift voor Economische en Sociale Geografie*, **67** 102–13.

**Janson, C-G.** (1971) A preliminary report on Swedish urban spatial structure, *Economic Geography*, **47**, 249–57.

**Jaye, M. C.** and **Watts, A. C. (eds.)** (1981) *Literature and the Urban Experience: essays on the city and literature*, Rutgers University Press, New Brunswick. NJ.

**Jephcott, P.** (1971) *Homes in High Flats*, Oliver & Boyd, Edinburgh.

**Johnson, J.** (ed.), (1974) *Suburban Growth*, Wiley, London.

**Johnston, R. J.** (1966) The location of high status residential areas, *Geografiska Annaler*, **48B**, 23–35.

**Johnston, R. J.** (1969a) Towards an analytical study of the townscape: the residential building fabric, *Geografiska Annaler*, **51B**, (1), 20–32.

**Johnston, R. J.** (1969b) Population movements and metropolitan expansion, *Transactions, Institute of British Geographers*, **46**, 69–91.

**Johnston, R. J.** (1969c) Some tests of a model of intra-urban population mobility: Melbourne, Australia, *Urban Studies*, **6**, 34–57.

**Johnston, R. J.** (1969d) Process of change in the high status residential districts of Christchurch, 1951–64, *New Zealand Geographer*, **25**, 1–15.

**Johnston, R. J.** (1970) On spatial patterns in the residential structure of cities, *Canadian Geographer*, **14**, 361–67.

**Johnston, R. J.** (1971) *Urban Residential Patterns: An Introductory Review*, Bell, London.

**Johnston, R. J.** (1973a) Social area change in Melbourne 1961–1966, *Australian Geographical Studies*, **11**, 79–98.

**Johnston, R. J.** (1973b) The factorial ecology of major New Zealand urban areas: a comparative study, *Institute of British Geographers, Special Publication*, **5**, 143–68.

**Johnston, R. J.** (ed.) (1973c) *Urbanization in New Zealand: Geographical Essays*, Reed, Wellington.

**Johnston, R. J.** (1973d) Spatial patterns in suburban evaluations, *Environment and Planning*, **5A**, 385–95.

**Johnston, R. J.** (1974) Local effects in voting at a local election, *Annals, Association of American Geographers*, **64**, 418–9.

**Johnston, R. J.** (1976a) Residential area characteristics: research methods for identifying urban sub-areas – social area analysis and factorial ecology, pp. 193–236 in Herbert, D. and Johnston R. J. (eds) *Social Areas in Cities*, Wiley, London.

**Johnston, R. J.** (1976b) *Classification in*

*Geography*, Catmog 6, of British Geographers, London.

**Johnston, R. J.,** (1977) Urban geography: city structures, *Progress in Human Geography*, **1**, 118–23.

**Johnston, R. J.** (1978) *Multivariate Statistical Analysis in Geography*, Longman, London.

**Johnston, R. J.** (1979a) Urban geography: city structures, *Progress in Human Geography*, **3**, 133–8.

**Johnston, R. J.** (1979b) *Political, Electoral and Spatial Systems*, Oxford University Press. Oxford.

**Johnston, R. J.** (1979c) The homes of callers to a telephone counselling service: towards a mapping of community in the city, *New Zealand Geographer*, **35**, 34–40.

**Johnston, R. J.** (1981a) The political element in suburbia, *Geography*, **66**, 286–96.

**Johnston, R. J.** (1981b) The management and autonomy of the local state: the role of the judiciary in the US, *Environment and Planning*, A **13**, 1305–15.

**Johnston, R. J.** (1981c) Local government, suburban segregation and litigation in US metropolitan areas, *American Studies*, **15**, 211–30.

**Johnston, R. J.** (1982a) Voice as a strategy in locational conflict: the Fourteenth Amendment and residential separation in the United States, pp. 111–26 in K. Cox and R. J. Johnston (eds) *Conflict, Politics and the Urban Scene*, Longman, London.

**Johnston, R. J.** (1982b) The local state and the judiciary: institutions in suburban America, pp. 255–88 in R. Flowerdew (ed.) *Institutions and Geographical Patterns*, Croom Helm, London.

**Johnston, R. J.** (1983) Texts, actors and higher managers: judges, bureaucrats and the political organization of space, *Political Geography Quarterly*, **2**, 3–19.

**Johnston, R. J.** (1984a) *City and Society*, 2nd edition, Hutchinson, London.

**Johnston, R. J.** (1984b) Marxist political economy, the state, and political geography, *Progress in Human Geography*, **8**, 473–92.

**Johnston, R. J.** and **Rimmer, P. J.** (1969) *Retailing in Melbourne*, Publication HG/3,

Department of Human Geography, Australian National University, Canberra.

**Jones, C.** (1978) Household movement, filtering and trading up within the owner-occupied sector, *Regional Studies*, **12**, 551–61.

**Jones, E.** (1958) The delimitation of some urban landscape features in Belfast, *Scottish Geographical Magazine*, **74**, 150–62.

**Jones, E.** (1980) London in the early seventeenth century: an ecological approach, *London Journal*, **6**, 123–33.

**Jones, E.** and **Eyles, J.** (1977) *An Introduction to Social Geography*, Oxford University Press, London.

**Jones, G. S.** (1971) *Outcast London*, Oxford University Press, London.

**Jones, G. S.** (1974) Working-class culture and working-class politics in London, 1870–1900, *Journal of Social History*, **7**, 485–97.

**Jones, G. S.** (1981) *Urbanization and class consciousness*, Arnold, London.

**Jones, G. W.** (1969) *Borough Politics: A Study of the Wolverhampton Town Council 1888–1964*, Macmillan, London.

**Jones, K.** and **Kirby, A.** (1982) Provision and well-being: an agenda for public resources research, *Environment and Planning A*, **14**, 297–310.

**Jones, P. N.** (1979) Ethnic areas in British cities, pp. 158–185 in D. Herbert and D. M. Smith (eds), *Social Problems and the City: Geographical Perspectives*, Oxford University Press, Oxford.

**Jones, P. N.** (1983) Ethnic population succession in a West German City 1974–80: The Case of Nuremburg, *Geography*, **68**, 121–32.

**Jones, T. P.** and **McEvoy D.** (1978) Race and space in cloud cuckoo land, *Area*, **10**, 162–6.

**de Jonge, D.** (1962) Images of urban areas: their structure and psychological foundations, *Journal of the American Institute of Planners*, **28**, 266–76.

**Joseph, A.** and **Phillips, D.** (1984) *Accessibility and Utilization*, Harper and Row, New York.

**Kain, J. F.** (1962) The journey to work as a determinant of residential location, *Papers and Proceedings, Regional Science Association*, **9**, 137–60.

**Kain, J. F.** and **Quigley, J. M.** (1972) Housing market discrimination, homeownership, and savings behaviour, *American Economic Review*, **62**, 263–77.

**Kain, J. F.** and **Quigley, J. M.** (1975) *Housing Markets and Racial Dicrimination*, Columbia University Press, New York.

**Kain R.** (ed.) (1981) *Planning for Conservation*, St Martin's Press, New York.

**Kaiser, E. J.** and **Weiss, S. F.** (1970) Public policy and the residential development process, *Journal of the American Institute of Planners*, **36**, 30–7.

**Kantor, A. C.** and **Nystuen, J. D.** (1982) De facto redlining: a geographic view, *Economic Geography*, **58**, 309–28.

**Kantrowitz, N.** (1973) *Ethnic and Racial Segregation in the New York Metropolis*, Praeger, New York.

**Kaplan, H.** (1967) *Urban Political Systems*, Columbia University Press, New York.

**Kaplan, S.** and **Kaplan, R.** (eds) (1978) *Humanscape: The environments for people*, Duxbury/Wadsworth, Mass.

**Karp, D. A., Stone, G. P.** and **Yoels, W. C.** (1977) *Being Urban: A Social Psychological View of City Life*, Heath, Lexington, Mass.

**Kasarda, J. D.** (1972) The impact of suburban population growth on central city service functions, *American Journal of Sociology*, **77**, 1111–24.

**Kasarda, J. D.** and **Janowitz, M.** (1974) Community attachment in mass society, *American Sociological Review*, **39**, 328–39.

**Kasperson, R. E.** and **Breitbart, M.** (1974) *Participation, Decentralization and Advocacy Planning*, Resource Paper No. 25, Commission on College Geography, Association of American Geographers, Washington, D.C.

**Kazin, A.** (1983) Fear of the city, 1783–1983, *American Heritage*, February, 14–23.

**Kearsley, G. W.** (1983) Teaching urban geography: the Burgess model, *New Zealand Journal of Geography*, **75**, 10–13.

**Kearsley, G. W.** and **Srivastava, S. R.** (1974) The spatial evolution of Glasgow's Asian community, *Scottish Geographical Magazine,* **90**, 110–24.

**Keller, S.** (1968) *The urban neighborhood: a sociological perspective*, Random House, New York.

**Kellerman, A.** (1984) Telecommunications and the geography of metropolitan areas, *Progress in Human Geography*, **8**, 222–46.

**Kellett, J. R.** (1969) *The Impact of Railways on Victorian cities*, Routledge & Kegan Paul, London.

**Kemeny, J.** (1980) *Home Ownership and the Family Life-cycle*, Working Paper 20, Centre for Urban and Regional Studies, University of Birmingham, Birmingham.

**Kemeny, J.** (1983) *The Privatised City: Critical Studies in Australian Housing and Urban Structure*, Occ. Pap. 10, Centre for Urban and Regional Studies, University of Birmingham, England.

**Kennedy, R** (1943) Premarital residential propinquity, *American Journal of Sociology*, **48**, 580–4.

**Kennedy, C. G.** (1962) Commuter services in the Boston area 1835–1860, *Business History Review*, **26**, 277–87.

**Kennedy, J. W.** (1975) *Adapting to new environments: residential mobility from the mover's point of view*, University of Toronto, Centre for Urban and Community Studies, Major Report No. 3, Toronto.

**Kennedy, M.** (1970) *Portrait of Manchester*, Hale, Manchester.

**Kilroy, B.** (1972) Improvement grants threaten North Kensington, *Housing Review*, **21**, 79–80.

**King, A. D.** (ed.) (1980a) *Buildings and Society: essays on the social development of the built environment*, Routledge and Kegan Paul, London.

**King, A. D.** (1980b) Historical patterns of reaction to urbanism; the case of Britain 1880–1939, *International Journal of Urban and Regional Research*, **4**, 453–69.

**King, A. D.** (1984) The social production of building form: theory and research, *Environment and Planning*, D, **2**, 429–46.

**King, R. L.** (1976) The evolution of international labor migration movements concerning the EEC, *Tijdschrift voor Economische en Sociale Geografie*, **67**, 66–82.

**Kirby, A. M.** (1976) Housing market studies: a critical review, *Transactions, Institute of British Geographers*, N.S., **1**, 2–9.

**Kirby, A. M.** (1977) *Housing Action Areas in Great Britain: 1975–1977*, Geographical Paper No. 60, Department of Geography, University of Reading.

**Kirby, A. M.** (1979a) *Towards an Understanding of the Local State*, Geographical Paper No. 70, Department of Geography, University of Reading.

**Kirby, A. M.** (1979b) *Education, Health and Housing*, Saxon House, Farnborough.

**Kirby, D. A.** *Slum Housing and Residential Renewal: The Case in Urban Britain*, Longman, London.

**Kirk, G.** (1980) *Urban Planning in a Capitalist Society*, Croom Helm, Beckenham.

**Kirk, W.** (1963) Problems in Geography, *Geography*, **48**, 357–71.

**Kirmeyer, S.** (1978) Urban density and pathology: a review of research, *Environment and Behaviour*, **10**, 247–270.

**Klein, H. J.** (1967) The delimitation of the town centre in the image of its citizens, pp. 286–306 in Brill, E. J. (ed.) *Urban Core and Inner City*, University of Leiden.

**Klein, J.** (1965) *Samples from English Culture*, Routledge & Kegan Paul, London.

**Kleniewsk, N.** (1984) From industrial to corporate city: the role of urban renewal, pp. 205–22 in W. K. Tabb and L. Sawers (eds) *Marxism and the Metropolis*, 2nd edition, Oxford University Press, New York.

**Knesl, J. A.** (1984) The powers of architecture, *Environment and Planning*, D, **2**. 3–22.

**Knox, P. L.** (1976) Fieldwork in urban geography: assessing environmental quality, *Scottish Geographical Magazine*, **92**, 101–7.

**Knox, P. L.** (1978a) Community councils, electoral districts and social geography, *Area*, **10**, 387–91.

**Knox, P. L.** (1978b) The intra-urban ecology of primary medical care: patterns of accessibility and their policy implications, *Environment and Planning*, A10, 415–35.

**Knox, P. L.** (1978c) Territorial social indicators and area profiles: some cautionary observations, *Town Planning Review*, **49**, 75–83.

**Knox P. L.** (1979a) Medical deprivation, area deprivation, and public policy, *Social Science and Medicine*, **13D**, 111–21.

**Knox, P. L.** (1979b) The accessibility of primary care to urban patients: a geographical analysis, *Journal of the Royal College of General Practitioners*, **29**, 160–8.

**Knox, P. L.** (1980a) Measures of accessibility as social indicators, *Social Indicators Research*, **7**, 367–77.

**Knox, P. L.** (1980b) Urban deprivation and health care provision, *Medicine in Society*, **5**, 54–9.

**Knox, P. L.** (1982a) The geography of medical care: an historical perspective, *Geoforum*, **13**, 245–51.

**Knox, P. L.** (1982b) Residential structure, facility location and patterns of accessibility, pp. 62–87 in K. Cox and R. J. Johnston (eds) *Conflict, Politics and the Urban Scene*, Longman, London.

**Knox, P. L.** (1984) Signs, symbolism and settings: the social production of the built environment, *Architecture et Comportement*, **2**, 107–122.

**Knox, P. L.** (1986a) The localization of disadvantaged households in Scottish cities, in G. Heinritz and E. Lichtenberger (eds) *The Crisis of the City and the Take-off of Suburbia*, Franz Steiner Verlag, Wiesbaden.

**Knox, P. L.** (1986b) Collective consumption and socio-spatial change, pp. 110–129 in M. Pacione (ed.) *Progress in Social Geography*, Croom Helm, London.

**Knox, P. L., Bohland, J. R.** and **Shumsky, N L.** (1983) The urban transition and the evolution of the medical care delivery system in America, *Social Science and Medicine*, **17D**, 37–43.

**Knox, P. L., Bohland, J. R.** and **Shumsky, N. L.** (1984) Urban development and the geography of personal services: the example of medical care in the United States, pp. 152–75 in A. Kirby, P. Knox and S. Pinch (eds) *Public Service Provision and Urban Development*, Croom Helm, London.

**Knox, P. L.** and **Cullen, J.** (1981a) Town planning and the internal survival mechanisms of urbanized capitalism, *Area*, **13**, 183–8.

**Knox, P. L.** and **Cullen, J. D.** (1981b) Planners as urban managers: an exploration of the attitudes and self-image of senior British planners, *Environment and Planning*, A, **13**, 885–98.

**Knox, P. L.** and **Pacione, M.** (1980) Locational behaviour, place preferences and the inverse care law in the distribution of primary medical care, *Geoforum*, **11**, 43–55.

**Knox, P. L.** and **MacLaran, A. C.** (1978) Values and perceptions in descriptive approaches to urban social geography, pp. 197–247 in Herbert, D. and Johnston, R. J. (eds) *Geography and the Urban Environment*, Vol. 1, Wiley, Chichester.

**Kohl, J. G.** (1841) *Der Verkehr und die Ansiedlung der Menschen in ihrer Abhängigkeit von der Gerstaltungder Erdoberfläche*, Arnoldische Buchhangdlung, Leipzig.

**Korte, C.** (1978) Helpfulness in the urban environment, in A. Baun *et al.* (eds) *Advances in Environmental Psychology, Volume 1: The Urban Environment*, Erlbaum, Hillsdale, New Jersey.

**Korte, C.** and **Kerr, N.** (1975) Response to altruistic opportunities in urban and non-urban settings, *Journal of Social Psychology*, **95**, 183–4.

**Kostof, S.** (1978) The Emperor and the Duce, pp. 270–25 in H. A. Millon and L. Nochlin (eds) *Art and Architecture in the Service of Politics*, MIT Press, Cambridge, Ma.

**Koutsopoulos, K. C.** and **Schmidt, C. G.** (1976) Mobility constraints of the carless,

*Traffic Quarterly*, **30**, 67–83.

**Kowinski, W. S.** (1978) The malling of America, *New Times*, 1 May, 31–55.

**Kramer, J. R.** (1970) *The American Minority Community*, Crowell, New York.

**Kramer, R. M.** (1969) *Participation and the Poor*, Prentice-Hall, Englewood Cliffs, N. J.

**Krampen, M.** (1979) *Meaning in the Urban Environment*, Pion, London.

**Kravitz, A. S.** (1970) Mandarinism: Planning as handmaiden to conservative politics, pp. 240–68 in T. L. Boyle and G. T. Lothrop (eds.) *Planning and Politics*, Odyssey Press, New York.

**Krier, L.** *et al.* (1978) *Rational Architecture: the reconstuction of the European City*, Archives d' Architecture Moderne, Paris.

**Kristoff, F. S.** (1970) Economic facets of New York City's housing problems, pp. 79–93 in Fitch, L. and Walsh, A. (eds) *Agenda for a City*, Institute for Public Administration, New York.

**Krueckeberg, D. A.** (ed.) (1983) *Introduction to planning history in the United States*, Center for Urban Policy Research, Rutgers University, New Brunswick, NJ.

**Kuper, L.** (ed.) (1953) *Living in Towns*, Cresset, London.

**Lake, R. L.** (ed.) (1986) *Resolving Locational Conflict*, Center for Urban Policy Research, Piscataway, N.J.

**Lambert, C.** (1976) *Building Societies, Surveyors and the Older Areas of Birmingham*, Working Paper No. 38, Centre for Urban and Regional Studies, University of Birmingham.

**Lambert, J., Paris, C.,** and **Blackaby, R.** (1978) *Housing Policy and the State*, Macmillan, London.

**Lambert, J. R.** (1970) *Crime, Police and Race Relations: A Study in Birmingham*, Oxford University Press, London.

**Lampard, E.** (1983) The nature of urbanization, pp. 3–53, in D. Fraser and A. Sutcliffe (eds) *The Pursuit of Urban History*, Arnold, London.

**Lanegran, D. A.** and **Palm, R.** (eds) (1978) *An Invitation to Geography*, McGraw-Hill, New York.

**Langton, J.** (1975) Residential patterns in pre-industrial cities: some case studies from seventeenth-century Britain, *Transactions*, Institute of British Geographers, **65**, 1–27.

**Lankford, P.** (1971) The changing location of physicians, *Antipode*, **3**, 68–72.

**Lansing, J. B., Clifton, C. W.** and **Morgan, J. N.** (1969) *New Homes and Poor People: A Study of Chains of Moves*, Institute for Social Research, University of Michigan, Ann Arbor.

**Lasswell, H.** (1979) *The Signature of Power*, Transaction Books, New Brunswick, NJ.

**Laumann, E. O.** (1966) *Prestige and Association in an Urban Community*, Bobbs Merrill, Indianapolis.

**de Lauwe, P. H. C.** (1952) *Paris et l'Agglomeration Parisienne*, Mouton, Paris.

**Lave, L. B.** (1970) Congestion and urban location, *Papers and Proceedings, Regional Science Association*, **25**, 133–50.

**Lavedan, P.** (1926–52) *Historie de l'urbanisme* (4 vols) Laureus, Paris.

**Lavedan, P.** (1941) *Historie de l'urbanisme: Renaisance et temps modernes*, Laureus, Paris.

**Lawless, P.** (1979) *Urban Deprivation and Government Initiative*, Faber & Faber, London.

**Lawton, R.** (1959) Irish immigration into England and Wales in the mid-nineteenth century, *Irish Geography*, **4**, 35–54.

**Lawton, R.** (1983) Urbanization and population change in nineteenth-century England, pp. 179–224 in J. Patten (ed.) *The Expanding City*, Academic Press, London.

**Lazarus, R. S.** (1969) *Patterns of Adjustment and Human Effectiveness*, McGraw-Hill, New York.

**Lazin, F. A.** (1980) Policy, perception, and program failure: the politics of public housing in Chicago and New York City, *Urbanism Past and Present*, **9**, 1–12.

**Leahy, P. J.** (1985) Race and the allocation of mortgage money: an aspect of discrimination, *American Journal of Sociology*, **44**, 185–96.

**Lee, B. A., Oropesa, R. S., Metch, B.** and **Guest, A. M.** (1984) Testing the decline-of-community thesis: neighbourhood organizations in Seattle, 1929 and 1979, *American Journal of Sociology*, **89**, 1161–88.

**Lee, J. M.** (1963) *Social Leaders and Public Persons*, Oxford University Press, London.

**Lee, R.** (1976) Public finance and urban economy: some comments on spatial reformism, *Antipode*, **8**, 44–50.

**Lee, T.** (1968) Urban neighbourhood as a socio-spatial schema, *Human Relations*, **21**, 241–68.

**Lee, T.** (1970) Perceived distance as a function of direction in the city, *Environment and Behaviour*, **20**, 40–51.

**Lee, T.** (1976) Cities in the mind, pp. 159–87 in Herbert, D. T. and Johnston, R. J. (eds), *Social Areas in Cities*, Vol. 2, Wiley, Chichester.

**Lee, T. R.** (1977) *Race and Residence*, Clarendon Press, Oxford.

**Lees, A.** (1985) *Cities Perceived: urban society in European and American thought*, Manchester University Press, Manchester.

**Lees, A** and **Lees, N.** (1976) *The urbanisation of European Society in the Nineteenth Century*, D. C. Heath, Lexington, Mass.

**de Leeuw, F.** (1972) *The Distribution of Housing Services*, Urban Institute, Washington, D.C.

**Le Gates, R. T.** and **Hartman, C.** (1981) Displacement, *Clearinghouse Review*, **15**, 207–47.

**Lehman-Wilzig, S.** (1981) Will cities become obsolete? *Telecommunications Policy*, **7**, 326–8.

**Leitner, H.** (1983) *Gastarbeiter in der Stadtischen Gesellschaft*, Campus Verlag, Frankfurt.

**Leonard, S.** (1982) Urban managerialism: a period of transition? *Progress in Human Geography*, **6**, 190–215.

**Leven, C.** (1979) Economic maturity and the metropolis's evolving physical form, pp. 21–45 in G. A. Tobin (ed.) *The Changing Structure of the City*, Sage, Beverly Hills.

**Levenstein, C.** (1981) The political economy

of suburbanization, *Review of Radical Political Economy*, **13**, 23–31.

**Lewin, K.** (1983) *The conceptual representation and the measurement of Psychological Forces*, Duke University Press, Durham, North Carolina.

**Lewis, C. R.** (1979) A Stage in the development of the industrial town: a case study of Cardiff, 1845–75, *Transactions, Institute of British Geographers*, New Series, **4**, 129–52.

**Lewis, G. J.** (1980) Urban Neighbourhood and community: explanatory studies in Leicester, *Leicester and Its Region*, University of Leicester Occasional Papers. 1.

**Lewis, J .P.** (1965) *Building cycles and Britain's Growth*, Macmillan, London.

**Lewis, N.** (1976) Council housing allocation: problems of discretion and control, *Public Administration*, **54**, 147–60.

**Lewis, O.** (1966) The culture of poverty, *Scientific American*, **215**, 19–25.

**Lewis, O.** (1952) Urbanisation without breakdown, *Scientific Monthly*, **75**, 311–41.

**Ley, D.** (1974) *The Black Inner City as Frontier Outpost: images and behavior of a Philadelphia neighborhood*, Monograph No. 7, Association of American Geographers, Washington, D.C.

**Ley, D.** (1977) Social geography and the taken-for-granted world, *Transactions, Institute of British Geographers*, **2**, 498–512.

**Ley, D.** (1980) Liberal ideology and the postindustrial city, *Annals, Association of American Geographers*, **70**, 238–58.

**Ley, D.** (1983) *A Social Geography of the City*, Harper and Row, New York.

**Ley, D.** and **Cybriwsky, R.** (1974) The spatial ecology of stripped cars, *Environment and Behaviour*, **6**, 63–7.

**Lichtenberger, E.** (1984) *Gastarbeiter: Leben in Zwei Gesellschaften*, Bohlaus, Vienna.

**Lieberson, S.** (1981) An asymmetrical approach to segregation, pp. 61–82 in C. Peach, V. Robinson and S. Smith (eds), *Ethnic Segregation in Cities*, Croom Helm, London.

**Liebow, E.** (1967) *Tally's Corner*, Little, Brown, Boston, Ma.

**Lincoln, H. R.** (1978) Community structure and industrial conflict, *American Sociological Review*, **43**, 199–219.

**Lindley, D. V.** (1961) Dynamic programming and decision theory, *Applied Statistics*, **10**, 39–51.

**Lineberry, R. L.** (1977) *Equality and Urban Policy*, Sage, Beverly Hills.

**Linton, Mields** and **Coston, Inc.** (1971) *A Study of the Problems of Abandoned Housing*, Report PB 212–198, National Technical Information Service, Springfield, Va.

**Lofland, L.** (1973) *A World of Strangers*, Basic Books, New York.

**Lojkine, J.** (1974) *La politique urbaine dans la région Lyonnaise 1945–1972*, Mouton, Paris.

**Lojkine, J.** (1984) The working class and the state, pp. 217–237 in I. Szelyeni (ed.) *Cities in Recession*, Sage, Beverly Hills.

**London Borough of Southwark** (1973) Preliminary Research, unpublished report, Planning Division, Southwark Development Department, London.

**London, B.** *et al.* (1981) Approaches to inner-city revitalization, *Urban Affairs Quarterly*, **15**, 373–80.

**Loney, M.** (1983) *Community Against Government: the British Community Development Project 1968–1978*, Heinemann, London.

**Lovrich, N. P.** (1974) Differing priorities in an urban electorate: service preferences among Anglo, Black and Mexican American voters, *Social Sciences Quarterly*, **4**, 704–17.

**Lowe, P. D.** (1977) Amenity and equity: a review of local environmental pressure groups in Britain, *Environment and Planning*, **A9**, 35–58.

**Lowe, P. D.** and **Goyder, J.** (1983) *Environmental Groups in Politics*, Allen and Unwin, London.

**Lowenthal, D.** (1961) Geography, experience and imagination: towards a geographic epistemology, *Annals, Association of American Geographers*, **51** 241–60.

**Lowenthal, D.** and **Prince, H. C.** (1964) The English landscape, *Geographical Review*, **54**, 309–46.

**Lowery, R. A.** (1973) A method for

analysing distance concepts of urban residents, pp. 338–60 in Downs, R. and Stea, D. (eds), *Image and Environment*, Aldine, Chicago.

Lowry, L. S. (1960) Filtering and housing standards: a conceptual analysis, *Land Economics*, **36**, 362–70.

Loyd, B. (1982) Women, home and status, pp. 181–97 in J. S. Duncan (ed.) *Housing and Identity*, Holmes and Meier, New York.

Lupton, J. and Mitchell, G. D. (1954) *Neighbourhood and Community*, Liverpool University Press, Liverpool.

Lynch, K. (1960) *The Image of the City*, M. I. T. Press, Cambridge, Mass.

Lynch, K. (1984) Reconsidering "The image of the City", pp. 151–62 in R. M. Hollister and L. Rodwin (eds) *Cities of the Mind*, Plenum, New York.

Lynd, R. S. and Lynd, H. M. (1956) *Middletown*, Harcourt, Brace and World, New York.

Lyon, D. (1970) Capital spending and the neighbourhoods of Philadelphia, *Business Review* (May), 16–27.

Lyon, S. and Wood, M. E. (1977) Choosing a house, *Environment and Planning*, **9**, 1169–76.

McCann, L. D. and Smith, P. J. (1972) Residential morphology and urban social structure  Paper presented to section XI of the I. G. U. Conference, Montreal, Canada (mimeo).

McCarthy, D. and Saegert, S. (1978) Residential density, social overload and social withdrawal, *Human Ecology*, **6**, 253–272.

McCarthy, M. P. (1977) on bosses, reformers and urban growth: some suggestions for a political typology of American cities, *Journal of Urban History*, **4**, 29–38.

McDowell, L. (1978) University accommodation officers: welfare workers or estate agents? *Higher Education Review*, **10**, 55–62.

McDowell, L. (1983a) Housing deprivation an intergenerational approach, pp. 172–91 in M. Brown (ed.) *The Structure of Disadvantage*, Heinemann, London.

McDowell, L. (1983b) Towards an understanding of the gender division of urban space, *Environment and Planning, D: Space & Society*, **1**, 59–72.

McElrath D. C. (1962) The social areas of Rome: A comparative analysis, *American Sociological Review*, **27**, 376–91.

McElrath, D. C. (1968) Societal scale and social differentiation, pp. 33–52 in Greer, S. *et al.* (eds) *The New Urbanization*, St. Martin's Press, New York.

McGregor, A. (1977) Intra-urban variations in unemployment duration: a case study, *Urban Studies*, **14**, 315–26.

McKay, J. P. (1976) *Tramways and Trolleys: the rise of urban mass transportation in Europe*, Princeton University Press, Princeton, NJ.

McKelvey, B. (1963) *The Urbanization of America, 1860–1915*, Rutgers University Press, New Brunswick. NJ.

McKenzie, R. (1968) *On Human Ecology*, University of Chicago Press, Chicago.

Mackenzie, S. (1980) Women and the reproduction of labour power in the industrial city, *Working paper 23*, Urban and Regional Studies, University of Sussex, Brighton.

McLafferty, S. (1982) Urban structure and geographical access to public services. *Annals, Association of American Geographers*, **72**, 347–54.

MacLaran, A. C. (1981) Area-based positive discrimination and the distribution of well-being, *Transactions, Institute of British Geographers*, **6**, 53–67.

MacLaran, A. C., Malone, P. and Beamish, C. (1985) *Property and the Urban Environment: Dublin*, Department of Geography, Trinity College, Dublin.

McLeod, H. (1974) *Class and Religion in Victorian Britain*, Croom Helm, London.

McLoughlin, J. B. (1969) *Urban and Regional Planning: A Systems approach*, Faber & Faber, London.

Malpass, P. (1975) Professionalism and the role of architects in local authority housing, *Journal, Royal Institute of British Architects*, **82**, 6–29.

Mandelbaum, S. (1982) *Boss Tweed's New York*, Greenwood Press, Westport, CT.

Mann, P. (1965) *An Approach to Urban*

*Sociology*, Routledge & Kegan Paul, London.

**Marcelloni, M.** (1979) Urban movements and political struggles in Italy, *Intenational Journal of Urban and Regional Research*, **3** 251–68.

**Marcuse, P.** (1980) Housing policy and city planning: the puzzling split in the US, 1893–1931, pp. 23–58 in G. E. Cherry (ed.) *Shaping an Urban World*, Mansell, London.

**Maris, R. W.** (1969) *Social Forces in Urban Suicide*, Dorsey Press, Illinois.

**Markusen, A. R.** (1984) Class and urban social expenditure: a Marxist theory of Metropolitan government, pp. 82–100 in W. K. Tabb and L. Sawers (eds) *Marxism and the Metropolis*, 2nd edition Oxford University Press, New York.

**Marris, P.** and **Rein, M** (1973) *Dilemmas of Social Reform*, Aldine, Chicago.

**Marshall, J. N.** (1985) Services in a postindustrial economy, *Environment and Planning*, A, **17**, 1155–68.

**Marston, S.** (1985) Women in US cities: urban captives, *Cities*, **2**, 120–23.

**Martens, M.** (1985) Owner-occupied housing in Europe: postwar developments and current dilemmas, *Environment and Planning*, A, **17**, 605–24.

**Marx, L.** (1984) The puzzle of antiurbanism in classic American literature, pp. 163–180 in L. Rodwin and R. M. Holister (eds) *Cities of the Mind*, Plenum Press, London.

**Maslow, A. H.** (1970) *Motivation and Personality*, Harper & Row, New York.

**Masotti, L. H.** and **Hadden, J. K.** (eds) (1973) *The Urbanization of the Suburbs*, Sage, Beverly Hills.

**Massam, B.** (1975) *Location and Space in Social Administration*, Arnold, London.

**Massey, D.** and **Catalano, A.** (1978) *Capital and Land: Landownership by Capital in Great Britain*, Arnold, London.

**Mawby, R. I.** (1977) Defensible space: a theoretical and empirical appraisal, *Urban Studies*, **14**, 169–79.

**Mayhew, H.** (1862) *London Labour and the London Poor*, Griffin, Bohn, London.

**Mayhew, P,** (1979) Defensible space: the current status of a crime prevention theory, *Howard Journal*, **18**, 150–9.

**Mays, J. B.** (1963) Delinquency areas: a re-assessment, *British Journal of Criminology*, **3**, 216–30.

**Means, R.** (1977) *Social Work and the 'Underserving' Poor*, Occasional Paper No. 37, Center for Urban and Regional Studies, University of Birmingham.

**Mearns, A.** (1883) *The Bitter Cry of Outcast London: An Inquiry into the Condition of the Abject Poor*, Publisher unspecified, London.

**Mechanic, D.** (1968) *Medical Sociology: A Selective View*, Free Press, New York.

**Megee, M.** (1976) Restructuring the health care delivery system in the United States, pp. 239–330 in Adams, J. S. (ed.) *Urban Policymaking and Metropolitan Dynamics*, Ballinger, Cambridge, Mass.

**Meier, R.** (1985) High tech and urban settlement, in J. Brotchie *et al.* (eds), *The Future of Urban Form*, Croom Helm, Beckenham.

**Melling, J. (ed.)** (1980) *Housing, Social Policy and the State*,

**Mellor, R.** (1973) Planning for housing: market processes and constraints, *Planning Outlook*, **13**, 45–9.

**Mercer, C.** (1975) *Living in Cities: Psychology and the Urban Environment*, Penguin, Harmondsworth.

**Mercer, J.** and **Hultquist, J.** (1976) National progress toward housing and urban renewal goals, pp. 101–622 in Adams, J. S. (ed.), *Urban Policymaking and Metropolitan Dynamics*, Ballinger, Cambridge, Mass.

**Merrett, S.** and **Gray, F.** (1982) *Owner-occupation in Britain*, Routledge and Kegan Paul, London.

**Merton, R.** (1957) *Social Theory and Social Structure*, Free Press, Glencoe, Illinois.

**Michelson W.** (1977) *Environmental Choice, Human Behaviour and Residential Satisfaction*, Oxford University Press, New York.

**Mik, G.** (1983) Residential segregation in Rotterdam: Background and Policy, *Tijdschrift voor Economische en Sociale Geografie*, **74**, 74–86.

**Milgram, S.** (1970) The experience of living in cities, *Science*, **167**, 1461–8.

**Milgram, S.** and **Jodelet, D.** (1976) Psychological maps of Paris, pp. 104–24 in Proshnasky, H., Rivlin, L. and Ittelson, W. H. (eds), *Environmental Psychology*, Holt, Rinehart and Winston, New York.

**Miliband, R.** (1969) *The state in capitalist society*, Weidenfeld & Nicolson, London.

**Miliband, R.** (1974) Politics and poverty, pp. 183–96 in Wedderburn, D. (ed.) *Poverty, Inequality and Class Structure*, Cambridge University Press, Cambridge.

**Miliband, R.** (1977) *Marxism and Politics*, Oxford University Press, London.

**Millas, A.** (1980) Planning for the elderly in the context of a neighbourhood, *Ekistics*, **47**, 273–76.

**Miller, R.** (1983) The Hoover in the garden: middle-class women and suburbanization, 1850–1920, *Environment and Planning D: Society and Space*, **1**, 73–87.

**Millon, H. A.** (1978) Some new towns in Italy in the 1930s, pp. 326–41 in H. A. Millon and L. Nochlin (eds) *Art and Architecture in the Service of Politics*, MIT Press, Cambridge, Mass.

**Mills, C.** (1959) *The Sociological Imagination*, Oxford University Press, London.

**Mills, E. S.** (1967) An aggregate model of resource allocation in a metropolitan area, *American Economic Review*, **57**, 197–211.

**Mills, E. S.** and **MacKinnon, J.** (1973) Notes on the new urban economics, *Bell Journal of Economics and Management Science*, **4**, 593–601.

**Mintz, N. L.** and **Schwarz, D. T.** (1964) Urban psychology and psychoses, *International Journal of Social Psychiatry*, **10**, 101–17.

**Mitchell, J. C.** (ed.), (1969) *Social networks in Urban Situations*, Manchester University Press, Manchester.

**Mladenka, K. R.** and **Hill, K. Q.** (1977) The distribution of benefits in an urban environment: parks and libraries in Houston, *Urban Affairs Quarterly*, **113**, 73–94.

**Mladenka, K. R.** and **Hill, K. Q.** (1978) The distribution of urban police services, *Journal of Politics*, **40**, 112–33.

**Moch, L. P.** (1983) *Paths to the City*, Sage, Beverly Hills.

**Moffatt, I.** (1984) Environmental quality in Sterling, pp. 75–88 in M. Pacione and G. Gordon (eds) *Quality of Life and Human Welfare*, Geo Books, Norwich.

**Mogey, J. M.** (1956) *Family and Neighbourhood*, Oxford University Press, London.

**Mollenkopf, J. H.** (1981) Neighbourhood political development and the politics of urban growth: Boston and San Francisco, 1958–78, *International Journal of Urban and Regional Research*, **5**. 15–39.

**Mollenkopf, J. H.** (1983) *The Contested City*, Princeton University Press, Princeton, NJ.

**Molotch, H.** (1972) *Managed Integration: Dilemmas of Doing Good in the City*, University of California Press, Berkeley.

**Montgomery R.** and **Mandelker, D.** (eds) (1979) *Housing in America*, 2nd edition, Bobbs-Merrill, Indianapolis.

**Moore, E. G.** (1969) The structure of intra-urban movement rates: an ecological model, *Urban Studies*, **6**, 17–33.

**Moore, E. G.** (1971) Comments on the use of ecological models in the study of residential mobility in the city, *Economic Geography*, **47**, 73–84.

**Moore, E. G.** (1972) *Residential Mobility in the City*, Association of Resource Paper, Commission on College Geography, American Geographers, No. 13, Washington, D.C.

**Moore, G. T.** and **Golledge, R. G.** (eds) (1976) *Environmental Knowing: Theories, Research and Methods*, Dowden, Hutchinson & Ross, Stroudsburg, Pa.

**Moore, P. W.** (1983) Public services and residential development in a Toronto neighborhood, 1880–1915, *Journal of Urban History*, **9**, 445–71.

**Morgan, B. S.** (1971) The morphological region as a social unit, *Tijdschrift voor Economische en Sociale Geografie*, **72**, 226–33.

**Morgan, B. S.** (1973) Housing type and the

social characteristics of residents: the case of Exeter, Devon, *Geografiska Annaler*, **55B**, 57–70.

**Morgan, B. S.** (1976) The bases of family status segregation: a case study in Exeter, *Transactions, Institute of British Geographers*, New Series, **1**, 83–107.

**Morgan, B. S.** (1979) Residential segregation, marriage and the evolution of the stratification system: a case study in Christchurch, New Zealand, *Environment and Planning*, **11A**, 209–17.

**Morgan, B. S.** (1980) Occupational segregation in metropolitan areas in the United States, 1970, *Urban Studies*, **17**, 63–9.

**Morgan, B. S.** (1981) A contribution to the debate on homogamy, propinquity and segregation, *Journal of Marriage and the Family*, **43**, 909–21.

**Morgan, D. J.** (1980) Residential housing abandonment in the US: the effect on those who remain, *Environment and Planning*, A, **12,**, 1343–56.

**Morrill, R. L.** (1965) The negro ghetto: problems and alternatives, *Geographical Review*, **55**, 339–61.

**Morris, A. E. J.** (1972) *History of Urban Form*, Godwin, London.

**Morris, D.** (1967) *The Naked Ape*, McGraw-Hill, New York.

**Morris, J.** (1976) Access to community health services in Melbourne, *Papers of the First Australia – New Zealand Regional Science Conference*, Australia – New Zealand Regional Science Association, Brisbane.

**Mortimore, M. J.** (1969) Landownership and urban growth in Bradford and its environs in the West Riding conurbation, *Transactions, Institute of British Geographers* **46**, 99–113.

**Mowrer, E. R.** (1958) The family in suburbia, pp. 186–201 in Dorbriner, W M (ed.) *The Suburban Community*, Putnam, London.

**Muller, P. O.** (1976a) *The Outer City*, Association of American Geographers, Resource Paper No. 22, Washington, D.C.

**Muller, P. O.** (1976b) Social transportation geography, *Progress in Geography*, **8**, 208–31.

**Muller, P. O.** (1981) *Contemporary Suburban America*, Prentice-Hall, Englewood Cliffs, NJ.

**Muller, T.** (1975) *Growing and Declining Urban Areas: A Fiscal Comparison*, The Urban Institute, Washington, D.C.

**Mullin, J. R.** (1981) The Architecture of the Third Reich, *Journal of the American Planning Association*, **47**, 35–47.

**Mullin, J. R.** (1982) Ideology, Planning theory and the German city in the inter-war years, *Town Planning Review*, **53**, 257–72.

**Mumford, L.** (1934) *Technics and Civilisation*, Routledge, London.

**Mumford, L.** (1940) *The Culture of Cities*, Secker & Warburg, London.

**Mumford, L.** (1961) *The City in History*, Secker & Warburg, London.

**Murdie, R. A.** (1969) *Factorial Ecology of Metropolitan Toronto 1951–1961*, Research Paper No. 116, Department of Geography, University of Chicago.

**Murdie, R. A.** (1976) Spatial form in the Residential Mosaic, pp. 237–72 in Herbert, D. and Johnston, R. J. (eds) *Social Areas in Cities*, Vol. 1, Wiley, Chichester.

**Murdock, G. P.** (ed.) (1973) *Studies in the Science of Society*, Yale University Press, New Haven.

**Murie, A.** (1982) Selling Council Houses, *Built Environment*, **8**, 12–19.

**Murie, A., Niner, P.** and **Watson, C.** (1976) *Housing Policy and the Housing System*, Urban and Regional Studies No. 7, University of Birmingham, Allen & Unwin, London.

**Murie A.** and **Forrest, R.** (1980) Wealth, inheritance and housing policy, *Policy and Politics*, **8**, 1–19.

**Muth, R. F.** (1969) *Cities and Housing*, University of Chicago Press, Chicago.

**Naparstek, A. J., Biegel, D. E.,** and **Spiro, H. R.** (1982) *Neighborhood Networks for Human Mental Health Care*, Plenum, New York.

**Nathan, P. R.** and **Adams, C.** (1976)

Understanding central city hardship, *Political Science Quarterly*, **91**, 47–62.

**National Urban League** (1971) *National Survey of Housing Abandonment*, The Centre for Community Change, New York.

**Neenan, W. B.** (1972) *Political Economy of Urban Areas*, Markham, Chicago.

**Nelson, H.** and **Clark, W. A. V.** (1976) *Los Angeles: The Metropolitan Experience*, Ballinger, Cambridge Mass.

**Neutze, M.** (1971) *People and Property in Randwick*, Urban Research Unit, Australian National University, Canberra.

**Nevitt, A. A.** (1978) Issues in housing, pp. 183–215 in Davies, R. and Hall, P. (eds), *Issues in Urban Society*, Penguin, Harmondsworth.

**Newman, D.** (1985) Integration and ethnic spatial concentration: changing spatial distribution of the Anglo-Jewish community, *Transactions, Institute of British Geographers*, **10**, 360–76.

**Newman, O.** (1972) *Defensible Space*, Macmillan, New York.

**Newson, J.** and **Newson, E.** (1965) *Patterns of Infant Care in an Urban Community*, Penguin, Harmondsworth.

**Newton, K.** (1975) Social class, political structure and public goods in American urban politics, *Urban Affairs Quarterly*, **11**, 241–64.

**Newton, K.** (1976) *Second City Politics*, Oxford University Press, London.

**Newton, K.** (1978) Conflict avoidance and conflict suppression: the case of urban politics in the United States, pp. 76–93 in Cox, K. R. (ed.) *Urbanization and Conflict in Market Societies*, Methuen, London.

**Newton, P. W.** and **Johnston, R. J.** (1976) Residential area characteristics and residential area homogeneity: further thoughts on extensions to the factorial ecology method, *Environment and Planning*, **A8**, 543–52.

**Newton, R.** (1968) Society and politics and in Exeter 1837–1941, pp. 301–14 in Dyos, H. J. (ed.) *The Study of Urban History*, Arnold, London.

**Nicholls, D. C., Turner, D. M., Kirby-Smith, R.** and **Cullen, J. D.,** (1982) The risk business: developers' perception and prospects for housebuilding in the inner city, *Urban Studies*, **19**, 331–41.

**Nicol, L.** (1983) *Information technology, information networks and on-line information services*, Working Paper, Institute of Urban and Regional Development, University of California. Berkeley.

**Niner, P.** (1975) *Local authority housing policy and practice: a case study approach*, Occasional Paper No. 31, Centre for Urban and Regional Studies, Universtiy of Birmingham.

**Niner, P.** (1980) *Transfer Policies: a case study in Harlow*, Research Memorandum 79, Centre for Regional Urban and Local Government Studies, University of Birmingham, England.

**Niner, P.** and **Watson, C. J.** (1978) Housing in British cities, pp. 319–51 in Herbert, D. T. and Johnston, R. J. (eds) *Geography and the Urban Environment*, Vol. 1, Wiley, Chichester.

**Norborg, K.** (ed.) (1962) *Proceedings of the I. G. U. Symposium in Urban Geography*, Lund Series B, No. 24, Lund, Sweden.

**Nordstrand, E. A.** (1973) Relationships between intra-urban migration and urban residential social structure, M. A. thesis, University of Minnesota, Minneapolis.

**Norman, P.** (1975) Managerialism: a review of recent work, pp. 62–86 in Harloe, M. (ed.), *Proceedings of the Conference on Urban Change and Conflict*, Centre for Environmental Studies, London.

**Norton, R. D.** (1983) Reindustrialization and the urban underclass, pp. 181–204 in D. A. Hicks and N. Glickman (eds) *Transition to the 21st Century*, JAI Press, Greenwich, CT.

**Nowotny, H.** (1981) The information society: the impact on the home, local community and marginal groups, *Eurosocial Occasional Papers*, **9**, Vienna.

**Noyelle, T. J.** (1983) The implications of industry restructuring for spatial organization in the US, pp. 113–34 in F. Moulaert and P. W. Salinas (eds)

*Regional analysis and the new international division of labour*, Kluwer Nijhof, The Hague.

**Oakland W. H.** (1979) Central cities: fiscal plight and prospects for reform, pp. 322–58 in P. Mieszkowski and M. Streszheim (eds) *Current issues in urban economics*, Johns Hopkins University Press, Baltimore.

**O'Connor, J.** (1973) *The fiscal crisis of the state*, St. Martin's Press, New York.

**OECD** (1977) *Measuring Social Well-Being*, OECD Social Indicator Development Programme Series, No. 3, Paris.

**Offe, C.** (1974) Structural problems of the capitalist state, pp. 79–93 in Beyme, K. (ed.) *German Political Studies*, Vol. 1, Sage, Beverly Hills.

**Offe, C.** (1976) Political authority and class structures, pp. 388–421 in Connerton, P. (ed.) *Critical Sociology*, Penguin, Harmondsworth.

**Office of Population Censuses and Surveys** (1976) *The General Household Survey: Introductory Report*, H.M.S.O., London.

**Office of Population Censuses and Surveys** (1978) *The General Household Survey 1976*, OPCS Social Survey Division, H.M.S.O., London.

**Ogden, P.** and **Winchester, S.** (1975) The residential segregation of provincial migrants in Paris in 1911, *Transactions, Institute of British Geographers*, **65**, 29–44.

**O'Loughlin, J.** (1976) Malapportionment and gerrymandering in the ghetto, pp. 539–65 in Adams, J. S. (ed.), *Urban Policymaking and Metropolitan Dynamics*, Ballinger, Cambridge, Mass.

**O'Loughlin, J.** (1980) Distribution and migration of foreigners in German cities, *Geographical Review*, **70**, 253–75.

**O'Loughlin, J.** (1982) The identification and evaluation of racial gerrymandering, *Annals, Associations of American Geographers*, **72**, 165–84.

**O'Loughlin, J.** and **Glebe, G.** (1984) Intraurban migration in West German cities, *Geographical Review*, **74**, 1–23.

**Olives, J.** (1976) The struggle against urban renewal in the 'Cité d'Aliarte' (Paris), pp. 174–97 in Pickvance, C. (ed.) *Urban Sociology*, Tavistock, London.

**Olsen, M. E.** (1968) Two categories of political alienation, *Social Forces*, **47**, 288–99.

**Olson, E.** (1969) A competitive theory of the housing market, *American Economic Review*, **59**, 612–22.

**Openshaw, S.** (1969) *Canonical correlates of social structure and urban building fabric: an explanatory study*, Seminar Paper No. 11, Department of Geography, University of Newcastle upon Tyne, Newcastle upon Tyne.

**Orbell, J. M.** and **Uno, T.** (1972) A theory of neighbourhood problem-solving: political action versus residential mobility, *American Political Science Review*, **66**, 471–89.

**Orleans, P.** (1973) Differential cognition of urban residents: effects of social scale on mapping, pp. 115–30 in Downs, R. and Stea, D. (eds) *Image and Environment*, Chicago, Aldine.

**Orr, D. M., Jr.** (1969) The persistence of the gerrymander in North Carolina congressional redistricting, *Southeastern Geographer*, **9**, 39–54.

**Ouichi, W. G.** (1981) *Theory Z*, Avon Books, New York.

**Paaswell, R. E.** and **Berechman, J.** (1976) The urban disadvantaged and the search for locational opportunity, *Traffic Quarterly*, **30**, 85–100.

**Pacione, M.** (1982) Evaluating the quality of the residential environment in a deprived council estate, *Geoforum*, **13**, 45–55.

**Pacione, M.** (1983) The temporal stability of perceived neighbourhood areas in Glasgow, *Professional Geographer*, **35**, 66–73.

**Pacione, M.** (1984) Local areas in the city, pp. 61–89 in D. T. Herbert and R. J. Johnson (eds) *Geography and the Urban Environment*, vol. 6, Wiley, Chichester.

**Pacione, M.** (1984) Revealed Preferences and Residential environment quality, pp. 51–64 in M. Pacione and G. Gordon (eds) *Quality of Life and Human Welfare*,

Geo Books, Norwich.

**Packard, V.** (1972) *A Nation of Strangers*, McKay, New York.

**Pahl, R. E.** (1969) Urban social theory and research, *Environment and Planning*, **A1**, 143–53.

**Pahl, R. E.** (1970a) *Whose City?* Longman, London.

**Pahl, R. E.** (1970b) *Patterns of Urban Life*, Longman, London.

**Pahl, R. E.** (1975) *Whose City?* Penguin, Harmondsworth (2nd ed.)

**Pahl, R. E.** (1977) Managers, technical experts and the state: forms of mediation, manipulation and dominance in urban and regional development, pp. 49–60 in Harloe, M. (ed.) *Captive Cities*, Wiley, London.

**Pahl, R. E.** (1979) Socio-political factors in resource allocation, pp. 33–46 in D. Herbert and D. M. Smith (eds), *Social Problems and the City*, Oxford University Press, Oxford.

**Pahl. R. E.** (1981) Employment, work and the domestic division of labour, pp. 142–63 in M. Harloe and E. Lebas (eds) *City, Class, and Capital*, Arnold, London.

**Palm, R.** (1973) Factorial ecology and the community of outlook, *Annals, Association of American Geographers*, **63**, 341–6.

**Palm, R.** (1976a) Real estate agents and geographical information, *Geographical Review*, **66**, 226–80.

**Palm, R.** (1976b) The role of the real estate agents as information mediators in two American cities, *Geografiska Annaler*, **58B**, 28–41.

**Palm, R.** (1978) Spatial segmentation of the urban housing market, *Economic Geography*, **54**, 210–21.

**Palm, R.** (1979) Financial and real estate institutions in the housing market: a study of recent house price changes in the San Francisco Bay area, pp. 83–123 in Herbert, D. and Johnston, R. J. (eds), *Geography and the Urban Environment*, Vol. 2, Wiley, Chichester.

**Palm, R.** and **Caruso, D.** (1972) Labelling in factorial ecology, *Annals, Association of American Geographers*, **62**, 122–23.

**Palmer, R.** (1955) Realtors, as social gatekeepers, Ph.D. thesis, Yale University, New Haven.

**Papageorgiou, G. J.** (1976) On spatial consumer equilibrium, pp. 145–76 in Papageorgiou, G. J. (ed.), *Mathematical Land Use Theory*, Lexington Books, Lexington, Mass.

**Paris, C.** (1984) Private rental housing in Australia, *Environment and Planning*, A, **16**, 1079–98.

**Park, R. E.** (1916) The city: suggestions for the investigation of human behaviour in an urban environment, *American Journal of Sociology*, **20**, 577–612.

**Park, R. E.** (1936) Human ecology, *American Journal of Sociology*, **42**, 1.

**Park, R. E., Burgess, E. W.** and **McKenzie, R. D.** (1925) *The City*, University of Chicago Press, Chicago.

**Parker, J.** and **Dugmore, K.** (1976) *Colour and the Allocation of G.L.C. housing: The Report of the G.L.C. Lettings Survey 1974–5*, Greater London Council, London.

**Parkin, F.** (1971) *Class, Inequality and Political Order*, Routledge and Kegan Paul, London.

**Parry, H. B.** (ed.) (1974) *Population and its problems*, Clarendon, Oxford.

**Parsons, T.** (1951) *The Social System*, Tavistock, London.

**Paterson, J.** (1976) The poet and the metropolis, pp. 93–108 in Watson, J. and O'Riordan, *The American Environment: Perceptions and Policies*, Wiley, London.

**Patrick, J.** (1973) *A Glasgow Gang Observed*, Eyre Methuen, London.

**Peach, G. C. K.** (1974) Ethnic segregation in Sydney and intermarriage patterns, *Australian Geographical Studies*, **12**, 219–29.

**Peach, G. C. K.** (1975) Immigrants in the inner city, *Geographical Journal*, **141**, 372–9.

**Peach, G. C. K.** (1984) The force of West Indian island identity in Britain, pp. 214–30 in C. Clarke, D. Ley and C. Peach (eds) *Geography and Ethnic Pluralism*, Allen and Unwin, London.

**Peach, G. C. K.** and **Shah, S.** (1980) The contribution of council house allocation to West Indian desegregation in London, 1961–1971, *Urban Studies*, **17**, 333–41.

**Pearson, P.** and **Henney, A.** (1972) *Home Improvement: People or Profit?* Shelter, London.

**Peattie, L.** (1968) Reflections on advocacy planning, *Journal of the American Institute of Planners*, **34**, 80–8.

**Peel, N.** *et al.* (1971) Racial Discrimination in Public Housing Site Selection, *Stanford Law Review*, **23**, 63–147.

**Peet, R.** (1975) The geography of crime: a political critique, *Professional Geographer*, **27**, 277–80.

**Peet, R.** (1976) Further comments on the geography of crime, *Professional Geographer*, **28**, 96–100.

**Perin, C.** (1977) *Everything in Its Place: Social Order and Land Use in America*, Princeton University Press, Princeton, N.J.

**Perle, E. D.** (1981) Perspectives on the changing ecological structure of suburbia, *Urban Geography*, **2**, 237–54.

**Peucker, T. K.** (1968) Johaan Georg Kohl, a theoretical geographer of the nineteenth century, *Professional Geographer*, **20**, 247–50.

**Philliber, W.** (1977) Patterns of alienation in inner city ghettos, *Human Relations*, **30**, 303–10.

**Phillips, D.** (1981) The social and spatial segregation of Asians in Leicester, pp. 101–122 in P. Jackson and S. Smith (eds) *Social Interaction and Ethnic Segregation*, Academic Press, London.

**Phillips, D. R.** (1979) Public attitudes to general practitioners services; a reflection of an inverse care law in intra-urban primary medical care? *Environment and Planning*, **A11**, 315–24.

**Phillips, M.** (1977) Earls Court: Top of the Pox, *The Guardian*, 19 August, p. 11.

**Phillips, M.** (1978) Health gap in a class of its own, *The Guardian*, 20 October, p. 3.

**Phillipson, M.** (1971) *Sociological aspects of crime and delinquency*, Routledge & Kegan Paul, London.

**Philpott, T. L.** (1978) *The Slum and The Ghetto: Neighbourhood Deterioration and Middle-class Reform, Chicago, 1880–1930*, Oxford University Press, New York.

**Pickup, L.** (1976) *A space-time approach to womens' quality of life and employment opportunity*, Department of Geography, University of Reading.

**Pickup, L.** (1984) Womens' gender role and its influence on their travel behaviour, *Built Environment*, **10**, 61–8.

**Pickvance, C.** (1976a) On the study of urban social movements, pp. 198–218 in Pickvance, C. (ed.) *Urban Sociology*, Tavistock, London.

**Pickvance, C.** (ed.) (1976) *Urban Sociology*, Tavistock, London.

**Pickvance, C.** (1985) The rise and fall of urban movements and the role of comparative analysis, *Environment and Planning*, D. *Society and Space*, **3**, 31–54.

**Pillai, V. K.** (1981) Ecology of intra-urban delinquency and crime: a reassessment, *Journal of Environmental Systems*, **11**, 101–11.

**Pinch, S. P.** (1979) Territorial justice in the city: a case study of the social services for the elderly in Greater London, pp. 201–23, in Herbert, D. and Smith, D. (eds), *Social Problems and the City: Geographical Perspectives*, Oxford University Press, Oxford.

**Pinch, S. P.** (1984) Inequality in pre-school provision: a geographical perspective, pp. 231–82 in A. Kirby, P. Knox and S. Pinch (eds) *Public Service Provision and Urban Development*, Croom Helm, London.

**Pinch, S. P.** (1985) *Cities and Services: The Geography of Collective Consumption*, Routledge and Kegan Paul, London.

**Pipkin, J., La Gory, M.** and **Blau, J. R.** (eds) (1982) *Professionals and Urban Form*, SUNY Press, Albany.

**Piven, F.** and **Cloward, R. A.** (1977) *Poor People's Movements: Why they Succeed, How they Fail*, Pantheon Books, New York.

**Piven, F. F.** and **Cloward, R. A.** (1984) The new class war in the US, pp. 26–45 in I. Szelyeni (ed.) *Cities in Recession*, Sage, Beverly Hills.

**Pocock, D.** (1970) Land ownership and urban growth in Scunthorpe, *East Midland Geographer*, **5**, 52–61.

**Pocock, D.** (1972) City of the mind: a review of mental maps of urban areas, *Scottish Geographical Magazine*, **88**, 115–24.

**Pocock, D.** (1975) *Durham: Images of a Cathedral City*, Occasional Publications, Department of Geography, University of Durham.

**Pocock, D.** (1976) Some characteristics of mental maps: an empirical study, *Transactions, Institute of British Geographers*, New Series, **1**, 493–512.

**Pocock, D.** and **Hudson, R.** (1978) *Images of the Urban Environment*, Macmillan, London.

**Pollins, H.** (1964) Transport lines and social divisions, pp. 27–54 in Glass, R., *et al.* (eds) *London: Aspects of Change*, McGibbon & Kee, London.

**Polk, K.** (1957) Juvenile delinquency and social areas, *Social Problems*, **5**, 214–17.

**Pons, V.** (1978) Contemporary interpretations of Manchester in the 1830s and 1840s, *Stanford Journal of International Studies*, **13**, 51–76.

**Poole, M. A.** and **Boal, F. W.** (1973) Religious residential segregation in Belfast in 1969: a multi-level analysis, pp. 1–40 in Clark, B. D. and Gleave, M. B. (eds) *Social Patterns in Cities*, Institute of British Geographers, Special Publication No. 5, London.

**Pooley, C. G.** (1979) Residential mobility in the Victorian city, *Transactions, Institute of British Geographers*, **4**, 258–77.

**Pooley, C. G.** (1984) Residential differentiation in Victorian cities: a reassessment, *Transactions, Institute of British Geographers*, **9**, 131–44.

**Pooley, C. G.** (1985) Housing for the poorest poor: slum clearance and rehousing in Liverpool, 1890–1908, *Journal of Historical Geography*, **11**, 70–88.

**Pooley, M. E.** and **Pooley, C. G.** (1984) Health, society and environment in nineteenth-century Manchester, pp. 148–75 in R. Woods and J. Woodward (eds) *Urban Disease and mortality in Nineteenth-Century England*, Batsford, London.

**Porteous, J. D.** (1976) Home: the territorial core, *Geographical Review*, **66**, 383–90.

**Poulantzas, N.** (1973) *Political power and social classes*, New Left Books, London.

**Powell, A. C.** (1973) Methodology in the strategy for the North West Region with special reference to evaluation, pp. 167–75 in *Urban and Regional Models*, PTRC, Seminar Proceedings, Planning and Transport Research and Computation, London.

**Pred, A.** (1973) Urbanization, domestic planning problems, and Swedish geographic research, *Progress in Geography*, **5**, 1–76.

**Pred, A.** and **Palm, R.** (1974) *A time-geographic perspective on problems of inequality for women*, Working Paper No. 236, Institute of Urban and Regional Development, University of California, Berkeley.

**Pred, A.** (1981a) Production, family and 'free-time' projects: a time-geographic perspective on the individual and societal change in nineteenth-century US cities, *Journal of Historical Geography*, **7**, 3–36.

**Pred, A.** (1981b) Social reproduction and the time-geography of everyday life, *Geografiska Annaler*, **63B**, 5–22.

**Pred, A.** and **Palm, R.** (1978) The status of American women: a time-geographic view, pp. 99–109 in Lanegran, D. A., and Palm, R. (eds), *An Invitation to Geography*, (2nd ed.), McGraw-Hill, New York.

**Pressman, N.** (1985) Forces for spatial change, pp. 349–61 in J. Brotchie *et al.* (eds) *The Future of Urban Form*, Croom Helm, London.

**Preteceille, E.** (1973) *La Production des Grands Ensembles*, Mouton, Paris.

**Preteceille, E.** (1986) Collective consumption, urban segregation and social classes, *Environment and Planning*, D, **4**, 145–54.

**Priemus, H.** (1983) Squatters in Amsterdam: urban social movement, urban managers or something else? *International Journal of Urban and Regional Research*, **7**, 417–28.

**Priest, R. F.** and **Sawyer, J.** (1967) Proximity and peership: bases of balance in interpersonal attraction, *American Journal of Sociology*, **72**, 633–49.

**Pritchard, R. M.** (1976) *Housing and the Spatial Structure of the City*, Cambridge University Press, Cambridge.

**Proshansky, H. M., Ittelson, W. H.** and **Rivlin, L. G.** (eds) (1976) *Environmental Psychology: People and Their Physical Settings*, Holt, Rinehart and Winston, New York.

**Pyle, G. F.** (ed.) (1974) *The Spatial Dynamics of Crime*, Research Paper No. 159, Department of Geography, University of Chicago.

**Pyle, G. F.** (1976) Geographic perspectives on crime and the impact of anticrime legislation, pp. 257–292 in Adams, J. (ed.), *Urban Policymaking and Metropolitan Dynamics*, Ballinger, Cambridge.

**Quinn, J. A.** (1939) The nature of human ecology: re-examination and redefinition, *Social Forces*, **18**, 166–72.

**Quinney, R.** (1980) *Class, State and Crime*, Longman, New York.

**Raban, J.** (1975) *Soft City*, Fontana, London.

**Radford, J. P.** (1979) Testing the model of the pre-industrial city: the case of ante-bellum Charleston, South Carolina, *Transactions, Institute of British Geographers*, **4**, 392–410.

**Radford, J. P.** (1981) The Social Geography of the nineteenth century US city, pp. 257–93 in D. T. Herbert and R. J. Johnston (eds) *Geography and the Urban Environment*, Volume IV, Wiley, Chichester.

**Rae, J. H.** (1983) *Social Deprivation in Glasgow*, City of Glasgow District Council, Glasgow.

**Rainwater, L.** (1966) Fear and the house-as-haven in the lower class, *Journal of the American Institute of Planners*, **32**, 23–31.

**Ramsøy, N. R.** (1966) Assortative mating and the structure of cities, *American Sociological Review*, **31**, 773–86.

**Rakove, M. L.** (1975) *Don't Make No Waves, Don't Back No Losers*, Indiana University Press, Bloomington.

**Rand, G.** (1984) Crime and environment: a review of the literature and its implications for urban architecture and planning, *Journal of Architecture and Planning Research*, **1**, 3–20.

**Rapoport, A.** (1977) *Human Aspects of Urban Form*, Pergamon, Oxford.

**Ratcliff, R. U.** (1949) *Urban Land Economics*, McGraw-Hill, New York.

**Raveau, F.** (1970) The use of minorities in the social sciences, *The New Atlantis*, **2**, 159–72.

**Ravetz, A.** (1980) *Remaking Cities*, Croom Helm, Beckehham.

**Rawcliffe, J. M.** (1982) Bromley: Kentish market town to London Suburb, 1841–81, pp. 27–92 in F. M. L. Thompson (ed.) *The Rise of Suburbia*, Leicester University Press, Leicester.

**Raynor, J.** *et al.* (1974) *The Urban Context*, Open University, Milton Keynes.

**Reade, E. J.** (1983) Town planning and sociology, in V. Pons and R. Francis (eds) *Urban Social Research: Problems and Prospects*, Sociological Review Monograph 30, Routledge and Kegan Paul, London, 146–70.

**Redburn, S.** *et al.* (1980) How representative are mandated citizen participation processes? *Urban Affairs Quarterly*, **15**, 345–52.

**Rees, G.** and **Lambert, J.** (1985) *Cities in Crisis*, Arnold, London.

**Rees, P.** (1970) Concepts of social space, pp. 306–94 in Berry, B. and Horton, F. E. (eds), *Geographic Perspectives on Urban Systems*, Prentice-Hall, Englewood Cliffs, New Jersey.

**Rees, P.** (1971) Factorial ecology: an extended definition, survey and critique, *Economic Geography*, **47**, 220–33.

**Rees, P.** (1972) Problems of classifying subareas as within cities, pp. 265–330 in Berry, B. (ed.), *City Classification Handbook: Methods and Applications*, Wiley, New York.

**Rees, P.** (1979) *Residential Patterns in American cities: 1960*, Research Paper No. 189, Department of Geography, University of Chicago.

**Reiser, R.** (1973) The territorial illusion and the behavioural sink, *Antipode*, **5**, 52–7.

**Reiss, A. J. Jr.** (1955) An analysis of urban phenomena, pp. 41–51 in Fisher, R. M. (ed.), *The Metropolis and Mental Life*, Doubleday, New York.

**Relph, E.** (1976) *Place and Placelessness*, Pion, London.

**Report of the Committee on Public Participation in Planning** (1969) *People and Planning* (Skeffington Report) H.M.S.O., London.

**Reps, J. W.** (1965) *The Making of Urban America*, Princeton University Press, Princeton.

**Rex, J.** (1968) The sociology of the zone of transition, pp. 211–31 in Pahl, R. E. (ed.), *Readings in Urban Sociology*, Pergamon, Oxford.

**Rex, J.** and **Moore, R.** (1967) *Race, Community and Conflict*, Oxford University Press, London.

**Reynolds, D. R.** (1976) Progress toward achieving efficient and responsive spatial-political systems in urban America, pp. 463–537 in Adams, J. S. (ed.), *Urban Policymaking and Metropolitan Dynamics*, Ballinger, Mass.

**Rich, R. C.** (1979a) Neglected issues in the study of urban service distributions: a research agenda, *Urban Studies*, **16**, 143–56.

**Rich, R. C.** (1979b) The roles of neighbourhood organizations in urban service delivery, *Urban Affairs Papers*, **1**, 81–93.

**Rich, R. C.** (1982a) The political economy of urban-service distribution, pp. 1–16 in R. C. Rich (ed.) *The Politics of Urban Public Services*, Lexington Books, Lexington, Mass.

**Rich, R. C.** (1982b) Problems of theory and methods in the study of urban-service distributions, pp. 3–18 in R. C. Rich (ed.) *Analyzing Urban-service Distribution*, Lexington Books, Lexington, Mass.

**Richardson, H. W.** (1971) *Urban Economics*, Penguin, Harmondsworth.

**Richardson, H. W.** (1977) *The New Urban Economics: and its Alternatives*, Pion, London.

**Riesman, I.** (1950) *The Lonely Crowd*, Yale University Press, New Haven.

**Roberts, J. T.** (1976) *General Improvement Areas*, Saxon House, Farnborough.

**Robertson, I. M. L.** (1984) Single parent lifestyle and peripheral estate residence, *Town Planning Review*, **55**, 197–213.

**Robinson, V.** (1981) The development of South Asian settlement in Britain and the myth of return, pp. 149–60 in C. Peach, V. Robinson and S. Smith (eds) *Ethnic Segregation in Cities*, Croom Helm, London.

**Robinson, V.** (1984) Asians in Britain: a study in encapsulation and marginality, pp. 231–57 in C. Clark, D. Ley and C. Peach (eds) *Geography and Ethnic Pluralism*, Allen and Unwin, London.

**Robson, B. T.** (1969) *Urban Analysis*, Cambridge University Press, Cambridge.

**Robson, B. T.** (1975) *Urban Social Areas*, Oxford University Press, London.

**Robson, B. T.** (1981) Social concern, planning and geography in Britain, in D. Stoddart (ed.) *Geography, Ideology and Social Concern*, Barnes and Noble, Totowa, NJ.

**Robson, B. T.** (1982) The Bodley barricade: social space and social conflict, pp. 45–61 in K. R. Cox and R. J. Johnston (eds) *Conflict, Politics and the Urban Scene*, Longman, London.

**Roettger, W. B.** (1980) The urban condition: resident perspectives, *Midwest Review of Public Administration*, **14**, 211–30.

**Roistacher, E. A.** (1984) A tale of two conservatives: housing policy under Reagan and Thatcher, *Journal of the American Planning Association*, **50**, 479–84.

**Roistacher, R. C.** (1974) A review of mathematical methods in sociometry, *Sociological Methods and Research*, **3**, 123–71.

**Romanos, M. C.** (1976) *Residential Spatial Structure*, Lexington Books, Lexington, Mass.

**Rose, H. M.** (1969) *Social Processes in the City: Race and Urban Residential Choice*, Resource Paper No. 6, Commission on College Geography, Association of American Geographers, Washington, D.C.

**Rose, H. M.** (1970) The development of an urban sub-system: the case of the negro ghetto, *Annals, Association of American Geographers*, **60**, 1–17.

**Rose, H. M.** (1971) *The Black Ghetto: A Spatial Behavioural Perspective*, McGraw-Hill, New York.

**Rosen, G.** (1973) Disease, debility and death, pp. 625–68 in Dyos, H. J. and Wolff, M. (eds), *The Victorian City: Images and Realities*, Routledge, London.

**Rosenberg, M.** (1983) Accessibility to health care: A North American Perspective, *Progress in Human Geography*, **7**, 78–87.

**Rosenberg, M.** (1984) Physician location behaviour in Metropolitan Toronto, *Canadian Geographer*, **28**, 156–70.

**Rosenthal, E.** (1961) Acculturation without assimilation? The Jewish community of Chicago, Illinois, *American Journal of Sociology*, **66**, 275–88.

**Rosser, C.** and **Harris, C.** (1965) *The Family and Social Change*, Routledge & Kegan Paul, London.

**Rossi, P. H.** (1980) *Why Families Move*, The Free Press, Glencoe, Illinois, 2nd edition.

**Rothenberg, J.** (1967) *Economic Evaluation of Urban Renewal*, Brookings Institution, Washington, D.C.

**Rowley, G.** (1975) Landownership in the spatial growth of towns: a Sheffield example, East Midland Geographer, **6**, 200–13.

**Royal Commission on Local Government in England** (1969) *Research Studies 9*, Community Attitudes Survey, H.M.S.O., London.

**Rubin, B.** (1977) A chronology of architecture in Los Angeles, *Annals, Association of American Geographers*, **67**, 521–37.

**Rubin, B.** (1979) Aesthetic ideology and urban design, *Annals, Association of American Geographers*, **69**, 339–61.

**Rubin, L.** (1967) Maximum feasible participation, *Poverty and Human Resources Abstracts*, **2**, 5–18.

**Rumley, D.** (1981) Spatial structural effects in voting behaviour: description and explanation, *Tijdschrift voor Economische en Sociale Geografie*, **72**, 214–23.

**Rummel, R. J.** (1967) Understanding factor analysis, *Journal of Conflict Resolution*, **40**, 440–80.

**Rutter, M.** and **Madge, N.** (1976) *Cycles of Disadvantage*, Heinemann, London.

**Ryker, R., Pol, L. G.** and **Guy, R. F.** (1984) Racial discrimination as a determinant of home improvement loans, *Urban Studies*, **21**, 177–82.

**Rykwert, J.** (1976) *The idea of a town: the anthropology of urban form in Rome, Italy and the Ancient World*, Faber & Faber, London.

**Sack, R. D.** (1980) *Conceptions of Space in Social Thought*, Macmillan, London.

**Salins, P. D.** (1971) Household location patterns in American metropolitan areas, *Economic Geography*, **47**, 234–48.

**Samuels, M. S.** (1981) An existential geography, pp. 115–32 in M. E. Harvey and B. P. Holly (eds) *Themes in Geographic Thought*, Croom Helm, London.

**Sandercock, L.** (1976) *Cities for Sale: Property, Politics and Urban Planning in Australia*, Heinemann, London.

**Sargent, C. S., Jr.** (1976) Land speculation and urban morphology, pp. 21–58 in Adams, J. S. (ed.), *Urban Policymaking and Metropolitan Dynamics*, Ballinger, Cambridge, Mass.

**Saunders, P.** (1978) Domestic property and social class, *International Journal of Urban and Regional Research*, **2**, 233–51.

**Saunders, P.** (1979) *Urban Politics: A Sociological Interpretation*, Hutchinson, London.

**Saunders, P.** (1981) *Social Theory and the Urban Question*, Hutchinson, London.

**Schacht, R.** (1971) *Alienation*, Doubleday: Anchor Press, New York.

**Scherer, J.** (1973) *Contemporary Community*, Tavistock, London.

**Schill, M. H.** and **Nathan, R.** (1983)

*Revitalizing America's Cities*, SUNY Press, Albany.

**Schmid, C. F.** (1960) Urban crime areas, *American Sociological Review*, **25**, 527–42, and 655–78.

**Schmid, C. F.** and **Schmid, S. E.** (1972) *Crime in the State of Washington*, Law and Justice Planning Office, Washington State Planning and Community Affairs Agency, Olympia.

**Schmid, C. F.** and **Tagashira, K.** (1965) Ecological and demographic indices: a methodological analysis, *Demography*, **1**, 194–211.

**Schmitt, R. C., Zane, L. Y. S.,** and **Nishi, S.** (1978) Density, health and social disorganization revisited, *Journal of the American Institute of Planners*, **44**, 201–12.

**Schnore, L. F.** (1965) *The Urban Scene*, Free Press, New York.

**Schroeter, E.** (1978) Rome's first national state architecture: the Pallazo delle Finanze, pp. 128–149 in H. A. Millon and L. Nochlin (eds) *Art and Architecture in the Service of Politics*, MIT Press, Cambridge, Mass.

**Schwartz, B.** (ed.) (1976) *The Changing Face of the Suburbs*, University of Chicago Press, Chicago.

**Scobie, R. S.** (1975) *Problem Tenants in Public Housing*, Praeger, New York.

**Scott, A. J.** (1985) Location processes, urbanization, and territorial development, *Environment and Planning*, A, **17**, 479–501.

**Scott, P.** (1972) The spatial analysis of crime and delinquency, *Australian Geographical Studies*, **10**, 1–18.

**Scottish Development Department** (1974) *Community Councils*, H.M.S.O., Edinburgh.

**Seamon, D.** (1979) *A Geography of the Lifeworld*, St Martin's, New York.

**Seamon, D.** (1981) Heidegger, Environment and Dwelling, *Environment and Planning*, A, **13**, 1121–33.

**Seeman, M.** (1971) Alienation studies, *Annual Review of Sociology*, **1**, 91–124.

**Sewel, J., Twine F.** and **Williams N.** (1984) The sale of council houses: some

empirical evidence, *Urban Studies*, **21**, 439–50.

**Shah, S.** (1979) Aspects of the geographical analysis of Asian immigrants in London. Unpublished D. Phil thesis, University of Oxford.

**Shannon, G. W.** and **Dever, G. E. A.** (1974) *Health care delivery: spatial perspectives*, McGraw-Hill, New York.

**Shannon, G. W., Spurlock, C. W., Gladin, S. T.** and **Skinner, J. L.** (1975) A method for evaluating the geographic accessibility of health services, *Professional Geographer*, **27**, 30–6.

**Sharpe, C. A.** (1978) New construction and housing turnover: vacancy chains in Toronto, *Canadian Geographers*, **22**, 130–44.

**Sharrod, D. R.** and **Downs, R.** (1974) Environmental determinants of altruism, *Journal of Experimental Social Psychology*, **10**, 468–79.

**Shaw, C. R.** and **McKay, H. D.** (1942) *Juvenile delinquency and urban areas*, University of Chicago Press, Chicago.

**Shaw, C. R.** *et al.* (1929) *Delinquency Areas*, University of Chicago Press, Chicago.

**Shaw, M.** (1979) Reconciling social and physical space: Wolverhampton, 1871, *Transactions, Institute of British Geographers*, **4**, 192–213.

**Shevky, E.** and **Bell, W.** (1955) *Social Area Analysis*, Stanford University Press, Stanford, California.

**Shevky, E.** and **Williams, M.** (1949) *The Social Areas of Los Angeles*, University of California Press, Los Angles.

**Short J. F.** (1971) *The Social Fabric of the Metropolis*, University of Chicago Press, Chicago.

**Short, J. R.** (1978a) Residential mobility, *Progress in Human Geography*, **2**, 418–47.

**Short, J. R.** (1978b) Residential mobility in the private housing market of Bristol, *Transactions, Institute of British Geographers*, N.S., **3**, 533–47.

**Short, J. R.** (1979) Landlords and the private rented housing sector: a case study, pp. 56–75 in Boddy, M. (ed.), *Land, Property and Finance*, Working

Paper No. 2, School for Advanced Urban Studies, University of Bristol.

**Short, J. R.** (1982) *Housing in Britain: The Post-War Experience*, Methuen, London.

**Shutt, J.** (1984) Tory enterprise zones and the Labour movement, *Capital and Class*, **23**, 19–44.

**Siegel, A.** (1981) *The Image of the American City in Popular Literature 1820–1870*, Kennikat Press, Port Washington, New York.

**Silk, J.** (1971) *Search behaviour*, Geographical Paper No. 7, Department of Geography, University of Reading.

**Simey, T.** (ed.) (1954) *Neighbourhood and Community*, Liverpool University Press, Liverpool.

**Simkus, A. E.** (1978) Residential segregation by occupation and race in the urbanized areas, 1950–1970, *American Sociological Review*, **43**, 81–93.

**Simmel, G.** (1905) The Metropolis and Mental Life, pp. 47–60 in Sennett, P. (ed.) *Classic Essays on the Culture of Cities*, Appleton-Century-Crofts, New York, 1969.

**Simmie, J. M.** (1974) *Citizens in Conflict*, Hutchinson, London.

**Simmie, J. M.** (1981) *Power, Property and Corporation: the Political Sociology of Planning*, Macmillan, London.

**Simmons, J.** (1973) The power of the railway, pp. 277–310 in Dyos, H. J. and Wolff, M. (eds), *The Victorian City: Images and Realities*, Routledge & Kegan Paul, London.

**Simmons, J. W.** (1968) Changing residence in the city: a review on intra-urban mobility. *Geographical Review*, **58**, 621–51.

**Sjoberg, W.** (1960) *The pre-industrial city, past and present*, Free Press, Glencoe, Illinois.

**Skellington, R.** (1981) How blacks lose out in council housing, *New Society*, January 29, 187–9.

**Skogan, W. G.** (1977) The changing distribution of big-city crime, *Urban Affairs Quarterly*, **13**, 33–47.

**Sly, D. F.** and **Tayman, J.** (1980) Changing metropolitan morphology and municipal service expenditures in cities and rings, *Social Science Quarterly*, **61**, 595–611.

**Smailes, A. E.** (1955) Some reflections on the geographical description and analysis of townscapes, *Transactions, Institute of British Geographers*, **21**, 99–115.

**Smailes, A. E.** (1964) Urban Survey, pp. 206–21 in Coppock, J. T. and Prince, H. C. (eds) *The Geography of Greater London*, Faber, London.

**Smailes, A. E.** (1966) *The Geography of Towns*, Hutchinson, London.

**Smith, C. A.** and **Smith, C. J.** (1978) Locating natural neighbours in the urban community, *Area*, **10**, 102–10.

**Smith, C. J.** (1978) Self-help and social networks in the urban community, *Ekistics*, **45**, 106–115.

**Smith, C. J.** (1980) Neighbourhood effects on mental health, pp. 363–415 in D. Herbert and R. J. Johnston (eds) *Geography and the Urban Environment*, Vol. 3, Wiley, Chichester.

**Smith, C. J.** (1984) Economic determinism and the provision of human services, pp. 176–212 in A. Kirby, P. Knox and S. Pinch (eds) *Public Service Provision and Urban Development*, Croom Helm, Beckenham.

**Smith, D. M.** (1973a) *An Introduction to Welfare Geography*, Occasional Paper No. 11, University of Witwatersrand, Johannesburg.

**Smith, D. M.** (1973b) *The Geography of Social Well-Being in the United States*, McGraw-Hill, New York.

**Smith, D. M.** (1974a) *Who gets what, where, and how*: a welfare focus for human geography, *Geography*, **59**, 289–97.

**Smith, D. M.** (1974b) *Crime rates as Territorial Social Indicators*, Occasional Paper No. 1, Department of Geography, Queen Mary College, London.

**Smith, D. M.** (1977) *Human Geography: A Welfare Approach*, Arnold, London.

**Smith, D. M.** (1979a) *Where the Grass Grows Greener*, Croom Helm, London.

**Smith, D. M.** (1979b) The identification of problems in cities: applications of social indicators, pp. 13–32 in Herbert, D. and Smith, D. M. (eds) *Social Problems and*

*The City: Geographical Perspectives*, Oxford University Press, Oxford.

**Smith, D. M.** (1979c) Inner-city deprivation: problems and policies in advanced capitalist countries, *Geoforum*, **10**, 297–310.

**Smith, G. C.** and **Ford, R. G.** (1985) Urban mental maps and housing estate preference of council tenants, *Geoforum*, **16**, 25–36.

**Smith, N.** (1979) Toward a theory of gentrification, *Journal of the American Planning Association*, **45**, 538–48.

**Smith, N.** (1982) Gentrification and uneven development, *Economic Geography*, **58**, 139–55.

**Smith, N.** and **Williams, P.** (eds) (1986) *Gentrification of the City*, Allen and Unwin, Winchester, MA.

**Smith, P. F.** (1977) *The Syntax of Cities*, Hutchinson, London.

**Smith, S. J.** (1981) Negative interaction: crime in the inner city, pp. 35–58 in P. Jackson and S. Smith (eds) *Social Interaction and Ethnic Segregation*, Institute of British Geographers Special Publication No. 12, Academic Press, London.

**Smith, W. F.** (1964) *Filtering and Neighborhood Change*, Research Report No. 24, Center for Real Estate and Urban Economics, University of California, Berkeley.

**Smyth, H.** (1985) *Property Companies and the Construction Industry in Britain*, Cambridge University Press, Cambridge.

**Soja, E. W.** (1971) *The Political Organization of Space*, Resource Paper No. 8, Commission on College Geography, Association of American Geographers, Washington, D.C.

**Sopher, D. E.** (1972) Place and location: notes on the spatial patterning of culture, *Social Science Quarterly*, **52**, 321–37.

**Southworth, M.** and **Southworth, S.** (1973) Environmental quality in cities and regions, *Town Planning Review*, **44**, 231–53.

**Spain, D.** and **Nock, S.** (1984) Two-career couples: a portrait, *American Demographics*, **6**, 24–27.

**Speare, A., Goldstein, S.** and **Frey, W. H.** (1975) *Residential Mobility, Migration and Metropolitan Change*, Ballinger, Cambridge, Mass.

**Spencer, D.** and **Lloyd, J.** (1974) *The Small Heath school session: mental maps of routes from home to school*, Working Paper No. 24, Centre for Urban and Regional Studies, University of Birmingham.

**Spring, D.** (1951) The English landed estate in the age of coal and iron: 1830–1880, *Journal of Economic History*, **11**, 3–24.

**Srole, L.** (1972) Urbanization and mental health, *American Scientist*, **60**, 576–83.

**Stacey, M.** (1960) *Tradition and Change*, Oxford University Press, London.

**Stacey, M.** (1969) The myth of community studies, *British Journal of Sociology*, **20**, 134–46.

**Stahura, J. M., Huff, C. R.** and **Smith, B. L.** (1980) Crime in the Suburbs: A Structural Model, *Urban Affairs Quarterly*, **15**, 291–316.

**Stanback, T. M. Jr** and **Noyelle, T. J.** (1982) *Cities in Transition*, Allanheld-Osmun, Totowa, NJ.

**Stanislawski, D.** (1946) The origin and spread of the grid pattern town, *Geographical Review*, **36**, 105–20.

**Stapleton, C.** (1980) reformulation of the family life-cycle concept: implications for residential mobility, *Environment and Planning*, A, **12**, 1103–18.

**Stave, B. M.** and **Stave, S. A.** (1981) *Urban Bosses, Machines and Progressive Reformers*, Krieger Publishers, Huntingdon, New York.

**Stein, M.** (1960) *The Eclipse of Community*, Harper & Row, New York.

**Stern, E.** (1983) Communication and future spatial structure, *Town and Regional Planning*, **15**, 19–22.

**Sternlieb, G.** and **Hughes, J. W.** (1984) *Income and Jobs USA: Diagnosing the reality*, Center for Urban Policy Research, Rutgers University, New Brunswick, NJ.

**Stetzer, D. F.** (1975) *Special districts in Cook County: toward a geography of local government*, Research Paper No. 169,

Department of Geography, University of Chicago.

**Stimpson, R. J.** (1970) Patterns of immigrant settlement in Melbourne, 1947–61, *Tijdschrift voor Economische en Sociale Geografie*, **61**, 114–26.

**Stimpson, R. J.** (1978) The spatial characteristics of health care services provision and utilisation in Australia, paper presented to the annual conference of the Institute of British Geographers, Kingston-upon-Hull.

**Stimpson, R. J.** (1982) *The Australian City: A Welfare Geography*, Longman Cheshire, Melbourne.

**Stokols, D.** (ed.) (1976) *Psychological Perspectives on Environment and Behaviour*, Plenum Press, New York.

**Stone, M. E.** (1978) Housing, mortgage lending, and the contradictions of capitalism, pp. 179–207 in Tabb, W. K. and Sawers, L. (eds), *Marxism and the Metropolis*, Oxford University Press, New York.

**Straszheim, M.** (1975) *An Econometric Analysis of the Housing Market*, National Bureau of Economic Research, New York.

**Stetzer, D. F.** (1975) *Special districts in Cook County: toward a geography of local government*, Research Paper No. 169, Department of Geography, University of Chicago.

**Stringer, P.** and **Taylor, M.** (1974) *Attitudes and Information in Public Participation: A case Study*, Working Paper No. 3, Centre for Environmental Studies, London.

**Stringer, P., Boaden, N., Goldsmith, M.** and **Hampton, W.** (1980) Planning and Participation in Practice, *Progress in Planning*, Pergamon, Oxford.

**Stutz, F. P.** (1976) *Social aspects of Interaction and transportation*, Resource Paper 76–2, Association of American Geographers, Washington, D.C.

**Sumner, W. G.** (1906) *Folkways*, Ginn, Boston.

**Susskind, L.** and **Elliot, M.** (eds) (1983) *Paternalism, Conflict and Coproduction*, Plenum Press, New York.

**Sutcliffe, A.** (ed.) (1980) *The Rise of Modern Urban Planning*, Mansell, London.

**Sutcliffe, A.** (1982) The growth of public intervention in the British urban environment in the nineteenth century: a structural approach, pp. 107–24 in J. H. Johnson and C. G. Pooley (eds) *The Structure of Nineteenth-Century Cities*, Croom Helm, London.

**Sutcliffe, D.** (1982) *British Black English*, Blackwell, Oxford.

**Suttles, G. D.** (1968) *The Social Order of The Slum: Ethnicity and Territory in the Inner City*, University of Chicago Press, Chicago.

**Suttles, G. D.** (1972) *The Social Construction of Communities*, University of Chicago Press, Chicago.

**Suttles, G. D.** (1975) Community design: the search for participation in an urban society, pp. 235–97 in Hawley, A. H. and Rock, V. P. (eds) *Metropolitan America in Contemporary Perspective*, Halstead Press, New York.

**Sweetser, F. L.** (1965a) Factorial ecology: Helsinki, *Demography*, **2**, 372–85.

**Sweetser, F. L.** (1965b) Factor structure as ecological structure in Helsinki and Boston, *Acta Sociologica*, **8**, 205–25.

**Taafe, E. J.** and **Gauthier, L.** (1973) *Geography of Transportation*, Prentice-Hall, Englewood Cliffs, New Jersey.

**Tabb, W. K.** (1984) The New York City fiscal crisis, pp. 323–45, in Tabb, W. K. and Sawers, L. (eds) *Marxism and the Metropolis*, Oxford University Press, New York, 2nd edition.

**Tabb, W. K.** and **Sawers, L.** (eds) (1984) *Marxism and the Metropolis*, Oxford University Press, New York, 2nd edition.

**Taeuber, K. E.** (1965) Residential segregation, *Scientific American*, **213**, 12–19.

**Taeuber, K. E.** and **Taeuber, A. F.** (1965) *Negroes in cities: Residential Segregation and Neighbourhood Change*, Aldine, Chicago.

**Tafuri, M.** (1976) *Architecture and Utopia: design and capitalist development*, MIT Press, Cambridge, Mass.

**Taggart, H.** and **Smith, K. W.** (1981) Redlining: An assessment of the evidence of disinvestment in metropolitan Boston, *Urban Affairs Quarterly*, **17**, 91–107.

**Talarchek, G.** (1982) A model of residential search and selection, *Urban Geography*, **3**, 34–57.

**Tallman, I.** and **Morgner, R.** (1970) Life-style differences among urban and suburban blue collar families, *Social Forces*, **48**, 334–48,

**Tarn, J. N.** (1973) *Five Per Cent Philanthropy*, Cambridge University Press, London.

**Tarn, J. N.** (1980) Housing reform and the emergence of town planning in Britain before 1914, pp. 71–98 in A. Sutcliffe (ed.) *The Rise of Modern Urban Planning 1800–1914*, St Martins, New York.

**Tarn, J. N.** (1985) Urban regeneration: the conservation dimension, *Town planning Review*, **56**, 245–68.

**Tata, R. J., Hurn, S.** and **Lee, D.** (1975) Defensible space in a housing project: a case study from south Florida, *Professional Geographer*, **27**, 297–303.

**Taylor, I., Walton, P.** and **Young, J.** (1973) *The New Criminology*, Routledge & Kegan Paul, London.

**Taylor, P. J.** (1978) '*Difficult to let*', '*Difficult to live in*', and sometimes '*Difficult to get out of*': An essay on the provision of council housing with special reference to Killingworth, Discussion Paper No. 16, Centre for Urban and Regional Development Studies, University of Newcastle Upon Tyne.

**Taylor, P. J.** and **Gudgin, G.** (1976) The myth of non-partisan cartography: a study of electoral biases in the English Boundary Commission's Redistribution for 1955–1970, *Urban Studies*, **13**, 13–25.

**Taylor, P. J.** and **Johnston, R. J.** (1979) *Geography of Elections*, Penguin, Harmondsworth.

**Taylor, P.** (1980) *Policies for deprived areas or deprived people?* Discussion Paper 8, Policy Analysis Research Unit, Glasgow College of Technology, Glasgow.

**Taylor, P.** and **Hadfield, H.** (1982) Housing and the State: a case study and structuralist interpretation, p. 241–63 in K. R. Cox and R. J. Johnston (eds) *Conflict, Politics and the Urban Scene*, Longman, London.

**Theodorson, G. A.** (ed.). (1961) *Studies in Human Ecology*, Harper & Row, New York.

**Thernstrom, S.** and **Sennett, R.** (eds) (1969) *Nineteenth-Century Cities*, Yale University Press, New Haven.

**Thomas, A. D.** (1986) *Housing and Urban Renewal: Residential Decay and Revitalisation in the Private Sector*, Allen and Unwin, London.

**Thomas, C. J.** (1968) Geographical aspects of the growth of the residential area of Greater Nottingham in the twentieth century, unpublished Ph.D. thesis, University of Nottingham.

**Thompson, D. L.** (1963) New concepts, subjective distance, *Journal of Retailing*, **39**, 1–6.

**Thompson, E. P.** (1967) Time, work discipline and industrial capitalism, *Past and Present*, **38**, 56–97.

**Thompson, E. P.** (1968) *The Making of the English Working Class*, Penguin, Harmondsworth.

**Thompson, F. M. L.** (1982) The rise of suburbia, pp. 1–26 in F. M. L. Thompson (ed.) *The Rise of Suburbia*, Leicester University Press, Leicester.

**Thorn, R.** (1980) Places of refreshment in the nineteenth century city, pp. 228–54 in A. D. King (ed.) *Buildings and Society*, Routledge and Kegan Paul, London.

**Thornhill Neighbourhood Project** (1978) *Health Care in Thornhill: A Case of Inner City Deprivation*, Thornhill Neighbourhood Project, London.

**Thorns, D. C.** (1981) Owner-occupation: its significance for wealth transfer and class formation, *Sociological Review*, **29**, 705–28.

**Tiebout, C. M.** (1956) A pure theory of local expenditures, *Journal of Political Economy*, **64**, 416–24.

**van Til, J.** (1980) A new type of city for an energy-short world? *Futurist*, June, 64–70.

**Tilly, C.** (1961) Occupational rank and grade of residence in a metropolis, *American Journal of Sociology*, **67**, 323–9.

**Tilly, L. A.** (1981) Three faces of capitalism: women and work in French cities, pp. 165–92 in J. M. Merriman (ed.) *French Cities in the Nineteenth Century*, Holmes and Meier, New York.

**Timms, D. W. G.** (1965) The spatial distribution of social deviants in Luton, England, *Australian and New Zealand Journal of Sociology*, **1**, 38–52.

**Timms, D. W. G.** (1969) The dissimilarity between overseas-born and Australian-born in Queensland, *Sociology and Social Research*, **3**, 363–74.

**Timms, D. W. G.** (1971) *The Urban Mosaic: Towards a Theory of Residential Differentiation*, Cambridge University Press, Cambridge.

**Timms, D. W. G.** (1976) Social bases to social areas, pp. 19–40 in Herbert, D. T. and Johnston, R. J. (eds) *Social Areas in Cities*, Vol. **1**, Wiley, Chichester.

**Timms, D. W. G.** (1977) Factorial ecologies in central Scotland, Final Report to SSRC.

**de Tocqueville, A.** (1946) *Democracy in America*, Knopf, New York.

**Toffler, A.** (1970) *Future Shock*, The Bodley Head, London.

**Toffler, A.** (1981) *The Third Wave*, Bantam, New York.

**Tomeh, A. K.** (1964) Informal group participation and residential pattern, *American Journal of Sociology*, **70**, 28–35.

**Tomlinson, H.** (1980) Design and Reform: The 'separate' system in the nineteenth century English prison, pp. 94–119 in A. D. King (ed.) *Buildings and Society*, Routledge and Kegan Paul, London.

**Tönnies, F.** (1887) *Community and Society*, translated by C. P. Loomis, Harper, New York, 1963.

**Tournier, R. E.** (1984) Cities as people, cities as places: urban revitalization and urban conflict, *Journal of Urban Affairs*, **6**, 141–50.

**Tranter, P.** and **Parkes, D.** (1979) Time and images in urban space, *Area* **11**, 115–20.

**Treen, C.** (1982) The process of suburban development in north Leeds, 1870–1914, pp. 157–210 in F. M. L. Thompson (ed.) *The Rise of Suburbia*, Leicester University Press, Leicester.

**Tuan, Y. F.** (1974) *Topophilia*, Prentice-Hall, Englewood Cliffs, New Jersey.

**Tuan, Y. F** (1975) Place: an experiential perspective, *Geographical Review*, **65**, 151–65.

**Tuan, Y. F.** (1976) Geopiety: a theme in man's attachment to nature and to place, pp. 11–39 in Lowenthal, D. and Bowden, M. J. (eds), *Geographies of the Mind*, Oxford University Press, London.

**Tuan, Y. F** (1977) *Space and Place: the perspective of experience*, University of Minnesota Press, Minneapolis.

**Tuan, Y. F.** (1978) The city: its distance from nature, *Geographical Review*, **68**, 1–12.

**Twine, Y. F.** and **Williams, N. J.** (1983) Social segregation and public sector housing: a case study, *Transactions, Institute of British Geographers*, **8**, 253–66.

**Tym, R.** and **Partners** (1982) *Monitoring the enterprise zones: year 2*, Roger Tym and Partners, London.

**Udry, J. R.** (1964) Increasing scale and spatial differentiation: new tests of two theories from Shevky and Bell, *Social Forces*, **42**, 404–13.

**Unit for Manpower Studies** (1976) *The Role of Immigrants in the Labour Market*, Department of Employment, London.

**United States Department of Health, Education and Welfare** (1969) *Toward a Social Report*, U.S.G.P.O., Washington, D.C.

**US National Commission on Neighborhoods** (1979) *People, Building Neighborhoods*, Final Report to the President and Congress of the United States, U.S.G.P.O, Washington, D.C.

**United States National Committee on Urban Problems** (1968) *Building the American City*, U.S. Government Printing Office, Washington, D.C.

**Van Arsdol, M. D., Camilleri, S. F.** and **Schmid, C. F.** (1958) The generality of urban social area indexes, *American Sociological Review*, **23**, 277–84.

**Van Arsdol, Jr. M. D., Sabagh, G.** and **Butler, E. W.** (1968) Retrospective and subsequent metropolitan residential mobility, *Demography*, **5**, 249–57.

**Vance, Jr. J. E.** (1964) *Geography and Urban Evolution in the San Francisco Bay Area*, Institute of Governmental Studies, University of California Press, Berkeley.

**Vance, Jr. J. E.** (1971) Land assignment in pre-capitalist, capitalist and post-capitalist cities, *Economic Geography*, **47**, 101–20.

**Vance, Jr. J. E.** (1976) Institutional forces that shape the city, pp. 81–110 in Herbert, D. T. and Johnston, R. J. (eds) *Social Areas in Cities*, Vol. 1, *Spatial Process and Form*, Wiley, Chichester.

**Vance, Jr. J. E.** (1977) *This scene of man: The role and structure of the city in the geography of Western civilization*, Harper & Row, New York.

**Vance, Jr. J. E.** (1978) Institutional forces that shape the city, pp. 97–125 in D. T. Herbert and R. J. Johnston (eds) *Social Areas in Cities*, Wiley, Chichester.

**Van den Berghe, P.** (1974) Bringing beasts back in: toward a biosocial theory of aggression, *American Sociological Review*, **39**, 777–88.

**Van Valey, T. L., Roof, W. C.** and **Wilcox, J. E.** (1977) Trends in residential segregation 1960–1970, *American Journal of Sociology*, **82**, 826–44.

**Verba, S.** (1961) *Small Groups and Political Behaviour*, Princeton University Press, New Jersey.

**Verba, S.** and **Nie, N. H.** (1972) *Participation in America: Political Democracy and Social Equality*, Harper & Row, New York.

**de Vise, P.** (1968) *Slum medicine: Chicago style: how the medical needs of the city's Negro poor are met*, Working Paper No. 3IV.7, Chicago Regional Hospital Study, Chicago.

**de Vise, P.** (1973 *Misused and Misplaced Hospitals and Doctors*, Resource Paper No. 22, Commission on College Geography, Association of American Geographers, Washington, D.C.

**de Vise, P.** (1976) The suburbanization of jobs and minority employment, Economic Geography, **52**, 348–62.

**de Vise, P.** and **Dewey, D. R.** (1972) *More money, more doctors, less care: Chicago's changing distribution of physicians, hospitals and population, 1950 to 1970*, Working Paper No. 1.19, Chicago Regional Hospital Study, Chicago.

**Wachs, M.** (1984) Autos, Transit and the Sprawl of Los Angeles: the 1920s, *Journal of the American Planning Association*, **50**, 297–310.

**Walker, R. A.** (1978) The transformation of urban structure in the nineteenth century and the beginnings of suburbanization, pp. 165–212 in Cox, K. (ed.) *Urbanization and Conflict in Market Societies*, Methuen, London.

**Walker, R. A.** (1981) A theory of suburbanization: capitalism and the construction of urban space in the United States, pp. 383–430 in M. Dear and A. J. Scott (eds) *Urbanization and Urban Planning in Capitalist Society*, Methuen, London.

**Wallis, C. P,** and **Maliphant, R.** (1967) Delinquent areas in the county of London: ecological factors, *British Journal of Criminology*, **7**, 250–84.

**Walmsley, J.** (1976) Territory and neighbourhood in metropolitan Sydney, *Journal of the Royal Australian Planning Institute*, **14**, 66–9.

**Ward, C.** (1978) *The Child in The City*, Architectural Press, London.

**Ward, D.** (1962) The pre-urban cadaster and the urban pattern of Leeds, *Annals, Association of American Geographers*, **52**, 150–66.

**Ward, D.** (1964) A comparative historical geography of streetcar suburbs in Boston, Massachusetts and Leeds, England: 1850–1920, *Annals, Association of American Geographers*, **54**, 477–89.

**Ward, D.** (1971) *Cities and Immigrants*, Oxford University Press, New York.

**Ward, D.** (1975) Victorian cities: how modern? *Journal of Historical Geography*, **1**, 135–51.

**Ward, D.** (1980) Environs and neighbours in the 'Two Nations': residential differentiation in mid-nineteenth century Leeds, *Journal of Historical Geography*, **6**, 133–162.

Ward, D. (1982) The ethnic ghetto in the United States: past and present, *Transactions, Institute of British Geographers*, **7**, 257–275.

Ward, D. (1983) The place of Victorian cities in developmental approaches to urbanization, pp. 355–380 in J. Patten (ed.) *The Expanding City*, Academic Press, London.

Ward, D. (1984) The progressives and the urban question: British and American responses to inner-city slums 1880–1920, *Transactions, Institute of British Geographers*, **9**, 299–315.

Warner, Jr. S. B. (1962) *Streetcar Suburbs: The Process of Growth in Boston, 1870–1900*, Harvard University and the M.I.T. Press, Cambridge, Mass.

Warner, Jr. S. B. (1972) *The Urban Wilderness: A History of the American City*, Harper & Row, New York.

Warner, Jr. S. B. (1984) Slums and skyscrapers: urban images, symbols and ideology, pp. 181–196 in L. Rodwin and R. M. Hollister (eds) *Cities of the Mind*, Plenum Press, London.

Warner, W. L. and Lunt, P. S. (1941) *The Social Life of a Modern Community*, Yale University Press, New Haven.

Warner, W. L. and Lunt, P. S. (1942) *Status system of a Modern Community*, Yale University Press, New Haven.

Warner, W. L. and Srole, L. (1945) *The Social System of American Ethnic Groups*, Yale University Press, New Haven.

Warnes, A. M. (1973) Residential patterns in an emerging industrial town, pp. 169–89 in Clark, B. D. and Gleave, M. G. (eds), *Social Patterns in Cities*, Special Publication No. 5, Institute of British Geographers, London.

Warren, D. I. (1981) *Helping Networks: How people cope with problems in urban communities*, University of Notre Dame Press, Notre Dame, IN.

Warren, R. L. (1963) *The Community in America*, Rand McNally, Chicago.

Watson, C. J. (1974) Vacancy chains,

filtering and the public sector, *Journal, Institute of American Planners*, **40**, 346–52.

Watson, J. W. (1972) Mental distance in geography: its identification and representation, paper presented to I.G.U. Symposium, Montreal.

Watson, J. W. and O'Riordan, T. (1976) *The American Environment: Perceptions and Policies*, Wiley, London.

Webb, S. D. and Colette, J. (1979) Rural-urban stress: new data and new conclusions, *American Journal of Sociology*, **84**, 1446–52.

Webber, M. M. (1963) Order diversity: community without propinquity, pp. 23–56 in Wingo, L. (ed.) *Cities and Space*, Johns Hopkins University Press, Baltmore.

Webber, M. M. (1964) The urban place and the nonplace urban realm, pp. 79–153 in Webber, M. M. *et al.* (eds), *Explorations Into Urban Structure*, University of Pennsylvania Press, Philadelphia.

Webber, M. M. (1980) *A communications strategy for cities of the twenty-first century*, Working Paper, Institute of Urban and Regional Development, University of California, Berkeley.

Webber, R. J. (1975) *Liverpool Social Area Study 1971 Data: Final Report*, Planning Research Applications Group, Centre for Environmental Studies, London.

Webber, R. J. (1977) An introduction to the national classification of wards and parishes, TP-23, Planning Research Action Group, CES, London.

Weber, A. F. (1899) *The Growth of Cities in the Nineteenth Century: a study in statistics*, Cornell University Press, Ithaca, New York, (reprint 1967).

Weber, M. (1947) *The Theory of Social and Economic Organization*, Free Press, Glencoe, Illinois.

Weicher, J. C. (1971) The allocation of police protection by income class, *Urban Studies*, **8**, 207–20.

Weir, S. (1976) Red Line Districts, *Roof*, **1**, 109–14.

Weisbrod, G. and Vidal, A. (1981) Housing search barriers for low-income renters,

*Urban Affairs Quarterly*, **16**, 465–82.

**Weiss, S. F., Smith, J. E., Kaiser, E. J.** and **Kenney, K. B.** (1966) *Residential Developer Decisions*, Centre for Urban and Regional Studies, University of North Carolina, Chapel Hill, North Carolina.

**Wellman, B.** (1979) The community question, *American Journal of Sociology*, **84**, 1201–31.

**Wellman, B.** and **Crump, B.** (1978) *Networks, Neighbourhoods and Communities*, Research Paper No. 97, Centre for Urban and Community Studies, University of Toronto.

**Wellman, B.** and **Leighton, B.** (1979) Networks, neighbourhoods and communities, *Urban Affairs Quarterly*, **14**, 363–90.

**Welsh Consumer Council** (1976) *Council Housing: A Survey of Allocation Policies in Wales*, Welsh Consumer Council, Cardiff.

**West, D. J.** (1967) *The Young Offender*, Duckworth, London.

**Westoff, C. F.** (1983) Fertility decline in the West: causes and prospects, *Population and Development Review*, **9**, 99–104.

**Wheatley, P.** (1975) The ancient Chinese city as a cosmological symbols, *Ekistics*, **39**, 147–58.

**Wheaton, W. L. C.** (1977) Income and urban residence: an analysis of consumer demand for locations, *American Economic Review*, **67**, 630–41.

**White, P.** (1984) *The West European City: a social geography*, Longman, London.

**White, P.** (1985) Levels of intra-urban migration in Western European cities: a comparative analysis, *Espace, Populations, Societies*, **1**, 129–137.

**Whitehand, J. W. R.** (1967) Fringe belts: a neglected aspect of urban geography, *Transactions, Institute of British Geographers*, **41**, 223–33.

**Whitehand, J. W. R.** (1972) Building cycles and the spatial pattern of urban growth, *Transactions, Institute of British Geographers*, **56**, 39–55.

**Whitehand, J. W. R.** (1974) The changing nature of the urban fringe, pp. 31–52 in Johnson, J. H. (ed.), *Suburban Growth:*

*Geographical Processes at the Edge of the Western City*, Wiley, London.

**Whitehand, J. W. R.** (1975) Building activity and the intensity of development at the urban fringe: the case of a London suburb in the nineteenth century, *Journal of Historical Geography*, **1**, 211–24.

**Whitehand, J. W. R.** (1977) The basis for a historico geographical theory of urban form, *Transactions, Institute of British Geographers*, N.S., **2**, 400–16.

**Whitehand, J. W. R.** (1983) Land-use structure, built form and agents of change, pp. 41–60 in R. L. Davies and A. G. Champion (eds) *The Future for the City Centre*, Institute of British Geographers Special Publication No. 14, Academic Press, London.

**Whitehand, J. W.R.** (1984) Commercial townscapes in the making, *Journal of Historical Geography*, **10**, 174–200.

**Whitehand, J. W. R.** and **Whitehand, S. M.** (1983) The study of physical change in town centres: research procedures and types of change, *Transactions, Institute of British Geographers*, **8**, 483–507.

**Whitehand, J. W. R.** and **Whitehand, S. M.** (1984) The physical fabric of town centres: the agents of change, *Transactions, Institute of British Geographers*, **9**, 231–47.

**Whitehead, C. M. E., Harloe, M.** and **Bovaird, A.** (1985) Prospects and strategies for for housing in the private rented sector, *Journal of Social Policy*, **14**, 151–74.

**Whyte, W. H.** (1956) *The Organization Man*, Doubleday, New York.

**Wiener, R.** (1976) *The Rape and Plunder of the Shankhill in Belfast*, Notaems Press, Belfast.

**Wilkinson, H.** *et al.* (1970) *Kingston-upon-Hull and Haltemprice – Social Area Analysis 1966: Part I – Atlas*, Miscellaneous Series No. 10, Department of Geography, University of Kingston-upon-Hull.

**Williams, N. J.** (1985) Crime Patterns in Aberdeen, *Scottish Geographical Magazine*, **101**, 49–59.

**Williams, P.** (1976a) The role of institutions

in the inner London housing market: the case of Islington, *Transactions, Institute of British Geographers*, N.S., **1**, 72–82.

**Williams, P.** (1976b) *The Role of Financial Institutions and Estate Agents in the Private Housing Market: A General Introduction*, Working Paper No. 39, Centre for Urban and Regional Studies, University of Birmingham, Birmingham.

**Williams, P.** (1978) Urban managerialism: a concept of relevance? *Area*, **10**, 236–40.

**Williams, P.** (1982) residential mortgage patterns and institutional structures: theory and reality, pp. 229–54 in R. Flowerdew (ed.) *Institutions and Geographical Patterns*, Croom Helm, London.

**Williams, P.** (1984) Economic processes and urban change: an analysis of contemporary patterns of residential restructuring, *Australian Geographical Studies*, **22**, 39–57.

**Williams, R.** (1973) *The Country and the City*, Chatto & Windus, London.

**Williams-Ellis, C.** (ed.) (1938) *Britain and the Beast*. Dent, London.

**Willmott, P.** and **Young, M.** (1960) *Family and Class in a London Suburb*, Routledge & Kegan Paul, London.

**Wilson, A. G.** (1970) *Entropy in Urban and Regional Modelling*, London.

**Wilson, A. G.** (1974) *Urban and Regional Models in Geography and Planning*, Wiley, London.

**Wilson, W.** (1980) The ideology, aesthetics and politics of the city beautiful movement, pp. 166–98 in A. Sutcliffe (ed.) *The Rise of Modern Urban Planning*, Mansell, London.

**Winchester, S. W. C.** (1974) Immigrant areas in Coventry in 1971, *New Community*, **4**, 97–104.

**Wing, J. K.** (1974) Housing environments and mental health, pp. 75–89 in Parry, H. (ed.) *Population and Its Problems*, Clarendon Press, Oxford.

**Wingo, L.** (1961) *Transportation and Urban Land*, Johns Hopkins University Press, Baltimore.

**Wingo, L.** (1963) *Cities and Space*, Johns Hopkins University Press, Baltimore.

**Wirth, L.** (1928) *The Ghetto*, University of Chicago Press, Chicago.

**Wirth, L.** (1938) Urbanism as a way of life, pp. 143–64 in Sennett, R. (ed.) *Classic Essays on the Culture of Cities*, Appleton-Century-Crofts, New York.

**Wohl, A. S.** (1977) *The Eternal Slum*, Arnold, London.

**Wohlenberg, E. H.** (1982) The geography of civility revisited: New York blackout looting, 1977, *Economic Geography*, **58**, 29–44.

**Wolch, J. R.** (1980) The residential location of the service-dependent poor, *Annals, Association of American Geographers*, **70**, 330–41.

**Wolch, J. R.** (1981) The location of service-dependent households in urban areas, *Economic Geography*, **57**, 52–67.

**Wolch, J. R.** (1982) Spatial consequences of social policy: the role of service-facility location in urban development patterns, pp. 19–35 in R. C. Rich (ed.) *Analyzing Urban-service Distributions*, Lexington Books, Lexington, Mass.

**Wolch, J. R.** and **Gabriel, S. A.** (1984) Development and decline of service-dependent population ghettos, *Urban Geography*, **5**, 111–29.

**Wolch, J. R.** and **Gabriel, S. A.** (1985) Dismantling the community-based human service system, *Journal of the American Planning Association*, **51**, 53–62.

**Wolf, E.** and **Lebeaux, C. N.** (eds) (1969) *Change and Renewal in an Urban Community*, Praeger, New York.

**Wolfe, T.** (1982) *From Bauhaus to Our House*, Farar, Strauss, Giroux, New York.

**Wolfinger, R. E.** and **Rosenstone, S. J.** (1980) *Who Votes?* Yale University Press, New Haven.

**Wolpert, J.** (1966) Migration as an adjustment to environmental stress, *Journal of Social Issues*, **22**, 92–102.

**Wolpert, J., Mumphrey, A.** and **Seley, J.** (1972) *Metropolitan Neighbourhoods: Participation and Conflict over Change*, Resource Paper No. 16, Association of American Geographers, Washington, D.C.

**Women and Geography Study Group** (1984) *Geography and Gender*, Hutchinson. London

**Wood, C. M., Lee, N., Loker, J. A.** and **Saunders, P. J. W.** (1974) *The Geography of Pollution: A Study of Greater Manchester*, Manchester University Press, Manchester.

**Woods, R.** (1984) Mortality and sanitary conditions in late nineteenth century Birmingham, pp. 176–202 in R. Woods and J. Woodward (eds) *Urban Disease and Mortality in Nineteenth Century England*, Batsford, London.

**Woods, R. I.** (1976) Aspects of the scale problem in the calculation of segregation indices: London and Birmingham 1961 and 1971, *Tijdschrift voor Economische en Sociale Geografie*, **69**, 169–74.

**Wright, G.** (1981) *Building the Dream*, Pantheon, New York.

**Wynn, M.** (ed.) (1984) *Housing in Europe*, Croom Helm, Beckenham.

**Yablonsky, L.** (1970) *The Violent Gang*, Penguin, Baltimore.

**Yago, G.** (1984) *The Decline of Transit: urban transportation in German and US cities, 1900–1970*, Cambridge University Press, Cambridge.

**Yancey, W. L.** (1971) Architecture, interaction and social control, *Environment and Behaviour*, **3**, 3–21.

**Yeates, M.** and **Garner, B.** (1976) *The North American City*, Harper & Row, New York.

**Yelling, J. A.** (1982) L.C.C. slum clearance policies 1889–1907, *Transactions, Institute of British Geographers*, **7**, 292–303.

**Young, K.** and **Kramer, J.** (1977) Local exclusionary policies in Britain: the case of suburban defence in a metropolitan system, pp. 229–51 in Cox, K. (ed.) *Urbanization and Conflict in Market Societies*, Methuen, London.

**Young, M.** and **Willmott, P.** (1957) *Family and Kinship in East London*, Routledge & Kegan Paul, London.

**Young, M.** and **Willmott, P.** (1962) *Family and Kinship in East London*, Penguin, Harmondsworth.

**Young, M.** and **Willmott, P.** (1973) *The Symmetrical Family*, Pantheon, New York.

**Zelinsky, W.** (1975) Personality and self-discovery: the future social geography of the United States, pp. 108–21 in Abler, R. *et al.* (eds) *Human Geography in a Shrinking World*, Duxbury Press, North Scituate, Mass.

**Zorbaugh, H. W.** (1929) *The Gold Coast and the Slum*, University of Chicago Press, Chicago.

**Zukin, S.** (1982) *Loft Living: culture and capital in urban change*, Johns Hopkins University Press, Baltimore.

**Zunz, O.** (1980) Residential segregation in the American metropolis, *Urban History Yearbook 1980*, Leicester University Press, Leicester, 23–33.

**Zunz, O.** (1982) *The Changing face of Inequality: urbanization, industrial development and immigrants in Detroit, 1880–1920*, University of Chicago Press, Chicago.

# Index